The Race for the Governor's Cup

To my big brothers, Walt and Bob,
who taught their little brother baseball

The Race for the Governor's Cup

The Pacific Coast League Playoffs, 1936–1954

by
DONALD R. WELLS

McFarland & Company, Inc., Publishers
Jefferson, North Carolina, and London

Library of Congress Online Catalog data:

Wells, Donald R., 1932–
    The race for the Governor's cup : the Pacific Coast League
playoffs, 1936–1954 / by Donald R. Wells.
      p.   cm.
    Includes index.
    ISBN 0-7864-0760-3 (softcover : 50# alkaline paper) ∞
    1. Pacific Coast League — History.   2. Pacific Coast League —
Statistics.   3. Governor's Cup — History.   I. Title.
GV875+

                                        00-25237

British Library cataloguing data are available

Manufactured in the United States of America

McFarland & Company, Inc., Publishers
  Box 611, Jefferson, North Carolina 28640
  www.mcfarlandpub.com

CONTENTS

ACKNOWLEDGMENTS

I want to acknowledge the following authors and newspaper sources that I relied on to write this book on the Pacific Coast League's experience with the Shaughnessy system of postseason playoffs:

Richard Beverage's *Los Angeles Angels* and his *Hollywood Stars;* John Spalding's *Sacramento Solons and Senators;* Gary Waddingham's *The Seattle Rainiers 1938–1942;* Ken Stadler's *The Pacific Coast League, One Man's Memories 1938–1957;* Bill O'Neal's *The Pacific Coast League 1903–1958,* and Ray Brandes and Bill Swank's two-volume work on *The San Diego Padres.*

The newspapers are: *The Sporting News, The Seattle Post Intelligencer, The Seattle Times, The Portland Oregonian, The Sacramento Bee, The Sacramento Union, The Oakland Tribune, The San Francisco Chronicle, The San Francisco Examiner, The Los Angeles Times, The Los Angeles Examiner,* and *The San Diego Union.*

Finally, I am grateful to Douglas McWilliams for providing many of the photographs that appear in this book.

INTRODUCTION

Before the Pacific Coast League adopted the Shaughnessy system of playoffs in 1936, they played three series against the American Association's champion in 1919, 1924 and 1925 and tried the split season format in 1904, 1905, 1918, 1928, 1929, 1930, 1931, 1934 and 1935. The weather and the travel distance discouraged the series with champions of the American Association. The Vernon Tigers beat the St. Paul Saints five out of nine games in 1919, but in 1924 St. Paul won the only game played in Seattle with the champion Indians before rain washed the rest of series away. In 1925, the Louisville Colonels lost five of nine games to the San Francisco Seals.

The league tried the split season format for four straight years beginning in 1928 after the 1927 Oakland Oaks had an easy time winning the pennant, causing attendance to drop late in the season. The winner of the first half played the winner of the second half of the season for the championship. In 1928 San Francisco beat Sacramento; in 1929 Hollywood beat the Missions; in 1930 Hollywood beat Los Angeles; and in 1931 San Francisco beat Hollywood. This system was dropped for the next two seasons but resumed in 1934, after the Los Angeles Angels had a huge midseason lead. When the Angels also won the second half, they were matched against an all star team from the other seven clubs and also won that series. The last split season was 1935 when San Francisco beat Los Angeles.

The playoffs were named for Frank J. "Shag" Shaughnessy, who had a long minor league playing career which ended in 1924. He played football, track and baseball at Notre Dame, but saw only limited major league action with the Washington Nationals in 1905 and the Philadelphia Athletics in 1908. Shaughnessy became associated with the Montreal Royals of the International League in the 1930s as general manager, field manager and radio announcer. After elected president of the International League in 1936, he argued strongly that the playoffs were the financial salvation of minor league baseball in those depressed times.

The idea of having the top four teams play for a postseason championship came from Canada's favorite sport, hockey, which in turn imported it from

1

England. But the idea was very controversial. A team could finish first by a wide margin after a 22-week schedule and be eliminated in a best of seven series by a team that finished fourth and did not even play .500 ball. Shaughnessy constantly had to argue with officials in the International League and the American Association who wanted to drop the playoffs and go to a split season. The famous Bill Veeck opposed the playoffs because so few first place teams from those two leagues made it to the Junior World Series. Only twice between 1933 and 1944 did the two first place teams meet in that Series. But Shaughnessy's main counterpoint was that the split season could cause the first half winner to lose incentive, as may have happened in the major leagues in 1981, when a strike led to a split season.

Shaughnessy also argued that the quality of play would be maintained more with a playoff system because teams would be less apt to sell key players if they are struggling to finish in the first division. He felt the top teams needed to play those games and not merely receive bonus money for finishing in the top four spots, as the Coast League tried in 1950. The players would then get a postseason reward without having to work for it.

For the first two years that the Pacific Coast League used the Shaughnessy system, the pennant winner was the team that won the playoffs and not the team finishing first. But as late as June 1936, league president W.C. Tuttle was still uncertain about this, believing that the pennant should go to the team finishing first. But Charles Graham, president of the San Francisco Seals, polled the other team presidents and they all agreed that the playoff winner would be crowned champion. The Portland Beavers settled the argument by winning it both ways in 1936, but 1937 was a different story.

After finishing last in 1935 and 1936, the Sacramento Solons received a lot of talent from their parent, the St. Louis Cardinals, and finished on top in 1937 for the first time in their history. But the Solons were eliminated in the first round of the playoffs by the eventual playoff winner, the San Diego Padres, who had finished in third place. Not only were the Solons and their fans miffed, but the owner of the Padres, Bill Lane, opposed the playoffs as a money loser. Lane did not feel a series between a third and a fourth place team would constitute a championship battle, even though his team was awarded the pennant. In 1954, when the Padres tied Hollywood and then beat them in a one game playoff for the pennant, *The San Diego Union* proclaimed that to be the Padres' first pennant. No one wanted to claim the "tainted" 1937 pennant won in the playoffs.

After the 1937 controversy, the league officials decided that the team finishing first would be the pennant winner, and the playoff winner would receive a cup from the league's president, as well as prize money. This prize money was actually more than what the pennant winner was to receive, giving the teams a strong incentive to win the playoffs.

Charles Graham of the Seals made a strong argument for the playoffs in

1942 even though his team failed to finish in the first division. Graham pointed out that the Seals drew 30,000 fans for their final home series with the Oakland Oaks because his team had a good chance of finishing fourth. He felt that the benefit of having the playoffs came during the regular season as teams struggled to make the first division, even if the playoffs themselves did not turn a profit.

THE PLAYOFFS

1936

The first season under the Shaughnessy plan provided fans with one of the closest races in Pacific Coast League history with only three games separating fourth place Seattle from first place Portland. With as little as two games left in the season, it would have been possible to have a four way tie for first. San Diego and Oakland tied for second, only a game and a half behind the Beavers. Even though the pennant was decided in the playoffs, Portland received $2,500 of the $10,000 prize money for finishing first. The playoff winner was to receive $3,000, the loser of the final round $2,000, and each first round loser $1,250.

The Mission Reds and the Los Angeles Angels made a run at the first division but came up short, finishing in a tie for fifth, 8.5 games behind Portland. The Missions led the league as late as the end of June and were as high as fourth in early September. The Angels' chances for first division were hurt when outfielder Marvin Gudat broke his leg in early September.

Seattle led the league in attendance with 400,000 even though the Indians, as the team was then called, played at old Civic Stadium, with its all-dirt infield. The newest team, San Diego, drew the next highest at 225,000. The owners reported the league finally turned a profit in this depression year, and the playoffs may have been a factor. At this early stage, president W. C. Tuttle was supportive of the new system.

Plans originally called for the first and third place teams to meet in the opening round, unlike the International League where the first and fourth place teams opened the postseason. However, to save travel costs, officials decided to have Portland to open with Seattle regardless of how each finished. As it turned out, it was natural for San Diego to play Oakland in the first round since those two ended tied for second. The team finishing higher in the standings could choose where the series was to start, so Portland chose to open at home. The San Diego–Oakland series opened in Oakland because the Padres ended the season at San Francisco while Oakland was in nearby Sacramento.

Two problems that dogged the playoffs through the years were competition with college, and later, pro football, and broadcasts of the World Series. Football was a big rival in Los Angeles, the Bay Area and Seattle, but the other teams did not have Pacific Coast Conference teams in their immediate area. In 1936 the playoffs ended on September 30, the day the World Series opened, so that should not have been a major distraction.

The Portland-Seattle Series

This was to be a two trip series with games three, four and five in Seattle, but it took the Beavers only four games to eliminate the Suds, as Seattle was often called. During the regular season, Portland won 12 and lost 10 to their northern rival.

Game One

The Beavers beat their nemesis, Kewpie Dick Barrett, 5–0, with George Caster pitching the shutout and going 2 for 3, with a double and a run batted in. Barrett had gone 12–2 against Portland the past two seasons, but this was not to be his series. Moose Clabaugh and Anthony Bongiovanni (called Nino Bongy in the papers) also got two hits each. Portland even pulled a triple play in the fourth inning.

Seattle	AB	R	H	RBI	O	A	E
Donovan RF	4	0	2	0	2	0	0
Shevlin 1B	3	0	0	0	7	0	1
Bassler C	4	0	1	0	1	2	0
Hunt LF	4	0	1	0	4	0	1
Muller 2B	4	0	0	0	3	5	0
Lawrence CF	3	0	2	0	1	0	0
Gyselman 3B	4	0	2	0	3	2	0
Smith SS	3	0	0	0	3	1	1
Barrett P	1	0	0	0	0	1	0
Lucas P	0	0	0	0	0	0	0
Spindell[a]	1	0	0	0	0	0	0
Osborn P	0	0	0	0	0	1	0
Michaels[b]	1	0	0	0	0	0	0
Wells P	0	0	0	0	0	0	0
	32	0	8	0	24	12	3

(a) Batted for Lucas in the fifth.
(b) Batted for Osborn in the eighth.

Portland	AB	R	H	RBI	O	A	E
Bongy CF[a]	4	0	2	0	1	0	0
Lee SS	3	0	1	2	5	5	0
Sweeney 1B	5	0	0	0	9	0	0
Frederick RF	4	0	0	0	1	0	0
Clabaugh LF	4	2	2	0	4	0	0
Brucker C	3	0	1	0	4	1	0
Bedore 3B	3	1	0	1	0	0	0
P. Coscarart 2B	4	1	2	0	3	3	0
Caster P	3	1	2	1	0	2	0
	33	5	10	4	27	11	0

(a) *Real Name was Bongiovanni, but was shortened for box scores.*

Losing Pitcher: Barrett. Runs Responsible For: Barrett 2, Osborn 1. Struck Out by Caster 3, By Barrett 2. Bases on Balls: Off Caster 2, off Barrett 3. Stolen Base: Donovan. Two Base Hits: Caster, Clabaugh. Sacrifices: Brucker, Lee, Caster. Triple Play: Lee to Sweeney. Wild Pitch. Barrett. Umpires: Powell, Hood, and Cole. Time: 1 hr. 43 min.

Seattle	000	000	000	0 –	8 –	3
Portland	002	210	00x	5 –	10 –	0

Game Two.

The Beavers pounded Lou Koupal early to win 10–5, but starter Ad Liska could not finish the fifth inning so the win went to Bill Radonits, even though Liska got two hits and drove in three runs. Fred Bedore had a three hit night for Portland and both Bongy and Dudley Lee each got two hits. Seattle's Mike Hunt got a double and two singles and drove in two runs in a losing cause.

Seattle	AB	R	H	RBI	O	A	E
Donovan RF	4	1	0	0	1	0	0
Shelvin 1B	4	2	2	1	9	0	0
Spindell C	3	1	0	0	3	0	0
Hunt LF	5	0	3	2	1	0	0
Muller 2B	5	0	3	1	4	2	0
Lawrence CF	4	0	1	0	2	0	0
Gyselman 3B	4	0	1	0	0	1	1
Smith SS	4	1	1	0	4	6	0
Koupal P	1	0	0	0	0	1	0
Osborn P	1	0	1	0	0	3	1
J. Campbell P	1	0	0	0	0	0	0
Basler[a]	1	0	0	0	0	0	0

Seattle	AB	R	H	RBI	O	A	E
Wells P	1	0	0	0	0	0	0
Michaels[b]	1	0	0	0	0	0	0
	39	5	12	4	24	13	2

(a) *Batted for J. Campbell in the eighth.*
(b) *Batted for Smith in the ninth.*

Portland	AB	R	H	RBI	O	A	E
Bongy CF	3	2	2	0	2	0	0
Lee SS	5	0	2	3	2	3	0
Sweeney 1B	5	0	0	0	8	1	0
Frederick RF	5	1	4	2	1	0	0
Clabaugh LF	5	1	1	0	1	0	0
Brucker C	2	2	0	0	8	0	1
Bedore 3B	4	2	3	2	3	0	1
P. Coscarart 2B	3	2	2	0	2	2	0
Liska P	2	0	2	3	0	1	0
Radonitz P	1	0	0	0	0	2	0
	35	10	16	10	27	9	2

Winning Pitcher: Radonitz. Losing Pitcher: Koupal. Struck Out By: Liska 5, Radonitz 3, J. Campbell 1, Wells 1. Bases on Balls Off: Liska 2, Koupal 2, Osborn 1, Radonitz 2. Two Base Hits: Clabaugh, Hunt. Sacrifices: P. Coscarart, Radonitz. Hit Batsman: By Koupal 1, Radonitz 1. Double Plays: Koupal to Smith To Shevlin; Mueller to Smith to Shevlin 2. Wild Pitch: Liska. Passed Ball: Brucker. Umpires: Hood, Cole and Powell. Time: 2 hrs.

Seattle	000	030	002	5 – 12 – 2
Portland	124	030	00x	10 – 16 – 2

Game Three.

Switching sites to Seattle, the Beavers made it three in a row with a 4–3 win, scoring all their runs in the top of the first inning. Kewpie Dick Barrett started for Seattle and gave up four straight hits and left without retiring a batter. The key blow was John Frederick's triple that drove in two runs. Manager Bill Sweeney and Moose Clabaugh each drove in a run that inning. Pitcher Paul Gregory shut the Beavers out the rest of the way, giving up just four hits and two walks, causing Seattle fans to question Manager Dutch Ruether why Gregory did not start. Sailor Bill Posedel went the distance for Portland and was saved by a game ending double play that killed an Indian rally.

Portland	AB	R	H	RBI	O	A	E
Bongy CF	5	1	2	0	3	0	0
Lee SS	3	1	1	0	0	3	0
Sweeney 1B	4	1	1	1	9	0	0
Frederick RF	4	1	2	2	2	1	0
Clabaugh LF	4	0	1	1	1	0	0
Brucker C	3	0	1	0	8	1	0
Bedore 3B	4	0	0	0	1	1	0
P. Coscarart 2B	3	0	0	0	3	2	0
Posedel P	4	0	0	0	0	2	0
	34	4	8	4	27	10	0

Seattle	AB	R	H	RBI	O	A	E
Donovan RF	5	0	2	0	1	0	0
Shevlin 1B	4	1	2	1	7	2	0
Bassler C	5	0	1	1	5	1	0
Hunt LF	4	0	1	0	0	0	0
Muller 2B	4	0	0	0	1	3	0
Lawrence CF	4	1	2	0	7	0	0
Gyselman 3B	3	0	1	0	2	0	0
Smith SS	2	0	1	1	4	1	0
Barrett P	0	0	0	0	0	0	0
Gregory P	2	0	0	0	0	1	0
Spindell [a]	0	1	0	0	0	0	0
Michael [b]	1	0	0	0	0	0	0
	34	3	10	3	27	8	0

(a) *Batted for Smith in the ninth.*
(b) *Batted for Gregory in the ninth.*

Losing Pitcher: Barrett. Runs Responsible For: Barrett 4, Posedel 3. Struck Out by: Gregory 3, Posedel 9. Bases on Balls Off: Gregory 2, Posedel 4. Hit by Pitcher: P. Coscarart by Gregory. Left on Bases: Portland 6, Seattle 9. Three Base Hit: Frederick. Two Base Hit: Bassler. Sacrifice: Gregory. Double Plays: Bassler to Muller; Lee to Coscarart to Sweeney. Umpires: Cole, Powell and Hood. Time: 1 hr. 44 min.

Portland	400	000	000	4	– 8	– 0
Seattle	011	000	001	3	– 10	– 0

Game Four.

This series' final game was a massacre, with Portland scoring seven runs in the fourth inning and three more in the fifth, on their way to an easy 13–3 win. Ray Lucas started for Seattle, yielding all seven runs in the fourth. Again, Ad Liska started but did not finish the fifth inning, so the win went to George Caster, who hit a ninth inning home run. Catcher Earle Brucker led the attack with three hits, while Sweeney, Clabaugh, Bedore and Bongy got two each. Dutch Ruether resigned as manager after Seattle was swept.

Portland	AB	R	H	RBI	O	A	E
Bongy CF	6	0	2	1	5	0	0
Lee SS	6	0	1	1	2	1	0
Sweeney 1B	3	1	2	2	4	0	1
Frederick RF	4	1	1	1	4	0	0
Clabaugh LF	4	1	2	1	2	0	0
Brucker C	5	3	3	0	4	1	1
Bedore 3B	4	3	2	1	1	4	0
P.Coscarart 2B	2	2	0	0	2	1	0
French P	0	0	0	0	0	0	0
Liska P	3	1	1	2	0	3	0
S. Coscarart 1B[a]	2	0	0	0	2	0	0
Caster P	2	1	1	3	1	0	0
	41	13	15	12	27	10	2

(a) Ran for Sweeney in the fourth.

Seattle	AB	R	H	RBI	O	A	E
Donovan RF	5	0	0	0	1	0	0
Shevlin 1B	3	1	0	0	15	0	0
Bassler C	1	0	0	0	2	0	0
Hunt LF	4	1	2	2	0	0	0
Muller 2B	1	0	0	0	1	1	0
Lawrence CF	2	0	1	0	2	0	1
Gyselman 3B	4	0	1	0	2	3	0
Smith SS	4	0	0	0	2	5	1
Lucas P	1	0	1	0	0	2	0
Wells P[a]	1	0	0	0	0	0	0
Duggan C	3	1	1	0	2	0	0
Michael 2B[b]	2	0	1	0	0	3	1
Bonetti CF[c]	2	0	1	0	0	0	0
Osborn P	1	0	0	0	0	0	0
Spindel[d]	1	0	0	0	0	0	0
Koupal P	0	0	0	0	0	1	0
Barrett P	0	0	0	0	0	1	0
	35	3	8	2	27	16	3

(a) *Batted for Lucas in the fourth.*
(b) *Batted for Muller in the fifth.*
(c) *Batted for Lawrence in the fifth.*
(d) *Batted for Osborn in the eighth.*

Winning Pitcher: Caster; Losing Pitcher: Lucas. Struck out by: Lucas 2, Wells 1, Caster 3, Osborn 1. Bases on Balls: French 4, Lucas 2, Wells 1, Caster 1, Osborn 1. Left on Base: Portland 7, Seattle 10. Home runs: Hunt, Caster. Two Base Hits: Hunt, Frederick. Sacrifice: P. Coscarart. Double Plays: Liska to Brucker to Sweeney; Lucas to Smith to Shevlin. Umpires: Hood, Powell, and Cole. Time: 1 hr. 55 min.

Portland	000	730	003	13 – 15 – 2
Seattle	100	020	000	3 – 8 – 3

This series ended on Friday night, September 18, preventing any weekend games which might have attracted more fans. The Beavers had almost a week to rest before the final series which began on September 24.

The San Diego–Oakland Series

San Diego had an unwarranted feeling of confidence going into this series because they had won the season series from the Oaks 17–11. This series' peculiar scheduling called for the first two games to be in Oakland and then for the teams to move to San Diego if one team won both games. But if the teams split the first two contests, the third game would also be at Oaks Park, making it difficult to sell advanced tickets for the third game.

The Padres were upset that one of their outfielders, Chuck Shiver, quit the team in a tight pennant race to take a coaching job down in Georgia, but in those depression days, job security meant a great deal. Nevertheless, Padre manager Frank Shellenback still had three good outfielders in Ted Williams, Vince DiMaggio and Cedric Durst. Because the playoffs were a new adventure and assumed to be a big draw, both clubs dropped ladies day and special passes for these games.

The Oaks had to share newspaper space with college football to a much greater extent than the Padres did because Bay Area fans were interested in the California–St. Marys and the Stanford–Santa Clara games. Even so, *The Oakland Tribune* reported that hundreds of fans were going south to see the Oaks play in San Diego and that many fans came to the depot to see the team off after the second game.

Game One.

Billy Meyer's Oaks won the opener 6–3, with Wee Willie Ludolph besting Manny Salvo. Third baseman Jimmy Hitchcock got three hits, two of them doubles, and drove in two runs for the Oaks. Centerfielder Earl Bolyard got a triple and a single and drove in a run while second baseman Dario Lodigiani got two singles. Catcher Willard Hershberger got a triple, but it did not figure in the scoring. Ted Williams homered in a losing cause, before a crowd of about 8,000.

San Diego	AB	R	H	RBI	O	A	E
Myatt SS	4	1	1	1	1	4	2
Doerr 2B	4	0	0	0	1	2	0
Williams LF	3	1	1	2	2	0	0
Holman 3B	4	0	3	0	2	2	0
Desautels C	4	0	1	0	4	1	0
Durst RF	4	0	1	0	1	0	0
DiMaggio CF	4	0	0	0	4	0	0
McDonald 1B	4	0	1	0	9	1	0
Salvo P	0	0	0	0	0	1	0
Horne P	3	1	0	0	0	1	0
Wirthman [a]	1	0	0	0	0	0	0
	35	3	8	3	24	12	2

(a) Batted for Horne in the ninth.

Oakland	AB	R	H	RBI	0	A	E
Hitchcock 3B	4	1	3	2	0	3	0
Bolyard CF	3	1	1	1	1	0	0
Glynn RF	5	0	1	1	3	0	0
Pool LF	4	0	1	1	5	0	0
Anton 1B	3	1	0	0	8	1	0
Gordon SS	4	0	0	0	1	0	1
Hershberger C	3	1	1	0	7	1	0
Lodigiani 2B	4	1	2	1	1	4	0
Ludolph P	2	1	0	0	1	1	0
Bell LF	0	0	0	0	0	0	0
	32	6	9	6	27	10	1

Losing Pitcher: Salvo. Hits off Salvo 3, Horne 6. Runs off Salvo 3, Horne 3. Bases on Balls: Salvo 2, Horne 2, Ludolph 1. Strikeouts: Horne 3, Ludolph 6. Hit by Pitcher: Hershberger by Horne. Home Run: Williams. Three Base Hits: Bolyard, Hershberger. Two Base Hits: Hitchcock 2, Glynn, McDonald, Myatt. Sacrifices: Bolyard, Hitchcock. Umpires: Snyder, Crawford And Valerio. Time: 2 hr. 20 min.

| San Diego | 000 | 000 | 030 | 3 | – | 8 | – | 2 |
| Oakland | 030 | 201 | 00x | 6 | – | 9 | – | 1 |

Game Two.

This game was controversial. The Padres and their hometown newspaper, *The San Diego Union,* were upset with umpire Sam Crawford's two calls in the seventh inning. In the top half, Vince DiMaggio was called out at the plate in a 3–3 tie trying to score from first on George McDonald's double. In the last half, shortstop Joe Gordon was called safe at the plate on pitcher Jack Tobin's fielder's choice. Crawford was dubbed, "Sleepy Sam, the Optician's Friend" by San Diego writers. Tobin, who relieved starter Jack LaRoca in that quarrelsome seventh, not only got credit for the win but drove in the winning run. Wally Hebert started and lost for San Diego, being relieved by Howard Craighead in the seventh.

San Diego	AB	R	H	RBI	O	A	E
Berkowitz SS	3	0	0	0	0	3	1
Doerr 2B	4	1	1	0	1	1	1
Williams LF	4	0	0	0	3	0	0
Holman 3B	4	1	1	1	1	0	0
Desautels C	4	1	3	1	6	0	0
Durst RF	4	0	0	0	2	0	0
DiMaggio CF	3	0	1	1	4	0	0
McDonald 1B	4	0	2	0	7	1	0
Hebert P	3	0	1	0	0	0	1
Craighead P	0	0	0	0	0	1	0
Myatt 1B[a]	0	0	0	0	0	0	0
	33	3	9	3	24	6	3

(a) *Ran for McDonald in eighth.*

Oakland	AB	R	H	RBI	O	A	E
Hitchcock 3B	5	0	1	0	1	1	0
Bolyard CF	4	1	2	0	2	2	0
Glynn RF	4	1	2	0	3	0	0
Bell LF	4	1	1	0	1	0	0
Anton 1B	4	1	2	1	8	1	1
Gordon SS	2	0	0	1	1	2	0
Hershberger C	3	0	0	1	7	2	0
Lodigiani 2B	4	0	0	0	3	6	0
LaRocca P	3	0	1	0	1	1	0
Tobin P	1	0	0	1	0	0	0
	34	4	9	4	27	15	1

Pitching Records	IP	H	R	ER	SO	BB
Hebert (L)	6+	9	3	1	3	4
Craighead	2	0	1	0	1	1
LaRocca	6.1	8	3	3	5	1
Tobin (W)	2.2	1	0	0	1	2

Wild Pitch: Hebert. Two Base Hits: Hebert, Holman, DiMaggio, Bell, Bolyard, McDonald. Sacrifices: Anton, Hershberger. Double Play: Bolyard to Anton. Umpires: Crawford, Valerio and Snyder. Time: 2hr. 15 min.

San Diego	010	002	000	3 – 9 – 2
Oakland	002	010	10x	4 – 9 – 1

Between the second and third game, two disputes broke out. The bad blood that flared up in game two caused president Tuttle to order the two teams to be in separate cars on the train to San Diego and not to mix with one another. Then Padre owner, Bill Lane, refused to allow Oakland to work out at Lane Field during the two off days before game three, which was moved back from Friday night to Saturday, September 19, to give the players an extra day of rest. Fans planning to attend Friday night were upset even though their tickets were honored on Saturday afternoon.

Game Three.

The Oaks made it three in a row with an unearned run in the ninth which broke a 4–4 tie. Oakland got three runs in the second off "Old Folks" Herman Pillette but the Padres tied it in the fourth when they knocked out starter Ken Douglas. Each team scored a run in the seventh, but an error by Joe Berkowitz, who was filling in for injured second baseman George Myatt, set up the winning run in the ninth. Dario Lodigiani was safe on that error and eventually came around to score on Earl Bolyard's infield hit. It looked as if San Diego was going to tie it in its half of the ninth when Vince DiMaggio reached third with no one out on a single and an error, but Vince was thrown out at the plate by Joe Gordon on Ray Jacobs' grounder. Both relief pitchers got the decision: Hal Haid in relief of Douglas, and Howard Craighead, who followed Pillette.

Oakland	AB	R	H	RBI	O	A	E
Hitchcock 3B	5	0	3	2	1	2	1
Bolyard CF	5	0	1	2	1	0	0
Glynn RF	5	0	1	0	4	0	0
Pool LF	4	0	1	0	2	0	0

Oakland	AB	R	H	RBI	O	A	E
Anton 1B	2	1	1	0	10	1	0
Gordon SS	4	1	1	0	0	5	0
Hershberger C	4	0	1	0	5	2	0
Lodigiani 2B	4	3	1	1	4	4	0
Douglas P	1	0	0	0	0	0	0
Haid P	0	0	0	0	0	3	0
Bell LF	0	0	0	0	0	0	1
	34	5	10	5	27	17	2

San Diego	AB	R	H	RBI	O	A	E
Berkowitz SS	4	1	2	0	3	3	1
Doerr 2B	4	1	1	0	3	2	0
Durst RF	4	1	1	1	1	0	0
Holman 3B	4	0	2	1	1	1	0
Desautels C	4	0	1	1	5	2	0
DiMaggio CF	3	0	1	0	4	0	0
Williams LF	3	1	0	0	4	0	0
Jacobs 1B	3	0	0	0	6	0	0
Pillette P	2	0	0	0	0	1	1
Craighead P	0	0	0	0	0	1	0
Wirthman [a]	1	0	1	1	0	0	0
Myatt [b]	1	0	0	0	0	0	0
Mulligan [c]	0	0	0	0	0	0	0
	33	4	9	4	27	10	2

(a) Batted for Pillette in the seventh.
(b) Batted for Craighead in the ninth.
(c) Ran for Jacobs in the ninth.

Pitching Records	IP	H	R	ER	SO	BB
Douglas	3+	5	3	3	2	0
Haid (W)	6	4	1	0	1	1
Pillette	7	9	4	3	4	0
Craighead (L)	2	1	1	0	1	0

Hit by Pitcher: Douglas and Anton hit by Pillette. Left on Base: Oakland 8, San Diego 5. Two Base Hit: Lodigiani. Sacrifices: Di Maggio, Anton, Haid 2, Jacobs. Stolen Base: Holman. Double Plays: Berkowitz to Jacobs; Hershberger to Lodigiani to Anton. Umpires: Valerio, Snyder and Crawford. Time: 2 hrs.

Oakland	030	000	101	5	–	10	– 2
San Diego	000	300	100	4	–	9	– 2

Game Four.

San Diego avoided the sweep by taking the fourth game on Sunday afternoon, 7–1. Dick Ward set the Oaks down with five hits. Catcher Gene Desautels got two hits, including a triple, while Bobby Doerr got a double. The Padres racked starter Willie Ludolph for five runs in the sixth. The Oaks had their bags packed in the hotel lobby ready to take the train north after this game, but had to check back in for one more game.

Oakland	AB	R	H	RBI	O	A	E
Hitchcock 3B	4	1	1	0	1	1	0
Bolyard CF	3	0	0	0	1	0	0
Glynn RF	4	0	0	0	3	0	0
Pool LF	4	0	1	1	2	0	0
Anton 1B	4	0	1	0	7	1	0
Gordon SS	4	0	1	0	2	0	0
Hershberger C	3	0	0	0	2	1	0
Lodigiani 2B	2	0	1	0	3	2	1
Ludolph P	2	0	0	0	1	2	0
Douglas[a]	1	0	0	0	0	0	0
Olds P	0	0	0	0	0	1	0
Hartje C	1	0	0	0	2	0	0
	32	1	5	1	24	8	1

(a) Batted for Ludolph in the seventh.

San Diego	AB	R	H	RBI	O	A	E
Myatt SS	4	0	0	1	0	1	0
Doerr 2B	4	1	1	0	0	3	0
Durst RF	4	1	2	1	5	0	0
Holman 3B	2	1	1	0	1	0	0
Desautels C	4	2	2	1	6	0	0
Williams LF	2	1	0	1	1	0	0
Di Maggio CF	4	1	1	1	9	0	1
McDonald 1B	4	0	2	1	5	0	0
Ward P	4	0	2	1	0	1	0
	32	7	11	7	27	5	1

Pitching Records	IP	H	R	ER	SO	BB
Ludolph (L)	6	9	7	6	2	2
Olds	2	2	0	0	2	0
Ward	9	5	1	1	6	2

Left on Bases: Oakland 6, San Diego 6. Three Base Hit: Desautels. Two Base Hits: Doerr, Holman. Sacrifices: Myatt, Holman 2. Umpires: Snyder, Valerio, Crawford. Time: 1hr. 38 min.

Oakland	000	001	000	1	–	5	–	1
San Diego	020	005	00x	7	–	11	–	1

Game Five.

The final game of this series was played on Monday afternoon, September 21, and the Oaks eliminated the Padres with a 7–6 win. Oakland starter Jack Tobin was knocked out when the Padres got five runs in the second, but Padre starter Manny Salvo was chased in the fourth when Oakland scored three to close the gap to 6–5. In the seventh, Archie Campbell, who took the loss, gave up singles to Ray Anton and Willard Hershberger and walked Dario Lodigiani to load the bases. Dick Ward relieved but gave up the game winning single to Fern Bell, who batted for winning pitcher Pudgy Gould. Hal Haid saved the game by pitching shutout ball for Oakland the last three innings.

Oakland	AB	R	H	RBI	O	A	E
Hitchcock 3B	5	0	1	1	0	4	0
Bolyard CF	5	0	2	0	3	0	0
Glynn RF	5	0	3	1	4	0	0
Pool LF	3	0	0	0	0	0	1
Anton 1B	5	1	1	0	10	1	0
Gordon SS	5	2	2	0	1	3	1
Hershberger C	5	2	2	0	5	0	0
Lodigiani 2B	4	1	3	2	2	3	0
Tobin P	1	0	0	1	0	0	0
LaRocca P	0	0	0	0	0	0	0
Douglas[a]	1	0	1	0	0	0	0
Olds[b]	0	1	0	0	0	0	0
Gould P	1	0	0	0	0	1	0
Bell LF[c]	2	0	1	2	1	0	0
Haid P	0	0	0	0	1	0	0
	42	7	16	7	27	12	2

(a) Batted for LaRocca in the fourth.
(b) Ran for Douglas in the fourth.
(c) Batted for Gould in the seventh.

San Diego	AB	R	H	RBI	O	A	E
Berkowitz SS	5	1	2	1	2	4	0
Doerr 2B	5	0	2	1	4	2	0
Durst RF	5	0	1	0	4	0	0
Holman 3B	5	0	1	0	0	1	0
Desautels C	4	2	2	0	6	0	0
Williams LF	4	1	2	0	3	0	0
Di Maggio CF	3	1	2	1	2	1	0
McDonald 1B	4	0	1	1	6	0	0
Salvo P	2	1	1	2	0	1	0
Campbell P	1	0	0	0	0	0	0
Ward P	0	0	0	0	0	1	0
Wirthman[a]	1	0	0	0	0	0	0
Hebert P	0	0	0	0	0	0	0
	39	6	14	6	27	10	0

(a) Batted for Ward in the eighth.

Pitching Records	IP	AB	H	R	ER	SO	BB
Tobin	1.1	10	7	4	5	1	0
LaRocca	1.2	7	3	2	1	1	0
Gould (W)	3	10	1	0	0	1	0
Haid	3	12	3	0	0	1	0
Salvo	3.1	18	8	3	5	4	0
Campbell (L)	3.1	15	5	2	2	2	2
Ward	1.1	5	2	2	0	0	0
Hebert	4	1	0	0	0	0	0

Left on Base: Oakland 11, San Diego 7. Three Base Hits: Bolyard, Berkowitz. Two Base Hits: Glynn, Gordon. Sacrifice: Haid. Stolen Bases: McDonald, Doerr. Double Plays: Hitchcock to Lodigiani to Anton; Lodigiani to Gordon to Anton. Umpires: Crawford, Snyder and Valerio. Time: 2 hr. 22 min.

Oakland	020	300	200	7 – 16 – 2	
San Diego	051	000	000	6 – 14 – 0	

The Final Series: Portland vs. Oakland

League president Tuttle tried to get the Beavers to open this final series in Oakland but Portland officials correctly pointed out they had the right to open at home because they finished higher than Oakland. While overflow crowds jammed Vaughan Street Park for the three games in Portland, the Oaks were unhappy because they arrived in San Francisco at noon on Tuesday, September 22, and had to leave from Oakland on the morning of the 23rd to begin play on Thursday night the 24th. *The Portland Oregonian* gave the Beavers good coverage but their lead story was on the opening game of the college football season between top ranked Minnesota Gophers at Seattle against the Washington Huskies. The Huskies were to win the conference that season and go to the Rose Bowl.

Game One.

These clubs played very close during the regular season, with Portland winning 15 and losing 13, and this opening game reflected how even these teams had played during the year. The Oaks broke a 3–3 tie in the 10th with two runs but the Beavers came back with three to pull it out before 8,199 fans. Ken Douglas started for Oakland but was relieved in the eighth by Jack La Rocca, who took the loss. George Caster staggered through all 10 innings and came out the winner. In the 10th, right fielder Jack Glynn doubled and scored on first baseman Ray Anton's single. After Anton stole second, Willard Hershberger singled him home. But in the last of the 10th, Moose Clabaugh doubled and scored on singles by Fred Bedore and Pete Coscarart. Bedore scored on Nino Bongy's single, and after a walk to Dudley Lee to load the bases, Manager Bill Sweeney singled in Coscarart to win the game.

Oakland	AB	R	H	RBI	O	A	E
Hitchcock 3B	4	1	1	0	1	2	0
Bolyard CF	3	0	0	1	2	0	0
Glynn RF	5	2	3	0	1	0	0
Bell LF	2	0	1	2	2	1	0
Anton 1B	5	1	1	1	12	1	0
Gordon SS	5	0	2	0	3	2	0
Hershberger C	5	0	1	1	7	0	0
Lodigiani 2B	5	1	2	0	0	3	0
Douglas P	3	0	0	0	1	5	0
LaRocca P	1	0	0	0	0	1	0
	38	5	11	5	29[a]	15	0

(a) Two outs when winning run scored.

Portland	AB	R	H	RBI	O	A	E
Bongy CF	5	0	2	1	3	0	0
Lee SS	5	0	1	0	1	2	0

Portland	AB	R	H	RBI	O	A	E
Sweeney 1B	6	1	3	1	8	0	0
Frederick RF	4	1	2	0	3	0	0
Clabaugh LF	4	1	3	2	1	0	0
Brucker C	4	1	1	0	10	2	1
Bedore 3B	4	1	1	0	0	0	1
P. Coscarart 2B	5	1	3	2	4	2	1
Caster P	4	0	0	0	0	4	0
Holt[a]	1	0	0	0	0	0	0
	42	6	16	6	30	10	3

(a) Batted for Caster in the 10th.

Losing Pitcher: LaRocca. Struck out by: Caster 9, Douglas 3, LaRocca 3. Bases on Balls off: Caster 2, Douglas 2, LaRocca 2. Stolen Base: Anton. Two Base Hits: Glynn 2, Brucker Lodigiani, Frederick 2, Clabaugh 3, Sweeney. Sacrifices: Hitchcock, Bell 2, Brucker, Frederick. Double Plays: Coscarart to Brucker to Sweeney, Lee to Sweeney. Umpires: Powell and Hood. Time: 2 hr. 19 min.

Oakland	210	000	000	2	5 – 11 – 0
Portland	010	001	010	3	6 – 16 – 3

Game Two.

There was no game on Friday, September 25, because of Yom Kippur and high school football. The teams played Saturday night before a crowd of 9,238, thus avoiding a conflict with college football. Sailor Bill Posedel shut the Oaks out on five hits while his mates were pounding four Oak pitchers for 10 runs, with starter Jack Tobin taking the loss. Nino Bongy got three hits while Bill Sweeney, John Frederick and Fred Bedore got two each. It was only 2–0 until the seventh when the Beavers erupted for five runs and then added three more in the eighth.

Oakland	AB	R	H	RBI	O	A	E
Hitchcock 3B	4	0	0	0	1	2	0
Bolyard CF	3	0	0	0	1	0	0
Glynn RF	4	0	1	0	1	0	0
Pool LF	4	0	0	0	2	0	0
Anton 1B	4	0	2	0	13	0	0
Gordon SS	3	0	1	0	2	5	0
Hershberger C	2	0	0	0	2	0	0
Lodigiani 2B	2	0	0	0	1	3	0
Tobin P	2	0	0	0	0	2	0

Oakland	AB	R	H	RBI	O	A	E
Douglas[a]	1	0	0	0	0	0	0
Haid P	0	0	0	0	0	0	0
Olds P	1	0	1	0	0	0	0
Hartje C	0	0	0	0	1	0	0
	30	0	5	0	24	12	0

(a) Batted for Hershberger in the seventh.

Portland	AB	R	H	RBI	O	A	E
Bongy CF	5	3	3	0	2	0	0
Lee SS	3	2	1	0	3	1	1
Sweeney 1B	3	2	2	0	9	1	0
Frederick RF	3	1	2	3	2	0	0
Clabaugh LF	2	2	0	0	2	0	0
Brucker C	5	0	2	3	4	0	0
Bedore 3B	4	0	0	0	2	0	0
P. Coscarart 2B	3	0	0	0	2	4	1
Posedel P	4	0	1	1	1	2	0
	32	10	11	7	27	8	2

Pitching Records	IP	H	R	ER	SO	BB
Tobin (L)	6.1	8	2	5	2	3
Haid	0.1	0	3	2	1	1
Olds	1.1	3	5	3	0	2
Posedel (W)	9	5	0	0	4	1

Hit by Pitcher: Clabaugh by Haid. Two Base Hits: Brucker, Bongy, Frederick. Double Plays: Coscarart to Lee to Sweeney; Gordon to Lodigiani to Anton. Umpires: Hood and Powell.

Oakland	000	000	000	0 –	5 –	0
Portland	010	010	53x	10 –	11 –	2

Game Three.

Portland fans knew that Sunday's game would be the last one played at Vaughan Street Park in 1936 regardless of the outcome, so 12,035 spilled over to a roped off area behind third and along the fence in left and left center. They were not disappointed. Leading 6–2 going into the last of the eighth, the Beavers had an old fashioned "dish denting" party as they scored eight runs, making the game a rout. Submariner Ad Liska, known as "the Bohemian Bowler of Bill Sweeney's Bending Brigade," not only went the distance but

The 1936 Portland Beavers finished on top of the Pacific Coast League standings and won the playoffs as well. *Top Row, left to right:* "Hobo" Carson, Tom Flynn, Steve Larkin, Steve Coscarart, Earle Brucker, "Moose" Claybaugh. *Middle Row:* Doc Meikle (Trainer), Bill Posedel, Pete Coscarart, Don French, Art McDougall, Fred Bedore, Bill Radonits, Johnnie Frederick, George Caster. *Bottom Row:* Bill Cronin, Nino Bongiovanni, Eddie Taylor, Goldie Holt, Bill Sweeney (Manager), Dudley Lee, Ad Liska, Sam Samhammer.

went four for five at the plate, including two doubles. Moose Clabaugh got three doubles, John Frederick two, and Bill Sweeney one. Sweeney and Pete Coscarart each got three hits. Willie Ludolph, the starter for Oakland, took the loss.

Oakland	AB	R	H	RBI	O	A	E
Hitchcock 3B	5	1	1	0	1	4	0
Bolyard CF	5	0	2	1	1	1	0
Glynn RF	4	0	0	0	3	0	0
Bell LF	4	0	0	0	0	0	0
Anton 1B	4	0	0	0	9	2	1
Gordon SS	4	1	3	0	4	3	0
Hershberger C	3	0	0	0	3	1	0
Lodigiani 2B	3	0	0	0	1	4	0
Ludolph P	1	1	0	0	2	2	0
Pool[a]	1	0	0	0	0	0	0
Gould P	0	0	0	0	0	1	0
Olds P	0	0	0	0	0	0	0
Hartje[b]	0	0	0	0	0	0	0
	34	3	6	1	24	18	1

(a) Batted for Ludolph in the seventh.
(b) Batted for Olds in the ninth.

Portland	AB	R	H	RBI	O	A	E
Bongy CF	6	1	4	2	2	0	1
Lee SS	6	2	1	0	2	1	0
Sweeney 1B	4	2	1	0	8	0	0
Frederick RF	5	2	2	2	2	0	0
Clabaugh LF	3	2	2	2	4	0	0
Brucker C	5	2	4	4	5	1	0
Bedore 3B	2	0	1	1	0	3	0
P. Coscarart 2B	4	1	1	1	2	1	0
Liska P	5	1	4	2	0	0	0
Holt 3B	3	1	1	0	2	0	0
	43	14	21	14	27	6	1

Pitching Records	IP	H	R	ER	SO	BB
Ludolph (L)	6	12	6	5	0	3
Gould	1.2	9	8	8	0	1
Olds	0.1	0	0	0	0	0
Liska (W)	9	6	3	1	5	4

Two Base Hits: Frederick 2, Brucker, Bedore, Liska 2, Bongy 2, Gordon, Clabaugh 2, Holt. Double Play: Ludolph to Gordon to Anton. Umpires: Hood and Powell.

Oakland	002	000	001	3 – 6 – 1
Portland	023	010	08x	14 – 21 – 1

Monday was a travel day, and many Oakland fans and civic officials, encouraged by *The Oakland Tribune*, came out to meet the Oaks as they arrived at the S. P. depot on 16th Street. The paper declared that Portland had the advantage of nearly a week's rest before this series while the Oaks had to travel all the way from San Diego to play them.

Game Four.

A crowd of 5,800 saw a great pitching duel in which Jack La Rocca gave up only one unearned run in beating George Caster 2–1. The Oaks' runs came in the second when Lodigiani, La Rocca and Jimmy Hitchcock all singled to load the bases, before Jack Glynn's single scored Lodigiani and La Rocca, who showed good speed for a pitcher.

Portland	AB	R	H	RBI	O	A	E
Bongy CF	3	1	1	0	1	0	0
Lee SS	3	0	0	0	0	1	0
Sweeney 1B	4	0	0	1	8	0	0
Frederick RF	3	0	1	0	3	0	0
Clabaugh LF	4	0	0	0	0	0	0
Brucker C	4	0	0	0	10	0	0
Holt 3B	4	0	2	0	1	1	0
P. Coscarart 2B	4	0	1	0	1	2	0
Caster P	3	0	1	0	0	2	0
Bedore[a]	1	0	0	0	0	0	0
	33	1	6	1	24	6	0

(a) Batted for Caster in the ninth.

Oakland	AB	R	H	RBI	O	A	E
Hitchcock 3B	4	0	1	0	1	1	0
Bolyard CF	3	0	0	0	0	0	0
Glynn RF	4	0	1	1	2	0	0
Pool LF	3	0	0	0	2	0	0
Anton 1B	3	0	0	0	13	1	0
Gordon SS	3	0	0	0	2	1	0
Hershberger C	3	0	1	0	4	2	0
Lodigiani 2B	3	1	1	0	2	5	0
LaRocca P	3	1	1	0	1	1	0
Bell LF	0	0	0	0	0	0	0
	29	2	5	1	27	11	0

Pitching Records	IP	H	R	ER	SO	BB
Caster (L)	8	5	2	2	8	1
LaRocca (W)	9	6	1	0	4	3

Passed Ball: Hershberger. Umpires: Powell and Hood.

Portland	000	100	000	1 – 6 – 0
Oakland	002	000	00x	2 – 5 – 0

Game Five.

The fifth and final game of the 1936 season was played on Wednesday night, September 30, before only 3,000 on a cold foggy night. This game was decided quickly when the Beavers pounced on Ken Douglas for five runs in the first, knocking him out of the game. Pete Coscarart got two hits includ-

ing a triple, while Bill Sweeney, Fred Bedore and Earle Brucker got two each.
Bill Posedel sailed to an easy victory.

Portland	AB	R	H	RBI	O	A	E
Bongy CF	4	1	1	1	2	0	0
Lee SS	3	1	0	0	0	1	0
Sweeney 1B	5	1	2	0	14	1	0
Frederick RF	5	0	1	0	1	0	0
Clabaugh LF	4	2	1	1	2	0	0
Brucker C	4	1	2	1	5	0	0
Bedore 3B	4	1	2	1	1	1	0
P. Coscarart 2B	4	1	2	2	1	5	0
Posedel P	3	0	0	0	1	4	0
	36	8	11	6	27	12	0

Oakland	AB	R	H	RBI	O	A	E
Hitchcock 3B	5	0	1	1	0	1	0
Bolyard CF	5	0	1	0	1	0	0
Glynn RF	4	1	2	0	4	0	0
Pool LF	3	1	1	1	1	0	0
Anton 1B	4	0	1	1	11	1	0
Gordon SS	3	0	0	0	1	4	0
Hershberger C	3	0	0	0	4	0	0
Lodigiani 2B	4	0	0	0	4	5	1
Douglas P	0	0	0	0	0	1	0
Tobin P	31	1	0	0	1	0	0
	34	3	6	3	27	12	1

Pitching Records	IP	H	R	ER	SO	BB
Posedel	9	6	3	3	5	4
Douglas (L)	0.2	3	4	3	0	1
Tobin	7.1	8	7	3	4	1

Two Base Hits: Clabaugh, Glynn, Anton, Hitchcock. Three Base Hit:
Coscarart. Sacrifice: Lee, Posedel. Double Play: Lodigiani to Gordon to
Anton. Umpires: Hood and Powell.

Portland	501	000	002	8	– 11	– 0
Oakland	001	001	001	3	– 6	– 1

The Beavers split $5,500 — $2,500 for finishing first and $3,000 for win-
ning the playoffs — which came to about $220 a man. This would amount to

about $1,594 in current dollars, but the players also received an extra 17 days' pay. Oakland divided up $2,000, or about $80 per man, while San Diego and Seattle both divided $1,250, or $40 each. In addition to Dutch Ruether resigning at Seattle, the popular Jack Lellivelt quit at Los Angeles after failing to make the playoffs.

Key Players on the 1936 Playoff Teams

Portland. *Pitchers:* George Caster, Ad Liska, and Bill Posedel.
Position Players: Moose Clabaugh, Bill Sweeney, John Frederick, Fred Bedore, Earle Brucker, and Anthony Bongiovanni (Nino Bongy).

Oakland. *Pitchers:* Ken Douglas, Willie Ludolph, Jack Tobin and Jack La Rocca.
Position Players: Jack Glynn, Joe Gordon, Fern Bell, Jimmy Hitchcock and Earl Boylard.

Seattle. *Pitchers:* Dick Barrett, Lou Koupal, Ray Lucas and Paul Gregory.
Position Players: Mike Hunt, Johnny Bassler, Dick Gyselman and Bill Lawrence.

San Diego. *Pitchers:* Wally Hebert, Manny Salvo, Dick Ward, and Howard Craighead.
Position Players: Bobby Doerr, Ted Williams, George McDonald, Gene Desautels, Ernie Holman and Vince DiMaggio.

1937

The same rules and prize money applied in 1937 as in 1936 but this time third place San Diego won the playoffs and was awarded the pennant, much to the annoyance of the fans in Sacramento, whose team finished on top for the first time. New rules were to apply after this year.

Three teams — the Sacramento Solons, the San Francisco Seals and the San Diego Padres — battled for first place most of the season, while being certain of playoff spots. San Diego led as late as September 2, but the Solons went on a very successful road trip and pulled away, winning by four games over the Seals. San Francisco won eight in a row the last week to overtake the Padres, but *The San Francisco Chronicle* correctly pointed out that it was immaterial if a team finished second, third or fourth.

The real battle was for fourth place between Portland and the Los Angeles Angels. On September 1, the Angels were 80 and 74 while Portland was 76 and 76, but in the last 24 games, the Angels went 10 and 14 while the Beavers went 14 and 10. Each team ended with 90 wins but Portland had two fewer losses and the Pacific Coast League did not require teams to make up rained out games. In 1905, 1911 and 1914, the second place team had more wins than the team finishing first, and in 1912 the top two teams had the same number of losses. In some future years, some fourth place teams made the playoffs by finishing only half a game ahead of the fifth place club.

Losing out on the playoffs was especially disappointing to the Angels because 1936 and 1937 were the only two seasons from 1909 through 1957 that they did not have to share their city with another team. They either had the Vernon or Venice Tigers, and then first or second Hollywood Stars to compete with for fans, except for those two years, and they were unable to capitalize on this situation.

The Sacramento–San Diego Series

The first place Solons exercised their right to open at home, but attendance on Tuesday, Wednesday and Thursday nights, September 21–23, was disappointing, especially after their fine season that saw an increase of over 100,000 from 1936, when they had finished last. The playoffs did come on a school night but *The Sacramento Bee's* editorial did not help in which it argued that the Solons could be cheated out of their first pennant by a system designed to make money for hockey. Ironically, if this system had remained in effect for two more years, the Solons would have won two pennants!

The Solons and Padres had battled on fairly even grounds during the season, with the Solons winning 13 and losing 12. The Padres had to play without injured second baseman Jimmy Reese, who was replaced by Joe Berkowitz.

Game One.

The Padres won the opener 6–4, as Jim Chaplin outpitched Tony Freitas before 4,902 fans. San Diego's big inning was the third when they got three runs on four straight hits, by Hal Padgett, George Detore, Ted Williams and Joe Berkowitz. All were doubles except for Williams' single, but Ted went four for five, including a triple and a double. Chaplin snuffed out a Solon rally in the eighth by striking out shortstop Johnny Vergez with the bases loaded.

San Diego	AB	R	H	RBI	O	A	E
Myatt SS	5	1	1	0	1	3	1
Thompson RF	4	0	1	1	4	1	0
Patchett CF	4	1	2	1	2	0	0
Detore C	5	1	1	1	9	0	0
T. Williams LF	5	2	4	0	2	0	0
Berkowitz 2B	4	0	1	1	1	0	0
McDonald 1B	4	0	2	1	7	0	0
Holman 3B	4	1	2	0	1	2	1
Chaplin P	3	0	1	0	0	2	0
	38	6	15	5	27	8	2

Sacramento	AB	R	H	RBI	O	A	E
Vergez SS	5	2	2	0	1	2	0
Adams CF	5	1	3	1	5	0	0
Vezilich LF	5	0	1	1	1	0	0
Garibaldi 3B	5	0	1	1	0	2	0

Sacramento	AB	R	H	RBI	O	A	E
Cullop RF	3	1	0	0	1	0	1
Orengo 2B	2	0	0	0	2	6	1
Prout 1B	4	0	0	0	11	2	0
Franks C	4	0	2	0	5	1	0
Freitas P	2	0	0	0	0	0	0
Schmidt P	1	0	0	0	0	1	0
Pippen P	0	0	0	0	1	2	0
D.Williams[a]	1	0	0	1	0	0	0
Newsome[b]	0	0	0	0	0	0	0
	37	4	9	4	27	16	2

(a) *Batted for Schmidt in the eighth.*
(b) *Ran for D. Williams in the eighth.*

Pitching Records	H	R	ER	SO	BB
Chaplin	9	4	3	8	3
Freitas (L)	13	6	5	3	0
Schmidt	1	0	0	1	0
Pippen	1	0	0	0	2

Three Base Hits: Adams, T. Williams. Two Base Hits: Vezelich, Patchett, Detore, Berkowitz, T. Williams, Vergez. Sacrifice: Chaplin. Stolen Bases: Myatt 2, Adams. Double Play: Vergez to Orengo to Prout. Time of Game: 2 hr. Umpires: Hood, Crawford, Engeln.

San Diego	013	110	000	6	– 15 –	2
Sacramento	200	010	010	4	– 9 –	2

Game Two.

Manny Salvo limited Sacramento to just one run on four hits and received all the support he would need in the top of the first when the Padres got two runs off Tommy Seats. George Detore's double scored Rupert Thompson, who had singled. Joe Berkowitz then singled in the Padre catcher for what became the game winner. Art Garibaldi's double plated the Solons' only run in the third.

There were only 2,260 fans there on Wednesday night, and considering what happened, it was a good thing more were not present. In the eighth, the Padres had two men on with two out when George McDonald grounded to first and Bill Prout had ample time to step on the bag, but umpire Bill Engeln ruled he missed it. As Prout and Seats argued strenuously, George Detore and Ted Williams both came around to score. Over 50 fans from the stands poured out onto the field and began throwing bottles and threatening the umpire. The police had to restore order while Seats and Prout were ejected.

San Diego	AB	R	H	RBI	O	A	E
Patchett CF	5	0	1	0	2	0	0
Thompson RF	3	1	2	0	1	0	0
Detore C	4	2	3	1	8	0	0
T. Williams LF	3	1	0	0	0	0	0
Berkowitz 2B	4	0	1	0	6	6	1
McDonald 1B	4	0	0	2	8	0	0
Holman 3B	4	0	0	0	1	0	0
Skelley SS	4	0	0	0	1	5	0
Salvo P	4	0	0	0	0	3	0
	35	4	7	3	27	14	1

Sacramento	AB	R	H	RBI	O	A	E
Vergez SS	5	1	0	0	3	0	0
Adams CF	4	0	0	0	0	0	0
Vezilich LF	3	0	0	0	1	0	0
Garibaldi 3B	4	0	2	1	2	2	0
Cullop RF	3	0	0	0	2	0	0
D.Williams 2B	3	0	0	0	1	3	0
Prout 1B	2	0	0	0	8	1	1
Franks C	3	0	2	0	8	0	1
Seats P	2	0	0	0	1	2	0
Klinger P	0	0	0	0	0	1	0
Cooper[a]	1	0	0	0	0	0	0
Orengo 1B	1	0	0	0	1	0	0
	31	1	4	1	27	9	2

(a) Batted for Klinger in the ninth.

Pitching Records	IP	H	R	ER	SO	BB
Salvo	9	4	1	1	8	7
Seats (L)	7.2	7	4	2	5	1
Klinger	1.1	0	0	0	1	0

Hit by Pitcher: T. Williams by Seats. Wild Pitches: Salvo, Seats. Left on Base: San Diego 6, Sacramento 10. Two Base Hits: Detore, Patchett, Garibaldi. Stolen Base: Garibaldi. Time of Game: 2hr. 19 min. Umpires: Crawford, Hood and Engeln.

San Diego	200	000	020	4 − 7 − 1
Sacramento	001	000	000	1 − 4 − 2

Before the third game was played, *The Sacramento Bee* announced that Sacramento fans could keep up with the play-by-play wire reports of the Solons and Padres from San Diego when the series shifted there for the fourth game by coming to a free baseball party at the city's auditorium. Bill Lane, Padre owner, was the only team owner who would not allow radio broadcasts or direct wire reports of games from Lane Field, but he relented for this playoff, but only for Sacramento, and not San Diego fans. Lane feared that radio kept fans from attending games, rather than enhancing fan interest.

Game Three.

Only 2,683 fans turned out on Thursday night, September 23, to see the last game played at Cardinal Field in 1937 when Dick Ward limited the Solons to just one run as the Padres took a 3–0 lead in the series with a 6–1 win. The Padre hero was Bill Skelly, who was filling in for the injured George Myatt at short. Since Myatt was the normal leadoff man, Manager Frank Shelleback had to juggle his lineup, putting Hal Padgett first and Skelly in the eighth spot. Skelly drove in the first run in the second and another in the fourth with singles. Rupert Thompson hit a two run homer off loser Dick Newsome.

San Diego	AB	R	H	RBI	O	A	E
Patchett CF	5	1	1	0	0	0	0
Thompson RF	4	1	2	2	1	0	0
T. Williams LF	5	0	0	0	0	0	0
Detore C	5	1	1	0	8	0	0
McDonald 1B	5	1	3	0	7	1	0
Berkowitz 2B	4	0	3	0	8	1	1
Holman 3B	3	1	0	0	2	5	0
Skelley SS	4	1	2	2	1	6	1
Ward P	4	0	3	1	0	0	1
	39	6	15	5	27	13	3

Sacramento	AB	R	H	RBI	O	A	E
Vergez SS	4	0	0	0	0	5	1
Adams CF	5	0	1	0	2	0	0
Vezilich LF	5	1	2	0	1	0	0
Zambach 3B	5	0	1	0	3	1	0
Cullop RF	4	0	1	0	0	1	0
D. Williams 2B	4	0	2	1	5	3	2
Prout 1B	4	0	1	0	11	0	0
Franks C	2	0	0	0	5	1	0
Newsome P	0	0	0	0	0	1	0
Stout P	2	0	0	0	0	2	0

Sacramento	AB	R	H	RBI	O	A	E
Orengo[a]	1	0	0	0	0	0	0
Klinger P	0	0	0	0	0	0	0
	36	1	8	1	27	14	3

(a) Batted for Stout in the eighth.

Pitching Records	IP	H	R	ER	SO	BB
Ward	9	8	1	0	7	5
Newsome (L)	3.1	8	6	6	1	0
Stout	4.2	6	0	0	4	1
Klinger	1	1	0	0	0	0

Wild Pitch: Stout. Passed Ball: Detore. Left on Base: San Diego 8; Sacramento 13. Home Run: Thompson. Two Base Hit: Vezilich. Double Plays: Holman to Berkowitz; Vergez to D. Williams to Prout. Time: 2hr. 25 min. Umpires: Engeln, Hood and Crawford.

San Diego	012	300	000	6 – 15 – 3
Sacramento	000	010	000	1 – 8 – 3

Game Four.

The teams took Friday off and resumed the series Saturday night, September 25, at Lane Field. About 7,000 fans saw a great pitching duel between Tony Freitas and Jim Chaplin. Ted Williams' fourth inning homer was the only run of the game until the top of the ninth when the Solons, facing elimination, tied the game on a double by Art Garibaldi and a single by Nick Cullop. But in the last of the 10th, Freitas' throwing error led to his downfall. The Portuguese southpaw fielded Bill Skelly's bunt and threw it into center field trying to get the runner at second. Hal Padgett later singled in the winning run, ruining the baseball party at the Sacramento auditorium.

Sacramento	AB	R	H	RBI	O	A	E
Vergez SS	5	0	1	0	2	2	0
Adams CF	5	0	1	0	3	0	0
Vezilich LF	5	0	1	0	1	0	0
Garibaldi 3B	4	1	2	0	1	2	0
Cullop RF	4	0	1	1	0	0	0
D. Williams 2B	4	0	0	0	2	4	0
Prout 1B	4	0	1	0	12	1	0
Franks C	4	0	0	0	7	1	0
Freitas P	3	0	1	0	1	1	2
	38	1	8	1	29*	11	2

*Two out when winning run scored.

San Diego	AB	R	H	RBI	O	A	E
Patchett CF	5	0	2	1	4	0	0
Thompson RF	4	0	1	0	4	0	0
Detore C	4	0	0	0	4	1	0
T. Williams LF	4	1	2	1	3	0	0
Berkowitz 2B	3	0	1	0	5	2	0
McDonald 1B	4	0	0	0	6	2	0
Holman 3B	4	0	1	0	2	2	0
Skelley SS	4	1	1	0	1	2	1
Chaplin P	4	0	0	0	1	2	0
	36	2	8	2	30	11	1

Pitching Records	IP	H	R	ER	SO	BB
Freitas	9.2	8	2	1	6	0
Chaplin	10	1	8	1	4	1

Passed Ball: Detore. Left on Base: Sacramento 8; San Diego 5. Home Run: T. Williams. Two Base Hits: Patchett, Garibaldi. Sacrifices: Berkowitz, Skelley. Stolen Base: Prout. Double Play: Vergezto D. Williams to Prout. Time: 2hr. 06 min. Umpires: Hood, Crawford and Engeln.

Sacramento	000	000	001	0	1 – 8 – 2
San Diego	000	100	000	1	2 – 8 – 1

The Portland–San Francisco Series

The Seals were disappointed that Portland edged the Angels for fourth place owing to the higher travel costs and because the Beavers played the Seals even in 24 games while the Seals won 16 of 24 from Los Angeles. Back in July when Portland won seven of eight from San Francisco, Manager Bill Sweeney said the Seals did not belong in the first division, but the Seals ended up seven games ahead of Portland.

The Seals also did not allow any passes or ladies day specials for the playoffs, but the three games in Seals Stadium were not well attended. The Seals had direct competition from college football, which was receiving a lot of media attention. California, which would go on to win the conference in 1937 and also the Rose Bowl, opened its season with St. Mary's, while Stanford was playing Santa Clara. In addition, the public was distracted by the move of the Mission Reds to Hollywood for the 1938 season.

Game One.

Portland's Bill Thomas beat Sad Sam Gibson 5–1 in the opener on Tuesday night, September 21. The Beavers broke a 1–1 tie with four runs in the eighth. An error by Harley Boss put two men on base before Pete Coscarart singled in one run, Nino Bongy doubled in another, and John Frederick tripled in the final two runs. The Seals had to use pitcher Gene Lillard at third base because Frank Hawkins was injured.

Portland	AB	H	RBI	O	A	E
Lee SS	5	0	0	5	1	0
P. Coscarart 2B	4	1	1	4	2	0
Bongy CF	4	2	1	2	0	0
Frederick 1B	4	1	2	7	1	0
Clabaugh LF	3	0	0	1	0	0
Bedore 3B	4	1	1	3	3	0
Tresh RF	4	1	0	1	0	0
Cronin C	4	2	0	3	1	0
Thomas P	4	1	0	1	1	0
	36	9	5	27	9	0

San Francisco	AB	H	RBI	O	A	E
Di Maggio CF	3	0	0	3	1	0
Holder RF	4	1	0	3	0	0
Jennings SS	4	0	0	0	0	0
Boss 1B	4	2	0	8	2	0
Norbert LF	4	0	0	1	0	0
Lillard 3B	3	0	0	2	1	0
Wright 2B	3	1	1	1	3	0
Monzo C	3	1	0	7	1	0
Gibson P	3	1	0	2	2	0
	31	6	1	27	10	0

Pitching Records	IP	H	R	ER	SO	BB
Thomas	9	5	1	1	3	1
Gibson	9	9	5	5	6	0

Stolen Base: Clabaugh. Three Base Hit: Frederick. Two Base Hits: Boss, Bongy. Double Play: Di Maggio to Monzo to Lillard. Time of Game: 1 hr. 43 min. Umpires: Snyder, Fanning and Cole.

Portland	000	000	140	5 – 9 – 0
San Francisco	000	010	000	1 – 5 – 0

Game Two.

This game, played on Wednesday afternoon, was one the Seals would like to forget. Portland pounded out 17 hits in a lopsided 13–3 win. Bill Radonits coasted on the mound while getting a three run double. Nino Bongy got four hits while Pete Coscarart and Fred Bedore got three each. Starter Bill Shores did not make it out of the third inning; things got so bad that Manager Lefty O'Doul grabbed a mitt in the eighth inning and took the mound without even warming up.

Portland	AB	R	H	RBI	O	A	E
Lee SS	5	2	1	0	1	3	1
P. Coscarart 2B	6	2	3	4	4	2	0
Bongy CF	4	0	4	1	7	0	0
Frederick 1B	5	0	1	0	7	0	0
Clabaugh LF	4	1	1	0	2	0	0
Bedore 3B	5	2	3	0	2	2	0
Tresh RF	3	3	1	2	1	0	0
Cronin C	3	2	2	0	3	0	0
Radonits P	3	1	1	3	0	1	0
	38	13	17	10	27	8	1

San Francisco	AB	R	H	RBI	O	A	E
Di Maggio CF	3	0	0	0	2	1	0
Holder RF	4	0	1	0	1	1	0
Jennings SS	4	1	1	0	1	3	0
Boss 1B	4	0	0	0	9	3	1
Norbert LF	3	1	1	0	3	0	0
Lillard 3B	4	0	0	1	2	2	0
Wright 2B	4	0	1	1	5	4	0
Woodall C	4	0	1	0	3	2	0
Shores P	0	0	0	0	0	0	0
Lamanske P	2	1	1	0	0	1	0
Cole P	1	0	0	0	0	0	0
O'Doul P	1	0	0	0	1	1	0
	34	3	6	2	27	18	1

Pitching Records	IP	H	R	ER	SO	BB
Radonits	9	6	3	3	3	1
Shores (L)	2.2	6	6	6	1	4
Lamanske	2.1	6	4	5	0	3

Pitching Records	IP	H	R	ER	SO	BB
Cole	2.2	3	2	2	1	4
O'Doul	1.1	2	1	0	0	0

Hit by Pitcher: Norbert. Wild Pitch: Lamanske. Passed Ball: Woodall. Stolen Base: Clabaugh. Home Run: Hawkins. Three Base Hit: P. Coscarart. Two Base Hits: Bongy, Radonits, Bedore 2, Norbert, Wright, Clabaugh. Sacrifices: Cronin, Clabaugh. Caught Stealing: Jennings, Frederick 2, Lee. Double Plays: Wright to Jennings to Boss; Woodall to Lillard. Time of Game: 1 hr. 58 min. Umpires: Fanning, Cole, and Snyder.

Portland	042	122	020	13 – 17 – 1
San Francisco	000	210	000	3 – 6 – 1

Game Three.

The last game at Seals Stadium in 1937 on Thursday night, September 23, saw the Beavers edge the Seals 9–8, in a sloppy game marred by five errors and ten walks. Seals starter Old Pard Win Ballou was wild, walking in a run, but his reliever, Ed Stutz, not only duplicated that feat but also hit a man with the bases loaded. Stutz got the loss, while Sailor Bill Posedel started and was the winner, even though Ad Liska had to relieve him. After Portland broke a 5–5 tie with four runs in the seventh, the Seals came back with three runs in their half, aided by catcher Mike Tresh dropping a fly in right field. Tresh was out there because Manager Bill Sweeney was hurt, necessitating John Frederick to move to first base. Fred Bedore got two hits and drove in four runs, while Frederick got three hits and drove in two runs.

Portland	AB	R	H	RBI	O	A	E
Lee SS	3	0	0	1	2	1	1
P. Coscarart 2B	4	3	1	0	1	4	0
Bongy CF	5	2	2	0	5	0	0
Frederick RF	5	1	3	2	8	0	0
Clabaugh LF	3	0	1	0	2	0	0
Bedore 3B	4	2	2	4	2	1	1
Tresh RF	5	1	1	1	3	1	1
Cronin C	4	0	0	0	4	0	0
Posedel P	3	0	0	1	0	1	0
Liska P	1	0	0	0	0	1	0
	37	9	10	9	27	9	3

San Francisco	AB	R	H	RBI	O	A	E
Di Maggio CF	5	1	2	0	1	0	1
Holder RF	4	3	1	0	2	0	0

San Francisco	AB	R	H	RBI	O	A	E
Jennings SS	4	2	2	1	1	2	0
Boss 1B	5	1	1	2	7	1	0
Norbert LF	5	0	1	1	4	0	0
Hawkins 3B-2B	5	1	2	1	5	3	1
Wright 2B	2	0	0	0	1	2	0
Woodall C	3	0	0	0	3	1	0
Ballou P	1	0	0	0	0	1	0
Stutz P	1	0	0	0	1	0	0
Gill [a]	0	0	0	0	0	0	0
O'Doul [b]	1	0	0	0	0	0	0
Sheehan P	1	0	0	0	0	0	0
Longacre 3B	0	0	0	0	0	0	0
Monzo C	0	0	0	0	2	0	0
Lillard P	1	0	0	0	0	0	0
	38	8	9	5	27	10	2

(a) Batted for Wright in the seventh.
(b) Batted for Woodall in the seventh.

Pitching Records	IP	H	R	ER	SO	BB
Posedel (W)	6.2	8	8	4	2	3
Liska	2.1	1	0	0	1	0
Ballou	4.2	6	5	5	2	4
Stutz (L)	2.0	3	4	4	0	3
Sheehan	1.1	1	0	0	1	0
Lillard	1.0	0	0	0	2	0

Home Run: Hawkins. Three Base Hit: Jennings. Two Base Hit: Tresh. Hit by Pitcher: Lee by Stutz. Double Play: Jennings to Boss. Time of Game: 2hr. 21 min. Umpires: Cole, Snyder and Fanning.

Portland	000	320	400	9 – 10 – 3
San Francisco	000	311	300	8 – 9 – 2

Friday was a travel day, and *The San Francisco Chronicle* reported that in the Seals' rail car the talk was more of the current college football season than of baseball. The Seals got off the train at 3:30 P.M. Saturday, and by 11 P.M. that night they were out of the playoffs. Portland had planned to play only one game on Sunday, if needed, instead of the usual doubleheader, but that point became moot. While the fourth game did not conflict with college football, the Beavers did have to share headlines with Oregon's loss on Friday night to UCLA in Los Angeles.

Game Four.

A crowd of 8,000 turned out at Vaughan Street Park on Saturday night, the 25th, to see the Beavers sweep the Seals with an 8–5 win. *The San Francisco Chronicle* said that more people saw this game than all three at Seals Stadium. The Seals chased starter Bill Thomas with four runs in the first on homers by Harley Boss and Ted Norbert. Reliever Joe Hare was the key for Portland, allowing only one run and one hit, while striking out seven until he had to come out in the seventh when he hurt his ankle. Bill Radonits finished up. Sad Sam Gibson could not hold that 4–0 lead, giving up two runs in the first, three more in the third, before being knocked out in the sixth, when Portland scored its final three runs. Dudley Lee, Nino Bongy and Pete Coscarart each got two hits.

San Francisco	AB	R	H	RBI	O	A	E
Di Maggio CF	5	0	0	0	8	0	0
Holder RF	4	1	3	0	1	1	0
Jennings SS	4	1	1	0	0	0	2
Boss 1B	4	1	1	3	7	0	0
Norbert LF	4	1	2	1	2	0	0
Hawkins 3B	4	0	0	0	1	2	1
Wright 2B	4	0	0	0	1	3	0
Monzo C	4	1	2	0	4	0	0
Gibson P	3	0	2	1	0	1	0
Lamanske P	0	0	0	0	0	0	0
O'Doul[a]	1	0	0	0	0	0	0
	37	5	11	5	24	7	3

(a) *Batted for Lamanske in the ninth.*

Portland	AB	R	H	RBI	O	A	E
Lee SS	5	1	2	0	0	3	0
P. Coscarart 2B	4	3	2	2	3	3	0
Bongy CF	5	1	2	1	2	0	0
Frederick 1B	3	1	1	1	12	0	0
Clabaugh LF	3	1	1	1	0	0	1
Bedore 3B	4	0	1	0	0	5	0
Tresh RF	3	1	1	0	2	0	0
Cronin C	3	0	0	0	8	0	0
Thomas P	0	0	0	0	0	0	0
Hare P	3	0	0	0	0	0	0
Radonits P	1	0	0	0	0	1	0
	34	8	10	5	27	12	1

Pitching Records	IP	H	R	ER	SO	BB
Gibson (L)	5.2	9	7	5	3	1
Lamanske P	2.1	1	1	0	1	2
Thomas	0.1	3	4	4	0	1
Hare (W)	5.2	7	1	1	7	1
Radonits	3	1	0	0	2	1

Home Runs: Boss, Norbert. Two Base Hits: Frederick, Clabaugh, Monzo, Holder, P. Coscarart. Sacrifice: Cronin. Double Play: Bedore to P. Coscarart to Frederick. Hit Batesman: Gibson 1. Time of Game: 2hr. 05 min. Umpires: Snyder, Cole and Fanning.

San Francisco	400	100	000	5 – 11 – 3
Portland	203	003	00x	8 – 10 – 1

This was the last playoff series Portland ever won. It would be six years before they would qualify for postseason play again, and each time thereafter, they would lose in the first round. On a favorable note, *The San Francisco Chronicle* pointed out the honesty of baseball when the lack of a Sunday game in San Diego and in Portland cost all four teams about $3,000 each. The Seals barely made expenses going to Portland for one game, and had to stay in a hotel Saturday night before taking the train home, arriving in Oakland on Monday. But the sweep allowed the Seals' Dominic DiMaggio to travel to New York to see brother Joe in the World Series. Until then, Dominic had never been East.

The Final Series: San Diego vs. Portland

The 1937 season was the first of three straight years that the final round of the playoffs would be contested between teams finishing third and fourth. This series began with a controversy because Portland wanted to start it at home, claiming cold and wet weather would be more likely the longer the teams waited to play there. But the third place Padres exercised their right to open at home so the Beavers left on the Sunday night train and did not arrive in San Diego until 12:35 P.M., Tuesday, just an hour and 40 minutes before game time. Manager Bill Sweeney wired Padre management to delay the start until at least 3 P.M., or even to play it at night, but San Diego insisted on keeping the 2:15 P.M. start.

Game One.

A crowd of 3,500 cheered their hero Rupert Thompson as his two homers drove in all four Padre runs in this 10 inning, 4–3 victory. With the Beavers up 1–0 in the third, Thompson socked a three-run homer off Ad Liska after Fred Bedore messed up a double play ball that would have ended the inning. Portland nicked Wally Hebert for single runs in the seventh and eighth innings to tie the game, but in the last of the tenth, Rupert Thompson blasted one of reliever Bill Thomas' pitches over the right field wall to win the game.

Portland	AB	R	H	RBI	O	A	E
Lee SS	2	0	1	0	1	1	0
P. Coscarart 2B	5	0	1	1	2	5	0
Bongy CF	5	1	1	0	2	0	0
Frederick 1B	5	0	1	0	6	1	0
Clabaugh RF	4	1	1	1	1	0	0
Bedore 3B	4	0	1	0	2	2	1
Tresh LF	2	0	0	0	4	0	0
Cronin C	4	0	0	1	9	1	0
Liska P	?	1	1	0	0	1	0
Sweeney[a]	0	0	0	0	0	0	0
Moncrief[b]	0	0	0	0	0	0	0
Montague SS	2	0	0	0	0	0	0
Thomas P	1	0	0	0	1	0	0
	36	3	7	3	28[c]	11	1

(a) *Batted for Liska in the seventh.*
(b) *Ran for Sweeney in the seventh.*
(c) *One out when winning run scored.*

San Diego	AB	R	H	RBI	O	A	E
Myatt SS	5	1	1	0	0	8	2
Thompson RF	3	2	2	4	3	0	0
Patchett CF	2	0	0	0	2	0	0
Williams LF	4	0	0	0	3	0	0
McDonald 1B	4	0	0	0	18	0	0
Berkowitz 2B	4	0	0	0	4	5	1
Holman 3B	2	0	0	0	0	4	0
Starr C	4	0	1	0	0	0	0
Hebert P	4	1	0	0	0	2	0
	32	4	4	4	30	19	3

Pitching Records	IP	H	R	ER	SO	BB
Liska	6	2	3	2	4	5
Thomas (L)	3.1	2	1	1	3	1
Hebert	10	7	3	1	0	0

Left on Base: Portland 7, San Diego 6. Home Runs: Thompson 2. Hit by Pitcher: Holman by Liska. Sacrifice: Tresh. Double Play: Myatt to Berkowitz to McDonald. Time of Game: 1 hr. 48 min. Umpires: Snyder, Hood, Fanning, Engeln.

Portland	001	000	110	0	3 – 7 – 1
San Diego	003	000	000	1	4 – 4 – 3

Game Two.

On Wednesday afternoon, September 29, Dick Ward hurled a three hitter and drove in the Padres' first run in a 3–1 victory. Moose Clabaugh's second inning homer was Portland's only run. Ted Williams got three hits and drove in a run for the Padres. Bill Posedel was the loser for Portland. Manager Bill Sweeney's bad leg did not prevent him from beating out an infield hit as a pinch hitter in the eighth, but Ward was able to get Pete Coscarart to bounce out with the bases loaded that inning to end Portland's major threat.

Portland	AB	R	H	RBI	O	A	E
Lee SS	3	0	0	0	5	4	0
P. Coscarart 2B	4	0	0	0	3	4	0
Bongy CF	4	0	0	0	1	0	0
Frederick 1B	4	0	0	0	7	0	1
Clabaugh RF	4	1	1	1	1	1	0
Bedore 3B	3	0	1	0	2	0	0
Tresh LF	3	0	0	0	3	0	0
Cronin C	3	0	1	0	2	1	1
Posedel P	1	0	1	0	0	1	0
Sweeney[a]	1	0	0	0	0	0	0
Thomas[b]	0	0	0	0	0	0	0
Carson P	0	0	0	0	0	0	0
	30	1	4	1	24	11	2

(a) Batted for Posedel in the eighth.
(b) Ran for Sweeney in the eighth.

San Diego	AB	R	H	RBI	O	A	E
Myatt SS	4	0	1	0	0	0	0
Thompson RF	4	0	0	0	1	0	0
Patchett CF	3	1	1	0	3	0	0
Williams LF	4	0	3	1	4	0	0
Detore C	3	0	0	0	6	0	0
McDonald 1B	3	0	0	0	11	2	0

San Diego	AB	R	H	RBI	O	A	E
Berkowitz 2B	3	0	0	0	1	3	0
Holman 3B	3	1	2	0	0	3	0
Ward P	4	1	1	1	1	3	0
	31	3	8	2	27	11	0

Pitching Records	IP	H	R	ER	SO	BB
Posedel	7	7	3	2	1	4
Carson	1	1	0	0	0	1
Ward	9	4	1	1	5	1

Hit by Pitcher: Thompson by Posedel. Left on Base: Portland 4, San Diego 11. Home Run: Clabaugh. Two Base Hit: Holman. Sacrifices: Posedel, Berkowitz. Stolen Bases: Myatt, Patchett. Time of Game: 1 hr. 42min. Umpires: Snyder, Engeln, Hood and Fanning.

Portland	010	000	000	1 – 4 – 1	
San Diego	002	010	00x	3 – 8 – 0	

Game Three.

A crowd of 9,000 turned out on Thursday night, September 30, knowing this would be the last game played at Lane Field in 1937. They were not disappointed. Rupert Thompson hit another crucial homer that wrecked the Beavers. But it was poor Portland's fielding in the second that gave Thompson his chance to be a hero. George McDonald was safe when Dudley Lee misplayed his grounder, but it was ruled a hit. Then Joe Berkowitz's hit also grounded to Lee, who again bobbled it, for an error. This might have been a double play. Fred Bedore then threw wildly on Ernie Holman's bunt, filling the bases. George Myatt's fielder's choice scored one run, and then Thompson hit a three-run shot, putting the Padres up 4–1. Manny Salvo allowed 12 hits but only one run, while going three for four at the plate. Bill Radonits pitched all eight innings for Portland. The Beavers' one chance came in the seventh when Moose Clabaugh lined into an inning-ending double play with the bases loaded.

Portland	AB	H	RBI	O	A	E
Lee SS	5	1	0	0	3	1
P. Coscarart 2B	5	2	0	2	2	0
Bongy CF	5	1	0	5	0	0
Frederick 1B	4	2	0	7	2	0
Clabaugh LF	4	0	0	1	0	0
Bedore 3B	4	2	0	0	0	1

Portland	AB	H	RBI	O	A	E
Tresh RF	3	1	1	2	0	0
Cronin C	4	1	0	5	0	0
Radonits P	3	1	0	2	2	0
Sweeney[a]	1	1	0	0	0	0
Moncrief[b]	0	0	0	0	0	0
	38	12	1	24	9	2

(a) Batted for Radonits in the ninth.
(b) Ran for Sweeney in the ninth.

San Diego	AB	H	RBI	O	A	E
Myatt SS	5	1	2	3	2	0
Thompson RF	3	1	3	3	0	0
Patchett CF	4	1	0	1	0	0
Williams LF	4	1	0	2	0	0
Detore C	4	1	0	1	0	0
McDonald 1B	4	2	0	12	2	0
Berkowitz 2B	4	0	0	3	7	0
Holman 3B	3	0	0	0	1	0
Salvo P	4	3	0	2	3	0
	35	10	5	27	15	0

Pitching Records	IP	H	R	ER	SO	BB
Radonits	8	10	5	1	5	1
Salvo	9	12	1	0	1	1

Left on Base: Portland 11; San Diego 8. Home Run: Thompson. Two Base Hit: Salvo. Sacrifice: Holman. Stolen Base: Myatt. Double Play: Berkowitz to Myatt to McDonald. Umpires: Engeln, Hood, Fanning and Snyder.

Portland	010	000	000	1 – 12 – 2	
San Diego	040	001	00x	5 – 10 – 0	

The two clubs could not leave San Diego until Friday morning, October 1, so did not arrive in Portland until 3:30 P.M. Saturday, for an 8:30 P.M. game. This was the same situation that confronted the Seals a week earlier but this time rain prevented the game from being played until Sunday afternoon. *The Portland Oregonian* had far more coverage on college football than on the upcoming playoff game.

Game Four.

Intermittent showers held the crowd down to 4,400 on Sunday, October 3, and the game had to be held up a couple of times. The wet grass allowed George Myatt's first inning hit off Ad Liska to go for a triple, as the outfielders slipped. A walk and a force play scored Myatt, then two stolen bases by Hal Padgett and a wild throw by catcher Bill Cronin brought in the second run. Ted Williams then doubled and scored on George McDonald's single, giving San Diego a three-run lead before Portland came to bat. After the Beavers narrowed the gap to 3–2 in the fourth, Rupert Thompson bashed a two-run homer in the fifth to restore the Padres three run lead. Wally Hebert was able to make that stand up, giving the Padres another four game sweep.

San Diego	AB	H	RBI	O	A	E
Myatt SS	5	2	0	1	2	1
Thompson RF	4	1	2	1	0	1
Patchett CF	5	1	1	3	0	0
Williams LF	4	1	0	2	0	0
McDonald 1B	4	2	1	13	1	0
Berkowitz 2B	3	0	0	3	3	0
Holman 3B	4	1	0	0	5	0
Starr C	4	2	0	4	1	0
Hebert P	4	1	0	0	2	0
	37	11	4	27	14	2

Portland	AB	H	RBI	O	A	E
Lee SS	5	2	0	4	4	0
P. Coscarart 2B	4	1	0	3	6	1
Bongy CF	4	1	1	3	0	0
Frederick 1B	4	1	1	9	1	0
Clabaugh LF	4	0	0	3	1	0
Bedore 3B	4	1	0	0	3	0
Tresh RF	4	1	0	1	0	0
Cronin C	3	0	0	3	0	1
Liska P	2	0	0	0	0	0
Sweeney[a]	1	1	1	0	0	0
Thomas P	0	0	0	1	0	0
Montague[b]	1	1	0	0	0	0
	36	9	3	27	15	2

(a) Batted for Liska in the seventh.
(b) Batted for Thomas in the eighth.

Pitching Records	IP	H	R	ER	SO	BB
Hebert	9	9	4	4	5	1
Liska (L)	7	8	5	4	2	1
Thomas	2	3	1	1	0	0

Stolen Bases: Patchett 2, McDonald. Home Run; Thompson. Three Base Hit: Myatt. Two Base Hits: Williams, Coscarart, Patchett, Bedore, Starr, Tresh. Sacrifice: Berkowitz. Umpires: Hood, Fanning, Snyder. Time of Game: 1 hr. 31 min.

San Diego	300	020	010	6 – 11 – 2	
Portland	000	200	101	4 – 9 – 2	

The fact that Portland was home for only two playoff games led owners to complain that the chief beneficiary of the playoffs was the Southern Pacific Railroad. The clubs did plan to play an exhibition game on Monday night for the Portland Community Chest and to defray the players' travel expenses, but it was called off because of likely rain. The Padres were anxious to leave for home, especially Rupert Thompson, who was getting married.

Even though Sacramento was eliminated in the first round, they split $3,750, compared to the Padres' $3,000. Each Solon share was $157.82, which would be worth about $1,103 today. Portland divided $2,000 and the Seals $1,250. Each Padre received about $136, each Beaver about $90, and each Seal about $54.

Key Players on 1937 Playoff Teams

Sacramento. *Pitchers:* Tony Freitas, Bob Klinger, Bob Schmidt, Tommy Seats. *Position Players:* Art Garibaldi (league's MVP), Lou Vezilich, Nick Cullop, Buster Adams.

San Diego. *Pitchers:* Wally Hebert, Manny Salvo, Dick Ward, Jim Chaplin. *Position Players:* Rupert Thompson, George Detore (batting champion), George McDonald, Ted Williams, Jimmie Reese, Hal Padgett.

San Francisco. *Pitchers:* Sam Gibson, Ed Stutz, Bill Shores, Gene Lillard. *Position Players:* Dominic DiMaggio, Brooks Holder, Ted Norbert, Frank Hawkins.

Portland. *Pitchers:* Ad Liska, Bill Posedel, Bill Radonits. *Position Players:* Moose Clabaugh, Bill Sweeney, Nino Bongy, John Frederick.

1938

The disappointment over Sacramento being deprived of the 1937 pennant caused league officials to change the pennant winner to the team finishing first rather than the playoff winner. The team winning the playoffs would now receive a cup from league president W.C. Tuttle and an increase in prize money from $3,000 to $5,000. The team losing in the final round would also get an increase from $2,000 to $2,500, but the other prize money would stay the same: $2,500 for the first place team and $1,250 for each of the two clubs eliminated in the first round. Thus, the total amount for the postseason was increased from $10,000 to $12,500. If the first place team were eliminated in the first round, as happened in 1938 and 1939, it would receive less money than the playoff winner, unlike Sacramento in 1937.

In 1938, the Mission Reds moved from Seals Stadium to Wrigley Field to become the new Hollywood Stars. The Angels gave them permission to play only one year at Wrigley, so the team constructed a new park, Gilmore Field, for the 1939 season. This was the last franchise shift until the 1956 season. Meanwhile in Seattle, the fortunes of that team brightened considerably when a wealthy brewer, Emil Sick, bought the club and immediately went after better players and built a new ball park. This team, now called the Rainiers instead of the Indians, had been forced to play in Civic Stadium with its hard dirt infield since July 4, 1932, when its old park, Dugdale Field, burned down. The team was able to move into its fine new facility, called Sick's Stadium, in mid–June 1938, which Mr. Sick built on the picturesque site of old Dugdale Field. The Rainiers won three pennants and three playoffs from 1939 through 1942 in their new park.

Unlike the major leagues, the 1938 Pacific Coast League schedule was not balanced; teams played between 24 and 27 games with opponents and did not have an equal amount of games at home and away. This could have affected the race, especially for fourth place.

The Sacramento Solons led the 1938 pennant chase by seven games in June but ran into a hot Angel club that beat them seven of nine in Los Angeles and then six of seven in Sacramento a couple of weeks later. Los Angeles won 32 of 41 games in June and July to vault from sixth place to the top, where they stayed for the rest of the season. After one very successful road trip, the team was welcomed home by 1,000 fans at the old Southern Pacific Arcade Depot on Alameda Street.

The Seattle Rainiers also had a hot streak, winning 28 of 31, including 14 in a row from the middle of August to September 15. They passed up San Diego, San Francisco and Sacramento to end up in second place, even putting heat on the Angels, who did not clinch the pennant until two days before the season ended. But with the Solons secure in third place, the closest race was for fourth , just as in 1937.

San Diego was either in third or fourth place throughout July and August, but the Seals began to close the gap by winning 13 of 14 in August. By September 14 the two were in a virtual tie, but the Seals moved a half game ahead on the 16th, and stayed that way as the season ended on the 18th. San Francisco finished 93–85 while the Padres were 92–85. As mentioned previously, the league did not permit postponed games to be made up, thus allowing teams to win by percentage points or by half a game. The fifth place finish for the Padres cost manager Frank Shellenback his job.

The first round of the playoffs began with the champion Angels hosting the third place Solons while San Francisco visited Seattle. The first three games in each series were played Tuesday through Thursday nights, September 20–22, before the teams moved to their opponent's park to finish that round.

College football was getting more coverage in the sports pages than the playoffs. In Seattle, fans were interested in the Washington Huskies' opening game at Minnesota, while in Los Angeles, both UCLA and USC were starting their seasons at home in the Coliseum. On Friday night, September 23, Iowa played UCLA, and on Saturday afternoon, Alabama, who had played in the 1938 Rose Bowl game, opposed USC, who was to win the 1939 Rose Bowl game. In the Bay Area, the Seals had to share the spotlight with Stanford and California, both of whom opened with two local colleges, Santa Clara and St. Mary's, respectively.

The Los Angeles–Sacramento Series

Regardless of how well a team does against another during the regular season, both clubs start even in the postseason. This was never more apparent than in this series, when the Solons manhandled the Angels after winning only 6 of 27 games from them during the pennant race.

Game One.

This series opened in direct competition with a college football game at Gilmore Stadium between Loyola University and Cal Tech, which was quite unusual for a Tuesday night. About 9,000 fans saw the football game while only 2,500 saw Tony Freitas beat the Angels, 10–6, at Wrigley Field. This game was a rout. The Solons led 10–1 going into the last of the ninth, when the Angels got five harmless runs. Angel ace Ray Prim was rocked for five runs and nine hits in six innings. Bill James and Johnny Vergez each homered for Sacramento while Joe Orengo got three hits. For the Angels, Paul Carpenter went five for five and Charlie English four for five in a losing cause.

Sacramento	AB	R	H	RBI	O	A	E
Marshall LF	5	0	2	1	2	0	0
Barton 1B	5	0	1	0	11	1	0
Williams 2B	5	0	0	0	3	2	0
Vergez 3B	5	2	2	1	1	2	1
Orengo SS	5	1	3	0	4	8	0
Cullop RF	4	3	2	0	0	0	0
Franks C	4	1	1	2	5	0	0
James CF	5	2	2	3	1	0	0
Freitas P	3	1	1	2	0	0	0
	41	10	14	9	27	13	1

Los Angeles	AB	R	H	RBI	O	A	E
Statz CF	5	1	1	0	1	0	0
Mayo 2B	5	1	3	0	1	1	0
Carpenter RF	5	1	5	1	3	0	0
Rothrock LF	4	1	1	1	1	0	0
Russell 1B	5	1	1	0	12	1	1
English 3B	5	1	4	2	2	3	1
Cihocki SS	5	0	3	0	0	3	0
Collins C	5	0	1	1	7	0	0
Prim P	2	0	0	0	0	1	0
Lieber P	1	0	0	0	0	2	0
Sueme [a]	1	0	0	0	0	0	0
Bush P	0	0	0	0	0	0	0
Dittmar [b]	1	0	0	0	0	0	0
	44	6	19	5	27	11	2

(a) Batted for Lieber in the eighth.
(b) Batted for Bush in the ninth.

Pitching Records	IP	H	R	ER	SO	BB
Freitas	9	19	6	4	3	1
Prim (L)	5.1	9	5	6	4	1
Lieber	2.2	3	4	0	2	1
Bush	1	2	1	1	1	0

Left on Base: Sacramento 7, Los Angeles 12. Home Runs: Vergez, James. Two Base Hits: Marshall, Carpenter, Cullop, Russell, English, Barton, Mayo, Orengo. Sacrifice: Franks. Double Plays: Orengo to Vergez to Williams; Barton to Orengo; Williams to Orengo to Barton. Time of Game: 2 hr. 25 min. Umpires: Hood, Falls, Fanning.

Sacramento	001	401	031	10 – 14 – 1
Los Angeles	000	100	005	6 – 19 – 2

Game Two.

Solon manager Bill Killefer, who announced his retirement before the regular season ended, started pitcher Lee Sherrill instead of Bill Walker as he had originally stated. The Angel starter was Jittery Joe Berry, but neither pitcher got the decision. The Angels got three runs in the fourth to take a 4–2 lead but could not hold it. The Solons scored three in the sixth to go up 5–4 but lost the lead for good in the seventh when the Angels scored three runs of their own. The Angel hero was Jigger Statz who went three for three, scoring two runs and driving in two. Joe Orengo and Nick Cullop homered for the Solons. Guy Bush, "the Mississippi Mudcat," who relieved Joe Berry, got the win, while Dick Newsome, second of three Sacramento pitchers, was charged with the loss. The crowd was about 2,500, almost the same as the previous night.

Sacramento	AB	R	H	RBI	0	A	E
Marshall LF	5	2	2	0	1	0	1
Barton 1B	5	0	3	2	5	1	1
Williams 2B	4	1	1	0	2	3	0
Vergez 3B	4	0	0	0	5	1	1
Orengo SS	4	1	1	2	3	1	0
Cullop RF	4	1	1	1	4	0	0
Franks C	2	0	0	0	2	1	2
James CF	4	0	1	0	2	0	0
Sherrill P	1	0	0	0	0	1	0
Malinosky[a]	1	0	0	0	0	0	0
Newsome P	1	0	0	0	0	1	0

Sacramento	AB	R	H	RBI	0	A	E
Schmidt P	0	0	0	0	0	0	0
Dieffenbach [b]	1	0	0	0	0	0	0
	36	5	9	5	24	9	5

(a) Batted for Sherrill in the fifth.
(b) Batted for Schmidt in the ninth.

Los Angeles	AB	R	H	RBI	O	A	E
Statz CF	3	2	3	2	1	0	0
Mayo 2B	3	0	0	1	4	3	0
Carpenter RF	5	0	1	0	0	0	0
Rothrock LF	4	1	0	0	7	0	0
Russell 1B	5	1	2	1	6	1	0
English 3B	4	1	2	1	3	1	0
Cihocki SS	3	0	1	1	1	0	0
Collins C	2	1	0	0	4	1	1
Berry P	1	2	1	1	1	1	0
Moore [c]	1	0	0	0	0	0	0
Bush P	1	0	0	0	0	1	0
	32	8	10	7	27	8	1

(c) Batted for Berry in the sixth.

Pitching Records	IP	H	R	ER	SO	BB
Sherrill	4	5	4	4	2	3
Newsome (L)	2.2	4	3	3	0	2
Schmidt	1.1	1	1	0	0	1
Berry	6	7	5	4	3	2
Bush (W)	3	2	0	0	2	0

Left on Base: Sacramento 6, Los Angeles 10. Home Runs: Orengo, Cullop. Three Base Hit: Marshall. Two Base Hits: Russell, Barton, English. Sacrifices: Cihocki, Mayo 2. Stolen Base: Carpenter. Double Play: Orengo to Williams to Barton. Time of Game: 2 hr. 45min. Umpires: Fanning, Falls, Hood.

Sacramento	101	003	000	5 – 9 – 5
Los Angeles	001	300	31x	8 – 10 – 1

Game Three.

Before this game, Sacramento president Phillip Bartelme announced that if the Angels won this game, the fourth game would not be played until Sunday at Cardinal Field, but if the Solons won, they would play on Saturday night, September 24. Bartelme also said that they would play a doubleheader

Sunday if both games were needed. There would indeed be a Saturday night game in the capital city. The Angels were humiliated by a 12–2 score, in the last game played in Wrigley Field in 1938. The Solons pounded out 16 hits including five doubles and a homer off of Fay "Scow" Thomas, Jack Salveson and Ed Carnett. Bill Walker had an easy time with the Angel hitters. The outcome was decided when the Sacs got five in the third and three more in the fourth. *The Sacramento Bee* remarked that the Solons showed more bat power against the Angels in this one game than they did all season long against them. Because of an American Legion convention, the Solons were unable to stay in their normal Los Angeles hotel and ended up in the Margann, but it certainly did not hurt their performance on the field.

Sacramento	AB	R	H	RBI	O	A	E
Marshall LF	5	2	3	0	2	1	0
Barton 1B	5	3	2	3	10	1	1
Williams 2B	6	2	4	0	4	5	0
Vergez 3B	5	1	2	3	0	2	0
Orengo SS	3	2	0	0	3	5	0
Cullop RF	3	1	0	0	4	0	0
Franks C	4	1	2	4	3	0	0
James CF	5	0	2	2	1	0	0
Walker P	5	0	1	0	0	1	0
	41	12	16	12	27	15	1

Los Angeles	AB	R	H	RBI	O	A	E
Statz CF	2	1	1	0	0	0	0
Mayo 2B	4	0	1	0	4	3	1
Carpenter RF	4	1	1	1	0	0	0
Rothrock LF	4	0	1	1	0	0	0
Russell 1B	4	0	1	0	5	0	0
English 3B	3	0	1	0	1	3	1
Cihocki SS	3	0	0	0	2	2	0
Collins C	4	0	1	0	15	2	0
Thomas P	1	0	0	0	0	0	0
Salveson P	0	0	0	0	0	0	0
Carnett P	2	0	0	0	0	1	0
Sueme[a]	1	0	0	0	0	0	0
	32	2	7	2	27	11	2

(a) *Batted for Carnett in the ninth.*

Pitching Records	IP	H	R	ER	SO	BB
Walker	9	7	2	1	3	3
Thomas (L)	2.2	6	5	6	3	4
Salveson	0.1	5	2	3	1	0
Carnett	6	5	5	2	10	3

Balk: Carnett. Passed Ball: Collins. Left on Base: Sacramento 9, Los Angeles 7. Home Run: Barton. Two Base Hits: Collins, Williams, Vergez 2, Franks, Rothrock, Barton. Double Plays: Mayo to Russell; Williams to Orengo to Barton; Williams to Barton; Mayo to Cihocki to Russell. Time of Game: 2 hr. 37 min. Umpires: Falls, Hood, Fanning.

Sacramento	015	320	001	12 – 16 – 1
Los Angeles	101	000	000	2 – 7 – 2

Game Four.

Even though Sacramento did not have major college football in their city, their fans may still have been more interested in football than baseball on Saturday night, September 24, because only 2,200 turned out to see the Solons take 3–1 lead in the series. Ray Prim faced Tony Freitas again and the result was no better for the Angel lefty, who could not finish the first inning. With men on first and second, Prim walked three batters in a row, forcing in two runs, and later wild pitched a third run home before manager Truck Hannah yanked him. Those were all the runs Freitas needed but Nick Cullops' two run homer in the fifth made it 5–1. Max Marshall got three hits for the Sacs, including a triple.

Los Angeles	AB	R	H	RBI	O	A	E
Statz CF	4	0	0	0	2	0	0
Mayo 2B	4	0	1	0	3	1	1
Carpenter RF	4	1	2	0	2	0	0
Rothrock LF	4	1	2	1	1	0	1
Russell 1B	4	0	1	0	4	0	0
English 3B	4	0	0	0	0	0	
Cihocki SS	3	0	1	1	1	1	0
Collins C	3	0	0	0	10	0	0
Prim P	0	0	0	0	0	0	0
Lieber P	3	0	0	0	0	1	0
Moore LF	0	0	0	0	1	0	0
	33	2	7	2	24	3	2

Sacramento	AB	R	H	RBI	O	A	E
Marshall LF	5	1	3	1	3	0	0
Barton 1B	3	1	0	0	8	0	0
Williams 2B	4	0	0	0	5	2	0
Vergez 3B	3	1	0	0	3	3	0
Orengo SS	3	1	1	1	0	2	0
Cullop RF	3	1	1	3	3	0	0
Franks C	3	0	0	0	4	0	0
James CF	4	1	1	0	1	0	0
Freitas P	4	0	0	0	0	1	0
	32	6	6	5	27	8	0

Pitching Records	IP	H	R	ER	SO	BB
Prim (L)	0.2	1	3	1	2	3
Lieber	7.1	5	3	3	8	2
Freitas	9	7	2	2	3	1

Wild Pitch: Prim. Left on Base: Los Angeles 5, Sacramento 8. Home Run: Cullop. Three Base Hit: Marshall. Two Base Hits: Carpenter, Orengo, James. Double Play: Orengo to Williams to Barton. Time of Game: 2 hr. Umpires: Fanning, Falls, Hood.

Los Angeles	000	100	100	2 – 7 – 2
Sacramento	300	020	01X	6 – 6 – 0

Game Five.

Only 3,993 fans showed up on Sunday hoping to see just one game, but sloppy play by the Solons made it necessary to play the seven-inning night-cap. In the opener, Fay Thomas held the Sacs to just one run until the ninth, when he was relieved by Guy Bush, who gave up a second run. Bill Schmidt, who also pitched well, deserved a better fate. In the second, the Angels scored twice when Dib Williams' wild throw allowed Charlie English to get to second base, from where he scored when Bill James lost Eddie Cihocki's fly in the sun. Cihocki scored on Fay Thomas' single. Then in the fifth, Eddie Mayo got a gift double when his pop fly fell between James and Williams and later scored on Johnny Moore's ground out.

Los Angeles	AB	R	H	RBI	O	A	E
Statz CF	5	0	3	0	3	0	0
Mayo 2B	3	1	1	0	3	0	0
Carpenter LF	4	0	1	0	3	0	0

Los Angeles	AB	R	H	RBI	O	A	E
Moore RF	4	0	0	1	0	0	0
Russell 1B	3	0	0	0	6	1	0
English 3B	4	1	0	0	2	3	0
Cihocki SS	4	1	2	1	0	1	0
Collins C	4	0	1	0	9	0	0
Thomas P	4	0	2	1	1	0	0
Bush P	0	0	0	0	0	0	0
	35	3	10	3	27	5	0

Sacramento	AB	R	H	RBI	O	A	E
Marshall LF	5	0	1	1	1	0	0
Barton 1B	5	0	1	0	6	1	0
Williams 2B	4	0	2	0	7	4	1
Vergez 3B	4	0	0	0	2	2	1
Urengo SS	4	1	1	0	3	3	0
Cullop RF	3	1	2	0	2	0	0
Franks C	3	0	1	0	5	0	0
James CF	4	0	1	1	1	0	0
Schmidt P	2	0	0	0	0	0	0
Malinosky[a]	1	0	1	0	0	0	0
Newsome P	0	0	0	0	0	0	0
Pippen[b]	0	0	0	0	0	0	0
Grube[c]	1	0	0	0	0	0	0
	36	2	10	2	27	10	2

(a) Batted for Schmidt in the seventh.
(b) Ran for Franks in the ninth.
(c) Batted for Newsome in the ninth.

Pitching Records	IP	H	R	ER	SO	BB
Thomas (W)	8+	10	1	2	8	2
Bush	1	0	1	0	1	0
Schmidt (L)	7	10	3	3	4	1
Newsome	2	0	0	0	1	0

Left on Base: Los Angeles 7, Sacramento 9. Two Base Hits: Cihocki, James, Mayo. Sacrifice: Mayo. Double Plays: Vergez to Williams to Barton; Vergez to Williams: English to Russell. Time of Game: 2 hr. 25 min. Umpires: Fanning, Falls and Hood.

Los Angeles	020	010	000	3 – 10 – 0
Sacramento	010	000	001	2 – 10 – 2

Game Six.

This was the first playoff series to go as far as a sixth game. Jittery Joe Berry started this seven inning game against Lefty Bill Walker and shut the Solons out with no hits for three innings before the roof fell in on him in the fourth. Sacramento scored nine runs that inning when Dib Williams hit two home runs, one a grand slam, and Johnny Vergez got two doubles. The Solons really put their hitting clothes on when Bill Walker took the mound for them, scoring 21 runs in his two starts.

Los Angeles	AB	R	H	RBI	O	A	E
Statz CF	3	0	0	0	0	0	0
Mayo 2B	2	0	0	0	1	2	0
Carpenter LF	2	0	0	0	1	0	0
Moore RF	2	0	0	0	1	0	0
Russell 1B	3	0	1	0	8	0	0
English 3B	3	0	1	0	0	1	0
Cihocki SS	3	1	1	1	1	1	0
Collins C	3	0	1	0	5	0	0
Berry P	1	0	1	0	0	2	0
Bush P	0	0	0	0	0	0	0
Salveson P	1	0	0	0	0	0	0
Wakeham RF[a]	0	0	0	0	1	0	0
Sueme[b]	1	0	0	0	0	0	0
	24	1	5	1	18	6	0

(a) Batted for Moore in the sixth.
(b) Batted for Salveson in the seventh.

Sacramento	AB	R	H	RBI	O	A	E
Marshall LF	3	2	1	0	1	0	0
Barton 1B	4	1	2	2	11	0	0
Williams 2B	4	2	2	5	3	1	0
Vergez 3B	3	1	2	0	0	7	0
Orengo SS	2	1	1	1	1	2	0
Cullop RF	3	1	1	1	1	0	0
Franks C	3	1	1	1	2	0	0
James CF	3	1	1	0	2	0	0
Walker P	3	0	0	0	0	2	0
	28	10	11	10	21	12	0

Pitching Records	IP	H	R	ER	SO	BB
Berry (L)	3.1	4	3	4	3	1

Pitching Records	IP	H	R	ER	SO	BB
Bush	0.1	3	3	4	0	1
Salveson	2	4	4	2	2	0
Walker	7	5	1	1	2	3

Left on Base: Los Angeles 5, Sacramento 6. Home Runs: Williams 2, Cihocki. Two Base Hits: Vergez 2, Cullop, Russell. Sacrifices: Statz, Orengo. Double Play: Vergez to Williams to Barton. Time of Game: 1 hr. 35 min. Umpires: Hood, Falls and Fanning.

Los Angeles	000	000	1	1 –	5 –	0
Sacramento	000	901	x	10 –	11 –	0

The Los Angeles Times remarked that Hannah's hired hands just could not come down to earth after winning the pennant. The paper gave the impression that the playoffs were anticlimatic after the struggle to finish first. The Angels divided $3,750 among the players and coaches, which amounted to about $150 to $170 per man, depending upon the number of shares. In current dollars this would come to between $1,063 and $1,205.

The Seattle–San Francisco Series

The Seattle Rainiers were on the verge of greatness; the 1938 season was a prelude to some happy times for their fans. Emil Sick not only purchased some good players but hired one of the Pacific Coast League's most successful managers in Jack Lelivelt. Lelivelt had managed the Angels to pennants in 1933 and 1934 and to first half wins in 1930 and 1935, only to lose the split season championship series. With Sick's Stadium opening in June, the Rainiers drew 437,161 fans for the season, allowing visiting teams to take home checks in amounts not seen since before 1929. With Seattle winning 28 of 31 games near the end of the season, it appeared they were primed for the playoffs, but this was not to be the case.

By contrast, the Seals barely made the playoffs with their half game edge over San Diego. The Seals and Rainiers, however, split evenly the 26 games played against each other during the season.

Game One.

Lelivelt started his sensational 18-year-old rookie, Freddie Hutchinson, who went to Seattle's Franklin High School and won 25 and lost 7 for the Rainiers in 1938. This was a natural choice because the youngster had beaten the Seals all three times he had faced them. But a crowd of only 5,500 turned out in Sick's Stadium on Tuesday, September 20, to see a pitcher who normally packed the park. The small crowd was blamed on the absence of ladies night and any free passes.

Lefty O'Doul started an ex–Seattle pitcher, Lou Koupal, who allowed only two runs and five hits over 7⅔ innings. The Seals got to Hutchinson in the first for a run on Dom DiMaggio's double and Ted Jennings' single. Seattle tied it in their half of the first but the Seals took the lead for good in the sixth when Frank Hawkins singled in Jennings and Ted Norbert. Seattle's best chance came in the eighth when Old Pard Win Ballou relieved Koupal and walked Dick Gyselman with the bases loaded, cutting the lead to 4–2. But Len Gabrielson grounded out to end the threat.

San Francisco	AB	R	H	RBI	O	A	E
DiMaggio CF	4	2	2	0	6	1	0
Jennings SS	3	1	1	1	1	3	0
Holder RF	4	0	2	1	1	0	0
Norbert LF	4	1	2	0	3	0	0
Hawkins 3B	3	0	1	2	1	2	0
Boss 1B	4	0	0	0	9	1	0
Wright 2B	4	0	0	0	4	2	0
Sprinz C	4	0	1	0	2	1	0
Koupal P	3	0	0	0	0	2	0
Frazier RF	0	0	0	0	0	0	0
Ballou P	0	0	0	0	0	0	0
	33	4	9	4	27	12	0

Seattle	AB	R	H	RBI	O	A	E
Vanni RF	3	0	1	0	0	0	0
Gyselman 3B	3	0	0	1	3	1	0
Gabrielson 1B	4	1	1	0	6	2	0
Muller 2B	4	0	1	1	7	2	0
Spindel C	4	0	0	0	1	1	0
Hunt LF	4	0	1	0	2	1	0
Lawrence CF	3	0	0	0	5	0	0
Strange SS	3	1	0	0	2	2	1
Hutchinson P	2	0	1	0	1	1	1
	30	2	5	2	27	10	2

Pitching Records	IP	H	R	ER	SO	BB
Koupal (W)	7.2	5	2	2	1	2

Pitching Records	IP	H	R	ER	SO	BB
Ballou	1.1	0	0	0	1	1
Hutchinson	9	9	4	4	1	3

Two Base Hits: DiMaggio, Norbert, Gabrielson, Sprinz. Stolen Bases: DiMaggio, Norbert. Double Plays: Hawkins to Wright to Boss; Muller to Strange. Time of Game: 2 hr. 2min. Umpires: Snyder, Engeln and Doran.

San Francisco	100	002	010	4 – 9 – 0
Seattle	100	000	010	2 – 5 – 2

Game Two.

Seattle evened the series with an 11–6 win, scoring seven runs in the third inning. Kewpie Dick Barrett coasted after that with his team up 9–2 after four innings. Seals' starter Bill Shores was wild and could not retire a batter in the third. Fred Mueller went four for four and Mike Hunt doubled and homered for the Rainiers. Lefty O'Doul ended up playing first base and Bill Lillard third for the Seals because Harley Boss and Frank Hawkins were ejected from the game. The crowd was only 2,500 on this Wednesday night. *The Seattle Post Intelligencer* believed this was because the playoffs were no longer for the championship as they were the two previous years.

San Francisco	AB	R	H	RBI	O	A	E
DiMaggio CF	4	1	1	0	2	0	0
Jennings SS	3	3	2	0	0	1	2
Holder RF	1	0	0	0	4	0	0
Norbert LF	3	1	2	1	0	0	0
Hawkins 3B	4	0	0	1	3	0	1
Boss 1B	3	0	1	1	9	0	0
Wright 2B	4	0	0	0	3	2	0
Sprinz C	1	0	0	0	1	0	0
Shores P	1	0	0	0	0	0	0
Hermann P	2	0	0	0	0	9	0
Koupal[a]	0	0	0	0	0	0	0
McIsaac C	2	0	0	0	1	0	0
Frazier LF	1	0	1	1	0	0	0
Storey RF	2	1	1	1	0	0	0
O'Doul 1B[b]	1	0	0	0	1	0	0
Lillard 3B	0	0	0	0	0	0	0
Gibson[c]	1	0	0	0	0	0	0
	33	6	8	5	24	12	3

(a) Ran for Sprinz in the fifth.

(b) Batted for Boss in the eighth.
(c) Batted for Hermann in the ninth.

Seattle	AB	R	H	RBI	O	A	E
Vanni RF	5	2	2	0	2	0	0
Gyselman 3B	5	1	1	0	0	0	0
Gabrielson 1B	4	1	1	0	9	1	0
Muller 2B	4	2	4	2	2	3	0
Spindel C	2	1	1	1	9	1	0
Hunt LF	4	2	2	4	0	0	0
Lawrence CF	4	1	1	2	4	0	0
Strange SS	4	0	2	0	0	5	0
Barrett P	5	1	1	1	1	1	0
Leishman 2B	0	0	0	0	0	0	0
	37	11	15	10	27	11	0

Pitching Records	IP	H	R	ER	SO	BB
Shores (L)	2+	5	5	5	1	3
Hermann	6	10	6	4	1	3
Barrett	9	8	6	6	8	6

Wild Pitch: Hermann. Left on Base: San Francisco 6, Seattle 9. Home Run: Hunt. Three Base Hits: Jennings, Lawrence. Two Base Hits: Hunt, Norbert, Frazier, Jennings. Sacrifices: Spindel 2. Double Plays: Strange to Muller to Gabrielson 2. Time of Game: 2 hr. 15 min. Umpires: Engeln, Doran, and Snyder.

San Francisco	100	101	030	6 – 8 – 3
Seattle	007	200	20X	11 – 15 – 0

Game Three.

The Rainers were now sharing the sports pages with Jimmy Phelen's Washington Huskies, who were opening their season in Minnesota. Unfortunately for Seattle, the hot-hitting Fred Mueller hurt his ankle and had to be replaced at second with Leishman and coach Eddie Taylor. This game was a thriller but a sad one for the 5,000 fans who witnessed the last game in Sick's Stadium in 1938. Ted Norbert hit two home runs, giving the Seals a 6–1 lead in the seventh. Trailing 7–3 in the last of the eighth, the Rainiers rallied for four runs to tie the game, knocking starter Ed Stutz out of the game. The key blow was a double by Alan Strange, which plated two runs. The game was then in the hands of the relievers, Sad Sam Gibson and Hal Turpin, who had relieved starter Paul Gregory. The tie was broken in the top of the 12th when Frank

Hawkins walked with the bases loaded. Harley Boss then hit a grand slam to ice the game.

San Francisco	AB	R	H	RBI	O	A	E
DiMaggio CF	6	2	2	1	2	0	0
Jennings SS	5	2	2	1	1	7	0
Holder RF	3	0	0	0	1	0	0
Norbert LF	5	3	2	1	3	0	0
Hawkins 3B	5	1	0	1	1	2	1
Boss 1B	6	2	3	4	19	1	0
Wright 2B	6	1	3	0	4	6	0
Sprinz C	6	1	2	0	2	0	0
Stutz P	2	0	1	2	0	3	0
Frazier RF	2	0	0	0	2	0	0
Gibson P	2	0	0	0	1	3	0
	40	12	15	10	36	22	1

Seattle	AB	R	H	RBI	O	A	E
Vanni RF	5	0	0	0	3	0	0
Gyselman 3B	6	2	2	0	2	5	0
Gabrielson 1B	6	1	2	1	14	2	0
Spindel C	5	2	2	1	6	2	0
Hunt LF	5	2	2	1	1	0	0
Lawrence CF	5	0	2	2	3	0	0
Strange SS	4	0	1	2	3	2	0
Leishman 2B	2	0	0	0	2	3	0
Gregory P	2	0	0	0	2	2	0
Fernandes [a]	1	0	0	0	0	0	0
Hutchinson [b]	1	0	0	0	0	0	0
Taylor 2B	2	0	0	0	0	0	0
Turpin P	2	0	1	0	0	1	0
	46	7	12	7	36	17	0

(a) Batted for Leishman in the seventh.
(b) Batted for Gregory in the seventh.

Pitching Records	IP	H	R	ER	SO	BB
Stutz	7.1	8	5	5	1	0
Gibson (W)	4.2	4	2	0	1	2
Gregory	7	9	6	6	2	2
Turpin (L)	5	6	6	6	1	2

Left on Base: San Francisco 5, Seattle 7. Home runs: Norbert 2, Boss. Three Base Hit: Jennings. Two Base Hits: Spindel, Lawrence, Hunt, Gabrielson, Strange. DiMaggio Sacrifices: Stutz, Spindel. Stolen Base: DiMaggio. Double Play: Wright to Boss. Time of Game: 2 hr. 45 min. Umpires: Doran, Snyder, and Engeln.

San Francisco	220	000	210	005	12	– 15	– 1
Seattle	100	000	240	000	7	– 12	– 0

The two teams left Seattle by train on Friday, September 23, and arrived at the Oakland depot on Saturday afternoon, ready for a doubleheader on Sunday. Saturday belonged to college football, especially with St. Mary's playing California at Berkeley. The Sunday paper devoted most of its coverage to football and only a small article on the matchup that afternoon at Seals Stadium. Nevertheless, a crowd of 17,534 saw the Seals eliminate Seattle in that twin bill, which was more than saw all three games in Seattle.

Game Four.

Freddie Hutchinson again lost to a team he had no trouble beating during the regular season. Leading 2–0 in the third, Hutchinson gave up two runs when Norbert doubled in DiMaggio and Hawkins singled in Jennings. But the key blow for the Seals was a two–out bloop single that drove in their final two runs in the fifth. This was crucial because Seattle rallied in the ninth, chasing starter Gibson when they scored two runs. Win Ballou came in and struck out Edo Vanni for the final out with the tying run on second. Hutchinson was allowed to bat in that ninth because of his .316 average, but he failed to deliver.

Seattle	AB	R	H	RBI	O	A	E
Vanni RF	5	0	1	0	3	0	1
Gyselman 3B	5	1	1	0	3	2	0
Gabrielson 1B	4	0	0	0	3	1	0
Spindel C	4	0	1	1	3	1	0
Hunt LF	3	0	1	0	2	0	1
Lawrence CF	4	2	2	0	4	1	0
Strange SS	3	1	2	1	1	1	0
Leishman 2B	3	0	1	1	5	2	0
Hutchinson P	4	0	0	0	0	1	0
Fernandez[a]	1	0	1	1	0	0	0
McCormick[b]	0	0	0	0	0	0	0
	36	4	10	4	24	9	2

(a) batted for Leishman in the ninth.
(b) Ran for Fernandes in the ninth.

San Francisco	AB	R	H	RBI	O	A	E
Dimaggio CF	5	2	2	0	3	0	0
Jennings SS	3	1	2	2	2	0	0
Holder RF	3	1	1	0	1	0	0
Norbert LF	3	0	1	2	3	0	0
Hawkins 3B	4	0	1	1	1	1	0
Boss 1B	4	0	2	0	6	1	0
Wright 2B	4	0	0	0	3	3	0
Sprinz C	3	1	1	0	7	0	0
Gibson P	4	0	1	0	0	0	0
Frazier RF	0	0	0	0	1	0	0
Ballou P	0	0	0	0	0	0	0
	33	5	11	5	27	5	0

Pitching Records	IP	H	R	ER	SO	BB
Ballou	1	0	0	0	1	0
Hutchinson	9	11	5	5	3	3
Gibson (W)	8+	10	4	4	5	2

Hit by Pitcher: Hutchinson by Gibson. Three Base Hit: Strange. Two Base Hits: Gyselman, Norbert, Jennings. Sacrifice: Holder. Double Plays: Lawrence to Gyselman; Wright to Boss. Time of Game: 1 hr. 47 min. Umpires: Snyder, Engeln, and Doran.

Seattle	011	000	002	4 – 10 – 2
San Francisco	002	012	00X	5 – 11 – 0

Game Five.

Lou Koupal beat his ex-teammates for the second time in this series with a ten-hit shutout in this seventh inning game. The Seals got five runs in the first three innings off Kewpie Dick Barrett to remove all doubt that the Rainier season was over. Seattle officials complained that their team traveled 1,700 miles just to play this one doubleheader and that the receipts even from this crowd of 17,534 were insufficient to cover expenses. The $1,250 awarded the Rainiers would be about $50 per man, or about $350 in current dollars. But the players did get an extra week's salary.

Seattle	AB	R	H	RBI	O	A	E
Vanni RF	4	0	0	0	1	0	0
Gyselman 3B	3	0	1	0	1	3	0
Gabrielson 1B	4	0	2	0	6	1	0

Seattle	AB	R	H	RBI	O	A	E
Spindel C	4	0	0	0	0	0	0
Hunt LF	4	0	1	0	6	0	0
Lawrence CF	3	0	2	0	1	0	0
Strange SS	3	0	3	0	0	2	0
Leishman 2B	2	0	0	0	2	2	0
Taylor 2B	0	0	0	0	0	0	0
Fernandes[a]	1	0	1	0	0	0	0
Barrett P	1	0	0	0	1	1	0
Turpin P	1	0	0	0	0	0	0
McCormick[b]	1	0	0	0	0	0	0
Pickrel P	0	0	0	0	0	0	0
	31	0	10	0	18	9	0

(a) *Batted for Leishman in the sixth.*
(b) *Batted for Turpin the sixth.*

San Francisco	AB	R	H	RBI	O	A	E
DiMaggio CF	2	2	2	0	4	0	0
Jennings SS	3	1	2	1	1	3	0
Holder RF	4	0	1	0	3	0	0
Frazier RF	0	0	0	0	0	0	0
Norbert LF	3	1	1	1	0	0	0
Hawkins 3B	4	0	0	1	1	0	0
Boss 1B	3	0	1	0	5	0	0
Wright 2B	3	2	1	1	3	2	0
Sprinz C	3	0	1	1	4	0	0
Koupal P	2	0	1	1	0	3	0
	27	6	10	6	21	8	0

Pitching Records	IP	H	R	ER	SO	BB
Barrett	2.2	6	5	5	0	2
Turpin	2.1	2	0	0	0	0
Pickrel	1	2	1	1	0	1
Koupal	7	10	0	0	2	1

Hit by Pitcher: Norbert by Barrett. Three Base Hit: DiMaggio. Two Base Hits: Gyselman, Wright, Boss, Gabrielson. Sacrifice: DiMaggio. Stolen Base: Jennings. Time of Game: 1 hr. 28 min. Umpires: Engeln, Doran, Snyder.

Seattle	000	000	0	0 – 10 – 0
San Francisco	212	001	x	6 – 10 – 0

The Final Series: San Francisco vs. Sacramento

The Solons, who split the 24 regular season games with the Seals, were allowed to open at home because they finished higher than the Seals. This was the second of three straight years when the final series was between teams finishing third and fourth. The series was scheduled to begin at Cardinal Field on Tuesday night, September 27, but rain prevented play that night. The Seals were just about to board a train for the 90 mile ride to Sacramento when they were informed of the postponement, so they spent an extra day at home. This was welcome news to catcher Joe Sprinz, who was forced to catch most of the games because Larry Woodall broke his thumb.

Game One.

Tony Freitas and Bill Shores each gave up an unearned run in the second but then pitched shutout ball until the last of the eighth inning. The Solons broke the tie when Max Marshall singled in Bill James, and then Larry Barton hit a two-run homer. Only 2,887 saw this Wednesday night game.

San Francisco	AB	R	H	RBI	O	A	E
DiMaggio CF	4	0	0	0	0	0	0
Lillard SS	4	0	1	0	1	0	0
Holder RF	2	0	0	0	3	2	0
Norbert LF	4	0	0	0	4	0	0
Hawkins 3B	4	1	1	0	1	2	1
Boss 1B	4	0	2	1	7	0	0
Wright 2B	4	0	1	0	5	1	1
Sprinz C	3	0	1	0	3	3	0
Shores P	3	0	0	0	0	1	0
	32	1	6	1	24	9	2

Sacramento	AB	R	H	RBI	O	A	E
Marshall LF	4	1	1	1	2	0	0
Barton 1B	4	1	1	2	9	0	0
Williams 2B	4	0	0	0	2	2	0
Vergez 3B	3	1	1	0	2	3	0
Orengo SS	3	0	0	0	1	3	0
Cullop RF	2	0	0	0	1	0	1
Franks C	3	0	1	0	8	0	0

Sacramento	AB	R	H	RBI	O	A	E
James CF	2	1	1	0	2	0	0
Freitas P	2	0	1	0	0	1	0
	27	4	6	3	27	9	1

Pitching Records	IP	H	R	ER	SO	BB
Shores	8	6	4	3	2	3
Freitas	9	6	1	0	6	2

Left on Base: Sacramento 2, San Francisco 6. Home Run: Barton. Two Base Hit: Wright. Sacrifice: Freitas. Stolen Base: Franks. Double Plays: Vergez to Barton; Orengo to Williams to Barton. Time of Game: 2 hr. Umpires: Snyder, Hood, Engeln and Fanning.

San Francisco	010	000	000	1 – 6 – 2
Sacramento	010	000	03x	4 – 6 – 1

Game Two.

The Seals evened the series with a 9–4 win, hitting Bill Walker and Henry "Cotton" Pippen rather hard. Harley Boss and Joe Sprinz each got three hits, while DiMaggio, Norbert, Hawkins and Al "A-1" Wright had two apiece. Joe Orengo homered and doubled for the losers. Ed Stutz went the whole way for the Seals before a small crowd of 2,484.

San Francisco	AB	R	H	RBI	O	A	E
DiMaggio CF	5	1	2	0	4	0	0
Lillard SS	5	1	1	1	2	3	1
Holder RF	4	2	1	0	3	0	0
Norbert LF	5	2	2	2	1	0	0
Hawkins 3B	5	1	2	2	0	2	1
Boss 1B	5	1	3	2	8	0	1
Wright 2B	5	0	2	2	6	3	0
Sprinz C	4	1	3	0	3	0	0
Stutz P	4	0	1	0	0	1	1
	42	9	17	9	27	9	4

Sacramento	AB	R	H	RBI	O	A	E
Marshall LF	5	0	0	0	1	0	0
Barton 1B	5	0	1	1	10	1	0
Williams 2B	5	0	1	0	4	0	0
Vergez 3B	4	1	2	0	1	6	0
Orengo SS	5	2	2	2	1	6	0

Sacramento	AB	R	H	RBI	O	A	E
Cullop RF	4	0	0	0	1	1	0
Franks C	4	0	0	0	7	0	0
James CF	4	0	3	1	2	0	0
Walker P	1	0	0	0	0	2	0
Newsome P	0	0	0	0	0	0	0
Pippen P	2	1	1	0	0	3	0
Malinosky[a]	1	0	0	0	0	0	0
	40	4	10	4	27	19	0

(a) Batted for Newsome in the fifth.

Pitching Records	IP	H	R	ER	SO	BB
Stutz	9	10	4	1	3	2
Walker (L)	4.2	9	5	5	2	2
Newsome	0.1	0	0	0	1	0
Pippen	4	8	4	4	2	1

Hit by Pitcher: Stutz by Walker. Passed Ball: Franks. Left on Base: Sacramento 8, San Francisco 12. Home Run: Orengo. Two Base Hits: DiMaggio, Norbert 2, James, Boss, Pippen, Orengo. Sacrifice: Lillard. Time of Game: 2 hr. 45min. Umpires: Fanning, Snyder, Hood and Engeln.

San Francisco	300	110	130	9 – 17 – 4
Sacramento	010	000	120	4 – 10 – 0

Game Three.

This Friday night game, on September 30, was the last one played in Sacramento in 1938 and one the Solons' fans would cherish, but a nightmare for the Seals. The Sacs won by the football score of 22–3, scoring seven runs in the third, four in the fifth, and three in each the seventh and eighth innings. Nick Cullop went five for five, driving in four runs, Dib Williams got four hits and drove in three runs, while Larry Barton also got four hits, including a homer and a double. Pitcher Bill Schmidt coasted to victory while Sam Gibson, Aldon Wilkie, and even Lefty O'Doul were shelled by the slugging Sacs for 23 hits. To make matters worse, the Seals committed five errors, four of them by shortstop Ted Jennings. After this fiasco, the Seals returned to San Francisco that night by bus.

San Francisco	AB	R	H	RBI	O	A	E
DiMaggio CF	4	0	0	0	0	0	0
Jennings SS	4	1	1	0	0	1	4
Holder RF	2	1	1	1	1	0	0

San Francisco	AB	R	H	RBI	O	A	E
Norbert LF	2	1	0	0	1	0	0
Hawkins 3B	4	0	2	1	3	2	1
Wright 2B	4	0	0	0	4	2	0
Boss 1B	4	0	1	1	6	1	0
Sprinz C	3	0	0	0	3	0	0
Gibson P	1	0	0	0	0	0	0
Wilkie P	1	0	1	0	0	1	0
McIssacs C	1	0	0	0	3	0	0
Storey LF	1	0	0	0	1	0	0
Frazier RF	1	0	0	0	1	0	0
Lilliard [a]	1	0	0	0	0	0	0
Ristau P	0	0	0	0	0	0	0
Woodall C	1	0	0	0	1	0	0
O'Doul P	1	0	0	0	0	0	0
	35	3	6	3	24	7	5

(a) *Batted for Wilkie in the seventh.*

Sacramento	AB	R	H	RBI	O	A	E
Marshall LF	7	3	2	0	5	0	0
Barton 1B	6	4	4	4	8	0	0
Williams 2B	7	3	4	3	0	3	0
Vergez 3B	8	2	2	1	3	1	0
Orengo SS	4	4	2	4	1	1	1
Cullop RF	5	2	5	4	3	0	0
Franks C	4	1	2	0	3	0	0
James CF	4	2	1	1	2	0	0
Schmidt P	6	1	1	1	1	0	0
Malinosky 3B	0	0	0	0	0	0	0
Grube C	1	0	0	0	1	0	0
Diffenbach RF	0	0	0	0	0	0	0
	52	22	23	18	27	5	1

Pitching Records	IP	H	R	ER	SO	BB
Gibson (L)	2+	6	4	3	2	2
Wilkie	4	12	12	4	2	2
Ristau	1	3	3	3	0	0
O'Doul	1	2	3	3	1	1
Schmidt	9	6	3	3	4	1

Wild Pitches: Gibson 2, Wilkie, O'Doul. Left on Base: Sacramento 11, San Francisco 6. Home Runs: Orengo, Barton. Two Base Hits: Barton, Williams 2, Jennings, Orengo, Marshall. Umpires: Engeln, Fanning, Snyder and Hood. Time of Game: 2 hr. 28 min.

San Francisco	201	000	000	3 –	6 –	5
Sacramento	227	041	33X	22 –	23 –	1

Saturday, October 1, was an off day while college football held center stage. *The San Francisco Chronicle* ran big stories on the Santa Clara at Stanford and the California at Washington State games. The Sunday paper devoted most of its coverage to those two games as well as other college games around the country. The small pre-game write-up stressed that the Solons could wrap up the playoffs with a doubleheader win that afternoon. But there was another college game for the Seals to compete with that day: Gonzaga was playing St. Mary's at Kezar Stadium while the Solons were playing the Seals. A heavy morning rain discouraged fans from going to either of those October 2 contests, but each managed to draw about 10,000.

Game Four.

The opener matched Tony Freitas against Lou Koupal, both of whom pitched brilliantly. The score was 1–1 after nine innings, but in the top of the tenth, Larry Barton walked, Dib Williams doubled, Joe Orengo singled in Barton, and Nick Cullop's fly scored Williams.

Sacramento	AB	R	H	RBI	O	A	E
Marshall LF	3	1	0	0	3	0	0
Barton 1B	4	1	1	0	14	0	0
Williams 2B	4	1	2	1	7	5	0
Vergez 3B	3	0	2	0	0	5	0
Orengo SS	5	0	2	1	1	3	2
Cullop RF	5	0	1	1	1	0	0
Franks C	5	0	0	0	1	1	1
James CF	4	0	1	0	1	0	0
Freitas P	4	0	0	0	2	2	0
	37	3	9	3	30	16	3

San Francisco	AB	R	H	RBI	O	A	E
DiMaggio CF	5	1	3	0	1	0	0
Lillard SS	5	0	0	0	4	5	1
Holder RF	4	0	3	1	1	0	0
Norbert LF	3	0	1	0	1	0	0
Hawkins 3B	4	0	0	0	2	1	0
Boss 1B	3	0	0	0	9	1	0
Wright 2B	4	0	0	0	6	2	0

San Francisco	AB	R	H	RBI	O	A	E
Sprinz C	4	0	0	0	5	0	0
Koupal P	3	0	2	0	1	5	0
Ballou P	0	0	0	0	0	0	0
Frazier [a]	1	0	0	0	0	0	0
	36	1	9	1	30	14	1

(a) Batted for Ballou in the tenth.

Pitching Records	IP	H	R	ER	SO	BB
Freitas	10	9	1	1	0	1
Koupal (L)	9.1	8	1	3	2	4
Ballou	0.2	1	2	0	1	1

Two Base Hits: Holder, Williams 2, Koupal, Norbert. Sacrifice: Williams. Stolen Base: Vergez. Double Plays: Vergez to Franks to Barton; Orengo to Williams to Barton 3; Wright to Lillard: Lillard to Wright to Boss. Time of Game: 2 hr. 2 min. Umpires: Fanning, Hood, Snyder and Engeln.

Sacramento	000	010	000	2	3 – 9 – 3
San Francisco	100	000	000	0	1 – 9 – 1

Game Five.

Bill Walker pitched a three-hitter in the seven-inning second game of the doubleheader, giving up a first inning homer to Ted Norbert. Sacramento scored in the third on doubles by Marshall and Barton; in the fourth on a walk, a sacrifice, and a single by Marshall; and two in the seventh on a walk, Johnny Vergez's triple, and Joe Orengo's single. Bill Shores went the distance for the losing Seals. The morning rain made the field unsteady and the infield very slow, but it is difficult to say which team was hurt more by these conditions.

Sacramento	AB	R	H	RBI	O	A	E
Marshall LF	4	1	3	1	2	0	0
Barton 1B	2	0	1	0	10	0	0
Williams 2B	3	1	2	1	0	2	0
Vergez 3B	4	1	1	1	0	2	0
Orengo SS	3	0	1	1	0	3	0
Cullop RF	2	0	0	0	2	0	0
Franks C	3	0	1	0	3	0	0
James CF	3	1	0	0	4	0	0
Walker P	1	0	0	0	0	1	0
	25	4	9	4	21	8	0

San Francisco	AB	R	H	RBI	O	A	E
DiMaggio CF	3	0	0	0	4	1	0
Lillard SS	2	0	0	0	1	2	0
Holder RF	3	0	0	0	2	0	0
Norbert LF	3	1	1	1	1	0	0
Hawkins 3B	3	0	1	0	0	0	0
Boss 1B	2	0	0	0	3	1	0
Wright 2B	3	0	1	0	6	0	0
Sprinz C	3	0	0	0	4	0	0
Shores P	2	0	0	0	0	3	0
Frazier 1B	0	0	0	0	0	0	0
	24	1	3	1	21	7	0

Pitching Records	IP	H	R	ER	SO	BB
Walker	7	3	1	1	3	2
Shores	7	9	4	4	1	7

Home Run: Norbert. Three Base Hit: Vergez. Two Base Hits: Marshall, Williams. Sacrifices: Barton, Walker, Vergez, Cullop. Time of Game: 1 hr. 39 min. Umpires: Snyder, Hood, Engeln and Fanning.

Sacramento	001	100	2	4 – 9 – 0
San Francisco	000	100	0	1 – 3 – 0

The winning Solons split $5,000, which was about $200 per man, or about $1,400 in current dollars. The runner up Seals got half that amount. Unlike 1937, the playoff winner received more than the team that finished first.

Even though the playoffs did not have to compete with the World Series broadcasts, which did not start until October 5, there was a great amount of controversy about whether these postseason games should continue. League president W. C. Tuttle wanted to drop them, stating that they were tried both when the pennant was decided in the playoffs, and when only bonus money was involved, and neither proved satisfactory. Tuttle wanted to reward the first four teams with descending sums of money without playing any games. He lamented that the geographical isolation of the Pacific Coast League from the other two AA leagues prevented it from playing a series with them such as the American Association and International League played with each other.

Sacramento and Seattle owners wanted to end the playoffs but the players liked not only the prize money, but the extended week or two of regular-season salary that could be earned. San Diego owner Bill Lane wanted to return to the split season format with bonuses for teams finishing in the first four spots of each half season, but only have the two winners play any postseason games. But the most persuasive argument was that of Charles Graham of the

Seals, who claimed that teams reap the benefit of higher attendance late in the season as clubs fight to get into first division. Thus, the playoffs were continued.

Key Players on 1938 Playoff Teams

Los Angeles. *Pitchers:* Ray Prim, Joe Berry, Fay Thomas, and Gene Lillard (out with broken leg).
Position Players: Eddie Mayo (Angels MVP), Paul Carpenter, Johnny Moore, Jigger Statz and Rip Russell.

Seattle. *Pitchers:* Freddie Hutchinson, Dick Barrett, Paul Gregory, and Hal Turpin.
Position Players: Dick Gyselman, Edo Vanni, Hal Spindell, Mike Hunt, and Len Gabrielson.

Sacramento. *Pitchers:* Bill Walker, Tony Freitas, Henry Pippen, and Bill Schmidt.
Position Players: Nick Cullop, Joe Orengo, Max Marshall, Larry Barton and Dib Williams.

San Francisco. *Pitchers:* Win Ballou, Sam Gibson, and Ed Stutz.
Position Players: Brooks Holder, Harley Boss, Ted Norbert, and Dom DiMaggio.

1939

The 1939 season was the most successful financially since before the depression as attendance soared to 2,277,176, an increase of 441,854 over 1938. Seattle won its first pennant since 1924 and set a team attendance record of 517,602 that stood until 1946. This was the first full season for the Rainiers to play in Sick's Stadium, having moved into it in June 1938. Another factor in increased attendance was the opening of the league's fourth new ball park since 1931, when the Hollywood Stars moved into new Gilmore Field, giving that franchise its own identity, which included a large following from the movie community. These newest parks followed the opening of Seals Stadium in 1931 and Lane Field, San Diego, in 1936. The World's Fair in San Francisco may also have helped Seals' attendance especially with catcher Joe Sprinz breaking his nose trying to catch a baseball dropped from a blimp as a stunt.

This season witnessed many streaks. The Angels won 19 in a row in April but then lost 11 of 15. The Solons began the season with 10 straight losses but later won 18 of 21 in late July and early August to move from eighth up to fourth place. Seattle won 7 in a row in July, taking over first place and never relinquished it. The Seals won 13 of 18 the last two weeks of the season to edge the Angels for second place by half a game.

The same four teams finished in the first division in 1939 as in 1938, but each in a different position. But unlike the previous season, there was no suspense as to which teams would qualify for the playoffs. No second division team threatened fourth place Sacramento, even though the Solons finished at the .500 mark. While the Seals passed the Angels, no team was a serious challenge to Seattle for the lead after early August. Since the Angels finished the season in Seattle, their slipping to third place meant they would not have to return to Los Angeles to open the playoffs with fourth place Sacramento, but remained in Seattle to open the first round of the playoffs with the Rainiers. It was the Seals who had to return from Portland to open at home against Sacramento.

The Seattle–Los Angeles Series

These two teams split evenly the 28 games between them during the regular season. This was to be the first of five times the Angels and Rainiers were to meet in the playoffs and the only time the Angels were to win. An acute and sometimes bitter rivalry developed between these two clubs that were the two most successful franchises from 1938 to the mid–1940s. Perhaps it was because Jack Lelivelt was fired by the Angels after the 1936 season and was hired by Seattle in 1938. Before this series began, Lelivelt asked manager Truck Hannah if the Rainiers could use their young infielder, Paul McGinnis, who joined the team after the August 31 deadline for the playoffs. Hannah said "sure, if we can use Lou Novikoff." Novikoff was a slugger who had joined the Angels after the deadline, hitting .452 with 8 homers in only 135 at-bats, after winning batting titles in the Three I League in 1938 and the Texas League in 1939. Lelivelt quickly withdrew his request.

The league restricted its team rosters to 20 players in 1939, so managers had little room to maneuver. Pitchers often had to bat with their team trailing in late innings and sometimes had to play other positions. Seattle was left with only one utility infielder, coach Eddie Taylor, while the Angels had only Eddie Mayo available. But Los Angeles had no spare outfielders because Johnny Moore broke his ankle and Novikoff was ineligible.

Game One.

The season ended on Sunday, September 17, so the teams took Monday off and opened the series in Sick's Stadium on Tuesday night, the 19th. The Angels started Julio Bonetti, who had the league's best won-lost percentage, while Seattle countered with Hal Turpin, "the Oregon farmer," whose 23 wins were the most in the league. Bonetti was 5–1 against the Rainiers during the season, while Turpin was 3–2 against L.A. Bonetti won the only time the two faced each other in Wrigley Field. Seattle got league permission to allow ladies to attend at reduced prices, unlike the 1938 playoffs, when resentment may have hurt attendance. A crowd of 8,400 saw the Angels take the first game 5–4, in 10 innings.

The batting star for the Angels was Jigger Statz, while in the field, Eddie Cihocki made several great plays that choked off Rainier rallies. With L.A. trailing 3–2 with two outs in the eighth, Statz drove Paul Carpenter home from second with a single. The same situation occurred in the 10th, and this time Jigger doubled Carpenter home and scored himself on Jack Rothrock's single. This last run was needed because in the last of the 10th, an error and a single put Alan Strange and Edo Vanni on base. George Archie sacrificed them along and Strange scored on Gilly Campbell's groundout before Bonetti struck out Bill Lawrence with the tying run on third base.

Los Angeles	AB	R	H	RBI	O	A	E
Stringer 2B	5	1	0	0	4	6	0
Statz CF	5	1	3	2	3	1	0
Rothrock RF	5	1	3	0	2	0	0
R. Collins C	5	0	1	0	3	0	0
J. Collins 1B	3	0	1	0	14	1	1
English 3B	4	0	1	0	1	2	0
Cihocki SS	4	0	0	0	1	6	0
Carpenter LF	4	2	2	2	2	0	0
Bonetti P	2	0	0	0	0	4	0
	37	5	11	4	30	20	1

Seattle	AB	R	H	RBI	O	A	E
White LF	3	2	1	0	4	0	0
Strange SS	4	1	1	1	3	3	1
Vanni RF	4	1	3	1	3	1	0
Archie 1B	4	0	2	1	8	0	0
Campbell C	4	0	1	1	3	1	0
Lawrence CF	5	0	1	0	4	0	0
Gyselman 3B	3	0	0	0	1	3	1
J. Coscarart 2B	4	0	0	0	4	0	0
Turpin P	4	0	1	0	0	3	0
	35	4	10	4	30	11	2

Pitching Records	IP	H	R	ER	SO	BB
Bonetti	10	10	4	3	3	2
Turpin	10	11	5	3	3	0

Left on Base: Seattle 8, Los Angeles 5. Two Base Hit: Statz. Sacrifices: Campbell, J. Collins, Vanni, Gyselman, Strange, Bonetti 2, Archie. Double plays: Turpin to Strange to Archie. Time of Game: 2hr. 4 min. Umpires: Powell, Engeln, Doran, Edwards.

Los Angeles	000	200	010	2	5 – 11 – 1
Seattle	101	010	000	1	4 – 10 – 2

Game Two.

On Wednesday night, September 20, the rollicking Rainiers routed Ray Prim, as writers of that period alliterated. In the first inning, Alan Strange and

Jo Jo White singled, moved up as catcher Bob Collins threw wildly on a pickoff attempt. George Archie doubled them home and went to third on a fly ball. When Prim wild pitched Archie home, Hannah brought in Jesse Flores to relieve. Flores did very well but the damage had already been done. Les Webber held the Angels to just one run and was never in danger after that three-run cushion in the first inning. A crowd of about 6,000 saw Seattle tie the series.

Los Angeles	AB	R	H	RBI	O	A	E
Stringer 2B	4	1	2	0	3	0	0
Statz CF	4	0	1	1	2	0	0
Rothrock RF	2	0	0	0	2	0	0
R. Collins C	4	0	0	0	5	0	0
J. Collins 1B	4	0	0	0	7	1	0
English 3B	4	0	1	0	1	6	1
Cihocki SS	3	0	0	0	0	0	1
Carpenter LF	4	0	0	0	3	0	0
Prim P	0	0	0	0	0	0	o
Flores P	3	0	1	0	1	3	0
	32	1	5	1	24	10	2

Seattle	AB	R	H	RBI	O	A	E
White CF	5	1	2	0	1	0	0
Strange SS	4	1	1	0	0	4	0
Vanni RF	4	0	1	0	3	0	0
Archie 1B	4	1	2	1	6	1	0
Lawrence CF	4	0	1	0	6	0	0
Gyselman 3B	4	1	2	0	2	3	1
J. Coscarart 2B	3	1	2	1	7	2	0
Hancken C	4	0	0	0	1	0	0
Webber P	4	0	1	1	1	2	0
	36	5	12	3	27	12	1

Pitching Records	IP	H	R	ER	SO	BB
Prim (L)	0.2	5	3	3	1	0
Flores	7.1	7	2	0	4	0
Webber	9	5	1	1	1	3

Wild pitch: Prim. Left on Base: Los Angeles 7, Seattle 8. Three Base hit: Stringer. Two Base Hits: Archie 2, Gyselman, Coscarart. Sacrifice: Coscarart. Stolen Base: White. Double Play: Gyselman to Coscarart to Archie. Time of game: 1 hr. 45 min. Umpires: Engeln, Doran, Edwards, Powell.

The 1939 Rainiers were Seattle's first pennant winner since 1924, but they were eliminated by Los Angeles in the first round of the playoffs.

Los Angeles	000	001	000	1 –	5 –	2
Seattle	300	000	02X	5 –	12 –	1

Game Three.

On Thursday night the 21st, the Rainiers took a 2–1 lead in the series as Kewpie Dick Barrett shut the Angels down 7–1. A crowd of 9,200 enjoyed themselves immensely as the running Rainiers stole six bases, got nine hits, and eight walks off Fay Thomas, who was unable to hold runners close. Edo Vanni got three hits and George Archie two. Joe Coscarart, Gilly Campbell and Tricky Dick Gyselman each drove in a pair of runs. Barrett endeared himself to the crowd, but not to the Angels, by strutting off the mound after retiring the side in the third inning. The Angels called the Rainiers "showboats" with their antics on the basepaths and one-handed catches. This was the last game played in Sick's Stadium in 1939 but the boisterous crowd was unaware of this. Just as in the opening game, neither team used any substitutes.

Los Angeles	AB	R	H	RBI	O	A	E
Stringer 2B	4	0	0	0	2	5	0
Statz CF	4	1	1	0	5	0	0
Rothrock RF	3	0	1	0	0	0	0
R. Collins C	2	0	1	1	2	1	0
J. Collins 1B	3	0	0	0	13	0	0
English 3B	4	0	0	0	1	3	0
Cihocki SS	4	0	0	0	0	2	1
Carpenter LF	4	0	0	0	1	0	0
Thomas P	2	0	0	0	0	1	1
	30	1	3	1	24	12	2

Seattle	AB	R	H	RBI	O	A	E
White LF	5	0	1	1	1	0	1
Strange SS	4	0	0	0	2	3	1
Vanni RF	5	2	3	0	1	0	0
Archie 1B	3	2	2	0	11	0	0
Campbell C	2	1	1	2	7	0	0
Lawrence CF	5	1	0	0	1	0	0
Gyselman 3B	1	1	1	2	1	3	0
J. Coscarart 2B	4	0	1	2	3	2	1
Barrett P	4	0	0	0	0	4	0
	33	7	9	7	27	12	3

Pitching Records	IP	H	R	ER	SO	BB
Thomas	8	9	7	5	2	3
Barrett	9	3	1	1	6	2

Left on Base: Los Angeles 7, Seattle 11. Two Base Hits: R. Collins, Gyselman, Statz, Campbell. Sacrifices: Thomas, Campbell, J. Collins, R. Collins. Stolen Bases: Vanni 3, Archie, White, Strange. Time of Game: 2hrs. Umpires: Doran, Edwards, Powell, Engeln.

Los Angeles	000	000	010	1 – 3 – 2
Seattle	011	000	32x	7 – 9 – 3

The Angels raced out of Sick's Stadium to make the night southbound train, thereby arriving in Los Angeles Saturday morning rather than Saturday evening, as the Rainiers did by waiting for Friday's train. Friday and Saturday were off days so a doubleheader was scheduled for Sunday, September 24. During the week of September 18–23, Los Angeles had been hit with a disastrous heat wave that caused many deaths. But by the 24th, the weather changed

dramatically. The heat was broken by a wind and rain storm that made playing conditions difficult.

Since the Pacific Coast Conference teams did not begin playing football
until the weekend of September 30, the first round of the playoffs did not have
the competition that occurred in other seasons. Nevertheless, football got pre-
game coverage in the sports pages.

Game Four.

A doubleheader was scheduled for Sunday, September 24, at Wrigley Field
and 7,500 fans sat through intermittent showers and strong winds that made
the field a quagmire by late in the nightcap, as the lights were turned on mid-
way through the second game.

Julio Bonetti again beat Hal Turpin as the Angels evened the series at two
games each with an impressive 12–3 win. However, it was only 5–2 going into
the last of the eighth when the Angels exploded for seven runs, three of them
on Lou Stringer's homer. The Angels got two runs in the first when Jimmy
"Ripper" Collins doubled in Jack Rothrock and Bob Collins, but in the top of
the third, doubles by Jo Jo White and George Archie cut the lead to 2–1. In
the fifth, Bob Collins doubled in Rothrock, but Seattle came right back to
make it 3–2 in the sixth when Archie scored on an infield out. L.A. increased
their lead to 5–2 in the bottom of the sixth when Paul Carpenter homered with
Charlie English on base. Hal Turpin was chased in the eighth during that
seven-run outburst and was relieved by Dwight Van Fleet, a pitcher the Angels
had released during the season.

The Rainiers had checked out of their hotel before the doubleheader and
made train reservations that night to leave for the north, but after that eighth
inning, they quickly called the depot to cancel those reservations and the hotel
to hold their rooms for them.

Seattle	AB	R	H	RBI	O	A	E
White LF	4	1	2	0	3	0	0
Strange SS	5	0	3	1	2	1	1
Vanni RF	4	0	0	1	2	0	0
Archie 1B	5	1	2	0	7	1	0
Campbell C	4	0	1	0	1	1	0
Lawrence CF	4	0	0	1	4	1	1
Gyselman 3B	4	0	0	0	2	0	0
J. Coscarart 2B	4	0	0	0	2	3	0
Turpin P	3	0	0	0	1	1	0
Van Fleet P	0	0	0	0	0	0	0

Seattle	AB	R	H	RBI	O	A	E
Selway P	0	0	0	0	0	0	0
Hancken[a]	1	1	1	0	0	0	0
	38	3	9	3	24	8	2

(a) Batted for Selway in the ninth.

Los Angeles	AB	R	H	RBI	O	A	E
Stringer 2B	5	1	3	3	4	3	1
Statz CF	3	1	1	0	5	0	0
Rothrock RF	4	3	1	0	2	0	0
R. Collins C	4	2	1	0	2	0	0
J. Collins 1B	4	0	2	3	9	1	0
English 3B	5	2	2	2	1	1	2
Cihocki SS	5	0	1	0	2	5	0
Carpenter LF	4	2	2	2	2	0	0
Bonetti P	4	1	1	0	0	0	0
	38	12	14	10	27	10	3

Pitching Records	IP	H	R	ER	SO	BB
Turpin (L)	7.2	9	6	6	1	3
Van Fleet	0+	4	6	1	0	2
Selway	0.1	1	0	0	0	0
Bonetti	9	9	3	2	1	1

Left on Base: Seattle 9, Los Angeles 8. Home Runs: Carpenter, Stringer, English. Two Base Hits: J. Collins, White, Archie. Sacrifices: Vanni, Statz. Time of Game: 2hr. 4 min. Umpires: Powell, Engeln, Doran.

Seattle	001	001	001	3	– 9	– 2
Los Angeles	200	012	07x	12	– 14	– 3

Game Five.

In this seven inning game, Jesse Flores, who had pitched well in relief of Prim in Seattle, held the Rainiers to just one run on Alan Strange's homer. Les Webber did not fare as well as he had in the second game of the series, giving up two runs in the first on Stringer's single and Rothrock's homer and another in the second when Cihocki doubled and scored on Paul Carpenter's single. Paul Gregory relieved Webber in the second and gave up L.A.'s final two runs in the fifth on Jimmie Collins' homer.

Seattle	AB	R	H	RBI	O	A	E
White LF	3	0	0	0	0	0	0
Strange SS	4	1	1	1	1	2	0
Vanni RF	3	0	0	0	2	0	0
Archie 1B	3	0	1	0	8	0	0
Campbell C	2	0	0	0	4	1	0
Lawrence CF	3	0	1	0	1	0	0
Gyselman 3B	3	0	0	0	1	3	1
J. Coscarart 2B	3	0	1	0	1	1	0
Webber P	0	0	0	0	0	0	0
Gregory P	2	0	0	0	0	1	0
Hancken [a]	1	0	1	0	0	0	0
	27	1	5	1	18	8	1

(a) Batted for Gregory in the seventh.

Los Angeles	AB	R	H	RBI	O	A	E
Stringer 2B	4	1	1	0	2	2	0
Statz CF	3	0	0	0	5	0	0
Rothrock RF	3	1	1	2	0	0	0
R. Collins C	3	1	1	0	4	0	0
J. Collins 1B	3	1	2	2	6	0	1
English 3B	3	0	0	0	1	1	0
Cihocki SS	3	1	2	0	0	2	1
Carpenter LF	3	0	2	1	3	0	0
Flores P	2	0	0	0	0	1	0
	27	5	9	5	21	6	2

Pitching Records	IP	H	R	ER	SO	BB
Webber (L)	1+	5	3	3	0	0
Gregory	5	4	2	2	3	0
Flores	7	5	1	1	3	2

Wild Pitches: Webber, Flores. Left on Base: Seattle 7, Los Angeles 5. Home Runs: J. Collins, Rockrock, Strange. Two Base Hit: Cihocki. Sacrifice: Flores. Double Play: English to J. Collins. Time of Game: 1 hr. 32 min. Umpires: Engeln, Doran and Powell.

Seattle	000	001	0　1 – 5 – 1
Los Angeles	210	020	x　5 – 9 – 2

　　Playing conditions were very bad in the second game with the rain and high wind. That Sunday night, the Los Angeles area was hit with 5.42 inches of rain and gale force winds up to 65 miles per hour. Instead of citizens dying from the heat, some were now being killed as small boats capsized along the coast. It would have been impossible to play at Wrigley Field on Monday night, so a doubleheader was scheduled for Tuesday night, the 26th, if a seventh game were necessary. Officials did not want this series to go beyond Tuesday night because Loyola University was playing football against Whittier at Gilmore Stadium on Wednesday night, the 27th. Furthermore, Sacramento had already eliminated the Seals in five games, so owners were anxious to get the final series started.

Game Six.

This game started at 7:30 instead of the usual 8:15 because of the possibility of a doubleheader but Ray Prim shut Seattle out 2–0 for L.A.'s first win in a playoff series. Prim made up for his poor showing in Seattle by pitching a five-hitter and striking out eight. Kewpie Dick Barrett, who annoyed the Angels with his strutting in game three, was the hard luck loser. Barrett walked with the bases loaded in the sixth, and with two outs, Paul Carpenter hit a "rainbow" single that eluded shortstop Alan Strange and center fielder Bill Lawrence. Things got exciting for the 4,000 fans in the top of the ninth, however, when Strange doubled and Lawrence walked. With two outs and the runners going, "Tricky" Dick Gyselman hit a slicing drive to deep right field on which Jack Rothrock made a game saving catch, sending the "Pride of Puget Sound" team home for the winter.

Seattle	AB	R	H	RBI	O	A	E
White LF	4	0	0	0	2	0	0
Strange SS	4	0	2	0	2	3	0
Vanni RF	3	0	0	0	5	1	0
Archie 1B	4	0	0	0	7	0	0
Lawrence CF	3	0	2	0	2	0	0
Gyselman 3B	4	0	0	0	0	1	0
J. Coscarart 2B	3	0	0	0	4	2	0
Hancken C	2	0	1	0	2	0	0
Barrett P	2	0	0	0	0	3	0
Hunt[a]	1	0	0	0	0	0	0
Selway[b]	1	0	0	0	0	0	0
Walker P	0	0	0	0	0	0	0
	31	0	5	0	24	10	0

(a) Batted for Barrett in the eighth.
(b) Batted for Vanni in the ninth.

Los Angeles	AB	R	H	RBI	O	A	E
Stringer 2B	4	0	2	0	1	2	0
Statz CF	3	0	0	0	3	0	0
Rothrock RF	2	0	1	0	5	0	0
R. Collins C	4	1	0	0	8	0	0
J. Collins 1B	3	1	0	0	4	0	0
English 3B	4	0	2	0	3	1	0
Cihocki SS	3	0	2	0	2	1	0
Carpenter LF	4	0	1	2	1	0	0
Prim P	3	0	0	0	0	1	0
	30	2	8	2	27	5	0

Pitching Records	IP	H	R	ER	SO	BB
Barrett (L)	7	7	2	2	2	4
Walker	1	1	0	0	0	0
Prim	9	5	0	0	8	2

Left on Base: Seattle 6, Los Angeles 9. Two Base Hits: Hancken, Strange. Sacrifice: Statz. Double Plays: Prim to Cihocki to J. Collins; Vanni to Archie. Time of Game: 2 hr. 10 min. Umpires: Doran, Powell, Engeln.

Seattle	000	000	000	0 – 5 – 0	
Los Angeles	000	002	00X	2 – 8 – 0	

The champion Rainiers received the same compensation as the Angels did in 1938: $2,500 for winning the pennant and $1,250 for losing the first round of the playoffs. With about 22 shares, this would amount to $170 per man, or about $1,226 in current dollars.

The Sacramento–San Francisco Series

Even though the Solons finished at .500 with 88 wins and losses, it did not prevent them from beating the same two teams they defeated in 1938 to win the president's cup. In fact, it took them the same number of games each year, five to beat the Seals and six to beat the Angels, but they played those teams in reverse order in 1939. No other team was ever to win the playoffs with this low a winning percentage, but three teams did qualify for the playoffs with losing records. The Solons won 16 and lost 9 to the Seals during the regular season.

Game One.

The second place Seals opened at home on Tuesday night, September 19, and were beaten by the little Portuguese left-hander, Tony Freitas, by a 4–1 score. Freitas himself drove in the Solons' second run in the sixth when he singled in Larry Barton. Sacramento's first run in the fourth came on Dib Williams' triple and Joe Orengo's single. Harvey Storey's error gave the Solons their third run in the eighth and Dib Williams' sacrifice fly scored their final run in the ninth. Sad Sam Gibson started and lost for the Seals, but was relieved by Old Pard Win Ballou. Rookie first baseman Bob Gibson of the Seals was hurt in the first inning, so the injured Harley Boss was forced into action. No attendance was reported.

Sacramento	AB	R	H	RBI	O	A	E
Marshall LF	3	1	0	0	3	0	0
Adams CF	5	0	1	0	3	0	0
Wieczorek RF	5	0	1	0	3	1	0
Garibaldi 3B	3	0	0	0	3	2	0
Williams 2B	3	2	1	1	3	1	0
Barton 1B	4	1	2	0	6	1	0
Orengo SS	2	0	1	1	2	1	0
Ogrodowski C	3	0	1	0	4	0	0
Freitas P	4	0	1	1	0	2	0
	32	4	8	3	27	8	0

San Francisco	AB	R	H	RBI	O	A	E
DiMaggio CF	4	0	0	0	3	1	0
Holder RF	4	0	2	0	3	0	0
Storey SS	4	0	1	0	1	1	1
Frazier LF	4	1	1	0	3	0	0
Warner 3B	4	0	2	0	1	1	0
B. Gibson 1B	0	0	0	0	1	0	0
Boss 1B	4	0	1	0	5	0	0
Wright 2B	4	0	1	0	2	1	0
Woodall C	4	0	1	0	8	0	0
S. Gibson P	2	0	1	0	0	1	0
Norbert[a]	1	0	0	0	0	0	0
Ballou P	0	0	0	0	0	0	0
	35	1	10	0	27	5	1

(a) Batted for S. Gibson in the eighth.

Five 1939 San Francisco Seals players buy tickets for a special performance at Seals Stadium. Lefty O'Doul is at the window and Dominic DiMaggio is with the glasses.

Pitching Records	IP	H	R	ER	SO	BB
Freitas	9	10	1	1	4	0
S. Gibson (L)	7	7	2	2	7	4
Ballou	2	3	2	1	0	3

Wild Pitch: S. Gibson. Passed Ball: Woodall. Three Base Hit: Williams. Two Base Hit: Frazier. Sacrifices: Orengo, Barton, Williams. Stolen Base: Marshall. Double Plays: Wieczorek to Barton; Freitas to Garibaldi to Barton to Garibaldi. DiMaggio to Boss. Time of Game: 2 hr. 5 min. Umpires: Snyder, Hood, Falls.

Sacramento	000	101	011	4 –	8 –	0
San Francisco	000	000	001	1 –	10 –	1

Game Two.

The Seals had trouble with left-handers in 1939, so manager Benny Borgmann, a former basketball player, decided to pitch Tommy Seats against them on Wednesday night. Tony Freitas had lost to San Francisco only once in three years, and Tommy Seats was 5–1 against the Seals in 1939. In addition, the Seals could not get their best lineup on the field because of injuries, so left fielder Ted Norbert was replaced by the rookie Keith Frazier and third baseman Ted Jennings gave way to the aging Jackie Warner. This game started out to be an easy one for Seats as his teammates got him three runs in the first and another in the second. In the first, Buster Adams and Chet Wieczorek singled, Art Garibaldi walked, before singles by Dib Williams and Larry Barton plated three runs. In the second, Brusie Ogrodowski singled, Seats sacrificed, and Max Marshall singled in the run. It was 4–1 going into the last of the ninth, when Seats gave up singles to Keith Frazier, Bob Gibson, Al Wright, and Larry Woodall. With two outs, Dom DiMaggio singled in the tying run but Brooks Holder grounded out to send the game to extra innings.

In the 10th, Lefty O'Doul brought in Orville Jorgens to pitch. Jorgens was the younger brother of Yankee back-up catcher Arndt Jorgens, giving the Seals two brothers on the world champions. In that inning, Art Garibaldi singled, was sacrificed to second, and after Larry Barton was passed, the runners pulled a double steal on the young catcher, Will Leonard, who replaced Larry Woodall, who was taken out for a pinch runner in the ninth. Garibaldi scored on Joe Orengo's sacrifice fly. In the last of the 10th, Seats was replaced by Ira Smith after giving up a double to Keith Frazier. Smith saved the game for Seats. Again, no attendance figures were given.

Sacramento	AB	R	H	RBI	O	A	E
Marshall LF	5	0	1	1	1	0	0
Adams CF	5	1	2	0	5	1	1

Sacramento	AB	R	H	RBI	O	A	E
Wieczokek RF	5	1	1	0	2	0	0
Garibaldi 3B	5	1	2	0	2	2	0
Williams 2B	4	1	2	1	3	3	0
Barton 1B	4	0	2	1	9	1	0
Orengo SS	4	0	0	1	1	5	1
Ogrodowski C	1	1	1	0	0	0	0
Seats P	4	0	2	0	0	1	0
Smith P	0	0	0	0	0	0	0
Grilk C	2	0	1	0	7	0	0
	39	5	14	4	30	13	2

San Francisco	AB	R	H	RBI	O	A	E
DiMaggio CF	5	0	3	0	0	1	0
Holder RF	4	0	1	0	0	0	0
Storey SS	5	0	0	0	0	2	0
Frazier LF	5	1	3	0	3	0	0
Warner 3B	4	1	1	0	0	4	0
B. Gibson 1B	5	1	1	0	13	1	0
Wright 2B	4	1	3	1	7	2	1
Woodall C	4	0	1	2	7	2	0
Stutz P	2	0	0	0	0	3	0
Norbert[a]	1	0	0	0	0	0	0
Jorgens P	1	0	0	0	0	1	0
Guay[b]	0	0	0	0	0	0	0
Leonard C	0	0	0	0	0	0	0
Boss[c]	1	0	0	0	0	0	0
	41	4	13	3	30	16	1

(a) Batted for Stutz in the eighth.
(b) Ran for Woodall in the ninth.
(c) Batted for Warner in the 10th.

Pitching Records	IP	H	R	RBI	SO	BB
Seats (W)	9.1	12	4	3	4	1
Smith	0.2	1	0	0	1	0
Stutz	8	12	4	3	7	1
Jorgens (L)	2	2	1	1	0	2

Three Base Hit: Barton. Two Base Hits: DiMaggio, Frazier, Grilk. Sacrifices: Orengo, Seats, Williams. Stolen Bases: DiMaggio, Garibaldi, Barton. Double Plays: Seats to Orengo to Barton. Time of Game: 2hr. 30min. Umpires: Hood, Falls, Snyder.

Sacramento	310	000	000	1	5 –	14 –	2
San Francisco	010	000	003	0	4 –	13 –	1

Game Three.

On Thursday night, September 21, rookie left-hander Larry Powell held the Solons to just three hits and one run as the Seals eked out a 2–1 win. The only run Sacramento got came on a bases loaded walk to Larry Barton in the fourth. The Seals tied the game in the sixth when Dom DiMaggio and Brooks Holder singled off Bill Schmidt, and then Ted Jennings, who returned to the lineup, drove in DiMaggio with a force out. The Seals got an unearned run in the seventh off the hard luck Schmidt when Al Wright singled and Larry Powell was safe on Barton's error at first. DiMaggio then singled in Wright with the deciding run.

Sacramento	AB	R	H	RBI	O	A	E
Marshall LF	4	1	2	0	2	0	0
Adams CF	4	0	0	0	4	0	0
Wieczorek RF	4	0	0	0	1	0	0
Garibaldi 3B	4	0	1	0	0	1	0
Williams 2B	1	0	0	0	3	3	0
Barton 1B	2	0	0	1	6	0	1
Orengo SS	3	0	0	0	3	4	0
Grilk C	3	0	0	0	5	1	0
Schmidt P	3	0	0	0	0	1	1
	28	1	3	1	24	10	2

San Francisco	AB	R	H	RBI	O	A	E
DiMaggio CF	4	1	2	1	3	0	0
Holder RF	4	0	1	0	1	0	0
Jennings 3B	4	0	1	1	1	2	0
Storey SS	4	0	0	0	0	2	0
Boss 1B	4	0	2	0	8	0	0
Frazier LF	4	0	0	0	2	0	0
Wright 2B	3	1	1	0	2	3	0
Woodall C	3	0	0	0	10	0	0
Powell P	3	0	1	0	0	2	0
	33	2	8	2	27	9	0

Pitching Records	IP	H	R	ER	SO	BB
Schmidt	8	8	2	1	4	0
Powell	9	3	1	1	10	3

Two Base Hit: Powell. Double Play: Jennings to Wright to Boss. Time of Game: 1 hr. 50 min. Umpires: Falls, Snyder, Hood.

Sacramento	000	100	000	1 –	3 –	2
San Francisco	000	001	10X	2 –	8 –	0

Game Four.

There was no off day because these two cities are only 90 miles apart. On Friday night, September 22, the Solons pounded the Seals 9–0 at Cardinal Field before a shirt sleeve crowd of 5,000, taking a commanding three games to one lead in the series. Nick Strincevich pitched a five hit shutout and walked only one while Bill Shores was knocked out in the first inning while the Solons scored three runs. Lou Koupal relieved for the Seals but was no better as the Solons got three more in the second, and two in the third to make the game a laugher for the Sacramento fans. Buster Adams got three hits, while Joe Orengo and Art Garibaldi got two each. Dib Williams drove in three runs.

San Francisco	AB	R	H	RBI	O	A	E
DiMaggio CF	3	0	2	0	3	0	0
Holder RF	4	0	0	0	2	0	0
Jennings 3B	4	0	0	0	0	0	0
Storey SS	3	0	1	0	2	2	1
Boss 1B	2	0	1	0	3	0	0
Frazier LF	1	0	0	0	2	0	1
Wright 2B	3	0	0	0	1	3	0
Woodall C	1	0	0	0	3	0	0
Shores P	0	0	0	0	0	0	0
Koupal P	1	0	0	0	0	1	0
B. Gibson 1B[a]	2	0	0	0	4	0	0
Leonard C	2	0	1	0	4	0	0
Wilkie LF	1	0	0	0	0	0	1
Raimondi[b]	1	0	0	0	0	0	0
Guay P	1	0	0	0	0	1	0
	29	0	5	0	24	7	3

(a) Batted for Frazier in the fourth.
(b) Batted for Koupal in the fifth.

Sacramento	AB	R	H	RBI	O	A	E
Marshall LF	3	1	0	1	1	0	0
Adams CF	4	2	3	1	2	0	0
Wieczorek RF	4	1	0	0	3	0	0

Sacramento	AB	R	H	RBI	O	A	E
Garibaldi 3B	4	2	2	2	0	0	0
Williams 2B	4	0	1	3	2	3	0
Barton 1B	4	0	0	0	8	1	0
Orengo SS	4	2	2	1	4	4	0
Grilk C	3	1	1	0	7	0	0
Strincevich P	4	0	0	0	0	1	0
	34	9	9	8	27	9	0

Pitching Records	IP	H	R	ER	SO	BB
Shores (L)	0.2	2	3	3	1	2
Koupal	3.1	6	5	5	4	1
Guay	4	1	1	0	2	0
Strincevich	9	5	0	0	6	1

Left on Base: San Francisco 3, Sacramento 6. Two Base Hits: Boss, Garibaldi, DiMaggio, Grilk. Sacrifice: Marshall. Double Plays: Barton to Orengo to Barton; Orengo to Barton. Time of Game: 1 hr. 42min. Umpires: Snyder, Hood, Falls.

San Francisco	000	000	000	0	– 5 – 3
Sacramento	332	010	00X	9	– 9 – 0

Game Five.

The teams took Saturday the 23rd off because of a football game between the College of Pacific Tigers and the University of South Dakota Coyotes. A doubleheader was scheduled for Sunday the 24th , but only if the Seals won the opener to extend the series.

Only one game was needed but it took extra innings to end the Seals' season. The same pitchers that started the opening game faced each other again, Freitas and Gibson, but Gibson was not around very long. O'Doul jerked him in the first inning after he gave up a walk to Adams and a homer to Wieczorek, and a double to Garibaldi. Young Larry Powell came in and gave up only one run and four hits in 5⅔ innings, before being lifted for a pinch hitter. Meanwhile, Freitas shut the Seals out until the seventh, when they erupted for three runs to tie the game. The Seals were hampered by so many injured players in their lineup who could not run that singles by Ted Norbert, Bob Gibson, Al Wright and Larry Woodall produced only one run. Finally, Dom DiMaggio's single did score two runs to tie the game.

Win Ballou pitched the rest of the game for the Seals and absorbed the loss. Freitas was taken out in the 10th inning for Ira Smith, who got the win.

In the last of the 11th, Ballou walked two men and then Ira Smith hit a grounder past the limping Harley Boss at first base into right field to score the winning run. Boss had to be put in when Gibson hurt his knee. The win gave the Solons three days of rest before they were to meet the Angels on Thursday the 28th.

San Francisco	AB	R	H	RBI	O	A	E
DiMaggio CF	5	0	4	2	4	1	0
Holder RF	5	0	1	0	4	0	0
Storey SS	5	0	0	0	3	2	0
Norbert LF	4	0	1	0	0	0	0
Warner 3B	5	1	1	0	2	2	0
B. Gibson 1B	3	1	1	0	4	1	0
Wright 2B	5	1	1	0	4	4	0
Woodall C	5	0	1	1	9	1	0
S. Gibson P	0	0	0	0	0	0	0
Powell P	2	0	0	0	0	0	0
Frazier[a]	1	0	0	0	0	0	0
Ballou P	1	0	0	0	0	0	0
Jennings[b]	0	0	0	0	0	0	0
Boss 1B	1	0	1	0	2	0	0
	42	3	11	3	32[c]	11	0

(a) Batted for Powell in the seventh.
(b) Batted for B. Gibson in the ninth.
(c) Two out when winning run scored.

Sacramento	AB	R	H	RBI	O	A	E
Marshall LF	5	0	0	0	5	0	0
Adams CF	4	2	3	1	3	0	0
Wieczorek RF	5	1	1	2	0	0	0
Garibaldi 3B	4	0	1	0	2	4	0
Williams 2B	4	1	0	0	4	4	0
Barton 1B	4	0	1	0	9	2	0
Orengo SS	5	0	1	0	4	3	1
Grilk C	4	0	0	0	5	2	0
Freitas P	2	0	1	0	1	0	1
Smith P	1	0	1	1	0	1	0
	38	4	9	4	33	16	2

Pitching Records	IP	H	R	ER	SO	BB
S. Gibson	0.1	2	2	2	0	1
Powell	5.2	4	1	1	5	1

Ballou (L)	4.2	3	1	1	1	5
Freitas	9.1	10	3	3	5	0
Smith (W)	1.2	1	0	0	0	1

Hit by Pitcher: B. Gibson by Freitas. Left on Base: San Francisco 8, Sacramento 9. Home Runs: Wieczorek, Adams. Two Base Hit: Garibaldi. Double Plays: Wright to Woodall to Warner; Garibaldi to Williams to Barton; Orengo to Williams to Barton. Time of Game: 2 hr. 25 min. Umpires: Hood, Falls, Snyder.

| San Francisco | 000 | 000 | 300 | 00 | 3 – 11 – 0 |
| Sacramento | 201 | 000 | 000 | 01 | 4 – 9 – 2 |

The Seals got practically nothing in playoff money. With 22 shares for the $1,250, it came to $57 per man, but when young outfielder Keith Frazier had $380 stolen from his car parked outside Cardinal Field on that Sunday, the Seals decided to make up Frazier's loss by chipping in their playoff money, leaving each man with very little.

The Final Series: Sacramento vs. Los Angeles

The Angels and Solons split their 28 seasonal games evenly. Although the Angels had the right to open this series at home, they decided to open at Sacramento to avoid any conflict with college football. On Friday night, September 29, UCLA opened their undefeated season with Texas Christian, and on Saturday afternoon, USC opened its undefeated season with Oregon. There was a lot of interest in these two fine college teams, that tied each other later on, sending the Trojans to the Rose Bowl. In addition, *The Los Angeles Times* was giving a lot of coverage to the Cincinnati Reds winning their first pennant in 20 years, making it difficult for the Angels to compete.

Game One.

Fay Thomas pitched the opener on Thursday night, September 28, for the Angels, which was his first outing since Thursday night, the 21st, in Seattle. This time Thomas pitched very well, allowing five hits and seven walks, while striking out seven in a ten-inning victory over Tommy Seats. Hannah's hired hands scored a run in the first when Jigger Statz tripled and scored on Jack Rothrock's single. Benny Borgmann's boys tied it up in the fourth when Chet Wiecorek walked, was safe at second on Thomas' wild throw, and scored on Dib Williams' single. The tie was broken in the top of the 10th on three straight singles by Jimmy Collins, Charlie English and Eddie Cihocki. No attendance was given for this game, which was played with no substitutions.

Los Angeles	AB	R	H	RBI	O	A	E
Stringer 2B	4	0	1	0	2	4	0
Statz CF	4	1	2	0	2	0	0
Rothrock RF	4	0	1	1	2	0	0
R. Collins C	4	0	0	0	8	0	0
J. Collins 1B	4	1	1	0	12	1	0
English 2B	4	0	1	0	2	2	1
Cihocki SS	4	0	1	1	0	5	0
Carpenter LF	4	0	0	0	2	0	0
Thomas P	4	0	0	0	0	1	2
	36	2	7	2	30	13	3

Sacramento	AB	R	H	RBI	O	A	E
Marshall LF	4	0	0	0	2	0	0
Adams CF	5	0	1	0	5	0	0
Wieczorek RF	2	1	0	0	1	0	0
Garibaldi 3B	5	0	0	0	0	1	0
Williams 2B	5	0	1	1	3	0	0
Barton 1B	4	0	1	0	7	0	0
Orengo SS	3	0	1	0	0	5	0
Grilk C	4	0	1	0	12	1	0
Seats P	3	0	0	0	0	0	0
	35	1	5	1	30	7	0

Pitching Records	IP	H	R	ER	SO	BB
Thomas	10	5	1	0	7	7
Seats	10	7	2	2	12	0

Left on Base: Los Angeles 7, Sacramento 12. Three Base Hit: Statz. Two Base Hits: Orengo, Adams, Statz. Sacrifice: Orengo. Double Plays: Cihocki to Stringer to J. Collins; Grilk to Williams. Umpires: Powell, Engeln and Doran.

Los Angeles	100	000	000	1	2 – 7 – 3
Sacramento	000	100	000	0	1 – 5 – 0

Game Two.

The fans knew that this Friday night doubleheader would be the last games played in Cardinal Field in 1939 so 5,298 turned out to see their Sacs take two one-run games from the Angels to go up 2–1 in the series. Julio Bonetti dueled Tony Freitas in the opener and had a 2–1 lead until the last of the sixth when the Solons struck for two runs. Doubles by Art Garibaldi and Dib Williams scored one run, and Joe Orengo's single plated the tie breaker. The Angels tied it in the eighth on three singles, with Lou Stringer scoring the tying run. Young Stringer went four for five with a double and two runs scored in a losing cause. The Solons won it in the ninth when Orengo got his third hit of the night, a single, and took second on Jim Grilk's sacrifice. Buster Adams looped a two-out single that eluded Stringer and Statz for the game winner.

Los Angeles	AB	R	H	RBI	O	A	E
Stringer 2B	5	2	4	1	5	4	0
Statz CF	5	0	2	0	1	0	0
Rothrock RF	2	0	1	1	2	0	0
R. Collins C	4	0	0	0	3	0	0
J. Collins 1B	4	0	1	1	9	4	0
English 3B	4	0	0	0	3	0	0
Cihocki SS	4	0	1	0	2	6	0
Carpenter LF	3	0	1	0	1	0	0
Bonetti P	4	1	1	0	0	2	0
	35	3	11	3	26[a]	16	0

(a) Two outs when winning run scored.

Sacramento	AB	R	H	RBI	O	A	E
Marshall LF	5	0	1	0	1	0	0
Adams CF	5	0	3	1	3	0	0
Wieczorek RF	4	0	2	0	2	0	0
Garibaldi 3B	3	1	1	0	2	1	0
Williams 2B	4	1	1	1	2	2	0
Barton 1B	4	1	1	0	9	2	0
Orengo SS	4	1	3	1	1	3	0
Grilk C	3	0	0	1	4	0	0
Freitas P	3	0	0	0	3	3	0
	35	4	12	4	27	11	0

Pitching Records	IP	H	R	ER	SO	BB
Bonetti	8.2	12	4	4	3	1
Freitas	9	11	3	3	4	1

Left on Base: Los Angeles 8, Sacramento 9. Two Base Hits: Adams, Bonetti, Stringer, Garibaldi, Williams. Sacrifices: Rothrock, Garibaldi, Carpenter,

Grilk. Double Play: Stringer to J. Collins to Cihocki. Time of Game: 1 hr. 31 min. Umpires: Engeln, Powell, Doran.

Los Angeles	002	000	010	3 –	11 –	0
Sacramento	010	002	001	4 –	12 –	0

Game Three.

The seven inning nightcap saw only one unearned run scored, but it was enough for Bill Schmidt to beat Jesse Flores. In the first, Buster Adams singled and Wieczorek walked. Garibaldi grounded into what might have been a double play but Lou Stringer threw wildly to first, allowing Adams to score. The Angels threatened in the seventh when Eddie Mayo got a pinch hit single, and with Ray Prim running for him, Jimmy Collins hit a smash to right field but Chet Wieczorek made a sensational catch, and doubled Prim off first.

Los Angeles	AB	R	H	RBI	O	A	E
Stringer 2B	2	0	0	0	4	0	1
Statz CF	3	0	1	0	2	0	0
Rothrock RF	3	0	0	0	1	0	0
R. Collins C	2	0	0	0	6	0	0
J. Collins 1B	3	0	0	0	2	1	0
English 3B	2	0	0	0	0	1	0
Cihocki SS	2	0	0	0	0	4	0
Carpenter LF	2	0	1	0	3	0	0
Flores P	1	0	0	0	0	0	0
Mayo [a]	1	0	1	0	0	0	0
Prim [b]	0	0	0	0	0	0	0
	21	0	3	0	18	6	1

(a) Batted for R. Collins in the seventh.
(b) Ran for Mayo in the seventh.

Sacramento	AB	R	H	RBI	O	A	E
Marshall LF	3	0	0	0	0	0	0
Adams CF	3	1	2	0	1	0	0
Wieczorek RF	1	0	0	0	2	1	0
Garibaldi 3B	2	0	1	0	0	0	0
Williams 2B	2	0	0	0	2	3	0
Barton 1B	2	0	0	0	7	2	0
Orengo SS	3	0	0	0	2	3	1

Sacramento	AB	R	H	RBI	O	A	E
Grilk C	3	0	1	0	5	1	0
Schmidt P	1	0	0	0	2	1	0
	20	1	4	0	21	11	1

Pitching Records	IP	H	R	ER	SO	BB
Flores	6	4	1	0	6	2
Schmidt	7	3	0	0	3	1

Hit by Pitcher: Wieczorek by Flores. Left on Base: Los Angeles 2, Sacramento 7. Two Base Hit: Garibaldi. Sacrifices: Schmidt, Flores, Garibaldi, Williams. Stolen Base: Garibaldi. Double Plays: Grilk to Garibaldi to Grilk; Williams to Orengo to Barton; Wieczorek to Orengo. Time of Game: 1 hr. 30 min. Umpires: Doran, Powell, Engeln.

Los Angeles	000	000	0	0 – 3 – 1
Sacramento	100	000	x	1 – 4 – 1

With Saturday a travel day while college football drew the attention, the Angels scheduled a doubleheader for Sunday, October 1, and if more games were needed, another doubleheader was on Tuesday night, the 3rd. This was the same arrangement the Angels made the week before when Seattle was in town. There was no reason given why Monday was an off night, but perhaps it was because the Coast League traditionally did not play on Mondays during the season, using that day to travel. It would have been impossible to play on Monday the 25th of September because of rain, but the weather was not a problem on October 2.

Game Four.

The Solons could have ended the playoffs with a doubleheader win over the Angels but an eighth inning rally in the opener allowed the Angels to tie the series at two games each. Nick Strincevich started for Sacramento against Ray Prim and was staked to a 2–0 lead. In the first, Garibaldi singled in Wieczorek and in the third, Strincevich singled and scored on Wieczorek's sacrifice fly. Jimmy Collins' homer in the sixth cut the lead to 2–1, but in the eighth, the Sacs looked like they were going to put the game away. The Solons tallied three runs on four hits and two Angel errors that inning to go up 5–1. But in the last of the eighth, the wheels came off the Solons' cart. Ripper Collins singled off reliever Ira Smith, and came all the way around to score on a single by Charlie English. After Cihocki was retired, Paul Carpenter walked and Ray Prim, was allowed to hit for himself, trailing 5–2. One reason may have been a depleted Angel bench. Eddie Mayo had already been used to hit for Bob

Collins in the seventh, and Hal Sueme was in the game catching. The right-handed batting Prim looped a single to score English, making it 5–3. After Stringer was retired, Jigger Statz stepped up and powered a three-run homer over the left field wall to put the Angels up 6–5.

Sacramento	AB	R	H	RBI	O	A	E
Marshall LF	3	1	1	0	3	0	0
Adams CF	4	1	3	2	3	0	0
Wieczorek RF	3	1	1	1	2	0	0
Garibaldi 3B	4	0	1	1	0	1	1
Williams 2B	4	0	1	0	2	4	0
Barton 1B	4	0	0	0	9	0	0
Orengo SS	4	0	0	0	2	5	0
Grilk C	4	1	1	0	3	0	0
Strincevich P	1	1	1	0	0	1	0
Smith P	2	0	0	0	0	0	0
	33	5	9	4	24	11	1

Los Angeles	AB	R	H	RBI	O	A	E
Stringer 2B	4	0	1	0	3	3	0
Statz CF	4	1	2	3	3	0	0
Rothrock RF	3	0	0	0	2	0	0
R. Collins C	2	0	0	0	1	0	0
J. Collins 1B	4	2	2	1	10	1	0
English 3B	4	1	2	1	2	4	0
Cihocki SS	4	0	0	0	0	4	1
Carpenter LF	2	1	1	0	4	1	1
Prim P	4	1	1	1	1	0	0
Mayo[a]	1	0	0	0	0	0	0
Sueme C	1	0	0	0	1	0	0
	33	6	9	6	27	13	2

(a) Batted for R. Collins in the seventh.

Pitching Records	IP	H	R	ER	SO	BB
Strincevich	6.1	5	1	1	3	5
Smith (L)	1.2	4	5	5	0	2
Prim	9	9	5	4	1	1

Left on Base: Sacramento 4, Los Angeles 10. Home Runs: J. Collins, Statz. Two Base Hits: Statz, J. Collins. Sacrifices: Marshall, Wieczorek. Double Plays: English to J. Collins; Williams to Orengo to Barton. Time of Game: 2hr. 3 min. Umpires: Powell, Engeln, Doran.

Sacramento	101	000	030	5 – 9 – 1
Los Angeles	000	001	05X	6 – 9 – 2

Game Five.

In the seven-inning nightcap, the Solons' John Hubbell, who was the younger brother of the Giants' famous Carl, stopped the Angels on three hits and only one run as Sacramento took the pivotal fifth game, to go up three games to two in the series. The Angels started Fay Thomas who had only two days rest after his 10 inning win on Thursday in Sacramento. In the top of the first, Max Marshall doubled and later scored on Dib Williams' single. In the third, Buster Adams homered, and in the fourth, Larry Barton singled, took second on a sacrifice, and scored on Jim Grilk's single. The only Angel tally came on Lou Stringer's sixth inning homer. No attendance was announced for this doubleheader.

Sacramento	AB	R	H	RBI	O	A	E
Marshall LF	3	1	1	0	0	0	0
Adams CF	4	1	1	1	6	0	0
Wieczorek RF	4	0	1	1	1	0	0
Garibaldi 3B	3	0	0	0	0	1	0
Williams 2B	3	0	2	0	3	2	0
Barton 1B	3	1	1	0	7	0	0
Orengo SS	2	0	0	0	2	2	0
Grilk C	3	0	1	1	2	0	0
Hubbell P	3	0	0	0	0	2	0
	28	3	7	3	21	7	0

Los Angeles	AB	R	H	RBI	O	A	E
Stringer 2B	2	1	1	1	4	2	0
Statz CF	3	0	1	0	1	0	0
Rothrock RF	3	0	0	0	0	0	0
R. Collins C	1	0	0	0	5	1	1
J. Collins 1B	3	0	0	0	5	1	0
English 3B	3	0	1	0	3	0	0
Cihocki SS	3	0	0	0	1	3	1
Carpenter LF	3	0	0	0	2	0	0
Thomas P	1	0	0	0	0	1	0
Mayo[a]	1	0	0	0	0	0	0
Berry P	0	0	0	0	0	0	0
	23	1	3	1	21	8	2

(a) Batted for Thomas in the sixth.

Pitching Records	IP	H	R	ER	SO	BB
Hubbell	7	3	1	1	1	3
Thomas (L)	6	7	3	3	4	0
Berry	1	0	0	0	1	1

Left on Base: Sacramento 6, Los Angeles 4. Home Runs: Adams, Stringer. Two Base Hit: Marshall. Sacrifice: Orengo. Stolen Base: Orengo. Double Play: Orengo to Williams to Barton. Time of Game: 1 hr. 25 min. Umpires: Engeln, Doran and Powell.

Sacramento	101	100	0	3 – 7 – 0
Los Angeles	000	001	0	1 – 3 – 2

Game Six.

Tommy Seats faced Julio Bonetti at 7:30 in what would have been the first game of this Tuesday night doubleheader, but Seats' three-hit shutout made the nightcap unnecessary. Larry Barton's second inning homer was all the support Seats needed but the Solons got two more in the sixth and five more in the eighth to make the game a rout. *The Los Angeles Times* had a bigger story on the firing of manager Truck Hannah than on the final playoff game. Hannah was told he was through after the team returned from Seattle during the opening playoff series, but the announcement was held up until the season ended. It was his failure to win the pennant after that 19 game winning streak in April that caused him to lose his job.

Sacramento	AB	R	H	RBI	O	A	E
Marshall LF	5	1	3	0	2	0	0
Adams CF	4	1	0	0	4	0	0
Wieczorek RF	5	2	3	2	2	0	0
Garibaldi 3B	4	1	1	2	0	2	0
Williams 2B	4	1	1	1	3	4	0
Barton 1B	4	1	3	2	7	0	0
Orengo SS	4	0	0	0	2	3	0
Grilk C	4	1	2	1	7	0	0
Seats P	1	0	0	0	0	0	0
	35	8	13	8	27	9	0

Los Angeles	AB	R	H	RBI	O	A	E
Stringer 2B	4	0	0	0	8	2	0
Statz CF	3	0	0	0	1	0	0
Rothrock RF	4	0	0	0	2	0	0

Los Angeles	AB	R	H	RBI	O	A	E
R. Collins C	3	0	1	0	7	2	0
J. Collins 1B	3	0	0	0	4	4	0
English 3B	3	0	1	0	2	1	1
Cihocki SS	3	0	1	0	2	5	1
Carpenter LF	3	0	0	0	1	0	0
Bonetti P	2	0	0	0	0	1	0
Flores P	1	0	0	0	0	0	0
	29	0	3	0	27	15	2

Pitching Records	IP	H	R	ER	SO	BB
Seats	9	3	0	0	7	0
Bonetti (L)	6.1	10	4	4	2	0
Flores	2.2	5	4	3	4	2

Passed Ball: R. Collins. Left on Base: Sacramento 6, Los Angeles 3. Home Runs: Barton, Garibaldi. Two Base Hits: R. Collins, Cihocki, Wieczorek. Sacrifices: Seats 3, Garibaldi. Double Plays: Cihocki to Stringer to J. Collins; Garibaldi to Williams to Barton. Time of Game: 1 hr. 45 min. Umpires: Doran, Powell and Engeln.

Sacramento	010	002	500	8	– 13 – 0
Los Angeles	000	000	000	0	– 3 – 2

The Angels announced they would have 22 shares for their $2,500 playoff money, 21 full shares, and the last one divided ¼ to Novikoff, ¼ to Dutch Lieber, and ½ to a part time trainer. A full share of $113.63 would amount to $817.53 in current value, so if the Solons also had 22 shares for their $5,000 prize, theirs would amount to $227, or $1,633 in today's funds. The 1939 season saw a team that finished at .500 receive more money than Seattle, who played .580 ball at 101–73.

The 1939 World Series did not begin until Wednesday October 4, the day after the playoffs ended, so its broadcasts did not compete with them.

Key Players on 1939 Playoff Teams

Seattle. *Pitchers:* Dick Barrett, Hal Turpin, Paul Gregory, Les Webber and Bill Walker.
   Position Players: Gilly Campbell, George Archie, Alan Strange, Jo Jo White, and Dick Gyselman.

San Francisco. *Pitchers:* Sam Gibson, Larry Powell, Ed Stutz and Win Ballou. *Position Players:* Dom DiMaggio, Brooks Holder, Ted Norbert, Ted Jennings, and Harvey Storey.

Los Angeles. *Pitchers:* Ray Prim, Fay Thomas, Julio Bonetti, and Jesse Flores. *Position Players:* Jigger Statz, Jimmy Collins, Bob Collins, Lou Stringer, Jack Rothrock, Charlie English and Johnny Moore (out with broken ankle).

Sacramento. *Pitchers:* Tony Freitas, Tommy Seats, Bill Schmidt, John Hubbell and Ira Smith.
Position Players: Chet Wieczorek, Larry Barton, Art Garibaldi, Joe Orengo and Dib Williams.

1940

The 1940 season was a Rainier romp. Manager Jack Lelivelt's 1940 Seattle team was the best club the Pacific Coast League had seen since his great Angel team of 1934, but unfortunately, this was to be his last team because Lelivelt died in January 1941. This team had an easier time winning the pennant than the 1939 Rainiers, and in addition, had no trouble winning the playoffs as well. After taking the lead from Oakland in May, Seattle was never challenged the rest of the season, leading by as much as 17 games at one point. Portland manager John Frederick commented that this was the first time he had seen seven teams in the second division.

The Rainiers were built on super pitching, great team speed, excellent defense and timely hitting, but with very little power. The whole club hit only 35 homers during the season while the Angel triple crown winner, Lou Novikoff, hit 41 alone. Even though Seattle was safely in first place in late June, they had scored the fewest runs in the league, while the Angels, then mired in seventh place, had scored 100 more runs than the Rainiers. But when the two teams met, Seattle rarely had trouble outscoring the Angels.

The Angels, now managed by the popular Jigger Statz, floundered until late June before righting themselves and began to climb in the standings. They reached third place in late July and finally overtook Oakland for second place in late August. They were anxious to finish second because the third place team had to open the playoffs against Seattle. The Angels had a winning record against every team in the league except the Rainiers.

The Oakland Oaks, finishing in the first division for the first time since 1936, were managed by Johnny Vergez, the former third baseman for Sacramento. They led the league until Seattle overtook them in late May and held that spot until the Angels passed them in late August. But the Oaks were never in danger of falling out of the first division.

The San Diego Padres, now managed by Cedric Durst, struggled to stay ahead of the Sacramento Solons until late August, when they pulled ahead to stay. The "Pounding Padres" had the highest batting average in the league but with little power, hitting only 38 homers all year, three fewer than Novikoff.

This was San Diego's first time in the playoffs since 1937, and the only season that Sacramento did not qualify for them between 1937 and 1942.

The Seattle-Oakland Series

The Rainiers gave up the right to open this series at home in order to have the weekend games in Sick's Stadium, where they normally drew large crowds. But Seattle was willing to play only two games in Oakland and the Oaks agreed. Seattle again led the league in attendance but did not reach the 1939 total because of some rainouts and the runaway race. Seattle won the season series from all their opponents; with Oakland it was 14 to 10.

Two sour notes put a damper on this series at the start. An article by Art Cohn in *The Oakland Tribune* blasted the playoffs as meaningless and a feeble attempt to extract some "additional coin" from the fans. He argued that Seattle had proven beyond all doubt that they were the league's best team and lamented that in 1939, a fourth place Sacramento team could win the president's cup while finishing at .500 and 14 games behind Seattle. Secondly, the Oaks Booster Club, which was organized to get fans behind their team, decided to hold its annual barbecue in San Jose the very night the playoffs were to open at Oaks Park.

The Bay Area sports pages were giving more coverage to the tight American League race between Detroit and Cleveland than they were to the playoffs. Preseason football articles in Seattle were more enthusiastic about the Washington Huskies than the Oakland and San Francisco papers were about California and Stanford, but it was the surprising Stanford team that had the perfect season and won the Rose Bowl.

Game One.

As great a team as Seattle was, and as great a manager as Jack "Old Lilly Foot" Lelivelt was, neither had ever won a playoff series before 1940. The Rainiers had been eliminated in the first round of the 1936, 1938 and 1939 playoffs, the last two managed by Lelivelt. The Angels also lost split season championship series under his direction in 1930 and 1935, but his great 1934 team won both halves of the season before beating an all-star team in the post-season.

It looked as if the jinx would continue against Seattle and Lelivelt when the Oaks took the opening game 2–1 before 5,200 fans in Oaks Park on Tuesday night, September 17. Kewpie Dick Barrett, who won 24 and lost 5 during the season despite being on the sidelines twice with injuries, started against Oakland's Stanley Corbett. "Richard the Lion Hearted," as the Seattle press called Barrett, deserved a better fate. In the first, Bill Lyman got a bloop double, Hugh Luby struck out but Gilly Campbell dropped the third strike and then threw wildly to first, allowing Luby to reach safely. With two outs, Marvin Gudat tripled them home for Oakland's only runs.

In the eighth, Seattle got three straight singles by Al Niemiec, pinch hitter Spencer Harris and Jo Jo White, which scored a run with no one out. But they were unable to get any more runs. In the ninth, Bill Lyman's two great defensive plays saved the game for Corbett.

Seattle	AB	R	H	RBI	O	A	E
White LF	3	0	1	1	0	0	0
Schuster SS	3	0	0	0	3	4	0
Vanni RF	4	0	0	0	4	0	0
Lawrence CF	4	0	0	0	0	0	0
Archie 1B	3	0	0	0	8	0	0
Campbell C	4	0	1	0	6	0	1
Gyselman 3B	4	0	1	0	2	0	0
Niemiec 2B	3	1	2	0	1	1	0
Barrett P	2	0	1	0	0	2	0
Harris[a]	1	0	1	0	0	0	0
Webber[b]	0	0	0	0	0	0	0
Scribner P	0	0	0	0	0	0	0
Kearse[c]	1	0	0	0	0	0	0
	32	1	7	1	24	7	1

(a) Batted for Barrett in the eighth.
(b) Ran for Harris in the eighth.
(c) Batted for Scribner in the ninth.

Oakland	AB	R	H	RBI	O	A	E
Lyman SS	4	1	2	0	3	7	0
Luby 2B	3	1	0	0	4	3	1
Christopher CF	3	0	1	0	0	0	0
Chapman RF	4	0	0	0	3	0	0
Gudat LF	3	0	2	2	0	0	0
Dunn 1B	3	0	0	0	11	1	0
E. Raimondi 3B	3	0	0	0	1	1	0
W. Raimondi C	3	0	0	0	4	1	0
Corbett P	3	0	0	0	1	2	0
	29	2	5	2	27	15	1

Pitching Records	IP	H	R	ER	SO	BB
Barrett (L)	7	5	2	0	6	1
Scribner	1	0	0	0	0	0
Corbett	9	7	1	1	2	2

Three Base Hit: Gudat. Two Base Hits: Lyman, Nieniec. Sacrifices: Schuster, Christopher. Stolen Bases: Niemiec, Gudat, Archie. Time of Game: 1hr. 53 min. Umpires: Snyder, Hood, Engeln, Falls.

Seattle	000	000	010	1 – 7 – 1
Oakland	200	000	00X	2 – 5 – 1

Game Two.

In another 2–1 game, Seattle evened the series behind Hal Turpin. A crowd of 6,700 came out on Wednesday night, September 18, and saw Ralph Buxton pitch the last home game for the Oaks in 1940. In the third, Turpin singled, moved around to third on two infield outs, and scored on Edo Vanni's single. The Oaks tied it in the fifth when Pete Chapman singled and came home when Marvin Gudat hit another triple. But Oakland could not get him home from third with no one out. Then in the top of the sixth, Seattle scored the winning run on a play of questionable judgment. George Archie, who had tripled, was on third with two outs when Dick Gyselman bunted, and Ralph Buxton elected to shovel the ball to catcher Billy Raimondi instead of throwing to first. Archie slid under the tag. Both teams left on the same train on Thursday morning, September 19, and arrived in Seattle on Friday afternoon for a game that night.

Seattle	AB	R	H	RBI	O	A	E
White LF	4	0	1	0	0	0	0
Schuster SS	4	0	0	0	1	6	0
Vanni RF	4	0	1	1	0	0	0
Lawrence CF	4	0	0	0	3	0	0
Archie 1B	4	1	2	0	13	0	0
Campbell C	4	0	1	0	7	1	0
Gyselman 3B	4	0	2	1	1	3	0
Niemiec 2B	4	0	0	0	2	1	0
Turpin P	3	1	1	0	0	1	0
	35	2	8	2	27	12	0

Oakland	AB	R	H	RBI	O	A	E
Lyman SS	4	0	0	0	1	2	0

Oakland	AB	R	H	RBI	O	A	E
Luby 2B	4	0	2	0	4	2	1
Christopher CF	4	0	0	0	2	0	0
Chapman RF	3	1	1	0	3	0	0
Gudat LF	3	0	1	1	3	0	0
Dunn 1B	3	0	0	0	9	1	0
E. Raimondi 3B	2	0	0	0	1	2	0
W. Raimondi C	3	0	0	0	3	0	0
Buxton P	2	0	0	0	1	1	0
DeVaurs[a]	1	0	0	0	0	0	0
Christoff[b]	1	0	0	0	0	0	0
Ambrose 3B	0	0	0	0	0	1	0
	30	1	4	1	27	9	0

(a) Batted for E. Raimondi in the eighth.
(b) Batted for Buxton in the ninth.

Pitching Records	IP	H	R	ER	SO	BB
Turpin	9	1	4	1	6	0
Buxton	9	8	2	2	3	0

Three Base Hits: Gudat, Archie. Two Base Hit: Campbell. Stolen Bases: Gyselman, White. Time of Game: 1hr. 33min. Umpires: Hood, Engeln, Falls, Snyder.

Seattle	001	001	000	2 – 8 – 0
Oakland	000	010	000	1 – 4 – 0

Game Three.

Playing the percentages, Lelivelt started right-hander Paul Gregory against the mainly right-handed-hitting Oaks. One of his lefties, Les Webber, was out for the season anyway after injuring his ankle as a pinch runner in the first game. Johnny Vergez called on the ailing Jack Salveson, who was unable to open the series because of a sore arm. Salveson was leading 1–0 after three innings but had to come out of this game after his arm bothered him. Ben "Cun'nul" Cantwell replaced Salveson and gave up three runs in the fifth. Gilly Campbell walked, Al Niemiec singled him to third, and Paul Gregory's fly ball scored his battery mate. Then Jo Jo White hit an inside-the-park homer to give Seattle a 3–1 lead. This lead was increased to 4–1 in the eighth when Bill Schuster walked, was sacrificed to second and scored on pinch hitter Ed Kearse's single. The Oaks' final run came in the ninth, but the smooth fielding of the Rainiers prevented a big inning. After Cecil "Dynamite" Dunn and

Ernie Raimondi both singled, Billy Raimondi hit into a double play. Pinch hitter Mike Christoff then singled in Dunn, but Lyman was retired to send 5,000 fans home happy.

Oakland	AB	R	H	RBI	O	A	E
Lyman SS	4	0	0	0	0	2	1
Luby 2B	4	0	0	0	4	1	0
Christopher CF	3	1	0	0	6	0	0
Chapman RF	4	0	2	0	4	0	0
Gudat LF	3	0	1	0	1	0	0
Dunn 1B	4	1	1	0	5	0	0
E. Raimondi 3B	4	0	3	0	0	3	0
W. Raimondi C	3	0	0	0	4	0	0
Salveson P	2	0	0	0	0	0	0
Cantwell P	0	0	0	0	0	1	0
DeVaurs [a]	1	0	0	0	0	0	0
Darrow P	0	0	0	0	0	1	0
Christoff [b]	1	0	1	1	0	0	0
	33	2	8	1	24	8	1

(a) Batted for Cantwell in the seventh.
(b) Batted for Christoff in the ninth.

Seattle	AB	R	H	RBI	O	A	E
White LF	4	1	1	2	2	0	0
Schuster SS	2	1	0	0	0	2	1
Vanni RF	3	0	0	0	2	0	0
Lawrence CF	4	0	2	0	2	0	0
Archie 1B	3	0	0	0	9	1	0
Campbell C	2	1	0	0	6	0	0
Gyselman 3B	4	0	0	0	0	5	0
Niemiec 2B	3	1	1	0	5	4	0
Gregory P	3	0	0	1	1	1	0
Kearse C [a]	1	0	1	1	0	0	0
	29	4	5	4	27	13	1

(a) Batted for Campbell in the eighth.

Pitching Records	IP	H	R	ER	SO	BB
Salveson	3	1	0	0	1	0
Cantwell (L)	3	3	3	3	0	2
Darrow	2	0	1	1	1	3
Gregory	9	8	2	1	5	3

Left on Base: Oakland 8; Seattle 6. Home Run: White. Sacrifices: W. Raimondi, Vanni. Stolen Bases: Archie, Chapman. Double Play: Gyselman to Niemiec to Archie; Schuster to Niemiec to Archie.

Oakland	100	000	001	2 – 8 – 1
Seattle	000	030	01X	4 – 5 – 1

Game Four.

On Saturday night, September 21, 14,000 fans jammed into Sick's Stadium to honor Jack Lelivelt. The game was delayed for speeches and presentation of gifts to the popular manager. Kewpie Dick Barrett pitched a five-hit shutout over Henry "Cotton" Pippen to put the Rainiers one win away from the final round. A second inning argument at the plate led to the ejection of Oak catcher Billy Raimondi and coach Duke Kenworthy when Gilly Campbell was called safe by umpire Cicero Falls when Pete Chapman caught Dick Gyselman's fly ball and threw to the plate. Even *Seattle Post Intelligencer* writer Royal Broughman agreed that Campbell should have been out, but since the Oaks did not score, it did not affect the outcome. Seattle got another run in the fifth when Schuster's fly scored Niemiec and a fourth one in the sixth when Campbell singled in Edo Vanni.

Oakland	AB	R	H	RBI	O	A	E
Lyman SS	4	0	0	0	0	4	0
Luby 2B	3	0	1	0	5	3	0
Chapman RF	4	0	0	0	3	0	0
Christopher CF	4	0	0	0	4	0	0
Gudat LF	4	0	1	0	1	0	1
Dunn 1B	3	0	1	0	9	0	0
E. Raimondi 3B	4	0	1	0	0	1	0
W. Raimondi C	0	0	0	0	1	0	0
Pippen P	2	0	1	0	0	3	0
Conroy C	3	0	0	0	1	2	0
Darrow P	0	0	0	0	0	0	0
DeVaurs[a]	1	0	0	0	0	0	0
	32	0	5	0	24	13	1

(a) Batted for Darrow in the ninth.

Seattle	AB	R	H	RBI	O	A	E
White LF	3	0	1	0	1	0	0
Schuster SS	4	0	0	1	3	1	0
Vanni RF	4	1	2	0	1	0	0

Seattle	AB	R	H	RBI	O	A	E
Lawrence CF	3	0	0	0	5	0	0
Archie 1B	4	1	2	0	9	0	0
Campbell C	3	1	3	1	6	0	0
Gyselman 3B	3	0	0	1	1	5	0
Niemiec 2B	3	1	1	0	1	2	0
Barrett P	2	0	0	0	0	3	0
	29	4	9	3	27	11	0

Pitching Records	IP	H	R	ER	SO	BB
Pippen (L)	6	8	4	2	1	1
Darrow	2	1	0	0	1	0
Barrett	9	5	0	0	6	2

Left on Base: Oakland 6, Seattle 5. Sacrifices: Barrett, Lawrence. Stolen Base: Niemiec. Double Play: Lyman to Luby to Dunn. Umpires: Snyder, Hood, Engeln and Falls.

Oakland	000	000	000	0 – 5 – 1
Seattle	020	011	00X	4 – 9 – 0

Game Five.

A doubleheader was scheduled for Sunday, September 22, if needed, but the Rainers won the opener, so the nightcap was canceled. If Oakland had won both games, the teams would have had to wait until Tuesday night to play because Wilkie was using the stadium for a speech Monday night. That was Wendell Wilkie, candidate for president, and not Aldon Wilkie, the Seattle left-handed pitcher from Canada.

A crowd of 6,700 saw Hal Turpin beat Stanley Corbett 3–1. The Oaks' run came in the first when Lyman doubled, went to third on Hugh Luby's infield out, and scored on Pete Chapman's fly ball. After that, the Oaks got only three hits off the Oregon farmer. Seattle tied the game in the second when Gyselman doubled and Niemiec singled, and took the lead for good in the third when White singled, Schuster sacrificed, and Vanni singled. Seattle got an insurance run in the eighth when George Archie doubled and scored on Campbell's triple. Archie played every inning of every game and was voted the league's MVP, much to the objection of Angel followers who felt Novikoff should have had that honor.

Oakland	AB	R	H	RBI	O	A	E
Lyman SS	4	1	2	0	1	4	0
Luby 2B	4	0	0	0	4	5	0
Chapman RF	3	0	0	1	0	0	0
Christoff CF	4	0	0	0	2	0	0
Gudat LF	4	0	1	0	1	0	0
Dunn 1B	3	0	0	0	10	0	0
E. Raimondi 3B	3	0	1	0	3	3	0
W. Raimondi C	3	0	0	0	3	0	0
Corbett P	2	0	0	0	0	0	1
Salveson[a]	1	0	0	0	0	0	0
Cantwell P	0	0	0	0	0	1	0
	31	1	4	1	24	13	1

(a) Batted for Corbett in the eighth.

Seattle	AB	R	H	RBI	O	A	E
White LF	3	1	1	0	3	0	0
Schuster SS	3	0	0	0	0	7	0
Vanni RF	3	0	1	1	0	0	0
Lawrence CF	4	0	0	0	2	0	0
Archie 1B	4	1	1	0	17	0	0
Campbell C	3	0	2	1	3	0	0
Gyselman 3B	4	1	1	0	0	5	0
Niemiec 2B	3	0	1	1	2	4	0
Turpin P	3	0	2	0	0	1	0
	30	3	9	3	27	17	0

Pitching Records	IP	H	R	ER	SO	BB
Corbett (L)	7	7	2	2	2	2
Cantwell	1	2	1	1	0	0
Turpin	9	4	1	1	1	1

Left on Base: Seattle 7, Oakland 4. Three Base Hit: Campbell. Two Base Hits: Lyman 2, Gyselman, Campbell, Gudat, Archie. Sacrifice: Schuster, White. Double Play: Lyman to Luby to Dunn. Time of Game: 1hr. 31 min. Umpires: Snyder, Hood, Engeln, Falls.

Oakland	100	000	000	1 – 4 – 1
Seattle	011	000	01x	3 – 9 – 0

In the aftermath of this series, Royal Broughman wrote that Washington football coach Jimmy Phelan should take his players out to watch the Rainiers and see what unselfish teamwork can accomplish. The Rainers had no great star but each sacrificed his own ambition for the good of the team. On another note, Leo Lassen, Seattle radio broadcaster and columnist, argued for the continuation of the playoffs, even though Emil Sick opposed them, because they gave teams a goal to shoot for and they kept up fan interest.

The Los Angeles–San Diego Series

This was the first playoff series to go seven games. These two teams had a bitter rivalry going back to the days when the Padres were the original Hollywood club sharing Wrigley Field with the Angels. During the 1940 season, the Angels won 12, lost 9 and tied 2 games with the Padres. This series matched the team with the highest batting average against the Angels, the one with the most home runs.

The Angels exercised their option to open at Wrigley Field for the first three games, which were held Wednesday through Friday nights, September 18–20. The Padres announced that if one team swept the first three games, the fourth would not be played until Sunday, to get a bigger crowd. Otherwise, game four would be at Lane Field on Saturday night. Each team was without one of its outfielders, Paul Carpenter for L.A. and Hal Patchett for San Diego. This year, the Padres allowed ladies to get in free to boost the gate.

Game One.

Ray Prim shut the Padres out 9–0 on Wednesday night, September 18, beating San Diego's ace "Cap'n Dick" Newsome. Newsome was 23 and 7 during the regular season and matched Prim goose egg for goose egg for six innings. After he retired the first two batters in the seventh, the roof fell in on "Cap'n Dick." Eddie Cihocki and Billy Holm singled and then Prim singled in the first run of the game. Statz' infield single filled the bases before Eddie Mayo singled in two more runs. Cedric Durst yanked Newsome and brought in "Professor" Howard Craighead, who passed Novikoff to fill the bases. Johnny Moore then singled in the fourth and fifth runs of the inning. In the eighth, Craighead was bombed for four more runs which sent most, but not all, of the 5,000 fans home happy. San Diego still had some die-hard fans in L.A. left over from their days as the original Hollywood team.

San Diego	AB	R	H	RBI	O	A	E
Jensen CF	4	0	2	0	7	1	0
Stewart RF	4	0	1	0	1	0	0

San Diego	AB	R	H	RBI	O	A	E
Garibaldi LF	3	0	0	0	2	0	0
Salkeld C	3	0	0	0	2	1	0
Haslin 3B	4	0	0	0	1	1	0
Mesner SS	3	0	2	0	0	3	1
Sperry 2B	3	0	0	0	4	4	0
McDonald 1B	3	0	0	0	7	2	0
Newsome P	3	0	1	0	0	1	0
Craighead P	0	0	0	0	0	0	0
	30	0	6	0	24	13	1

Los Angeles	AB	R	H	RBI	O	A	E
Statz CF	4	1	1	1	2	0	0
Mayo 3B	4	2	1	2	2	1	0
Novikoff LF	4	0	2	0	3	1	0
Moore RF	5	0	2	3	3	0	0
Collins 1B	4	0	0	0	8	1	0
Stringer 2B	4	1	2	1	1	2	1
Cihocki SS	3	1	1	0	5	3	0
Holm C	4	2	2	0	3	1	0
Prim P	3	2	2	1	0	3	0
	35	9	13	8	27	12	1

Pitching Records	IP	H	R	ER	SO	BB
Newsome (L)	6.2	7	3	5	0	1
Craighead	1.1	6	6	2	0	1
Prim	9	6	0	0	3	2

Wild Pitch: Craighead. Passed Ball: Salkeld. Left on Base: San Diego 6, Los Angeles 7. Home Run: Stringer. Two Base Hit: Misner. Sacrifices: Prim, Cihocki, Garibaldi, Mayo. Double Plays: Stringer to Collins to Cihocki; Novikoff to Stringer. Time of Game: 1 hr. 55 min. Umpires: Fanning, Powell, Doran, Edwards.

San Diego	000	000	000	0 –	6 –	1
Los Angeles	000	000	54x	9 –	13 –	1

Game Two.

San Diego evened the series on Thursday night with an 8–2 win. Bill Thomas beat Lee Stine who was shelled to cover in the fourth inning. The Padres got two in the first when Swede Jensen walked and Bill Salkeld doubled him home. Mickey Haslin then singled in the Padre catcher. The five runs in the fourth made the game a San Diego stampede. Stan Sperry walked, George McDonald doubled, Swede Jensen singled in one, Ed Stewart tripled in two, Art Garibaldi walked, Salkeld singled in the fourth run of the inning and Haslin singled in the fifth. Bill Thomas' shutout was ruined by Johnny Moore's two run homer in the sixth. This Padre win allowed the team to sell tickets for Saturday night's fourth game.

San Diego	AB	R	H	RBI	O	A	E
Jensen CF	4	2	1	1	1	0	0
Stewart RF	5	1	2	2	0	0	0
Garibaldi LF	3	1	0	0	3	0	0
Salkeld C	5	1	3	2	4	0	0
Haslin 3B	5	1	3	2	0	4	0
Mesner SS	4	0	0	0	1	6	0
Sperry 2B	3	1	1	0	3	5	0
McDonald 1B	5	1	1	0	15	0	0
Thomas P	3	0	2	0	0	0	0
	37	8	13	7	27	15	0

Los Angeles	AB	R	H	RBI	O	A	E
Statz CF	4	0	1	0	4	0	0
Mayo 3B	4	0	1	0	1	0	0
Novikoff LF	4	1	1	0	2	0	0
Moore RF	4	1	1	2	4	0	0
Collins 1B	4	0	2	0	11	0	0
Stringer 2B	4	0	0	0	2	2	1
Cihocki SS	4	0	0	0	1	5	0
Holm C	4	0	1	0	2	2	0
Stine P	1	0	0	0	0	0	0
Fallon P	2	0	1	0	0	3	0
Carroll[a]	1	0	0	0	0	0	0
	36	2	8	2	27	12	1

(a) Batted for Fallon in the ninth.

Pitching Records	IP	H	R	ER	SO	BB
Thomas	9	8	2	2	3	0
Stine (L)	3.2	7	5	6	2	2
Fallon	5.1	6	3	1	0	2

Wild Pitch: Stine. Left on Base: San Diego 8, Los Angeles 7. Home Run: Moore. Three Base Hits: Mayo, Stewart. Two Base Hits: Salkeld, Haslin.

Sacrifices: Thomas, Mesner, Garibaldi. Time of Game: 1 hr. 45 min. Umpires: Powell, Edwards, Doran, Fanning.

San Diego	200	500	100	8 –	13 –	0
Los Angeles	000	002	000	2 –	9 –	1

Game Three.

This Friday night game on September 20 had to compete with Loyola University's 13–0 win over Redlands at Gilmore Stadium. There were 12,000 at the football game, which got better coverage than the Angels' 5–2 win over San Diego. For the second night in a row, no attendance was announced at Wrigley Field. Lefty Bob Weiland beat Wally Hebert but Jittery Joe Berry had to relieve the Angel starter in the seventh inning. The Angels got to Hebert for four runs in the third when Cihocki and Holm singled, Weiland sacrificed, and manager Jigger Statz doubled them both home. Mayo then singled in Statz and took second on a wild pitch, and scored on Novikoff's single. In the Padre seventh, Sperry walked and took third on McDonald's single. Joe Berry relieved at this point and gave up a run scoring single to Wally Hebert. Hebert was considered a fair hitter but with the 1940 rosters limited to 20 players, managers had little room to maneuver. Hebert took second and McDonald third when Moore muffed the ball in right field. Swede Jensen's fly scored McDonald. The Angels added an unearned run in the bottom of the seventh when Sperry's wild throw on Statz' grounder allowed Holm to score from second base.

San Diego	AB	R	H	RBI	O	A	E
Jensen CF	4	0	1	1	0	0	0
Stewart RF	5	0	0	0	1	0	0
Garibaldi LF	3	0	0	0	5	0	0
Detore C	3	0	0	0	0	1	0
Haslin 3B	4	0	2	0	0	1	0
Mesner SS	4	0	1	0	1	7	0
Sperry 2B	1	1	0	0	6	6	1
McDonald 1B	4	1	2	0	11	1	0
Hebert P	4	0	1	1	0	0	0
Salkeld C	1	0	0	0	0	0	0
	33	2	7	2	24	16	1
Los Angeles	AB	R	H	RBI	O	A	E
Statz CF	4	1	2	2	3	0	0
Mayo 3B	3	1	2	1	1	1	0

Los Angeles	AB	R	H	RBI	O	A	E
Novikoff LF	4	0	2	1	2	0	0
Moore RF	4	0	0	0	1	1	1
Collins 1B	4	0	0	0	9	0	1
Stringer 2B	4	0	2	0	5	4	0
Cihocki SS	4	1	1	0	3	6	1
Holm C	3	2	2	0	3	0	0
Weiland P	1	0	0	0	0	0	0
Berry P	0	0	0	0	0	0	0
	31	5	11	4	27	12	3

Pitching Records	IP	H	R	ER	SO	BB	
Hebert	8	11	5	4	0	1	
Weiland (W)	6+	6	0	1	1	3	
Berry	3	1	2	0	1	1	

Hit by Pitcher: Jensen by Weiland. Wild Pitch: Hebert. Left on Base: San Diego 9, Los Angeles 5. Two Base Hits: Jensen, Statz. Sacrifices: Weiland, Berry. Double Plays: Moore to Cihocki to Stringer; Mesner to Sperry to McDonald 2; Stringer to Cihocki to Collins. Time of Game: 1 hr. 47 min. Umpires: Doran, Edwards, Fanning, Powell.

San Diego	000	000	200	2 – 7 – 1
Los Angeles	004	000	10x	5 – 11 – 3

Game Four.

The teams took the 125 mile train ride south for Saturday night's game which saw the Padres even the series with a 3–2 win. "Old Folks" Herman Pillette, born in December 1895, started for San Diego against the 1939 Angel ace, Julio Bonetti, who had declined to a 14–10 season in 1940. The 4,000 fans cheered when Swede Jensen opened the first inning with a triple and scored on Ed Stewart's ground out. The Angels tied the game in the fourth when Jimmy "Ripper" Collins doubled in Novikoff who had gotten an infield single. The Angels went up 2–1 the next inning and could have had another run but for a questionable call at first. Holm walked, Bonetti sacrificed, Statz singled Holm to third, and Mayo singled in Holm, sending Statz to third. Then Novikoff grounded into an inning-ending double play, but Al Wolf of *The Los Angeles Times* reported that Novikoff clearly beat the throw to first. It was discovered years later that first base was only 87 feet from home plate in Lane Field, so if it had been the regulation 90 feet, Novikoff may have been out without an argument.

The Padres tied the game in the sixth when Salkeld, Haslin and Steve Mesner singled, with Salkeld scoring on a very close play which again went against the Angels. The runners took second and third on the throw home, and there were no outs. Statz removed Bonetti and brought in Jittery Joe Berry who retired the side with no further scoring, only to lose the game the next inning. Doubles by Ed Stewart and Art Garibaldi scored the decisive run. In the top of the ninth, Statz slid into Steve Mesner trying to break up a double play, and a fight erupted between former teammates in Los Angeles in 1935–1937. Statz, who was born in October 1897, was not reluctant to fight a man born in January 1918. Neither man was ejected.

Los Angeles	AB	R	H	RBI	O	A	E
Statz CF	4	0	2	0	4	0	0
Mayo 3B	5	0	1	1	0	2	0
Novikoff LF	5	1	1	0	1	0	0
Moore RF	4	0	1	0	1	0	0
Collins 1B	4	0	2	1	10	1	0
Stringer 2B	4	0	1	0	3	4	0
Cihocki SS	4	0	1	0	1	2	0
Holm C	2	1	0	0	4	1	0
Bonetti P	2	0	1	0	0	1	0
Berry P	0	0	0	0	0	1	0
Carroll[a]	1	0	0	0	0	0	0
Hernandez C	0	0	0	0	0	0	0
Lowrey[b]	1	0	0	0	0	0	0
	36	2	10	2	24	12	0

(a) Batted for Holm in the eighth.
(b) Batted for Berry in the ninth.

San Diego	AB	R	H	RBI	O	A	E
Jensen CF	4	1	1	0	1	0	0
Stewart RF	3	1	1	1	0	0	0
Garibaldi LF	4	0	2	1	1	0	0
Salkeld C	3	1	1	0	5	0	0
Haslin 3B	4	0	3	0	0	4	1
Mesner SS	4	0	2	1	4	3	0
Sperry 2B	4	0	1	0	5	7	0
McDonald 1B	3	0	0	0	11	2	0
Pillette P	4	0	0	0	0	1	0
	33	3	11	3	27	17	1

Pitching Records	IP	H	R	ER	SO	BB
Bonetti	5	8	2	2	2	2
Berry (L)	3	3	1	1	1	1
Pillette	9	10	2	2	3	2

Left on Base: Los Angeles 10, San Diego 9. Three Base Hit: Garibaldi. Two Base Hits: Collins, Stewart, Mayo. Sacrifice: Bonetti. Double Plays: Haslin to Sperry to McDonald; Mayo to Stringer to Collins. Time of Game: 2 hr. 2 min. Umpires: Edwards, Fanning, Powell.

Los Angeles	000	110	000	2 – 10 – 0
San Diego	100	001	10x	3 – 11 – 1

Game Five.

Saturday night in his San Diego hotel, Statz had a dream that the Angels would lose the opening game of Sunday's doubleheader and then come back to win the next two, and take the series. He told this to his players, and that is precisely what happened.

There were 6,000 fans on Sunday, September 22, to see Dick Newsome edge Ray Prim in the opener, 3–1, to give the Padres the pivotal fifth game. In the second, San Diego took a 1–0 lead when George Detore doubled and came around to score on fly balls by Haslin and Mesner. The Angels tied it in the third when Statz and Mayo singled and Novikoff hit into a double play. That was the extent of the Angel scoring. The Padres got the winning run in the last of the third when Jensen singled, Stewart sacrificed and Detore doubled home the run. They added an insurance run the next inning when Mesner singled, stole second, went to third on Holm's overthrow, and scored on McDonald's single.

Los Angeles	AB	R	H	RBI	O	A	E
Statz CF	4	1	1	0	3	0	0
Mayo 3B	4	0	2	0	0	3	0
Novikoff LF	4	0	0	0	1	0	0
Moore RF	4	0	0	0	3	0	0
Collins 1B	4	0	1	0	13	1	0
Stringer 2B	4	0	1	0	2	3	0
Cihocki SS	4	0	2	0	0	3	0
Holm C	4	0	2	0	1	0	1
Prim P	2	0	0	0	0	2	0
Carroll[a]	1	0	0	0	0	0	0
Berry P	0	0	0	0	1	1	0

Los Angeles	AB	R	H	RBI	O	A	E
Hernandez[b]	1	0	0	0	0	0	0
	36	1	9	0	24	13	1

(a) Batted for Prim in the seventh.
(b) Batted for Berry in the ninth.

San Diego	AB	R	H	RBI	O	A	E
Jensen CF	4	1	2	0	4	0	0
Stewart RF	3	0	1	0	5	0	0
Garibaldi LF	3	0	0	0	2	0	0
Detore C	4	1	2	1	1	0	0
Haslin 3B	4	0	1	0	1	3	0
Mesner SS	4	1	1	1	2	2	0
Sperry 2B	3	0	1	0	1	4	1
McDonald 1B	3	0	2	1	11	1	0
Newsome P	2	0	0	0	0	1	0
	30	3	10	3	27	11	1

Pitching Records	IP	H	R	ER	SO	BB
Prim (L)	6	8	3	3	0	1
Berry	2	2	0	0	0	0
Newsome	9	9	2	1	1	0

Left on Base: Los Angeles 8, San Diego 6. Two Base Hits: Detore 2, Stringer. Sacrifices: Stewart, Newsome. Stolen Base: Mesner. Double Plays: Mayo to Stringer to Collins; McDonald to Mesner to McDonald; Stringer to Collins. Time of Game: 1 hr. 35 min. Umpires: Fanning, Doran, Powell, Edwards.

Los Angeles	001	000	000	1	–	9	–	1
San Diego	011	100	00x	3	–	10	–	1

Game Six.

Los Angeles tied the series for the third time by shutting the Padres out 8–0 in this seven inning game. Bill Thomas, who won the second game, faced Jesse Flores and the two served up only goose eggs until the fifth inning. Eddie Cihocki tripled and later scored on Statz' clutch two-out single. But in the sixth, the Padres fell apart as the Angels enjoyed a "dish denting" party at their expense. Eleven Angels trotted to the plate and seven of them scored. Moore homered, Collins and Stringer singled, Cihocki was passed but catcher Chico Hernandez singled in two, Flores was hit by a pitch to reload the bases, before singles by Statz, Mayo and Novikoff plated the rest.

Los Angeles	AB	R	H	RBI	O	A	E
Statz CF	4	1	2	3	2	0	0
Mayo 3B	4	0	2	0	0	1	0
Novikoff LF	4	0	1	2	0	0	0
Moore RF	4	1	2	1	2	0	0
Collins 1B	3	1	1	0	7	2	0
Stringer 2B	4	1	1	0	1	3	0
Cihocki SS	3	2	1	0	3	0	0
Hernandez C	3	1	1	2	4	0	0
Flores P	2	1	0	0	2	1	0
	31	8	11	8	21	7	0

San Diego	AB	R	H	RBI	O	A	E
Jensen CF	3	0	0	0	3	0	0
Stewart RF	2	0	0	0	1	0	0
Garibaldi LF	3	0	2	0	2	0	0
Salkeld C	3	0	0	0	4	0	0
Haslin 3B	3	0	1	0	0	1	0
Mesner SS	2	0	0	0	1	4	0
Sperry 2B	3	0	0	0	1	1	0
McDonald 1B	3	0	1	0	9	0	0
Thomas P	2	0	0	0	0	1	0
Craighead P	0	0	0	0	0	0	0
Olsen P	0	0	0	0	0	0	0
	24	0	4	0	21	7	0

Pitching Records	IP	H	R	ER	SO	BB
Flores	7	4	0	0	4	1
Thomas (L)	5.1	7	4	7	4	2
Craighead	0+	3	4	1	0	0
Olsen	1.2	1	0	0	0	0

Hit by Pitcher: Flores by Thomas. Left on Base: Los Angeles 5, San Diego 5. Home Run: Moore. Three Base Hit: Cihocki. Two Base Hit: Garibaldi. Sacrifice: Mesner. Stolen Base: Stringer. Double Play: Sperry to Mesner to McDonald. Time of Game: 1 hr. 35 min. Umpires: Powell, Doran, Edwards, and Fanning.

Los Angeles	000	017	0	8 – 11 – 0
San Diego	000	000	0	0 – 4 – 0

Game Seven.

The Angels won the deciding game on Monday afternoon, September 23, in just one hour and 35 minutes. Bob Weiland almost had a no-hitter, giving up only a scratch hit in the first to Jensen, which Mayo bobbled. Mayo said it should have been an error. The Angels got the only run they needed off Wally Hebert in the first when Novikoff doubled and scored on Moore's single. In the third, "the Clouting Cossack" blasted a home run over the right field wall. Novikoff, whose 41 homers were more than the 38 hit by the whole Padre team, particularly enjoyed that one because the Padres had been heckling him and the rest of the team that their homers were easy to hit in Wrigley Field, but the Angels hit two in each park in the series, and the "Pounding Padres" none. In addition, the team with the highest team batting average was shut out three times in this series.

Los Angeles	AB	R	H	RBI	O	A	E
Statz CF	4	0	0	0	5	0	0
Mayo 3B	4	0	1	0	1	1	0
Novikoff LF	3	2	2	1	2	0	0
Moore RF	4	0	2	1	1	0	0
Collins 1B	4	0	1	0	11	1	0
Stringer 2B	3	0	0	0	2	3	0
Cihocki SS	4	0	0	0	1	2	0
Holm C	2	0	0	0	3	2	0
Weiland P	3	0	0	0	1	2	0
	31	2	6	2	27	11	0

San Diego	AB	R	H	RBI	O	A	E
Jensen CF	4	0	1	0	4	0	0
Stewart RF	3	0	0	0	0	1	0
Garibaldi LF	3	0	0	0	0	0	0
Detore C	3	0	0	0	5	0	0
Haslin 3B	3	0	0	0	1	2	0
Mesner SS	3	0	0	0	3	3	1
Sperry 2B	2	0	0	0	1	5	0
McDonald 1B	3	0	0	0	12	0	0
Hebert P	2	0	0	0	1	2	0
Berkowitz[a]	1	0	0	0	0	0	0
	27	0	1	0	27	13	1

(a) Batted for Hebert in the ninth.

Pitching Records	IP	H	R	ER	SO	BB
Weiland	9	1	0	0	3	1
Hebert	9	6	2	2	3	3

Left on Base: Los Angeles 5, San Diego 2. Home Run: Novikoff. Two Base Hit: Novikoff. Sacrifice: Stewart. Stolen Base: Moore. Double Plays: Sperry to Mesner to McDonald; Hebert to Mesner to McDonald. Time of Game: 1 hr. 35 min. Umpires: Doran, Edwards, Fanning, Powell.

Los Angeles	101	000	000	2 – 6 – 0
San Diego	000	000	000	0 – 1 – 1

With this win, Statz' Saturday night dream came true, but the nightmare of playing Seattle lay just ahead. With the game over at 3:05 P.M., the Angels were able to make the 4:05 P.M. train to L.A. to connect with the 7:30 P.M. train to Seattle, arriving on Wednesday afternoon, September 25, for a game that night.

The Padres, like the Oaks, divided $1,250. San Diego had 21 shares of $55 and two others of $50. The $55 would be worth about $357 today. Oakland did not mention the number of its shares.

The Final Series: Seattle vs. Los Angeles

While the Rainiers had Monday and Tuesday off, the Angels played Monday afternoon and then had a 1,200 mile train ride to get to Seattle Wednesday afternoon, just a few hours before the game that night. The schedule called for a single game Wednesday night and then a doubleheader Thursday night, September 26, at Sick's Stadium. But the Thursday doubleheader was rained out, so only one game was played in Seattle and the Angels traveled all that way, spending two nights in a hotel just to play a single game. A crowd of 5,000 watched Wednesday night's game but it seems likely that a larger crowd would have come out the next night, knowing that it would be their last chance to see their champion Rainiers in 1940.

These two teams did not like each other. The Angels, who won only 7 of 20 from Seattle, felt that Seattle showed them up in the last series in Los Angeles by running wild on the bases. Manager Lelivelt delighted in making his former team look bad and reveled in calling his team the "showboats," a name the Angels had pinned on them in 1939.

Game One.

Kewpie Dick Barrett faced Julio Bonetti in the opener, which was played in a fog that seemed to engulf the Angels all evening. L.A. made four errors, two by the usually sure-handed Lou Stringer, as the Rainiers romped, 8–2. Seattle opened the scoring in the fourth when Bill Lawrence singled, Gilly Campbell was safe on Bonetti's error, and Dick Gyselman singled. The Angels took a brief lead in the fifth when Ripper Collins singled, Stringer tripled and scored on Eddie Cihocki's fly ball. But in the last of the fifth, the Rainiers took charge. Jo Jo White was safe on Stringer's error, Schuster and Vanni singled, Lawrence tripled and scored on Archie's hit. In the sixth, White doubled in Al Niemiec, and in the eighth, White's second double plated Gyselman and Dick Barrett.

Los Angeles	AB	R	H	RBI	O	A	E
Statz CF	4	0	1	0	3	1	0
Mayo 3B	4	0	0	0	1	1	0
Novikoff LF	4	0	0	0	1	0	0
Moore RF	4	0	0	0	0	0	0
Collins 1B	4	1	2	0	9	1	0
Stringer 2B	3	1	1	1	5	5	2
Cihocki SS	2	0	0	1	1	1	1
Holm C	2	0	0	0	4	1	0
Bonetti P	1	0	0	0	0	1	1
Fallon P	1	0	0	0	0	1	0
Carroll[a]	1	0	0	0	0	0	0
Flores P	0	0	0	0	0	1	0
	30	2	4	2	24	13	4

(a) Batted for Fallon in the eighth.

Seattle	AB	R	H	RBI	O	A	E
White LF	5	1	2	2	2	0	0
Schuster SS	4	1	1	0	2	0	0
Vanni RF	5	1	1	1	1	0	0
Lawrence CF	4	2	3	2	5	0	0
Archie 1B	4	0	1	1	9	0	0
Campbell C	4	0	0	0	5	1	0
Gyselman 3B	4	1	2	1	1	1	0
Niemiec 2B	2	1	1	0	2	4	0
Barrett P	1	1	0	0	0	4	0
	33	8	11	7	27	10	0

Pitching Records	IP	H	R	ER	SO	BB
Bonetti (L)	4.1	7	5	5	1	1
Fallon	2.2	2	1	1	0	0
Flores	1	2	2	2	0	2
Barrett	9	4	2	2	5	2

Wild Pitch: Bonetti. Left on Base: Seattle 7, Los Angeles 3. Three Base Hits: Lawrence 2; Stringer. Two Base Hits: White 2. Sacrifices: Barrett, Niemiec. Stolen Base: Archie. Double Plays: Statz to Stringer; Cihocki to Stringer to Holm to Mayo to Holm. Time of Game: 2 hr. 1 min. Umpires: Snyder, Powell, Fanning, Engeln.

Los Angeles	000	020	000	2 – 4 – 4
Seattle	000	141	02x	8 – 11 – 0

Sport pages in both Seattle and Los Angeles were devoting more coverage to college football than to this playoff. The Washington game at Minnesota drew a lot of attention up north, while in Los Angeles there were two games to distract fans. On Friday night, September 27, 70,000 fans saw Southern Methodist beat UCLA 9–6, and then on Saturday afternoon, 40,000 saw Washington State tie USC 14–14 in the Coliseum. While both Los Angeles schools were to have poor years in 1940, there was anticipation and excitement at the beginning of the season.

Game Two.

The two teams traveled to Los Angeles on Friday and Saturday, ready to play a doubleheader on Sunday, September 29. The two pitchers that faced each other in the final game of the 1939 playoffs, Dick Barrett and Ray Prim, were matched again in another great pitching dual that was scoreless until the ninth inning. Then Seattle struck. With one out, White singled and stole second. Frank Kelleher walked, Lawrence singled in White and the runners moved up to second and third on Moore's throw to the plate. Jittery Joe Berry relieved Prim and gave up a two run single to Archie, for a 3–0 Seattle win.

Seattle	AB	R	H	RBI	O	A	E
White LF	4	1	1	0	4	0	0
Schuster SS	4	0	0	0	4	5	0
Kelleher RF	3	1	0	0	3	0	0
Lawrence CF	4	1	1	1	5	0	0
Archie 1B	4	0	2	2	8	0	0
Kearse C	4	0	0	0	2	0	0
Gyselman 3B	3	0	1	0	1	2	0

Seattle	AB	R	H	RBI	O	A	E
Niemiec 2B	3	0	1	0	0	2	0
Barrett P	3	0	0	0	0	0	0
	32	3	6	3	27	9	0

Los Angeles	AB	R	H	RBI	O	A	E
Statz CF	4	0	0	0	6	0	0
Mayo 3B	4	0	0	0	0	4	0
Novikoff LF	4	0	2	0	1	0	0
Moore RF	3	0	0	0	2	0	0
Collins 1B	2	0	0	0	7	0	0
Stringer 2B	3	0	0	0	1	1	0
Cihocki SS	3	0	0	0	1	2	0
Holm C	3	0	0	0	9	1	0
Prim P	3	0	0	0	0	0	0
Berry P	0	0	0	0	0	0	0
	29	0	2	0	27	8	0

Pitching Records	1P	H	R	ER	SO	BB
Barrett	9	2	0	0	2	1
Prim	8.2	5	1	3	8	1
Berry	0.1	1	2	0	1	0

Wild Pitch: Barrett. Two Base Hit: Novikoff. Stolen Base: White. Time of Game: 1 hr. 54 min. Umpires: Powell, Fanning, Engeln, Snyder.

Seattle	000	000	003	3 – 6 – 0
Los Angeles	000	000	000	0 – 2 – 0

Game Three.

In the seventh inning nightcap, Hal Turpin faced Jesse Flores. L.A. got a run in the first on singles by Eddie Mayo, Johnny Moore and a double by Ripper Collins. But Seattle went ahead 2–1 in the second when Campbell singled, Gyselman doubled, and Niemiec singled. The Rainiers increased this lead to 4–1 the next inning when Lawrence singled and Archie homered. This score stood up until the last of the sixth inning. Just when it looked as if the Rainiers were going to sweep the doubleheader and ruin the day for 12,000 Los Angeles fans, the Angels erupted for eight runs, displaying their only real punch in this series. Novikoff and Collins hit solo homers to cut the lead to 4–3. After Stringer walked and Cihocki singled, Lelivelt yanked Turpin and brought in

Bill Walker, who had beaten the Angels twice in the 1938 playoffs when he was with Sacramento. This was not Walker's day: He walked Holm, gave up a bases-loaded double to Statz and a single to Mayo before being relieved by Paul Gregory. Gregory gave up singles to Novikoff, Moore and Collins, to put the Angels up 9–4. Joe Berry set the Rainiers down in the ninth, to cut their lead in the series to 2–1.

Seattle	AB	R	H	O	A	E
White LF	4	0	0	1	0	0
Schuster SS	4	0	1	2	2	0
Vanni RF	3	0	0	1	0	0
Lawrence CF	3	1	1	4	0	0
Archie 1B	3	1	1	5	0	0
Campbell C	2	1	1	5	0	0
Gyselman 3B	3	1	1	0	3	0
Niemiec 2B	2	0	1	0	0	0
Turpin P	1	0	0	0	0	0
Walker P	0	0	0	0	0	0
Gregory P	0	0	0	0	0	0
Harris[a]	0	0	0	0	0	0
	25	4	6	18	5	0

(a) Batted for Gregory in the seventh.

Los Angeles	AB	R	H	O	A	E
Statz CF	4	1	1	1	0	0
Mayo 3B	4	2	2	2	0	0
Novikoff LF	4	2	3	2	0	0
Moore RF	4	0	2	3	0	0
Collins 1B	4	1	3	7	0	0
Stringer 2B	3	1	0	2	1	0
Cihocki SS	3	1	1	1	2	0
Hernandez C	2	0	0	2	0	0
Flores P	1	0	0	1	3	0
Carroll[b]	0	0	0	0	0	0
Holm C[c]	0	1	0	0	0	0
Lowrey[d]	1	0	0	0	0	0
Berry P	0	0	0	0	0	0
	30	9	12	21	6	0

(b) Announced for Hernandez in the sixth.
(c) Batted for Carroll in the sixth.
(d) Batted for Flores in the sixth.

Pitching Records	IP	H	R	ER	SO	BB
Turpin (L)	5.1	7	3	4	4	2
Walker	0.1	2	4	3	0	1
Gregory	0.1	0	2	1	0	0
Flores (W)	6	6	4	4	1	2
Berry	1	0	0	0	0	0

Left on Base: Seattle 4; Los Angeles 6. Home Runs: Archie, Novikoff, Collins. Two Base Hits: Gyselman, Collins, Statz. Umpires: Doran, Powell, Fanning, Engeln.

Seattle	022	000	0	4 – 6 – 0
Los Angeles	100	008	x	9 – 12 – 0

Game Four.

The Monday night game on September 30 was a Seattle slaughter. The Rainers got 18 runs on 21 hits, 6 of them for extra bases, while the Angels committed 6 errors. In addition the 6,000 fans saw a near riot in the sixth when Angel reliever Jack Fallon charged over to the first base coaching box to take on coach Eddie Taylor, who had been needling the Angels all night. It took a while to restore order, with Fallon being ejected. The Rainiers knocked starter Lee Stine out of the box in the third, after he had given up five runs. This lead reached 9–2 in the turbulent sixth, when Seattle got three more runs. Fay Thomas gave up the 10th run in the seventh before the Angels suffered a complete melt down in the eighth, when Seattle got eight runs off Joe Berry and Charles Strada. Ira Scribner pitched the whole game for the winners, getting a double and driving in a run.

Seattle	AB	R	H	RBI	O	A	E
White LF	6	3	3	4	5	1	0
J. Coscarart SS	6	2	2	0	0	2	0
Vanni RF	5	4	4	1	2	0	0
Lawrence CF	4	1	2	3	2	0	0
Archie 1B	4	1	2	2	4	0	0
Campbell C	5	0	0	0	7	1	0
Gyselman 3B	6	3	4	1	0	0	0
Niemiec 2B	5	3	3	2	6	1	0
Scribner P	4	1	1	1	1	2	0
	45	18	21	14	27	7	0

Los Angeles	AB	R	H	RBI	O	A	E
Statz CF	4	2	3	1	2	0	0
Mayo 3B	5	0	2	0	1	0	0
Novikoff LF	5	0	3	1	1	0	0
Moore RF	4	0	1	1	1	0	1
Collins 1B	3	1	1	0	14	2	2
Stringer 2B	4	0	1	0	3	6	0
Cihocki SS	5	0	1	1	0	3	1
Holm C	3	0	0	0	5	2	1
Stine P	1	0	1	0	0	1	0
Fallon P	1	0	0	0	0	2	0
Thomas P	0	0	0	0	0	0	0
Carroll[a]	1	0	0	0	0	0	0
Berry P	0	0	0	0	0	0	0
Strada P	1	1	1	0	0	1	0
	37	4	14	4	27	17	5

(a) Batted for Thomas in the seventh.

Pitching Records	IP	H	R	ER	SO	BB
Scribner	9	14	4	4	6	6
Stine (W)	2.2	7	5	5	2	1
Fallon	3.0	7	4	3	2	0
Thomas	0.1	1	1	1	1	0
Berry	0.1	5	5	6	0	1
Strada	2.2	1	3	0	1	2

Wild Pitches: Stine, Scribbner. Left on Base: Seattle 9, Los Angeles 12. Home Run: Gyselman. Two Base Hits: Lawrence, Niemiec, Scribner, White 2, Strada, Statz, Novikoff. Sacrifices: Scribner 2, Lawrence 2. Double Plays: Cihocki to Stringer to Collins; Scribner to Niemiec; Coscarart to Niemiec to Archie. Time of Game: 2 hr. 45 min. Umpires: Engeln, Snyder, Powell, Fanning.

Seattle	221	103	180	18 – 21 – 0
Los Angeles	100	100	002	4 – 14 – 5

Game Five.

A doubleheader was scheduled for Tuesday night, October 1, but only the first game was needed to finish the series. The World Series began the next day in Cincinnati so those broadcasts did not conflict with the playoffs. The Angels blew a golden opportunity to have a really big inning in the first, and let Seattle off the hook.

Two left-handers started this game but neither was involved in the decision. Seattle started the Canadian Aldon Wilkie, while Bob Weiland was making his first start since his one-hitter in San Diego. Wilkie retired no one. Statz walked, Mayo was safe on an error, Novikoff doubled them home, Moore and Collins singled, scoring Novikoff, and Stringer walked to load the bases. Wilkie got a 3–0 count on Eddie Cihocki before Lelivelt relieved him with Leftie Bill Walker. Unlike Sunday, this was Bill Walker's night. He got Cihocki and Holm on pop ups and struck out Weiland to leave three Angels stranded. Seattle got one back in the second on Gyselman's double and Niemiec's single. They tied the game the next inning on homers by Lawrence and Kelleher. Jesse Flores relieved after Kelleher's blast.

Mayo's homer gave the Angels a brief lead in the fifth, but the Suds tied it again in the sixth when Niemiec doubled, went to third on Walker's sacrifice, and scored on White's outfield fly. Seattle took the lead for good in the eighth when Gyselman homered, then Niemiec singled, Walker sacrificed and White singled. George Archie's two-run homer in the ninth made the final score 8–5. The Rainiers delighted in saying that they beat the Angels at their own game by hitting four home runs.

Seattle	AB	R	H	RBI	O	A	E
White LF	5	0	1	2	3	0	0
Schuster SS	4	0	0	0	1	6	0
Kelleher RF	3	1	1	1	0	1	0
Lawrence CF	4	2	1	1	4	0	0
Archie 1B	5	1	2	2	8	0	0
Kearse C	4	0	1	0	5	0	1
Gyselman 3B	4	2	3	1	2	1	1
Niemiec 2B	4	2	3	1	4	4	1
Wilkie P	0	0	0	0	0	0	0
Walker P	2	0	0	0	0	0	0
Vanni RF	2	0	1	0	0	0	0
	37	8	13	8	27	12	3
Los Angeles	AB	R	H	RBI	O	A	E
Statz CF	3	1	0	0	2	0	0
Mayo 3B	5	2	2	1	1	1	0
Novikoff LF	5	1	1	1	3	1	0
Moore RF	4	1	3	0	0	0	0
Collins 1B	4	0	3	1	7	2	0
Stringer 2B	3	0	0	0	5	2	0
Cihocki SS	4	0	0	1	2	4	1
Holm C	4	0	0	0	7	0	0

Los Angeles	AB	R	H	RBI	O	A	E
Weiland P	1	0	0	0	0	0	0
Flores P	2	0	0	0	0	4	0
Lowrey[a]	1	0	0	0	0	0	0
	36	5	9	4	27	14	1

(a) Batted for Flores in the ninth.

Pitching Records	IP	H	R	ER	SO	BB
Wilkie	0+	3	3	2	0	2
Walker (W)	9	6	2	1	3	1
Weiland	2+	5	3	3	1	2
Flores (L)	7	8	5	5	5	1

Left on Base: Seattle 9, Los Angeles 7. Home Runs: Kelleher, Mayo, Lawrence, Gyselman, Archie. Two Base Hits: Gyselman, Collins, Niemiec. Sacrifices: Kearse, Walker 2. Stolen Bases: Statz, Mayo, White. Double Plays: Schuster to Niemiec to Archie; Niemiec to Schuster to Archie. Time of Game: 2 hr. 31 min. Umpires: Snyder, Powell, Fanning, Engeln.

Seattle	012	001	022	8 – 13 – 3
Los Angeles	300	010	010	5 – 9 – 1

This great Seattle team disbanded at Wrigley Field that night, with manager Jack Lelivelt remaining at his Van Nuys home until the winter meetings. But this was his last game; he had just 3½ months to live. The Rainiers divided up $7,500, which came to about $357 a man, or $2,430 in current dollars. The Angels shared $2,500, which would be about $119 each, or $810 in today's money.

Key Players on 1940 Playoff Teams

Seattle. *Pitchers:* Dick Barrett, Hal Turpin, Ira Schribner, Aldon Wilkie, and Bill Walker.
  Position Players: George Archie (PCL's MVP), Edo Vanni, Ed Kearse, Jo Jo White, Bill Schuster, Dick Gyselman, and Gilly Campbell.

Los Angeles. *Pitchers:* Ray Prim, Bob Weiland, Jesse Flores, and Julio Bonetti.
  Position Players: Lou Novikoff (Triple Crown winner), Jigger Statz, Johnny Moore, Eddie Mayo, Lou Stringer and Jimmy Collins.

Oakland. *Pitchers:* Jack Salveson, Stanley Corbett, Ralph Buxton, and Henry Pippen.

Position Players: Mike Christoff (injured), Lloyd Christopher, Cecil Dunn, Hugh Luby, Marvin Gudat, Bill Lyman, Ernie Raimondi and Billy Raimondi.

San Diego. *Pitchers:* Dick Newsome, Bill Thomas, Wally Hebert, and Herman Pillette.

Position Players: Steve Mesner, George Detore, Ed Stewart, Mickey Haslin, Stan Sperry, Swede Jensen, George McDonald, Art Garibaldi, and Hal Patchett (injured).

1941

In this last pre-war season for the United States, the Rainiers won it all again but this time they did it the hard way. They clinched the pennant the second to the last day of the season after trailing Sacramento by 15 games in mid-season. Then, they won the playoffs after trailing three games to two in both the opening and the final series.

Seattle hired Bill Skiff, a former catcher, to replace the late Jack Lelivelt. Skiff won his only pennant with the Rainiers in 1941, but won the playoffs again in 1942. Skiff was a stern taskmaster and less willing than Lelivelt to put up with problem players. He dealt Broadway Bill Schuster to the Angels and traded catchers with that club, sending them Gilly Campbell for Bob Collins. He also picked up some older players such as Sylvester Johnson, Spencer Harris and Earl Averill, and got good performances from them, which gave further credence to the belief that the Pacific Coast League was an old man's league.

The Sacramento Solons led the league for about 95 percent of the season, only to falter at the end. The Cardinals sent them "The Wild Hoss of the Ossage," John "Pepper" Martin, as playing manager. Martin instilled in the Sacs the reckless base running and diving catches that the Gas House Gang was famous for in St. Louis. The team began with a 50–19 run, only to fall to a 51–56 record from that point until the end of the season. Martin's managerial tactics were praised and envied when the team was on a terror, but were called into question when the Solons slumped. The team became dog tired late in the season especially because rosters were limited to 20 players. Pepper admitted that the most inexcusable thing that he did during the season was to hit another motorist after a traffic accident, which dislocated a finger on his right hand. Martin was hitting well at the time and had been filling in for his outfielders, giving them some needed rest, but this injury sidelined him at a crucial time.

The San Diego Padres were the only team to have a winning record over the Solons and they played Seattle even in 26 meetings. It was the Padres' seven wins out of nine over Sacramento in a series split between those two cities in

Pepper Martin of the Sacramento Solons connects with the ball during the 1941 play-offs (Dick Dubbins collection).

late August and early September that put the skids under the Solons. San Diego went into first place on September 6, only to lose it the next day to Seattle.

These three teams dominated the league; Seattle finished 34 games over .500 while Sacramento and San Diego both ended up 26 games over. The fourth place Hollywood Stars were 6 games under .500 at 85–91, which was the lowest percentage that any playoff team was to have. Hollywood was the last of the eight teams to qualify for the playoffs. This occurred in the sixth year of the Shaughnessy system; the other seven clubs had appeared at least once by 1938, the third year of this system.

There was a close race among three clubs with losing records for fourth place, with the Stars edging out the Seals and Oaks, who ended up tied at 81–95. Bill Sweeney, former Portland manager, was in his second year as Hollywood's playing manager. The fourth place finish did not save his job, however. He was released at the end of the season and became a coach with the Angels in 1942.

While the Angels were totally out of the race, finishing a dismal seventh, they did play an important part in the outcome by being such easy marks for the Seattle Rainiers. Seattle won 21 of the first 26 games from the Angels before losing a meaningless doubleheader on the last day of the season, after the pennant was clinched. The Seattle fans chipped in and sent the Rainiers a 20 foot long telegram to their clubhouse at Wrigley Field, urging them on to victory that last week of the season.

Originally, plans called for Seattle to open the playoffs with two games at San Diego and Hollywood to play three at Sacramento. The reasoning behind this was that Seattle ended the season in L.A. while the Padres finished at home. The Padres wanted three games at home but Seattle argued that they could demand to open at home, and would do so, if San Diego insisted upon a third game. But all this became academic when Sacramento and San Diego ended up tied for second place with 101 wins and 75 losses. President Tuttle then ordered Sacramento to open at San Diego for three games and Seattle to open at Hollywood for two games. He further stated that the first game of the Solon-Padre series would decide second place in the standings and that all statistics would count in the regular season.

The Sacramento–San Diego Series

The Solons evened up the score with the Padres in this series by sweeping them in four games just as San Diego had done to first place Sacramento in 1937. This was the only year that a playoff game counted as a regular season game to determine second place. This was not done in 1936 when Oakland and San Diego tied for second. Luck appeared to be with the Padres in this series, not only because they did not have to start with Seattle, but they began with three games at home against a team they defeated 15 out of 23 times during the season.

Game One.

The odds further moved into San Diego's favor when the starting pitchers were announced for this game. The Padres called on their ace, Yank Terry, who was 26–8 and 5–0 against the Solons. Pepper Martin called on Tony Freitas who was 0–6 while facing the Padres that season. The Padres had to play the first game without center fielder Hal Patchett, who was injured, so Mel Mazzera moved from right to center, and Art Garibaldi played right field for San Diego. Garibaldi had the misfortune to be on the losing side of the Solon-Padre sweeps in both 1937 and 1941.

Neither team allowed any radio broadcast of this series nor any ladies' days. A crowd of 6,000 showed up at Lane Field on Tuesday night, September 23, and saw the Solons prevail in 11 innings, 5–4. San Diego took a 1–0 lead in the second on singles by Swede Jensen and Mel Mazzera and Stan Sperry's ground out. This lead was increased to 3–0 in the sixth on George Detore's walk, Jensen's double, and a fly ball by Mazzera that was dropped by Chet Wieczorek for an error. That was the second dropped fly ball by the Solon right fielder in this game.

In the seventh, the Solons got the bases loaded but only one run scored on Bobby Blattner's fly ball. But in the eighth, Wieczorek got a chance to redeem himself. Pinch hitter Frank Scalzi was safe on Mickey Haslin's error and scored on Don Gutteridge's triple. The next two batters could not get the run home but Wieczorek homered to put the Solons up 4–3. Haslin made up for his error by doubling off reliever Bill Caplinger, who was promptly relieved by Bill Schmidt. After being sacrificed to third, Haslin scored on Mazzera's fly to tie the game. It remained tied until the 11th, when Clyde Klutz tripled and scored on Blattner's long fly. The Solons finished second and had a game lead in the playoffs.

Sacramento	AB	R	H	RBI	O	A	E
Gutteridge 3B	5	1	2	1	2	1	0
Handley SS	5	0	1	0	3	2	0
Sturdy 1B	4	1	1	0	4	0	0
Wieczorek RF	4	1	2	2	2	0	2
Martin CF	5	0	1	0	3	0	0
Klutz C	5	1	2	0	10	0	0
Blattner 2B	5	0	0	2	2	2	0
Endicott LF	5	0	0	0	3	0	0
Freitas P	2	0	0	0	1	0	0
Scalzi[a]	1	1	0	0	0	0	0
Caplinger P	0	0	0	0	0	0	0
Schmidt P	1	0	0	0	0	1	0
Adams RF	1	0	0	0	3	0	0
	43	5	9	5	33	6	2

(a) Batted for Freitas in the eighth.

San Diego	AB	R	H	RBI	O	A	E
Pellargrini SS	5	0	1	0	3	3	0
McDonald 1B	5	0	2	0	16	0	0
Garibaldi RF	5	0	1	0	0	0	0
Detore C	4	1	0	0	3	0	0
Haslin 3B	5	1	1	0	0	3	1

San Diego	AB	R	H	RBI	O	A	E
Jensen LF	4	2	2	0	3	0	0
Mazzera CF	5	0	1	1	7	0	0
Sperry 2B	5	0	1	1	1	4	0
Terry P	4	0	0	0	0	3	0
Salkeld[a]	1	0	0	0	0	0	0
	43	4	9	2	33	13	1

(a) Batted for Terry in the 11th.

Pitching Records	IP	H	R	ER	SO	BB
Freitas	7	7	3	1	5	1
Caplinger	0+	1	0	1	0	0
Schmidt (W)	4	1	1	0	4	0
Terry	11	9	5	2	3	1

Left on Base: Sacramento 6, San Diego 8. Two Base Hits: Jensen, Haslin. Three Base Hits: Gutteridge, Klutz. Home Run: Wieczorek. Sacrifice: Jensen. Stolen Base: Gutteridge. Time of Game: 2 hr. 35 min. Umpires: Doran, Fanning, Powell, Jordan.

Sacramento	000	000	130	01	5 – 9 – 2
San Diego	010	002	010	00	4 – 9 – 1

Game Two.

Al Hollingsworth's seven-hit shutout put the Solons up by two games on Wednesday night, September 24. The Sacramento lefty had trouble only with Eddie Pellagrini and Stan Sperry, who each got three hits. The game had to be held up for 15 minutes at the end of the fifth inning because the field was covered with a dense fog from the bay and smoke from a Santa Fe engine. When play was resumed in the sixth, the Solons got to Wally Hebert, breaking the scoreless tie, when Clyde Klutz' fly scored Gene Handley from third. Their second run came in the eighth when Wieczorek singled, Pepper Martin sacrificed, and Klutz doubled home Lincoln Blakely, who ran for Wieczorek. The final run came in the ninth when Blakely tripled and scored on Martin's single.

Sacramento	AB	R	H	RBI	O	A	E
Gutteridge 3B	5	0	0	0	0	1	0
Handley SS	5	1	1	0	1	7	0
Sturdy 1B	3	0	0	0	16	1	0
Wieczorek RF	4	0	2	0	1	0	0

Sacramento	AB	R	H	RBI	O	A	E
Martin CF-LF	2	0	1	1	1	0	0
Klutz C	5	0	1	2	3	3	0
Blattner 2B	3	0	1	0	3	3	0
Endicott LF	2	0	1	0	1	0	0
Hollingsworth P	4	0	1	0	1	2	0
Adams CF[a]	1	0	0	0	0	0	0
Blakely RF[b]	1	2	1	0	0	0	0
	35	3	9	3	27	17	0

(a) Batted for Endicott in the sixth.
(b) Ran for Wieczorek in the eighth.

San Diego	AB	R	H	RBI	O	A	E
Pellargrini SS	4	0	3	0	1	1	1
McDonald 1B	4	0	0	0	14	1	0
Sperry 2B	4	0	3	0	2	1	0
Detore C	3	0	0	0	4	0	0
Garibaldi 3B	3	0	0	0	0	4	0
Jensen LF	4	0	0	0	1	0	0
Mazzera RF	4	0	0	0	1	0	0
Patchett CF	3	0	1	0	3	0	0
Hebert P	3	0	0	0	1	5	0
	32	0	7	0	27	12	1

Pitching Records	IP	H	R	ER	SO	BB
Hollingsworth	9	7	0	0	4	2
Hebert	9	9	3	2	2	3

Wild Pitch: Hebert. Left on Base: Sacramento 10; San Diego 7. Three Base Hit: Blakely. Two Base Hits: Pellargrini, Klutz. Sacrifices: Sturdy, Martin. Stolen Base: Martin. Double Play: Handley to Blattner to Sturdy. Time of Game: 2 hr. 5 min. Umpires: Powell, Doran, Jordan, Fanning.

Sacramento	000	001	011	3 – 9 – 0
San Diego	000	000	000	0 – 7 – 1

Game Three.

The last game at Lane Field in 1941 was another disappointment for Padre fans. Tony Freitas came back to beat San Diego for the first time this season after pitching seven innings against them two nights before. This loss was especially frustrating for manager Cedric Durst because the Padres put their leadoff man on base the first six innings, and again in the eighth, but could not score him.

Sacramento took the lead in the third off loser Bill Thomas on singles by Bill Endicott, Don Gutteridge and Gene Handley. They went up 2–0 in the seventh when Bobby Blattner, the Ping Pong Champion, singled, stole second, and scored on Endicott's single. In the ninth, the Solons got their final run off reliever Woody Rich. With two outs, Blattner again singled and again stole second. He took third on Detore's overthrow and scored on Rich's wild pitch. This run was crucial because the Padres scored two runs in the last of the ninth. George McDonald and Hal Patchett singled, Art Garibaldi singled in one run, and Jensen the other, but Mel Mazzera grounded out to end the game.

Sacramento	AB	R	H	RBI	O	A	E
Gutteridge 3B	4	0	3	0	1	4	0
Handley SS	4	0	1	1	1	2	1
Sturdy 1B	4	0	0	0	11	0	0
Wieczorek RF	4	0	1	0	3	0	0
Martin CF	2	0	0	0	1	0	0
Klutz C	4	0	0	0	3	2	0
Blattner 2B	4	2	2	0	6	2	1
Endicott LF	3	1	2	1	1	1	0
Freitas P	3	0	0	0	0	2	1
Adams CF	2	0	0	0	0	0	0
Blakely RF	0	0	0	0	0	0	0
	34	3	9	2	27	13	3

San Diego	AB	R	H	RBI	O	A	E
Pellargrini SS	4	0	1	0	4	7	0
McDonald 1B	5	1	2	0	16	0	0
Patchett CF	5	1	3	0	2	0	0
Detore C	5	0	1	0	0	1	1
Garibaldi 3B-2B	5	0	2	1	1	7	0
Jensen LF	5	0	2	1	0	0	0
Mazzera RF	4	0	0	0	1	0	0
Sperry 2B	3	0	1	0	3	1	0
Thomas P	2	0	1	0	0	2	1
Haslin 3B[a]	1	0	0	0	0	0	0
Salkeld[b]	1	0	0	0	0	0	0
Rich P	0	0	0	0	0	1	0
	40	2	13	2	27	19	2

(a) Batted for Sperry in the eighth.
(b) Batted for Thomas in the eighth.

Pitching Records	IP	H	R	ER	SO	BB
Freitas	9	13	2	2	2	2
Thomas (L)	8	8	2	2	0	0
Rich	1	1	1	1	0	1

Wild Pitch: Rich. Left on Base: Sacramento 8, San Diego 15. Two Base Hit: Gutteridge. Sacrifices: Freitas, Thomas. Stolen Bases: Blattner 2, Endicott. Double plays: Garibaldi to Detore to Garibaldi to Sperry; Handley to Blattner to Sturdy; Pellargrini to Sperry to McDonald. Time of Game: 1 hr. 59 min. Umpires: Doran, Jordan, Fanning, Powell.

Sacramento	001	000	101	3 –	9 –	3
San Diego	000	000	002	2 –	13 –	2

Game Four.

The two teams left by train on Friday, September 26, for Sacramento and resumed the series on Saturday night at Cardinal Field. Only 2,103 turned out that night to see the Solons eliminate the Padres from postseason play. If they had waited until Sunday, they might have attracted more fans, but the capital city folk may have been so disappointed with the Solons blowing the pennant, that they may have stayed home anyway.

George Munger faced Yank Terry in this game, and the Solons scored first in the second on Blattner's homer. But in the fourth, the Padres got to Munger for three runs and three hits, the key blows being delivered by Swede Jensen and Stan Sperry. But in the last of the fourth, the Solons knocked Terry out of the game with four runs that wrapped up the series. Blattner singled and Lincoln Blakely tripled him home. Bill Endicott singled in the tying run, Munger sacrificed, Gutteridge reached base on an error, and both scored on what was described as a "comedy of errors" that involved some weird base running. Munger, who weathered the fourth inning storm, was removed when he gave up a leadoff hit in the fifth, so reliever Bill Schmidt was credited with the win. Rex Dilbeck relieved Terry and gave up the Solons' final run in the fifth when Blakely singled in Blattner. This small Saturday night crowd saw Sacramento win a series for the last time in the playoffs.

San Diego	AB	R	H	RBI	O	A	E
Pellargrini SS	5	0	1	0	1	3	1
McDonald 1B	2	0	0	0	5	0	0
Patchett CF	4	1	1	0	3	0	0

San Diego	AB	R	H	RBI	O	A	E
Salkeld C	4	0	1	0	7	1	0
Garibaldi 3B	4	0	1	0	0	2	1
Jensen LF	3	1	1	1	1	0	0
Mazzera RF	4	1	1	0	2	0	0
Sperry 2B	4	0	1	1	2	0	0
Terry P	2	0	0	0	0	1	1
Dillbeck P	0	0	0	0	0	0	0
Durst 1B	1	0	0	0	3	0	0
Haslin [a]	0	0	0	0	0	0	0
Rich P	0	0	0	0	0	0	0
Ballinger [b]	1	0	0	0	0	0	0
	34	3	7	2	24	7	3

(a) batted for Dillbeck in the seventh.
(b) Batted for Rich in the ninth.

Sacramento	AB	R	H	RBI	O	A	E
Gutteridge 3B	4	1	0	0	0	0	1
Handley SS	5	0	1	0	5	3	0
Sturdy 1B	5	0	2	0	7	1	0
Wieczorek RF	4	0	1	0	2	0	1
Klutz C	4	0	1	0	9	1	0
Blattner 2B	3	3	2	1	0	2	1
Blakely CF	4	1	2	1	1	0	0
Endicott LF	3	1	2	1	3	0	0
Munger P	1	0	0	0	0	2	0
Schmidt P	2	0	0	0	0	0	0
	35	6	11	3	27	9	3

Pitching Records	IP	H	R	ER	SO	BB
Terry (L)	4.1	9	6	4	3	2
Dillbeck	1.2	1	0	0	3	0
Rich	2	1	0	0	1	1
Munger	4+	5	3	2	5	2
Schmidt (W)	5	2	0	0	5	1

Left on Base: San Diego 5, Sacramento 9. Two Base Hits: Wieczorek, Jensen, Sperry, Sturdy, Klutz. Three Base Hit: Blakely. Home Run: Blattner. Sacrifice: Munger. Stolen Bases: Blattner, Endicott. Double Plays: Blattner to Handley to Sturdy; Sturdy to Handley to Sturdy to Handley. Time of Game: 2 hr. 2 min. Umpires: Jordan, Fanning, Powell, Doran.

San Diego	000	300	000	3 – 7 – 3
Sacramento	010	410	00x	6 – 11 – 3

The Seattle-Hollywood Series

With the champion Rainiers finishing the season in Los Angeles, it made sense for them to begin this series at Gilmore Field, rather than go to Seattle for the first three games. But with Hollywood finishing 20 games behind Seattle and beating the Rainiers only 10 of 26 games, the Stars were in no position to ask for a third game to be played at Gilmore Field. President Tuttle did say that if the Seattle forecast called for rain, all games would have to be played in Hollywood, but this was not the case.

Game One.

The Stars, regardless of their poor record, proved to be no pushovers for Seattle. Bill Skiff had to play without Jo Jo White, who was hospitalized after getting hit by a foul tip on the last day of the regular season. The 40 year old Spencer Harris filled in for him.

On Tuesday night, September 23, Kewpie Dick Barrett beat Hiram Bithorn 5–2, with all of Seattle's runs being unearned. The Stars made five errors, three of them by shortstop Joe Hoover, which ended up costing Hollywood the series. A scoreless tie was broken in the sixth when Lynn King was safe on Hoover's error. After the next two batters were retired, Les Scarsella doubled King to third, and Bob Collins was walked to fill the bases. Ned Stickle hit a fly to right center that Frenchie Uhalt called for but Johnny Barrett ran into him, knocking the ball loose, and all three runners scored. The butterfingered Stars were not through. In the seventh, Gyselman reached first when Hoover booted another one. After a sacrifice and a ground out, Spencer Harris singled in Gyselman. The fifth run came in the eighth, when Collins and Stickle walked, Al Niemiec hit into a force play, and then Joe Hoover let Gyselman's grounder go through his legs. Both of the Stars runs were earned: in the sixth, Uhalt doubled and later scored on Johnny Dickshots' fly ball, and in the ninth, Bob Kahle tripled in Fred Gay, who was running for Babe Herman, who had walked. No attendance was announced.

Seattle	AB	R	H	RBI	O	A	E
King CF	5	1	1	0	4	0	0
Harris LF	5	0	1	1	1	0	0
Matheson RF	5	0	0	0	3	0	0
Scarsella 1B	4	1	2	0	10	0	0
Collins C	1	2	1	0	6	0	0
Stickle SS	3	0	0	0	0	3	0

Seattle	AB	R	H	RBI	O	A	E
Niemiec 2B	4	0	0	0	3	4	0
Gyselman 3B	4	1	1	0	0	3	0
D. Barrett P	3	0	0	0	0	2	0
	34	5	6	1	27	12	0

Hollywood	AB	R	H	RBI	O	A	E
Uhalt CF	3	1	1	0	1	1	1
J. Barrett RF	4	0	0	0	2	0	0
Dickshot LF	4	0	0	1	0	0	0
Herman 1B	3	0	1	0	10	1	0
Kahle 3B	4	0	2	1	1	2	0
Dapper C	4	0	0	0	3	0	0
Schulte 2B	4	0	0	0	2	5	0
Hoover SS	3	0	1	0	7	2	3
Bithorn P	1	0	0	0	1	1	1
Rosenberg[a]	1	0	0	0	0	0	0
Osborne P	0	0	0	0	0	0	0
Gay[b]	0	1	0	0	0	0	0
	31	2	5	2	27	12	5

(a) Batted for Bithorn in the eighth.
(b) Ran for Herman in the ninth.

Pitching Records	IP	H	R	ER	SO	BB
D. Barrett	9	5	2	2	6	2
Bithorn (L)	8	6	5	0	2	4
Osborne	1	0	0	0	1	0

Left on Base: Seattle 7, Hollywood 5. Three Base Hit: Kahle. Two Base Hits: Scarsella, Uhalt. Sacrifices: Bithorn, D. Barrett. Stolen Base: Kahle. Double Plays: Hoover to Schulte to Herman; Schulte to Hoover to Herman. Time of Game: 2 hr. 10 min. Umpires: Snyder, Hood, Engeln, Widner.

Seattle	000	003	110	5 – 6 – 0	
Hollywood	000	001	001	2 – 6 – 5	

Game Two.

Again, no attendance was mentioned for this last game played in Gilmore Field in 1941. Hollywood tied the series, winning 4–1, with all the scoring in the first inning. Seattle broke the ice when catcher Chuck Fallon doubled, after Bill "Highpockets" Lawrence and Bill Matheson had singled. But Hal Turpin did not survive the last of the first inning. Frenchie Uhalt and Johnny Barrett singled and both scored on Dickshot's triple. After Babe Herman doubled, Ira Scribner replaced Turpin. Bob Kahle singled Herman to third and Ham Schulte's force out scored Herman with the final run. Fred Gay went all the way for Hollywood, pitching scoreless ball after the opening inning.

Seattle	AB	R	H	RBI	O	A	E
Lawrence CF	4	1	1	0	8	0	0
Harris LF	4	0	0	0	1	0	0
Matheson RF	4	0	2	0	1	0	0
Scarsella 1B	4	0	2	0	3	0	1
Fallon C	3	0	1	1	4	1	0
Stickle SS	3	0	2	0	2	3	0
Niemiec 2B	4	0	0	0	5	2	0
Gyselman 3B	4	0	0	0	0	0	0
Turpin P	0	0	0	0	0	0	0
Scribner P	2	0	0	0	0	0	0
Farrell[a]	1	0	0	0	0	0	0
Soriano P	0	0	0	0	0	0	0
Webber[b]	1	0	0	0	0	0	0
Collins[c]	1	0	0	0	0	0	0
	35	1	8	1	24	6	1

(a) Batted for Scribner in the sixth.
(b) Batted for Soriano in the ninth.
(c) Batted for Harris in the ninth.

Hollywood	AB	R	H	RBI	O	A	E
Uhalt CF	4	1	1	0	2	0	0
J. Barrett RF	4	1	1	0	3	0	0
Dickshot LF	3	1	1	2	5	0	0
Herman 1B	4	1	1	1	9	0	0
Kahle 3B	3	0	1	0	0	3	0
Dapper C	3	0	0	0	4	0	0
Schulte 2B	3	0	0	1	2	3	0
Hoover SS	3	0	0	0	2	3	0
Gay P	2	0	1	0	0	0	0
	29	4	6	4	27	9	0

Pitching Records	IP	H	R	ER	SO	BB
Turpin (L)	0+	4	3	4	0	0

Pitching Records	IP	H	R	ER	SO	BB
Scribner	5	2	1	0	3	0
Soriano	3	0	0	0	0	0
Gay	9	8	1	1	4	3

Left on Base: Seattle 10, Hollywood 4. Two Base Hits: Fallon, Herman, J. Barrett. Three Base Hits: Dickshot. Time of Game: 1 hr. 58 min. Umpires: Hood, Engeln, Widner, Snyder.

Seattle	100	000	000	1 – 8 – 1
Hollywood	400	000	00x	4 – 6 – 0

The two teams left Thursday morning, the 25th, for Seattle, with the injured Jo Jo White accompanying his teammates. The papers in both Los Angeles and Seattle were giving more coverage to the tight National League race between St. Louis and Brooklyn and to college football than to the playoffs. That coming weekend, three games were played in L.A. A crowd of 45,000 saw UCLA beat Washington State Friday night at the Coliseum, and 50,000 saw USC beat Oregon State there on Saturday afternoon. There were also 7,000 fans at Gilmore Stadium on Friday night to see Loyola University beat Redlands.

Seattle scheduled the third game for Saturday night, September 27, so it would not conflict with the Washington–Minnesota game that drew 43,000 to Husky Stadium that afternoon. Rainier fans did plan a big welcome for the team that was supposed to arrive at King Street Station on Friday night at 9:30 P.M. , but a rock slide on the tracks prevented the train from arriving until 6:30 A.M. Saturday. But the city made up for this by having a big celebration at Sick's Stadium prior to the third game.

Over 10,000 fans were in the park as the players paraded single file through the stands while Jackie Sounders' band played, "Hail, Hail, The Gang's All Here" and Mayor Earl Millikin gave a speech, and manager Bill Skiff even said a few words, praising the team. There was a display of fireworks, sky rockets, and a spectacular floral display of "Welcome Rainiers" on the field. In addition, Kewpie Dick Barrett was given a trophy for being selected Seattle's top athlete in all sports for 1940, with the three previous winners all present. This was a great night for Seattle, except that Hollywood won the game.

Game Three.

As often happens, when a player is given a special day or award, he has a poor game. In this game, Seattle's "Little Round Man" gave up no earned runs but lost 5–3, as the Rainiers made three crucial errors behind him. Barrett gave up only four hits but walked five, which hurt. In the first, he walked Uhalt , Dickshot, and Herman, with Uhalt scoring on Scarsella's error on Kahle's grounder. In the fourth, two more walks and another Scarsella error gave Hollywood a 2–0 lead, but the Stars still had no hits. Seattle cut the lead to 2–1 in the seventh when Gyselman walked and Lawrence and Harris singled.

It was still 2–1 going into the ninth, when Hollywood got three more unearned runs. With two out, Joe Hoover singled and pitcher Leftie Louie Tost struck out, but Bob Collins dropped the third strike and could not throw the pitcher out at first. (This was just eight days before Mickey Owens' famous drop of a third strike in the World Series.) Uhalt then singled in Hoover, and Johnny Barrett (no relation to Dick Barrett) tripled in the other two runners. Seattle scored two runs in the last of the ninth, knocking out Tost, but Hiram Bithorn came in and put the fire out.

Hollywood	AB	R	H	RBI	O	A	E
Uhalt CF	4	2	1	1	3	0	0
J. Barrett RF	5	0	2	2	3	0	0
Dickshot LF	3	0	0	0	4	0	0
Herman 1B	3	0	0	0	7	1	1
Kahle 3B	3	0	0	0	1	3	0
Dapper C	4	1	0	0	4	0	0
Schulte 2B	4	0	0	0	1	2	0
Hoover SS	3	1	1	0	4	1	0
Tost P	4	1	0	0	0	1	0
Bithorn P	0	0	0	0	0	0	0
	33	5	4	3	27	8	1

Seattle	AB	R	H	RBI	O	A	E
Lawrence CF	5	1	4	0	6	0	0
Harris LF	4	0	2	1	3	0	0
Matheson RF	4	0	0	0	3	0	0
Scarsella 1B	5	0	1	1	5	0	2
Collins C	5	0	0	0	3	0	0
Stickle SS	3	0	1	0	2	1	0
Niemiec 2B	4	0	0	0	4	3	0
Gyselman 3B	3	2	2	0	1	0	0
D. Barrett P	3	0	0	0	0	3	1
Fallon[a]	1	0	1	0	0	0	0
Webber[b]	0	0	0	0	0	0	0
	37	3	11	2	27	7	3

(a) Batted for D. Barrett in the ninth.
(b) Ran for Harris in the ninth.

Pitching Records	IP	H	R	ER	SO	BB
Tost (W)	8.1	10	3	1	2	4
Bithorn	0.2	1	0	0	1	0
D. Barrett	9	4	5	0	4	5

Left on Base: Hollywood 7, Seattle 11. Passed Ball: Collins. Three Base Hit: J. Barrett. Sacrifice: Dickshot. Double Play: Hoover to Herman. Time of Game: 2 hr. 2 min. Umpires: Jordan, Fanning, Powell, Doran.

Hollywood	100	100	005	5 –	4 – 1
Seattle	000	000	102	3 –	11 – 3

Game Four.

A doubleheader was scheduled for Sunday, September 28, but the opening game was played in a constant drizzle, so the field was too muddy to play a second game. Seattle proved to be better mudders than Bill Sweeney's Stars, outfitted in their navy blue uniforms which they wore at home and on the road. Lefty Fred Gay started for the Stars but did not last the first inning. The Rainiers got four runs on Lawrence's single, Scarsella's double, Fallon's walk, and Stickle's double. Wayne Osborne relieved and gave up the last run on Niemiec's single. Les Webber started for Seattle and gave up two runs in the third when Hoover singled, Osborne walked, Johnny Barrett doubled, and Dickshot hit a long fly. Hollywood narrowed the gap to 4–3 in the fifth when Dickshot doubled and scored on Herman's single. Forty-year-old Sylvester Johnson relieved at that point, and got credit for the win. Seattle made it 5–3 in their half of the fifth when Kahle's error allowed 40-year-old Spencer Harris to reach base. After a force play and a walk, Stickle singled in the run. Hollywood again closed the gap to one run in the sixth on Hoover's triple and Wayne Osborne's single. This was another case of forcing a pitcher to bat when trailing, because of the 20-man roster. However, Seattle blew the game open in the seventh with four runs on three singles, two walks and a long fly. Osborne was chased that inning and relieved by Pappy Roy Joiner. In the ninth, Sylvester Johnson fractured his pitching elbow and had to be relieved by Hal Turpin. That was the nineteenth injury for the Rainiers in 1941, and the third broken bone.

Hollywood	AB	R	H	RBI	O	A	E
Uhalt CF	5	0	0	0	2	0	0
J. Barrett RF	5	1	2	1	3	0	0

Hollywood	AB	R	H	RBI	O	A	E
Dickshot LF	5	1	3	1	2	0	0
Herman 1B	3	0	1	1	8	0	0
Kahle 3B	5	0	3	1	1	5	1
Brenzel C	5	0	0	0	1	0	0
Schulte 2B	4	0	0	0	5	3	0
Hoover SS	4	2	2	0	2	4	0
Gay P	0	0	0	0	0	0	0
Osborne P	2	1	1	1	0	2	0
Joiner P	0	0	0	0	0	0	0
	38	5	12	5	24	14	1

Seattle	AB	R	H	RBI	O	A	E
Lawrence CF	4	1	2	0	3	0	0
Harris LF	4	1	1	0	4	0	0
Matheson RF	4	1	0	0	4	0	0
Scarsella 1B	3	2	2	1	6	0	0
Fallon C	4	2	2	1	2	0	0
Stickle SS	3	2	2	3	2	2	1
Niemiec 2B	4	0	3	3	4	1	0
Gyselman 3B	3	0	0	1	2	3	0
Webber P	2	0	0	0	0	0	0
Johnson P	2	0	0	0	0	1	0
Turpin P	0	0	0	0	0	0	0
	33	9	12	9	27	7	1

Pitching Records	IP	H	R	ER	SO	BB
Gay (L)	0.2	3	3	4	0	1
Osborne	5.2	6	5	4	1	4
Joiner	1.2	3	1	0	0	0
Webber	4.1	7	3	3	2	2
Johnson (W)	4	5	2	2	1	1
Turpin	0.2	0	0	0	0	0

Wild Pitch: Osborne. Left on Base: Hollywood 10, Seattle 8. Two Base Hits: Scarsella, Stickle, J. Barrett, Fallon, Dickshot, Kahle. Three Base Hit: Hoover. Sacrifices: Harris, Gyselman, Matheson. Double Plays: Gyselman to Niemiec to Scarsella; Hoover to Schulte to Herman. Time of Game: 2 hr. 15 min. Umpires: Snyder, Hood, Edwards, Engeln.

Hollywood	002	011	001	5 – 12 – 1
Seattle	400	010	40x	9 – 12 – 1

Game Five.

With the series tied at two games each, Hiram Bithorn faced Ira Scribner in the pivotal fifth game on Monday night, September 29. The Stars got two in the first when Uhalt walked, Johnny Barrett singled, and Herman doubled them home. Scribner had to come out after three innings because of a sore ankle, and was relieved by Paul Gregory, who pitched scoreless ball until the ninth. Seattle tied the game with two runs in the fourth when Scarsella doubled, Collins walked, Stickle sacrificed, Niemiec singled in one and Gyselman's fly scored Collins, who barely beat the throw to the plate. But in the ninth, the Stars erupted for five runs, when Barrett walked, Dickshot and Herman singled, and Kahle homered. After Cliff Dapper doubled, Dewey Soriano relieved Gregory and gave up a run scoring double to Ham Schulte. Seattle was now down three games to two. No attendance was given for any games other than Saturday night's extravaganza.

Hollywood	AB	R	H	RBI	O	A	E
Uhalt CF	4	1	1	0	1	0	0
J. Barrett RF	3	2	3	0	1	0	0
Dickshot LF	3	1	2	0	3	0	0
Herman 1B	5	1	3	3	9	0	0
Kahle 3B	4	1	1	3	0	1	1
Dapper C	5	1	1	0	4	1	0
Schulte 2B	5	0	2	1	7	3	0
Hoover SS	5	0	2	0	2	5	0
Bithorn P	4	0	1	0	0	2	0
	38	7	16	7	27	12	1

Seattle	AB	R	H	RBI	O	A	E
King CF	5	0	0	0	3	0	0
Harris LF	4	0	1	0	2	0	0
Matheson RF	4	0	1	0	1	0	0
Scarsella 1B	4	1	1	0	12	1	0
Collins C	3	1	1	0	2	1	0
Stickle SS	2	0	1	0	3	5	0
Niemiec 2B	3	0	1	1	4	5	0
Gyselman 3B	3	0	1	1	0	1	0
Scribner P	0	0	0	0	0	0	0
Averill[a]	1	0	0	0	0	0	0
Gregory P	2	0	0	0	0	1	0
Soriano P	1	0	0	0	0	1	0
	32	2	7	2	27	15	0

(a) *Batted for Scribner in the third.*

Pitching Records	IP	H	R	ER	SO	BB
Bithorn	9	7	2	2	3	3
Scribner	3	4	2	2	1	3
Gregory (L)	5.1	11	4	5	3	4
Soriano	0.2	1	0	0	0	0

Two Base Hits: Herman, J. Barrett, Scarsella, Matheson, Dapper, Schulte. Home Run: Kahle. Sacrifices: Dickshot, Kahle, Stickle, Niemiec. Double Plays: Hoover to Schulte to Herman; Stickle to Niemiec to Scarsella 2; Niemiec to Stickle to Scarsella. Time of Game: 2 hr. 15 min. Umpires: Hood, Edwards, Engeln, Snyder.

Hollywood	200	000	005	7 – 16 – 1	
Seattle	000	200	000	2 – 7 – 0	

Game Six.

A doubleheader was played on Tuesday night, September 30, the day before the World Series started. Manager Bill Sweeney complained that the Pacific Coast League schedule was too long, resulting in rainouts in April and again in September, especially in the north. In addition, he felt there was too much competition from football during the playoffs. In any event, the season was two games too long for Hollywood because Seattle shut them out in both games of this doubleheader to capture the series. Both games were 2–0. In the opener, Ed Cole, "the Silent Pole," beat Lefty Louie Tost. Seattle's two runs came in the second when Fallon homered and Neimiec doubled and scored when Joe Hoover booted Gyselman's grounder. Fred Gay, who was to pitch the nightcap, got a pinch single in this game.

Hollywood	AB	R	H	RBI	O	A	E
Uhalt CF	4	0	1	0	2	0	0
J. Barrett RF	3	0	0	0	2	0	0
Dickshot LF	4	0	0	0	2	0	0
Herman 1B	3	0	0	0	11	0	0
Kahle 3B	3	0	0	0	1	1	0
Dapper C	3	0	0	0	4	1	0
Schulte 2B	3	0	1	0	1	4	0
Hoover SS	2	0	0	0	1	4	1
Tost P	2	0	0	0	0	1	0
Gay[a]	1	0	1	0	0	0	0

Hollywood	AB	R	H	RBI	O	A	E
Bittner P	0	0	0	0	0	1	0
Lillard SS	0	0	0	0	0	0	0
Rosenberg[b]	1	0	0	0	0	0	0
	29	0	3	0	24	12	1

(a) Batted for Hoover in the eighth.
(b) Batted for Tost in the eighth.

Seattle	AB	R	H	RBI	O	A	E
Lawrence CF	4	0	0	0	2	0	0
Harris LF	4	0	1	0	3	0	0
Matheson RF	4	0	0	0	3	0	0
Scarsella 1B	3	0	1	0	7	1	0
Fallon C	3	1	2	1	6	0	0
Stickle SS	2	0	0	0	1	1	1
Niemiec 2B	3	1	1	0	4	4	0
Gyselman 3B	2	0	0	0	0	3	0
Cole P	3	0	0	0	1	0	0
	28	2	5	1	27	9	1

Pitching Records	IP	H	R	ER	SO	BB
Tost (L)	7	3	2	1	4	1
Bittner	1	2	0	0	0	0
Cole	9	3	0	0	6	1

Left on Base: Hollywood 3, Seattle 4. Two Base Hits: Niemiec, Scarsella. Home Run: Fallon. Double Plays: Gyselman to Niemiec to Scarsella 2; Kahle to Herman. Time of Game: 1 hr. 45 min. Umpires: Edwards, Snyder, Hood, Engeln.

Hollywood	000	000	000	0 – 3 – 1
Seattle	020	000	00x	2 – 5 – 1

Game Seven.

Had Hollywood won the opener, this game would not have been played. Dick Barrett limited Hollywood to four hits in this seven inning finale. In the second, Collins singled and Joe Hoover booted Stickle's grounder for his fifth error of the series. Collins was out when hit by Niemiec's batted ball but Gyselman's single scored Stickle. The final run of the series was scored in the fourth when Stickle walked and came around on singles by Niemiec and Gyselman. Stickle scored both runs and Gyselman drove both home.

Hollywood	AB	R	H	RBI	O	A	E
Uhalt CF	2	0	0	0	3	0	2
J. Barrett RF	3	0	1	0	1	0	0
Dickshot LF	3	0	1	0	2	0	0
Herman 1B	3	0	0	0	5	0	0
Kahle 3B	3	0	0	0	1	1	0
Brenzel C	3	0	1	0	3	0	0
Schulte 2B	3	0	1	0	2	2	0
Hoover SS	1	0	0	0	1	1	1
Gay P	3	0	0	0	0	2	0
Rosenberg[a]	1	0	0	0	0	0	0
Lillard SS	1	0	0	0	0	0	0
	26	0	4	0	18	6	3

(a) Batted for Hoover in the fifth.

Seattle	AB	R	H	RBI	O	A	E
Lawrence CF	3	0	1	0	1	0	0
Harris LF	2	0	1	0	1	0	0
Matheson RF	3	0	0	0	2	0	0
Scarsella 1B	3	0	0	0	5	1	0
Collins C	3	0	1	0	6	0	0
Stickle SS	2	2	0	0	2	1	1
Niemiec 2B	3	0	2	0	3	2	0
Gyselman 3B	3	0	2	2	0	1	0
D. Barrett P	2	0	0	0	1	1	0
	24	2	7	2	21	6	1

Pitching Records	IP	H	R	ER	SO	BB
Gay	6	7	2	1	3	0
D. Barrett	7	4	0	0	6	0

Left on Base: Hollywood 6; Seattle 6. Double Play: Hoover to Schulte to Herman. Time of Game: 1 hr. 25 min. Umpires: Engeln, Snyder, Hood, Edwards.

Hollywood	000	000	0	0 – 4 – 3
Seattle	010	100	x	2 – 7 – 1

The Stars, like the Padres, split $1,250 prize money, which came to about $50 per man. This would be worth about $340 in current dollars. Of course, the extra week's pay was worth more to the players on teams eliminated in the first round.

The Final Series: Seattle vs. Sacramento

The World Series between the Yankees and the Dodgers was in full swing before the final round of the playoffs could begin. The Solons arrived in Seattle on Thursday night, October 2, for the opener, which was scheduled for Friday night. Single games were planned for Saturday night and Sunday afternoon before the teams were to depart for Sacramento, but rain prevented them from playing Friday, so they played a doubleheader on Saturday night. Rain had dogged the Rainiers throughout 1941, causing them to play 47 doubleheaders when they were scheduled for only 32. In addition, they played 46 innings of baseball that was washed out by rain. Even so, the 393,542 fans they drew still topped every team in the league, but it was down from 1940, which in turn was down from their record year of 1939. The Solons, by contrast, drew just 165,738, but that was their all time high up until that point.

Game One.

The Solons won 15 of the 24 games played with Seattle during the season but they lost this Saturday night doubleheader to fall behind in the playoffs. Hal Turpin, with the aid of two three-run innings, defeated Bill Schmidt in the opener, 6–3. The first three-run inning erased a 2–0 Sacramento lead, while the second one broke a 3–3 tie. The Sacs got a run in the first when Chet Wieczorek singled in Don Gutteridge. Gutteridge scored again in the fifth when Jo Jo White dropped his long fly ball, ahead of Jack Sturdy's single. But in the last of the fifth, singles by Gyselman, Turpin, White, Harris and Scarcella, the latter a bunt, put the Rainiers up 3–2. The Solons quickly tied it in the sixth on Blattner's single, Charley Fallon's two-base throwing error, and Endicott's fly ball. But in the seventh, Seattle put the game away with its second three-run inning. White tripled, Harris and Scarsella singled, and Fallon doubled.

Sacramento	AB	R	H	RBI	O	A	E
Gutteridge 3B	5	2	3	0	0	1	1
Handley SS	4	0	1	0	2	1	0
Sturdy 1B	5	0	1	1	9	1	0
Wieczorek RF	4	0	2	1	4	0	0
Klutz C	4	0	1	0	4	1	0
Blattner 2B	3	1	1	0	2	2	0
Blakely CF	4	0	0	0	1	0	0
Endicott LF	4	0	1	1	2	0	0

Sacramento	AB	R	H	RBI	O	A	E
Schmidt P	3	0	0	0	0	2	0
Hollingsworth P	1	0	0	0	0	2	0
	37	3	10	3	24	10	1

Seattle	AB	R	H	RBI	O	A	E
White CF	4	2	2	1	2	0	1
Harris LF	5	1	3	2	3	0	0
Matheson RF	3	0	0	0	2	0	0
Scarsella 1B	4	1	2	3	8	1	1
Fallon C	4	0	1	0	6	0	1
Stickle SS	4	0	2	0	0	3	0
Niemiec 2B	4	0	0	0	3	1	0
Gyselman 3B	4	1	2	0	0	3	1
Turpin P	4	1	2	0	1	3	0
Lawrence CF	1	0	1	0	2	0	0
	37	6	15	6	27	11	4

Pitching Records	IP	H	R	ER	SO	BB
Schmidt (L)	6.1	12	5	5	3	0
Hollingsworth	1.2	3	1	0	1	0
Turpin	9	10	3	1	6	1

Passed Ball: Klutz. Left on Base: Sacramento 10, Seattle 8. Two Base Hit: Fallon. Three Base Hit: White. Sacrifices: Blattner, Handley, Matheson. Stolen Base: Gutteridge. Time of Game: 1 hr. 25 min. Umpires: Snyder, Hood, Edwards, Engeln.

Sacramento	100	011	000	3	– 10	– 1
Seattle	000	020	30x	6	– 15	– 4

Game Two.

Sacramento again jumped into the lead in this seven-inning nightcap with a run in the first off Les Webber, but they were to get no more. Jack Sturdy doubled and scored on Wieczorek's single. George "Red" Munger also pitched very well for Sacramento, but in the third he gave up a single to his mound opponent, followed by a game winning homer to Jo Jo White. A crowd of 5,000 saw this doubleheader.

Sacramento	AB	R	H	RBI	O	A	E
Gutteridge 3B	3	0	1	0	0	1	0
Handley SS	2	0	0	0	1	3	0
Sturdy 1B	3	1	2	0	8	1	0
Wieczorek RF	2	0	1	1	3	0	0
Klutz C	3	0	1	0	2	1	0
Blattner 2B	3	0	0	0	1	3	0
Adams CF	3	0	0	0	2	0	1
Endicott LF	2	0	0	0	0	0	0
Munger P	2	0	0	0	1	1	0
Blakely[a]	0	0	0	0	0	0	0
Martin[b]	1	0	0	0	0	0	0
	24	1	5	1	18	10	1

(a) *Ran for Endicott in the seventh.*
(b) *Batted for Munger in the seventh.*

Seattle	AB	R	H	RBI	O	A	E
White CF	3	1	2	2	1	0	0
Harris LF	3	0	0	0	1	0	0
Matheson RF	3	0	0	0	1	1	0
Scarsella 1B	3	0	2	0	10	1	0
Collins C	3	0	0	0	6	0	0
Stickle SS	2	0	0	0	1	0	0
Niemiec 2B	2	0	0	0	1	3	0
Gyselman 3B	2	0	0	0	0	1	0
Webber P	2	1	2	0	0	5	0
	23	2	6	2	21	11	0

Pitching Records	IP	H	R	ER	SO	BB
Munger	6	6	2	2	2	0
Webber	7	5	1	1	6	2

Left on Base: Sacramento 5, Seattle 3. Two Base Hit: Sturdy. Home Run: White. Sacrifice: Handley. Double Play: Matheson to Scarsella. Time of Game: 1hr. 35min. Umpires: Hood, Edwards, Engeln, Snyder.

Sacramento	100	000	0	1 – 5 – 1
Seattle	002	000	x	2 – 6 – 0

Game Three.

Over 6,000 fans turned out on Sunday afternoon, October 5, for what they knew would be the last game in Sick's Stadium in 1941. Dick Barrett faced

Tony Freitas but neither pitcher was involved in the decision. Seattle broke the scoreless tie in the fifth when Stickle walked, was sacrificed to second by Niemiec, but had to remain there as Gyselman grounded to Gutteridge at third, but "Tricky Dick" was safe on a poor throw. Dick Barrett then singled but Wieczorek threw Stickle out at the plate. Jo Jo White then singled in Gyselman. In the seventh, Stickle again walked and again Niemiec sacrificed him to second, and again Barrett singled to right, but this time Stickle beat the throw to the plate for a 2–0 lead.

The Solons cut the lead to 2–1 in the eighth on a double by Frank Scalzi, who batted for Freitas. He came around to score on a bunt and a ground out. But Dick Barrett had only himself to blame for Sacramento tying the game in the ninth. Klutz got a scratch single off Barrett's glove, taking second on Gyselman's bad throw. He was on third with two outs and two strikes on Endicott, when Barrett uncorked a wild pitch, allowing Klutz to score the tying run. In the 11th, Wieczorek doubled off reliever Ira Scribner and scored the winning run on Klutz' single. Al Hollingsworth pitched the final four innings for the Solons to get the win.

Sacramento	AB	R	H	RBI	O	A	E
Gutteridge 3B	5	0	3	0	3	1	1
Handley SS	5	0	0	0	1	3	0
Sturdy 1B	5	0	1	1	10	2	1
Wieczorek RF	5	1	1	0	5	1	0
Klutz C	4	1	3	1	3	1	0
Blattner 2B	4	0	1	0	7	4	0
Adams CF	4	0	0	0	2	0	0
Endicott LF	5	0	2	0	1	0	0
Freitas P	2	0	0	0	1	4	0
Scalzi [a]	1	1	1	0	0	0	0
Hollingsworth P	2	0	0	0	0	1	0
	42	3	12	2	33	17	2

(a) Batted for Freitas in the eighth.

Seattle	AB	R	H	RBI	O	A	E
White LF	5	0	2	1	0	1	0
Lawrence CF	5	0	2	0	3	0	0
Matheson RF	5	0	0	0	6	0	0
Scarsella 1B	5	0	1	0	9	1	0
Collins C	5	0	0	0	5	2	0
Stickle SS	3	1	2	0	2	2	0
Niemiec 2B	2	0	0	0	6	2	0

Seattle	AB	R	H	RBI	O	A	E
Gyselman 3B	3	1	0	0	1	4	1
Barrett P	3	0	2	1	1	4	0
Fallon [a]	1	0	0	0	0	0	0
Scribner P	0	0	0	0	0	1	0
	37	2	9	2	33	17	1

(a) Batted for Barrett in the ninth.

Pitching Records	IP	H	R	ER	SO	BB
Freitas	7	6	2	1	1	2
Hollingsworth (W)	4	3	0	0	1	1
Barrett	9	9	2	1	3	1
Scribner (L)	2	3	1	1	0	1

Wild Pitch: Barrett. Left on Base: Sacramento 9, Seattle 6. Two Base Hits: Endicott, Scalzi, Wieczorek. Sacrifices: Niemiec 3, Blattner. Stolen Base: Gutteridge. Double Plays: Klutz to Blattner; Gutteridge to Sturdy to Blattner to Sturdy. Time: 2 hr. 35 min. Umpires: Edwards, Hood, Snyder, Engeln.

Sacramento	000	000	011	01	3 – 12 – 2
Seattle	000	010	100	00	2 – 9 – 1

Game Four.

With the World Series ending on Monday, October 6, the Pacific Coast League was the last to conclude the 1941 season. The two clubs traveled south to Sacramento on that Monday and played the fourth game, Tuesday night, the 7th at Cardinal Field. Red Munger shut the Suds out 3–0 to tie the series. Ed Cole gave up an unearned run in the second when Klutz reached second base when Scarsella dropped Gyselman's throw. Blattner singled in Klutz. Cole gave up a homer to Lincoln Blakely in the seventh, and another run in the eighth on Sturdy's double and Klutz' single. These games in Sacramento were not on radio because the Solons were not broadcasting and Seattle only did their home games. No attendance was announced.

Seattle	AB	R	H	RBI	O	A	E
White CF	3	0	1	0	5	0	1
Harris LF	3	0	0	0	2	0	0
Matheson RF	3	0	0	0	0	0	0
Scarsella 1B	3	0	1	0	9	2	1
Collins C	3	0	0	0	5	1	1

Seattle	AB	R	H	RBI	O	A	E
Stickle SS	3	0	0	0	1	2	0
Gyselman 3B	3	0	0	0	0	5	0
Berger 2B	3	0	0	0	2	1	0
Cole P	2	0	0	0	0	0	0
King[a]	1	0	0	0	0	0	0
	27	0	2	0	24	11	3

(a) Batted for Cole in the ninth.

Sacramento	AB	R	H	RBI	O	A	E
Gutteridge 3B	4	0	0	0	0	0	0
Handley SS	4	0	1	0	3	3	1
Sturdy 1B	2	1	1	0	6	0	0
Wieczorek RF	2	0	0	0	1	0	0
Klutz C	4	1	1	1	7	2	0
Blattner 2B	4	0	2	1	2	2	0
Endicott LF	4	0	0	0	4	0	0
Blakely CF	3	1	2	1	4	0	0
Munger P	3	0	0	0	0	1	0
	30	3	7	3	27	8	1

Pitching Records	IP	H	R	ER	SO	BB
Cole	8	7	3	2	4	2
Munger	9	2	0	0	7	2

Left on Base: Seattle 2, Sacramento 7. Two Base Hit: Sturdy. Home Run: Blakely. Sacrifices: Sturdy, Wieczorek. Stolen Base: White. Double Plays: Munger to Handley to Sturdy; Collins to Stickle. Time of Game: 1 hr. 57 min. Umpires: Engeln, Snyder, Hood, Powell.

Seattle	000	000	000	0 – 2 – 3
Sacramento	010	000	11x	3 – 7 – 1

Game Five.

On Wednesday night, October 8, the Solons won their third straight game to take a 3–2 lead in the series. Tony Freitas beat Hal Turpin 4–1 before a small gathering of 1,635. The little Portuguese left-hander retired the final 15 batters in a row. The Solons' first run came in the third when Gutteridge beat out an infield hit and raced around to score on a hit-and-run double by Gene Handley. Seattle tied the game in the fourth when Bill Matheson doubled, went to third on Scarsella's grounder and scored as Fallon flied out. Matheson was the last Rainer base runner. Sacramento took the lead for good in the sixth on Sturdy's double and two fly balls by Wieczorek and Klutz. In the seventh, Blakely doubled and scored on Gutteridge's single, and in the eighth, the final run scored when Sturdy singled, stole second ahead of Blattner's single. The game took only an hour and 31 minutes to play.

Seattle	AB	R	H	RBI	O	A	E
White LF	4	0	0	0	1	0	0
Lawrence CF	4	0	0	0	8	0	0
Matheson RF	4	1	2	0	3	0	0
Scarsella 1B	4	0	0	0	8	0	0
Fallon C	3	0	1	1	4	0	0
Stickle SS	3	0	0	0	0	2	0
Gyselman 3B	3	0	1	0	0	0	0
Berger 2B	3	0	0	0	0	1	0
Turpin P	2	0	0	0	0	1	0
Collins[a]	1	0	0	0	0	0	0
Soriano P	0	0	0	0	0	0	0
	31	1	4	1	24	4	0

(a) Batted for Turpin in the eighth.

Sacramento	AB	R	H	RBI	O	A	E
Gutteridge 3B	4	1	2	1	1	0	0
Handley SS	4	0	2	1	3	2	0
Sturdy 1B	4	2	3	0	9	1	0
Wieczorek RF	3	0	0	0	2	0	1
Klutz C	4	0	0	1	6	1	0
Blattner 2B	4	0	1	1	1	2	0
Endicott LF	4	0	0	0	2	0	0
Blakely CF-RF	3	1	1	0	2	0	0
Freitas P	3	0	0	0	1	2	0
Adams CF	0	0	0	0	0	0	0
	33	4	9	4	27	8	1

Pitching Records	IP	H	R	ER	SO	BB
Turpin (L)	7	7	3	3	3	1
Soriano	1	2	1	1	1	0
Freitas	9	4	1	1	6	0

Left on Base: Seattle 3, Sacramento 6. Two Base Hits: Handley, Matheson, Sturdy, Blakely. Three Base Hit: Matheson. Stolen Bases: Gyselman, Study, Blattner. Time of Game: 1 hr. 31 min. Umpires: Snyder, Hood, Powell, Engeln.

Seattle	000	100	000	1 – 4 – 0		
Sacramento	001	001	11x	4 – 9 – 1		

Game Six.

Attendance picked up a bit to 2,039 on Thursday night, October 9, but the fans were disappointed that the Solons could not finish off the Rainiers. Les Webber beat Bill Schmidt to end Seattle's three-game losing streak with a 4–3 win. For the third game in a row Seattle was forced to use Boze Berger at second base because Al Niemiec was down with the flu. Sacramento took a 1–0 lead in the first on Handley's triple and Sturdy's ground out, but in the third, Seattle took the lead for good, scoring three runs. Schmidt retired the first eight batters, making 23 Rainiers in a row go down before Webber singled and scored on White's triple. Spencer Harris was hit by a pitch, and despite his advanced age, stole second. Matheson then singled both runners home. The last and decisive Seattle run came off Al Hollingsworth in the fifth when White doubled and scored on Harris' single. The Solons got two unearned runs in the sixth but fell short.

Seattle	AB	R	H	RBI	O	A	E
White CF	5	2	2	1	3	0	0
Harris LF	3	1	1	1	5	0	0
Matheson RF	4	0	1	2	1	0	0
Scarsella 1B	4	0	1	0	8	2	0
Collins C	4	0	1	0	4	1	1
Stickle SS	4	0	0	0	0	3	1
Gyselman 3B	3	0	0	0	1	1	0
Berger 2B	3	0	0	0	3	2	1
Webber P	4	1	1	0	2	1	0
	34	4	7	4	27	10	3

Sacramento	AB	R	H	RBI	O	A	E
Gutteridge 3B	4	1	0	0	3	1	0
Handley SS	4	1	1	0	0	3	2
Sturdy 1B	4	0	0	1	9	0	0
Wieczorek RF	4	1	1	1	3	0	0
Klutz C	4	0	1	1	5	2	0
Blattner 2B	4	0	0	0	1	2	0

Sacramento	AB	R	H	RBI	O	A	E
Endicott LF	3	0	0	0	2	0	0
Blakely CF	3	0	1	0	4	0	0
Schmidt P	1	0	1	0	0	0	0
Hollingsworth P	2	0	0	0	0	0	0
	33	3	5	3	27	8	2

Pitching Records	IP	H	R	ER	SO	BB
Webber	9	5	3	1	0	0
Schmidt (L)	3.2	4	3	3	2	1
Hollingsworth	5.1	3	1	1	2	0

Hit by Pitcher: Harris by Schmidt. Left on Base: Seattle 6, Sacramento 2. Two Base Hits: White, Wieczorek. Three Base Hits: White, Handley. Sacrifice: Berger. Stolen Bases: Harris 2. Double Play: Gutteridge to Sturdy. Time of Game: 1 hr. 15 min. Umpires: Hood, Engeln, Powell, Snyder.

Seattle	003	010	000	4 – 7 – 3
Sacramento	100	002	000	3 – 5 – 2

Game Seven.

In the final baseball game of 1941, on Friday, October 10, at Cardinal Field, 2,639 disappointed fans saw Kewpie Dick Barrett beat George Munger to give Seattle its second straight playoff triumph. Seattle's "Little Round Man" got all the runs he needed in the second when Collins walked and Al Niemiec, back from his sick bed, singled. Gyselman doubled both men home. The Solons cut the lead to 2–1 in the third on Gutteridge's single, Harris' error, and Handley's double. Seattle got the final run of the season the next inning on Stickle's double and White's single. Manager Bill Skiff had boldly predicted his team, even when trailing Sacramento by 15 games, would overtake them and win the pennant. His team also came from behind in each round of the playoffs to win the President's Cup.

Seattle	AB	R	H	RBI	O	A	E
White CF-LF	5	0	1	1	3	0	0
Harris LF	2	0	0	0	0	0	1
Matheson RF	4	0	0	0	2	0	0
Scarsella 1B	4	0	2	0	11	0	0
Collins C	3	1	0	0	2	2	0
Stickle SS	4	1	1	0	1	5	0
Niemiec 2B	3	1	1	0	2	3	0

Seattle	AB	R	H	RBI	O	A	E
Gyselman 3B	3	0	1	2	3	1	0
Barrett P	3	0	0	0	0	4	0
Lawrence CF[a]	2	0	1	0	3	0	0
	33	3	7	3	27	15	1

(a) Batted for Harris in the fourth.

Sacramento	AB	R	H	RBI	O	A	E
Gutteridge 3B	4	1	1	0	1	0	0
Handley SS	4	0	1	1	2	2	0
Sturdy 1B	4	0	1	0	4	1	0
Wieczorek RF	4	0	0	0	4	0	0
Klutz C	4	0	1	0	6	1	0
Blattner 2B	2	0	1	0	6	2	0
Endicott LF	3	0	1	0	2	0	0
Blakely CF	3	0	0	0	2	0	0
Munger P	1	0	0	0	0	0	0
Freitas P	0	0	0	0	0	1	0
Martin b[a]	1	0	0	0	0	0	0
Hollingsworth P	0	0	0	0	0	0	0
	30	1	6	1	27	7	0

(a) Batted for Freitas in the eighth.

Pitching Records	IP	H	R	ER	SO	BB
Barrett	9	6	1	1	3	1
Munger (L)	3.2	5	3	3	5	3
Freitas	4.1	2	0	0	1	0
Hollingsworth	1	0	0	0	1	0

Left on Base: Seattle 7, Sacramento 5. Two Base Hits: Gyselman, Handley, Stickle. Sacrifices: Niemiec, Freitas. Double Play: Barrett to Stickle to Scarsella. Time of Game: 2 hr. Umpires: Powell, Engeln, Snyder, Hood.

Seattle	020	100	000	3 – 7 – 1
Sacramento	001	000	000	1 – 6 – 0

Seattle received $7,500 prize money: $2,500 for first place, and $5,000 for the playoffs. They had 22 shares of $340, or about $2,313 in current dollars. The Sacs earned $2,500, or about $114 per man, which would be $775 in today's money. The consolation prize money had to be disappointing to Sacramento, which blew leads in both the pennant race and in the playoffs.

Key Players on 1941 Playoff Teams

Seattle. *Pitchers:* Dick Barrett, Hal Turpin, Sylvester Johnson, Ed Cole, Les
   Webber, and Ira Scribner.
   Position Players: Les Scarsella, Jo Jo White, Bill Matheson, Spencer Harris,
   Bob Collins, Bill Matheson, and Al Niemiec.

Sacramento. *Pitchers:* Tony Freitas, Bill Schmidt, George Munger, Al Hol-
   lingsworth and Norb Kleinke.
   Position Players: Jack Sturdy, Don Gutteridge, Pepper Martin, Lincoln
   Blakely, Bill Endicott and Clyde Klutz.

San Diego. *Pitchers:* Yank Terry, Wally Hebert, Rex Dilbert, and Al Olsen.
   Position Players: George Detore, Mel Mazzera, Hal Patchett, Swede Jensen,
   and Mickey Haslin.

Hollywood. *Pitchers:* Fred Gay, Lou Tost, Hiram Bithorn, and Frankie Dasso.
   Position Players: Babe Herman, Johnny Dickshot, Johnny Barrett, Bob Kahle
   and Bernard "Frenchie" Uhalt.

1942

The first wartime season saw Sacramento win the last five games in a row from Los Angeles to win the pennant by a single game, while San Diego eliminated the Seals from the first division by beating them in a doubleheader on the last day of the season. But the war required some drastic changes. Many players had to go into the armed services or were waiting to be called. But unlike 1943–1945, there were still enough regulars to give the fans a quality of baseball they had enjoyed in the past. But later in the season, night games were forbidden because of blackouts, causing attendance to suffer. Portland and Seattle tried 5 P.M. starts to try and get more fans, with limited success.

After the successful 1941 season, owners had planned to expand rosters to 25 players, with 5 rookies and 20 veterans, but after baseball was given the green light to play in 1942, the rosters were reduced to 20 without regard to status. The military had travel priority. Rail fares were increased, and no longer were separate dining cars and sleepers set aside for players; they would have to take berths wherever they could find them and carry their own luggage. Train delays often caused teams to play doubleheaders after postponements. Radio announcers could no longer mention the weather on the air, so games were postponed or delayed because of "unplayable conditions."

Seattle jumped into an early lead, going for their fourth pennant in a row, but faltered in late May and fell to second behind Los Angeles, and later to third behind the Angels and Sacramento. The Solons were in seventh place in May before winning 38 of 47 to take the top spot from the Angels in June. But when the Sacs went into L.A., they could win only one of ten games played there. But up in Sacramento, it was a different story. In late June, the Angels won the first two games of a series at Cardinal Field and then lost the last five. History repeated itself the last week of the season.

With nine games to go, Sacramento and L.A. were tied for first at 100–69 and San Diego and San Francisco were tied for fourth at 85–84. But the next day, Sunday, September 13, the Angels won two from Hollywood while Sacramento was losing two to Seattle, and San Diego won two from Portland while

163

Tommy Thompson, Buster Adams and Deb Garms were Sacramento teammates in 1942 (Dick Dobbins collection).

San Francisco lost two to Oakland. So with seven games to go, the Angels and Padres each led their rivals by two games.

In the final week, the Angels were at Sacramento for seven games while the Seals were at San Diego for seven. Unfortunately, this head to head competition did not attract large crowds until the last Sunday in Sacramento, when an overflow crowd witnessed the Solons win the pennant. Sacramento officials blamed the small crowds on the need to play in the daytime, while in San Diego, it was blamed on a "who cares?" attitude about making the playoffs, which San Diego writers called anticlimatic and a sure money loser. But Seal owner Charles Graham credited this close race for fourth place for the Seals being able to draw 30,000 in their final home series against the Oaks. Graham felt the real benefit of the playoffs came while teams struggled to make the first division.

Manager Pepper Martin was concerned that the Cardinals would call up a key player in September, as happened in 1941 when catcher Charlie Marshall was taken with no replacement. But this time the Cardinals sent him vital help that allowed the Solons to overtake the tired and injury-plagued Angels. Sacramento received pitcher John Pintar, who went 3–0, and infielder-pitcher Gene Lillard, the former Angel, who hit .340 and helped beat his former teammates twice that last week, with a pinch single and a pinch homer. These two helped in the pennant drive but Lillard was ineligible for the playoffs. Meanwhile, the parent Chicago Cubs gave the Angels no help at all. Right fielder Johnny Moore was unable to play that last week, and then left fielder Barney Olsen went down after the second game of that crucial series, and then the Angels lost the last five games. L.A. had to play utility infielder Glen "Gabby" Stewart in left field and manager Jigger Statz, whom the Sacramento press uncharitably described as "a decrepit 45 year old man," in right field during those last five decisive games.

By winning the first two games in Sacramento, the Angels had a four-game lead with five to play and then lost all five. This was the all-time great moment for Sacramento fans and close to the all-time low for Angel followers. Certainly it was for manager Statz, who resigned after the season. The Sacramento bench was described as a college cheering section while the Angel bench was a morgue.

Meanwhile, down in San Diego the Seals lost the first two games to the Padres to fall four behind. They then won three in a row to get to within one game, going into the last Sunday doubleheader. But San Diego swept that doubleheader to clinch fourth place.

The Sacramento-Seattle Series

The Rainiers finished the season at Oakland and were at the S.P. station on 16th Street waiting to get a night train to Los Angeles when they got word that the Solons won the pennant. So they checked back into their Oakland hotel and left the next morning for Sacramento to open the playoffs. Because of wartime travel restrictions, Seattle was told they would have to play all their playoff games in California. There was even talk of reducing the series to a best of five instead of a best of seven series, but Angel president Clarence

"Pants" Rowland insisted upon keeping faith with the players who received additional salaries while the games were being played.

The schedule called for single games on Tuesday, Wednesday, Thursday and Saturday afternoons, and then if needed, a doubleheader on Sunday. No game was to be played Friday, because that night the Solon players were to be honored with a victory dinner at the Eagle Theater. Fans were invited to this dinner, which cost $1.50, and were asked to contribute to a fund to give each player a war bond.

Game One.

The Solons won 16 and lost 11 to Seattle over the regular season. On Tuesday afternoon, September 22, Seattle ace Kewpie Dick Barrett faced Frank Nelson, as Sacramento took a 1–0 lead in the series with a 3–2 win in 11 innings. Seattle scored a run in the second when Bob Collins' fly scored Bill Matheson, who had doubled. Buster Adams' homer tied it in the third, but in the top of the fifth, Seattle took the lead on an unearned run. With two outs, Jo Jo White was safe on Gene Handley's error, and scored on Earl Torgeson's double. "Torgy" went 4-for-4 in a losing cause. The Solons got even in the seventh when Jack Sturdy singled and scored on Deb Garms' triple. The score remained deadlocked until the last of the 11th when Eddie Lake singled, Mel Serafini doubled, Sturdy was walked intentionally, and Garms won it with a single.

The Sacramento Bee was premature in bragging that the Solons had a winning spirit and did not know how to lose, after winning six in a row. But this was to be the high water mark for Sacramento baseball. They were about to lose the next four in a row and be eliminated from the playoffs. The following two seasons would be abysmal. In 1943, the Sad Sacs had the lowest winning percentage of any PCL team in history (.265) and would draw only 31,600 fans the entire season.

Seattle	AB	R	H	RBI	O	A	E
Stickle SS	5	0	0	0	2	4	0
King CF	6	0	0	0	4	0	0
White LF	5	1	1	0	1	0	0
Torgeson 1B	4	0	4	1	14	1	0
Matheson RF	5	1	1	0	0	0	0
Gyselman 3B	4	0	0	0	1	6	0
Niemiec 2B	4	0	2	0	2	3	0
Collins C	4	0	2	1	5	3	0
Barrett P	5	0	0	0	2	3	0

Seattle	AB	R	H	RBI	O	A	E
Harris[a]	1	0	0	0	0	0	0
Kearse C	0	0	0	0	0	0	0
	43	2	10	2	31[b]	20	0

(a) Batted for Collins in the ninth.
(b) One out when winning run scored.

Sacramento	AB	R	H	RBI	O	A	E
Lake SS	5	1	1	0	2	1	0
Handley 2B	4	0	2	0	2	2	1
Sturdy 1B	4	1	2	0	12	0	0
Garms RF	4	0	2	2	2	0	0
Thompson LF	4	0	0	0	2	0	0
Mesner 2B-3B	4	0	0	0	0	3	0
Adams CF	2	1	1	1	10	0	0
Mueller C	4	0	0	0	2	3	0
Nelson P	4	0	1	0	0	4	0
Serafini 3B	1	0	1	0	1	0	0
	36	3	10	3	33	13	1

Pitching Records	IP	H	R	ER	SO	BB
Barrett	10.1	10	3	3	5	4
Nelson	11	10	2	1	2	5

Left on Base: Seattle 12, Sacramento 7. Two Base Hits: Matheson, Torgeson, Collins, Nelson, Serafini. Three Base Hit: Garms. Home Run: Adams. Stolen Base: Stickle. Double Plays: Stickle to Niemiec to Torgeson 2. Time of Game: 2 hr. 24 min. Umpires: Fanning, Engeln, Edwards, McDonald.

Seattle	010	010	000	00	2 – 10 – 0
Sacramento	001	000	100	01	3 – 10 – 1

Game Two.

Seattle held on in the ninth to tie the series at a game each on Wednesday afternoon, September 23. Solon starter Kemp Wicker was knocked out in the first inning as Seattle gave Hal Turpin a 4–0 lead. Walks to Ned Stickle and Jo Jo White, sandwiched around a Bill Lawrence single, loaded the bases. Gene Handley then threw low on Earl Torgeson's grounder, scoring a run and keeping the bases loaded. Bill Matheson doubled in two runs but Torgy was thrown out at the plate. John Pintar relieved at that point and gave up an infield single to Dick Gyselman and a run-scoring fly ball to Al Niemiec. The Solons cut the lead to 4–2 in the second when Pintar himself singled in two runs. Each team got a run in the fourth: Seattle's came on a Bob Collins double, Hal Turpin's bunt single, and a force out, while Sacramento's came on Buster Adams' homer. The Solons narrowed it to 5–4 in the fifth on singles by Jack Study, Deb Garms and Averett "Tommy" Thompson.

Seattle's unearned run in the eighth turned out to be the key to the game. Bill Matheson doubled and scored on shortstop Eddie Lake's crucial error to put the Rainiers up 6–4. Then in the last of the ninth, Bill Skiff used four pitchers to subdue the Sacs. Turpin gave up a single to Ray Mueller, who stole second while Mel Serafini was striking out. Lake doubled in Mueller to cut the lead to 6–5. Larry Guay relieved and retired Handley but walked Sturdy. Ed Carnett then relieved Guay and walked Garms to load the bases. Skiff then called on 41-year-old Sylvester Johnson, who retired Thompson to save the game. As with the first game, no attendance was mentioned.

Seattle	AB	R	H	RBI	O	A	E
Stickle SS	4	1	0	1	3	7	0
Lawrence CF	5	1	2	0	4	1	0
White LF	4	1	1	0	1	0	0
Torgeson 1B	5	0	0	1	8	1	0
Matheson RF	5	2	2	2	3	0	0
Gyselman 3B	3	0	3	0	1	2	0
Niemiec 2B	4	0	0	1	4	2	0
Collins C	2	1	1	0	3	1	0
Turpin P	3	0	0	0	0	1	0
Guay P	0	0	0	0	0	0	0
Carnett P	0	0	0	0	0	0	0
Johnson P	0	0	0	0	0	0	0
	35	6	9	5	27	15	0

Sacramento	AB	R	H	RBI	O	A	E
Lake SS	5	0	1	1	2	6	1
Handley 2B	5	0	0	0	3	2	1
Sturdy 1B	4	1	2	0	8	1	0
Garms RF	4	0	2	0	2	0	0
Thompson LF	5	1	2	1	2	0	0
Mesner 3B	4	0	1	0	0	0	0
Adams CF	3	2	1	1	6	1	0
Mueller C	2	1	1	0	3	1	0
Wicker P	0	0	0	0	0	0	0

Sacramento	AB	R	H	RBI	O	A	E
Pintar P	3	0	1	2	1	2	0
Serafini[a]	1	0	0	0	0	0	0
	36	5	11	5	27	13	2

(a) Batted for Pintar in the ninth.

Pitching Records	IP	H	R	ER	SO	BB
Turpin (W)	8.1	11	5	5	3	3
Guay	0.1	0	0	0	0	1
Carnett	0+	0	0	0	0	1
Johnson	0.1	0	0	0	0	0
Wicker (L)	0.1	2	3	2	0	2
Pintar	8.2	7	3	1	2	2

Left on Base: Seattle 8, Sacramento 9. Two Base Hits: Matheson 2, Gyselman 2, Collins, Lake. Home Run: Lake. Sacrifices: Turpin, Gyselman. Stolen Base: Mueller. Time of Game: 2 hr. 4 min. Umpires: Engeln, Edwards, McDonald, Fanning.

Seattle	400	100	010	6 –	9 –	0
Sacramento	020	110	001	5 –	11 –	2

Game Three.

On Thursday afternoon, September 24, a sparse crowd of 725 saw Seattle take a 2–1 lead in the series, with Carl Fischer beating Bill Schmidt. Fischer gave up only four hits, three of which came in the first inning when the Solons got their only run. Singles by Handley, Sturdy and Garms brought home that run. Tommy Thompson's eighth inning single was the Solons' only other hit. Bill Schmidt allowed Seattle only seven hits, but they eked out two runs to win the game. In the sixth, ex–Solon Lynn King was credited with a double when Eddie Lake dropped Garms' throw from right field as King slid into second. Bill Matheson's single tied the game. In the seventh, Niemiec got an infield single and was safe at second when Schmidt threw too late on Collins' bunt. Fischer sacrificed them along and Niemiec scored on Stickle's fly ball.

Seattle	AB	R	H	RBI	O	A	E
Stickle SS	5	0	0	1	1	1	1
King CF	4	1	1	0	5	0	0
White LF	4	0	1	0	3	0	0
Torgeson 1B	3	0	1	0	12	0	0

Seattle	AB	R	H	RBI	O	A	E
Matheson RF	4	0	1	1	0	0	0
Gyselman 3B	4	0	0	0	0	3	1
Niemiec 2B	4	1	1	0	3	4	0
Collins C	2	0	1	0	3	0	0
Fischer P	3	0	1	0	0	3	0
	33	2	7	2	27	11	2

Sacramento	AB	R	H	RBI	O	A	E
Lake SS	4	0	0	0	0	5	0
Handley 2B	4	1	1	0	5	3	1
Sturdy 1B	4	0	1	0	12	1	0
Garms RF	4	0	1	1	1	0	0
Mesner 3B	4	0	0	0	1	3	0
Adams CF	3	0	0	0	2	0	0
Mueller C	3	0	0	0	3	0	0
Thompson LF	3	0	1	0	3	0	0
Schmidt P	3	0	0	0	0	2	0
	32	1	4	1	27	14	1

Pitching Records	IP	H	R	ER	SO	BB
Fischer	9	4	1	1	3	0
Schmidt	9	7	2	2	2	2

Left on Base: Seattle 8, Sacramento 4. Two Base Hits: White, King, Torgeson. Sacrifices: Collins, Fischer. Double Play: Gyselman to Niemiec to Torgeson. Time of Game: 1 hr. 44 min. Umpires: Edwards, McDonald, Fanning, Engeln.

Seattle	000	001	100	2 – 7 – 2
Sacramento	100	000	000	1 – 4 – 1

Game Four.

The off day on Friday gave Sacramento sports writers another opportunity to criticize the playoffs, calling them anticlimatic and sure money losers. They also stated that Seattle cared so little for them that they were willing to play all their games on the road, ignoring the fact that this was necessitated by wartime travel restrictions.

On Saturday the 26th Kewpie Dick Barrett faced Tony Freitas, who had a tired arm from being used so extensively that last hectic week against the Angels. Freitas lasted only three innings and gave up three of Seattle's four

The 1942 Sacramento team took the pennant in a miracle finish. From left (back) trainer Jack Downey, Ken Penner, Pepper Martin, Clarence Beers, Bill Shewey, Jack Sturdy, Kemp Wicker, Gene Handley, John Pintar; (middle) Charlie Marshall, Herschel Lyons, Bill Schmidt, Buster Adams, Steve Mesner, Frank Nelson; (front) Blix Donnelly, Tommy Thompson, Ray Mueller, Tony Freitas, Mel Serafini, Deb Garms, Eddie Lake (Dick Dobbins collection).

runs. Barrett himself drove in the first run in the second with a single, scoring Collins, who had doubled. In the third, Lawrence singled, White was safe on Sturdy's error, Torgeson doubled in Lawrence, and Matheson was safe on a fielder's choice as White was thrown out at the plate. Torgeson was then thrown out trying to steal third, but Gyselman's double scored Matheson. Seattle's fourth run came off Herschel Lyons in the fourth as Lawrence doubled in Collins. Barrett was helped by four double plays behind him, and gave up only one run in the seventh, when Thompson walked and came around on singles by Steve Mesner and Ray Mueller. No attendance was announced.

Seattle	AB	R	H	RBI	O	A	E
Stickle SS	5	0	0	0	4	5	0
Lawrence CF	5	1	1	1	2	0	1
White LF	3	0	2	0	1	0	0
Torgeson 1B	4	0	2	1	10	0	1
Matheson RF	4	1	0	0	0	0	0
Gyselman 3B	4	0	1	1	1	5	0
Niemiec 2B	4	0	0	0	5	2	0

Seattle	AB	R	H	RBI	O	A	E
Collins C	4	2	2	0	4	0	0
Barrett P	3	0	2	1	0	2	0
	36	4	10	4	27	14	2

Sacramento	AB	R	H	RBI	O	A	E
Lake SS	4	0	0	0	0	3	0
Handley 2B	4	0	2	0	1	1	2
Sturdy 1B	4	0	0	0	12	0	1
Garms RF	3	0	0	0	1	0	0
Thompson LF	3	1	0	0	2	0	0
Mesner 3B	4	0	2	0	2	6	0
Adams CF	4	0	1	0	5	0	0
Mueller C	3	0	3	1	4	2	0
Freitas P	0	0	0	0	0	1	0
Marshall [a]	1	0	0	0	0	0	0
Lyons P	0	0	0	0	0	0	0
Serafini [b]	1	0	0	0	0	0	0
Beers P	0	0	0	0	0	1	0
Martin [c]	1	0	0	0	0	0	0
Pintar P	0	0	0	0	0	1	0
	32	1	8	1	27	15	3

(a) Batted for Freitas in the third.
(b) Batted for Lyons in the fifth.
(c) Batted for Beers in the seventh.

Pitching Records	IP	H	R	ER	SO	BB
Barrett	9	8	1	1	4	2
Freitas (L)	3	5	3	2	0	0
Lyons	2	3	1	1	1	0
Beers	2	1	0	0	1	0
Pintar	2	1	0	0	2	0

Two Base Hits: Collins, Torgeson, Gyselman, Lawrence. Double Plays: Niemiec to Torgeson; Stickle to Niemiec to Torgeson; Stickle to Torgeson; Barrett to Niemiec to Torgeson. Umpires: Edwards, Fanning, McDonald, Engeln.

Game Five.

A doubleheader was scheduled on Sunday, September 27, but Seattle needed only one game to eliminate the Solons before 2,829 fans. Sacramento, behind Blix Donnelly, was leading Hal Turpin 1–0 after five innings but things fell apart for the Sacs in the sixth. With two outs and King on second, Matheson's single tied the game. Gyselman walked and then Niemiec and Collins followed with doubles, bringing on Tony Freitas, who walked Turpin to load the bases before Stickle singled in the fifth run of the inning. After the Solons cut the lead to 5–2 with a run in the last of the sixth, the Rainiers blew the game open with four more runs in the seventh off Clarence Beers and Kemp Wicker. Matheson's two-run double was the key blow of that inning.

Seattle	AB	R	H	RBI	O	A	E
Stickle SS	6	0	2	2	4	5	0
King CF	4	1	1	0	3	0	0
White LF	6	1	2	0	4	0	0
Torgeson 1B	5	1	1	0	5	0	0
Matheson RF	6	2	4	2	4	0	0
Gyselman 3B	4	2	2	1	1	0	0
Niemiec 2B	3	1	1	2	4	3	0
Collins C	4	1	2	1	2	1	1
Turpin P	4	0	0	0	0	1	0
	42	9	15	8	27	10	1

Sacramento	AB	R	H	RBI	O	A	E
Lake SS	4	1	2	0	2	5	1
Handley 2B	4	0	1	0	1	6	0
Sturdy 1B	4	0	1	1	12	1	0
Garms RF	4	0	1	0	1	0	0
Thompson LF	4	1	1	0	1	0	1
Mesner 3B	3	0	1	0	2	0	0
Adams CF	4	0	2	0	5	0	0
Mueller C	2	0	1	1	1	0	0
Donnelly P	2	0	0	0	1	1	0
Freitas P	0	0	0	0	0	0	0
Serafini 3B	2	0	1	0	1	1	0
Beers P	0	0	0	0	0	0	0
Wicker P	0	0	0	0	0	1	0
Pintar[a]	1	0	0	0	0	0	0
Marshall C	1	0	0	0	0	0	0
Lyons P	0	0	0	0	0	0	0
	35	2	11	2	27	15	2

(a) Batted for Wicker in the eighth.

Pitching Records	IP	H	R	ER	SO	BB
Turpin	9	11	2	2	5	2
Donnelly (L)	5.2	6	4	5	1	2
Freitas	0.1	1	1	0	0	1
Beers	0+	2	2	3	0	1
Wicker	2	4	2	1	0	2
Lyons	1	2	0	0	0	0

Left on Base: Seattle 14, Sacramento 9. Two Base Hits: Matheson 2, Collins 2, Niemiec, Gyselman, Thompson. Sacrifices: Handley, Niemiec. Stolen bases: Adams, Torgeson. Double Plays: Stickle to Torgeson; Turpin to Stickle to Torgeson. Time of Game: 2 hr. 7 min. Umpires: Fanning, Engeln, Edwards, McDonald.

Seattle	000	005	400	9 – 15 – 1
Sacramento	100	001	000	2 – 11 – 2

Sacramento writers tried to put a good spin on this postseason failure after the Solons had won their only pennant. They claimed that the Solons could have beaten Seattle if they played the way they did against the Angels, but that it was hard to fire the team up after that fantastic finish. The Solons gave Gene Lillard $100 of their $2,500 pennant winning money, so they had a total of $3,650 to divide among 20 players. Each received about $182.50, which would come close to $1,126 today.

The Los Angeles–San Diego Series

The Angels, having just blown the pennant, were in poor shape to begin the playoffs. Barney Olsen was in the hospital, Johnny Moore was hurting, and their pitching staff had been raked over the coals by Sacramento's mad dash to the pennant. The Padres, having knocked the Seals out of the first division, were in a better frame of mind. The second place Angels were taking on the fourth place Padres just as in 1940, but this year the Angels gave up the right to open at home to avoid a direct conflict with a Friday afternoon football game at the Coliseum between UCLA and TCU. With USC scheduled to play Tulane there on Saturday, the L.A. papers were devoting more coverage to football and to the tight National League race between the Cardinals and Dodgers than to the Angels and Padres. The Angels had won 16 and lost 10 to the Padres during the season.

Game One.

The series began on Wednesday, September 23, at 4:30 P.M. The late start was designed to attract fans after normal working hours, but since it lasted 11 innings, it was almost dark when the game ended at 7 P.M. Jesse Flores faced Norm Brown and each gave up a run in the first inning and again in the sixth inning. L.A.'s first run was unearned, when they benefited from two errors, a sacrifice and a ground out. San Diego tied the game on singles by Johnny Hill, Mel Mazzera and Bill Salkeld. The Angels' second run came on Roy Hughes' triple and Johnny Moore's foul fly, which some San Diego writers felt should have been allowed to drop. But in the last of the sixth, Hill's double and Mazzera's single tied the game. The game went into extra innings, and in the 10th the Angels went up 3–2 on Peanuts Lowrey's triple and Hughes's grounder. But San Diego tied it quickly on Hal Patchett's double and Hughes' throwing error. But L.A. broke the tie again in the 11th as darkness approached. Statz, who had replaced "Gabby" Stewart, tripled, Flores doubled, and Lowrey singled, bringing in Rex Dilbeck to relieve Brown. An error by Jack Whipple allowed Lowrey to move to second, from where he scored on Hughes' single. But the Padres made it interesting in the last half. Frank Stinson and Del Ballinger singled, bringing Red Lynn to relieve Flores. After Jack Calvey was unable to beat out a bunt, Hal Patchett singled in two runs to cut the lead to 6–5. The Padres later loaded the bases with two outs, but Swede Jensen struck out to end the game.

Los Angeles	AB	R	H	RBI	O	A	E
Lowrey CF	6	3	2	1	7	1	0
Waitkus 1B	6	0	1	0	11	0	0
Hughes 2B	5	1	2	1	6	5	1
Moore RF	6	0	1	2	0	0	0
Mayo 3B	4	0	1	0	0	1	0
Schuster SS	2	0	0	0	2	5	0
Stewart LF	4	0	0	0	2	0	0
Campbell C	2	0	0	0	5	0	0
Flores P	3	1	1	1	0	2	0
Statz LF	1	1	1	0	0	0	0
Lynn P	0	0	0	0	0	1	0
	39	6	9	5	33	15	1

San Diego	AB	R	H	RBI	O	A	E
Calvey SS	4	0	0	1	5	4	0
Patchett CF	6	1	3	2	3	0	0
Hill 3B	3	2	3	0	0	4	0

San Diego	AB	R	H	RBI	O	A	E
Mazzera RF	4	0	2	1	1	1	0
Salkeld C	3	0	1	1	2	2	1
Jensen LF	4	0	0	0	2	0	0
Skelley 2B	4	0	0	0	6	4	1
Stinson 1B	5	1	2	0	12	1	1
Brown P	3	0	1	0	2	3	1
Detore [a]	1	0	0	0	0	0	0
Whipple 2B	0	0	0	0	0	1	1
Garibaldi 3B	0	0	0	0	0	1	0
Dilbeck P	0	0	0	0	0	1	0
Balinger [b]	1	1	1	0	0	0	0
	38	5	13	5	33	22	5

(a) Batted for Skelley in the 10th.
(b) Batted for Dilbeck in the 11th.

Pitching Records	IP	H	R	ER	SO	BB
Flores (W)	10+	12	3	4	3	5
Lynn	1	1	2	0	1	2
Brown (L)	10.1	8	4	2	1	6
Dilbeck	0.2	1	2	0	1	2

Left on Base: Los Angeles 12, San Diego 13. Two Base Hits: Hill, Moore, Patchett, Flores. Three Base Hits: Hughes, Lowrey, Statz. Sacrifices: Hughes, Flores 2, Brown, Salkeld, Hill 2, Mazzera, Calvey, Schuster. Stolen Base: Stewart. Double Plays: Lowrey to Waitkus; Schuster to Hughes to Waitkus 2; Hughes to Schuster to Waitkus; Salkeld to Whipple to Salkeld; Garibaldi to Dilbeck to Calvey. Time of Game: 2 hr. 25 min. Umpires: Powell, Snyder, Hood, Widner.

Los Angeles	100	001	000	13	6 – 9 – 1
San Diego	100	001	000	12	5 – 13 – 5

Game Two.

The Angels took a two game lead in the series when Ray Prim shut out the Padres 1–0. The only run came in the first when Lowrey singled, moved around to third on two ground outs, and scored on Johnny Moore's hit back to the mound that Wally Hebert could not handle. Broadway Bill Schuster made a game saving play in the sixth: With Jack Calvey on second, Patchett hit a sharp grounder over second base that Schuster grabbed, wheeled around, and fired to Eddie Mayo, who tagged Calvey as he rounded third.

Los Angeles	AB	R	H	RBI	O	A	E
Lowrey CF	4	1	2	0	4	0	0
Waitkus 1B	3	0	0	0	8	2	0
Hughes 2B	4	0	0	0	3	2	0
Moore RF	4	0	2	1	1	0	0
Mayo 3B	2	0	0	0	1	2	0
Schuster SS	4	0	0	0	3	2	0
Stewart LF	3	0	0	0	2	0	0
Todd C	2	0	1	0	4	2	0
Prim P	3	0	0	0	0	3	0
Statz LF	1	0	0	0	1	0	0
	30	1	5	1	27	13	0

San Diego	AB	R	H	RBI	O	A	E
Calvey SS	4	0	2	0	1	2	0
Patchett CF	4	0	1	0	1	0	0
Hill 3B	4	0	0	0	0	5	0
Mazzera RF	3	0	0	0	2	0	0
Detore C	2	0	0	0	6	0	0
Jensen LF	3	0	1	0	2	0	0
Skelley 2B	2	0	0	0	1	5	0
Stinson 1B	3	0	0	0	13	1	0
Hebert P	2	0	0	0	1	0	0
Whipple[a]	1	0	0	0	0	0	0
Dasso P	0	0	0	0	0	1	0
	28	0	4	0	27	14	0

(a) Batted for Hebert in the eighth.

Pitching Records	IP	H	R	ER	SO	BB
Prim	9	4	0	0	3	2
Hebert (L)	8	4	1	1	5	2
Dasso	1	1	0	0	1	0

Left on Base: Los Angeles 6; San Diego 4. Two Base Hit: Calvey. Sacrifices: Skelley, Waitkus, Mayo. Time of Game: 1 hr. 29 min. Umpires: Snyder, Hood, Widner, Powell.

Los Angeles	100	000	000	1 – 5 – 0
San Diego	000	000	000	0 – 4 – 0

Game Three.

The final game at Lane Field in 1942 was played on Friday afternoon, September 25, as San Diego edged L.A. 2–1 to cut the Angels' series lead. The Los Angeles papers gave more coverage to UCLA's 7–6 loss to TCU before only 15,000 and to the upcoming USC game with Tulane than to the playoffs. Despite the Bruin loss, they did manage to win their conference and go to the Rose Bowl for the first time.

The Padres' two runs came in the first after the first two batters were retired. Hill singled, Mazzera walked and Salkeld doubled both men home off loser Red Lynn. Al Olson pitched out of a couple of tight spots to get the win. The Angel run came in the fourth when Lowrey tripled and scored on a wild pitch. Lowrey got to third base with one out in the sixth on Salkeld's two-base throwing error, but neither Waitkus nor Hughes could score him. In the ninth, Hughes got to second with no one out, but could not score. No attendance figures were announced for any of the games in San Diego.

Los Angeles	AB	R	H	RBI	O	A	E
Lowrey CF	4	1	2	0	2	0	0
Waitkus 1B	4	0	0	0	11	0	0
Hughes 2B	4	0	1	0	4	5	0
Moore RF	4	0	1	0	1	0	0
Mayo 3B	3	0	0	0	2	2	0
Schuster SS	4	0	0	0	2	2	0
Stewart LF	3	0	2	0	1	0	0
Todd C	3	0	0	0	1	0	0
Lynn P	2	0	0	0	0	2	1
Statz LF[a]	1	0	1	0	0	0	0
Prim[b]	0	0	0	0	0	0	0
Dobernic P	0	0	0	0	0	1	0
Sweeney[c]	1	0	0	0	0	0	0
	33	1	7	0	24	12	1

(a) Batted for Lynn in the eighth.
(b) Ran for Stewart in the eighth.
(c) Batted for Dobernic in the ninth.

San Diego	AB	R	H	RBI	O	A	E
Calvey SS	4	0	0	0	3	1	0
Patchett CF	3	0	1	0	3	0	1
Hill 3B	4	1	2	0	0	2	0
Mazzera RF	2	1	0	0	7	0	0
Salkeld C	2	0	1	2	1	0	0

San Diego	AB	R	H	RBI	O	A	E
Jensen LF	4	0	0	0	4	0	0
Skelley 2B	3	0	0	0	1	4	1
Stinson 1B	2	0	0	0	6	2	1
Olson P	2	0	0	0	2	1	0
	26	2	4	2	27	10	3

Pitching Records	IP	H	R	ER	SO	BB
Lynn (L)	7	3	2	2	1	4
Dobernic	1	1	0	0	0	2
Olson	9	7	1	1	1	1

Wild Pitch: Olson. Left on Base: Los Angeles 6, San Diego 4. Two Base Hit: Salkeld. Three Base Hit: Lowrey. Sacrifice: Olson. Double Plays: Hill to Skelley to Stinson; Olson to Calvey to Stinton; Hughes to Schuster to Waitkus; Mayo to Hughes to Waitkus. Time of Game: 1 hr. 30 min. Umpires: Hood, Widner, Powell, Snyder.

Los Angeles	000	100	000	1 – 7 – 1
San Diego	200	000	00x	2 – 4 – 3

Game Four.

A doubleheader was played on Sunday, September 27, because Saturday belonged to college football. Tulane beat USC 27–13 before 45,000 at the Coliseum while Loyola beat Occidental at Gilmore Stadium before "practically nobody." Despite the small pregame coverage of this doubleheader, 6,000 showed up at Wrigley Field to see the two teams split. The Angels went up three games to one with a 2–1 win in the opener. Jesse Flores again beat Norm Brown, as he did in game one. Swede Jensen's second inning homer accounted for San Diego's only run and half of their two hits. Eddie Mayo's homer tied it in the seventh, and in the eighth Lowrey singled in Statz, who at age 45 ran for Gilly Campbell. Brown, as Flores, pitched superbly, allowing just four hits.

San Diego	AB	R	H	RBI	O	A	E
Calvey SS	4	0	0	0	1	4	0
Patchett CF	4	0	0	0	2	0	0
Hill 3B	4	0	0	0	2	0	0
Mazzera RF	1	0	0	0	3	0	0
Salkeld C	2	0	0	0	1	0	0
Jensen LF	3	1	2	1	3	0	0
Skelley 2B	2	0	0	0	3	0	0

San Diego	AB	R	H	RBI	O	A	E
Stinson LF	3	0	0	0	7	2	0
Brown P	3	0	0	0	2	2	0
	26	1	2	1	24	8	0

Los Angeles	AB	R	H	RBI	O	A	E
Lowrey CF	3	0	1	1	2	0	0
Waitkus 1B	4	0	1	0	15	2	0
Hughes 2B	4	0	0	0	1	5	0
Moore RF	3	0	0	0	1	0	0
Mayo 3B	3	1	1	1	0	1	0
Schuster SS	3	0	1	0	3	3	0
Stewart LF	3	0	0	0	0	0	0
Campbell C	2	0	0	0	2	0	0
Flores P	2	0	0	0	2	1	0
Statz LF[a]	0	1	0	0	0	0	0
Todd C	0	0	0	0	1	0	0
	27	2	4	2	27	12	0

(a) Ran for Campbell in the eighth.

Pitching Records	IP	H	R	ER	SO	BB
Brown	8	4	2	2	1	2
Flores	9	2	1	1	3	3

Passed Ball: Salkeld. Left on Base: San Diego 2, Los Angeles 4. Two Base Hit: Lowrey. Home Runs: Jensen, Mayo. Sacrifices: Flores, Skelley. Double Plays: Waitkus to Schuster; Hughes to Schuster to Waitkus. Time of Game: 1 hr. 40 min. Umpires: Widner, Powell, Snyder, Hood.

San Diego	010	000	000	1 – 2 – 0
Los Angeles	000	000	11x	2 – 4 – 0

Game Five.

With their backs to the wall, the Padres were able to stay alive by beating L.A. 7–4 in the seven inning nightcap. San Diego got single runs in the second, third, and fifth innings off loser Paul Gehrman to take a 3–0 lead into the final inning. In that seventh, the Padres lit up reliever Jess Dobernic for four runs, on two-run homers by both Mazzera and Jensen. Trailing 7–0 in the last of the seventh, the Angels scored four runs, knocking out starter Frankie Dasso. Rex Dilbeck came in with the tying run at the plate, and got the final out.

San Diego	AB	R	H	RBI	O	A	E
Calvey SS	4	0	1	0	1	2	1
Patchett CF	4	2	2	0	2	0	0
Hill 3B	3	1	1	0	2	3	0
Mazzera RF	4	1	2	3	1	0	0
Salkeld C	2	2	0	0	3	0	0
Jensen LF	4	1	3	3	2	0	0
Detore 1B	2	0	0	0	6	2	0
Skelley 2B	2	0	0	1	2	2	0
Dasso P	3	0	0	0	1	0	0
Dilbeck P	0	0	0	0	1	0	0
	28	7	9	7	21	9	1

Los Angeles	AB	R	H	RBI	O	A	E
Lowrey CF	4	1	1	1	4	0	0
Waitkus 1B	4	1	1	2	4	0	0
Hughes 2B	2	0	0	0	3	2	0
Moore RF	3	0	2	1	2	0	0
Mayo 3B	3	0	0	0	1	2	1
Schuster SS	3	0	0	0	1	1	0
Stewart LF	3	0	1	0	2	0	0
Todd C	3	1	1	0	4	1	0
Gehrman P	1	0	0	0	0	1	1
Campbell[a]	1	0	0	0	0	0	0
Dobernic P	0	0	0	0	0	0	0
Statz[b]	0	1	0	0	0	0	0
	27	4	6	4	21	7	2

(a) batted for Gehrman in the fifth.
(b) Batted for Dobernic in the seventh.

Pitching Records	IP	H	R	ER	SO	BB
Dasso (W)	6.2	5	3	4	2	5
Dilbeck	0.1	1	1	0	0	0
Gehrman (L)	5	6	3	2	4	3
Dobernic	2	3	4	4	0	1

Hit by Pitcher: Detore by Gehrman. Left on Base: San Diego 5, Los Angeles 7. Two Base Hits: Patchett, Stewart, Lowrey. Home Runs: Mazzera, Jensen. Sacrifices: Skelley, Hill. Double Play: Calvey to Skelley to Detore. Time of Game: 1 hr. 38 min. Umpires: Powell, Snyder, Hood, Widner.

San Diego	011	010	4	7 – 9 – 1
Los Angeles	000	000	4	4 – 6 – 2

Game Six.

Since Seattle eliminated Sacramento on Sunday, the two teams played another doubleheader on Monday, September 28, to finish this series a day sooner. The victorious Rainiers were on hand to watch the Angels and Padres fight it out. If L.A. had won the opener, there would have only been one game played, but this time Wally Hebert was able to beat Ray Prim 3–2. Al Todd's homer put the Angels up 1–0 in the fifth, but San Diego quickly erased that lead with three runs in the sixth. Hill singled, stole second, and scored on Jensen's single. Salkeld then homered to give the Padres a 3–1 lead. The Angels cut the lead to 3–2 in their half of the sixth on Eddie Waitkus' double and Eddie Mayo's single. Johnny Moore had to come out in this game and was unable to play after that, leaving Stewart and Statz to flank Lowery in the outfield. For the rest of the playoffs, the Angels had only 38-year-old coach Bill Sweeney and the back-up catcher to pinch hit. No attendance was mentioned for this Monday afternoon doubleheader.

San Diego	AB	R	H	RBI	O	A	E
Calvey SS	3	0	0	0	3	6	0
Patchett CF	4	0	1	0	2	0	0
Hill 3B	4	1	1	0	2	2	0
Mazzera RF	4	0	0	0	0	0	0
Jensen LF	4	1	2	1	5	0	0
Salkeld C	3	1	1	2	1	0	0
Detore C	4	0	2	0	12	0	0
Skelley 2B	2	0	0	0	2	4	0
Hebert P	4	0	0	0	0	1	0
	32	3	7	3	27	13	0

Los Angeles	AB	R	H	RBI	O	A	E
Lowrey CF	4	0	1	0	4	0	0
Waitkus 1B	4	1	2	0	9	0	0
Hughes 2B	3	0	0	0	1	3	0
Moore RF	1	0	0	0	0	0	0
Mayo 3B	4	0	2	1	1	3	0
Schuster SS	3	0	0	0	4	0	0
Statz LF-RF	3	0	0	0	1	0	0
Todd C	3	1	1	1	6	0	0
Prim P	3	0	0	0	0	4	0
Stewart LF	3	0	0	0	1	0	0
	31	2	6	2	27	10	0

Pitching Records	IP	H	R	ER	SO	BB
Hebert	9	6	2	2	0	2
Prim	9	7	3	3	5	2

Left on Base: San Diego 6, Los Angeles 4. Two Base Hits: Detore, Waitkus. Home Runs: Todd, Salkeld. Sacrifices: Salkeld, Skelley. Stolen Base: Hill. Double Plays: Calvey to Skelley to Detore, 2. Time of Game: 1 hr. 40 min. Umpires: Snyder, Hood, Widner, Powell.

San Diego	000	003	000	3 – 7 – 0
Los Angeles	000	011	000	2 – 6 – 0

Game Seven.

Just as in 1940, the Angels eliminated the Padres from the first round of the playoffs by winning the seventh game. The same pitchers faced each other as in game three, but this time Red Lynn beat Al Olson 5–1 in the seven inning nightcap. The Angels got single runs in the second and third to take a 2–0 lead into the fifth when the Padres got their only run. George Detore, playing first base, walked, went to third on Mel Skelly's single and scored as pinch hitter Del Ballinger was being retired. Boots Poffenberger came in to pitch the last of the fifth as Olson had been lifted for a hitter. Boots lasted only two-thirds of an inning before being replaced by Rex Dilbeck, who retired no one. Norm Brown finally got the third out, but by then the Angels had a 5–1 lead and the series locked up. Bill Schuster's two-run single was the key blow of that inning. Schuster and Hughes also made great defensive plays to help out Lynn.

San Diego	AB	R	H	RBI	O	A	E
Calvey SS	3	0	0	0	1	3	0
Patchett CF	2	0	0	0	2	0	0
Hill 3B	3	0	1	0	0	0	0
Mazzera RF	2	0	1	0	1	0	0
Salkeld C	3	0	0	0	5	0	0
Jensen LF	3	0	0	0	2	0	0
Detore 1B	2	1	0	0	4	0	0
Skelley 2B	3	0	1	0	2	2	1
Olson P	1	0	0	0	1	1	0
Ballinger[a]	1	0	0	1	0	0	0
Poffenberger P	0	0	0	0	0	0	0
Dillbeck P	0	0	0	0	0	0	0
Brown P	0	0	0	0	0	1	0
	23	1	3	1	18	7	1

(a) Batted for Olson in the fifth.

Los Angeles	AB	R	H	RBI	O	A	E
Lowrey CF	2	0	0	0	2	0	0
Waitkus 1B	3	1	2	0	7	1	0
Hughes 2B	2	1	0	1	2	3	0
Mayo 3B	2	2	1	1	1	1	0
Schuster SS	3	0	2	2	1	0	0
Stewart LF	3	0	0	1	1	0	0
Statz RF	3	0	0	0	4	0	0
Campbell C	3	0	0	0	2	0	0
Lynn P	3	1	1	0	1	0	0
	24	5	6	5	21	5	0

Pitching Records	IP	H	R	ER	SO	BB
Olson (L)	4	3	2	2	2	1
Poffenberger	0.2	1	1	2	1	1
Dilbeck	0+	1	1	1	0	0
Brown	1.1	2	1	0	2	0
Lynn	7	3	1	1	1	1

Left on Base: San Diego 4, Los Angeles 4. Two Base Hits: Skelley, Mayo. Sacrifice: Lowrey. Stolen Base: Waitkus. Double Play: Waitkus unassisted. Time of Game: 1 hr. 20 min. Umpires: Hood, Widner, Powell, Snyder.

San Diego	000	010	0	1 – 3 – 1
Los Angeles	011	030	x	5 – 6 – 0

The Padres divided $1,250 among 20 players, which came to $62.50 a man, or about $386 in current funds. San Diego would not be in another playoff until 1949. They had been in five of the first seven, but were about to experience a drought.

The Final Series: Seattle vs. Los Angeles

Even though all games had to be played at Wrigley Field, Seattle was in much better shape than the Angels going into this deciding series. The Rainiers were coming off four straight wins at Sacramento and did not have to play any doubleheaders, while the Angels had to struggle to beat San Diego in seven games and had just finished two doubleheaders on consecutive days. Furthermore, the Angels had to play without two regulars, Johnny Moore and Barney Olsen, leaving them with very little bench strength.

As mentioned before, these two clubs had been antagonists since 1938 when the Angels beat them out of the pennant. This was also the first season since 1938 that L.A. had finished higher than Seattle and had been able to win the season series over them. The Angels won 15 of the 23 games played with Seattle in 1942, including a crucial series five games to two, which culminated on August 2, with L.A. beating Dick Barrett and Hal Turpin in a doubleheader. That series went a long way to prevent Seattle from finishing any higher than third place.

Game One.

There was no off day for the Angels after the Padre series, so these teams met on Tuesday, September 29, before a sparse crowd. Unlike San Diego, the Angels started their games at 2:15 P.M., so it was very hard to draw families with schools in session. Carl Fischer beat Pete Mallory 2–1, as Schuster's baserunning blunder cost his team a run. In the second, Broadway Bill walked and stole second, and then tried to score on Al Todd's infield single, and was throw out by a block and a half. Singles by "Gabby" Stewart and Statz got Todd home but that was all L.A. could score. In the fourth, Matheson singled and Gyselman hit a home run for Seattle's two runs.

Seattle	AB	R	H	RBI	O	A	E
Stickle SS	4	0	0	0	0	2	0
King CF	3	0	0	0	3	0	0
White LF	4	0	1	0	2	0	0
Torgeson 1B	3	0	0	0	8	0	0
Matheson RF	4	1	2	0	1	0	0
Gyselman 3B	4	1	1	2	2	3	0
Niemiec 2B	3	0	0	0	4	3	0
Kearse C	2	0	0	0	7	2	0
Fischer P	3	0	1	0	0	2	0
Lawrence CF[a]	1	0	0	0	0	0	0
	31	2	5	2	27	12	0

(a) Batted for King in the eighth.

Los Angeles	AB	R	H	RBI	O	A	E
Lowrey CF	4	0	0	0	2	0	0
Waitkus 1B	4	0	0	0	10	1	0
Hughes 2B	4	0	1	0	1	7	0
Mayo 3B	4	0	0	0	1	0	0

Los Angeles	AB	R	H	RBI	O	A	E
Schuster SS	3	0	2	0	4	3	0
Todd C	3	1	1	0	3	1	0
Stewart LF	4	0	2	0	3	0	0
Statz RF	3	0	1	1	3	0	0
Mallory P	2	0	1	0	0	1	0
Sweeney[b]	1	0	0	0	0	0	0
Raffensberger P	0	0	0	0	0	0	0
	32	1	8	1	27	13	0

(b) Batted for Mallory in the seventh.

Pitching Records	IP	H	R	ER	SO	BB
Fischer	9	8	1	1	6	1
Mallory (L)	7	3	2	2	1	1
Raffensberger	2	2	0	0	2	0

Hit by Pitcher: Kearse by Mallory. Left on Base: Seattle 4, Los Angeles 7. Home Run: Gyselman. Sacrifices: Statz, Todd. Stolen Bases: White, Schuster, Stickle. Time of Game: 1 hr. 55 min. Umpires: Widner, Powell, Snyder, Hood.

Seattle	000	200	000	2 – 5 – 0
Los Angeles	010	000	000	1 – 8 – 0

Game Two.

This Wednesday afternoon game, and the one the next day, had direct competition from the World Series broadcast, which began at 11 A.M. Pacific War Time, and was still going on as this game started. There was far more coverage of the Yankees and Cardinals than of the Rainiers 6–1 win over the Angels. Dick Barrett beat Paul Gehrman, who was relieved by Jess Dobernic, Ken Raffensberger and Ray "Peaches" Davis. Seattle broke it open with four runs in the fourth, chasing Gehrman. Two walks and a single loaded the bases before Torgeson singled in two runs. Dobernic relieved, walked Gyselman and gave up a double to Al Niemiec for two more runs. Seattle scored two more in the ninth on singles by Niemiec, Collins, Barrett, and Lawrence. The Angel run came in the seventh on two singles and a passed ball. The only radio broadcast was heard in L.A.; these games were not recreated back to Seattle.

Seattle	AB	R	H	RBI	O	A	E
Stickle SS	4	1	0	0	5	5	0
King CF	2	1	0	0	1	1	0

Seattle	AB	R	II	RBI	O	A	E
White LF	5	0	2	0	2	0	0
Torgeson 1B	5	1	1	2	11	2	0
Matheson RF	3	0	2	0	1	0	0
Gyselman 3B	3	1	0	0	0	3	0
Niemiec 2B	4	1	3	2	3	6	0
Collins C	4	1	1	0	2	1	0
Barrett P	4	0	2	1	1	2	0
Lawrence CF	2	0	2	1	1	0	0
	36	6	13	6	27	20	0

Los Angeles	AB	R	H	RBI	O	A	E
Lowrey CF	2	0	1	0	3	2	0
Hughes 2B	4	0	1	0	2	4	0
Waitkus 1B	3	0	0	0	9	2	0
Mayo 3B	4	0	1	0	1	1	0
Schuster SS	4	1	1	0	3	6	0
Stewart LF	4	0	1	0	1	1	0
Campbell C	3	0	1	1	4	1	0
Statz RF	3	0	1	0	3	0	0
Gehrman P	1	0	0	0	1	1	0
Dobernic P	0	0	0	0	0	0	0
Moore[a]	1	0	0	0	0	0	0
Raffensberger P	0	0	0	0	0	0	0
Todd[b]	1	0	1	0	0	0	0
Flores[c]	0	0	0	0	0	0	0
Davis P	0	0	0	0	0	0	0
	30	1	8	1	27	18	0

(a) Batted for Dobernic in the fifth.
(b) Batted for Raffensberger in the eighth.
(c) Ran for Todd in the eighth.

Pitching Records	IP	H	R	ER	SO	BB
Barrett	9	8	1	1	0	4
Gehrman (L)	3.1	3	2	3	0	2
Dobernic	1.2	2	2	1	1	1
Raffensberger	3	3	0	0	3	1
Davis	1	5	2	2	0	0

Wild Pitch: Barrett. Passed Ball: Collins. Left on Base: Seattle 7, Los Angeles 6. Two Base Hit: Niemiec. Stolen Base: Matheson. Double Plays: Barrett to Stickle to Torgeson; Gyselman to Niemiec to Torgeson 2; Stickle to Niemiec to Torgeson. Time of Game: 2 hr. 16 min. Umpires: Powell, Snyder, Hood, Widner.

Seattle	000	400	002	6 – 13 – 0		
Los Angeles	000	000	100	1 – 8 – 0		

Game Three.

On Thursday, October 1, the Rainiers won their seventh straight playoff game to take a commanding 3–0 lead in this final series. The smallest crowd of the year, 669, saw the Angels again lose a game that could have gone their way. Jesse Flores faced Hal Turpin as L.A. took a 1–0 lead in the fourth on a walk to Hughes and a Waitkus double. They increased this lead to 2–0 the next inning when successive singles by Statz, Flores and Lowrey filled the bases, but they only scored one run on Hughes' fly.

Seattle took a 3–2 lead in the sixth when White doubled and scored on Matheson's single. Gyselman then doubled home the tying run and ex–Angel Bob Collins then singled in Gyselman to give Seattle the lead. Eddie Mayo's homer tied the game in the last of the sixth, and it remained tied until the ninth. With Ned Stickle on first with two outs, White got an infield single, on which Stickle was able to go to third. White promptly stole second, and with 18-year-old Earl Torgeson up with a 2–2 count, catcher Al Todd and Flores thought they had him struck out, but umpire Ray Snyder called it a ball. On the next pitch, "The Second Earl of Snohomish" doubled home the two runs that won the game.

Seattle	AB	R	H	RBI	O	A	E
Stickle SS	5	1	1	0	3	2	0
Lawrence CF	4	0	1	0	4	0	0
White LF	4	2	3	0	2	0	0
Torgeson 1B	4	0	1	2	10	0	1
Matheson RF	5	1	1	1	3	0	0
Gyselman 3B	4	1	2	1	0	4	0
Niemiec 2B	3	0	1	0	2	3	0
Collins C	4	0	1	1	3	1	0
Turpin P	4	0	0	0	0	2	0
Harris[a]	1	0	0	0	0	0	0
King CF	0	0	0	0	0	0	0
	38	5	11	5	27	12	1

(a) *Batted for Lawrence in the ninth.*

Los Angeles	AB	R	H	RBI	O	A	E
Lowrey CF	4	0	1	0	4	0	1
Hughes 2B	2	1	1	1	2	3	0
Waitkus 1B	4	0	1	1	6	1	0
Mayo 3B	4	1	1	1	0	2	0
Schuster SS	4	0	1	0	2	0	0
Todd C	4	0	0	0	5	0	0
Stewart LF	4	0	0	0	2	0	0
Statz RF	4	1	1	0	5	0	0
Flores P	3	0	1	0	1	1	0
	33	3	7	3	27	7	1

Pitching Records	IP	H	R	ER	SO	BB
Turpin	9	7	3	3	2	2
Flores	9	11	5	5	4	3

Left on Base: Seattle 9, Los Angeles 5. Two Base Hits: White, Gyselman, Torgeson, Waitkus. Home Run: Mayo. Stolen Bases: Gyselman, Stickle, Collins, White. Double Play: Gyselman to Nieniec to Torgeson. Time of Game: 2 hr. Umpires: Snyder, Hood, Widner, Powell.

Seattle	000	003	002	5 – 11 – 2
Los Angeles	000	111	000	3 – 7 – 1

Game Four.

On Friday, October 2, the playoffs did not have to compete with the World Series because that was a travel day. But there were a lot of pregame writeups in both L.A. and Seattle papers on USC's game in Seattle against Washington and UCL.A.'s game in the Coliseum against St. Mary's Pre-Flight on Saturday. The Angels finally broke Seattle's win streak with a 7–4 triumph, as Ray Prim went the distance, while Larry Guay did not survive the first inning. L.A. pushed four runs over in that inning, as Lowrey walked, Hughes sacrificed, and Waitkus singled. Then Mayo singled, and after Schuster was retired, Glen Stewart doubled in two runs, sending Guay to the showers. Mike Budnick relieved and gave up a run-scoring single to Gilly Campbell.

The Rainiers closed the gap to 4–3 in the fourth when Lawrence singled, White walked, and both scored on Matheson's triple. Gyselman's fly ball scored Matheson. Lowrey scored for L.A. on a passed ball in the fifth for a 5–3 lead, and with Ed Carnett pitching in the seventh, the Angels made it 7–3 on Mayo's single, walks to Schuster and Stewart, and Campbell's single. Seattle got its final run in the eighth. No attendance was announced.

Seattle	AB	R	H	RBI	O	A	E
Stickle SS	3	1	2	0	4	4	1
Lawrence CF	4	1	2	1	1	0	0
White LF	3	1	0	0	2	0	0
Torgeson 1B	4	0	0	0	11	2	0
Matheson RF	4	1	1	2	1	0	0
Gyselman 3B	4	0	0	1	0	4	0
Niemiec 2B	4	0	1	0	3	3	0
Collins C	3	0	0	0	2	1	0
Guay P	0	0	0	0	0	0	0
Budnick P	2	0	0	0	0	0	1
Harris[a]	1	0	0	0	0	0	0
Carnett P	0	0	0	0	0	2	0
	32	4	6	4	24	16	2

(a) Batted for Budnick in the seventh.

Los Angeles	AB	R	H	RBI	O	A	E
Lowrey CF	2	2	0	0	4	0	1
Hughes 2B	2	0	0	0	2	4	0
Waitkus 1B	4	1	2	1	10	0	0
Mayo 3B	3	2	3	0	0	3	0
Schuster SS	3	1	0	0	1	1	0
Stewart LF	3	1	2	2	0	0	0
Campbell C	3	0	2	3	5	1	0
Statz RF	2	0	0	0	5	0	0
Prim P	3	0	0	0	0	2	0
	25	7	9	6	27	11	1

Pitching Records	IP	H	R	ER	SO	BB
Guay (L)	0.2	3	3	4	1	1
Budnick	5.1	3	1	0	1	5
Carnett	2	3	2	2	0	1
Prim	9	6	4	3	4	2

Passed Ball: Collins 2. Left on Base: Seattle 3, Los Angeles 7. Two Base Hit: Stewart. Three Base Hit: Matheson. Sacrifices: Hughes 2, Campbell, Prim, Lowrey. Stolen Base: Mayo. Double Plays: Torgeson to Stickle; Niemiec to Stickle. Time of Game: 2 hr. 17 min. Umpires: Hood, Snyder, Powell, Widner.

Seattle	000	300	010	4 – 6 – 2
Los Angeles	400	010	20x	7 – 9 – 1

Game Five.

The teams took Saturday off, avoiding a conflict with football and the World Series broadcast, but the latter did interfere with the opening game on Sunday. A doubleheader was scheduled for 1:30 and the World Series, which began at 11 A.M. on the coast, ended just as Seattle and the Angels were to start. Only 3,500 came out to see the Angels prolong the series by winning the opener 8–3, but the home team was crushed by the visitors from Puget Sound, 10–1 in the nightcap. Barrett had nothing in the opener, getting shelled for five runs and six hits, while failing to survive the first inning, before Mike Budnick relieved Seattle's "Little Round Man." The Angels got single runs in the fifth, sixth and the eighth, while Seattle scored a run in the first and two in the seventh. Red Lynn went the distance and got three hits, including a double. Peanuts Lowrey also got three hits while Roy Hughes got a triple and a single. Jo Jo White went 4-for-4, including three doubles, in a losing cause.

Seattle	AB	R	H	RBI	O	A	E
Stickle SS	3	2	1	0	0	3	0
Lawrence CF	2	0	0	0	4	0	0
White LF	4	0	4	3	2	0	0
Torgeson 1B	3	0	1	0	9	0	0
Matheson RF	4	0	0	0	2	0	0
Gyselman 3B	4	0	0	0	1	1	0
Niemiec 2B	4	0	0	0	2	3	0
Collins C	3	0	0	0	4	1	0
Barrett P	0	0	0	0	0	0	0
Budnick P	2	0	0	0	0	1	1
Harris[a]	0	1	0	0	0	0	0
Libke P	0	0	0	0	0	1	0
King[b]	1	0	0	0	0	0	0
Carnett[c]	1	0	0	0	0	0	0
	31	3	6	3	24	10	1

(a) Batted for Budnick in the seventh.
(b) Batted for Collins in the ninth.
(c) Batted for Libke in the ninth.

Los Angeles	AB	R	H	RBI	O	A	E
Lowrey CF	3	2	3	1	3	1	0
Hughes 2B	5	1	2	2	2	2	0
Waitkus 1B	4	1	1	0	7	1	0
Mayo 3B	4	1	1	2	1	2	0
Schuster SS	4	1	1	1	1	2	0

Los Angeles	AB	R	H	RBI	O	A	E
Stewart LF	3	1	1	1	2	0	0
Campbell C	3	0	0	0	6	0	0
Statz RF	3	0	0	0	4	0	0
Lynn P	4	1	3	1	1	1	0
	33	8	12	8	27	9	0

Pitching Records	IP	H	R	ER	SO	BB
Barrett (L)	0.2	6	5	5	1	2
Budnick	5.1	5	2	1	2	0
Libke	2	1	1	1	0	2
Lynn	9	6	3	3	5	5

Left on Base: Seattle 7, Los Angeles 7. Two Base Hits: White 3, Lynn. Three Base Hit: Hughes. Sacrifices: Lawrence, Lowrey 2. Stolen Bases: Mayo, Stewart. Double Play: Stickle to Niemiec to Torgeson. Time of Game: 2 hr. 5 min. Umpires: Widner, Powell, Snyder, Hood.

Seattle	100	000	200	3 – 6 – 1
Los Angeles	500	011	01x	8 – 12 – 0

Game Six.

Had Seattle won the opener, this second game would not have been played. Carl Fischer again stopped the Angels on just one run, but his mound opponent from game one, Pete Mallory, got pounded this time, along with Raffensberger, Gehrman and Dobernic for 10 runs on 15 hits. Seattle got a run off Mallory in the second on a triple by Matheson and a double by Niemiec. They got two more in the third when Stickle singled and White homered. Jo Jo White went 7-for-8 in this doubleheader, with four doubles, a homer and two singles. In the fifth, the Rainiers got six runs off Raffensberger and Gehrman to make the game a rout.

Seattle	AB	R	H	RBI	O	A	E
Stickle SS	4	2	2	0	2	1	0
King CF	2	0	1	0	1	0	0
White LF	4	2	3	2	4	0	0
Torgeson 1B	3	1	1	2	4	0	0
Matheson RF	4	2	3	1	3	0	0
Gyselman 3B	2	1	1	0	1	0	0
Niemiec 2B	2	1	2	1	1	2	0
Kearse C	3	0	1	2	4	1	0

Seattle	AB	R	H	RBI	O	A	E
Fischer P	4	0	0	0	0	2	0
Lawrence CF	2	1	1	1	1	0	0
	30	10	15	9	21	6	0

Los Angeles	AB	R	H	RBI	O	A	E
Lowrey CF	3	0	2	0	1	0	0
Waitkus 1B	3	1	1	0	4	1	0
Hughes 2B	3	0	2	1	2	1	0
Mayo 3B	2	0	0	0	2	0	0
Schuster SS	3	0	0	0	1	1	0
Stewart LF	3	0	0	0	1	0	0
Statz RF	3	0	1	0	1	0	0
Campbell C	3	0	0	0	8	4	0
Mallory P	0	0	0	0	1	0	0
Moore [a]	1	0	0	0	0	0	0
Raffensberger P	0	0	0	0	0	2	0
Gehrman P	0	0	0	0	0	2	0
Todd [b]	1	0	0	0	0	0	0
Dobernic P	0	0	0	0	0	0	1
Sweeney [c]	1	0	0	0	0	0	0
	26	1	6	1	21	11	1

(a) Batted for Mallory in the third.
(b) Batted for Gehrman in the sixth.
(c) Batted for Dobernic in the seventh.

Pitching Records	IP	H	R	ER	SO	BB
Fischer	7	6	1	1	4	1
Mallory (L)	3	5	3	3	3	0
Raffensberger	1	5	3	4	0	2
Gehrman	2	3	3	2	2	2
Dobernic	1	2	1	0	2	0

Passed Ball: Campbell. Left on Base: Seattle 5, Los Angeles 5. Two Base Hits: Niemiec, Waitkus, White, Gyselman. Three Base Hits: Matheson, Stickle. Home Run: White. Sacrifices: Niemiec, Gyselman. Stolen Base: Torgeson. Double Plays: Raffensberger to Campbell to Waitkus; Campbell to Mayo. Time of Game: 1 hr. 40 min. Umpires: Powell, Snyder, Hood, Widner.

Seattle	012	060	1	10 – 15 – 0
Los Angeles	000	100	0	1 – 6 – 1

Seattle divided their $5,000 playoff money among 20 players plus five other shares to give each man $200, which would be worth about $1,227 today. The Angels split $2,500 but it is not certain how many shares there were because some players were with the team part of the year. It was a bitter end for the Angels, who felt they had the best team in the league, having won the regular season series from each of the seven opponents. With only 20 men on the team, it was impossible to replace two outfielders the caliber of Moore and Olsen.

Seattle writer Royal Brougham called for an end to the playoffs because of the low attendance and the fact that Seattle had to play all of the games on the road. He felt a series with the International League or American Association would have more meaning.

Key Players on the 1942 Playoff Teams

Sacramento. *Pitchers:* Tony Freitas, Bill Schmidt, Blix Donnelly, Kemp Wicker and Clarence Beers.
   Position Players: Jack Sturdy, Steve Mesner, Averett "Tommy" Thompson, Deb Garms, Buster Adams and Ray Mueller.

Los Angeles. *Pitchers:* Ray Prim, Red Lynn, Jesse Flores, Paul Gehrman, and Pete Mallory.
   Postion Players: Eddie Waitkus, Roy Hughes, Bill Schuster, Eddie Mayo, Harry "Peanuts" Lowery, Barney Olson and Johnny Moore.

Seattle. *Pitchers:* Dick Barrett, Hal Turpin, Carl Fischer and Larry Guay.
   Position Players: Earl Torgeson, Al Niemiec, Dick Gyselman, Bill Lawrence, Jo Jo White, and Bill Matheson.

San Diego. *Pitchers:* Wally Hebert, Al Olson, Frankie Dasso, and Rex Dilbeck.
   Position Players: Mel Mazzera, Hal Patchett, Swede Jensen, John Hill, Bill Salkeld, and George Detore.

1943

By 1943, the war really hit baseball hard. Many minor leagues shut down, including the Texas League. The rosters of the Coast League teams were often revolving doors with players leaving for military service and others playing just part-time while working in defense plants or on farms. Many career-type Coast League players got a chance to play in the majors, such as Dick Barrett, Eddie Mayo, Jesse Flores, Jack Salveson, and Steve Mesner, while some former major leaguers, such as Jo Jo White, were able to return to the big leagues.

The 1943 schedule was reduced to 155 games from 178, with teams playing opponents 21 to 24 times, rather than the normal 28. Therefore, teams would go to some cities for just a one-week series, but that particular opponent would come to their park twice, while the reverse was true with the other opponents. Two exceptions were made to attract bigger gates: Los Angeles gave up seven games with San Francisco to play Hollywood 28 times and Oakland gave up seven games with Hollywood to play the Seals 28 times. Night games were again forbidden, but teams experimented with starting games at noon, at 5 P.M., and just about every hour in between.

There was no pennant race at all as the Angels took off and never looked back. They were the first PCL team to be in first place from opening day until the end, finishing 21 games ahead of the second place Seals. On their first road trip to Hollywood, Portland and Seattle, the Angels won 18 straight games and came home to win two more before this 20 game streak ended. Throughout the season, L.A. lost only two series, both five games to four at home, to Portland over Memorial Day and to Seattle over the Fourth of July weekend. But after reaching a peak of 100 wins and 35 losses, the Angels played only .500 ball over their last 20 games of the season. This team was now managed by Bill Sweeney, who moved up from coach after Jigger Statz resigned. Outfielders Andy Pakfo and Johnny Ostrowski helped power this team, the former winning the batting and RBI titles, while the latter led in homers.

Lefty O'Doul got his San Francisco Seals into second place and into the playoffs for the first time since 1939. Even though this team finished 21 games behind the Angels, they were about to win four playoffs in a row. O'Doul was

195

especially successful with wartime players, even talking Gus Suhr out of retirement.

Bill Skiff did a very good job wheeling and dealing during the season to change a poor Seattle club into a very good one at the end. In early June the Rainiers were 18–31 and in last place, and a month later, they moved only to seventh place at 34–44. But from that point on, they played .662 ball, finishing in third place at 85–70, four games behind the Seals, and 25 behind Los Angeles. Skiff was also able to get good mileage out of older players, talking Bill Lawrence out of retirement to play center field.

The Portland Beavers, managed by catcher Marvin Shea, finished in the first division for the first time since 1937, after four dismal seasons in the cellar. The Beavers spent most of the season in third place until Seattle overtook them in mid–August. Portland ended up six games behind third place Seattle and six games ahead of Hollywood and Oakland, who were tied for fifth. There was only a faint glimmer of hope that either Stars or Oaks could catch Portland, so this race lacked suspense.

The runaway pennant race caused more interest in the playoffs than ever before. Now sportswriters were saying that the playoffs were made to order to show up a pennant winner that might go stale and that they can reward "Johnny-come-latelys" by giving them a chance to redeem themselves. Otherwise, what would it matter if Seattle went from last to third place? The attendance in the first two rounds of the 1943 playoffs surpassed that of both rounds in 1942. The final series between the Seals and Rainiers drew 27,000 fans, with all games played at Seals Stadium.

The Los Angeles–Seattle Series

The Angels won the season series from all seven opponents in 1943, beating Seattle fifteen times and losing nine, but after sweeping the Rainiers seven straight in May, the Angels won only eight and lost nine to them afterwards. The two teams had just concluded a season ending series in Seattle, splitting the eight games. It was therefore natural for the playoffs to open at Sick's Stadium for two games, before playing the remainder at Wrigley Field. The champion Angels had to play only two games on the road just as the champion 1941 Rainiers had to play only two games at Hollywood, after ending the season in Los Angeles. Manager Bill Skiff was outspoken in his belief that Seattle was the best team in the league at the end of the season, and that they would beat the Angels in this series. He further stated that his 1941 championship team was much better than this "wartime" Angel outfit.

Game One.

Bill Skiff was honored before this game as 5,000 fans gathered for the 5 P.M. start. Fans contributed money which was used to buy the skipper various gifts. Seattle got a run off Red Lynn in the third when former pitcher Ed Carnett doubled and scored on Bill Matheson's triple.

The Angels quickly tied it in the fourth off Frank Tincup and missed a chance to take the lead. Roy Hughes singled and scored on Andy Pafko's double. Pafko was on third with one out and tried to score on Rip Russell's fly but Ed Carnett's throw to Hal Sueme nailed him at home. The game was still tied in the eighth, when a near riot broke out. The Angels loaded the bases with one out, with Bill Schuster the runner on first. Hughes hit an infield grounder that forced Schuster at second, while the run scored, but Schuster went hard into Ford "Moon" Mullen at second, who came up swinging, because he felt there was no chance for a double play. It took a while to restore order but there were no ejections. In the last of the eighth, the fans' booing of Schuster may have intimidated him because he took Frank Tincup's ground ball and threw it into the dugout, allowing the Seattle pitcher to go to second base. This was another case of a pitcher batting for himself in late innings with his team trailing, but Tincup was considered a fair hitter. Bill Katz ran for Tincup and scored on Mullen's bloop single, which delighted the crowd. After Carnett sacrificed, Mullen scored the winning run on Matheson's double. The Seattle right fielder went 3-for-4 with and drove in two runs with a double and a triple. John Yelovic set the Angels down in the ninth to save the win.

Los Angeles	AB	R	H	RBI	O	A	E
Schuster SS	3	0	0	0	1	2	1
Hughes 2B	4	1	2	1	3	3	0
Pafko CF	4	0	1	1	2	0	0
English 3B	3	0	1	0	0	6	0
Russell LF-1B	2	0	0	0	1	0	0
Ostrowski RF	4	0	0	0	1	0	0
Quinn 1B	2	0	0	0	12	0	0
Holm C	3	0	2	0	2	1	0
Lynn P	3	0	0	0	0	5	0
Moore[a]	0	0	0	0	0	0	0
Garriott LF[b]	1	1	0	0	2	0	0
	29	2	6	2	24	17	1

(a) *Batted for Quinn in the eighth.*
(b) *Ran for Moore in the eighth.*

Seattle	AB	R	H	RBI	O	A	E
Mullen 2B	3	1	1	1	3	3	0
Carnett LF	3	1	1	0	2	1	0
Matheson RF	4	0	3	2	4	1	0
Dobbins SS	4	0	0	0	2	4	0
Christopher CF	4	0	2	0	3	0	0
Gabrielson 1B	3	0	0	0	9	0	0
Gyselman 3B	1	0	0	0	1	1	0
Sueme C	3	0	0	0	2	0	0
Tincup P	3	0	0	0	1	2	0
Katz[a]	0	1	0	0	0	0	0
Yelovic P	0	0	0	0	0	0	0
	28	3	7	3	27	12	0

(a) Ran for Tincup in the eighth.

Pitching Records	IP	H	R	ER	SO	BB
Lynn	8	7	3	2	2	1
Tincup (W)	8	6	2	2	0	2
Yelovic	1	0	0	0	0	1

Left on Base: Los Angeles 5, Seattle 5. Two Base Hits: Carnett, Christopher, Matheson. Three Base Hit: Matheson. Sacrifices: English, Carnett, Gyselman 2, Russell. Stolen Base: Holm. Double Plays: Carnett to Sueme; Matheson to Mullen. Time of Game: 1 hr. 43 min. Umpires: Edwards and Engeln.

Los Angeles	000	100	010	2 – 6 – 1
Seattle	001	000	02x	3 – 7 – 0

Game Two.

Seattle fans were told that this would be the last game at Sick's Stadium in 1943 unless the final series were between Portland and the Rainiers because of military restrictions on travel. On Wednesday, September 15, Seattle went up 2–0 in the series as Carl Fischer beat Jodie Phipps by a 4–1 score. Phipps at 17–5 had led the league in winning percentage but had not been very effective late in the season. In the first, the Rainers lit up Phipps for two runs on Ed Carnett's single, a stolen base, Bill Matheson's single and Lloyd Christopher's double. Bill Sweeney yanked Phipps in the second after he gave up a lead off single to Len Gabrielson, and brought in Don Osborn. The Angels almost tied the game in the fifth, but again the strong arm of Ed Carnett nailed a man at the plate. Billy Holm and Bill Schuster singled, and Hughes forced Holm at third. Andy Pakfo doubled Schuster home but Carnett's throw to Sueme nailed

Hughes to keep it at 2–1. The Rainers got a run in the sixth on Joe Dobbins' double and Dick Gyselman's triple, and another one in the seventh when Matheson singled in Mullen. In the ninth, Los Angeles loaded the bases with one out but neither Cecil Garriott nor Bill Schuster could deliver.

Los Angeles	AB	R	H	RBI	O	A	E
Schuster SS	5	1	3	0	1	5	0
Hughes 2B	4	0	1	0	2	0	0
Pafko CF	4	0	1	1	2	0	0
English 3B	4	0	1	0	3	3	0
Russell LF	4	0	1	0	5	0	0
Ostrowski RF	3	0	0	0	0	0	
Quinn 1B	4	0	0	0	10	0	0
Holm C	3	0	1	0	1	1	0
Phipps P	0	0	0	0	0	0	0
Osborn P	2	0	1	0	0	3	0
Garriott[a]	1	0	0	0	0	0	0
	34	1	9	1	24	12	0

(a) Batted for Osborn in the ninth.

Seattle	AB	R	H	RBI	O	A	E
Mullen 2B	4	1	2	0	3	1	0
Carnett LF	4	1	1	0	1	1	0
Matheson RF	4	1	2	2	5	1	0
Dobbins SS	4	1	1	0	1	3	0
Christopher CF	4	0	1	1	4	0	0
Gyselman 3B	4	0	1	1	1	3	0
Gabrielson 1B	3	0	2	0	6	0	0
Sueme C	4	0	0	0	6	0	0
Fischer P	3	0	1	0	0	0	0
	34	4	11	4	27	9	0

Pitching Records	IP	H	R	ER	SO	BB
Phipps (L)	1+	4	2	2	0	0
Osborn	7	7	2	2	1	1
Fischer	9	9	1	1	4	3

Left on Base: Los Angeles 9, Seattle 7. Two Base Hits: Christopher, Pafko, Dobbins, Osborn. Three Base Hit: Gyselman. Double Plays: Holm to Hughes; Gyselman to Mullen to Gabrielson. Time of Game: 2 hr. 3 min. Umpires: Engeln and Edwards.

Los Angeles	000	010	000	1 – 9 – 0
Seattle	200	001	10x	4 – 11 – 0

Game Three.

The teams left Seattle on the Thursday morning train and arrived in Los Angeles on Friday evening, September 17. They played on Saturday afternoon, the 18th, because college football had not yet started. Before the game, there was a ceremony honoring the champion Angels, with each player getting a $100 war bond. That ceremony was the highlight of the day for the 6,000 fans at Wrigley Field.

Seattle's "second wind" Suds gave the "suddenly inept" Seraphs a humiliating whipping by a score of 8–2. The Angels could not hit, field, pitch or run. Spot starter Joe Demoran handcuffed Los Angeles while Red Lynn had nothing on the ball. Jody Phipps relieved and was just as ineffective. The Rambunctious Rainiers scored in each of the first four innings, building up a 6–0 lead. In the first, Carnett doubled home Mullen, who had singled. In the second, Christopher doubled, Gyselman got an infield single, and Sueme's fly scored Christopher. In the third, Mullen and Carnett singled, sending Lynn to unwrap a bar of soap. Matheson greeted Phipps with a run-scoring single, and Dobbins got an infield single, loading the bases. Gyselman later singled in two runs to make it 5–0. In the sixth, Sueme singled and went to third as Phipps threw Demoran's bunt into right field. Carrett's single made it 6–0. Relievers Oren Baker and Garmen "Pete" Mallory each gave up a run over the last two innings. Andy Pafko's homer with Hughes aboard prevented Demoran from getting a shutout.

Seattle	AB	R	H	RBI	O	A	E
Mullen 2B	5	2	2	0	3	2	0
Carnett LF	5	1	3	2	3	0	0
Matheson RF	4	2	2	1	1	0	0
Dobbins SS	5	0	2	0	2	1	0
Christopher CF	5	1	1	1	2	1	0
Gyselman 3B	5	1	3	2	2	5	0
Gabrielson 1B	4	0	1	0	7	0	0
Sueme C	3	1	2	2	7	0	0
Demoran P	4	0	0	0	0	1	0
	40	8	16	8	27	10	0
Los Angeles	AB	R	H	RBI	O	A	E
Schuster SS	3	0	1	0	2	2	0
Hughes 2B	4	1	1	0	3	3	0

Los Angeles	AB	R	H	RBI	O	A	E
Pafko CF	4	1	2	2	2	0	0
English 3B	4	0	0	0	3	1	0
Russell LF	4	0	0	0	3	0	0
Ostrowski RF	3	0	1	0	0	0	0
Quinn 1B	3	0	0	0	7	0	0
Holm C	3	0	0	0	7	4	0
Lynn P	0	0	0	0	0	0	0
Phipps P	1	0	0	0	0	1	1
Garriott[a]	1	0	0	0	0	0	0
Baker P	0	0	0	0	0	0	0
Moore[b]	1	0	0	0	0	0	0
Mallory P	0	0	0	0	0	0	1
	31	2	5	2	27	11	2

(a) Batted for Phipps in the sixth.
(b) Batted for Baker in the eighth.

Pitching Records	IP	H	R	ER	SO	BB
Demoran	9	5	2	2	7	1
Lynn (L)	2+	6	2	4	1	1
Phipps	4	5	4	1	3	2
Baker	2	3	1	1	1	0
Mallory	1	2	1	1	2	0

Left on Base: Seattle 8, Los Angeles 3. Two Base Hits: Carnett, Christopher, Matheson. Home Run: Pafko. Double Plays: Holm to English 2; Hughes to Quinn. Time of Game: 2 hr. Umpires: Powell and McDonald.

Seattle	113	100	011	8 – 16 – 0
Los Angeles	000	000	002	2 – 5 – 2

Game Four.

A doubleheader was scheduled for Sunday, September 19, and both games were played, but the second game was only an exhibition because the Rainiers completed the four game sweep by winning the opener, 7–3. This was the first time in playoff history that a meaningless second game of a doubleheader was played after one team had won the series, but with 15,000 fans in the stands, the owners may have felt obligated to give the crowd the promised second game. Pete Jonas, who faced the Angels' Paul Gehrman, gave up a run in the last of the first when Schuster stole home. Seattle tied it in the third when catcher Hal Sueme, whom the Angels released after spring training, blasted a homer off Gehrman. Seattle went up 2–1 in the fourth when Matheson and Dobbins singled and Rip Russell dropped Christopher's fly ball. But Charley English, who went 4-for-4, hit a game tying homer in the bottom of that inning. Each team got a run in the sixth: Seattle's came on a Dobbins double and a wild throw by Gehrman on Christopher's bunt, while the Angels got theirs on Johnny Moore's pinch hit sacrifice fly.

With the game tied in the ninth, Paul Gehrman blew up after making a poor decision. With Gyselman on second and one out, the Angels discussed whether or not to pitch to Hal Sueme, the catcher they had discarded. They pitched to him and Sueme blasted a double, scoring Gyselman. Then pitcher Pete Jonas singled in Sueme, Mullen singled, and both moved up on a ground out and scored on Matheson's single. For the first time in 1943, the Angels had lost four games in a row. Bill Skiff undiplomatically boasted his Rainiers outplayed the Angels in every phase of the game and that he would not be afraid to play the Yankees with this team. L.A. won the exhibition game 5–0.

Seattle	AB	H	RBI	O	A	E
Mullen 2B	5	3	0	3	2	0
Carnett LF	5	1	0	3	0	0
Matheson RF	5	2	2	1	0	0
Dobbins SS	4	2	0	3	5	0
Christopher CF	3	0	1	5	0	0
Gyselman 3B	3	1	0	2	2	0
Gabrielson 1B	3	0	0	8	0	0
Sueme C	4	2	2	2	0	0
Jonas P	4	1	1	0	0	0
	36	12	6	27	9	0

Los Angeles	AB	H	RBI	O	A	E
Schuster SS	4	1	0	3	4	0
Hughes 2B	5	0	0	3	2	0
Pafko CF	4	1	0	1	1	0
English 3B	4	4	1	1	2	0
Russell LF-1B	3	1	0	5	0	1
Ostrowski RF	3	0	0	2	1	0
Quinn 1B	1	0	0	7	2	0
Holm C	3	0	0	5	1	0
Gehrman P	3	0	0	0	1	1
Moore[a]	1	0	1	0	0	0
Garriott LF	1	0	0	0	0	0
Fernandes[b]	1	1	0	0	0	0
	33	8	2	27	14	2

(a) *Batted for Quinn in the sixth.*
(b) *Batted for Gehrman in the ninth.*

Pitching Records	IP	H	R	ER	SO	BB
Jonas	9	8	3	3	2	3
Gehrman	9	12	7	6	3	2

Wild Pitch: Gehrman. Left on Base: Seattle 5 Los Angeles 3. Two Base Hits: English, Dobbins, Sueme, Fernandes. Home Runs: Sueme, English. Sacrifices: Holm, Christopher, Gyselman, Russell, Gabrielson. Stolen Bases: Schuster, English, Mullen. Time of Game: 2 hr. 12 min. Umpires: McDonald and Powell.

Seattle	001	101	004	7 – 12 – 0	
Los Angeles	100	101	000	3 – 8 – 2	

This great Angel team, second only to the 1934 club in winning percentage and in games ahead of the second place team, sadly disbanded after the Seattle debacle. The players had $3,750 to divide among themselves and other players who were with the team sometime during the season. If this amounted to 25 shares, it would give each player $150, which would be about $867 in current-day funds.

The San Francisco–Portland Series

The Seals ended the season in Portland so they were willing to play the first two games of the playoffs there in order to cut travel costs and to have the remaining games at Seals Stadium. A fire had damaged some of the stands at the ancient Vaughan Street Park on the last Sunday of the season, September 12, but firefighters were able to extinguish it before a lot of damage was done. Some of the stands had to be roped off for these two playoff games. The Seals had been stumbling at the season's end, having lost 14 of their last 20, including seven of the last nine to the Beavers. But San Francisco still won the season series from Portland, 14 games to 10.

Game One.

Portland started its games at 3:30 P.M., rather than 5 P.M. as Seattle did. The series began on Wednesday, September 15, before 2,500 fans. Al Lien, on military leave, started for the Seals against Sid Cohen but neither was involved in the decision. Jimmie Adair's homer gave the Seals a 1–0 lead in the first, but the Beavers went up 2–1 in the fourth on Ted Gullic's homer, Johnny Gill's double and Larry Barton's single. The Seals tied it in the sixth on a walk to Charley Petersen and a double by Henry Steinbacher. The Seals took a 5–2 lead with three runs in the seventh on three singles, a walk and two squeeze plays, one by Al Lien and one by Jimmie Adair. Sid Cohen twisted his knee throwing Lien out at first, and was replaced by Marino Pieretti.

The Beavers closed the gap to 5–4 with two runs in the last of the eighth on a single by Johnny O'Neil and a bunt single by Ted Gullic, before Gill hit a bouncer that hopped over Adair's head at short, scoring O'Neil. Barton then singled in Gullic. The Seals increased the lead to 6–4 in the ninth with three straight singles by Frenchie Uhalt, Adair and Petersen off Earl Cook. But in the last of the ninth, Portland scored three runs off Al Epperly to win. Packy Rogers doubled, Spencer Harris walked, Rupert Thompson singled in Rogers, Earl Floyd's ground out scored Harris to tie the game, and Gullic singled in Thompson to send the Portland fans home happy.

San Francisco	AB	H	RBI	O	A	E
Uhalt CF	5	2	0	7	0	0
Adair SS	4	3	2	2	2	0
Petersen 3B	4	1	1	1	1	0
Steinbacher LF	5	2	1	3	0	0
Rosenberg RF	4	1	0	4	0	0
Suhr 1B	3	1	0	5	1	0
Young 2B	3	0	0	3	4	0
Sprinz C	3	1	1	0	0	0
Lien P	2	0	1	0	2	0
Epperly P	1	0	0	1	0	0
	34	11	6	26[a]	10	0

(a) Two out when winning run scored.

Portland	AB	H	RBI	O	A	E
Thompson RF	4	1	1	3	1	0
Floyd SS	5	0	1	3	3	1
Gullic CF	5	3	2	2	0	0
Gill LF	4	2	1	4	0	0
Barton 1B	4	2	2	7	0	0
Owen 3B	4	0	0	2	1	0
Rogers 2B	4	2	0	3	4	0
Adams C	4	1	0	3	3	0
Cohen P	1	0	0	0	2	0

Portland	AB	H	RBI	O	A	E
Pieretti P	0	0	0	0	0	0
O'Neil[a]	1	1	0	0	0	0
Cook P	0	0	0	0	0	0
Harris[b]	0	0	0	0	0	0
	36	12	7	27	14	1

(a) Batted for Pieretti in the eighth.
(b) Batted for Cook in the ninth.

Pitching Records	IP	H	R	ER	SO	BB
Lien	7.2	9	4	4	0	1
Epperly (L)	1.0	3	3	3	0	0
Cohen	6.1	6	4	5	1	4
Pieretti	1.2	2	1	0	0	1
Cook (W)	1	3	1	1	2	0

Wild Pitch: Epperly. Left on Base: San Francisco 6, Portland 6. Home Runs: Adair, Gullic. Two Base Hits: Rosenberg, Gill, Steinbacher, Rogers. Double Plays: Adair to Young to Suhr; Thompson to Owen. Sacrifices: Cohen, Lien. Time of Game: 2 hr. 2 min. Umpires: Hood and Widner.

San Francisco	100	001	301	6 – 11 – 0
Portland	000	200	023	7 – 12 – 1

Game Two.

This Thursday afternoon game turned out to be the last game in Portland in 1943 but Beaver fans, as Rainier fans, were hoping for a final series between the two Northwest teams, which would have insured each city of hosting some of the games. This game was a great pitching duel between submariner Al Liska and Bob Joyce, with all runs coming on solo home runs. Portland won 2–1 on Gill's homer in the fourth and Thompson's blast in the sixth. Liska lost his shutout in the ninth when Steinbacher connected for the Seals. No crowd figure was announced.

San Francisco	AB	R	H	RBI	O	A	E
Uhalt CF	4	0	1	0	5	0	0
Adair SS	3	0	0	0	1	0	0
Petersen 3B	4	0	1	0	1	4	0
Steinbacher LF	3	1	1	1	1	0	0
Rosenberg RF	4	0	0	0	4	0	0
Suhr 1B	3	0	1	0	5	0	0

San Francisco	AB	R	H	RBI	O	A	E
Young 2B	3	0	1	0	3	0	1
Sprinz C	2	0	0	0	4	0	0
Joyce P	3	0	0	0	0	2	0
Hooper[a]	1	0	0	0	0	0	0
Ogrodowski C	0	0	0	0	0	0	0
	30	1	5	1	24	6	1

(a) Batted for Sprinz in the eighth.

Portland	AB	R	H	RBI	O	A	E
Thompson RF	4	1	1	1	3	1	0
Floyd SS	4	0	1	0	0	1	0
Gullic CF	4	0	1	0	1	0	0
Gill LF	4	1	2	1	1	0	0
Barton 1B	3	0	1	0	14	1	0
Owen 3B	3	0	1	0	2	2	1
Rogers 2B	2	0	0	0	1	6	0
Adams C	3	0	0	0	5	0	0
Liska P	3	0	0	0	0	2	0
	30	2	7	2	27	13	1

Pitching Records	IP	H	R	ER	SO	BB
Joyce	8	7	2	2	2	0
Liska	9	5	1	1	4	0

Home Runs: Gill, Thompson, Steinbacher. Two Base Hits: Floyd, Barton, Owen, Gullic. Sacrifices: Adair, Steinbacher, Rogers. Left on Base: San Francisco 4, Portland 5. Double Play: Petersen to Suhr. Time of Game: 1 hr. 21 min. Umpires: Widner and Hood.

San Francisco	000	000	001	1 – 5 – 1
Portland	000	101	00x	2 – 7 – 1

The two teams left on the morning train on Friday, September 17, and arrived in Oakland late that evening. Even though the Seals had just lost nine of the last eleven to Portland, they felt better about returning to spacious Seals Stadium, where the Beavers would have more trouble hitting homers than in the smaller Vaughan Street Park.

Game Three.

On Saturday afternoon, September 18, the Seals hosted their first playoff game since 1939. Fans had a choice of this game or a football game at Kezar

Stadium between College of the Pacific and the Alameda Coast Guard. The Seals drew 2,500 compared to 10,000 at the football game.

Tommy Seats shut out the Beavers 3–0, with all runs coming in the first off Earl Cook. Uhalt, Adair, and Petersen singled for one run, Steinbacher sacrificed and Gus Suhr singled in the last two runs. The Seals now trailed two games to one.

Portland	AB	R	H	RBI	O	A	E
Thompson RF	4	0	0	0	6	0	0
Floyd SS	4	0	2	0	4	2	0
Gullic CF	4	0	1	0	1	0	0
Gill LF	4	0	1	0	1	0	0
Barton 1B	4	0	0	0	8	0	0
Owen 3B	3	0	1	0	1	2	0
Rogers 2B	2	0	0	0	2	2	0
Adams C	3	0	1	0	1	0	0
Cook P	2	0	0	0	0	1	0
O'Neil[a]	1	0	0	0	0	0	0
Wilson P	0	0	0	0	0	0	0
	31	0	6	0	24	7	0

(a) Batted for Cook in the eighth.

San Francisco	AB	R	H	RBI	O	A	E
Uhalt CF	4	1	2	0	3	0	0
Adair SS	4	1	2	0	3	4	0
Petersen 3B	4	1	2	1	1	1	0
Steinbacher LF	2	0	1	0	1	0	0
Rosenberg RF	4	0	1	0	3	0	0
Suhr 1B	4	0	2	2	9	1	0
Young 2B	4	0	0	0	3	4	0
Ogrodowski C	3	0	1	0	4	0	0
Seats P	2	0	0	0	0	1	0
	31	3	11	3	27	11	0

Pitching Records	IP	H	R	ER	SO	BB
Cook (L)	7	10	3	3	0	0
Wilson	1	1	0	0	3	1
Seats	9	6	0	0	3	1

Sacrifices: Steinbacher 2, Seats. Double Plays: Adair to Young to Suhr to Ogrodowski; Floyd to Barton; Adair to Young to Suhr. Time of Game: 1 hr. 27 min. Umpires: Hood and Widner.

Portland	000	000	000	0 –	6 –	0
San Francisco	300	000	00x	3 –	11 –	0

Game Four.

A crowd of 10,661 came out to Seals Stadium on Sunday, September 19, to see the home team sweep a twin bill from Portland, to go up three games to two. The opener was decided quickly when the Seals pounded Ad Liska for six runs in the first, with the key blow a bases loaded double by Joe Sprinz. That was preceded by singles by Uhalt, Petersen, Steinbacher, Harry Rosenberg and Gus Suhr. Suhr's hit drove in two of the runs. Manager Marv Shea started at catcher for the Beavers, but after that initial inning, he put Eddie Adams behind the plate and part-time outfielder Frank Shone in to pitch. Bob Joyce coasted to an easy victory.

Portland	AB	R	H	RBI	O	A	E
Thompson RF	4	0	2	1	4	0	0
Floyd SS-2B	4	0	1	0	3	5	0
Harris LF	4	0	0	0	1	0	0
Gill RF	4	0	0	0	0	0	0
Barton 1B	4	0	3	0	10	1	0
Owen 3B	3	0	2	0	1	1	0
Rogers 2B-3B	4	0	0	0	0	2	0
Shea C	0	0	0	0	0	0	0
Liska P	0	0	0	0	0	0	0
Adams C	4	0	0	0	4	1	0
Shone P	4	1	1	0	0	1	1
O' Neil SS[a]	0	0	0	0	1	1	0
	35	1	9	1	24	12	1

(a) Ran for Owen in the seventh.

San Francisco	AB	R	H	RBI	O	A	E
Uhalt CF	5	1	1	1	5	0	1
Adair SS	4	0	1	0	3	6	0
Petersen 2B	4	1	2	1	3	3	0
Steinbacher LF	4	1	2	0	2	0	0
Rosenberg RF	4	2	2	0	1	0	0
Suhr 1B	4	1	2	2	6	1	0
Paul 3B	3	2	2	0	2	1	1
Sprinz C	4	0	2	4	3	0	0
Joyce P	4	0	1	0	2	1	0
	36	8	15	8	27	12	2

Pitching Records	IP	H	R	ER	SO	BB
Liska (L)	1	7	6	6	0	0
Shone	7	8	2	1	3	0
Joyce	9	9	1	0	3	1

Wild Pitches: Shone, Joyce. Three Base Hit: Steinbacher. Two Base Hits: Sprinz, Thompson, Joyce. Sacrifices: Adair, Paul. Stolen Base: Uhalt. Double Play: Petersen to Adair to Suhr. Time of Game: 1 hr. 50 min. Umpires: Widner and Hood.

Portland	000	000	010	1 – 9 – 1	
San Francisco	600	000	02x	8 – 15 – 2	

Game Five.

This was private Al Lien's last game before his leave was over. He made it a winning occasion by holding Portland to two runs and seven hits, while Marino Pieretti was racked for four runs and 12 hits. The Seals took a 1–0 lead in the first on singles by Adair and Petersen ahead of Steinbacher's fly ball. The Seals upped this lead to 3–0 in the third on a Steinbacher single, a throwing error by Pieretti, a single by Rosenberg and a bloop double by Babe Paul. The Seals made it 4–0 in the fifth on doubles by Steinbacher and Rosenberg. Portland's two runs came in the sixth on walks to Gill and Barton, a ground out, and Packy Rogers' single.

Portland	AB	R	H	RBI	O	A	E
Thompson RF	2	0	0	0	2	0	0
Floyd SS	4	0	2	0	0	1	0
Gullic CF	3	0	1	0	2	0	0
Gill RF-LF	3	1	0	0	0	0	0
Barton 1B	3	1	0	0	10	0	0
Owen 3B	3	0	0	0	0	3	1
Rogers 2B	2	0	1	2	2	1	0
Adams C	3	0	1	0	2	0	0
Pieretti P	3	0	2	0	0	5	1
Harris LF	1	0	0	0	0	0	0
	27	2	7	2	18	10	2

San Francisco	AB	R	H	RBI	O	A	E
Uhalt CF	3	0	1	0	3	0	0
Adair SS	3	1	2	0	2	2	0
Petersen 2B	3	0	1	0	3	3	0

San Francisco	AB	R	H	RBI	O	A	E
Steinbacher LF	3	2	2	1	0	0	0
Rosenberg RF	3	0	2	1	2	0	0
Suhr 1B	3	1	1	1	7	0	0
Paul 3B	3	0	1	1	0	1	0
Ogrodowski C	3	0	1	0	4	0	0
Lien P	3	0	1	0	0	2	0
Hooper RF[a]	1	0	0	0	0	0	0
	28	4	12	4	21	8	0

(a) Ran for Rosenberg in the fifth.

Pitching Records	IP	H	R	ER	SO	BB
Pieretti	6	12	4	4	2	2
Lien	7	7	2	2	4	4

Two Base Hits: Paul, Pieretti, Steinbacher, Rosenberg. Sacrifices: Adair, Petersen. Double Play: Adair to Petersen to Suhr. Time of Game: 1 hr. 51 min. Umpires: Hood and Widner.

Portland	000	002	0	2 –	7 –	2
San Francisco	102	010	x	4 –	12 –	0

Game Six.

A sweltering crowd of 2,500 on Monday, September 20, saw the Seals eliminate Portland by hanging on to a 6–5 win. The Beavers' eighth inning rally fell short mainly because Larry Barton tripped over second base, preventing Marvin Owen from getting a bases-loaded triple. Ad Liska started and gave up the six Seals' runs, two in each of the third, fifth and seventh innings. Al Epperly, who got the win, helped himself at bat, but needed relief help in the eighth.

The Seals' runs in the third came on a Sprinz single, an Epperly triple, and Uhalt's single. In the fifth, Epperly beat out a bunt, and got to second when Barton failed to cover first base. Uhalt again singled in his pitcher, and scored on Petersen's double. In the seventh, Adair's fly to right was misjudged by the 43-year-old Spencer Harris for a gift double. Steinbacher singled but when the ball rolled through Rupert Thompson's legs, Henry was able to circle the bases with the run that proved decisive.

In the top of the eighth, Rogers singled, Adams walked, and Bill Krueger ran for Adams. Gullic hit for Liska and doubled in Rogers. Thompson's fly scored Krueger and moved Gullic to third, allowing him to score on Earl Floyd's grounder. Epperly now had a 6–3 lead with two outs and no one on base, but he ran out of gas. Harris walked, Gill singled, bringing in Tommy Seats to relieve. Barton walked to load the bases and Owen smashed one that should have cleared the bases, but Barton fell flat on his face, going around second. Barton was able to make it only to third, keeping Owen at second. Bob Joyce relieved and walked Rogers to reload the bases. Johnny O'Neil batted for the pinch runner Krueger and hit a sharp grounder on which Jimmie Adair made a game-saving play. Joyce was able to set Portland down in the ninth, to send the Seals to the final round.

Portland	AB	R	H	RBI	O	A	E
Thompson CF	5	0	1	1	2	0	1
Floyd SS	5	0	0	1	4	2	0
Harris RF	3	1	0	0	3	0	0
Gill LF	4	1	1	0	1	0	0
Barton 1B	3	0	0	0	5	1	1
Owen 3B	4	0	1	2	4	2	0
Rogers 2B	3	1	2	0	2	2	0
Adams C	2	0	0	0	2	1	0
Liska P	2	0	1	0	0	0	0
Gullic 2B[a]	2	1	1	1	1	1	0
Krueger[b]	0	1	0	0	0	0	0
O'Neil[c]	1	0	0	0	0	0	0
Cook P	0	0	0	0	0	0	0
Shea C	0	0	0	0	0	1	0
	34	5	7	5	24	10	2

(a) Batted for Liska in the eighth.
(b) Batted for Adams in the eighth.
(c) Batted for Krueger in the eighth.

San Francisco	AB	R	H	RBI	O	A	E
Uhalt CF	4	1	2	2	3	0	0
Adair SS	3	1	1	0	0	4	0
Petersen 2B	2	0	1	1	1	5	1
Steinbacher LF	4	1	2	1	2	0	0
Rosenberg RF	3	0	0	0	4	0	0
Suhr 1B	3	0	0	0	14	1	0
Paul 3B	4	0	1	0	0	2	0
Sprinz C	4	1	1	0	3	0	0
Epperly P	3	2	2	1	0	2	0
Seats P	0	0	0	0	0	0	0
Joyce P	0	0	0	0	0	0	0
	30	6	10	5	27	14	1

Pitching Records	IP	H	R	ER	SO	BB
Liska (L)	7	10	6	5	1	1
Cook	1	0	0	0	0	1
Epperly (W)	7.2	6	3	5	2	2
Seats	0+	1	2	0	0	1
Joyce	1.1	0	0	0	0	1

Hit by Pitcher: Rosenberg by Liska. Three Base Hit: Epperly. Two Base Hits: Paul, Petersen, Adair, Owen, Gullic. Sacrifices: Petersen, Adair. Double Play: Suhr to Adair to Suhr. Time of Game: 2 hr. 1 min. Umpires: Widner and Hood.

Portland	000	000	050	5 – 7 – 2
San Francisco	002	020	20x	6 – 10 – 1

The Portland players had just $1,250 prize money to divide, and depending upon the number of shares voted, it may have amounted to only $50 per man. In today's money, it would be worth about $290.

The Final Series: San Francisco vs. Seattle

Seattle tried to get some of the final round games in Sick's Stadium but Seals president Charles Graham was adamant about the Seals having the weekend games at home, and since the series began on Thursday, September 23, there would not have been enough time to get to Seattle and back. The Seals had the right to choose the site because they finished higher than the Rainiers. Seattle had won 13 and lost 12 to the Seals during the season.

Game One.

The Seals rallied with four runs in the ninth to take the opener from Seattle by a 6–5 score. Carl Fischer faced Tommy Seats but neither got the decision. The Seals scored first on a bases loaded walk to Uhalt in the second, but Seattle took a 2–1 lead in the fifth on two hits and two errors. Sueme and Fischer singled, Mullen forced Fischer, and then stole second as Ambrose "Brusie" Ogrodowski threw the ball into center field, allowing Sueme to score and Mullen to reach third. Ed Carnett grounded to Suhr, who booted the ball, allowing Mullen to score. In the seventh, Seattle increased the lead to 4–1 on singles by Jimmy Jewell and Hal Sueme, a force play by Fischer, a double by Mullen, which plated Jewell, and a single by Carnett, which scored Fischer, but Harry Rosenberg threw Mullen out at the plate, which later proved to be crucial. Seattle's fifth and final run came in the eighth when Christopher got on base on Babe Paul's error and scored on singles by Jewell and Sueme. The Rainier catcher went 3-for-4 in a losing cause.

The Seals scored an unearned run in the eighth to cut the lead to 5–2. Steinbacher beat out a bunt and Rosenberg was safe on Gyselman's error. Ogrodowski's two-out single drove in the run. The Seals batted for Seats in the eighth, so Bill Werle pitched a scoreless ninth. Carl Fischer was tiring as he began the last of the ninth with a three run lead. He walked two and gave up a single to load the bases, before being replaced by the 42-year-old Sylvester Johnson. After Rosenberg popped up, Gus Suhr doubled two men home, putting the tying run on third and the winner on second. Del Young walked to reload the bases before Ogrodowski singled in the tying run, but the 37-year-old Suhr was nailed at the plate by Ed Carnett's strong arm. On the play, pinch runner Bob Joyce reached third, and scored the winning run when Dick Gyselman booted pinch hitter Logan Hooper's ground ball.

Seattle	AB	R	H	RBI	O	A	E
Mullen 2B	5	1	1	1	2	6	0
Carnett LF	5	0	1	1	4	1	0
Matheson RF	5	0	2	0	0	0	0
Dobbins SS	5	0	0	0	3	4	0
Christopher CF	3	1	0	0	2	0	0
Gyselman 3B	4	0	1	0	1	1	2
Jewell 1B	4	0	3	0	8	0	0
Sueme C	4	2	3	1	6	0	0
Fischer P	4	1	1	0	0	1	0
Johnson P	0	0	0	0	0	0	0
	39	5	12	3	26[a]	13	2

(a) Two outs when winning run scored.

San Francisco	AB	R	H	RBI	O	A	E
Uhalt CF	4	0	1	1	3	0	0
Adair SS	4	1	0	0	1	5	0
Petersen 2B	5	1	2	0	2	2	0
Steinbacher LF	4	2	2	0	1	0	0
Rosenberg RF	5	0	1	0	1	1	1
Suhr 1B	4	1	2	2	12	0	1
Paul 3B	4	0	3	0	3	3	0
Ogrodowski C	5	0	3	2	4	1	1
Seats P	3	0	0	0	0	3	0

San Francisco	AB	R	H	RBI	O	A	E
Enos[a]	0	0	0	0	0	0	0
Epperly[b]	0	0	0	0	0	0	0
Werle P	0	0	0	0	0	0	0
Young[c]	0	0	0	0	0	0	0
Joyce[d]	0	1	0	0	0	0	0
Hooper[e]	1	0	0	0	0	0	0
	39	6	14	5	27	15	3

(a) Batted for Seats in the eighth.
(b) Ran for Enos in the eighth.
(c) Batted for Paul in the ninth.
(d) Ran for Young in the ninth.
(e) Batted for Werle in the ninth.

Pitching Records	IP	H	R	ER	SO	BB
Fischer	8+	12	2	1	5	5
Johnson (L)	0.2	2	4	3	0	1
Seats	8	11	5	2	2	1
Werle (W)	1	1	0	0	0	0

Three Base Hit: Rosenberg. Two Base Hits: Matheson, Steinbacher, Mullen, Suhr. Sacrifice: Mullen. Double Plays: Mullen to Dobbins to Jewell; Gyselman to Mullen to Jewell. Time of Game: 2 hr. 15 min. Umpires: Widner, Hood, Doran.

Seattle	000	020	210	5 – 12 – 2		
San Francisco	010	000	014	6 – 14 – 3		

Game Two.

A Friday afternoon crowd of 2,500 saw Seattle tie the series on Joe Demoran's two-hit shutout. Lloyd Christopher hit a fifth inning homer off loser Bob Joyce to give Demoran all the support he would need. But Seattle added an insurance run the next inning when Moon Mullen singled, moved around on a sacrifice and an error, and scored on Joe Dobbin's single.

Seattle	AB	R	H	RBI	O	A	E
Mullen 2B	3	1	2	0	2	7	1
Carnett LF	2	0	0	0	4	0	0
Matheson RF	3	0	0	0	0	0	0
Dobbins SS	4	0	1	1	0	4	0
Christopher CF	4	1	1	1	3	0	0

Scattle	AB	R	H	RBI	O	A	E
Gyselman 3B	3	0	1	0	0	2	0
Gabrielson 1B	3	0	0	0	14	2	0
Sueme C	3	0	0	0	2	0	0
Demoran P	3	0	0	0	2	1	0
	28	2	5	2	27	16	1

San Francisco	AB	R	H	RBI	O	A	E
Uhalt CF	4	0	1	0	6	0	0
Adair SS	3	0	0	0	1	1	0
Petersen 2B	3	0	1	0	1	3	0
Steinbacher LF	3	0	0	0	3	0	1
Rosenberg RF	3	0	0	0	2	0	0
Suhr 1B	3	0	0	0	11	0	0
Paul 3B	3	0	0	0	0	4	0
Sprinz C	3	0	0	0	2	0	0
Joyce P	2	0	0	0	1	2	1
Hooper[a]	1	0	0	0	0	0	0
	28	0	2	0	27	10	2

(a) Batted for Joyce in the ninth.

Pitching Records	IP	H	R	ER	SO	BB
Demoran	9	2	0	0	2	0
Joyce	9	5	2	1	1	0

Home Run: Christopher. Sacrifices: Carnett, Matheson. Double Play: Gyselman to Mullen to Gabrielson. Time of Game: 1 hr. 29 min. Umpires: Doran, Widner, Hood.

Seattle	000	011	000	2 – 5 – 1
San Francisco	000	000	000	0 – 2 – 2

Game Three.

On Saturday afternoon, September 25, Bay Area fans had a choice of two football games besides this playoff game. A crowd of 35,000 saw California beat St. Mary's 27–12 in Berkeley, and 3,000 saw Pleasanton Naval Center beat the University of San Francisco Dons 13–0 at Kezar Stadium. The Seals and Rainiers outdrew the latter game when 4,000 witnessed Cowboy Ray Harrell outduel Frank Tincup 2–1, to put the Seals a game up on Seattle in the series. San Francisco got only three hits (which made it a total of five in two days), but they got two extra base blows in the fourth when they scored both their runs. Charley Petersen doubled and scored on Henry Steinbacher's triple. The latter scored as Rosenberg grounded out. Seattle got an unearned run in the second when Gyselman was safe on Babe Paul's error, stole second, and scored on Len Gabrielson's single.

This 2–1 game was far from dull. Seattle had many chances to score. In the fourth, Sueme hit into a double play with the bases loaded. In the seventh, Frenchie Uhalt made a shoestring catch with two outs and runners on first and second. An inning later, Uhalt made a sensational catch on Matheson's drive that had triple written all over it. He dove parallel to the ground, landed on his head, rolled over, and came up holding the ball for all to see. In the ninth, the Rainiers had runners on second and third when Tincup, batting for himself because he was a good hitter, grounded out to end the game.

Seattle	AB	R	H	RBI	O	A	E
Mullen 2B	4	0	1	0	0	0	0
Carnott LF	4	0	0	0	4	0	0
Matheson RF	4	0	0	0	3	0	0
Dobbins SS	3	0	0	0	3	3	1
Christopher CF	4	0	2	0	1	0	0
Gyselman 3B	4	1	0	0	1	0	0
Gabrielson 1B	3	0	2	1	6	2	0
Sueme C	3	0	1	0	4	2	0
Tincup P	4	0	0	0	2	2	0
Katz[a]	0	0	0	0	0	0	0
	33	1	6	1	24	9	1

(a) Ran for Gabrielson in the ninth.

San Francisco	AB	R	H	RBI	O	A	E
Uhalt CF	3	0	0	0	3	0	1
Adair SS	3	0	0	0	3	3	1
Petersen 2B	3	1	1	0	3	2	0
Steinbacher LF	2	1	1	1	2	0	1
Rosenberg RF	4	0	0	1	2	0	0
Suhr 1B	3	0	1	0	8	0	0
Paul 3B	2	0	0	0	1	2	1
Sprinz C	2	0	0	0	5	1	0
Harrell P	3	0	0	0	0	1	0
	25	2	3	2	27	9	4

Pitching Records	IP	H	R	ER	SO	BB
Tincup	9	3	2	2	3	5
Harrell	9	6	1	0	5	2

Hit by Pitcher: Uhalt by Tincup. Three Base Hit: Steinbacher. Two Base Hits: Petersen, Christopher. Sacrifices: Sueme, Petersen. Stolen Bases: Christopher, Mullen, Gyselman, Sueme. Double Play: Paul to Petersen to Suhr. Time of Game: 1 hr. 41 min. Umpires: Widner, Hood, Doran.

Seattle	010	000	000	1 – 6 – 1
San Francisco	000	200	00x	2 – 3 – 4

Game Four.

A crowd of 14,301 saw the teams split a doubleheader, giving the Seals a 3–2 series lead. The baseball crowd surpassed the 9,000 that saw two service teams play football at Kezar. Seattle took the opener, temporarily tying the series, with Pete Jonas squaring off against Al Epperly. Four Seal errors made four of Seattle's seven runs unearned, but not unwelcome. Seattle got a run in the second when Gyselman got on base via Petersen's error and came around to score on Gabrielson's single and Jonas' fly ball. But Jonas was wracked for three runs in the Seal second on singles by Adair and Steinbacher and doubles by Rosenberg and Paul. Seattle quickly went back on top 4–3 in the third on singles by Carnett, Dobbins, and Christopher, plus a walk to Gabrielson, and another single by Sueme, but the Rainiers left the bases loaded. In the last of the third, Jonas was relieved by John Yelovic, who gave up a run-scoring fly ball to Rosenberg to tie the game at 4–4.

Seattle got the winning runs in the sixth when Uhalt, who made great catches Saturday, dropped Carnett's fly ball with two out. This opened the flood gates. Matheson doubled, and Dobbins singled, bringing in the 44-year-old Sad Sam Gibson to relieve Epperly. Gibson gave up singles to Christopher and Gyselman to give Seattle a 7–4 lead. Yelovic got the win but he was relieved in the eighth by Sylvester Johnson, as the Seals scored their fifth run.

Seattle	AB	R	H	RBI	O	A	E
Mullen 2B	5	0	2	0	1	2	0
Carnett LF	5	1	2	0	1	0	1
Matheson RF	5	2	1	1	6	0	0
Dobbins SS	5	2	2	2	3	4	1
Christopher CF	5	1	3	1	1	0	0
Gyselman 3B	5	1	3	1	0	3	0
Gabrielson 1B	4	0	3	0	12	1	0
Sueme C	5	0	1	1	3	1	0
Jonas P	1	0	0	1	0	0	0
Yelovic P	3	0	0	0	0	3	0
Johnson P	0	0	0	0	0	0	0
	43	7	17	7	27	14	2

San Francisco	AB	R	H	RBI	O	A	E
Uhalt CF	5	0	1	0	0	0	1
Adair SS	5	1	1	0	6	5	1
Petersen 2B	3	1	2	0	2	1	1
Steinbacher LF	3	1	2	0	3	1	0
Suhr 1B	2	0	0	1	9	0	1
Rosenberg RF	4	1	1	2	3	1	0
Paul 3B	4	1	2	1	1	2	0
Sprinz C	3	0	0	0	3	3	0
Epperly P	2	0	1	0	0	1	0
Gibson P	1	0	0	0	0	0	0
Young[a]	1	0	0	0	0	0	0
Ogrodowski C	0	0	0	0	0	1	0
Hooper[b]	1	0	0	0	0	0	0
	34	5	10	4	27	15	4

(a) Batted for Sprinz in the eighth.
(b) Batted for Gibson in the ninth.

Pitching Records	IP	H	R	ER	SO	BB
Jonas	2+	5	3	3	0	0
Yelovic (W)	5+	4	1	1	1	3
Johnson	2	1	1	0	2	0
Epperly (L)	2.2	12	5	3	0	1
Gibson	6.1	5	2	0	0	0

Two Base Hits: Rosenberg, Paul, Gyselman, Matheson, Petersen. Sacrifice: Steinbacher. Stolen Bases: Carnett 2. Double Plays: Gabrielson to Dobbins; Dobbins to Mullen to Gabrielson. Time of Game: 1 hr. 48 min. Umpires: Hood, Doran, Widner.

Seattle	013	003	000	7 – 17 – 2
San Francisco	031	000	010	5 – 10 – 4

Game Five.

The Seals took the seven-inning nightcap 9–3, to take a 3–2 series lead. Glen Elliott started for Seattle and gave up two runs in the first on singles by Adair and Petersen and a double by Rosenberg. He was lifted for a hitter in the third, so the Seals got to John Babich for three runs in the fourth. Del Young walked, Ogrodowski was safe on Dobbins' error, Uhalt tripled and Adair squeezed in Uhalt. The Seals went up 6–0 the next inning, but in the sixth, Seattle touched up starter Tommy Seats for three runs to cut the lead in half. Carnett singled, Matheson homered, Dobbins singled and Gyselman tripled. But Seats weathered the storm and the Seals put the game away with three runs of their own in the bottom of the sixth off John Yelovic, the winner in the opener.

Seattle	AB	R	H	RBI	O	A	E
Mullen 2B	4	0	0	0	2	3	0
Carnett LF	4	1	2	0	1	0	0
Matheson RF	4	1	1	2	0	0	0
Dobbins SS	3	1	1	0	3	1	1
Christopher CF	2	0	1	0	2	0	0
Gyselman 3B	3	0	1	1	0	2	0
Jewel 1B	3	0	1	0	9	2	0
Sueme C	3	0	1	0	1	0	0
Elliott P	0	0	0	0	0	1	0
Lawrence[a]	1	0	0	0	0	0	0
Babich P	0	0	0	0	0	1	0
Katz[b]	1	0	1	0	0	0	0
Speece P	0	0	0	0	0	0	0
Demoran[c]	1	0	0	0	0	0	0
Yelovic P	0	0	0	0	0	0	0
	29	3	9	3	18	10	1

(a) Batted for Elliott in the third.
(b) Batted for Babich in the fifth.
(c) Batted for Speece in the sixth.

San Francisco	AB	R	H	RBI	O	A	E
Uhalt CF	4	1	3	1	2	0	0
Adair SS	3	2	1	2	1	2	0
Petersen 3B	3	2	2	0	1	2	0
Steinbacher LF	4	0	2	1	1	1	1
Rosenberg RF	3	1	1	1	2	0	0
Suhr 1B	4	0	1	1	7	1	0
Young 2B	2	1	1	0	2	2	0
Ogrodowski C	3	1	0	0	4	0	0
Seats P	3	1	1	1	1	0	0
	29	9	12	7	21	8	1

Pitching Records	IP	H	R	ER	SO	BB
Elliott (L)	2	5	2	2	0	0
Babich	2	1	3	1	0	2

Pitching Records	IP	H	R	ER	SO	BB
Speece	1	2	1	1	0	0
Yelovic	1	4	3	3	1	0
Seats	7	9	3	3	2	1

Home Run: Matheson. Three Base Hits: Uhalt, Suhr, Gyselman. Two Base Hits: Rosenberg, Steinbacher. Sacrifices: Rosenberg, Adair. Stolen Base: Adair. Umpires: Doran, Widner, Hood.

Seattle	000	003	0	3 – 9 – 1
San Francisco	200	313	x	9 – 12 – 1

Game Six.

A doubleheader was scheduled for Monday, September 27, but became unnecessary when the Seals won the first game 5–4. There was no exhibition game as occurred in Los Angeles when the Rainiers clinched the opening series. A crowd of 4,308 had plenty of excitement in this one game anyway, as Bob Joyce held on by his fingernails in the ninth as Seattle scored three runs and had the bases loaded with one out, before a double play ended the series.

Joe Demoran went all the way for Seattle, giving up a run in the second, three in the third and the last one in the seventh. In the second, Joe Sprinz singled in Suhr, who had walked. In the third, Adair doubled, Petersen singled, and Steinbacher got aboard when Gabrielson threw too late to get Adair at the plate. Rosenberg then doubled in two runs to make it 4–0. Seattle got a run on a double play in the fourth, while the Seals got their fifth, and decisive, run in the seventh when Petersen squeezed in Uhalt. Ford Mullen's throwing error helped Uhalt get into scoring position.

Joyce was tiring but he managed to weather the ninth inning storm. Carnett walked, Matheson doubled, Dobbins flied out, and Christopher doubled to make it 5–3. Gyselman singled in Christopher to make it 5–4. O'Doul went out to talk to Joyce but the whole team wanted to stay with their starter. This appeared to be a poor decision when Gabrielson doubled Gyselman to third and Sueme walked to load the bases. Frank Tincup, Saturday's tough-luck loser, batted for Demoran and hit a grounder to short. Adair fired to Sprinz, forcing Gyselman, and the throw to first nailed Tincup because he had fallen down on his way to first.

Seattle	AB	R	H	RBI	O	A	E
Mullen 2B	4	1	1	0	2	3	1
Carnett LF	3	1	1	0	2	0	0
Matheson RF	4	1	1	0	2	1	0

Seattle	AB	R	H	RBI	O	A	E
Dobbins SS	4	0	0	1	3	1	0
Christopher CF	3	1	1	1	2	0	0
Gyselman 3B	4	0	2	1	1	6	0
Gabrielson 1B	3	0	1	0	11	1	0
Sueme C	3	0	0	0	1	0	0
Demoran P	3	0	0	0	0	3	0
Katz[a]	0	0	0	0	0	0	0
Tincup[b]	1	0	0	0	0	0	0
	32	4	7	3	24	15	1

(a) Ran for Gabrielson in the ninth.
(b) Batted for Demoran in the ninth.

San Francisco	AB	R	H	RBI	O	A	E
Uhalt CF	4	1	1	0	3	0	0
Adair SS	3	1	2	0	2	4	0
Petersen 3B	2	1	1	1	0	0	1
Steinbacher LF	3	1	1	1	2	0	0
Suhr 1B	3	1	0	0	13	0	0
Rosenberg RF	4	0	1	2	4	0	0
Young 2B	3	0	2	0	2	6	0
Sprinz C	4	0	1	1	1	2	0
Joyce P	3	0	0	0	0	2	0
	29	5	9	5	27	14	1

Pitching Records	IP	H	R	ER	SO	BB
Demoran	8	9	5	4	1	3
Joyce	9	7	4	4	0	4

Two Base Hits: Mullen, Adair, Rosenberg, Matheson, Christopher, Gabrielson. Sacrifices: Adair, Petersen. Double Plays: Adair to Young to Suhr; Adair to Sprinz to Suhr. Time of Game: 1 hr. 32 min. Umpires: Widner, Hood, Doran.

Seattle	000	100	003	4 – 7 – 1
San Francisco	013	000	10x	5 – 9 – 1

The San Francisco fans and sports writers were delighted by this playoff win, which came after the team lost the pennant by 21 games. This was the only time that a team finishing in second place won the playoffs. The writers could not help "rubbing it in" to manager Bill Skiff, who felt his team could beat the Yankees. The 27,000 fans who saw the final series demonstrated that the playoffs seemed to be more popular when there was no tight pennant race.

By contrast, the exciting 1942 pennant race appeared to sap all the fans' enthusiasm, leaving nothing for the playoffs.

The Seals split their $5,000 among 30 players because so many came and went during the season. This would be about $168 per man, or about $1,000 in today's money. Seattle split $2,500, which if divided 25 ways, would be $100, or about $600 in current funds.

Key Players on 1943 Playoff Teams

Los Angeles. *Pitchers:* Jodie Phipps, Red Lynn, Ken Raffensberger, Paul Gehrman, Don Osborn, and Oren Baker.
 Position Players: Andy Pakfo (batting champ), Johnny Ostrowski (home run champ), Bill Schuster (team's MVP), Roy Hughes, Charlie English, Billy Holm, and Rip Russell.

San Francisco. *Pitchers:* Al Epperly, Bob Joyce, Tommy Seats and Al Lien.
 Position Players: Henry Steinbacher, Charley Petersen, Frenchy Uhalt, and Gus Suhr.

Seattle. *Pitchers:* Carl Fischer, Frank Tincup, Byron Speece, and Joe Demoran.
 Position Players: Joe Dobbins, Len Gabrielson, Ed Carnett, Bill Matheson, Dick Gyselman, Hal Sueme, and Lloyd Christopher.

Portland. *Pitchers:* Ad Liska, Sid Cohen, and Wayne Osborne.
 Position Players: John Gill, Marvin Owen, Larry Barton, Rupert Thompson and Spencer Harris.

1944

Looking only at the end results, one could be misled into thinking that 1944 was a rerun of 1943 because the Angels again won the pennant and the Seals again won the playoffs. But, unlike the previous year, there was a good pennant race in 1944 until mid–August when the Angels began to pull away, and a very close race for the first division, which went down to the final two days of the season. The number of games was increased from 155 to 169 and the improved war situation allowed the return of night games. Attendance more than doubled over 1943, rising from 1,155,034 to 2,358,352, an all time high, which did not count the servicemen allowed in free. The team with the largest attendance gain was seventh place Sacramento which drew 199,808, up from a mere 31,694 in 1943. A group of fans in that city banded together to save the club from being sold to Tacoma interests. Even last place San Diego drew 245, 795 because they were in contention until late June, when they sold pitcher Rex Cecil to the Red Sox.

The Angels, who lost most of their star players from their 1943 team, floundered in sixth place until late June, but finally received some help from the parent Chicago Cubs, and picked up the pace, moving into a four-way tie for fourth place on the Fourth of July. From then on, L.A. was on a roll, taking the lead for good in late July. By the end of August, they had a ten game lead over second place Portland, causing attention to turn to five teams competing for the other three first-division spots. Besides the Beavers, the Seals, Oaks, Rainiers and Stars stayed in contention for the playoffs right into the last week of the season.

Manager Bill Sweeney had his chance to even the score with Seattle's outspoken Bill Skiff, who humiliated the great Angel team of 1943 in the playoffs. The Rainiers finished the season with an eight game series at Wrigley Field. Even though Seattle won the first game, the Angels clinched the pennant when Portland lost at Oakland, but Bill Sweeney said that L.A. would still go all out to win every game, and not rest up for the playoffs. L.A. won six of the last seven, knocking the Rainiers out of the postseason for the first time since 1937, and causing them to finish under .500 at 84–85.

223

The Portland Beavers improved from fourth place in 1943 to second this season under playing manager Marvin Owen, who was the team's sixth manager in six years. This team led the league in May for the first time since early 1937 and was rarely out of contention for the first division. However, this race was so tight in the middle of the pack that the Beavers slid to seventh place in early August. Portland ended up 12 games behind the Angels but only one game ahead of the Seals and Oaks, who were tied for third. Since Seattle finished two games behind the Bay Area teams and Hollywood ended up only a game behind Seattle, there were only four games separating the sixth place Stars from second place Portland.

Lefty O'Doul had his Seals in the lead from early June through late July, and were never far from the lead until the Angels turned up the heat, and pulled away in August. As with the other clubs, the Seals lost key players to the service but were able to get good performances out of older players. Unlike 1943, the Seals did quite well against the Angels, beating them 14 out of 22 times.

The Oakland Oaks made the playoffs for the first time since 1940 under playing manager Dolph Camilli. Camilli was normally a first baseman but played mostly in the outfield because Les Scarsella, the league's batting champion, also played first base. The Oaks lost one of their best hitters, Frank Hawkins, when he got hurt in mid-season, but picked up Charley English from Los Angeles in August, which helped fill a void. The Oaks finished strong by beating the Seals the next-to-last week of the season, and then pounded Portland six out of eight times the last week. Oakland also won the season series from the Angels 17–13, but had an astonishingly poor record against Hollywood, winning only 2 of 22 games with the Stars.

The Pacific Coast League had a new president, Clarence "Pants" Rowland, formerly of the Angel front office, who replaced W. C. Tuttle. Rowland changed the cup for winning the playoffs to the Governors' Cup and had the governors of Washington, Oregon, and California engrave their names on the trophy which was given to the victorious team.

The Los Angeles–Portland Series

Because of wartime travel restrictions, all games were played in California because Portland was the only northwest club in the playoffs. The Beavers were scheduled to open at Los Angeles after Oakland and the Seals tied for third place. This was the first time in the playoffs that a team was allowed to act as home team (bat last) in another's park, as the Angels allowed Portland to be the home club after the third game. This privilege was not afforded

Seattle in 1942 or 1943. According to *The Oakland Tribune* the Beavers talked the Angels into paying their hotel bill in Los Angeles as compensation for not having any games in Portland. The Angels won 14 of the 21 games played with Portland during the season.

Game One.

This series opened on a cool Wednesday night, September 20, before 4,623 fans. The submariner Ad Liska faced another veteran, Ray Prim, as the Beavers won 4–2. The hero for Portland was catcher Eddie Adams, who drove in three of those runs with a homer and a single. In the second, manager Marvin Owen singled before Adams' big blast. In the seventh, Adams drove in Ted Gullic with the third run. Frank Demaree drove in the Beavers' last run in the eighth. The Angels got their first run in the seventh on singles by Stan Gray, Cecil Garriott and Rip Russell and their last run in the eighth on a double by Reggie Otero and a single by Tony York.

Portland	AB	H	RBI	O	A	E
Shone CF	3	0	0	2	0	0
O'Neil SS	4	1	0	6	2	0
Demaree RF	4	0	1	1	0	0
DeWeese LF-RF	4	2	0	3	0	0
Gullic 1B	4	0	0	10	1	1
Owen 3B	4	2	0	0	2	0
E. Adams C	4	2	3	3	0	0
Nunes 2B	4	0	0	1	2	0
Liska P	3	0	0	1	3	0
Harris LF	0	0	0	0	0	0
	34	7	4	27	10	1

Los Angeles	AB	H	RBI	O	A	E
Garriott CF	4	1	0	3	0	0
Russell 2B	5	1	1	1	2	0
Ostrowski 3B	5	0	0	2	2	0
Norbert LF	4	1	0	1	0	0
Sauer RF	4	1	0	1	0	0
Otero 1B	4	2	0	11	0	0
Miller SS	2	1	0	1	1	0
Fernandes C	3	0	0	7	1	0
Prim P	2	0	0	0	1	0
Gray[a]	1	1	0	0	0	0

Los Angeles	AB	H	RBI	O	A	E
Moore [b]	1	0	0	0	0	0
York SS	1	1	1	0	0	0
Comellas P	0	0	0	0	2	0
Willingham [c]	1	0	0	0	0	0
	37	9	2	27	9	0

(a) Batted for Miller in the seventh.
(b) Batted for Prim in the seventh.
(c) Batted for Comellas in the ninth.

Pitching Records	IP	H	R	ER	SO	BB
Liska	9	9	2	2	1	2
Prim (L)	7	5	3	3	7	0
Comellas	2	2	1	1	1	1

Left on Base: Portland 4, Los Angeles 10. Two Base Hits: Otero, DeWeese. Home Run: E. Adams. Time of Game: 1 hr. 47 min. Umpires: Engeln and Doran.

Portland	020	000	110	4 – 7 – 1
Los Angeles	000	000	110	2 – 9 – 0

Game Two.

The Beavers went up two games to none with a 3–2 win on Thursday night the 21st before 4,322 fans. Little Marino Pieretti limited L.A. to five hits while Red Adams and Claude Horton were giving up ten. The Angels got a run in the first without a hit on two walks, a wild pitch and Ted Norbert's fly ball. Portland tied it in the second when Eddie Adams singled, Mel Nunes doubled, and Johnny O'Neil singled. The Angels went up 2–1 on an unearned run in the third when Marvin Owen dropped Garriott's high pop fly, allowing the Angel center fielder to reach second base. Johnny Ostrowski singled in Garriott. Portland quickly tied it in the fourth on singles by Pieretti and centerfielder Frank Shone, a wild pitch, and O'Neil's grounder. Portland scored the winning run in the seventh when O'Neil singled and scored on 44-year-old Spencer Harris' double.

Portland	AB	H	RBI	O	A	E
Shone CF	4	1	0	3	0	0
O'Neil SS	5	2	2	1	6	0
Harris LF	4	1	1	0	0	0

Portland	AB	H	RBI	O	A	E
Gill RF	4	4	0	1	0	0
Gullic 1B	5	0	0	12	0	0
Owen 3B	4	0	0	1	5	1
E. Adams C	3	0	0	6	0	0
Nunes 2B	4	1	0	2	2	0
Pieretti P	4	1	0	1	2	0
	37	10	3	27	15	1

Los Angeles	AB	H	RBI	O	A	E
Garriott CF	4	0	0	5	0	0
Russell 2B	5	0	0	4	2	0
Ostrowski 3B	3	1	1	1	4	0
Norbert LF	4	1	1	0	0	0
Sauer RF	4	1	0	4	0	0
Otero 1B	3	1	0	9	0	0
Miller SS	2	0	0	1	3	1
Moore[a]	1	0	0	0	0	0
York SS	0	0	0	0	0	0
Fernandes C	0	0	0	2	0	0
Sarni C	2	0	0	1	1	0
Willingham[b]	1	0	0	0	0	0
C. Adams P	2	0	0	0	1	0
Gray[c]	1	0	0	0	0	0
Horton P	0	0	0	0	0	0
Grigg[d]	1	1	0	0	0	0
	33	5	2	27	11	1

(a) Batted for Miller in the eighth.
(b) Batted for Sarni in the ninth.
(c) Batted for C. Adams in the seventh.
(d) Batted for Horton in the ninth.

Pitching Records	IP	H	R	ER	SO	BB
Pieretti	9	5	2	1	6	5
C. Adams (L)	7	9	3	3	3	4
Horton	2	1	0	0	0	0

Wild Pitches: Pieretti 2, C. Adams 1. Left on Base: Portland 11 Los Angeles 9. Two Base Hits: Harris, Gill, Sauer. Stolen Base: Gill. Time of Game: 1 hr. 53 min. Umpires: Engeln and Doran.

Portland	010	100	100	3 – 10 – 1
Los Angeles	101	000	000	2 – 5 – 1

Game Three.

The Angels finally broke a seven game losing streak in the playoffs that went back to the last round of 1942, by beating Portland 5–4 on Friday night, September 22. No attendance was mentioned but this game had to compete with a speech by Presidential candidate Thomas E. Dewey, who was at the Coliseum, just a mile west of Wrigley Field. In addition, the writeup of this game was relegated to the second page of Saturday's sports section because UCLA was playing USC in the Coliseum that afternoon. Those two schools played twice a season during the war years.

This was a bad game for shortstops. Johnny O'Neil's three errors gave the Angels two unearned runs and Guy Miller's two errors gave the Beavers one. Roy Helser went all the way for Portland while Don Osborn started for the Angels, but was relieved by Pancho Comellas in the sixth. L.A. got two in the first when Garriott walked, O'Neil muffed Russell's grounder, Ostrowski singled to load the bases, before Reggie Otero singled in two runs. But Portland came right back to tie it in the second on four singles by John Gill, Marvin Owen, Eddie Adams and Roy Helser. The Angels went up 4–2 in the third when Russell doubled and scored on a two-base error by O'Neil. Ted Norbert then homered. The Beavers got one of those back in the fifth when Guy Miller made successive errors on balls hit by Helser and Frank Shone. The run scored on a sacrifice and Spencer Harris' ground out. Osborn was knocked out in the sixth when Portland tied the game on singles by Owen, Adams and pinch hitter Larry Barton. Pancho Jorge Comellas shut the Beavers down the rest of the way, getting credit for the win. Eddie Sauer drove in the winning run in the seventh after Garriott walked and was sacrificed by Russell.

Portland	AB	H	RBI	O	A	E
Shone CF	5	0	0	5	0	0
O'Neil SS	4	0	0	0	7	3
Harris LF	5	0	1	1	0	0
Gill RF	3	2	0	0	0	0
Gullic 1B-2B	4	0	0	8	0	0
Owen 3B	4	3	0	0	1	0
E. Adams C	3	2	1	3	0	0
Nunes 2B	2	0	0	1	2	0
Helser P	4	1	1	1	4	0
Barton 1B[a]	1	1	1	5	1	0
	35	9	4	24	15	3

(a) Batted for Nunes in the sixth.

Los Angeles	AB	H	RBI	O	A	E
Garriott CF	2	0	0	3	1	0
Russell 2B	2	1	0	6	1	0
Ostrowski 3B	3	1	0	1	3	0
Norbert LF	3	1	1	1	0	0
Sauer RF	4	1	1	3	0	0
Otero 1B	4	2	2	7	2	0
Miller SS	4	1	0	0	5	2
Sarni C	4	0	0	4	1	0
Osborn P	2	0	0	1	1	0
Comellas P	2	0	0	1	1	0
	30	7	4	27	15	2

Pitching Records	IP	H	R	ER	SO	BB
Helser	8	7	5	3	2	4
Osborn	5.1	9	4	3	1	1
Comellas (W)	3.2	0	0	0	2	3

Passed Ball: E. Adams. Left on Base: Portland 8, Los Angeles 7. Home Run: Norbert. Two Base Hit: Russell. Sacrifices: O'Neil, Ostrowski, Russell. Double Play: Miller to Russell to Otero. Time of Game: 1 hr. 44 min. Umpires: Engeln and Doran.

Portland	020	011	000	4 – 9 – 3
Los Angeles	202	000	10x	5 – 7 – 2

The two teams took Saturday off while 60,000 fans saw UCLA tie USC in an exciting finish at the Coliseum. USC was to go undefeated and win the Rose Bowl that season. But college football was not the only competition the playoffs faced in 1944. A new American Professional Football League began playing in early September with eight teams from Seattle to San Diego, including three in the L.A. area. This new league was drawing competing crowds during the last three Sundays of the season. The teams in the Los Angeles area used Gilmore Stadium.

Game Four.

On Sunday, September 24, 13,166 fans went to Wrigley Field to see the Angels take a 3–2 lead in the series by winning a doubleheader over Portland, while only 4,000 went to Gilmore Field to see the professional football game. Being the home team was of no benefit to the Beavers. The Angels blasted Ad

Liska and two relievers for 14 runs on 20 hits in the opener, as L.A. coasted to a 14–3 win. Claude Horton started for the Angels but had to leave in the first after being hit on the shin by a line drive. Pancho Comellas came in and pitched 8⅓ innings after pitching 3⅔ innings on Friday night. Ted Norbert hit two homers and drove in five runs, Garriott homered and drove in two, and Russell doubled and singled, also driving in a pair of runs. Even Comellas drove in three runs with two singles. Catcher Eddie Fernandes returned to action after being hit on the arm on Thursday night.

Los Angeles	AB	H	RBI	O	A	E
Garriott CF	5	2	2	3	0	0
Russell 2B	4	2	0	0	3	0
Ostrowski 3B	6	0	0	0	2	0
Norbert LF	4	4	5	1	0	0
Sauer RF	6	1	0	2	0	0
Otero 1B	5	4	1	12	0	0
York SS	5	3	0	3	5	0
Sarni C	1	0	0	5	0	0
Horton P	0	0	0	0	0	0
Comellas P	5	2	3	0	2	0
Moore[a]	1	1	1	0	0	0
Fernandes C	3	1	0	1	1	0
	45	20	12	27	13	0

(a) Batted for Sarni in the fifth.

Portland	AB	H	RBI	O	A	E
Shone CF	3	0	0	1	0	0
O'Neil SS	3	2	0	0	3	0
Harris LF	3	0	0	1	0	0
Gill RF	4	1	0	0	0	0
Barton 1B	3	1	0	7	0	0
Owen 3B	2	1	0	2	3	0
E. Adams C	2	0	0	4	0	1
Nunes 2B	4	2	2	5	2	0
Liska P	1	0	0	0	1	0
Demaree[a]	1	0	0	0	0	0
Federmeyer P	0	0	0	0	0	0
Windsor P	1	0	0	0	0	0
Gullic[b]	1	0	0	0	0	0
DeWeese CF	2	0	0	2	0	0
Daniels 3B	2	0	0	2	0	0

Portland	AB	H	RBI	O	A	E
Eddington SS-3B	2	1	0	1	0	0
Cook C	2	1	1	2	0	0
	36	9	3	27	9	1

(a) *Batted for Demaree in the fourth.*
(b) *Batted for Windsor in the ninth.*

Pitching Records	IP	H	R	ER	SO	BB
Horton	0.1	1	0	0	1	0
Comellas (W)	8.2	8	3	3	4	2
Liska (L)	4	7	5	5	3	1
Federmeyer	0.1	4	4	6	0	3
Windsor	4.2	9	5	3	2	1

Hit by Pitcher: Norbert by Liska. Home Runs: Garriott, Norbert 2. Two Base Hits: Russell, Nunes, O'Neil, Eddington. Left on Base: Los Angeles 8, Portland 12. Sacrifices: Sarni, Otero. Stolen Base: Garriott. Time of Game: 2 hr. 10 min. Umpires: Doran and Engeln.

Los Angeles	121	160	201	14	– 20 –	0
Portland	000	200	010	3	– 9 –	1

Game Five.

The seven inning nightcap was just as one-sided. Ray Prim beat Sid Cohen 11–1 as Rip Russell drove in five runs with a homer and two singles. The Angels got five doubles, including two by Johnny Ostrowski, while Portland made three errors that led to four unearned runs for the Angels, who were now just a game away from going to the final round.

Los Angeles	AB	H	RBI	O	A	E
Garriott CF	4	1	0	2	0	0
Russell 2B	5	3	5	5	2	1
Ostrowski 3B	5	2	1	1	4	0
Norbert LF	4	2	0	1	0	0
Sauer RF	5	2	0	1	0	0
Otero 1B	4	1	2	5	0	0
York SS	4	2	1	1	3	0
Fernandes C	2	0	0	5	0	0
Prim P	3	1	0	0	1	0
	36	14	9	21	10	1

Portland	AB	H	RBI	O	A	E
Shone CF	3	1	0	0	0	0
O'Neil SS	3	1	0	3	3	1
Gullic CF	2	0	0	3	0	0
DeWeese LF	3	0	1	1	0	1
Owen 3B	3	0	0	2	1	1
E. Adams C	3	0	0	4	0	0
Barton 1B	3	1	0	7	1	0
Nunes 2B	2	0	0	1	1	0
Cohen P	2	0	0	0	2	0
Pulford P	0	0	0	0	0	0
	24	3	1	21	8	3

Pitching Records	IP	H	R	ER	SO	BB
Prim	7	3	1	1	4	0
Cohen (L)	5.1	11	7	7	3	4
Pulford	1.2	3	4	0	1	0

Wild Pitch: Pulford. Left on Base: Los Angeles 9, Portland 3. Home Run: Russell. Two Base Hits: York, Sauer, Ostrowski 2, Norbert. Sacrifices: Gullic, Prim. Double Play: Ostrowski to Russell to Otero. Time of Game: 1 hr. 45 min. Umpires: Engeln and Doran.

Los Angeles	021	103	4	11	–	14	– 1
Portland	100	000	0	1	–	3	– 3

Game Six.

On Monday night, September 25, a crowd of 5,303 watched the Angels edge Portland 3–2, to eliminate the Beavers from the playoffs. Red Adams and Marino Pieretti each went the route while giving up 10 hits. The Angels went up 2–0 in the second when Eddie Sauer, Reggie Otero and Tony York got successive singles, before the 16-year-old catcher, Bill Sarni, grounded out. The Beavers got one of those back in the third when O'Neil doubled and Spencer Harris singled. They tied it in the last of the seventh when pitcher Marino Pieretti, who was allowed to bat with Frank Demaree on the bench, came through with a single and then stole second base. He then scored the tying run on Frank Shone's single. In the top of the ninth, Johnny Moore pinch hit for Bill Sarni, who had gotten two hits. Moore singled and Stan Gray ran for him. Red Adams sacrificed Gray to second, and Cecil Garriott singled him home. This was Garriott's last game before going into the army. He was originally supposed to report after Sunday's game but was given permission to

finish this opening round of the playoffs. For the Beavers, catcher Eddie Adams
went 4-for-4 in a losing cause.

Los Angeles	AB	H	RBI	O	E
Garriott CF	5	1	1	2	0
Russell 2B	4	2	0	3	0
Ostrowski 3B	4	1	0	1	0
Norbert LF	2	0	0	1	0
Sauer RF	4	1	0	0	0
Otero 1B	3	1	0	6	0
York SS	4	1	1	6	0
Sarni C	3	2	1	6	0
C. Adams P	2	0	0	1	0
Moore[a]	1	1	0	0	0
Gray[b]	0	0	0	0	0
Grigg C	0	0	0	1	0
	32	10	3	27	0

(a) Batted for Sarni in the ninth.
(b) Ran for Moore in the ninth.

Portland	AB	H	RBI	O	E
Shone CF	4	1	1	3	1
O'Neil SS	4	1	0	3	0
Harris LF	4	2	1	2	0
Gill RF	2	0	0	1	0
Barton 1B	4	0	0	10	0
Owen 3B	4	0	0	1	0
E. Adams C	4	4	0	2	0
Nunes 2B	2	1	0	5	0
Pieretti P	4	1	0	0	0
DeWeese[a]	0	0	0	0	0
Gullic[b]	1	0	0	0	0
	33	10	2	27	1

(a) Ran for E. Adams in the ninth.
(b) Batted for Nunes in the ninth.

Pitching Records	IP	H	R	ER	SO	BB
C. Adams	9	10	2	2	5	2
Pieretti	9	10	3	3	2	2

Left on Base: Los Angeles 7, Portland 7. Two Base Hits: O'Neil, Russell. Sacrifices: Nunes, C. Adams 2, Norbert. Stolen Bases: E. Adams, Sauer, Pieretti. Double Plays: Otero to York; O'Neil to Nunes to Barton; Russell to York to Otero. Umpires: Doran and Engeln.

Los Angeles	020	000	001	3 – 10 – 0	
Portland	001	000	100	2 – 10 – 1	

The Beavers split $1,250 but the number of shares was not published. If there had been about 25 full shares, each $50 share would come to about $284 in current dollars. The players earned more by getting an extra week's pay.

The San Francisco–Oakland Series

This turned out to be a bitterly contested series between the cross-bay rivals. Oakland finished with a rush to tie the Seals for third place, edging Seattle by two games and Hollywood by three games. During the season, the Seals won 16 and lost 14 to Oakland. It was decided that the first three games would be played at Oaks Park and the rest at Seals Stadium. If one team did not sweep the first three games, they planned to play a Saturday night game at Seals Stadium, but otherwise, they would wait until Sunday to play the fourth game, because the teams drew very well on Sundays. Instead of both team's announcers doing the games on radio, the Seals announcer called all the games.

Plans sometimes do not work out. The series opened in Oakland on Wednesday, September 20, and 6,000 fans were treated to an exciting 13-inning game. The Seals got two runs in the top of the 13th only to have the Oaks come back and score three to win the game. Or so the Oaks thought! Lefty O'Doul protested the game and president "Pants" Rowland upheld the protest, ordering the game to be replayed Saturday night in Oakland, much to the extreme disappointment and bitterness of Oakland players and fans.

The Protested Game.

Oakland's mid-season pickup, Damon Hayes, faced Bob Joyce and both pitchers went the distance, with Hayes giving up 20 hits, five walks and one hit batsman, while Joyce yielded 13 hits, and five walks. Oakland scored a run in each of the first three innings but the Seals came back with two runs in the fourth and tied it in the seventh on Neil Sheridan's solo homer. The 3–3 tie was not broken until the top of the 13th when Sheridan and Gus Suhr singled,

Ben Guintini sacrificed them along, and Del Young was passed to load the bases. John Trutta, who had replaced John Cavalli at third in the 11th, came through with a ground-rule double to put the Seals up 5–3, but the Seals could score no more. In the last of the 13th, successive singles by Chet Rosenlund, Charlie English, and Les Scarsella scored one run, and put runners at the corners with one out. Dolph Camilli almost grounded into a double play but Gus Suhr dropped the throw, as the tying run scored. John Kreevich singled Camilli to third, and Jake Caufield was walked to load the bases. Billy Raimondi's long fly scored Camilli with the run that the Oaks thought won the game.

But in the top of the second, Bob Joyce hit a grounder that hit first baseman Gus Suhr's mitt that was lying in foul ground. The ball ricocheted off the mitt into fair ground and Scarsella picked it up and stepped on first to retire Joyce. Manager O'Doul argued the ball should have been foul, and umpire Powell was uncertain, but allowed it to be fair. That successful protest led to the game being replayed Saturday night in Oakland. The Oakland players were so angry that they threatened to go on strike before the next game unless the gate receipts were given to charity, or made available to the players. However, nothing came of this protest.

San Francisco	AB	R	H	RBI	O	A	E
Uhalt CF	7	0	3	1	3	0	0
Futernick SS	6	0	1	0	2	5	0
Sheridan RF	7	2	4	1	3	0	0
Suhr 1B	6	1	2	0	23	1	1
Guintini LF	5	1	3	0	2	0	0
Young 2B	5	1	2	1	1	11	0
Cavalli 3B	4	0	1	0	0	2	0
Ripple[a]	1	0	0	0	0	0	0
Trutta 3B	1	0	1	2	1	0	0
Sprinz C	6	0	1	0	2	1	0
Joyce P	7	0	2	0	1	2	0
	55	5	20	5	38[b]	22	1

(a) Batted for Cavalli in the 11th.
(b) Two outs when winning run scored.

Oakland	AB	R	H	RBI	O	A	E
Mailho LF	5	2	2	0	2	0	1
Rosenlund 3B	6	1	2	0	0	0	0
English 2B	6	1	1	1	4	4	0
Scarsella 1B	6	0	2	2	11	1	0
Camilli RF	6	2	3	0	2	0	0
Kreevich CF	5	0	1	1	7	0	0

Oakland	AB	R	H	RBI	O	A	E
Caulfield SS	5	0	0	0	4	7	0
Raimondi C	6	0	2	2	7	3	0
Hayes P	5	0	0	0	2	2	0
	50	6	13	6	39	17	1

Pitching Records	IP	H	R	ER	SO	BB
Joyce	12.2	13	6	5	1	2
Hayes	13	20	5	5	6	5

Wild Pitch: Joyce. Hit by Pitcher: Guintini by Hayes. Left on Base: San Francisco 19, Oakland 9. Two Base Hits: Mailho, Guintini, Camilli, Cavalli, Trutta. Home Run: Sheridan. Stolen Bases: Mailho 2. Sacrifices: Kreevich, Sprinz, Sheridan. Double Play: English to Caulfield to Scarsella. Time of Game: 2 hr. 50 min. Umpires: Powell and Edwards.

San Francisco	000	200	100	000	2	5 – 20 – 1
Oakland	111	000	000	000	3	6 – 13 – 1

These pitchers were not recorded with either a win or a loss because of the protest.

Game One.

On Thursday night, September 21, Manny Salvo of the Oaks beat Tom Seats of the Seals 5–1, before 9,000 belligerent fans. Verbal abuse was heaped upon O'Doul and many of the Seal players by the irate Oakland fans. The Oaks scored a run in the first when Emil Mailho singled and scored on hits by Charley English and John Kreevich. The Oaks increased this lead to 3–0 with runs in the sixth and seventh off Seats before the Seals scored a run in the eighth with Joe Futernick driving in Henry Steinbacher. But with Bill Werle on the mound in the bottom of the eighth, Oakland put the game away with two runs on Scarsella's single, a sacrifice, a double by Jack Devincenzi, and a single by Jake Caufield.

San Francisco	AB	R	H	RBI	O	A	E
Uhalt CF	4	0	1	0	3	0	0
Futernick SS	4	0	2	1	0	1	1
Sheridan RF	4	0	1	0	2	0	0
Suhr 1B	4	0	1	0	7	1	0
Guintini lF	4	0	1	0	2	1	1
Young 2B	4	0	0	0	4	2	0

San Francisco	AB	R	H	RBI	O	A	E
Cavalli 3B	4	0	1	0	2	2	0
Ogrodowski C	3	0	0	0	4	0	0
Seats P	2	0	0	0	0	2	0
Steinbacher[a]	1	1	0	0	0	0	0
Werle P	0	0	0	0	0	0	0
	34	1	7	1	24	9	2

(a) Batted for Seats in the eighth.

Oakland	AB	R	H	RBI	O	A	E
Mailho LF	4	1	1	0	4	1	1
Rosenlund 3B	3	0	1	1	2	4	0
English 2B	4	0	2	0	3	4	0
Scarsella 1B	4	2	2	0	10	0	0
Kreevich CF	3	0	2	2	2	0	1
Devincenzi RF	4	1	1	1	1	0	0
Caulfield SS	4	0	1	0	2	1	0
Raimondi C	4	1	1	0	3	0	0
Salvo P	3	0	1	0	0	2	0
	33	5	12	4	27	12	2

Pitching Records	IP	H	R	ER	SO	BB
Seats (L)	7	9	3	3	4	1
Werle	1	3	2	1	0	0
Salvo	9	7	1	0	3	0

Left on Base: San Francisco 6, Oakland 8. Two Base Hit: Devincenzi. Sacrifices: Rosenlund, Salvo, Kreevich. Umpires: Edwards and Powell.

San Francisco	000	000	010	1 – 7 – 2
Oakland	100	001	12x	5 – 12 – 2

Game Two.

On Friday night, the 22nd, the Seals evened the series at a game apiece with a 1–0 win before 9,100 fans, some of whom misbehaved. Ben Guintini of the Seals was hit with a bottle, causing no injury but a great deal of anger. An umpire's decision hurt the Oaks in the third when Joe Futernick singled, stole second, and when Billy Raimondi's throw went into center field, the Seal shortstop raced to third. The throw by Kreevich to Chet Roselund may have had him but umpire Edwards was out of position. Only two umpires were used in each game of the first round of the playoffs, unlike four before the war. This call further angered the crowd when Gus Suhr singled in the only run of the game. "Cowboy" Ray Harrell pitched a five-hit shutout for the Seals, while Jack Lotz lost a heartbreaker.

San Francisco	AB	R	H	RBI	O	A	E
Uhalt CF	4	0	0	0	3	0	0
Futernick SS	3	1	1	0	2	1	0
Sheridan RF	4	0	0	0	3	0	0
Suhr 1B	3	0	1	1	6	1	0
Guintini LF	4	0	0	0	4	0	0
Young 2B	4	0	4	0	3	1	0
Cavalli 3B	3	0	0	0	3	1	0
Ogrodowski C	4	0	2	0	3	2	0
Harrell P	3	0	0	0	0	1	0
	32	1	8	1	27	7	0

Oakland	AB	R	H	RBI	O	A	E
Mailho LF	4	0	1	0	4	0	0
Rosenlund 3B	4	0	1	0	1	4	0
English 2B	4	0	1	0	4	0	0
Scarsella 1B	3	0	1	0	10	2	0
Camilli RF	3	0	0	0	2	0	0
Kreevich CF	3	0	0	0	1	0	0
Caulfield SS	3	0	1	0	3	3	1
Raimondi C	3	0	0	0	1	2	1
Lotz P	2	0	0	0	1	2	0
Storti[a]	1	0	0	0	0	0	0
	30	0	5	0	27	13	2

(a) Batted for Lotz in the ninth.

Pitching Records	IP	H	R	ER	SO	BB
Harrell	9	5	0	0	1	0
Lotz	9	8	1	1	2	4

Left on Base: San Francisco 10, Oakland 3. Two Base Hit: Rosenlund. Sacrifices: Futernick, Cavalli. Double Play: Rosenlund to Scarsella. Time of Game: 1 hr. 55 min. Umpires: Powell and Edwards.

San Francisco	001	000	000	1 – 8 – 0
Oakland	000	000	000	0 – 5 – 2

Game Three.

On Saturday night, September 23, these teams were making up the protested game in Oaks Park, rather than having this game in Seals Stadium as originally planned. A crowd of 7,500 turned out to see the final game in Oaks Park in 1944 as the Seals pounded the Oaks 9–3. That afternoon in Berkeley, a crowd of 30,000 saw the California Bears beat St. Mary's 31–7, which was why this game was played at night. Bob Joyce went all the way while Floyd Stromme was belted out in the fourth, followed by Kenny Gables and Elmer Phillips. A 2–0 Oakland lead was wiped out by an eight-run Seal outburst in the fourth, mostly after two were out. Johnny Cavalli homered to cut the lead to 2–1, Joe Sprinz popped up, Joyce walked, and Uhalt singled him to third, but Frenchy was nailed when he rounded first base too far. So with two outs and a man on third, the Seals went to town. Futernick singled in Joyce, Sheridan walked, Suhr singled, but when the ball skipped past Kreevich in center field, Sheridan scored and Suhr went to third. Ben Guintini doubled in Suhr, bringing in Kenny Gables to relieve Stromme. Del Young singled in Guintini and Cavalli, up for the second time in the inning, singled. Sprinz tripled in Young and Cavalli before Joyce mercifully made the third out. The Seals were now up 2–1 in the series.

San Francisco	AB	R	H	RBI	O	A	E
Uhalt CF	4	0	2	0	8	1	0
Futernick SS	5	2	2	1	0	1	0
Sheridan RF	5	1	3	1	2	0	0
Suhr 1B	3	1	1	1	10	0	0
Guintini LF	5	1	2	1	1	0	0
Young 2B	5	1	1	1	2	5	0
Cavalli 3B	5	2	3	1	1	2	0
Sprinz C	5	0	3	2	3	0	0
Joyce P	4	1	1	0	0	2	0
	41	9	18	8	27	11	0
Oakland	**AB**	**R**	**H**	**RBI**	**O**	**A**	**E**
Mailho LF	3	0	0	0	2	0	0
Storti 3B	4	0	0	0	1	2	0
English 2B	4	1	2	0	0	4	0
Scarsella 1B	3	1	1	0	11	1	0
Camilli RF	3	1	1	1	0	0	0
Kreevich CF	4	0	0	1	1	2	0
Caulfield SS	4	0	3	0	6	2	0
Raimondi C	2	0	0	0	5	1	0

Oakland	AB	R	H	RBI	O	A	E
Stromme P	1	0	0	0	1	0	0
Gables P	1	0	0	0	0	0	0
Phillips P	1	0	0	0	0	2	0
Campbell C	2	0	0	0	0	1	0
Devincenzi RF	1	0	0	0	0	0	0
Hayes[a]	1	0	0	0	0	0	0
	34	3	7	2	27	15	0

(a) Batted for Phillips in the ninth.

Pitching Records	IP	H	R	ER	SO	BB
Joyce	9	7	3	3	3	3
Stromme (L)	3.2	8	5	6	4	4
Gables	0.2	4	4	3	1	2
Phillips	4.2	6	0	0	0	1

Left on Base: San Francisco 12, Oakland 7. Home Run: Cavalli. Three Base Hits: Camilli, Sprinz. Two Base Hits: English, Guintini, Sprinz. Stolen Bases: Uhalt, Futernick. Double Plays: English to Caulfield to Scarsella; Kreevich to Scarsella. Time of Game: 2 hr. 5 min. Umpires: Edwards and Powell.

San Francisco	000	810	000	9 – 18 – 0
Oakland	002	010	000	3 – 7 – 0

Game Four.

The teams moved across the bay to Seals Stadium for a Sunday double-header on September 24, that attracted 15,200 fans, outdrawing the 15,000 that saw two service teams play football at Kezar Stadium that day. In the opener, Tommy Seats again faced Manny Salvo but this time the results were different. While both pitchers were hit hard, they each pitched the entire game. The Seals broke the ice with a run in the first on Sheridan's double and Suhr's single. They increased this lead to 4–0 in the second, but again a major umpiring decision went against Oakland. Bruisie Ogrodowski singled and scored on Tommy Seats' double. Two outs later, Seats ran home on Sheridan's swinging bunt, but the Oaks claimed that Salvo's throw to Raimondi was in time. Sheridan then stole second and scored on Suhr's double.

Oakland went ahead 5–4 with a big five run fifth inning. Devincenzi doubled, Raimondi, Salvo and English singled, and errors were committed by Young, Guintini and Futernick. But this lead did not last. In the bottom of the fifth, Suhr walked, and Guintini and Young singled to fill the bases. Ogrodowski's fly scored the tying run. Then Tommy Seats stepped up to the plate

Seals Stadium was the scene of four straight Seals' playoff triumphs, from 1943 to 1946.

and bashed a three-run homer, putting the Seals up 8-5. Seats drove in four runs with a double and a homer. The Oaks cut the lead to 8–7 in the seventh, but the Seals added an insurance run in the eighth, to win 9–7 and take a commanding three games to one lead in the series.

Oakland	AB	R	H	RBI	O	A	E
Mailho LF	4	1	2	0	4	0	0
Rosenlund 3B	4	2	0	1	1	1	0
English 2B	5	1	3	2	1	3	0
Scarsella 1B	5	0	1	1	8	0	0
Kreevich CF	5	0	0	1	4	0	0
Devincenzi RF	4	1	2	0	2	0	0
Caulfield 3B	4	0	0	0	0	3	1
Raimondi C	4	1	1	0	4	0	0
Salvo P	4	1	2	0	0	1	0
	39	7	11	5	24	8	1
San Francisco	AB	R	H	RBI	O	A	E
Uhalt CF	5	0	1	0	2	0	0
Futernick SS	4	0	0	0	3	3	1

San Francisco	AB	R	H	RBI	O	A	E
Sheridan RF	5	2	3	2	1	0	0
Suhr 1B	4	1	2	2	8	1	0
Guintini LF	3	1	2	0	6	0	1
Young 2B	3	1	1	0	2	3	1
Cavalli 3B	4	0	0	0	1	2	0
Ogrodowski C	4	2	2	1	4	0	0
Seats P	4	2	2	4	0	4	0
	36	9	13	9	27	13	3

Pitching Records	IP	H	R	ER	SO	BB
Salvo	8	13	9	9	2	3
Seats	9	11	7	3	3	2

Left on Base: Oakland 7, San Francisco 6. Two Base Hits: Suhr, Devincenzi, Sheridan, Guintini, Seats. Home Run: Seats. Stolen Base: Sheridan. Sacrifice: Rosenlund. Double Play: Raimondi to English to Scarsella. Time of Game: 2 hr. 5 min. Umpires: Powell and Edwards.

Oakland	000	050	200	7 – 11 – 1
San Francisco	130	040	01x	9 – 13 – 3

Game Five.

Ray Harrell pitched his second shutout of the series as the Seals beat the victimized Damon Hayes 2–0 to win the series four games to one. Hayes deserved better. In the third inning, Joe Sprinz singled and was sacrificed to second. Frenchie Uhalt then hit a grounder to Scarsella, who threw wildly past Hayes trying to cover first, allowing Sprinz to score. In the sixth, the Seals got another tainted run when Sheridan and Suhr walked, and moved up on a balk, as Hayes dropped the ball while on the mound. The upset Hayes then wild pitched the run in from third. Lefty O'Doul said he was never so glad to win a series as this one because of the viciousness of the Oakland fans after the protest was upheld. The Oakland players split the same amount as the Portland Beavers, $1,250.

Oakland	AB	R	H	RBI	O	A	E
Mailho LF	3	0	1	0	0	0	0
Rosenlund 3B	3	0	0	0	0	0	0
English 2B	3	0	2	0	1	2	0
Scarsella 1B	2	0	0	0	9	2	1
Kreevich CF	2	0	0	0	2	0	0

Oakland	AB	R	H	RBI	O	A	E
Devincenzi RF	3	0	1	0	0	0	0
Caulfield SS	3	0	0	0	3	3	0
Raimondi C	3	0	1	0	3	1	0
Hayes P	3	0	0	0	0	2	0
	25	0	5	0	18	10	1

San Francisco	AB	R	H	RBI	O	A	E
Uhalt CF	3	0	1	0	0	0	0
Futernick SS	3	0	0	0	1	5	0
Sheridan RF	2	1	1	0	3	0	0
Suhr 1B	1	0	0	0	9	0	0
Guintini LF	2	0	0	0	4	0	0
Young 2B	2	0	0	0	0	1	0
Cavalli 3B	2	0	1	0	1	2	0
Sprinz C	2	1	1	0	3	1	0
Harrell P	1	0	0	0	0	0	0
	18	2	4	0	21	9	0

Pitching Records	IP	H	R	ER	SO	BB
Hayes	6	4	2	0	2	5
Harrell	7	5	0	0	2	2

Hit by Pitcher: Guintini by Hayes. Wild Pitch: Hayes. Balk: Hayes. Left on Base: Oakland 6, San Francisco 6. Sacrifice: Harrell. Stolen Base: Mailho. Time of Game: 1 hr. 15 min. Umpires; Edwards and Powell.

Oakland	000	000	0	0 – 5 – 1
San Francisco	001	001	x	2 – 4 – 0

The Final Series: San Francisco vs. Los Angeles

The Angels gave up the right to open this series at home so they could play a Sunday doubleheader at Wrigley Field. During the season, the Seals beat the Angels 14 times while losing 8. The Angels left on the night train on Tuesday, September 26, without Cecil Garriott, their MVP, who had to go into the army, but they did take pitcher Claude Horton along, even though Horton could only relieve in the first game before reporting for military service. The loss of Garriott forced the Angels to move Johnny Ostrowski to center field and to play Stan Gray at third, because they had sold Charley English to Oakland in August.

Because the Angels lost Garriott, they would not let the Seals use Neil Sheridan in this series. Sheridan had joined the Seals after the August 1 deadline, but Oakland allowed San Francisco to use him because they wanted to use English. The Seals then tried to prevent the Angels from using shortstop Tony York, whom the Cubs had sent down to L.A., because he did not sign his contract until after August 1, but the Angels were allowed to use him because the deal was made before that date.

Game One.

On a very chilly Wednesday night, September 27, Bob Joyce shut the Angles out, 4–0, before 4,000 shivering fans. The four umpires assigned to the playoffs were all used in this series, after being split into two-man teams for the opening round. Henry Steinbacher, who replaced Sheridan in the outfield, got two hits and scored two runs. Ben Guintini drove in two runs, yet he went hitless in four at-bats. With Garriott gone, Tony York was moved to the leadoff spot. Rip Russell went 3-for-4, including a double and a triple, in a losing cause. The Angels lost a run in the ninth when Stan Gray missed third base trying to score on Eddie Fernandes' double. Claude Horton relieved starter Don Osborn and pitched two hitless innings in his farewell before reporting to Uncle Sam.

Los Angeles	AB	H	RBI	O	E
York SS	4	0	0	2	0
Russell 2B	4	3	0	3	0
Ostrowski CF	4	1	0	3	0
Norbert LF	3	0	0	1	0
Sauer RF	4	1	0	0	0
Otero 1B	4	0	0	12	0
Gray 3B	4	1	0	0	0
Fernandes C	3	2	0	3	0
Osborn P	2	0	0	0	0
Moore [a]	1	0	0	0	0
Horton P	0	0	0	0	0
Willingham [b]	0	0	0	0	0
	33	8	0	24	0

(a) *Batted for Osborn in the seventh.*
(b) *Batted for Horton in the ninth.*

San Francisco	AB	H	RBI	O	E
Uhalt CF	3	1	1	4	0
Futernick SS	4	2	0	3	0
Steinbacher RF	4	2	0	1	0
Suhr 1B	2	1	0	10	0
Guintini LF	4	0	2	4	0
Young 2B	4	1	0	2	0
Cavalli 3B	4	2	0	2	0
Sprinz C	2	0	0	1	0
Joyce P	4	0	0	0	0
	31	9	3	27	0

Pitching Records	IP	H	R	ER	SO	BB
Osborn (L)	6	8	4	4	0	4
Horton	2	1	0	0	2	0
Joyce	9	8	0	0	1	2

Left on Base: Los Angeles 8, San Francisco 8. Two Base Hits: Suhr, Russell, Fernandes. Three Base Hit: Russell. Sacrifice: Sprinz. Stolen Base: Uhalt. Umpires: Doran, Powell, Engeln, Edwards.

Los Angeles	000	000	000	0 – 8 – 0
San Francisco	001	021	00x	4 – 9 – 0

Game Two.

The Seals shut the Angels out again 5–0 on Thursday night before 4,000 fans as Tommy Seats beat Ray Prim. The Seals got all the runs they needed when they scored two in the first on a double by Bill Enos and singles by Ben Guintini and Del Young. Seats continued his good hitting as he drove in a run with a double, and Enos later drove in another run with a triple.

Los Angeles	AB	R	H	RBI	O	A	E
York SS	4	0	2	0	2	2	0
Russell 2B	4	0	2	0	3	2	0
Ostrowski CF	4	0	2	0	1	0	0
Norbert LF	4	0	0	0	2	0	0
Sauer RF	4	0	0	0	0	0	0
Otero 1B	4	0	0	0	11	0	1
Gray 3B	4	0	0	0	1	1	0
Fernandes C	3	0	1	0	4	0	0
Prim P	3	0	0	0	0	4	1
	34	0	7	0	24	9	2

San Francisco	AB	R	H	RBI	O	A	E
Uhalt CF	4	1	1	0	3	0	0
Futernick SS	5	0	1	0	3	2	1
Enos RF	4	1	2	1	3	0	0
Suhr 1B	3	1	1	0	8	0	0
Guintini LF	4	1	2	1	4	0	0
Young 2B	3	0	1	1	2	3	0
Cavalli 3B	3	1	1	0	2	4	0
Ogordowski C	4	0	0	0	2	0	0
Seats P	4	0	1	0	0	0	0
	34	5	10	3	27	9	1

Pitching Records	IP	H	R	ER	SO	BB
Prim	8	10	5	3	3	3
Seals	9	7	0	0	1	0

Left on Base: Los Angeles 7, San Francisco 9. Two Base Hits: Enos, Seats. Three Base Hit: Enos. Stolen Base: Futernick. Sacrifice: Young. Double Plays: Russell to York to Otero; Cavalli to Suhr. Time of Game: 1 hr. 55 min. Umpires: Engeln, Doran, Powell, Edwards.

Los Angeles	000	000	000	0 –	7 –	2
San Francisco	200	000	12x	5 –	10 –	1

Game Three.

On Friday night, September 29, 6,000 fans saw the Seals go up three games to none in the last game played at Seals Stadium in 1944. "Cowboy" Ray Harrell beat Pancho Jorge Comellas 5–1. Comellas had pitched a seven-inning no-hitter in Seals Stadium earlier in the season but this was not his night. The Seals got to him for two runs in the first inning on a walk, a triple by Suhr and a single by Guintini. Del Young went 3-for-3 and also drove in a run. Johnny Ostrowski hit two triples, one of which drove in the Angels' only run in San Francisco in 27 innings of baseball. This was the first run allowed by the Seals in 33 innings.

Los Angeles	AB	H	RBI	O	E
York SS	4	0	0	4	0
Russell 2B	4	1	0	2	0
Ostrowski CF	4	2	0	3	1
Norbert LF	4	1	0	1	0
Sauer RF	4	0	0	0	0

Los Angeles	AB	H	RBI	O	E
Otero 1B	4	1	0	9	0
Gray 3B	3	1	1	1	0
Sarni C	3	0	0	3	0
Comellas P	2	0	0	1	0
Fernandes [a]	0	0	0	0	0
Phipps P	0	0	0	0	0
Moore [b]	1	0	0	0	0
	33	6	1	24	1

(a) Batted for Comellas in the seventh.
(b) Batted for Sarni in the ninth.

San Francisco	AB	H	RBI	O	E
Uhalt CF	3	0	0	4	0
Futernick SS	3	0	0	2	0
Steinbacher RF	4	0	1	0	0
Suhr 1B	3	1	1	9	0
Guintini LF	4	2	1	2	0
Young 2B	3	3	1	1	0
Cavalli 3B	2	1	1	1	0
Ogrodowski C	3	0	0	7	0
Harrell P	3	0	0	1	0
	28	7	5	27	0

Pitching Records	IP	H	R	ER	SO	BB
Comellas (L)	6	7	5	3	1	3
Phipps	2	0	0	0	1	0
Harrell	9	6	1	1	7	0

Passed Ball: Sarni. Left on Base: Los Angeles 7, San Francisco 3. Two Base Hit: Guintini. Three Base Hits: Suhr, Ostrowski 2. Sacrifice: Futernick. Double Plays: Russell to Otero to York; Comellas to York to Russell. Umpires: Edwards, Doran, Engeln, Powell.

Los Angeles	000	001	000	1 – 8 – 1
San Francisco	200	111	00x	5 – 7 – 0

The two teams rode the day train south to L.A. on Saturday, September 30, arriving that evening. The series resumed at Wrigley Field on Sunday, October 1, with a doubleheader. The Angels announced that two games would be played even if the Seals won the opener, just as was done in 1943 when Seattle swept the Angels.

Game Four.

A crowd of 12,092 turned out at Wrigley Field on the first day of October with the hope that the Angels could stay alive in this series. The opening game began as if the Scals were going to pull a sweep, as they built up a 3–0 lead off Red Adams in two innings. Gus Suhr drove in a run in the first , and in the second, Frenchy Uhalt and Joe Futernick each drove in a run. Adams was lifted for a hitter in the second, bringing in Pancho Comellas, who gave up a solo homer to Ben Guintini in the sixth. The Angels got their first run off Bob Joyce in the fifth when the young Bill Sarni, who replaced Eddie Fernandes behind the plate, doubled and scored on Tony York's single. In the sixth, L.A. cut the lead to 4–3 when Eddie Sauer doubled, then Reggie Otero, Stan Gray, and pinch hitter John Moore all singled. Jodie Phipps came in and held the Seals scoreless in the seventh and eighth innings. In the last of the eighth, the Angels finally got even when Reggie Otero, who went 4-for-4, singled and eventually came around to score on a fielder's choice. Ray Prim pitched a scoreless ninth, and got the win when Johnny Ostrowski homered off Bob Joyce in the last half.

San Francisco	AB	H	RBI	O	E
Uhalt CF	4	2	1	2	0
Futernick SS	3	1	1	3	0
Steinbacher RF	4	0	0	3	0
Suhr 1B	4	1	0	8	0
Guintini LF	4	1	1	1	0
Young 2B	4	1	0	3	0
Cavalli 3B	4	1	0	1	0
Sprinz C	3	0	0	4	0
Joyce P	3	0	0	0	0
	33	7	3	25[a]	0

(a) One out when winning run scored.

Los Angeles	AB	H	RBI	O	E
York SS	5	1	1	0	0
Russell 2B	5	1	0	3	0
Ostrowski CF	5	3	1	5	0
Norbert LF	4	1	0	3	0
Sauer RF	4	1	0	0	0
Otero 1B	4	4	0	10	1
Gray 3B	3	2	1	1	0
Fernandes C	0	0	0	0	0

Los Angeles	AB	H	RBI	O	E
Adams P	0	0	0	0	0
Sarni C	4	2	0	4	0
Willingham[a]	1	0	0	0	0
Comellas P	1	0	0	0	0
Moore[b]	1	1	1	0	0
Miller[c]	0	0	0	0	0
Phipps P	0	0	0	1	0
Grigg[d]	1	0	1	0	0
Prim P	0	0	0	0	0
	38	16	5	27	1

(a) Batted for Adams in the second.
(b) Batted for Comellas in the sixth.
(c) Ran for Moore in the sixth.
(d) Batted for Phipps in the eighth.

Pitching Records	IP	H	R	ER	SO	BB
Joyce	8.1	16	5	5	4	2
Adams	2	5	3	3	0	1
Comellas	4	2	1	1	0	1
Phipps	2	0	0	0	3	0
Prim (W)	1	0	0	0	1	0

Left on Base: San Francisco 5, Los Angeles 9. Two Base Hits: Suhr, Norbert, Sarni, Cavalli, Sauer. Home Runs: Guintini, Ostrowski. Sacrifices: Futernick, Gray. Double Plays: Futernick to Suhr; Sarni to Russell. Umpires: Doran, Engeln, Edwards, Powell.

San Francisco	120	001	000	4 –	7 –	0
Los Angeles	000	012	011	5 –	16 –	1

Game Five.

Don Osborn, pitching much better than he did on Wednesday night in Seals Stadium, held the Seals to one run and four hits as the Angels edged Tommy Seats, 2–1, to cut their series deficit from three games to two. The only run Osborn gave up came in the first when Uhalt singled, stole second, went to third on a grounder and scored on Steinbacher's fly ball. The Angels tied it in the third on Russell's single and Ostrowski's double. L.A. got the deciding run in the fifth when Sarni singled, moved up on Osborn's sacrifice, and scored on Russell's double.

San Francisco	AB	H	RBI	O	E
Uhalt CF	2	1	0	3	0
Futernick SS	3	0	0	2	0
Steinbacher RF	3	0	1	0	0
Suhr 1B	3	1	0	6	0
Guintini LF	3	2	0	2	0
Young 2B	2	0	0	1	0
Cavalli 3B	3	0	0	0	0
Ogrodowski C	3	0	0	4	0
Seats P	2	0	0	0	1
Enos [a]	1	0	0	0	0
	25	4	1	18	1

(a) Batted for Seats in the seventh.

Los Angeles	AB	H	RBI	O	E
York SS	3	0	0	1	0
Russell 2B	3	2	1	2	0
Ostrowski CF	3	2	1	4	0
Norbert LF	3	1	0	2	0
Sauer RF	3	1	0	0	0
Otero 1B	3	0	0	8	0
Gray 3B	3	0	0	0	0
Sarni C	2	1	0	3	1
Osborn P	2	0	0	1	0
	25	7	2	21	1

Pitching Records	IP	H	R	ER	SO	BB
Seats	6	7	2	2	3	1
Osborn	7	4	1	1	2	2

Left on Base: San Francisco 5, Los Angeles 6. Two Base Hits; Guintini, Ostrowski 2, Sauer, Russell. Sacrifice: Osborn. Stolen bases: Uhalt 2, Gray. Umpires: Doran, Powell, Edwards, Engeln.

San Francisco	100	000	0	1 – 4 – 1
Los Angeles	001	010	x	2 – 7 – 1

Game Six.

On Monday night, October 2, a crowd of 8,250 saw the Angels tie the series with their third straight win over the Seals, 2–1 in 10 innings. Ray Prim, who got the win in the opener the previous day, pitched ten strong innings to beat Bill Werle, who left immediately after the game for his induction into the army. During the season, Prim was only 1–5 against the Seals, but he pitched nine shutout innings against them after giving up a first inning run. Uhalt again got things going for the Seals with a leadoff double and was driven home by Gus Suhr. The rest of the night belonged to Prim. L.A. tied the game in the fifth when Russell singled and Ostrowski tripled, and then in the 10th, Prim singled, Guy Miller singled, and Ostrowski singled in Prim with the winning run.

San Francisco	AB	H	RBI	O	E
Uhalt CF	5	3	0	4	0
Futernick SS	5	2	0	2	0
Enos RF	5	0	0	1	1
Suhr 1B	5	1	1	10	0
Guintini LF	5	2	0	2	0
Young 2B	4	1	0	1	0
Cavalli 3B	4	0	0	0	0
Ogrodowski C	3	1	0	4	0
Sprinz C	1	0	0	5	0
Werle P	4	0	0	0	0
	41	10	1	29[a]	1

(a) Two outs when wining run scored.

Los Angeles	AB	H	RBI	O	E
Miller SS	5	1	0	1	0
Russell 2B	5	1	0	4	0
Ostrowski CF	5	3	2	3	0
Norbert LF	3	0	0	2	0
Sauer RF	4	1	0	3	0
Otero 1B	4	1	0	8	0
Gray 3B	3	1	0	0	2
Sarni C	4	0	0	9	0
Prim P	4	1	0	0	0
	37	9	2	30	2

Pitching Records	IP	H	R	ER	SO	BB
Werle	9.2	9	2	2	9	2
Prim	10	10	1	1	9	0

Left on Base: San Francisco 10, Los Angeles 8. Two Base Hits: Uhalt, Guintini. Three Base Hit: Ostrowski. Umpires: Powell, Edwards, Doran, Engeln.

| San Francisco | 100 | 000 | 000 | 0 | 1 – 10 – 1 |
| Los Angeles | 000 | 010 | 000 | 1 | 2 – 9 – 2 |

Game Seven.

On October 3, a crowd of 13,385, (large by Tuesday night's standards) went to Wrigley Field hoping to see the Angels pull a miracle comeback in this series, but L.A. was done in by one of the weirdest plays that sportswriters in both Los Angeles and San Francisco had seen in their entire careers. Home runs by Russell and Ostrowski had given the Angels a 2–1 lead after three innings, with Ray Harrell pitching against Pancho Comellas. But in the fifth, Steinbacher and Suhr opened with singles. Ben Guintini, attempting to sacrifice, laid down a poor bunt which Comellas fielded and threw to third, where he assumed he had an easy force on Steinbacher. But third baseman Stan Gray started in for the bunt and then tried to go back to cover third. But Gray's feet got tangled up and he fell on this back with his feet up in the air and his arms waving as Comellas' throw whizzed past him down into the left field corner. Writers concentrated on the helpless Gray but it was Ted Norbert, in left field, who was slow retrieving the ball, which allowed even the batter Guintini to circle the bases for a 4–2 Seal lead. San Francisco writers likened this play to Ernie Lombardi's famous snooze in the 1939 World Series, but once the ball got past Gray, his immobility was immaterial. It was up to Norbert to get the ball back in. Oakland writers chided the Angels for getting rid of Charley English, whom they felt, would have made that play, but English had angered Bill Sweeney by taking his car on a road trip to San Francisco. But it was the acquisition of Eddie Sauer that made English expendable, because Sauer replaced Ostrowski in right field, while the latter moved to third. L.A. could not foresee the untimely loss of Garriott. The only other threat Harrell faced came in the ninth when the Angels loaded the bases with one out, but Stan "Goat" Gray struck out and John Moore fouled out.

San Francisco	AB	H	RBI	O	E
Uhalt CF	3	0	0	5	0
Futernick SS	5	2	0	0	0
Steinbacher RF	4	2	0	2	0
Suhr 1B	5	2	0	7	0
Guintini LF	5	2	1	4	0
Young 2B	5	1	0	1	1
Cavalli 3B	5	3	0	1	0
Sprinz C	4	1	0	6	0
Harrell P	4	0	0	0	0

San Francisco	AB	II	RBI	O	E
Enos[a]	1	0	0	0	0
Hooper RF	0	0	0	1	0
	41	13	1	27	1

(a) Batted for Steinbacher in the ninth.

Los Angeles	AB	H	RBI	O	E
Miller SS	4	0	0	2	0
Russell 2B	4	1	1	4	0
Ostrowski CF	4	2	1	5	0
Norbert LF	4	0	0	1	0
Sauer RF	4	2	0	3	0
Otero 1B	3	1	0	6	0
Gray 3B	3	0	0	0	1
Sarni C	3	0	0	5	0
Comellas P	2	0	0	1	0
Fernandes[a]	1	0	0	0	0
Prim P	0	0	0	0	0
Moore[b]	1	0	0	0	0
	33	6	2	27	1

(a) Batted for Comellas in the eighth.
(b) Batted for Moore in the ninth.

Pitching Records	IP	H	R	ER	SO	BB
Harrell	9	6	2	2	5	1
Comellas (L)	8	11	4	1	4	2
Prim	1	2	0	0	1	0

Left on Base: San Francisco 12, Los Angeles 6. Home Runs: Ostrowski, Russell. Sacrifice: Otero. Time of Game: 2 hr. 5 min. Umpires: Doran, Edwards, Powell, Engeln.

San Francisco	100	030	000	4 –	13 –	1
Los Angeles	101	000	000	2 –	6 –	1

The 1944 playoffs were very successful financially, and Charles Graham wanted to increase the amount paid to players from gate receipts. This was the only time that a pennant winner lost the final round of the playoffs — champions either won them or were eliminated in the opening round. Both the Angels and Seals received $5,000 prize money, and while the number of shares is uncertain, if there were 25, each would come to $200, which would be worth about $1,136 currently.

Key Players on 1944 Playoff Teams

Los Angeles. *Pitchers:* Ray Prim, Pancho Comellas, Claude Horton, Red Adams and Don Osborn.
Position Players: Johnny Ostrowski, Cecil Garriott (L.A.'s MVP), Reggie Otero, Rip Russell, and Ted Norbert.

Portland. *Pitchers:* Ad Liska, Roy Helser, and Marino Pieretti.
Position Players: Eddie Adams, John Gill, Marvin Owen, and Frank Shone.

San Francisco. *Pitchers:* Bob Joyce, Ray Harrell, Tommy Seats, and Bill Werle.
Position Players: Frenchy Uhalt, Neil Sheridan, Ben Guintini, Gus Suhr, and Johnny Cavalli.

Oakland. *Pitchers:* Manny Salvo, Damon Hayes, and Jack Lotz.
Position Players: Les Scarsella (league's MVP and batting champ), Billy Raimondi, Charley English, Chet Rosenlund, Jake Caufield and Frank Hawkins (injured).

1945

In this last wartime season, players were still leaving for military service but some veterans were rejoining their former teams. Any returning serviceman was allowed to participate in postseason play, regardless of when he rejoined his club. For the second year in a row, the Pacific Coast League set an all-time attendance record of 2,919,470, which was almost 25 percent higher than 1944. This record was probably attributable more to economic prosperity and to the success of winning the war than to the pennant race, because this season provided little suspense.

The Portland Beavers won their eighth and last pennant in 1945, continuing their improvement in each of their last three seasons. In 1942, they finished eighth; in 1943, they were fourth; in 1944, they moved up to second, and in 1945 they reached the top. The Beavers were in first place all but one week of the season and continually since late April. Their closest rival, Seattle, closed to within a game and a half in August, but Portland pulled away and led by five games on Labor Day and continued to move ahead, winning by eight and a half games. Pitcher Ad Liska was the only Beaver player left over from their previous pennant winner nine years earlier.

Sportswriter L. H. Gregory of *The Portland Oregonian* lamented that the 1936 championship Beavers did not have a memento of that great season, so he suggested that fans contribute to a fund for engraved watches for this 1945 team, and the fans did so. On September 24, the fans were invited to a dinner honoring the team at the Multnomoah Hotel, which was given by the chamber of commerce. The players received their watches and also a gold and diamond ring, which the team furnished.

The second place Seattle Rainiers had four pitchers over 40 years old plus some position players who were a little long in the tooth. They were never in danger of falling below second place, finishing eight and a half games ahead of third place Sacramento, the same distance by which they trailed Portland. This was Bill Skiff's last good team; he was fired in mid–1946 with his team in the cellar. Skiff said that the 1945 Rainiers were forced to play too many doubleheaders late in the season, and had too many older players to catch Portland.

JoJo White of the 1945 Sacramento Solons (Dick Dobbins collection).

The Sacramento Solons, after two very poor seasons, surprised everyone by finishing third under manager Earl Sheely. The Solons never got any higher than third, but after falling to sixth place in early June, they were never lower than fourth after early July. This team was bolstered by pitcher "Grumpy" Guy Fletcher, who won 24 games, and by the acquisition of former Seattle star Jo Jo White, who led the league in batting. This team set an attendance record of 310,741 in Double Day Park, the third of four names that playing field was to have. When it opened in 1922, it was called Moreling Field and then changed to Cardinal Field when the Sacs were a St. Louis farm club, and became Double Day Park in 1943, and finally Edmonds Field after this season.

The San Francisco Seals finished a half game behind the Solons but were not seriously challenged by Oakland, who was six games behind them in fifth place, so there was no suspense about which teams would finish in the first division. Pitcher Bob Joyce had a sensational season, winning 31 games plus four more in the playoffs. Joyce won the Triple Crown, having the highest winning percentage, the most strikeouts and the lowest ERA. Lefty O'Doul still was able to get good performances out of older players; his Seals struggled in May and early June, falling as low as seventh place, but by the end of June, they reached the first division and were not threatened thereafter by any second division team.

The war had ended about a month before the season was over, so the postseason games were played in peace time. However, railroads were still heavily burdened with traffic, so in order to cut down on travel, the first round was scheduled to be between the teams that were close to one another. Seattle opened at Portland, and San Francisco at Sacramento. Even the 1945 World Series was restricted to just one trip between Detroit and Chicago.

This was a sad season for Los Angeles area fans: the Angels finished seventh and Hollywood dead last.

The Portland-Seattle Series

The Beavers won 15 and lost 14 to the Rainiers during the season, but the statistic that stood out was Portland's great road record. Away from that ancient firetrap known as Vaughan Street Park, or Lucky Beaver Stadium, Portland played .656 ball with 61 wins and 32 losses, while at home, their pace was a more modest .586, with 51 wins and 36 losses. So after Portland won the first three playoff games at home, the trip to Seattle seemed to pose no problem for them, but as happens so often in postseason play, the regular season is a poor indicator of how the playoffs will unfold.

Game One.

Four umpires were assigned to all playoff games in 1945. This series opened on Tuesday night, September 25, at Vaughan Street Park before 4,015 fans. A heavy rain that afternoon delayed the start of this game, as the ground crew worked on the field, and may have held the attendance down. Jake Mooty of the Beavers pitched a three-hit shutout to put Portland up in the series. The Beavers got to Carl Fischer in the sixth for all three of their runs. Larry Barton singled and scored on Charley English's double. English moved to third on the throw home and scored on Frank Demaree's fly ball. Then successive singles by manager Marvin Owen, Ted Gullic, and Johnny O'Neil brought home the third run. Hal Sueme got two of the three Seattle hits.

Seattle	AB	H	RBI	O	A	E
Gorbould 2B	3	0	0	3	2	0
Patchett CF	4	0	0	2	0	0
Matheson RF	4	1	0	6	0	0
McDonald 1B	4	0	0	5	2	0
Dobbins SS	3	0	0	3	1	0
Norbert LF	4	0	0	1	0	0
Aleno 3B	3	0	0	0	1	0
Sueme C	3	2	0	3	0	0
Fischer P	0	0	0	1	1	0
Kats[a]	0	0	0	0	0	0
C. Johnson P	0	0	0	0	0	0
	28	3	0	24	7	0

(a) Batted for Fischer in the eighth.

Portland	AB	H	RBI	O	A	E
Shone CF	4	0	0	3	0	0
Barton 1B	4	1	0	5	0	0
English 2B	4	2	1	4	2	0
Demaree LF	4	2	1	3	0	0
Owen 3B	3	1	0	0	0	0
Gullic RF	3	1	0	1	0	0
O'Neil SS	4	1	1	3	3	0
Adams C	2	0	0	8	1	0
Mooty P	3	0	0	0	2	0
	31	8	3	27	8	0

Pitching Records	IP	H	R	ER	SO	BB
Fischer (L)	7	7	3	3	3	2
C. Johnson	1	1	0	0	0	0
Mooty	9	3	0	0	8	4

Runs Scored: Barton, English, Owen. Wild Pitch: Fischer. Passed Ball: Adams. Left on Base: Seattle 6, Portland 7. Two Base Hits: English, Demaree, O'Neil. Sacrifices: Fischer, Owen. Time of Game: 2 hr. Umpires: Powell, Engeln, Doran, Edwards.

Seattle	000	000	000	0 – 3 – 0
Portland	000	003	00x	3 – 8 – 0

Game Two.

With better weather, 8,149 fans showed up to see their beloved Beavers overcome a 3–0 Seattle lead with four runs in the eighth, to take a two games to none lead in the series. Joe Demoran faced Ad Liska, and until the fateful eighth it looked as if the Seattle ace might have a shutout. Demoran was a hitting hero but a baserunning goat in this game. In the third, he singled and came around to score on Bob Gorbould's sacrifice and Bill Matheson's single. In the seventh, he singled in Seattle's second run. Chuck Aleno singled, Bob Finley bunted, but catcher Eddie Adams threw high into center field, allowing Aleno to take third. Demoran then singled in Aleno and Gorbould singled in Finley, to make it 3–0, still with no one out. When Matheson grounded out second to first, Demoran was trapped off third base, killing the inning.

In the last of the eighth, Portland struck with one out. Frank Demaree was safe on Joe Dobbins' error, Marvin Owen doubled him home, and Ted Gullic singled in his manager to cut the lead to 3–2. After O'Neil made the second out, Danny Escobar was sent up to bat for Eddie Adams. Escobar had just gotten out of the navy so was eligible for the playoffs. Escobar blasted a two-run homer putting the Beavers ahead, 4–3, that delighted the fans so much they showered the playing field with coins that amounted to $81 for their returning slugger. In the top of the ninth, the Rainiers had the tying run on second with no one out, but Ad Liska pitched out of trouble.

Seattle	AB	H	RBI	O	A	E
Gorbould 2B	4	2	1	2	0	0
Patchett CF	3	0	0	2	0	0
Matheson RF	4	1	1	2	0	0
McDonald 1B	4	0	0	9	1	1
Dobbins SS	4	3	0	1	6	1
Norbert LF	4	1	0	4	0	0
Aleno 3B	4	2	0	0	3	0
Finley C	2	0	0	4	0	0
Demoran P	2	1	1	0	2	0
Lyman[a]	0	0	0	0	0	0
Gill[b]	1	0	0	0	0	0
	32	10	3	24	12	2

(a) Ran for Aleno in the ninth.
(b) Batted for Demoran in the ninth.

Portland	AB	H	RBI	O	A	E
Shone CF	4	3	0	2	0	0
Barton 1B	4	1	0	11	1	0
English 2B	4	0	0	5	4	0
Demaree LF	4	0	0	5	0	0
Owen 3B	3	1	1	0	4	0
Gullic RF	4	3	1	0	0	0
O'Neil SS	4	0	0	1	5	0
Adams C	2	0	0	3	0	1
Liska P	4	1	0	0	0	0
Escobar[a]	1	1	2	0	0	0
Sousa C	0	0	0	0	0	0
	34	10	4	27	14	1

(a) Batted for Adams in the eighth.

Pitching Records	IP	H	R	ER	SO	BB
Demoran	8	10	4	1	4	2
Liska	9	10	3	2	3	1

The 1945 Portland Beavers won the PCL pennant but were eliminated by Seattle in the first round of the playoffs, despite winning the first three games of the series. *Back Row, left to right:* George Emich (trainer), Jack Tising, Don Pulford, Marvin Owen (Mgr.), Syd Cohen, Frank Shone, Roy Younker, Tedd Gullic, Robert Caviness, Bill Klepper (Gen. Mgr.). *Middle Row:* Carl Gunnarson, Wandell Mossor, Roy Helser, Danny Escobar, Hank Souza, Frank Demaree, Larry Barton, Charley English. *Front Row:* unidentified ballboy, Eddie Adams, Ad Liska, Johnnie O'Neil, Glenn Crawford, Frank Lucchesi, Jake Mooty, Nick Rhabe.

Runs Scored: Demoran, Aleno, Finley, Demaree, Owen, Gullic, Escobar. Left on Base: Seattle 6, Portland 6. Two Base Hits: Gullic, Gorbould, Owen. Home Run: Escobar. Sacrifices: Gorbould, Finley 2, Patchett. Double Plays: English to Barton; O'Neil to English to Barton. Time of Game: 1 hr. 53 min. Umpires: Doran, Edwards, Englin, Powell.

Seattle	001	000	200	3 – 10 – 2
Portland	000	000	04x	4 – 10 – 2

Game Three.

The third game was no contest. The 9,569 fans that came out on Thursday night, September 27, had a great time but never suspected that this would be the last game in Portland in 1945. Roy Helser had a no-hitter until two were out in the eighth, while his teammates were pounding Hal Turpin, Keith Frazier and Glen Elliott for 11 runs and 18 hits, including two doubles, a single and four RBIs by Helser himself. Charley English went 4-for-4, with a triple and two RBIs, and Marvin Owen had three hits. Everyone but Frank Demaree hit safely. The teams took two days off before resuming the series in Seattle on Sunday because they wanted a bigger crowd and did not want to compete with college football on Saturday.

Seattle	AB	H	RBI	O	A	E
Garbould 2B	4	0	0	1	1	0
Patchett CF	2	0	0	2	0	0
Matheson RF	4	0	0	6	0	0
McDonald 1B	4	0	0	5	1	0
Dobbins SS	3	0	0	3	3	0
Norbert LF	2	0	0	3	1	0
Aleno 3B	3	1	0	0	0	0
Sueme C	3	1	0	3	0	0
Turpin P	1	0	0	1	0	0
Kats [a]	1	0	0	0	0	0
Frazier P	0	0	0	0	1	0
Lyman [b]	1	0	0	0	0	0
Elliott P	0	0	0	0	0	0
	28	2	0	24	7	0

(a) Batted for Turpin in the sixth.
(b) Batted for Frazier in the eighth.

Portland	AB	H	RBI	O	A	E
Shone CF	5	2	1	4	0	0
Barton 1B	5	2	1	4	0	0
English 2B	4	4	2	3	2	1
Demaree LF	5	0	1	4	0	0
Owen 3B	4	3	0	0	1	0
Gullic RF	3	1	0	2	0	0
O'Neil SS	5	2	0	2	2	0
Adams C	4	1	1	8	1	0
Helser P	5	3	4	0	0	0
	40	18	10	27	6	1

Pitching Records	IP	H	R	ER	SO	BB
Turpin (L)	5	8	3	3	2	0
Frazier	2	8	7	7	0	4
Elliott	1	2	1	1	1	0
Helser	9	2	0	0	7	2

Wild Pitch: Elliott. Hit by Pitcher: Patchett by Helser. Left on Base: Seattle 4, Portland 10. Two Base Hits: Helser 2, Gullic. Three Base Hit: English.

Stolen Base: Shone. Sacrifice: Gullic. Double Plays: Adams to O'Neil; Norbert to Dobbins; O'Neil to English to Barton. Time of Game: 1 hr. 50 min. Umpires: Doran, Edwards, Powell and Engeln.

Game Four.

The rivalry between the two northwest cities extended beyond baseball. On Saturday, September 29, Washington Huskies beat the University of Oregon Ducks 20–6 at Husky Stadium before 35,000 fans. Meanwhile, *Seattle Post Intelligencer* writer Royal Brogham was conceding the series to Portland, lamenting that the Beavers were the superior team. He also hinted that Bill Skiff was upset with his team for quitting in that last game in Portland. Nevertheless, a crowd of 8,500 fans went to Sick's Stadium on Sunday, September 30, hoping to see a doubleheader, if the Rainiers could win the first game. The Portland players were so confident of wrapping up the series quickly, they brought very few changes of clothing with them.

Seattle took the opening game 7–4, with Joe Demoran getting the win with relief help from 44-year-old Sylvester Johnson. Lefty Wandel Mossor was knocked around for nine hits in six innings, yielding all seven runs. Portland's 1–0 lead in the second was quickly erased by Ted Norbert's two-run homer in the last half of that inning. Chuck Aleno's error let Portland tie the game in the top of the third, but Seattle scored one in the last half to take a 3–2 lead. The Rainiers blew the game open with a four-run sixth inning when Matheson doubled, George McDonald got a bunt single, and Norbert singled in one run before Bob Finley hit a three-run homer. The Beavers chased Demoran with four successive singles in the eighth, but old Syl Johnson put the fire out.

Portland	AB	R	H	RBI	O	E
Shone CF	5	1	1	0	3	0
Barton 1B	4	1	1	0	6	0
English 2B	4	1	1	0	2	0
Demaree LF	4	1	3	1	1	0
Owen 3B	4	0	1	1	5	0
Gullic RF	4	0	2	1	1	0
O'Neil SS	4	0	0	0	4	0
Younker C	3	0	1	0	2	0
Mossor P	2	0	0	0	0	0
Escobar [a]	1	0	0	0	0	0
Luccuesi [b]	0	0	0	0	0	0
Tising P	1	0	0	0	0	1
Souza C	0	0	0	0	0	0

Portland	AB	R	H	RBI	O	E
Helser[c]	1	0	0	0	0	0
	37	4	10	3	24	1

(a) Batted for Mossor in the seventh.
(b) Ran for Younker in the seventh.
(c) Batted for Souza in the ninth.

Seattle	AB	R	H	RBI	O	E
Gorbould 2B	4	1	0	0	0	0
Patchett CF	3	0	1	0	3	0
Matheson RF	4	1	1	1	1	0
McDonald 1B	4	1	2	0	10	1
Dobbins SS	4	1	2	1	3	0
Norbert LF	3	2	2	3	3	0
Aleno 3B	4	0	0	0	1	1
Finley C	4	1	1	2	6	0
Demoran P	2	0	1	0	0	0
S. Johnson P	1	0	0	0	0	0
Kats LF[a]	0	0	0	0	0	0
	33	7	10	7	27	2

(a) Ran for Norbert in the eighth.

Pitching Records	IP	H	R	ER	SO	BB
Mossor (L)	6	9	7	7	2	1
Tising	2	1	0	0	0	2
Demoran (W)	7.1	10	4	3	4	0
S. Johnson	1.2	0	0	0	2	0

Left on Base: Portland 6, Seattle 5. Two Base Hits: Matheson, Shone, McDonald. Home Runs: Norbert, Finley. Double Plays: O'Neil to English to Barton; Matheson to McDonald; Gorbould to Dobbins to McDonald; Owen to Barton. Umpires: Powell, Edwards, Engeln, Doran.

Portland	011	000	020	4 – 10 – 1
Seattle	021	004	00x	7 – 10 – 2

Game Five.

The Rainiers closed the series gap to 3–2 with a 4–2 win in the seven inning nightcap. Carl Fischer beat Don Pulford, who was relieved by Jack Tising in the third. Chuck Aleno's homer put Seattle up 1–0 in the second, but

Portland tied it in the third on walks to Adams and Pulford, a single by Frank Shone, and Larry Barton's fly ball. But Seattle came right back with three runs in their half of the third, chasing Pulford. Doubles by Bob Gorbould, Bill Matheson and Joe Dobbins brought in two runs and Jack Tising to pitch. Ted Norbert greeted the reliever with a run scoring single to provide the home team with a 4–1 lead. Portland got its last run in the fifth on three singles, with Charlie English driving in the run.

Portland	AB	R	H	RBI	O	E
Shone CF	4	1	1	0	2	0
Barton 1B	3	0	1	1	8	1
English 2B	3	0	1	1	0	0
Demaree LF	3	0	0	0	1	0
Owen 3B	3	0	2	0	2	0
Gullic RF	3	0	0	0	2	0
O'Neil SS	3	0	0	0	0	0
Adams C	2	1	1	0	3	0
Pulford P	0	0	0	0	0	0
Tising P	1	0	0	0	0	0
Younker[a]	1	0	0	0	0	0
	26	2	6	2	18	1

(a) Batted for Tising in the seventh.

Seattle	AB	R	H	RBI	O	E
Garbould 2B	4	1	1	0	2	0
Patchett CF	4	0	2	0	2	0
Matheson RF	3	1	1	1	2	0
McDonald 1B	3	0	1	0	7	0
Dobbins SS	3	1	1	1	3	0
Norbert LF	3	0	1	1	2	0
Aleno 3B	3	1	2	1	0	0
Sueme C	3	0	1	0	3	0
Fischer P	3	0	0	0	0	0
	29	4	10	4	21	0

Pitching Records	IP	H	R	ER	SO	BB
Pulford (L)	2.2	6	4	4	1	0
Tising	3.1	4	0	0	1	0
Fischer	7	6	2	2	3	2

Left on Base: Portland 5, Seattle 7. Two Base Hits: Gorbould, Matheson, Patchett, Owen, Dobbins. Home Run: Aleno. Double Play: Gorbould to Dobbins to McDonald. Umpires: Doran, Engeln, Edwards, Powell.

Portland	001	010	0	2	–	6	– 1
Seattle	013	000	x	4	–	10	– 0

Game Six.

With Portland's ace, Jake Mooty, on the mound, it looked as if this night, Monday, October 1, would be the night the Beavers would eliminate the Rainiers in the playoffs. Mooty, who had won nine straight games, was facing the Oregon farmer, Hal Turpin. In the top of the first, the first three Portland batters scored. Frank Shone singled, Larry Barton grounded to Chuck Aleno, who heaved the ball over George McDonald's head at first, allowing the runners to go to second and third. Charley English singled both men home, and then Frank Demaree singled English to third. Marvin Owen grounded into a force play, allowing English to score the third run of the inning. That, however, was the extent of the Portland scoring. Hal Turpin survived that rocky start and allowed the champion Beavers only five hits and no runs the rest of the evening.

It was still 3-0 until the sixth inning when Bill Matheson, who went 3-for-3, tripled and scored on George McDonald's fly. Then, in the last of the seventh, the 6,237 Seattle fans got what they came to see. Ted Norbert blooped a single, moved to second on Aleno's ground out and scored on Bob Finley's single. It was now 3–2. Finley's smash through the box hit Mooty on his pitching hand, but Jake tried to stay in the game. This proved to be the mistake of the series. Mooty walked Hal Turpin, who was allowed to bat that late in the game with his team trailing by a run, and facing elimination. Bob Gorbould then doubled off Frank Demaree's glove, scoring Finley with the tying run, and sending Turpin to third. Jack Tising relieved, and purposely walked Hal Patchett to load the bases. Bill Matheson singled in the go-ahead run. Roy Helser relieved Tising and got an inning ending double play, but the damage had been done. Portland came close to tying the game in the ninth when Ted Gullic reached second base on Dobbins' throwing error, but Bill Matheson made a game saving catch on pinch hitter Roy Younkers' long drive. The Rainiers, reportedly, were inspired by the talk of their quitting in game three in Portland, and were anxious to prove otherwise.

Portland	**AB**	**R**	**H**	**RBI**	**O**	**E**
Shone CF	4	1	2	0	2	0
Barton 1B	4	1	0	0	9	0
English 2B	4	1	1	2	6	0

Portland	AB	R	H	RBI	O	E
Demaree LF	4	0	2	0	2	0
Owen 3B	4	0	1	1	2	0
Escobar RF	4	0	0	0	1	0
O'Neil SS	3	0	1	0	1	1
Adams C	3	0	1	0	1	0
Mooty P	3	0	0	0	0	0
Tising P	0	0	0	0	0	0
Helser P	1	0	0	0	0	0
Lucchesi P	0	0	0	0	0	0
Gullic [a]	1	0	0	0	0	0
Pulford [b]	0	0	0	0	0	0
Younker [c]	1	0	0	0	0	0
	36	3	8	3	24	1

(a) Batted for Adams in the ninth.
(b) Ran for Gullic in the ninth.
(c) Batted for Lucchesi in the ninth.

Seattle	AB	R	H	RBI	O	E
Gorbould 2B	5	0	2	1	2	0
Patchett CF	2	0	0	0	3	0
Matheson RF	3	1	3	1	6	0
McDonald 1B	4	0	0	1	7	0
Dobbins SS	4	0	1	0	5	1
Norbert LF	4	1	2	0	0	0
Aleno 3B	3	0	0	0	1	1
Finley C	3	1	2	1	1	0
Turpin P	3	1	0	0	2	0
Kats LF [a]	0	0	0	0	0	0
	31	4	10	4	27	2

(a) Ran for Norbert in the eighth.

Pitching Records	IP	H	R	ER	SO	BB
Mooty (L)	6.1	8	3	4	1	3
Tising	0+	1	1	0	0	1
Helser	1.1	1	0	0	0	1
Lucchesi	0.1	0	0	0	0	0
Turpin	9	8	3	2	1	1

Left on Base: Portland 7, Seattle 9. Two Base Hits: Norbert, Gorbould. Three Base Hit: Matheson. Stolen Base: Shone. Sacrifice: Aleno. Double Plays: O'Neil

to English to Barton 2; Owen to Barton. Umpires; Engeln, Doran, Powell,
Edwards.

Portland	300	000	000	3 –	8 –	1
Seattle	000	001	30x	4 –	10 –	2

Game Seven.

On Tuesday night, October 2, 9,326 fans at Sick's Stadium saw their
Rainiers pull off the most remarkable comeback in Pacific Coast League history. Manager Bill Skiff tricked the Beavers by announcing lefty Chester Johnson as his starter, but came back with right hander Joe Demoran, who had
pitched the opening game on Sunday. The Portland players took batting practice against lefty Carl Gunnarson, expecting to face Johnson. Demoran held
the champion Beavers to just two hits and one run, as Seattle won the game,
3–1. Ad Liska was staked to a 1–0 lead in the second on Ted Gullic's homer,
but that was the last run Portland was to score in 1945. Liska, who was the
victim of three unearned runs in the fourth, retired the first two batters in
that fateful inning. Then McDonald tripled and Dobbins walked. Norbert then
hit a grounder to Johnny O'Neil at short, who fumbled it for an error, as
McDonald scored the tying run. Chuck Aleno then singled in Dobbins with
the winning run and Finley singled in Norbert with the insurance run.
Demoran shut Portland down the rest of the night to send Seattle to the final
round.

Portland	AB	R	H	RBI	O	E
Shone CF	4	0	0	0	1	0
Barton 1B	4	0	1	0	9	0
English 2B	3	0	0	0	3	0
Demaree LF	3	0	0	0	2	0
Owen 3B	4	0	0	0	1	0
Gullic RF	3	1	1	1	1	1
O'Neil SS	3	0	0	0	3	1
Adams C	2	0	0	0	2	0
Liska P	2	0	0	0	1	0
Helser [a]	1	0	0	0	0	0
Escobar [b]	1	0	0	0	0	0
Souza C	0	0	0	0	1	0
Tising P	0	0	0	0	0	0
	30	1	2	1	24	2

(a) Batted for Adams in the eighth.
(b) Batted for Liska in the eighth.

Seattle	AB	R	H	RBI	O	E
Garbould 2B	4	0	2	0	3	1
Patchett CF	3	0	0	0	2	0
Matheson RF	4	0	0	0	2	0
McDonald 1B	4	1	1	0	13	0
Dobbins SS	3	1	0	0	0	1
Norbert LF	3	1	2	0	1	0
Aleno 3B	3	0	1	1	1	0
Finley C	3	0	1	1	5	0
Demoran P	3	0	0	0	0	0
	30	3	7	2	27	2

Pitching Records	IP	H	R	ER	SO	BB
Liska (L)	7	7	3	0	2	1
Tising	1	0	0	0	1	0
Demoran	9	2	1	1	5	2

Left on Base: Portland 4, Seattle 5. Three Base Hit: McDonald. Home Run: Gullic. Stolen Base: Patchett. Sacrifice: Patchett. Double Plays: O'Neil to English to Barton; Gorbould to McDonald.

Portland	010	000	000	1 – 2 – 2
Seattle	000	300	00x	3 – 7 – 2

Portland's great road record went for naught in this series which saw the home team win all seven games. The league champs said they felt like chumps, or tailenders. The playoffs clearly left a bad taste in the mouth of Portland fans, just as happened with Angel fans after the 1943 season. But the games were well attended and gave some other team's fans a chance to celebrate and to look back on the 1945 season with happy memories.

The Pacific Coast League, at the insistence of new president Clarence Rowland, now provided more money for postseason play. Pennant winners now received $5,000, double what previous winners received. Other prize money was also doubled. Teams eliminated in the first round now received $2,500, while the playoff winner got $10,000 and the runner-up $5,000. So the Portland players split $7,500, which would be about $300 per player, or about $1,667 in current dollars.

The San Francisco–Sacramento Series

The Solons won 15 and lost 14 from the Seals in the regular season with each team doing much better in its own park. But that experience did not carry over to the playoffs. The fans in Sacramento were so enthusiastic for this series, after the two previous dismal years, that they purchased all the reserve seats for the first three games. The Sacs' regular shortstop, Jack Calvery, was unable to play in the first three games because he had injured his hand in an auto accident in Portland, when the Solons last played up there.

Game One.

On Wednesday night, September 26, a crowd of 6,063 saw the Seals eke out a 6–5 come-from-behind win, with 31-game-winner Bob Joyce beating Grumpy Guy Fletcher. The Sacs led 4–0 after three innings and 5–2 after five frames, but the Solon lead could have been greater if not for some base running blunders. In the first, singles by Gene Handley, Jo Jo White and Ed Zipay plated a run, but White was caught off first base. Then in the second, Barney Bridges, filling in for the injured Calvey, was trapped off third base, so the Solons were only able to get one run that inning despite a walk, a sacrifice, a single and three Seal errors. In the third, Jesse Landrum singled and George Mandish homered to give Sacramento a 4–0 lead.

The Seals cut that lead to 4–2 in the fourth on a double by Gus Suhr and a booming home run by Neil Sheridan. In the next inning the Solons scored their fifth and last run when White singled, stole second, went to third on catcher Sprinz' overthrow, and scored on Zipay's fly ball. Fletcher's wildness allowed the Seals to tie the game in the seventh. Sprinz singled and Joyce, who was allowed to bat with his team three runs behind, doubled. Uhalt's single cut the lead to 5–3. Walks to Del Young and Emil Mailho forced in the fourth run before Gus Suhr grounded into a double play, which allowed Uhalt to score the tying run. Then in the ninth, a mental lapse allowed the Seals to score the decisive run. With Uhalt on third and Mailho on first, Suhr struck out for the second out of the inning, but Mailho took off for second and was able to evade Bridges' tag long enough for Uhalt to score.

San Francisco	AB	R	H	RBI	O	A	E
Uhalt CF	4	2	1	1	1	0	0
Young 2B	3	0	0	0	3	0	0
Mailho LF	4	0	3	1	2	0	0
Suhr 1B	5	1	1	1	9	0	0
Sheridan RF	3	1	1	2	4	0	0
Perry 3B	4	0	0	0	1	6	0
Nicely SS	4	0	1	0	1	4	2
Sprinz C	3	1	1	0	6	1	1
Joyce P	4	1	1	0	0	2	1
	34	6	9	5	27	13	4

Sacramento	AB	R	H	RBI	O	A	E
Handley 2B	5	1	1	0	4	4	0
White CF	4	1	2	0	1	0	0
Landrum RF	4	1	1	0	3	0	0
Zipay 1B	4	0	1	1	11	0	0
Mandish LF	4	1	2	2	1	0	0
Marcucci 3B	4	1	1	0	0	3	0
Bridges SS	3	0	0	0	1	3	0
Schlueter C	4	0	0	0	6	1	0
Fletcher P	3	0	2	0	0	1	0
McElreath[a]	1	0	0	0	0	0	0
	36	5	10	3	27	12	0

(a) Batted for Fletcher in the ninth.

Pitching Records	IP	H	R	ER	SO	BB
Joyce	9	9	5	4	4	0
Fletcher	9	10	6	6	4	6

Left on Base: San Francisco 7, Sacramento 5. Two Base Hits: Suhr, Joyce. Home Runs: Mandish, Sheridan. Stolen Bases: Landrum, Sheridan. Double Play: Handley to Zipay. Time of Game: 2 hrs. Umpires: Kober, Dempsey, Ford, Floresi.

San Francisco	000	200	301	6 –	9 – 4
Sacramento	112	010	000	5 –	10 – 0

Game Two.

A smaller crowd of 3,961 turned out on Thursday night to see the Seals go up by two games in the series with a 3–1 win. Frank Seward beat John Pintar, with both teams leaving nine men on base. The Seals scored the first run in the fourth on three singles, with Roy Nicely driving in the run. The lead went to 3–0 in the seventh when Ray Perry singled and Ogrodowski was safe on Lilio Marcucci's two base throwing error, which put men on second and third. Pitcher Frank Seward singled in Perry, and Uhalt singled in "Oggie." The Solon run came in the last of the seventh on Al McElreath's walk, a wild pitch and Gene Handley's single.

San Francisco	AB	R	H	RBI	O	A	E
Uhalt CF	5	0	2	1	4	0	0
Young 2B	5	0	1	0	3	5	0
Mailho LF	5	0	2	0	1	0	0

San Francisco	AB	R	H	RBI	O	A	E
Suhr 1B	4	1	0	0	9	1	0
Sheridan RF	3	0	0	0	2	0	0
Perry 3B	3	0	2	0	0	0	0
Nicely SS	4	1	1	1	2	2	0
Ogrodowski C	4	1	1	0	6	0	0
Seward P	4	0	2	1	0	1	0
	37	3	11	3	27	9	0

Sacramento	AB	R	H	RBI	O	A	E
Handley 2B	5	0	2	1	4	4	0
White CF-RF	4	0	2	0	4	1	0
Landrum 2B	4	0	1	0	1	2	1
Zipay 1B	4	0	2	0	7	1	0
Mandish RF	3	0	0	0	3	0	0
Marcucci 3B	4	0	1	0	0	2	1
McElreath LF	3	1	1	0	2	0	0
Schlueter C	4	0	1	0	5	0	0
Pintar P	2	0	0	0	0	1	0
Greenhalgh CF	0	0	0	0	1	0	0
McCarthy[a]	1	0	0	0	0	0	0
	34	1	10	1	27	11	2

(a) Batted for Pintar in the ninth.

Pitching Records	IP	H	R	ER	SO	BB
Seward	9	10	1	1	5	2
Pintar	9	11	3	2	3	1

Left on Base: San Francisco 9, Sacramento 9. Two Base Hits: White, Seward. Sacrifices: Pintar, Sheridan. Double Plays: Young to Suhr; Nicely to Suhr; Handley to Zipay. Time of Game: 1 hr. 56 min. Umpires: Ford, Kober, Floresi, Dempsey.

San Francisco	000	100	200	3 – 11 – 0
Sacramento	000	000	100	1 – 10 – 2

Game Three.

A somewhat unruly crowd of 5,708 saw the last game played in Sacramento in 1945 on Friday night, September 28, as the Seals took a commanding three games to none lead in the series. Losing pitcher Jim McCarthy was hard luck loser in this 4–3 game, because of some sloppy play behind him. Seal starter Elmer Orella did not pitch the required five innings to get the win, so reliever Bob Barthelson, who slammed the door on the Solons, got credit for the victory. The Seals' four runs all came in the second when Sheridan and Perry opened with singles, Nicely bunted, but everyone was safe on an unwise throw to second base. Ogrodowski grounded to Handley, who was playing short, but Gene booted the ball, allowing Sheridan to score. Elmer Orella grounded to Zipay at first but the throw to the plate hit Orella on the shoulder, allowing Perry and Nicely to score. Young then singled in "Oggie."

In the third, Norm Schlueter singled and the pitcher McCarthy hit a two-run homer to cut the lead to 4–2. Then in the fourth, Jess Landrum's homer made it 4–3, but that was all the scoring. When Orella gave up two singles after the homer, Barthelson came in and shut the Sacs down. But trouble erupted later when Marcucci was called out on a close play at first. An argument followed and two fans separately ran out on the field to attack umpire Al Floresi. One was locked up in Sacramento's "hotel for the wicked."

San Francisco	AB	R	H	RBI	O	A	E
Uhalt CF	5	0	2	0	3	0	0
Young 2B	4	0	2	1	2	4	0
Mailho LF	1	0	0	0	0	0	0
Suhr 1B	4	0	0	0	8	0	0
Sheridan RF	4	1	2	0	5	0	0
Perry 3B	4	1	1	0	2	4	0
Nicely SS	3	1	1	0	3	1	0
Ogrodowski C	4	1	0	1	3	1	0
Orella P	2	0	1	1	0	0	0
Barthelson P	2	0	0	0	1	0	0
Guintini LF	1	0	0	0	0	0	0
	34	4	9	3	27	10	0

Sacramento	AB	R	H	RBI	O	A	E
Handley SS	3	0	0	0	4	3	1
White RF	3	0	0	0	2	0	0
Landrum 2B	3	1	1	1	2	2	0
Marcucci 3B	4	0	0	0	3	1	0
Mandish LF	4	0	0	0	1	0	0
Zipay 1B	4	0	2	0	5	1	1
Greenhalgh CF	3	0	1	0	4	0	0
Schlueter C	4	1	2	0	5	0	0
McCarthy P	4	1	1	2	1	1	0
McElreath[a]	1	0	0	0	0	0	0

Sacramento	AB	R	H	RBI	O	A	E
Bridgers[b]	0	0	0	0	0	0	0
	33	3	7	3	27	8	2

(a) *Batted for Greenhalgh in the ninth.*
(b) *Ran for Schlueter in the ninth.*

Pitching Records	IP	H	R	ER	SO	BB
Orella	3.1	5	3	3	1	0
Barthelson (W)	5.2	2	0	0	1	2
McCarthy	9	9	4	2	5	3

Hit by Pitcher: Handley by Barthelson. Left on Base: San Francisco 7, Sacramento 6. Two Base Hits: Sheridan, Zipay. Home Runs: McCarthy, Landrum. Sacrifices: Nicely, Mailho. Double Plays: Landrum to Handley; Handley to Marcucci. Time of Game: 2 hr. 6 min. Umpires: Dempsey, Ford, Floresi, Kober.

San Francisco	040	000	000	4 – 9 – 0
Sacramento	002	100	000	3 – 7 – 2

The two teams moved to San Francisco to finish the series, taking Saturday off because of college football. On Saturday the 29th, 60,000 fans at Berkeley saw USC beat California, 13–2. Then on Sunday, the Seals and Solons had to compete with a game at Kezar in which St. Mary's beat Stockton Army Air Base 26–0, before 30,000. This St. Mary's team, with its All-American Herman Wedemeyer was to go to the Sugar Bowl that season.

Game Four.

A crowd of 11,000, despite the competition from football, came out to Seals Stadium on Sunday, September 30, hoping to see the Seals knock Sacramento out of the playoffs in the first game, making the nightcap unnecessary. But Joe Wood held the Seals to just one run, while Floyd Ehrman and his reliever, Elmer Orella, gave up four. Wood himself scored Sacramento's first run in the third when he walked, moved up on a sacrifice, and scored on Landrum's single. The Seals tied it in the fourth when Sheridan beat out a bunt and scored on Nicely's double. But Sacramento won it with three in the eighth when two walks and a bunt single loaded the bases with one out. Lilio Marcucci singled in one run, after which O'Doul replaced Ehrman with the lefty Orella. Manager Earl Sheely then replaced the left-handed hitting McElreath with the right-handed Ted Greenhalgh, who singled in two runs to make it 4–1. Solon shortstop Jack Calvey returned to the lineup with 20 stitches in his hand, but was ejected in the fourth for arguing a call.

Sacramento	AB	R	H	RBI	O	A	E
Handley 2B	3	0	0	0	0	5	0
White CF-LF	2	0	0	0	3	0	0
Landrum 3B	5	1	2	1	1	2	0
Zipay 1B	4	1	0	0	11	3	0
Mandish RF	2	1	0	0	2	0	0
Marcucci C	4	0	1	1	1	1	0
McElreath LF	2	0	1	0	3	0	0
Calvey SS	2	0	0	0	0	0	0
Wood P	3	1	0	0	3	1	0
Bridgers SS	1	0	0	0	3	3	0
Greenhalgh CF[a]	1	0	1	2	0	0	0
	29	4	5	4	27	15	0

(a) Batted for McElreath in the eighth.

San Francisco	AB	R	H	RBI	O	A	E
Uhalt CF	4	0	2	0	5	0	0
Young 2B	3	0	0	0	6	1	0
Mailho LF	3	0	0	0	3	1	0
Suhr 1B	4	0	0	0	6	1	0
Sheridan RF	3	1	1	0	4	0	0
Perry 3B	4	0	1	0	2	3	0
Nicely SS	3	0	2	1	1	2	0
Ogrodowski C	3	0	0	0	0	0	0
Ehrman P	2	0	0	0	0	4	0
Guintini LF	0	0	0	0	0	0	0
Orella P	0	0	0	0	0	0	0
Sanders[a]	1	0	1	0	0	0	0
Enos[b]	1	0	0	0	0	0	0
	31	1	7	1	27	12	0

(a) Batted for Nicely in the ninth.
(b) Batted for Ogrodowski in the ninth.

Pitching Records	IP	H	R	ER	SO	BB
Wood	9	7	1	1	1	3
Ehrman (L)	7.1	4	4	4	0	8
Orella	1.2	1	0	0	0	0

Two Base Hit: Nicely. Sacrifices: Handley, Bridgers, Ehrman. Double Plays: Handley to Bridgers to Zipay 2; Time of Game: 1 hr. 59 min. Umpires: Floresi, Kober, Ford, Dempsey.

| Sacramento | 001 | 000 | 030 | 4 – 5 – 0 |
| San Francisco | 000 | 100 | 000 | 1 – 7 – 0 |

Game Five.

Unlike the Seattle-Portland series, the nightcap of this doubleheader was scheduled for nine innings. Bob Joyce, the league's MVP, again faced Guy Fletcher but this time the Solons beat Joyce for the first time in 1945. Each team scored two runs in the third. The Sacs got theirs on hits by Fletcher, White and Landrum and the Seals answered with two walks, an error by Zipay, and Mailho's two-run single. In the fifth, the Solons took the lead for good when Handley singled, White tripled and Zipay singled. Three singles in the ninth by McElreath, Schlueter and Handley gave Sacramento an insurance run.

Sacramento	AB	R	H	RBI	O	A	E
Handley 2B	4	1	3	1	3	2	0
White CF-RF	5	2	2	2	4	0	0
Landrum 3B	4	0	1	0	1	0	0
Zipay 1B	4	0	2	2	8	1	1
Mandish RF	4	0	1	0	4	0	0
McElreath LF	4	1	1	0	1	0	0
Calvey SS	4	0	0	0	2	5	0
Schlueter C	4	0	1	0	1	0	0
Fletcher P	4	1	1	0	2	3	0
Greenhalgh CF	0	0	0	0	1	0	0
	37	5	12	5	27	11	1

San Francisco	AB	R	H	RBI	O	A	E
Uhalt CF	5	1	2	0	1	0	0
Young 2B	4	0	0	0	6	4	0
Mailho LF	2	0	2	2	2	0	0
Suhr 1B	4	0	1	0	7	1	1
Sheridan RF	5	0	0	0	1	0	0
Perry 3B	4	0	1	0	3	2	0
Nicely SS	3	0	0	0	2	2	0
Sprinz C	2	1	0	0	3	1	0
Joyce P	4	0	1	0	1	2	0
Sanders[a]	0	0	0	0	0	0	0
Futernick SS	0	0	0	0	1	0	0
Enos[b]	1	0	0	0	0	0	0
Ogrodowski C	0	0	0	0	0	0	0
	34	2	7	2	27	12	1

(a) Batted for Nicely in the eighth.
(b) Batted for Sprinz in the eighth.

Pitching Records	IP	H	R	ER	SO	BB
Fletcher	9	7	2	2	1	7
Joyce	9	12	5	5	2	0

Wild Pitch: Fletcher. Three Base Hit: White. Two Base Hit: Uhalt. Sacrifice: Handley. Time of Game: 1 hr. 56 min. Umpires: Kober, Ford, Floresi, Dempsey.

Sacramento	002	020	001	5 – 12 – 1
San Francisco	002	000	000	2 – 7 – 1

Game Six.

The Solons really made this an interesting series with an exciting 1–0 win on Monday night, October 1, to pull even with the Seals. A crowd of 7,000 was treated to a scoreless duel by the two pitchers who faced each other in game two, John Pintar and Frank Seward. The Solons broke through in the top of the ninth when Zipay got aboard on a bad hop single, George Mandish struck out, failing to sacrifice, McElreath singled Zipay to third, and Calvey's grounder scored him. Then came the bottom of the ninth: Manager Sheely took McElreath out, putting Ted Greenhalgh in center field and moved White to right. Greenhalgh made this move look brilliant with a sensational catch on Perry's long smash to open the inning. Bones Sanders hit for Nicely and singled, and went to second as White bobbled the ball in right. Bill Enos popped up, and then the third straight pinch hitter, Charley Petersen, singled to right and Jo Jo White's throw nipped Sanders at the plate, saving the game.

Sacramento	AB	R	H	RBI	O	A	E
Handley 2B	4	0	0	0	5	5	0
White CF-RF	2	0	1	0	0	1	1
Landrum 3B	4	0	1	0	0	1	0
Zipay 1B	4	1	2	0	12	0	0
Mandish RF	3	0	0	0	2	0	0
McElreath LF	3	0	1	0	2	0	0
Calvey SS	4	0	0	1	1	6	0
Schlueter C	4	0	0	0	4	0	0
Pintar P	3	0	0	0	0	2	0
Greenhalgh CF	0	0	0	0	1	0	0
	31	1	5	1	27	15	0

San Francisco	AB	R	H	RBI	O	A	E
Uhalt CF	4	0	0	0	2	0	0
Young 2B	4	0	3	0	5	2	1
Mailho LF	4	0	1	0	1	0	0
Suhr 1B	3	0	2	0	11	1	0
Sheridan RF	4	0	0	0	2	0	0
Perry 3B	4	0	1	0	0	2	0
Nicely SS	2	0	1	0	3	7	0
Ogrodowski C	3	0	0	0	3	1	0
Seward P	3	0	0	0	0	1	1
Guintini LF	0	0	0	0	0	0	0
Sanders[a]	1	0	1	0	0	0	0
Enos[b]	1	0	0	0	0	0	0
Petersen[c]	1	0	1	0	0	0	0
	34	0	10	0	27	14	2

(a) Batted for Nicely in the ninth.
(b) Batted for Ogrodowski in the ninth.
(c) Batted for Seward in the ninth.

Pitching Records	IP	H	R	ER	SO	BB
Pintar	9	10	0	0	2	1
Seward	9	5	1	1	2	3

Sacrifices: Nicely, Mandish. Double Plays: Pintar to Calvey to Zipay; Seward
to Nicely to Suhr; Calvey to Handley to Zipay. Time of Game: 1 hr. 52 min.
Umpires: Ford, Dempsey, Floresi, Kober.

Sacramento	000	000	001	1	–	5	– 0
San Francisco	000	000	000	0	–	10	– 2

Game Seven.

On Tuesday night, October 2, the day before the World Series began in
Detroit, the Seals came from behind to defeat Sacramento 9–6, to win the
series before 8,795 relieved fans. This was the only game the home team won
in this series. A six-run outburst by the Seals in the fifth prevented the Solons
from pulling off the miracle that Seattle performed against Portland.

Bob Joyce started against Jim McCarthy but neither pitcher was involved
in the decision. After 2½ innings, it looked as if the Solons were going to pull
off this miracle, roughing up Joyce for a 4–0 lead. They got a run in the second on Mandish's double and Calvey's single and three more in the third on
a walk to McCarthy, a single by Landrum, a double by Zipay and a single by

McElreath. But the Seals cut this lead to 4–2 with two runs in the last of the third, chasing McCarthy. Nicely singled, Uhalt doubled, Young walked and Guintini singled. After Sanders walked, Guy Fletcher was brought in and retired the side. In the fifth, the Solons went up 5–2 and chased Joyce. Landrum tripled and scored on Zipay's single. Elmer Orella relieved, got the side out, and was pitcher of record when his team struck for six runs in the last of the fifth.

Fletcher stayed in for the six-run onslaught. Uhalt singled, Young and Guintini walked, Sanders singled in one run, Enos forced Sanders, with Young scoring. Perry's infield hit scored Guintini to tie the game. Nicely was safe on Calvey's throwing error, allowing Enos to score the go ahead run. Petersen hit for Sprinz and singled in Perry, moving Nicely to third. Suhr hit for Orella and hit a fly, scoring Nicely. Bob Barthleson held the Sacs to just one run the last four innings to save the series for the Seals.

Sacramento	AB	R	H	RBI	O	A	E
Handley 2B	4	0	2	0	6	4	1
White CF	5	0	1	1	1	0	0
Landrum 3B	5	2	2	1	1	0	0
Zipay 1B	5	1	2	2	11	0	0
Mandish RF	5	1	3	0	1	0	0
McElreath LF	4	0	1	1	2	0	0
Calvey SS	5	0	1	1	0	5	1
Schlueter C	3	0	0	0	2	1	0
McCarthy P	0	1	0	0	0	0	0
Fletcher P	2	0	0	0	0	2	0
Greenhalgh [a]	1	1	1	0	0	0	0
Marcucci C [b]	1	0	1	0	0	0	0
Babbitt P	0	0	0	0	0	2	1
	40	6	14	6	24	14	3

(a) *Batted for Schlueter in the eighth.*
(b) *Batted for Fletcher in the eighth.*

San Francisco	AB	R	H	RBI	O	A	E
Uhalt CF	4	2	2	0	3	1	0
Young 2B	3	2	2	0	3	3	1
Guintini RF	3	1	2	1	3	0	0
Sanders 1B	4	0	1	1	11	1	0
Enos LF	5	1	1	1	0	0	0
Perry 3B	4	1	1	1	3	5	1
Nicely SS	4	2	3	0	1	3	0
Sprinz C	2	0	0	0	1	0	0

San Francisco	AB	R	H	RBI	O	A	E
Joyce P	2	0	0	1	1	1	0
Petersen[a]	1	0	1	1	0	0	0
Suhr[b]	1	0	0	1	0	0	0
Orella P	0	0	0	0	0	0	0
Ogrodowski C	0	0	0	0	1	0	0
Barthleson P	1	0	0	0	0	2	0
	34	9	13	7	27	16	2

(a) Batted for Sprinz in the fifth.
(b) Batted for Orella in the fifth.

Pitching Records	IP	H	R	ER	SO	BB
McCarthy	2.2	4	2	2	0	2
Fletcher (L)	4.1	7	6	4	1	1
Babbitt	1	2	1	0	0	0
Joyce	4.2	9	5	4	1	1
Orella (W)	0.1	0	0	0	0	0
Barthleson	4	5	1	I	1	0

Balk: Joyce. Three Base Hit: Landrum. Two Base Hits: Handley, Mandish, Zipay, Nicely. Sacrifices: Handley, Guintini, Ogrodowski. Double Play: Joyce to Young to Sanders. Time of Game: 2 hr. 15 min. Umpires: Dempsey, Floresi, Kober, Ford.

Sacramento	013	010	010	6 – 14 – 3
San Francisco	002	060	01x	9 – 13 – 2

The Solons received $2,500 prize money, which if divided into 25 shares, would be $100 per man. In current funds, it would amount to approximately $555.

The Final Series: San Francisco vs. Seattle

Since both first round series ended on Tuesday, October 2, and Seattle was entitled to open the final series at home, the Seals decided to fly to Seattle on Wednesday and open the series that night at Sick's Stadium. Plans called for single games Wednesday through Friday nights, and then for the teams to fly to San Francisco on Saturday and play a doubleheader at Seals Stadium on Sunday, October 7. All these plans went by the boards, because with the war's end, it was difficult to get space on airplanes, so the Seals had to take the train north on Wednesday morning, the third, arriving in Seattle on Thursday afternoon, the fourth. The Rainiers, therefore, decided to play a doubleheader that night, hoping to get three games in by Friday night. A crowd of over 8,000 fans was on hand that Thursday night in Sick's Stadium, hoping Seattle could continue its hot streak. Both the Rainiers and Seals were there but the Seals' equipment was not. It had gotten lost by the railroad. The Rainiers offered to let the Seals use their visiting uniforms and use their mitts, but there was no way the sporting goods stores could come up with 25 pairs of baseball shoes, so the disappointed crowd had to be sent home.

This completely changed plans for the rest of the series. The Seals had sold quite a few tickets to the doubleheader that was supposed to be played on Sunday, October 7, but now had to tell fans to exchange them for later in the week. The Rainiers had leased Sick's Stadium for a Sunday afternoon exhibition game between Bob Feller's all-stars and Satchel Paige's Negro League stars, so the third game of the playoffs had to be played on Sunday night, a rarity for the Coast League. In addition, the Seals had leased their ball park to those same two teams for an exhibition game on Tuesday night, October 9, so they could not host any playoff games until Wednesday, the 10th, which was the day the 1945 World Series ended.

Game One.

On Friday night, October 5, the final round got underway at Sick's Stadium before a crowd of 7,858 fans. Frank Seward of the Seals faced Carl Fischer but neither pitcher got the decision. The Seals got an unearned run in the second when Bill Enos was safe on Dobbins' error and came around to score on Bones Sanders' double. The next inning, the Seals went up 2–0 when Neil Sheridan doubled and scored on Enos' single. Three double plays prevented Seattle from scoring in the fourth, fifth and sixth innings, but they broke through in the seventh with two runs to tie the game.

Bob Finley's fly was misjudged by Ben Guintini and it fell for a triple. Pinch hitter John Gill doubled and took third as Bob Gorbould fouled out. Hal Patchett got a two-out, infield single to score Gill. Floyd Ehrman relieved Seward in the eighth, and gave up the game winning homer to Ted Norbert. Keith Frazier pitched the last two innings for the Rainiers to get the win. Hal Pachett made a gave-saving catch with two men on in the ninth on Guintini's line smash.

San Francisco	AB	R	H	RBI	O	E
Guintini CF	5	0	0	0	0	0
Nicely SS	4	0	0	0	3	0
Sheridan RF	3	1	1	0	1	0

San Francisco	AB	R	H	RBI	O	E
Enos LF	4	1	1	1	2	0
Perry 2B	4	0	0	0	6	0
Sanders 1B	4	0	1	1	5	0
Trutta 3B	4	0	1	0	4	0
Ogrodowski C	1	0	0	0	2	0
Seward P	3	0	0	0	0	0
Ehrman P	0	0	0	0	0	0
Mailho[a]	1	0	0	0	0	0
Suhr[b]	0	0	0	0	0	0
Futernick[c]	0	0	0	0	0	0
Young[d]	1	0	1	0	0	0
Uhalt CF	0	0	0	0	1	0
	34	2	5	2	24	0

(a) Batted for Trutta in the ninth.
(b) Batted for Ogrodowski in the ninth.
(c) Ran for Suhr in the ninth.
(d) Batted for Ehrman in the ninth.

Seattle	AB	R	H	RBI	O	E
Gorbould 2B	4	0	1	0	4	0
Patchett CF	2	0	1	1	2	0
Matheson RF	2	0	1	0	4	0
McDonald 1B	4	0	1	0	12	0
Dobbins SS	4	0	0	0	0	1
Norbert LF	4	1	3	1	0	0
Aleno 3B	3	0	1	0	1	0
Finley C	4	1	2	0	4	0
Fischer P	2	0	1	0	0	0
Gill[a]	1	1	1	1	0	0
Frazier P	1	0	0	0	0	0
Kats LF	0	0	0	0	0	0
	31	3	12	3	27	1

(a) Batted for Fischer in the seventh.

Pitching Records	IP	H	R	ER	SO	BB
Seward	6.2	11	2	2	1	3
Ehrman (L)	1.1	1	1	1	0	1
Fischer	7	4	2	1	1	2
Frazier (W)	2	1	0	0	2	1

Balk: Fischer. Left on Base: San Francisco 8, Seattle 9. Two Base Hits: Sanders, Sheridan, Gill. Three Base Hit: Finley. Home Run: Norbert. Stolen Base: Patchett. Double Plays: Perry to Nicely to Sanders; Perry to Sanders; Seward to Perry to Ogrodowski. Umpires: Edwards, Powell, Engeln, Doran.

San Francisco	011	000	000	2	–	5	– 0
Seattle	000	000	21x	3	–	12	– 1

Game Two.

On Saturday night, October 6, Bob Joyce beat Hal Turpin 4–2 to tie the series before 7,500 fans. After giving up two first inning runs, Joyce shut the Rainiers out the rest of the way, while getting three hits himself, including a triple. Seattle scored after two outs in the first when Matheson walked, went to third on McDonald's single and scored on a wild pitch. McDonald came home when Roy Nicely threw Joe Dobbins' grounder away. The Seals took a 3–2 lead in the fifth when Joyce singled and Bob Gorbould threw wildly on Uhalt's grounder, allowing them to go to second and third. Del Young singled in Joyce, and Emil Mailho's fly scored Uhalt. Bone Sanders drove in Young to put the Seals ahead. They added their final run in the sixth when Joyce tripled and scored on Uhalt's infield single.

A good many Seattle and San Francisco fans may have had their attention diverted that afternoon as California beat the University of Washington 27–14, in Berkeley before 50,000 fans.

San Francisco	AB	R	H	RBI	O	A	E
Uhalt CF	5	1	1	1	7	0	0
Young 2B	5	1	3	1	6	4	0
Mailho LF	3	0	0	1	4	0	0
Sanders 1B	4	0	1	1	7	0	0
Sheridan RF	3	0	1	0	1	0	0
Perry 3B	4	0	1	0	0	1	0
Nicely SS	4	0	1	0	1	2	1
Sprinz C	4	0	0	0	1	2	0
Joyce P	4	2	3	0	0	1	0
Guintini LF	1	0	1	0	0	0	0
	37	4	12	4	27	10	1

Seattle	AB	R	H	RBI	O	A	E
Gorbould 2B	3	0	1	0	2	2	1
Patchett CF	4	0	2	0	3	0	0
Matheson RF	3	1	0	0	2	0	0

Seattle	AB	R	H	RBI	O	A	E
McDonald 1B	4	1	1	0	12	0	0
Dobbins SS	4	0	0	0	4	6	0
Norbert LF	3	0	1	0	1	1	0
Aleno 3B	4	0	0	0	0	2	0
Finley C	3	0	0	0	3	1	1
Turpin P	3	0	0	0	0	2	0
Kats[a]	0	0	0	0	0	0	0
	31	2	5	0	27	14	2

(a) *Ran for Norbert in the ninth.*

Pitching Records	IP	H	R	ER	SO	BB
Joyce	9	5	2	1	2	3
Turpin	9	12	4	1	3	2

Wild Pitch: Joyce. Hit by Pitcher: Mailho by Turpin. Left on Base: San Francisco 11, Seattle 3. Two Base Hit: Guintini. Three Base Hit: Joyce. Stolen Bases: McDonald, Dobbins, Patchett, Uhalt. Double Play: Nicely to Young to Sanders. Time of Game: 1 hr. 55 min. Umpires: Engeln, Doran, Edwards, Powell.

San Francisco	000	031	000	4 – 12 – 1	
Seattle	200	000	000	2 – 5 – 2	

Game Three.

On Sunday night, October 7, 6,501 fans went to Sick's Stadium to see their Rainiers take a 2–1 lead in this series, by beating the Seals 7–5, in the last game played there in 1945. But a larger crowd was there that afternoon to see Bob Feller and Satchel Paige. Joe Demoran won the game with relief help from Sylvester Johnson. Bob Barthelson started and took the loss for the Seals, being followed by three relievers. The Seals scored in the first on Young's triple and Mailho's infield out. Chuck Aleno's homer tied it in the second but the Seals went up 2–1 in the fourth when Perry was safe on Aleno's error, and scored on Nicely's triple. But in the last of the fourth, the roof caved in on Barthelson. Seattle scored six runs when Matheson singled, McDonald bunted, but was safe as Barthelson threw too late to second. After Dobbins' sacrifice, Norbert was passed to load the bases, but Aleno doubled all three runners home. Elmer Orella relieved and retired Finley but then walked Demoran, Gorbould and Patchett on 12 straight pitches, forcing in the fourth run of the inning. Floyd Ehrman relieved and gave up a two-run single to Matheson to make it 7–2. The Seals closed the gap to 7–5 in the eighth, but Sylvester Johnson came in and shut the door.

San Francisco	AB	R	H	RBI	O	E
Uhalt CF	4	0	0	0	1	0
Young 2B	5	2	2	0	5	0
Mailho LF	4	1	1	1	3	0
Sanders 1B	5	0	1	0	9	0
Sheridan RF	4	1	1	1	1	0
Perry 3B	4	1	2	1	2	0
Nicely SS	3	0	1	1	0	0
Ogrodowski C	3	0	0	0	3	0
Barthleson P	1	0	0	0	0	0
Orella P	0	0	0	0	0	0
Ehrman P	2	0	0	0	0	0
Suhr [a]	0	0	0	0	0	0
Futernick SS [b]	1	0	0	0	0	0
Enos [c]	1	0	1	1	0	0
White [d]	0	0	0	0	0	0
Sarant C	0	0	0	0	0	0
Piercey P	0	0	0	0	0	0
	37	5	9	5	24	0

(a) *Batted for Nicely in the eighth.*
(b) *Batted for Ogrodowski in the eighth.*
(c) *Batted for Ehrman in the eighth.*
(d) *Ran for Suhr in the eighth.*

Seattle	AB	R	H	RBI	O	E
Garbould 2B	2	1	1	0	2	0
Patchett CF	3	0	1	0	1	0
Matheson RF	4	1	2	2	0	0
McDonald 1B	2	1	0	0	13	0
Dobbins SS	3	0	0	0	1	0
Norbert LF	3	1	1	0	1	0
Aleno 3B	3	2	2	4	0	1
Finley C	4	0	0	0	7	0
Demoran P	2	1	0	0	1	0
S. Johnson P	1	0	0	0	0	0
Kats LF	0	0	0	0	1	0
	27	7	7	6	27	1

Pitching Records	IP	H	R	ER	SO	BB
Barthelson (L)	3.1	5	4	5	1	1
Orella	0.1	0	2	2	0	3
Ehrman	3.1	2	1	0	2	1

Pitching Records	IP	H	R	ER	SO	BB
Piercey	1	0	0	0	0	1
Demoran (W)	7.2	8	5	4	6	3
S. Johnson	1.1	1	0	0	1	0

Passed Ball: Finley. Hit by Pitcher: McDonald by Ehrman. Left on Base: San Francisco 8, Seattle 5. Two Base Hits: Nicely, Aleno, Sheridan. Three Base Hit: Young. Home Run: Aleno. Umpires: Doran, Edwards, Powell, Engeln.

San Francisco	100	100	030	5 – 9 – 0
Seattle	010	600	00x	7 – 7 – 1

Game Four.

Even though they were going on the road, the Rainiers felt confident because they had beaten the Seals 16 of 28 times during the season, including 9 of 15 at Seals Stadium. The two teams left by train on Monday morning and arrived Tuesday, October 9, at the Oakland depot. This fourth game was played Wednesday night, the tenth, after Detroit had won the World Series from the Cubs that afternoon. The Coast League started before any other league in 1945 and finished later than any of them that year.

The same pitchers who faced each other in the opening game of this series met again, but this time Frank Seward pitched a six-hitter, beating Carl Fischer 6–1 to tie the series. The Seals got their first run in the second on doubles by Perry and Nicely but Seattle tied it in the fifth when Matheson doubled in Patchett. Then in the last of the fifth, the Seals scored four times to ace the game. The key blows were doubles by Guintini, Sheridan and Enos while they also got an infield single, a sacrifice and an outfield fly. They added their final run the next inning. No attendance was reported.

Seattle	AB	R	H	RBI	O	E
Gorbould 2B	4	0	0	0	2	0
Patchett CF	4	1	1	0	2	0
Matheson RF	2	0	1	1	2	0
McDonald 1B	4	0	0	0	8	0
Dobbins SS	4	0	0	0	2	0
Norbert LF	3	0	2	0	1	0
Aleno 3B	4	0	2	0	0	0
Finley C	3	0	0	0	4	0
Fischer P	1	0	0	0	2	0
Passero [a]	1	0	0	0	0	0
Elliott P	0	0	0	0	0	0

Seattle	AB	R	H	RBI	O	E
Whipple LF[b]	0	0	0	0	1	0
Gill[c]	1	0	0	0	0	0
	31	1	6	1	24	0

(a) *Batted for Fischer in the sixth.*
(b) *Ran for Norbert in the eighth.*
(c) *Batted for Elliott in the ninth.*

San Francisco	AB	R	H	RBI	O	E
Guintini CF	5	1	1	0	4	0
Peterson 2B	4	1	3	0	2	0
Sheridan RF	4	1	3	2	1	0
Enos LF	4	1	1	2	2	0
Perry 3B	2	1	2	0	2	0
Sanders 1B	3	0	0	1	7	0
Nicely SS	4	0	1	1	3	0
Ogrodowski C	3	1	1	0	5	0
Seward P	4	0	0	0	0	0
Uhalt CF	0	0	0	0	1	0
Young 2B	0	0	0	0	0	0
	33	6	12	6	27	0

Pitching Records	IP	R	ER	SO	BB
Fischer (L)	5	5	5	2	1
Elliott	3	1	1	2	1
Seward	9	1	1	5	4

Two Base Hits: Aleno, Perry, Nicely, Matheson, Guintini, Sheridan, Enos. Sacrifices: Matheson, Perry, Sanders. Umpires: Engeln, Powell, Doran, Edwards.

Seattle	000	010	000	1 –	6 – 0
San Francisco	010	041	00x	6 –	12 – 0

Game Five.

A crowd of 5,600 saw the Seals, behind Bob Joyce, take the pivotal fifth game in dramatic fashion, as Neil Sheridan blasted a three-run homer in the ninth. Seattle blew a 4–0 lead with Hal Turpin on the mound. Seattle's first two runs came in the fifth when Dobbins singled, Norbert bunted but Joyce threw too late to second. Aleno singled in one run and Hal Sueme singled in Norbert. They got their last two runs in the seventh when Norbert doubled,

Aleno beat out a bunt, Sueme was safe on a fielder's choice, which scored Norbert and Gorbould then squeezed Aleno home.

The Seals cut the lead to 4–2 in their half of the seventh when Perry doubled, Nicely singled, Uhalt singled, and pinch hitter Bill Enos hit an outfield fly. Turpin was chased in the eighth when the Seals tied the game on doubles by Perry and Nicely and a single by Petersen. Keith Frazier finished the eighth and put two runners on in the ninth before Neil Sheridan won the game 7–4 with a three-run homer, putting the Seals up in the series, three games to two.

Seattle	AB	R	H	RBI	O	E
Gorbould 2B	4	0	0	1	0	0
Patchett CF	5	0	2	0	2	0
Matheson RF	4	0	1	0	3	0
McDonald 1B	4	0	1	0	9	0
Dobbins SS	4	1	1	0	2	0
Norbert LF	3	2	2	0	3	0
Aleno 3B	4	1	2	1	2	0
Sueme C	4	0	1	2	4	0
Turpin P	1	0	0	0	0	0
Frazier P	1	0	1	0	0	0
Kats LF	0	0	0	0	1	0
	34	4	11	4	26[a]	0

(a) Two outs when winning run scored.

San Francisco	AB	R	H	RBI	O	E
Uhalt CF	4	1	3	0	2	0
Young 2B	3	0	0	0	4	0
Mailho LF	5	0	1	0	1	0
Sanders 1B	3	1	1	0	8	0
Sheridan RF	5	1	1	3	2	0
Perry 3B	4	2	2	0	1	0
Nicely SS	4	1	2	2	3	1
Sprinz C	2	0	0	0	3	0
Joyce P	4	0	2	0	1	0
Suhr[a]	1	0	0	0	0	0
Miller[b]	0	1	0	0	0	0
Enos[c]	1	0	0	1	0	0
Ogrodowski C	0	0	0	0	1	0
Peterson 2B	1	0	1	1	1	0
	37	7	13	7	27	1

(a) Batted for Sprinz in the seventh.

(b) Ran for Suhr in the seventh.
(c) Batted for Young in the seventh.

Pitching Records	IP	R	ER	SO	BB
Turpin	7.2	4	4	4	1
Frazier (L)	1	3	3	0	2
Joyce	9	4	4	3	0

Two Base Hits: Patchett, Norbert, Perry 2, Nicely. Home Run: Sheridan. Sacrifices: Turpin 2, Norbert, Gorbould, Ogrodowski. Umpires: Doran, Edwards, Powell, Engeln.

Seattle	000	020	200	4 – 11 – 0	
San Francisco	000	000	223	7 – 13 – 1	

Game Six.

On Friday night, October 12, the Seals and Rainiers each blew leads before the Seals were able to outlast Seattle 6–5, to win this hard-fought series four games to two. Had Seattle won, the final game would have been played on Sunday, the 14th. The Seals got to starter Joe Demoran for three runs in the first, but Seattle tied it with three of their own in the fourth chasing starter Bob Barthelson. It was Norbert's pinch single that brought in Floyd Ehrman. In the fifth, the Rainiers took a lead 4–3 when Matheson was safe on Ray Perry's error and eventually scored on Chuck Aleno's single. Lefty Chet Johnson relieved for Seattle and pitched three shutout innings, until he gave up the tying run in the seventh. O'Doul sent in his ace, Bob Joyce, to pitch the ninth, and Joyce gave up a run that could have made him the losing pitcher, but his mates bailed him out. In the Seattle ninth, George McDonald doubled and John Gill singled. With old Sylvester Johnson on the mound in the last of the ninth, Uhalt, Guintini and Suhr singled to tie the game, but Guintini was trapped between second and third, but stayed in the run down long enough for Suhr to take second. Neil Sheridan then became the Seal hero for the second night in a row by singling in Suhr to win the series. No attendance was mentioned.

Seattle	AB	R	H	RBI	O	E
Gorbould 2B	5	0	0	0	2	0
Patchett CF	4	0	1	0	3	0
Matheson RF	5	1	0	0	2	0
McDonald 1B	5	1	1	0	9	0
Dobbins SS	4	1	2	0	2	0

Seattle	AB	R	H	RBI	O	E
Gill LF	5	0	3	1	4	0
Aleno 3B	5	1	1	1	1	0
Finley C	3	1	1	0	3	1
Demoran P	1	0	1	0	0	1
Norbert[a]	1	0	1	2	0	0
Passero[b]	0	0	0	0	0	0
C. Johnson P	1	0	1	0	0	0
S. Johnson P	1	0	1	0	0	0
Kats LF	0	0	0	0	0	0
	40	5	13	4	26[c]	2

(a) Batted for Demoran in the fourth.
(b) Ran for Norbert in the fourth.
(c) Two outs when winning run scored.

San Francisco	AB	R	H	RBI	O	E
Uhalt CF	4	2	1	0	2	0
Young 2B	5	0	2	1	3	1
Mailho LF	2	1	1	0	1	0
Sanders 1B	1	1	0	0	5	1
Sheridan RF	3	0	1	1	3	0
Perry 3B	4	0	1	1	0	0
Nicely SS	4	0	1	0	2	0
Ogrodowski C	1	0	0	0	3	0
Barthleson P	1	0	1	0	0	0
Ehrman P	1	0	0	0	0	0
Guintini LF	2	0	1	0	5	0
Enos[a]	1	0	0	0	0	0
Peterson[b]	1	1	1	0	0	0
Trutta[c]	0	0	0	0	0	0
Suhr 1B	2	1	1	0	3	0
Sprinz C	1	0	0	0	0	0
Joyce P	1	0	0	0	0	0
	34	6	11	3	27	2

(a) Batted for Ogrodowski in the seventh.
(b) Batted for Ehrman in the seventh.
(c) Batted for Sanders in the seventh.

Pitching Records	IP	R	ER	SO	BB
Demoran	3	3	1	0	1
C. Johnson	4	1	1	2	3

Pitching Records	IP	R	ER	SO	BB
S. Johnson (L)	1.2	2	2	1	0
Barthleson	3.2	3	2	2	2
Ehrman	4.1	1	0	0	0
Joyce (W)	1	1	1	0	0

Two Base Hits: Gill, Finley, McDonald. Stolen Bases: Passero, Nicely. Sacrifice: Uhalt. Umpires: Edwards, Powell, Engeln, Doran.

Seattle	000	310	001	5 – 13 – 2
San Francisco	300	000	102	6 – 11 – 2

As in the two opening round series, a team's regular season performance meant nothing in the postseason. Seattle's fine record against the Seals, especially at Seals Stadium, was of no more value than Portland's fine road record was to the Beavers when they went to Sick's Stadium with a three game lead in the playoffs.

In the 1945 postseason, the three playoff series resulted in 20 games being played, more than any other year. This year was the second and last time that a fourth place team won the playoffs, but the third of four straight years that San Francisco was to win them. The Seals split $10,000, double what they earned by winning the two previous years. If 25 players shared this amount, each player would have received $400, which would come to about $2,220 today. Seattle's $5,000 would amount to half what the Seals earned, if the number of shares were the same.

Key Players on 1945 Playoff Teams

Portland. *Pitchers:* Ad Liska, Jake Mooty, Don Pulford, Roy Helser, Sid Cohen, and Wandel Mossor.
Position Players: Larry Barton, Charley English, Johnny O'Neil, Marvin Owen, Frank Shone and Frank Demaree.

Seattle. *Pitchers:* Joe Demoran, Chet Johnson, Hal Turpin, and Carl Fischer.
Position Players: George McDonald, Bob Gorbould, Joe Dobbins, Chuck Aleno, Ted Norbert (league's home run leader), Hal Patchett and Bill Matheson.

Sacramento. *Pitchers:* Guy Fletcher, Bud Beasley, John Pintar, and Jim McCarthy.

Position Players: Jo Jo White (batting champion), Ed Zipay, Gene Handley, Lilio Marcucci, George Mandish, Al McElreath and Jess Landrum.

San Francisco. *Pitchers:* Bob Joyce (31 game winner and league's MVP), Frank Seward, and Bob Barthelson.

Position Players: Joe Sprinz, Bones Sanders, Neil Sheridan, Frenchy Uhalt, Ben Guintini, and Bill Enos.

1946

The first postwar season began the Pacific Coast League's golden age of popularity, which lasted until the end of the 1940s. With star players returning from the military and people spending more money, the league set another attendance record of 3,722,843, an increase of 27 percent over 1945. The San Francisco Seals set a club record of 670,568, which was an all-time minor league record that stood for many decades.

The Seals did as well on the field as they did at the box office, winning their first pennant in 11 years, their fourth straight playoff cup, and beat an all-star team from the other seven clubs in a mid-season exhibition. Sportswriters in San Francisco wrote that this was the Seals' first "real" pennant since 1925, because the titles they won in 1928, 1931 and 1935 occurred under a split season format.

As great a year as the Seals had, they might not have won the pennant if not for an injury to a key Oakland player, Les Scarsella. Under their new manager, Casey Stengel, Oakland led the league for eight straight weeks, but in July, Scarsella was lost for the rest of the season with a hernia operation. He did return for some playoff games, but was not at full strength. Even without Scarsella, the Oaks crept to within a game and a half of the Seals on September 14, but never got closer. The Seals clinched the pennant on the last Saturday of the season, the 21st.

The Oaks, with an old ball park half the size of Seals Stadium, drew only 36,000 fewer fans than the Seals, so over 1.3 million people saw the two Bay Area teams play. Enthusiasm was so great when these two teams played each other they split their Sunday doubleheaders, playing a morning game in one city and the afternoon game in the other.

The Hollywood Stars finally finished over the .500 mark for the first time since the team moved to the Los Angeles area in 1938. Jimmy Dykes, the ex–White Sox manager, replaced Buck Fawcett in August and guided the team to a third place finish, passing up the Angels in September. This team outdrew the Angels by 12,000 but both clubs drew over half a million each, and could have drawn more, if not for a prolonged transit strike in the spring.

The Los Angeles Angels spent most of the season in third place but went into a tailspin the last four weeks of the season, almost falling out of the first division. They lost the last four series of the year, three of them on a prolonged road trip. They did not clinch fourth place until they won the last game of the season, staying ahead of the surging Sacramento Solons. The Angels and Sacs each won 94 games, but L.A. had three fewer losses because they did not make up all of their rained out games.

Unlike other clubs, the Angels were not helped by returning veterans. Three former PCL stars were on this team but seemed to have lost their ability while in the service. Yank Terry had been a big winner at San Diego, George Archie was the league's MVP at Seattle, and Barney Olsen was a star on the 1942 Angels, but none of these had good years in 1946.

This record attendance was set despite very strong competition from both college and professional football in September. Returning veterans

Les Scarsella played a key role on the 1948 Oakland Oaks club (Doug Mc-Williams collection).

strengthened that sport too. At the college level, Santa Clara, Stanford and USF resumed play after a wartime hiatus, while in Los Angeles, UCLA had an undefeated regular season and went to the Rose Bowl. But the big change came with professional football. The old Pacific Coast teams, the San Francisco Rockets, the Oakland Bears, the Los Angeles Bulldogs, and Hollywood Bears now had to compete with the new All America Conference's San Francisco 49ers and Los Angeles Dons. In addition, the established National Football League permitted its champion, the Cleveland Rams, to move to Los Angeles.

The San Francisco–Hollywood Series

The two playoff series opened on Wednesday night, September 25, in Seals Stadium and in Wrigley Field. The first place Seals and fourth place Angels hosted the first three games to prevent the two Bay Area teams and the two Los Angeles area teams from being home at the same time. During the regular season, the Seals won ten and lost nine to the Stars.

Game One.

The Seal ace, Larry Jansen, whose 30–6 record was tops in the league, pitched a 3–0 shutout in an hour and 38 minutes, beating Aldon Wilkie, the former Rainier. The Seals got two runs in the first when Don Trower and Hugh Luby singled and Neil Sheridan doubled them home. Sheridan, who went 3-for-4, scored the Seals last run in the third when he singled, moved to third on a sacrifice and an error, and scored when Alf Anderson fell down while catching Roy Nicely's pop up.

Hollywood	AB	R	H	RBI	O	A	E
Richardson 3B	4	0	0	0	0	4	1
Anderson SS	4	0	1	0	3	5	0
Lupien 1B	4	0	2	0	11	0	0
Rickard CF	4	0	0	0	2	0	1
Kelleher RF	3	0	1	0	2	0	0
E. Stewart LF	4	0	0	0	0	0	0
G. Stewart 2B	3	0	0	0	3	3	0
Unser C	3	0	1	0	3	2	0
Wilkie P	2	0	0	0	0	2	0
O'Brien[a]	1	0	1	0	0	0	0
Perez P	0	0	0	0	0	1	0
	32	0	6	0	24	17	2

(a) Batted for Wilkie in the eighth.

San Francisco	AB	R	H	RBI	O	A	E
Trower 3B	3	1	2	0	0	2	0
Luby 2B	4	1	1	0	1	7	0
Sheridan RF	4	1	3	2	1	1	0
Fain 1B	2	0	0	0	13	0	0
White LF	4	0	1	0	1	0	0
DiMaggio CF	2	0	0	0	2	0	0
Nicely SS	4	0	0	1	1	3	0
Sprinz C	3	0	1	0	8	0	0
Jansen P	2	0	0	0	0	1	0
	28	3	8	3	27	14	0

Pitching Records	IP	H	R	ER	SO	BB
Wilkie (L)	7	7	3	2	2	3
Perez	1	1	0	0	0	0
Jansen	9	8	0	0	8	1

Wild Pitch: Wilkie. Two Base Hits: Sheridan, Kelleher. Sacrifices: Fain 2, Jansen, DiMaggio. Time of Game: 1 hr. 38 min.

Hollywood	000	000	000	0 – 6 – 2
San Francisco	201	000	00x	3 – 8 – 0

Game Two.

A crowd of 5,029 came out Thursday night, the 26th, to see the Seals take a two game lead in the series by squelching a ninth inning Hollywood rally. Eddie Erautt, who won 20 games for the Stars, was locked in a scoreless duel with Al Lien until the last of the seventh, when the Seals got an unearned run. Nicely singled and moved to second when 44-year-old Joe Sprinz grounded out. Bones Sanders batted for Lien and hit a fly ball which Frank Kelleher dropped, allowing Nicely to score. Dale Mathewson set the Stars down in the eighth and seemed to have things well in hand when his team got two runs in the last of that inning. A walk to Hugh Luby, a double by Ferris Fain and a squeeze bunt by Don White put the Seals up 3–0. But in the ninth, Hollywood got three straight pinch hits from Cully Rickart, Hollis Sheely and Ed Stewart to load the bases. Mathewson then walked Kenny Richardson to force in a run and bring in Frank Seward to relieve. Alf Anderson's long fly plated the second run but Tony Lupien and Tommy O'Brien were retired to end the game.

Hollywood	AB	R	H	RBI	O	A	E
Richardson 3B	4	0	0	1	0	4	0
Anderson SS	5	0	1	1	2	2	0
Lupien 1B	5	0	0	0	9	1	1
O'Brien RF	5	0	0	0	0	0	0
Kelleher LF	4	0	2	0	2	0	1
Kalin CF	4	0	1	0	0	0	1
G. Stewart 2B	3	0	2	0	1	3	0
Unser C	2	0	1	0	9	0	0
Erautt P	3	0	0	0	1	1	0
Rickard[a]	1	1	1	0	0	0	0
Sheely[b]	1	1	1	0	0	0	0
E. Stewart[c]	1	0	1	0	0	0	0
Cavalli[d]	0	0	0	0	0	0	0
	38	2	10	2	24	11	3

(a) Batted for G. Stewart in the ninth.
(b) Batted for Unser in the ninth.
(c) Batted for Erautt in the ninth.
(d) Ran for Richardson in the ninth.

San Francisco	AB	R	H	RBI	O	A	E
Uhalt CF	4	0	0	0	4	0	0
Luby 2B	3	0	1	0	2	2	0
Jennings 3B	3	0	2	0	1	2	0
Fain 1B	4	1	1	1	8	0	0
Taormina RF	2	0	0	0	3	0	0
White LF	4	0	1	1	5	0	0
Nicely SS	4	1	1	0	1	4	1
Sprinz C	4	0	1	0	2	0	0
Lien P	2	0	0	0	0	0	0
Sanders[a]	1	0	0	0	0	0	0
Hoover[b]	0	0	0	0	0	0	0
Mathewson P	0	0	0	0	0	0	0
Trower 3B	0	0	0	0	0	0	0
Sheridan RF	0	1	0	0	1	0	0
	31	3	7	2	27	8	1

(a) Batted for Lien in the seventh.
(b) Ran for Sanders in the seventh.

Pitching Records	IP	H	R	ER	SO	BB
Erautt	8	7	3	2	9	3
Lien (W)	7	7	0	0	1	1
Mathewson	2	3	2	2	0	1

Two Base Hits: Jennings, Anderson, Fain. Sacrifices: Jennings 2, Mathewson 2.

Hollywood	000	000	002	2 – 10 – 3	
San Francisco	000	000	12x	3 – 7 – 1	

Game Three.

On Friday night, September 27, a crowd of 9,972 came out to see the Seals overcome a 5–0 deficit to win 7–5, and take a commanding three games to none lead in the series. Cowboy Ray Harrell started against Art "Cookie" Cuccurullo but neither pitcher was involved in the decision. In the second, Al Unser doubled in one run and Kenny Richardson singled in two more. In the fifth, the Stars went up 5–0 when Tony Lupien homered with Johnny Cavalli on base. Harrell was lifted for a hitter in the fifth and Frank Russo and Bill Werle shut the Stars down completely the last four innings.

In the last of the sixth, the Seals erupted for four runs to get within a run. Neil Sheridan led off with a home run, Ferris Fain walked, and Don White tripled. Vince DiMaggio walked, bringing in Manny Perez to relieve Cuccurullo. Nicely's fly scored White with the third run of the inning. DiMaggio got to second on Sprinz' ground out and scored on Bones Sanders' pinch single. Bill Werle took over the mound and was pitcher of record when the Seals got the winning runs in the eighth off loser Paul Gregory. Joe Sprinz singled and Joe Hoover ran for him. Werle, with his team trailing that late in the game, was allowed to bat and drew a walk. Ted Jennings singled in Hoover to tie the game. After Luby grounded out for the second out, O'Doul sent up Frenchy Uhalt to bat for Sheridan, who had two hits, including a homer. Frenchy made O'Doul look good by doubling home Werle and Jennings, for a 7–5 victory.

Hollywood	AB	H	RBI	O	A	E
Richardson 3B	4	1	2	1	4	0
Cavalli SS	4	1	0	1	1	1
Lupien 1B	5	3	2	10	0	0
Rickard CF	4	1	0	2	0	0
Kelleher RF	2	0	0	1	0	0
E. Stewart LF	3	0	0	3	0	0
G. Stewart 2B	3	0	0	1	2	0
Unser C	4	1	0	5	2	0
Cuccurullo P	3	0	0	0	0	0
Perez P	0	0	0	0	0	0
Gregory P	1	0	0	0	0	0
O'Brien[a]	1	0	0	0	0	0
	34	7	4	24	9	1

(a) Batted for Rickard in the ninth.

San Francisco	AB	H	RBI	O	A	E
Trower 3B	3	2	0	0	1	1
Luby 2B	4	1	0	3	2	1
Sheridan RF	3	2	1	0	0	0
Fain 1B	1	0	0	13	0	1
White LF	2	1	1	1	0	0
DiMaggio CF	2	0	0	3	0	0
Nicely SS	4	0	1	1	7	0

San Francisco	AB	H	RBI	O	A	E
Sprinz C	4	1	0	4	2	0
Harrell P	1	0	0	0	1	0
Restelli[a]	1	0	0	0	0	0
Rosso P	0	0	0	0	0	0
Sanders[b]	1	1	1	0	0	0
Mathewson[c]	0	0	0	0	0	0
Jennings 3B[d]	2	1	1	1	3	0
Werle P	0	0	0	0	0	0
Uhalt CF[e]	1	1	2	0	0	0
Taormina RF[f]	1	0	0	0	0	0
Hoover[g]	0	0	0	0	0	0
Ivy C	0	0	0	1	0	0
	30	10	7	27	16	3

(a) Batted for Harrell in the fifth.
(b) Batted for Rosso in the sixth.
(c) Ran for Sanders in the sixth.
(d) Batted for Trower in the sixth.
(e) Batted for Sheridan in the seventh.
(f) Batted for DiMaggio in the seventh.
(g) Ran for Sprinz in the eighth.

Pitching Records	IP	H	R	ER	SO	BB
Cuccurullo	5+	5	4	4	2	4
Perez	1.1	2	0	0	1	2
Gregory (L)	1.2	3	3	3	2	1
Harrell	5	5	5	5	2	4
Rosso	1	0	0	0	1	1
Werle (W)	3	2	0	0	2	1

Two Base Hits: Unser, Trower. Three Base Hit: White. Home Run: Lupien. Stolen Bases: E. Stewart, Lupien 2. Sacrifice: Uhalt. Double Plays: Richardson to G. Stewart to Lupien; Richardson to Lupien.

Hollywood	030	020	000	5 – 7 – 1
San Francisco	000	004	03x	7 – 10 – 3

Game Four.

Earlier in the week, Hollywood general manager Oscar Reichow had urged fans to get their tickets early for Sunday's doubleheader, which he felt could be a sellout. However, with the Stars down three games to none and on a rainy day, only 6,218 fans showed up at Gilmore Field to see the Seals sweep the Stars in the series. This game had to compete with the Rams, who drew 30,553 at the Coliseum in their loss to the Philadelphia Eagles. In addition, the Coliseum hosted USC's win over Washington State on Friday night and UCLA's win over Oregon State on Saturday afternoon, which could have drained sports dollars away from the Stars.

Cliff Melton started against Frankie Dasso but it was the relief pitchers who got the decisions. In the first, the Seals looked as if they would put Hollywood away quickly as they scored three runs, with Ferris Fain and Sal Taormina driving in the runs. But Hollywood began to peck away at this lead. In the second, Larry Jansen relieved Melton and gave up the Stars' first run. Hollywood cut the lead to 3–2 the next inning and tied the game in the fifth on Frankie Kelleher's solo home run. Then in the last of the seventh, Kelleher came up with Tommy O'Brien on base and hit another homer to put the Stars up 5–3.

Larry Jansen pitched for the San Francisco Seals in 1946 (Dick Dobbins collection).

In the eighth, the Seals rallied but a rain delay threatened to wash out these runs. Luby and Jennings singled, Sal Taormina doubled, scoring Luby and sending Ted to third. Don White was walked, and Paul Gregory relieved Dasso and gave up a run-scoring fly ball to pinch hitter Sanders. The teams waited out the rain delay, and in the top of the ninth, pitcher Larry Jansen hit a game winning homer to give the Seals a 6–5 win. No second game exhibition was played, as in the 1943 playoffs.

San Francisco	AB	H	RBI	O	A	E
Uhalt CF	4	1	0	2	0	0
Luby 2B	4	2	0	2	2	0
Jennings 3B	4	1	0	0	0	1
Fain 1B	5	2	1	12	0	0

San Francisco	AB	H	RBI	O	A	E
Taormina RF	4	2	2	1	0	0
White LF	3	0	1	4	0	0
Nicely SS	3	0	0	0	2	0
Sprinz C	4	1	0	4	0	0
Melton P	1	0	0	0	0	0
Jansen P	3	2	1	0	2	0
Sheridan RF[a]	0	0	0	2	0	0
Sanders[b]	1	0	1	0	0	0
Trower SS	0	0	0	0	1	0
	36	11	6	27	7	1

(a) Ran for Taormina in the eighth.
(b) Batted for Nicely in the eighth.

Hollywood	AB	H	RBI	O	A	E
Richardson 3B	4	2	0	2	1	0
Anderson SS	5	0	1	1	2	1
Lupin 1B	5	1	0	7	3	0
O'Brien RF	3	0	0	2	0	0
Kelleher LF	4	3	3	4	0	0
Kalin CF	4	1	0	5	0	0
G. Stewart 2B	4	0	0	2	2	0
Unser C	2	0	0	1	1	0
Dasso P	2	0	0	2	2	0
Gregory P	1	0	0	1	0	0
	34	7	4	27	11	0

Pitching Records	IP	H	R	ER	SO	BB
Melton	1.1	2	0	1	0	3
Jansen (W)	7.2	5	5	4	4	1
Dasso	7.1	9	4	5	0	3
Gregory (L)	1.2	2	1	1	0	0

Hit by Pitcher: Unser by Jansen. Left on Base: San Francisco 7, Hollywood 8. Two Base Hits: Taormina, Lupien. Three Base Hit: Richardson. Home Runs: Kelleher 2, Jansen. Sacrifice: Jennings. Stolen Bases: Fain, Kalin, Kelleher. Double Play: Dasso to Unser to Richardson.

San Francisco	300	000	021	6 – 11 – 1
Hollywood	011	010	200	5 – 7 – 0

The losing Stars each received $100 prize money, which would be worth about $513 in current dollars.

The Oakland–Los Angeles Series

Oakland had won 14 and lost only 8 to Bill Sweeney's Angels during the season. Oak fans were excited about Les Scarsella's return because he had done very well against the Angels in Wrigley Field before he went out in July. These games at Wrigley Field were broadcast live back to the Bay Area in competition with the Seals-Stars series, and *The Oakland Tribune* sent a writer down to cover the series. But *The Los Angeles Times* sent its baseball reporter, Al Wolf, to cover the exciting National League race between the Cardinals and Dodgers, so Los Angeles fans had to settle for an abbreviated wire report taken from the Oakland reporter.

Game One.

On Wednesday night, September 25, a crowd of 7,240 saw Frank Shea beat Red Adams 3–1, with all the scoring coming in the fifth inning. In the top half, Billy Raimondi and Ray Hamrick singled, and "Spec" Shea walked, to load the bases. Brooks Holder singled in two runs and Shea later scored when Reggie Otero misplayed Mickey Burnett's bunt. In the last half of that inning, Otero, who went 3-for-4, singled, Albie Glossop walked and pinch hitter Stu Martin singled in Otero. Jess Dobernic and Oren Baker finished up on the mound for the Angels.

Oakland	AB	R	H	RBI	O	A	E
Holder LF	3	0	2	2	3	0	0
Brunett 2B	3	0	0	0	3	1	1
Westlake CF	4	0	0	0	3	0	0
Scarsella 1B	4	0	1	0	3	1	0
Marshall RF	4	0	1	0	2	0	0
Hart 3B	4	0	0	0	0	1	0
Raimondi C	4	1	1	0	9	0	0
Hamrick SS	3	1	1	0	3	2	0
Shea P	2	1	0	0	1	1	0
	31	3	6	2	27	6	1
Los Angeles	AB	R	H	RBI	O	A	E
Treadway CF	4	0	0	0	1	0	0
Schuster SS	4	0	0	0	3	2	0
Sauer RF	4	0	1	0	0	0	0
Christopher LF	3	0	0	0	3	0	0

Los Angeles	AB	R	H	RBI	O	A	E
Archie 3B	4	0	0	0	0	1	0
Otero 1B	4	1	3	0	9	0	1
Glossop 2B	3	0	0	0	3	4	0
Spindel C	3	0	0	0	8	0	0
Adams P	1	0	0	0	0	2	0
Martin [a]	1	0	1	1	0	0	0
Mallory [b]	0	0	0	0	0	0	0
Baker P	0	0	0	0	0	0	0
Tyack [c]	1	0	1	0	0	0	0
Dobernic P	0	0	0	0	0	0	0
	32	1	6	1	27	9	1

(a) Batted for Adams in the fifth.
(b) Ran for Martin in the fifth.
(c) Batted for Baker in the eighth.

Pitching Records	IP	H	R	ER	SO	BB
Shea	9	6	1	1	8	1
Adams (L)	5	6	3	3	2	2
Baker	3	0	0	0	2	0
Dobernic	1	0	0	0	1	0

Hit by Pitcher: Christopher by Shea. Left on Base: Oakland 4, Los Angeles 6. Sacrifice: Burnett. Double Plays: Archie to Glossop to Otero; Schuster to Glossop to Otero; Shea to Hamrick to Scarsella. Time of Game: 1 hr. 31 min. Umpires: Sears, Warneke, Somers.

Oakland	000	030	000	3 – 6 – 1
Los Angeles	000	010	000	1 – 6 – 1

Game Two.

The Angels tied the series with Cliff Chambers going the distance in a 5–4 win before 5,735 fans on Thursday night. Bryan Stephens started for Oakland but pitched only three innings after giving up a solo homer to Joe Stephenson in the second and a two-run homer to Lloyd Christopher in the third. But the Oaks tied it with two in the fourth and one in the fifth. Bill Sweeney showed great patience with Chambers in the fourth when he gave up singles to Scarsella, Bill Hart and Raimondi to load the bases, with one out. Chambers then walked Hamrick to force in a run, and after Burnett struck out, pinch hitter Joe Biggs walked to force in the second run. But Brooks Holder left the bases loaded. Hart doubled in Scarsella to tie the game in the

Team photo of the 1946 San Francisco Seals. *Top Row, left to right:* Cliff Melton, Rino Restelli, Joe Sprinz, Al Lien, Bill Werle, Bones Sanders, Larry Jansen, Frank Seward, Ray Harrell, Doug Loane, Jim Tobin, Emmett O'Neil, Leo Hughes (trainer). *Middle Row:* Frank "Lefty" O'Doul (manager), Bernie Uhalt, Don White, Sal Taormina, Ted Jennings, Roy Nicely, Joe Hoover, Mel Ivy, Del Young. *Bottom Row:* Ed Stutz, Neill Sheridan, Bruce Ogrodowski, Don Trower, Ferris Fain, "Winky" Morris (mascot), Hugh Luby, Frank Rosso, Vince DiMaggio, "Chuck" Matzen, ball boy.

fifth but the Angels grabbed the lead back in the last half, when pinch hitter Jim Tyack flied out with the bases loaded.

Oakland tied it again in the sixth on singles by relief pitcher Floyd Speer, Holder and Tony Sabol, but L.A. again took the lead in the last half on Leon Treadway's single and Eddie Sauer's double. Reggie Otero saved the game in the ninth by leaping up and stabbing Les Scarsella's line smash.

Oakland	AB	R	H	RBI	O	A	E
Holder LF	4	0	2	0	2	0	0
Sabol RF	4	0	1	1	2	0	0
Westlake CF	4	0	0	0	1	0	0
Scarsella 1B	5	2	1	0	6	1	0
Hart 3B	4	1	2	1	1	2	0
Raimondi C	4	0	1	0	7	4	0
Hamrick SS	3	0	1	1	2	3	0
Burnett 2B	3	0	0	0	2	1	0
Stephens P	1	0	0	0	0	0	0
Biggs [a]	0	0	0	1	0	0	0
Speer P	1	1	1	0	0	0	0
Beardon P	1	0	0	0	1	1	0
Fox [b]	1	0	0	0	0	0	0
	35	4	9	4	24	12	0

(a) Batted for Stephens in the fourth.
(b) Batted for Burnett in the eighth.

Los Angeles	AB	R	H	RBI	O	A	E
Treadway CF	4	1	1	0	1	0	0
Schuster SS	3	1	1	0	3	3	0
Sauer RF	4	0	1	1	0	0	0
Christopher LF	2	2	2	2	2	0	0
Archie 3B	4	0	2	0	1	2	0
Otero 1B	4	0	2	0	6	0	0
Glossop 2B	2	0	0	0	1	0	1
Stephenson C	3	1	2	1	13	0	0
Chambers P	3	0	0	0	0	1	0
Tyack[a]	1	0	0	1	0	0	0
Mallory 2B	1	0	0	0	0	0	0
	31	5	11	5	27	6	1

(a) Batted for Glossop in the fifth.

Pitching Records	IP	H	R	ER	SO	BB
Stephens	3	5	3	3	3	3
Speer (L)	3	5	2	2	1	2
Beardon	2	1	0	0	1	0
Chambers	9	9	4	2	13	2

Two Base Hits: Hart, Sauer. Home Runs: Stephenson, Christopher. Sacrifices: Chambers, Westlake, Sabol. Double Play: Beardon to Sabol. Time of Game: 2 hr. 15 min. Umpires: Somers, Warneke, Sears.

Oakland	000	211	000	4 – 9 – 0
Los Angeles	012	011	00x	5 – 11 – 1

Unfortunately, readers of *The Oakland Tribune* had to contend with Lee Dunbar's column that said that fans don't care about the playoffs because all interest stops when the season ends. He did not feel Charles Graham's plan to increase the payout for players would rekindle interest.

Game Three.

The Oaks took a 2–1 lead in the series Friday night, September 27, before 6,920 fans, which was a very good crowd considering that USC was beating Washington State 13–7 before 68,282 at the Coliseum, just a mile away. Rugger Ardizoia started but Will Hafey got the win, pitching the last four innings.

Red Lynn started and lost but was relieved by Baker and Dobernic. It was a close 3–3 game after six innings, but the visitors blew it open with three runs on Scarsella's homer in the seventh and four more in the eighth. In the last of the fifth, Bill Schuster and Bill Sweeney were ejected after the umpire reversed himself and called Schuster out for interference, after first calling the interference on Raimondi. The Angels lost leads of 2–0 and 3–2; it was Max Marshall's sixth inning homer that tied it at 3–3. Marshall went 4-for-4 in the last game played at Wrigley Field in 1946.

Oakland	AB	R	H	RBI	O	A	E
Holder LF	2	2	1	1	1	0	0
Hamrick SS	4	1	1	2	4	3	1
Westlake CF	5	2	1	1	3	0	1
Scarsella 1B	5	1	1	3	9	2	0
Marshall RF	4	1	4	2	0	0	0
Hart 3B	4	0	0	0	1	0	0
Raimondi C	4	1	3	0	4	1	0
Burnett 2B	2	1	0	0	2	1	0
Ardizoia P	1	1	1	0	1	0	0
H. Martin[a]	1	0	0	0	0	0	0
Biggs 2B	2	1	2	0	1	1	0
Hafey P	3	0	0	0	1	2	0
	37	11	14	9	27	10	2

(a) Batted for Burnett in the sixth.

Los Angeles	AB	R	H	RBI	O	A	E
Treadway CF	5	2	3	1	0	0	0
Schuster SS	3	0	1	0	2	2	0
Sauer RF	5	0	2	1	2	1	0
Christopher LF	4	1	1	1	1	0	0
Archie 3B	4	0	1	0	1	4	0
Otero 1B	5	0	1	0	8	0	0
Mallory 2B	4	1	1	1	6	3	1
Stephenson C	3	1	2	1	6	2	1
Lynn P	2	0	0	0	1	1	0
Glossop 2B	2	0	2	0	0	0	0
Baker P	0	0	0	0	0	0	0
Dobernic P	0	0	0	0	0	0	0
Tyack[b]	1	0	0	0	0	0	0
	38	5	14	5	27	13	2

(b) Batted for Dobernic in the ninth.

Pitching Records	IP	H	R	ER	SO	BB
Ardizoia	5	6	3	3	1	1
Hafey (W)	4	8	2	2	2	1
Lynn (L)	6.2	8	6	5	5	7
Baker	1	3	3	2	1	1
Dobernic	1.1	3	2	1	0	2

Left on Base: Oakland 10, Los Angeles 10. Home Runs: Marshall, Scarsella. Sacrifices: Archie, Lynn. Double Plays: Schuster to Mallory to Otero; Hafey to Scarsella; Stephenson to Mallory; Sauer to Otero; Mallory to Otero. Time of Game: 2 hr. 49 min. Umpires: Warnekee, Sears, Somers.

Oakland	000	021	341	11 – 14 – 2
Los Angeles	020	010	101	5 – 14 – 2

The two teams both rode the S.P. Daylight north on Saturday, September 28, while UCLA was beating Oregon State 50–7 at the Coliseum and Wisconsin was beating California at Berkeley.

Game Four.

A doubleheader was scheduled at Oaks Park on Sunday, September 29, and the Angels surprisingly won both games to take a 3–2 lead in the series. A crowd of 8,933 saw this twin bill while, over at Kezar Stadium, 30,000 people saw USF beat the University of Nevada.

Red Adams beat Spec Shea in the opener, 3–2. L.A.'s first run came in the second on George Archie's single, Otero's sacrifice and Stephenson's single. Oakland tied it in the third when Archie's error allowed Raimondi to get to second base and Joe "Arky" Biggs singled him home. The Angels went up 3–1 in the fourth, when Otero doubled, Mallory sacrificed him to third, and Stephenson walked. While Red Adams was striking out, the Angels pulled off a double steal. *The Tribune* stated that the slow footed Stephenson would have been out if Biggs had not vainly thrown home trying to get Otero. But "Lead Foot" Stephenson then scored from second on Leon Treadway's single. The Oaks cut the lead to 3–2 in the seventh when Scarsella doubled and Bill Hart singled.

Los Angeles	AB	R	H	RBI	O	A	E
Treadway CF	4	0	1	0	1	0	0
Schuster SS	4	0	2	0	3	3	0
Sauer RF	4	0	1	0	2	0	0
Christopher LF	4	0	1	0	2	0	0

Los Angeles	AB	R	H	RBI	O	A	E
Archie 3B	4	1	1	0	0	0	1
Otero 1B	3	1	2	0	7	2	0
Mallory 2B	3	0	0	0	2	2	0
Stephenson C	2	1	1	1	8	1	0
Adams P	4	0	1	1	2	1	0
	32	3	10	2	27	9	1

Oakland	AB	R	H	RBI	O	A	E
Holder LF	3	0	2	0	1	0	0
Biggs 2B	3	0	1	0	4	2	0
Westlake CF	3	0	0	0	3	0	0
Scarsella 1B	3	1	1	0	13	0	0
Marshall RF	4	0	1	0	0	0	0
Hart 3B	4	0	1	1	1	4	0
Hamrick SS	4	0	0	0	0	3	0
Raimondi C	4	1	1	0	4	1	0
Shea P	2	0	0	0	1	3	0
Martin CF	1	0	0	0	0	0	0
Beardon[a]	1	0	1	0	0	0	0
Burnett[b]	0	0	0	0	0	0	0
Hayes P	0	0	0	0	0	0	0
Fox[c]	1	0	0	0	0	0	0
	33	2	8	1	27	13	0

(a) Batted for Shea in the eighth.
(b) Ran for Beardon in the eighth.
(c) Batted for Hayes in the ninth.

Pitching Records	IP	H	R	ER	SO	BB
Adams	9	8	2	2	8	3
Shea (L)	8	10	3	3	3	3
Hayes	1	0	0	0	0	0

Two Base Hits: Otero 2, Schuster, Scarsella. Sacrifices; Otero, Mallory. Double Plays: Schuster to Otero; Schuster to Mallory to Otero. Time of Game: 1 hr. 55 min. Umpires: Engeln, Doran, Kober.

Los Angeles	010	200	000	3 − 10 − 1
Oakland	001	000	100	2 − 8 − 0

Game Five.

The second game of the doubleheader was a nine-inning game in which Bill Fleming beat Bryan Stephens 2–1 to put the Angels up in the series, three games to two. A key play occurred in the last of the fourth when Oakland took a 1–0 lead, but might have scored more. Holder walked and Scarsella singled ahead of Max Marshall's double. Holder scored but Scarsella tried to run over catcher Hal Spindell, but was thrown out. The collision caused ill will between the two, and Spindell later tried to step on Scarsella's foot at first base, but was no match for the Oakland slugger.

Los Angeles tied the game in the fifth when Archie doubled and came around to score on infield singles by Elmer Mallory and Bill Fleming. The Angels got the winning run the next inning when Schuster singled, Sauer sacrificed and Christopher singled. Fleming walked only one batter and gave up just four hits.

Los Angeles	AB	R	H	RBI	O	A	E
Treadway CF	4	0	1	0	3	1	0
Schuster SS	3	1	1	0	1	2	0
Sauer RF	1	0	0	0	2	0	0
Christopher LF	4	0	1	1	6	0	0
Archie 3B	4	1	2	0	2	1	0
Otero 1B	3	0	0	0	9	0	0
Mallory 2B	4	0	1	0	1	4	0
Spindel C	4	0	0	0	3	0	0
Fleming P	3	0	1	1	0	0	0
	30	2	7	2	27	8	0

Oakland	AB	R	H	RBI	O	A	E
Burnett 2B	4	0	0	0	5	3	0
Martin CF	4	0	0	0	3	0	0
Holder LF	3	1	1	0	7	0	0
Scarsella 1B	4	0	1	0	6	1	0
Marshall RF	3	0	1	1	3	0	0
Hart 3B	3	0	0	0	1	1	0
Hamrick SS	3	0	1	0	1	2	0
Raimondi C	3	0	0	0	1	1	0
Stephens P	2	0	0	0	0	0	0
Beardon P[a]	1	0	0	0	0	1	0
	30	1	4	1	27	9	0

(a) Batted for Stephens in the eighth.

Pitching Records	IP	H	R	ER	SO	BB
Fleming	9	4	1	1	1	1
Stephens (L)	8	6	2	2	1	2
Beardon	1	1	0	0	0	0

Left on Base: Los Angeles 6, Oakland 3. Two Base Hits: Archie, Marshall. Stolen Base: Sauer. Sacrifices: Sauer, Schuster, Otero. Time of Game: 1 hr. 40 min. Umpires: Doran, Kober, Engeln.

Los Angeles	000	011	000	2 – 7 – 0
Oakland	000	100	000	1 – 4 – 0

Game Six.

On Monday night, September 30, the Oaks tied the series with a 2–0 win, as Ralph Buxton, a relief pitcher, beat Cliff Chambers. The smallest crowd of the year, 2,445, saw the fastest game of the year, one hour and 29 minutes. Each team got only three hits but the Oaks got all theirs in the fourth inning. Holder led off with a homer, Wally Westlake singled, stole second and scored on Bill Hart's double.

Los Angeles	AB	R	H	RBI	O	A	E
Treadway CF	4	0	0	0	4	0	0
Schuster SS	4	0	1	0	0	1	0
Sauer RF	4	0	0	0	3	0	0
Christopher LF	3	0	0	0	1	0	0
Archie 3B	3	0	1	0	0	2	0
Otero 1B	4	0	0	0	6	1	0
Mallory 2B	2	0	0	0	2	1	1
Stephenson C	3	0	1	0	7	0	0
Chambers P	3	0	0	0	1	2	0
	30	0	3	0	24	7	1

Oakland	AB	R	H	RBI	O	A	E
Holder LF	4	1	1	1	1	0	0
Hamrick SS	3	0	0	0	1	3	0
Westlake CF	3	1	1	0	2	0	0
Scarsella 1B	3	0	0	0	11	2	0
Hart 3B	2	0	1	1	2	3	1
Sabol RF	3	0	0	0	2	0	0
Kearse C	3	0	0	0	4	0	1
Burnett 2B	3	0	0	0	3	3	0
Buxton P	3	0	0	0	1	0	0
	27	2	3	2	27	11	2

Pitching Records	IP	H	R	ER	SO	BB
Chambers	8	3	2	2	6	1
Buxton	9	3	0	0	4	3

Two Base Hit: Hart. Home Run: Holder. Stolen Bases: Sauer, Westlake. Time of Game: 1 hr. 29 min. Umpires: Engeln, Doran, Kober.

Los Angeles	000	000	000	0 – 3 – 1
Oakland	000	200	00x	2 – 3 – 2

Game Seven.

On Tuesday night, October 1, only 2,839 fans came out to see the Oaks win the series with an exciting 6–5 victory, a game in which the lead changed four times and the score was tied four separate times. The Angels used Red Lynn and Bill Fleming on the mound, with the latter getting the loss, while

Casey Stengel used Rugger Ardizoia, Gene Beardon, Will Hafey, Frank Shea and Bryan Stephens, with the win going to Stephens.

In the first, Hershel Martin hit a solo homer, but the Angels tied it in the second. Then Mickey Burnett homered in the last of the second to put Oakland up 2–1, but the Angels again tied it with a run in the third. The Oaks grabbed a 3–2 lead in the fourth only to have the Angels take their first lead of the night, 4–3 in the top of the fifth. When Stengel brought in lefty Gene Beardon to face the left-handed pitch hitter, Tyack, Sweeney countered with the right-handed Barney Olsen, who singled in those two runs. Oakland tied it in the sixth, but L.A. again went up 5–4 in the seventh when Holder dropped Stephenson's fly ball, allowing Archie to score. But in the last of the eighth, Mickey Burnett, who went 3-for-4, singled in Bill Hart with the tying run. Then in the last of the ninth,

Casey Stengel managed the Oakland Oaks from 1946 to 1948 (Doug McWilliams collection).

Hamrick doubled, Tony Sabol sacrificed him to third, and after two men were walked to fill the bases, Max Marshall singled to send the Oaks into the final round against the Seals.

Los Angeles	AB	R	H	RBI	O	A	E
Treadway CF	4	0	0	0	4	0	0
Schuster SS	3	0	0	0	1	1	1
Sauer RF	5	2	2	0	2	0	1
Christopher LF	4	2	1	1	3	1	1
Archie 3B	4	1	1	0	3	1	0
Otero 1B	2	0	0	0	1	0	0
Mallory 2B	1	0	1	0	0	0	0
Stephenson C	3	0	1	1	3	0	0
Lynn P	4	0	0	0	0	2	0
S. Martin[a]	0	0	0	0	0	0	0
Quinn 1B	2	0	1	0	3	1	0
Tyack[b]	0	0	0	0	0	0	0
Olson[c]	1	0	1	2	0	0	0
Glossop 2B	2	0	0	0	5	1	0
Fleming P	0	0	0	0	0	3	0
	35	5	8	4	25[d]	10	3

(a) Batted for Otero in the fifth.
(b) Batted for Mallory in the fifth.
(c) Batted for Tyack in the fifth.
(d) One out when winning run scored.

Oakland	AB	R	H	RBI	O	A	E
Hamrick SS	5	1	1	0	2	1	1
H. Martin CF	2	1	1	1	3	0	0
Holder LF	3	0	0	0	2	0	1
Scarsella 1B	3	0	0	0	9	2	0
Marshall RF	5	1	1	1	1	0	0
Hart 3B	2	2	0	0	1	0	0
Raimondi C	3	0	1	0	5	1	0
Burnett 2B	4	1	3	2	3	3	0
Ardizoia P	2	0	0	0	0	2	0
Beardon P	0	0	0	0	0	0	0
Hafey P	0	0	0	0	0	0	0
Westlake[a]	1	0	1	1	0	0	0
Shea P	0	0	0	0	1	0	0
Sabol CF[b]	0	0	0	0	0	0	0
Biggs[c]	1	0	0	0	0	0	0

Oakland	AB	R	H	RBI	O	A	E
Stephens P	0	0	0	0	0	0	0
	31	6	8	5	27	9	2

(a) *Batted for Hafey in the sixth.*
(b) *Ran for H. Martin in the seventh.*
(c) *Batted for Shea in the eighth.*

Pitching Records	IP	H	R	ER	SO	BB
Lynn	6+	5	4	3	2	4
Fleming (L)	2.1	3	2	2	1	3
Ardizoia	4.2	5	2	3	1	3
Beardon	0.1	1	2	0	0	0
Hafey	1	0	0	0	0	1
Shea	2	2	1	0	2	1
Stephens (W)	1	0	0	0	2	0

Wild Pitch: Lynn. Left on Base: Los Angeles 11, Oakland 7. Two Base Hits: Stephenson, Sauer, Burnett, Hamrick. Home Runs: H. Martin, Burnett. Stolen Base: Sauer. Sacrifices: Stephenson, Holder, Schuster, Raimondi, Sabol. Time of Game: 2 hrs. 30 min. Umpires: Doran, Engeln, Kober.

Los Angeles	011	020	100	5 – 8 – 3
Oakland	110	101	011	6 – 8 – 2

The Angels, as the Stars, received $2,500 to divide, which came close to $100 per player. Meanwhile, the Seals remained in their Hollywood hotel from Sunday night until Wednesday morning, awaiting the outcome of this series. The Seals wanted to open the final series on the road in order to have the Sunday doubleheader at Seals Stadium. On Wednesday, October 2, the team flew to Oakland to open the final series that night, but rain delayed the start of that series until Thursday night, the third.

The Final Series: San Francisco vs. Oakland

The Wednesday night rainout caused this series to start on Thursday night, October 3, at Oaks Park, thus eliminating the planned off-day on Saturday. The third game of this series was played in direct competition with two college football games on Saturday, October 5, which probably hurt attendance. Both teams' announcers broadcast these games, and four umpires were used in this series, whereas only three were employed in the opening round.

Game One.

A former Oakland second baseman, Hugh Luby, returned to Oaks Park as a member of the Seals and made life miserable for this former team as the Seals took the opening game by a score of 5–2. Al Lien got all the support he needed in the first two innings as he defeated Gene Beardon, who was followed by three relievers. In the first, Trower walked and Luby homered. In the second, the Seals had a runner on first with one out and Mickey Burnett dropped a double-play ball at second, allowing both men to be safe. Al Lien then doubled in one run, and after a walk to fill the bases, Luby singled in two runs to make it 5–0. Damon Hayes of the Oaks pitched six innings of shutout ball in relief but the Oaks could manage only two runs, one of which came on Bill Hart's seventh inning homer. A crowd of 6,670 took in this game.

San Francisco	AB	R	H	RBI	O	A	E
Trower 3B	0	1	0	0	0	0	0
Luby 2B	4	1	2	4	1	2	0
Sheridan RF	1	0	1	0	1	0	0
Fain 1B	4	0	2	0	6	0	0
White LF	5	0	0	0	4	0	0
DiMaggio CF	5	0	1	0	4	0	0
Nicely SS	3	1	1	0	0	2	0
Sprinz C	4	1	1	0	7	0	0
Lien P	4	1	1	1	0	1	0
Sanders[a]	0	0	0	0	0	0	0
Taormina RF[b]	4	0	0	0	2	0	1
Hoover 3B[c]	2	0	1	0	2	1	0
	36	5	10	5	27	6	1

(a) Batted for Trower in the second.
(b) Batted for Sheridan in the second.
(c) Ran for Sanders in the second.

Oakland	AB	R	H	RBI	O	A	E
Hamrick SS	4	0	2	0	0	2	1
Sabol RF	4	0	1	0	1	0	0
Holder LF	4	0	1	0	3	0	0
Scarsella 1B	4	0	0	0	7	0	0
Westlake CF	4	0	0	0	1	0	0
Hart 3B	3	2	2	1	5	2	0
Raimondi C	4	0	1	1	7	0	0
Burnett 2B	4	0	0	0	3	4	1
Beardon P	0	0	0	0	0	2	0

Oakland	AB	R	H	RBI	O	A	E
Hafey P	0	0	0	0	0	0	0
Hayes P	2	0	0	0	0	1	0
Fox[a]	1	0	0	0	0	0	0
Speer P	0	0	0	0	0	1	0
Kearse[b]	1	0	0	0	0	0	0
	35	2	7	2	27	12	2

(a) Batted for Hayes in the eighth.
(b) Batted for Speer in the ninth.

Pitching Records	IP	H	R	ER	SO	BB
Lien	9	7	2	2	6	1
Beardon (L)	1.1	4	3	4	0	1
Hafey	0.2	1	2	0	1	2
Hayes	6	4	0	0	6	2
Speer	1	1	0	0	0	0

Hit by Pitcher: Hoover by Hayes. Left on Base: San Francisco 10, Oakland 7. Two Base Hits: Sheridan, DiMaggio, Lien, Hamrick. Home Runs: Luby Hart. Stolen Base: Hoover. Double Plays: Hart to Burnett to Scarsella; Burnett to Scarsella. Time of Game: 2 hr. 8 min. Umpires: Engeln, Doran, Kober, Sears.

San Francisco	230	000	000	5 –	10 –	1
Oakland	000	000	101	2 –	7 –	2

Game Two.

The Oaks evened the series on Friday night, the 4th, with a 5–4 win as Frank Shea beat Cliff "Mountain Music" Melton. Shea was nicked for two runs in the first when Frenchy Uhalt singled, Luby doubled and Ferris Fain singled them home. But after that, Shea shut the Seals down until the eighth. Meanwhile, Oakland finally got to Melton for its first run in the sixth on doubles by Ray Hamrick and Billy Raimondi. Then in the seventh, Melton was chased as the Oaks exploded for four runs. Brooks Holder walked and Wally Westlake homered, putting the Oaks up 3–2. Hart and Raimondi then singled, bringing in Dale Mathewson to relieve Melton. After Burnett walked to load the bases, Shea himself singled in two runs to make it 5–2. These runs proved to be decisive because the Seals scored two runs in the eighth to cut the lead to 5–4. After two were out, Fain doubled and Sal Taormina singled, but Burnett threw wildly past first, allowing Fain to score and Taormina to take second, from where he scored on Don White's single. Attendance for this tight game was 6,796.

San Francisco	AB	R	H	RBI	O	A	E
Uhalt CF	3	1	3	0	3	0	0
Luby 2B	5	1	1	1	2	3	0
Jennings 3B	4	0	0	0	1	3	0
Fain 1B	3	1	2	1	8	0	0
Taormina RF	4	1	1	0	4	0	0
White LF	4	0	1	1	0	0	0
Nicely SS	2	0	0	0	3	2	0
Sprinz C	3	0	0	0	2	0	0
Melton P	3	0	0	0	0	0	0
Mathewson P	0	0	0	0	0	0	0
Sanders[a]	1	0	0	0	0	0	0
Trower SS	0	0	0	0	1	1	0
Sheridan[b]	1	0	0	0	0	0	0
Perry[c]	1	0	0	0	0	0	0
	34	4	8	3	24	9	0

(a) Batted for Nicely in the eighth.
(b) Batted for Sprinz in the ninth.
(c) Batted for Mathewson in the ninth.

Oakland	AB	R	H	RBI	O	A	E
Hamrick SS	4	0	1	1	2	1	1
Sabol RF	3	0	0	0	4	0	0
Holder LF	3	1	0	0	1	0	0
Scarsella 1B	4	0	0	0	4	3	0
Westlake CF	4	1	2	2	4	0	0
Hart 3B	4	1	1	0	3	1	0
Raimondi C	4	2	3	0	5	1	0
Burnett 2B	2	0	0	0	1	0	0
Shea P	3	0	1	2	3	0	0
Martin CF	0	0	0	0	0	0	0
Marshall[a]	0	0	0	0	0	0	0
Biggs 2B	1	0	0	0	0	1	0
	32	5	8	5	27	7	1

(a) Batted for Burnett in the seventh.

Pitching Records	IP	H	R	ER	SO	BB
Melton (L)	6.1	5	3	5	2	1
Mathewson	1.2	3	2	0	0	1
Shea	9	8	4	4	2	3

Wild Pitch: Melton. Passed Ball: Sprinz. Two Base Hits: Luby, Uhalt, Raimondi 2, Hamrick, Fain. Home Run: Westlake. Time of Game: 2 hr. 3 min. Umpires: Kober, Sears, Doran, Engeln.

San Francisco	200	000	020	4 – 8 – 0
Oakland	000	001	40x	5 – 8 – 1

Game Three.

On Saturday afternoon the Oaks took a 2–1 lead in the series with an exciting 4–3 win before a smaller crowd of 4,267. While this game was being played, 35,000 saw the Oregon Ducks beat California 14–13 at Berkeley, and 45,000 saw Stanford beat USF 33–7 at Palo Alto. The Oaks probably played in the afternoon because they had rented their ball park to the Oakland Giants for a football game Sunday afternoon and there might not have been enough time to convert the field for football if the Oaks and Seals played on Saturday night.

Byran Stephens went the route for Oakland while Larry Jansen started for the Seals but was relieved by Bill Werle, who took the loss. Jansen gave up two runs in the second when he walked Max Marshall before Hart and Raimondi got infield singles to load the bases. Burnett's fly scored Marshall and sent Hart to third, and then Jansen's wild pitch scored Hart. Bill Werle, who replaced Jansen in the third, came up to bat in the fifth with Roy Nicely on base and hit a two-run homer to tie the game. Werle and Jansen each homered in these playoffs; however, Werle would lose this game because he gave up one more homer than he hit. In the sixth, Hart's homer put Oakland ahead 3–2, a lead which Stephens took into the ninth, but the Seals "stole" a run on him to tie the game. With Fain on third and White on first with two outs, the Seals pulled a double steal to make it 3–3. This was the second time in the playoffs the Oaks were victimized by a run-scoring double steal. But in the last of the ninth, Werle served up a home-run ball to Mickey Burnett, and the Oaks went home with a 4–3 victory in the last baseball game played in Oakland in 1946.

San Francisco	AB	R	H	RBI	O	A	E
Uhalt CF	4	0	1	0	2	0	0
Luby 2B	3	0	2	0	3	0	0
Jennings 3B	4	0	0	0	0	1	1
Fain 1B	3	1	1	0	5	0	0
Taormina RF	4	0	0	0	2	0	0
White LF	4	0	2	0	2	0	0
Nicely SS	3	1	1	0	3	4	0
Ogrodowski C	3	0	0	0	7	0	0

San Francisco	AB	R	H	RBI	O	A	E
Jansen P	1	0	0	0	0	0	0
Werle P	2	1	1	2	0	0	0
Trower 3B	0	0	0	0	0	0	1
Sanders[a]	1	0	0	0	0	0	0
Sheridan[b]	1	0	0	0	0	0	0
Hoover SS	0	0	0	0	0	0	0
Sprinz C	0	0	0	0	0	0	0
	33	3	8	2	24[c]	5	2

(a) Batted for Nicely in the ninth.
(b) Batted for Ogrodowski in the ninth.
(c) None out when winning run scored.

Oakland	AB	R	H	RBI	O	A	E
Hamrick SS	4	0	0	0	2	4	0
Westlake CF	3	0	0	0	3	0	0
Holder LF	4	0	2	0	0	0	0
Scarsella 1B	1	0	0	0	5	0	0
Marshall RF	2	1	0	0	3	0	0
Hart 3B	4	2	2	1	0	0	0
Raimondi C	3	0	1	0	6	0	0
Burnett 2B	4	1	1	2	0	4	0
Stephens P	3	0	0	0	0	3	0
Beardon 1B	2	0	0	0	8	0	0
Fox RF	1	0	0	0	0	0	0
Sabol RF	0	0	0	0	0	0	0
	31	4	6	3	27	11	0

Pitching Records	IP	H	R	ER	SO	BB
Jansen	2.1	4	2	2	2	1
Werle (L)	5.2+	2	2	2	4	1
Stephens	9	8	3	3	4	1

Hit by Pitcher: Beardon by Werle. Wild Pitch: Jansen. Two Base Hits: White, Holder, Uhalt. Home Runs: Werle, Hart, Burnett. Double Plays: Burnett to Hamrick to Beardon; Nicely to Fain. Time of Game: 1 hr. 54 min. Umpires: Kober, Sears, Engeln, Doran.

San Francisco	000	020	001	3 – 8 – 2
Oakland	020	001	001	4 – 6 – 0

Game Four.

Just as a week earlier, the Oaks took a 2–1 series lead into the Sunday doubleheader and lost both games to fall behind in the series, only this time the Oaks could not come back. A crowd of 14,797 went to Seals Stadium and saw the Seals win the opener 6–3 and the nightcap 4–1. While these games were going on, 25,000 saw St. Mary's smash Alameda Naval Air Station 73–0 at Kezar Stadium, and less than 4,000 saw the Oakland Giants lose to the Tacoma-Seattle Indians in a Coast League football game at Oaks Park.

Gene Beardon played first base for the Oaks in both games because Scarsella was slumping after his long layoff. In the opener, Frank Seward, with ninth inning relief help from Dale Mathewson, beat Ralph Buxton, who did not have the success he did against the Angels. In the second, the Seals got a run on Sheridan's single, a stolen base and White's single. They went up 3–0 in the third when Seward got an infield single, took second on Ed Kearse's wild throw and scored on Uhalt's single. Luby's single and a fielder's choice got Uhalt home. Buxton gave up two more runs in the fourth on an error, and doubles by White and Ogrodowski, giving the Seals a 5–0 lead.

Seward had a no-hitter through six innings but gave up a run in the seventh when Hershel Martin singled in Wally Westlake. It was 6–1 going into the ninth, and then the Oaks rallied for two runs, and had two men on base with only one out before Mathewson relieved Seward and got Raimondi to hit into a double play.

Oakland	AB	R	H	RBI	O	A	E
Hamrick SS	3	0	1	0	3	1	0
Westlake RF	4	2	1	0	3	0	0
Holder LF	3	0	0	1	4	0	0
Beardon 1B	2	1	0	0	6	3	0
Martin CF	4	0	2	1	0	0	0
Hart 3B	4	0	1	1	1	2	1
Kearse C	2	0	0	0	4	1	1
Buxton P	1	0	0	0	0	0	0
Burnett 2B	3	0	0	0	2	4	0
Speer P	0	0	0	0	0	1	0
Sabol[a]	0	0	0	0	0	0	0
Marshall[b]	1	0	0	0	0	0	0
Scarsella[c]	1	0	0	0	0	0	0
Biggs SS	1	0	0	0	0	1	1
Raimondi C	1	0	0	0	1	0	0
Palica P	0	0	0	0	0	0	0
	30	3	5	3	24	13	3

(a) Ran for Kearse in the eighth.
(b) Batted for Speer in the eighth.
(c) Batted for Hamrick in the eighth.

San Francisco	AB	R	H	RBI	O	A	E
Uhalt CF	5	1	2	1	1	0	0
Luby 2B	4	0	2	0	4	2	0
Jennings 3B	4	0	0	1	1	2	0
Fain 1B	2	0	0	0	10	2	0
Sheridan RF	4	2	1	0	0	0	0
White LF	4	2	3	1	1	0	0
Nicely SS	3	0	1	1	3	5	0
Ogrodowski C	4	0	2	1	6	0	0
Seward P	4	1	1	0	1	1	0
Trower 3B	0	0	0	0	0	0	0
Mathewson P	0	0	0	0	0	0	0
	34	6	12	5	27	12	0

Pitching Records	IP	H	R	ER	SO	BB
Buxton (L)	4+	7	5	4	1	0
Speer	3	3	0	0	3	3
Palica	1	2	1	0	0	0
Seward (W)	8.2	5	3	3	6	3
Mathewson	0.1	0	0	0	0	0

Hit by Pitcher: Luby by Speer. Wild Pitch: Seward. Two Base Hits: White, Ogrodowski, Westlake. Sacrifice: Nicely. Double Play: Fain to Nicely; Nicely to Luby to Fain. Time of Game: 2 hrs. 1 min. Umpires; Sears, Engeln, Doran, Kober.

Oakland	000	000	102	3 –	5 –	3
San Francisco	012	200	01x	6 –	12 –	0

Game Five.

In the nightcap, which was scheduled for nine innings, Oakland's best chance to regain the lead in this series was snuffed out in the first inning when Seal third baseman Ted Jennings leaped up and speared Bill Hart's line drive with the bases loaded, and stepped on third for an inning-ending double play. The Oaks had one run in already and that drive may have cleared the bases. Instead, this was Oakland's last gasp for 1946. Ray Harrell shut the Oaks out for the rest of the game, while the Seals scored four runs off Rugger Ardizoia.

In the second, the Seals took a 2–1 lead on Sheridan's single, White's triple and Nicely's infield out. In the third, Luby hurt his former team again with a solo homer, and in the fourth, Nicely's fly ball brought in Ferris Fain with the final run of the game. Even though the Oaks outhit the Seals 10–5, they could score no more runs in this game nor the next. These two games had to compete with the start of the World Series.

Oakland	AB	R	H	RBI	O	A	E
Hamrick SS	5	1	3	0	2	3	0
Beardon 1B	4	0	0	0	8	0	0
Holder LF	3	0	1	0	2	0	0
Marshall RF	4	0	1	0	1	0	0
Westlake CF	4	0	2	1	5	0	0
Hart 3B	4	0	0	0	0	1	0
Raimondi C	4	0	1	0	3	0	0
Burnett 2B	3	0	2	0	2	3	0
Ardizoia P	2	0	0	0	0	0	0
Hayes P	0	0	0	0	0	1	0
Scarsella[a]	1	0	0	0	0	0	0
Pippen P	0	0	0	0	0	0	0
Martin[b]	1	0	0	0	0	0	0
Fox[c]	1	0	0	0	0	0	0
Hafey P	0	0	0	0	0	0	0
Biggs 2B	0	0	0	0	1	2	0
	36	1	10	1	24	10	0

(a) Batted for Hayes in the sixth.
(b) Batted for Burnett in the eighth.
(c) Batted for Pippen in the eighth.

San Francisco	AB	R	H	RBI	O	A	E
Uhalt CF	4	0	0	0	3	0	0
Luby 2B	2	1	1	1	0	4	1
Jennings 3B	3	0	0	0	2	1	0
Fain 1B	4	1	1	0	10	1	0
Sheridan RF	2	1	1	0	1	0	0
White LF	3	1	2	1	2	0	0
Nicely SS	3	0	0	2	4	2	0
Ogrodowski C	2	0	0	0	5	0	0
Harrell P	3	0	0	0	0	2	0
Trower 3B	1	0	0	0	0	0	0
	27	4	5	4	27	10	1

Pitching Records	IP	H	R	ER	SO	BB
Ardizoia (L)	3.2	4	4	4	1	2
Hayes	1.1	0	0	0	1	1
Pippen	2	1	0	0	1	0
Hafey	1	0	0	0	0	0
Harrell	9	19	1	1	1	2

Wild Pitch: Ardizoia. Hit by Pitcher: Luby by Hafey. Left on Base: Oakland 11, San Francisco 3. Two Base Hit: Raimondi. Three Base Hit: White. Home Run: Luby. Sacrifice: Holder. Double Plays: Jennings unassisted; Hamrick to Beardon; Hart to Biggs to Beardon. Umpires: Doran, Kober, Sears, Engeln.

Oakland	100	000	000	1 – 10 – 0
San Francisco	021	100	00x	4 – 5 – 1

Game Six.

On Monday night, October 7, the San Francisco Seals set a record by winning their fourth playoff in a row when Al Lien shut out the Oaks 6–0, beating Gene Beardon before a small crowd of 4,905. The cold wind and fog probably held the crowd down. The Seals gave Lien the only run he would need in the first when Don Trower singled and went all the way to third on Uhalt's sacrifice, and scored on Beardon's wild pitch. Their second run came in the fourth when White doubled and scored on Nicely's single. In the sixth, White singled in Fain, who had doubled. The Seals tallied three more runs in the eighth off reliever Damon Hayes, but by then, the game was well in hand.

Oakland	AB	R	H	RBI	O	A	E
Hamrick SS	4	0	1	0	2	9	0
Biggs 1B	3	0	0	0	9	0	0
Holder LF	3	0	1	0	1	1	0
Westlake CF	3	0	0	0	2	0	1
Hart 3B	3	0	1	0	1	2	0
Sabol RF	3	0	1	0	2	1	0
Raimondi C	3	0	0	0	5	2	0
Burnett 2B	4	0	0	0	2	2	0
Beardon P	2	0	0	0	0	1	0
Hayes P	1	0	0	0	0	0	0
	29	0	4	0	24	18	1

San Francisco	AB	R	H	RBI	O	A	E
Trower 3B	4	1	2	0	1	1	0
Uhalt CF	3	0	0	0	4	0	0

San Francisco	AB	R	H	RBI	O	A	E
Luby 2B	4	1	1	0	2	2	0
Fain 1B	1	2	1	0	9	0	0
Sheridan RF	3	1	2	0	2	0	0
White LF	3	1	2	2	2	0	0
Nicely SS	4	0	3	1	2	1	0
Ogrodowski C	4	0	0	1	5	0	0
Lien P	4	0	0	0	0	2	0
	30	6	11	4	27	6	0

Pitching Records	IP	H	R	ER	SO	BB
Beardon (L)	7	8	3	3	5	2
Hayes	1	3	3	1	0	1
Lien	9	4	0	0	4	2

Left on Base. Oakland 4, San Francisco 10. Two Base Hits. White, Fain, Luby. Sacrifice: Uhalt. Double Plays: Hamrick to Beardon; Trower to Fain; Fain unassisted. Time of Game: 1 hr. 46 min. Umpires: Doran, Sears, Kober, Engeln.

Oakland	000	000	000	0	–	4	– 1
San Francisco	100	101	03x	6	–	11	– 0

This was the high water mark for Lefty O'Doul as Seal manager. While he had good teams the following two years, the Seals would finish a close second in each pennant race and lose in the first round of the playoffs. After that, the team tumbled into the second division. San Francisco would not win the playoffs again and would have to wait until 1957 to win another pennant, the last year of its existence.

In the seven seasons from 1940 through 1946, only Seattle and San Francisco won the playoffs. The next three years would see the three teams that had yet to win them, Los Angeles, Oakland and Hollywood, not only win the playoffs, but also the pennant.

The winning Seals in 1946 split $15,000 among 25 players, which came to $600 per man, or about $3,077 in current dollars. The Oaks received $5,000 or $200 per man, which would be worth about $1,026 today.

Key Players on 1946 Playoff Teams

San Francisco. *Pitchers:* Larry Jansen (30 game winner), Al Lien, Bill Werle, Frank Seward and Cliff Melton.
Position Players: Ferris Fain, Ted Jennings, Hugh Luby, and Neil Sheridan.

Oakland. *Pitchers:* Frank Shea, Gene Beardon, Rugger Ardizoia, Ralph Buxton, Floyd Speer and Henry Pippen.
Position Players: Les Scarsella (the league's MVP), Wally Westlake, Bill Raimondi, and Brooks Holder.

Hollywood. *Pitchers:* Eddie Erautt, Frankie Dasso, Paul Gregory, Aldon Wilkie, and Xavier Rescigno.
Position players: Frank Kelleher, Frank Kalin, Cully Rickard, Tony Lupien, and Alf Anderson.

Los Angeles. *Pitchers:* Cliff Chambers, Red Adams, Red Lynn, Jess Dobernic, Oren Baker and Bill Fleming.
Position Players: Lloyd Christopher (league's home run leader), Bill Schuster, Leon Treadway, and Eddie Sauer.

1947

For the first time in its 45 year history, the Pacific Coast League race ended in a tie that was decided by a single tie-breaker game played at Wrigley Field in which the Angels beat the Seals 5–0. Furthermore, Portland edged Oakland for third place on the last day of the season, thereby avoiding an extra game to decide that spot. In previous years, ties for second or third place were not settled by an extra game but the deadlocked teams met in the first round of the playoffs. In 1941, the first game of the playoffs between Sacramento and San Diego was used to decide second place. However, in 1947 if the Oaks and Beavers had tied for third, Portland would have had to go to Oakland to play an extra regular season game.

As exciting as the race for the championship was, there was little chance that fifth place Seattle could overtake Oakland or Portland to get into the first division. Nevertheless, Seattle broke its all-time attendance record, as did several other clubs, giving the league a fourth straight new attendance mark. The 4,068,300 was 9.2 percent more than 1946 and nearly twice as much as the combined attendance of the American Association and International leagues.

The Los Angeles Angels were heavy preseason favorites to win the pennant because they received some good talent from their parent Chicago Cubs. L.A. won, but it was not easy. The Cubs replaced the popular manager Bill Sweeney with Bill Kelly, a former umpire who had managed only two years, one in Class D and one in Class B. This move was questioned by many of the Los Angeles sportswriters. The Angels led most of the way until the Seals passed them on September 14, and then it took until September 25, before L.A. could catch the Seals. The two teams remained deadlocked the last four games of the season.

Lefty O'Doul's Seals gave the Angels quite a battle despite suffering many key injuries during the year. They swept a seven game series from San Diego in early September to overtake the Angels, but both contenders lost the last game of the season to end up tied. O'Doul felt that a poor decision by the plate umpire cost him the pennant. Before Max West hit a three run homer to beat the Seals in that final game in extra innings, the Seals had the bases loaded

324

with one out, and a 3–1 count on Roy Nicely. Dino Restelli, who was on third, broke for the plate and was called out. O'Doul claimed that Restelli slid under the tag, that the catcher interfered with Nicely's swing, and that the pitch was ball four. The umpire belatedly called the pitch a strike after calling Restelli out, and Nicely flied out to end the inning. Thus, the season ended in a tie.

The surprise team of 1947 was the Portland club that was picked to finish last, as it had done in 1946. Under its new manager, Jim "Milkman" Turner, Portland rose from last place in late July to third by winning nine series in a row. This was accomplished even though the Yankees called up Portland's best pitcher, Vic Raschi, in mid-season.

The Oakland Oaks, under Casey Stengel, finished fourth, but only a game behind Portland and five games ahead of Seattle. Stengel did quite well with so many older players, who were finishing their careers in the Coast League.

Casey Stengel helmed the 1946–1948 Oakland Oaks (Doug McWilliams collection).

Les Scarsella again was hurt, and missed a good part of the season. But Oakland acquired Nick Etten, former Yankee and Phillie, to play first base.

The Tie Breaker Game.

The Angels won the coin toss and chose to play this game at Wrigley Field. The two clubs were not only tied in the standings but also in seasonal play, with each winning 15 games from the other. A crowd of 22,996 packed the park on Monday night, September 29, to see the clash. Among the crowd were the Portland Beavers, who had finished the season at Hollywood and were waiting to see if they were going to stay in Los Angeles to play the Angels or fly to San Francisco the next morning to open the playoffs with the Seals.

Bill Schuster of the 1947 Los Angeles Angels (Dick Dobbins collection).

The pitchers, Cliff Chambers for the Angels and Jack Brewer for the Seals, were each pitching on one day's rest. The game was scoreless until the bottom of the eighth when Cecil Garriott walked, Bill Schuster singled and Eddie Sauer was hit by a pitch, to load the bases. Clarence Maddern then became an all-time Angel hero when he hit a grand slam homer. One out later, Larry Barton hit a solo homer to make it 5–0. A few years later, Angel fans were upset when Maddern was traded to San Diego for Max West, but it was West's homer, and an umpire's call, that made this game possible.

There were two coincidences with this season-ending tie. Manager Bill Kelly's Davenport team tied for its pennant in 1946 and also won that game on a homer. Secondly, the winning pitcher for San Diego in the game that caused the Seals to end the season tied was Bob Kerrigan, who in 1954, would pitch his Padre team to its only first place finish against Hollywood in another tie-breaking game, for his manager, Lefty O'Doul.

San Francisco	AB	R	H	RBI	O	A	E
White CF	4	0	0	0	2	1	0
Luby 2B	3	0	1	0	3	4	1
Sheridan RF	4	0	0	0	1	0	0
Restelli LF	4	0	0	0	0	0	0
Orteig 3B	4	0	1	0	1	2	0
Matheson 1B	4	0	1	0	9	0	1
Nicely SS	3	0	1	0	0	3	0
Gladd C	3	0	1	0	8	0	0
Brewer P	2	0	0	0	0	1	0
	31	0	5	0	24	11	2

Los Angeles	AB	R	H	RBI	O	A	E
Garriott CF	2	1	0	0	0	0	0
Schuster SS	4	1	1	0	2	8	0
Sauer RF	2	1	0	0	3	0	1
Maddern LF	3	1	1	4	0	0	0
Ostrowski 3B	4	0	0	0	0	2	1
Barton 1B	4	1	2	1	11	0	0
Stringer 2B	4	0	1	0	5	4	1
Malone C	3	0	0	0	5	0	0
Chambers P	3	0	1	0	1	0	0
	29	5	6	5	27	14	3

Pitching Records	IP	H	R	ER	SO	BB
Brewer	8	6	5	5	7	3
Chambers	9	5	0	0	5	2

Hit by Pitcher: Sauer by Brewer. Left on Base: San Francisco 6, Los Angeles 5. Home Runs: Maddern, Barton. Double Plays: Stringer to Schuster to Barton; Luby to Matheson; Ostrowski to Stringer to Barton; Schuster to Stringer to Barton.

San Francisco	000	000	000	0 – 5 – 2
Los Angeles	000	000	05x	5 – 6 – 3

The Los Angeles–Portland Series

Even though the league had set an all-time attendance record in 1947, the playoffs were not well attended. *The Los Angeles Times* had sent its baseball reporter, Al Wolf, to cover the World Series leaving Dick Hyland, primarily a football reporter, to cover the Angels in the closing days of the season and in the playoffs. Hyland argued that the Coast League season was about three weeks too long; that it should start one week later and end two weeks earlier. He was convinced that Los Angeles fans were more interested in the World Series, which was starting, and in football, now that October had arrived.

As evidence of this, on the Friday night before the season ended, September 26, 89,800 went to the Coliseum to see UCLA beat Iowa 22–7, and the next afternoon, 48,173 turned out to see USC beat Washington State, 21–0. Apparently, L.A. fans believed the old adage, "there's a time to bunt and a time to punt."

Game One.

Only 2,870 turned out on Tuesday night, September 30, to see the Angels edge Portland, 2–1 in 11 innings. The Beavers, who were in the packed stands the night before, must have wondered where everyone went. Tommy Bridges faced the Angels' Bob "Dutch" McCall, and each hurler was magnificent. Portland's only run came in the first when Danny Escobar singled and scored on Dick Wenner's double. The Angels tied the game in the third on Lou Stringer's double and Eddie Malone's single. Jess Dobernic relieved McCall in the eighth and got credit for the win. The 40-year-old Bridges was victimized by the exhaustion of Portland's reserve outfielders. Escobar played all three outfield positions as Mayo Smith and John Lazor were substituted for Dick Wenner and Herman Reich. In the top of the 11th, Escobar sprained his ankle getting back to second base on a Dobernic pickoff attempt. Because all the outfielders had been used, Escobar stayed in the game, but moved to right. In the last of the 11th, with two outs, Eddie Sauer singled and Clarence Maddern hit a pop fly down the right field line that fell in front of the hobbling Escobar. Danny's throw to the plate beat Sauer but the Angel rightfielder bowled over Charley Silvera, knocking the ball from his mitt. Sauer was called out at first, until the umpire saw that the ball had come loose. The game was recreated back to Portland.

Portland	AB	R	H	RBI	O	A	E
Ratto SS	3	0	1	0	1	3	0
Escobar CF-RF-LF	3	1	1	0	2	0	0
Wenner CF	3	0	1	1	0	1	0
Reich RF	4	0	1	0	1	0	0
Storey 3B	5	0	0	0	1	1	0
Basinski 2B-SS	5	0	1	0	5	3	1
Silvera C	4	0	0	0	14	2	0
Vico 1B	3	0	1	0	8	0	0
Bridges P	4	0	0	0	0	1	0
Lazor LF[a]	1	0	0	0	0	0	0
Mullen 2B[b]	0	0	0	0	0	1	0
Smith CF[c]	0	0	0	0	0	0	0
	35	1	6	1	32[d]	12	1

(a) Batted for Wenner in the eighth.
(b) Batted for Ratto in the eleventh.
(c) Batted for Reich in the eleventh.
(d) Two outs when winning run scored.

Los Angeles	AB	R	H	RBI	O	A	E
Garriott CF	5	0	0	0	0	0	0

Los Angeles	AB	R	H	RBI	O	A	E
Schuster SS	5	0	1	0	4	1	0
Sauer RF	4	1	2	0	1	0	0
Maddern LF	4	0	1	0	5	0	0
Ostrowski 3B	4	0	0	0	2	2	0
Barton 1B	4	0	1	0	5	1	0
Stringer 2B	2	1	1	0	4	2	0
Malone C	3	0	1	1	11	4	0
McCall P	2	0	0	0	1	0	0
Dobernic P	2	0	0	0	0	0	0
	35	2	7	1	33	10	0

Pitching Records	IP	H	R	ER	SO	BB
Bridges	10.2	7	2	1	14	4
McCall	7.1	4	1	1	6	2
Dobernic (W)	3.2	1	0	0	3	3

Left on Base: Portland 8, Los Angeles 6. Two Base Hits: Wenner, Stringer. Sacrifices: Stringer, Escobar, Lazor. Stolen Base: Schuster. Double Plays: Malone to Stringer 2; Ratto to Basinski to Vico.

Portland	100	000	000	00	1 – 6 – 1
Los Angeles	001	000	000	01	2 – 7 – 0

Game Two.

The Angels won again, 4–3, to take a two games to none lead on Wednesday night, October 1, before a small gathering of 3,236 fans. Russ Bauers went the route for Los Angeles while the Beavers used Vince DiBiasi, Edson Baher, and Jack Salveson, with the latter taking the loss. The Angels got to DiBiasi for three runs in the first after the first two men were retired. Sauer doubled, Maddern grounded to third but Harvey Storey threw the ball away, allowing Sauer to score. Johnny Ostrowski doubled in Maddern and Larry Barton singled in Ostrowski. After Lou Stringer singled, Edsor Bahr replaced DiBiasi and stopped the Angels cold, but was taken out for a pinch hitter in the seventh. Portland got one run back in the fourth when George Vico singled and Larry Barton let Johnny Lazor's ball go through his legs, sending Vico to third. Eddie "The Fiddler" Basinski's infield single scored Vico. In the seventh, Portland tied the game when Basinski was hit by a pitch and Charley Silvera homered. But in the last of the eighth, Salveson gave up singles to Bill Schuster and Eddie Sauer, and two outs later, ex–Beaver Larry Barton singled in Schuster with the winning run.

Portland	AB	R	H	RBI	O	A	E
Mullen RF	4	0	1	0	1	1	0
Ratto SS	4	0	1	0	1	1	0
Smith CF	4	0	0	0	3	0	0
Storey 3B	4	0	1	0	1	3	1
Vico 1B	4	1	1	0	7	0	0
Lazor LF	4	0	1	0	1	0	0
Basinski 2B	3	1	1	1	2	1	0
Silvera C	4	1	1	2	7	0	0
DiBiasi P	0	0	0	0	0	0	0
Baher P	2	0	0	0	0	0	0
Radulovich [a]	1	0	0	0	0	0	0
Salveson P	0	0	0	0	1	0	0
Reich [b]	1	0	0	0	0	0	0
	35	3	7	3	24	6	1

(a) Batted for Baher in the seventh.
(b) Batted for Salveson in the ninth.

Los Angeles	AB	R	H	RBI	O	A	E
Garriott CF	4	0	0	0	2	0	0
Schuster SS	4	1	1	0	1	3	0
Sauer RF	4	1	2	0	2	0	0
Maddern LF	4	1	1	0	2	0	0
Ostrowski 3B	4	1	2	1	0	5	0
Barton 1B	3	0	2	2	12	1	2
Stringer 2B	4	0	1	0	1	2	0
Gillespie C	3	0	0	0	7	0	1
Bauers P	3	0	1	0	0	2	0
	33	4	10	3	27	13	3

Pitching Records	IP	H	R	ER	SO	BB
DiBiasi	0.2	5	3	0	0	0
Bahr	5.1	2	0	0	5	1
Salveson (L)	2	3	1	1	1	0
Bauers	9	6	3	2	7	7

Hit by Pitcher: Basinski by Bauers. Left on Base; Portland 6, Los Angeles 6.
Two Base Hits: Sauer, Ostrowski. Home Run: Silvera. Stolen Base: Ratto.
Double Plays: Barton to Schuster to Barton; Storey to Basinki to Vico.

Portland	000	100	200	3 – 7 – 1
Los Angeles	300	000	01x	4 – 10 – 3

Game Three.

Before the third game was played, both the Portland and Los Angeles papers stated that the Beavers would leave on the Friday morning train for Portland, arriving Saturday evening while the Angels were going to take the Friday night train and arrive Sunday morning for a doubleheader that afternoon at Vaughan Street Park. But when weather reports called for rain in Portland, it was decided to play the entire series at Wrigley Field but to allow Portland to bat last starting with game four, which was moved up to Friday night.

On Thursday night, October 2, a crowd of 4,452 saw the Angels take a three games to none series lead with a 6–3 win. Lou Stringer was the Angel hero with his two-out, three-run homer in the ninth inning. Red Adams started against Ad Liska but neither got the decision. Jake Mooty was the loser while Jess

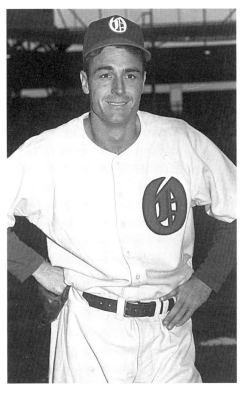

Gene Bearden took the mound for the 1946–1947 Oaks (Doug McWilliams collection).

Dobernic, who shared the Angel MVP award with Johnny Ostrowski, was the winner. Ostrowski's two-out triple scored Garriott and Sauer in the first to give L.A. the lead. They went up 3-0 in the sixth when Red Adams singled, went to second on Garriott's single, to third on Schuster's force of Garriott, and scored when George Vico threw too late to the plate on Eddie Sauer's grounder. But the Beavers tied the game the next inning when Harvey Storey walked, Vico doubled, Mayo Smith got an infield single that scored Storey, Charley Silvera singled in Vico, bringing in Jess Dobernic to relieve Adams. Ford Mullen's single scored Smith with the tying run. With Mooty pitching in the ninth, Sauer was on second with two outs when the decision was made to walk Larry Barton to get to Lou Stringer, who homered to win the game.

Portland	AB	R	H	RBI	O	A	E
Mullen 2B	3	0	1	1	7	3	0
Basinski SS	4	0	0	0	3	4	0

Portland	AB	R	H	RBI	O	A	E
Lazor RF	4	0	0	0	2	0	0
Storey 3B	2	1	0	0	0	3	0
Vico 1B	4	1	3	0	5	4	0
Wenner LF	4	0	0	0	2	0	0
Smith CF	4	1	1	1	2	0	0
Silvera C	4	0	1	1	3	0	0
Liska P	2	0	0	0	2	0	0
Radulovich[a]	1	0	0	0	0	0	0
Mooty P	1	0	0	0	0	1	0
	33	3	6	3	26[b]	15	0

(a) Batted for Liska in the seventh.
(b) Two outs when winning run scored.

Los Angeles	AB	R	H	RBI	O	A	E
Garriott CF	2	1	2	0	1	0	0
Schuster SS	5	0	0	0	1	0	0
Sauer RF	4	2	1	1	1	0	0
Maddern LF	4	0	2	0	3	0	0
Ostrowski 3B	5	0	1	2	0	1	0
Barton 1B	2	1	0	0	6	2	0
Stringer 2B	4	1	1	3	1	2	0
Gillespie C	3	0	1	0	9	1	0
Adams P	2	1	1	0	2	0	0
Dobernic P	0	0	0	0	0	2	0
Malone C	1	0	1	0	2	0	0
Sarni C	0	0	0	0	1	0	0
	32	6	10	6	27	8	0

Pitching Records	IP	H	R	ER	SO	BB
Liska	6	7	3	3	2	5
Mooty (L)	2.2	3	3	3	0	2
Adams	6.1	4	2	3	8	3
Dobernic (W)	2.2	2	1	0	4	0

Hit by Pitcher: Barton by Liska. Left on Base: Portland 6, Los Angeles 11. Two Base Hit: Vico. Three Base Hit: Ostrowski. Home Run: Stringer. Sacrifices: Adams, Dobernic, Maddern. Stolen Base: Garriott. Double Plays: Basinski to Mullen to Vico; Mooty to Basinski to Vico.

Portland	000	000	300	3 – 6 – 0
Los Angeles	200	001	003	6 – 10 – 0

Game Four.

On Friday night, October 3, only 3,380 fans turned out to see Portland avoid a sweep by beating the Angels 4–2 behind Roy Helser. Since this was supposed to be a travel day and a night usually devoted to high school football, the small turnout was not a surprise. In addition, Loyola University drew 12,000 that night at Gilmore Stadium for its 25–7 win over College of the Pacific. With the Beavers batting last, Helser himself hit a two-run homer off loser Red Lynn in the fifth to put his team up 3–2, a lead they never relinquished. The Angels scored first in the top of the third when Clarence Maddern singled in Garriott and Schuster, both of whom had singled. The Beavers cut the lead to 2–1 in their half of the third when Ford "Moon" Mullen singled in Charley Silvera, who had walked. Portland scored an insurance run in the eighth, with Reggie Otero's throwing error allowing Mullen to go to third before Vico singled him home.

Los Angeles	AB	R	H	RBI	O	A	E
Garriott CF	5	1	3	0	2	1	0
Schuster SS	5	1	1	0	4	4	0
Sauer RF	3	0	1	0	3	0	0
Maddern LF	3	0	1	2	1	0	0
Ostrowski 3B	3	0	1	0	1	0	0
Stringer 2B	3	0	0	0	3	3	0
Barton 1B	2	0	0	0	5	0	0
Sarni C	2	0	0	0	2	1	0
Lynn P	2	0	0	0	0	1	0
Christopher[a]	0	0	0	0	0	0	0
Glossop[b]	1	0	0	0	0	0	0
Stainback[c]	1	0	0	0	0	0	0
Otero 1B	1	0	0	0	2	0	1
Gillespie C	1	0	0	0	1	1	0
Fleming P	0	0	0	0	0	0	0
Mallory[d]	1	0	0	0	0	0	0
	33	2	7	2	24	11	1

(a) Batted for Barton in the sixth.
(b) Batted for Sarni in the sixth.
(c) Batted for Lynn in the sixth.
(d) Batted for Fleming in the ninth.

Portland	AB	R	H	RBI	O	A	E
Mullen 2B	2	1	1	1	3	2	0
Basinski SS	4	0	0	0	1	2	1

Portland	AB	R	H	RBI	O	A	E
Vico 1B	4	0	1	1	7	0	0
Storey 3B	3	0	1	0	1	1	0
Wenner LF	3	0	0	0	4	0	0
Reich RF	3	1	1	0	0	0	0
Smith CF	3	0	0	0	1	0	0
Silvera C	2	1	0	0	10	0	0
Helser P	2	1	1	2	0	1	0
	26	4	5	4	27	6	1

Pitching Records	IP	H	R	ER	SO	BB
Lynn (L)	5	3	3	3	2	3
Fleming	3	2	1	1	1	1
Helser	9	7	2	2	10	2

Passed Ball: Sarni. Left on Base: Los Angeles 9, Portland 2. Home Run: Helser. Sacrifice: Stringer. Stolen Base: Reich. Double Play: Schuster to Barton.

Los Angeles	002	000	000	2 – 7 – 1
Portland	001	020	01x	4 – 5 – 1

Game Five.

The teams waited until Sunday, the fifth, to resume the series because college football captured the fans' attention Saturday afternoon. On that Saturday, USC and Rice tied 7–7 before 64,231 at the Coliseum. The Trojans were to win their conference and go to the Rose Bowl that season. But on Sunday, the playoffs had to battle the World Series broadcast and professional football. A crowd of 36,087 saw the L.A. Dons beat the Buffalo Bills 27–25 at the Coliseum, while only 3,398 saw the Angels eliminate the Beavers with a 5–4 win. Had Portland won this game, the teams would have played a double-header.

Cliff Chambers, the Angels' ace, made his first start since his win over the Seals. Jack Salveson, who had lost four times to the Angels in 1947, lost again. The Angels struck for three runs in the top of the third when Paul Gillespie singled, was sacrificed by Chambers, and scored on Garriott's double. Schuster then singled in Garriott and Sauer doubled in Schuster. Portland cut the lead to 3–2 in the last of the fourth when Len Ratto singled and Dick Wenner homered. In the next inning, Los Angeles increased its lead to 4–2 off Vince DiBiasi when Sauer singled in Garriott, who had walked. The last Angels' run came in the top of the eighth off Andy Sierra when Ostrowski doubled and scored on Jess Dobernic's two-out single. This run proved to be decisive because the Beavers scored two in the last of the ninth. Storey singled, Basinski doubled, Mayo Smith singled in Storey, and Roy Helser, used as a pinch hitter, singled in Basinski. But Ford Mullen flied out to end the Beavers' season. During that regular season, the Angels had beaten Portland 14 times and lost 12 to them.

Los Angeles	AB	R	H	RBI	O	A	E
Garriott CF	4	2	1	1	5	0	0
Schuster SS	4	1	3	1	0	2	0
Sauer RF	5	0	3	2	3	0	0
Maddern LF	4	0	0	0	3	0	0
Ostrowski 3B	5	1	1	0	1	2	0
Barton 1B	3	0	1	0	4	1	0
Stringer 2B	3	0	1	0	3	0	0
Gillespie C	4	1	1	0	7	1	0
Chambers P	2	0	0	0	0	0	0
Dobernic P	1	0	1	1	1	0	0
	35	5	12	5	27	6	0

Portland	AB	R	H	RBI	O	A	E
Ratto SS	3	1	1	0	3	1	0
Vico 1B	4	0	2	0	6	3	0
Wenner LF	4	1	2	2	1	0	0
Reich RF	4	0	0	0	1	0	0
Storey 3B	4	1	1	0	0	3	0
Basinski 2B-SS	4	0	1	0	7	3	0
Silvera C	3	0	0	0	3	2	0
Smith CF	2	1	1	1	4	0	0
Salveson P	1	0	0	0	1	2	0
DiBiasi P	1	0	0	0	1	0	0
Radulovich[a]	1	0	0	0	0	0	0
Mullen 2B[b]	2	0	0	0	0	0	0
Sierra P	0	0	0	0	0	0	0
Mooty P	0	0	0	0	0	0	0
Lazor[c]	1	0	0	0	0	0	0
Helser[d]	1	0	1	1	0	0	0
	35	4	9	4	27	14	0

(a) Batted for DiBiasi in the seventh.
(b) Batted for Ratto in the eighth.
(c) Batted for Silvera in the ninth.
(d) Batted for Mooty in the ninth.

Pitching Records	IP	H	R	ER	SO	BB
Chambers (W)	5.1	5	2	2	3	1
Dobernic	3.2	4	2	2	3	1
Salveson (L)	3	6	3	3	2	2
DiBiasi	4	3	1	1	0	1
Sierra	1	2	1	1	1	1
Mooty	1	1	0	0	1	0

Left on Base: Los Angeles 9, Portland 9. Two Base Hits: Garriott, Sauer 2, Vico, Wenner, Ostrowski, Basinski. Home Run: Wenner. Sacrifices: Chambers, Schuster. Double Plays: Storey to Basinski to Vico; Basinski to Vico.

Los Angeles	003	010	010	5 – 12 – 0	
Portland	000	200	002	4 – 9 – 0	

The Oakland–San Francisco Series

It was a sad group of Seals that flew home to take on their crossbay rivals, the Oaks, in the playoffs. Not only had they lost the tie-breaker game but they believed a bad umpire call cost them the pennant in Sunday's second game in San Diego. From Oakland's viewpoint, this series was an opportunity to make up for their losses to the Seals in the 1944 and 1946 playoffs. During the regular season, Oakland won 15 and lost 13 to the Seals, winning 10 of 14 in San Francisco but only 5 of 14 in Oakland. *The Oakland Tribune* lamented that both team presidents, Charles Graham and Brick Laws, and league president Clarence Rowland, were not at the playoffs, but at the World Series. Rowland even missed the tie-breaker game.

Game One.

It may have been the start of the World Series, or the very cold weather, but only 3,202 fans showed up at Seals Stadium for the opening game on Tuesday night, September 30. These two teams really packed in the fans during the season, even splitting their doubleheaders by playing one at each park, but the enthusiasm for the postseason was clearly lacking. Will Hafey of the Oaks faced Bob Joyce and both pitched shutout ball until the top of the ninth, when Oakland came through with two runs to win. Dario Lodigiani singled, Billy Raimondi doubled him home, and Will Hafey, who was a very good hitting pitcher, singled in his catcher with the second run. Hafey held the Seals to just two hits. Both teams' announcers broadcast these games.

Oakland	AB	R	H	RBI	O	A	E
Crawford 3B	4	0	0	0	1	2	0
Workman RF	4	0	1	0	4	0	0
Holder LF	4	0	2	0	1	0	0
Etten 1B	4	0	1	0	11	0	0
Martin CF	4	0	0	0	0	0	0
Lodigiani 2B	4	1	1	0	3	3	0
Hamrick SS	4	0	0	0	0	0	1
Raimondi C	3	1	1	1	7	0	0
W. Hafey P	4	0	2	1	0	1	0
	35	2	8	2	27	6	1

San Francisco	AB	R	H	RBI	O	A	E
White CF	4	0	0	0	5	0	0
Luby 2B	4	0	1	0	1	4	0
Sheridan RF	4	0	0	0	3	0	0
Restelli LF	4	0	0	0	1	0	0
Orteig 3B	3	0	0	0	0	1	0
Matheson 1B	3	0	0	0	8	0	0
Nicely SS	3	0	1	0	6	2	0
Gladd C	2	0	0	0	3	0	0
Joyce P	3	0	0	0	0	0	0
	30	0	2	0	27	7	0

Pitching Records	IP	H	R	ER	SO	BB
W. Hafey	9	2	0	0	7	1
Joyce	9	8	2	2	3	2

Passed Ball: Gladd. Left on Base: Oakland 8, San Francisco 4. Two Base Hits: Luby, Holder, Raimondi, W. Hafey. Umpires: Warneke, Powell, Somers.

Oakland	000	000	002	2 – 8 – 1
San Francisco	000	000	000	0 – 2 – 0

Game Two.

On Wednesday night, October 1, a crowd of 3,821 went to Seals Stadium to see the ace of the staff, Bob Chesnes, face Damon Hayes of the Oaks. The Seals staked Chesnes to a 5–0 lead after 6 innings, scoring four runs in the sixth. Dino Restelli went 3-for-5 with two doubles and Bill Matheson went

Ralph Buxton of the 1947 Oakland Oaks (Dick Dubbins collection).

4-for-4, with a double and two runs batted in. Will Leonard also drove in two runs with a sixth inning single. Hayes was lifted for a pinch hitter in the seventh, when the Oaks struck for four runs to get within a run. Nick Etten homered, Charley Workman walked, Dario Lodigiani was safe on Ray Orteig's error, Ray Hamrick doubled home two runs to make it 5–3, and after Chesnes uncorked a wild pitch, sending Hamrick to third, Raimondi's grounder made it a 5–4 game.

Ralph Buxton came in to pitch for Oakland and held the Seals to just one run the rest of the way. Meanwhile, in the eighth, Hershel Martin homered to tie the game. Brooks Holder singled and Nick Etten homered to put the Oaks up 7–5. This was the first time that two homers were ever hit to right field in Seals Stadium in the same inning, and Etten was the first man to hit two consecutive homers in this big ball park.

Oakland	AB	H	RBI	O	A	E
Crawford 3B	4	1	0	0	0	0
Martin CF	4	1	1	2	0	1
Holder LF	4	2	0	5	1	0
Etten 1B	4	2	3	7	0	1
Workman RF	3	0	0	3	0	0
Lodigiani 2B	4	0	0	2	3	0
Hamrick SS	3	1	2	0	6	0
Raimondi C	4	1	1	7	2	0
Hayes P	2	0	0	0	0	0
W. Hafey[a]	1	0	0	0	0	0

Oakland	AB	H	RBI	O	A	E
Buxton P	1	0	0	0	0	0
Hughes 3B	1	0	0	1	0	0
DiMaggio CF	0	0	0	0	0	0
	35	8	7	27	12	2

(a) Batted for Hayes in the seventh.

San Francisco	AB	H	RBI	O	A	E
White CF	5	0	0	1	0	0
Luby 2B	5	2	0	0	1	0
Sheridan RF	3	0	0	6	0	0
Restelli LF	5	3	0	3	0	0
Orteig 3B	4	1	0	0	2	1
Matheson 1B	4	4	3	10	0	0
Nicely SS	3	0	0	4	2	0
Leonard C	3	1	2	3	1	0
Chesnes P	4	0	0	0	4	0
Taormina[a]	1	0	1	0	0	0
Gladd C	0	0	0	0	0	0
Mathewson P	0	0	0	0	0	0
	37	11	6	27	10	1

(a) Batted for Leonard in the eighth.

Pitching Records	IP	H	R	ER	SO	BB
Hayes	6	7	5	4	6	1
Buxton (W)	3	4	1	1	1	3
Chesnes (L)	8.2	8	7	5	3	2
Mathewson	0.1	0	0	0	0	0

Wild Pitch: Chesnes. Left on Base: Oakland 3, San Francisco 7. Two Base Hits: Hamrick, Leonard, Restelli 2, Matheson, Luby. Home Runs: Etten 2, Martin. Umpires: Powell, Somers, Warneke.

Oakland	000	000	430	7 – 8 – 2
San Francisco	000	104	010	6 – 11 – 1

Game Three.

On Thursday night, October 2, a slightly larger crowd of 4,344 fans saw the last game played in Seals Stadium in 1947. This time it was Oakland that blew a lead and lost in 11 innings. Gene Beardon went the distance for Oakland while Mike Budnick, in relief of Bill Werle, got the win. The Oaks got a run in the second when Etten walked and later came around on Lodigiani's single. They went up 2–0 in the fifth when Beardon singled, Holder walked and Tony Sabol singled in his pitcher. The third Oakland run came in the sixth on singles by Vince DiMaggio, Ray Hamrick and Billy Raimondi.

But in the last of the sixth, Ray Orteig and Bill Matheson both singled and scored on Roy Nicely's triple. Jim Gladd then singled in Nicely to tie the game. There was no further scoring until the 11th when Hugh Luby doubled and scored on Ray Orteig's single.

Oakland	AB	R	H	RBI	O	A	E
Holder LF	4	0	0	0	2	0	0
Sabol RF	4	0	2	1	1	0	0
Hughes 3B	4	0	0	0	1	6	0
Etten 1B	4	1	0	0	7	2	0
DiMaggio CF	4	1	1	0	0	0	0
Lodigiani 2B	4	0	1	1	9	3	1
Hamrick SS	5	0	1	0	4	4	0
Raimondi C	4	0	1	1	6	0	0
Beardon P	4	1	2	0	0	1	0
	37	3	8	3	30[a]	16	1

(a) None out when winning run scored.

San Francisco	AB	R	H	RBI	O	A	E
White CF	6	0	1	0	3	0	0
Luby 2B	5	1	2	0	3	2	0
Sheridan RF	5	0	2	0	4	0	0
Restelli LF	5	0	2	0	1	0	0
Orteig 3B	5	1	2	1	0	3	0
Matheson 1B	4	1	1	0	10	2	0
Nicely SS	5	1	2	2	4	4	0
Leonard C	2	0	1	0	2	3	0
Werle P	2	0	1	0	2	2	0
Gladd C	1	0	1	1	4	0	0
Joyce[a]	1	0	0	0	0	0	0
Budnick P	0	0	0	0	0	0	0
	41	4	15	4	33	16	0

(a) Batted for Werle in the 10th.

Pitching Records	IP	H	R	ER	SO	BB
Beardon	10+	15	4	4	4	8
Werle	10	8	3	3	5	4
Budnick (W)	1	0	0	0	0	1

Left on Base: Oakland 7, San Francisco 15. Three Base Hit: Nicely. Two Base Hits: Leonard, Sheridan, Luby. Sacrifices: Werle 2, Sheridan. Double Plays: Nicely to Matheson; Leonard to Nicely; Hamrick to Lodigiani to Etten; Lodigiani to Hamrick. Time of Game: 2 hr. 56 min. Umpires: Warneke, Powell, Somers.

Oakland	010	011	000	00	3 – 8 – 1	
San Francisco	000	003	000	01	4 – 15 – 0	

Game Four.

The scene shifted to Oaks Park for the Friday night game on October 3, and the largest crowd of the series, 7,725, turned out to see the Oaks go up three games to one with an 8–4 win. Vince DiMaggio tormented his 1946 team by going 3-for-4 with two homers and a double, driving in five runs. His first inning homer gave the Oaks a 1–0 lead, and in the fourth, his double put Oakland up 2–0. Then in the fifth, he homered with Brooks Holder and Roy Hughes on base to make it 5–0. Oakland also got single runs in the sixth, seventh and eighth, while the Seals scored their four runs over the last three innings. Don White drove in Nicely in the seventh, Orteig drove in two in the eighth, and Luby drove in White in the ninth. Floyd Speer went all the way for the Oaks, while Cliff Melton started and lost for the Seals.

San Francisco	AB	R	H	RBI	O	A	E
White CF	5	1	2	1	2	1	0
Luby 2B	5	0	2	1	0	1	0
Sheridan RF	5	1	1	0	1	0	0
Restelli lF	5	1	1	0	0	0	0
Orteig 3B	3	0	1	2	0	2	0
Matheson 1B	4	0	0	0	12	1	0
Nicely SS	4	1	1	0	2	6	0
Gladd C	4	0	1	0	6	1	0
Melton P	1	0	0	0	0	1	0
Jennings[a]	0	0	0	0	0	0	0
Rosso P	0	0	0	0	1	1	0
Taormina[b]	1	0	0	0	0	0	0
	37	4	9	4	24	14	0

(a) Batted for Melton in the seventh.
(b) Batted for Rosso in the ninth.

Oakland	AB	R	H	RBI	O	A	E
Holder LF	2	2	1	0	2	0	0
Hughes 3B	3	1	1	0	3	2	1
DiMaggio CF	4	3	3	5	2	0	0
Van Robays 1B	3	0	1	1	6	1	0
Lodigiani 2B	3	2	1	0	2	1	0
Lillard RF	3	0	1	1	5	0	0
Hamrick SS	4	0	2	1	3	4	0
Raimondi C	3	0	0	0	1	0	0
Speer P	4	0	0	0	0	1	0
Etten 1B	1	0	0	0	2	0	0
Workman RF	1	0	0	0	1	0	0
	31	8	10	8	27	9	1

Pitching Records	IP	H	R	ER	SO	BB
Melton (L)	6	8	6	6	3	3
Rosso	2	2	2	2	2	1
Speer	9	9	4	3	2	3

Hit by Pitcher: Orteig by Speer. Left on Base: San Francisco 10, Oakland 5. Two Base Hits: DiMaggio, Van Robays, Nicely, Lillard, Hamrick, Orteig, Luby, Lodigiani. Home Runs: DiMaggio 2. Sacrifice: Hughes. Stolen Base: Holder. Double Play: Van Robays to Hamrick. Time of Game: 2 hr. 6 min. Umpires; Powell, Somers, Warneke.

San Francisco	000	000	121	4 –	9 –	0
Oakland	100	131	11x	8 –	10 –	1

Game Five.

The teams took Saturday off and resumed the series on Sunday, October 5, with a scheduled doubleheader, but only one game was played. A crowd of 5,864 went to Oaks Park to see the Seals eliminated on a 4–0 shutout by Will Hafey, his second shutout of the Seals in this series. Meanwhile, 18,000 fans went to Kezar Stadium to see USF beat Duquesne 51–0. In the second, Maurice Van Robays led off with a homer off loser Al Lien, and then Lodigiani walked, Hamrick and Will Hafey both singled for another run. In the third, DiMaggio singled, Van Robays walked and Lodigiani singled in the third run for Oakland. Roy Hughes drove in Hamrick the next inning for Oakland's fourth run.

San Francisco	AB	R	H	RBI	O	A	E
White CF	4	0	2	0	4	0	0
Luby 2B	3	0	0	0	2	1	0
Sheridan RF	3	0	0	0	3	0	0
Restelli LF	4	0	0	0	0	0	0
Orteig 3B	4	0	1	0	3	2	0
Matheson 1B	3	0	0	0	6	1	0
Nicely SS	3	0	0	0	1	1	0
Gladd C	3	0	0	0	4	1	0
Lien P	1	0	0	0	0	0	0
Mathewson P	0	0	0	0	1	0	0
Taormina [a]	1	0	0	0	0	0	0
Werle P	0	0	0	0	0	0	0
Jennings [b]	1	0	1	0	0	0	0
Budnick P	0	0	0	0	0	1	0
	30	0	4	0	24	7	0

(a) Bated for Mathewson in the sixth.
(b) Batted for Werle in the eighth.

Oakland	AB	R	H	RBI	O	A	E
Holder LF	2	0	0	0	4	0	0
Hughes 3B	5	0	2	1	4	2	0
DiMaggio CF	4	1	1	0	3	0	0
Van Robays 1B	1	1	1	1	4	0	0
Lodigiani 2B	3	1	2	1	1	1	0
Lillard RF	1	0	0	0	0	0	0
Hamrick SS	4	1	3	0	2	4	0
Raimondi C	2	0	0	0	4	0	0
W. Hafey P	4	0	1	1	0	1	0
Workman RF	3	0	1	0	1	0	0
Etten 1B	2	0	0	0	4	0	0
	31	4	11	4	27	8	0

Pitching Records	IP	H	R	ER	SO	BB
Lien (L)	2.1	5	3	3	0	3
Mathewson	2.2	4	1	1	1	1
Werle	2	1	0	0	1	0
Budnick	1	1	0	0	1	0
W. Hafey	9	4	0	0	4	1

Hit by Pitcher: Luby by W. Hafey. Two Base Hit: White. Home Run: Van Robays. Sacrifices: Raimondi 2. Double Plays: Orteig to Luby to Matheson;

Hamrick to Etten; Hughes to Etten. Time of Game: 1 hr. 56 min. Umpires: Somers, Warneke, Powell.

San Francisco	000	000	000	0	–	4	–	0
Oakland	021	100	00x	4	–	11	–	0

The Final Series: Los Angeles vs. Oakland

Even though Oakland finished fourth, they were the only team to have a winning record against the champion Angels during the season, winning 14 and losing 11. Since Oakland was the team that eliminated the Angels from the 1946 playoffs, Los Angeles fans were a bit anxious before this series began. This series opened at Wrigley Field on Tuesday night, October 7, the day after the World Series ended.

Game One.

A crowd of 4,715 saw the Angels draw first blood in this series by coming from behind to beat the Oaks, 4–2. Bob "Dutch" McCall was starter and winner with relief help from Jess Dobernic. Gene Beardon started and lost, and was relieved by Tom Hafey, Will's brother. The Oaks took the lead in the second on Lodigiani's walk and Tony Sabol's double. This lead stood up until the seventh when Sauer walked, Maddern sacrificed, Ostrowski singled, but Holder's throw nailed Sauer at the plate. Then Stringer tripled in Ostrowski to tie the game. On the next play, Barton hit a long fly to right field on which Tony Sabol made a fine catch, but he crashed into the brick wall, hurting himself so badly he was taken by ambulance to the hospital. Sabol played no more in 1947. In the eighth, the Oaks broke the tie on a Van Robays homer, but the Angels came back with three runs in their half to win the game. Pinch hitter Lloyd Christopher singled, Schuster doubled him to third and Sauer tripled them home. Tom Hafey relieved at this point and gave up a run-scoring single to Clarence Maddern.

Oakland	AB	R	H	RBI	O	A	E
Holder LF-RF	2	0	0	0	1	1	0
Hughes 3B	4	0	0	0	0	4	0
DiMaggio CF	4	0	0	0	2	0	0
Van Robays 1B	4	1	2	1	9	1	1
Lodigiani 2B	2	1	0	0	3	3	0

Oakland	AB	R	H	RBI	O	A	E
Sabol RF	2	0	2	1	3	0	0
Hamrick SS	4	0	2	0	0	3	0
Raimondi C	2	0	1	0	6	0	0
Beardon P	2	0	0	0	0	1	0
Martin LF[a]	1	0	0	0	0	0	0
Etten 1B	0	0	0	0	0	0	0
T. Hafey P	0	0	0	0	0	0	0
Workman[b]	1	0	0	0	0	0	0
Crawford[c]	1	0	0	0	0	0	0
	29	2	7	2	24	13	1

(a) Batted for Sabol in the eighth.
(b) Batted for Raimondi in the ninth.
(c) Batted for T. Hafey in the ninth.

Los Angeles	AB	R	H	RBI	O	A	E
Garriott CF	3	0	0	0	4	0	0
Schuster SS	4	1	1	0	3	3	0
Sauer RF	3	1	1	2	1	0	0
Maddern LF	3	0	1	1	1	0	0
Ostrowski 3B	3	1	1	0	0	1	0
Stringer 2B	3	0	1	1	2	3	0
Barton 1B	3	0	0	0	6	1	0
Malone C	2	0	0	0	7	2	0
McCall P	2	0	1	0	0	1	0
Gillespie C	1	0	0	0	3	1	0
Christopher CF[a]	1	1	1	0	0	0	0
Glossop[b]	1	0	0	0	0	0	0
Dobernic P	0	0	0	0	0	0	0
	29	4	7	4	27	12	0

(a) Batted for McCall in the eighth.
(b) Batted for Garriott in the eighth.

Pitching Records	IP	H	R	ER	SO	BB
Beardon (L)	7.2	6	3	4	4	2
T. Hafey	0.1	1	1	0	1	0
McCall (W)	8	7	2	2	6	7
Dobernic	1	0	0	0	2	0

Wild Pitch: T. Hafey. Left on Base: Oakland 8, Los Angeles 4. Two Base Hits: Sabol, McCall, Schuster. Three Base Hits: Stringer, Sauer. Home Run: Van

Robays. Sacrifices: Beardon, Maddern. Double Plays: Malone to Schuster; Schuster to Barton to Malone; Hamrick to Lodigiani to Van Robays; McCall to Schuster to Stringer. Umpires: Somers, Ford, Warneke, Powell.

Oakland	010	000	010	2 – 7 – 1
Los Angeles	000	000	13x	4 – 7 – 0

Game Two.

A crowd of 5,588 came out on Wednesday, October 8, and were treated to a tight pitching duel between Damon Hayes and Red Adams. Each pitcher gave up just five hits. It was scoreless until the last of the eighth, when Cecil Garriott doubled, went to third on Schuster's sacrifice and scored on Angel hero Clarence Maddern's fly ball. In the top of the ninth, Garriott saved Adams' shutout with a sensational catch on Brooks Holder's long drive. Paul Gillespie was the only Angel catcher available on this night because Eddie Malone reinjured his finger and Bill Sarni was sick.

Oakland	AB	R	H	RBI	O	A	E
Crawford 3B	4	0	0	0	1	5	0
Workman RF	4	0	1	0	1	0	0
Holder LF	3	0	0	0	2	0	0
Etten 1B	4	0	0	0	11	0	0
Martin CF	4	0	2	0	2	0	0
Lodigiani 2B	4	0	0	0	2	1	0
Hamrick SS	2	0	1	0	1	4	0
Raimondi C	2	0	0	0	4	1	1
Hayes P	3	0	1	0	0	1	0
Burnett[a]	0	0	0	0	0	0	0
	30	0	5	0	24	12	1

(a) Ran for Martin in the ninth.

Los Angeles	AB	R	H	RBI	O	A	E
Garriott CF	4	1	1	0	2	0	0
Schuster SS	3	0	0	0	3	3	1
Sauer RF	3	0	1	0	0	0	0
Maddern LF	4	0	0	1	3	0	0
Ostrowski 3B	4	0	1	0	1	1	0
Barton 1B	3	0	1	0	7	1	0
Stringer 2B	2	0	1	0	6	4	1
Gillespie C	2	0	0	0	4	0	0
Adams P	3	0	0	0	1	2	0
	28	1	5	1	27	11	2

Pitching Records	IP	H	R	ER	SO	BB
Hayes	8	5	1	1	5	3
Adams	9	5	0	0	4	1

Left on Base: Oakland 6, Los Angeles 7. Two Base Hits: Sauer, Ostrowski, Stringer, Garriott. Sacrifices: Hamrick, Raimondi, Schuster. Stolen Bases: Workman, Burnett. Double Plays: Schuster to Stringer to Barton; Stringer to Schuster to Barton. Time of Game: 1 hr. 55 min. Umpires: Ford, Somers, Warneke, Powell.

Oakland	000	000	000	0	– 5 –	1
Los Angeles	000	000	01x	1	– 5 –	2

Game Three.

The largest crowd of the series came out on Thursday night, October 9, knowing that this would be the last game the champion Angels would play at home in 1947. The 8,567 fans got their money's worth if they enjoyed long games. This one took three hours and 15 minutes and lasted 12 innings, saw nine pitchers yield 21 walks, a hit batsman, 16 hits and 15 runs. At least no one made an error. The only home run was by the Angel starting pitcher, Cliff Chambers, who was long gone by the time the game ended. Oakland starter Floyd Speer was pounded for four runs in the first but the last of those runs was walked in by Will Hafey. Chambers gave back two of those runs in the fourth but his homer in the last half of that stanza made it 5–2. L.A. got another run in the fifth so Chambers took a 6–2 lead into the seventh, but was unable to retire a batter. The Oaks got a double and three walks, forcing in a run. The usually reliable Jess Dobernic got a double play on which the second run scored, making it 6–4, but in the eighth, Dobernic completely lost it. He walked four batters and Dutch McCall came in and walked another before Bill Fleming came in and got the side out, but only after Oakland had taken a 7–6 lead.

But Oakland could not hold this lead very long. In the last of the eighth, Clarence Maddern came to the rescue. With pinch hitter Albie Glossop on second with two outs, the Angel hero singled in the tying run. The game went into extra innings, and in the 10th, a Pacific Coast League rule was invoked that other leagues did not use. Dario Lodigiani was hit by reliever Oren Baker and needed some medical attention. Rather than delay the game, a courtesy runner was used while Dario was being attended to, and he then could stay in the game. The opposing manager was allowed to pick the runner, so Bill Kelly chose pitcher Aldon Wilkie, who also could have been used later as a pitcher if needed. The Angels went up three games to none in this series when they scored a run in the last of the 12th, for a 8–7 victory. Garriott doubled and

The 1947 Los Angeles Angels won the pennant in a one game tiebreaker with the Seals and then won the franchise's only playoff championship.

scored on Sauer's single. Gene Beardon, who lost the opening game, pitched 7⅔ innings only to lose again. Oren Baker was credited with the win.

Oakland	AB	H	RBI	O	A	E
Holder LF	5	1	0	2	0	0
Burnett 3B	3	1	0	2	1	0
DiMaggio CF	3	1	0	3	0	0
Van Robays 1B	4	0	1	17	0	0
Lodigiani 2B	4	1	1	4	5	0
Lillard RF	2	0	0	0	0	0
Hamrick SS	2	0	1	0	2	0
Raimondi C	5	0	0	6	0	0
Speer P	0	0	0	0	0	0
W. Hafey P	1	0	0	0	0	0
Beardon P	4	1	0	1	5	0
Crawford SS[a]	2	0	0	0	1	0
Martin CF	2	1	0	0	0	0
Workman[b]	0	0	0	0	0	0
Duezabou RF[c]	1	0	1	0	0	0
Etten[d]	1	0	1	0	0	0
T. Hafey 3B	1	0	0	0	2	0
Wilkie[e]	0	0	0	0	0	0
	40	6	5	35[f]	16	0

(a) Batted for Burnett in the eighth.
(b) Announced for Lillard in the eighth.
(c) Batted for Workman in the eighth.
(d) Batted for Hamrick in the eighth.
(e) Courtesy runner for Lodigiani in the 10th.
(f) Two outs when winning run scored.

Los Angeles	AB	H	RBI	O	A	E
Garriott CF	4	1	0	1	0	0
Schuster SS	7	1	0	0	3	0
Sauer RF	4	2	1	6	0	0
Maddern LF	4	1	1	4	0	0
Ostrowski 3B	5	1	2	0	3	0
Barton 1B	5	2	0	10	2	0
Stringer 2B	4	0	1	2	1	0
Gillespie C	4	1	1	9	0	0
Chambers P	3	1	1	1	1	0
Dobernic P	0	0	0	0	0	0
McCall P	0	0	0	0	0	0
Fleming P	0	0	0	1	0	0
Glossop[a]	0	0	0	0	0	0
Lynn P	0	0	0	1	0	0
Stainback[b]	1	0	0	0	0	0
Christopher[c]	0	0	0	0	0	0
Baker P	1	0	0	0	0	0
Sarni C	1	0	0	1	1	0
	43	10	7	36	11	0

(a) Batted for Fleming in the eighth.
(b) Batted for Gillespie in the ninth.
(c) Batted for Lynn in the ninth.

Pitching Records	IP	H	R	ER	SO	BB
Speer	0.1	2	3	4	0	3
W. Hafey	4	3	3	2	3	5
Beardon (L)	7.1	5	2	2	2	4
Chambers	6+	4	3	4	5	3
Dobernic	1.1	0	1	3	2	4
McCall	0+	0	1	0	0	1
Fleming	0.2	0	1	0	0	0
Lynn	1	1	0	0	2	0
Baker (W)	3	1	0	0	2	1

Hit by Pitcher: Lodigiani by Baker. Left on Base: Oakland 7, Los Angeles 14. Two Base Hits: Sauer, DiMaggio, Lodigiani, Barton, Garriott. Three Base Hit: Beardon. Home Run: Chambers. Sacrifices: Sauer, Garriott. Double Plays: Schuster to Stringer to Barton; Sarni to Stringer. Time of Game: 3 hr. 15 min. Umpires: Somers, Warneke, Powell, Ford.

Oakland	000	200	230	000	7 – 6 – 0	
Los Angeles	400	110	010	001	8 – 10 – 0	

The Oaks took the train north on Friday while the Angels took the train on Saturday, the 11th. A doubleheader was scheduled for Oaks Park on Sunday, the 12th, leaving Saturday for college football. On Saturday, Santa Clara beat Stanford at Palo Alto before 19,000 and Mississippi State beat USF at Kezar Stadium before 20,000. But on Sunday, the playoffs had to compete with professional football as 23,200 went to Kezar and saw the 49ers beat the Chicago Rockets 42–28.

Game Four.

A crowd of 5,684 came to Oaks Park on Sunday, October 12, hoping to see a doubleheader but, if the Angels won the opener, there would be no night-cap. This game was being broadcast live back to L.A. by Fred Haney, just as the games in L.A. were broadcast up to Oakland. Angels fans wanted to be in on the winning of the playoffs that had eluded them seven times. It looked as if there would only be one game played this afternoon because the Angels were sailing along with a 9–1 lead, going into the last of the sixth. Garriott and Maddern had each hit home runs, Schuster had two doubles, while Sauer, Maddern and Ostrowski had one each.

The Oaks got one run in the sixth and one in the seventh to cut the lead to 9–3. In the last of the eighth, Russ Bauers could not retire a single batter. Cliff Chambers came in and gave up three walks and two hits before retiring the side after Oakland had scored four runs to cut the lead to 9–7. Then in the ninth, Jess Dobernic, ace reliever, came in and served up a triple to Gene Lillard with Mickey Burnett and Charley Workman on base to tie the game. Vince DiMaggio then singled in Lillard to give the Oaks a 10–9 win and keep their playoff hopes alive. Tom Hafey was the beneficiary of the ninth inning runs and got the win.

Los Angeles	AB	R	H	RBI	O	A	E
Garriott CF	5	3	3	2	2	0	0
Schuster SS	5	3	2	1	2	3	0
Sauer RF	5	1	2	2	1	0	0
Maddern LF	5	1	2	3	1	0	0
Ostrowski 3B	5	0	2	1	2	1	0
Barton 1B	4	0	1	0	10	0	0
Stringer 2B	4	0	0	0	4	3	0
Gillespie C	3	1	1	0	3	3	0
Bauers P	4	0	0	0	1	1	0
Chambers P	0	0	0	0	0	0	0
Dobernic P	0	0	0	0	0	0	0
	40	9	13	9	26[a]	11	0

(a) Two outs when winning run scored.

Oakland	AB	R	H	RBI	O	A	E
Holder LF	5	0	3	1	0	0	0
DiMaggio CF	6	0	3	2	2	0	0
Crawford 3B	4	0	0	1	2	5	0
Etten 1B	5	1	1	0	12	0	0
Workman RF	2	2	1	0	1	0	0
Lodigiani 2B	5	1	2	1	2	4	0
Hamrick SS	3	1	1	0	2	1	0
Burnett SS	1	1	1	0	0	0	0
Raimondi C	4	1	0	0	6	0	0
Speer P	0	0	0	0	0	0	0
W. Hafey P	1	0	0	0	0	0	0
Wilkie P	1	0	0	0	0	0	0
Buxton P	0	0	0	0	0	0	0
Martin [a]	0	1	0	0	0	0	0
Mulcahy P	0	0	0	0	0	0	0
Van Robays [b]	1	1	1	1	0	0	0
Duezabou [c]	1	0	0	0	0	0	0
T. Hafey P	0	0	0	0	0	1	0
Lillard 3B	1	1	1	2	0	0	0
	40	10	14	8	27	11	0

(a) Batted for Buxton in the seventh.
(b) Batted for Hamrick in the eighth.
(c) Batted for Crawford in the eighth.

Pitching Records	IP	H	R	ER	SO	BB
Bauers	7+	9	5	5	2	4
Chambers	1+	2	2	2	1	3
Dobernic (L)	0.2	3	3	3	0	0
W. Hafey	3	5	4	4	0	4
Speer	1.2	4	3	3	2	3
Wilkie	1.1	3	2	2	1	0
Buxton	1.2	1	0	0	1	2
Mulcahy	0.1	0	0	0	0	0
T. Hafey (W)	1	0	0	0	1	0

Two Base Hits: Holder, Schuser 2, Sauer, Maddern, Ostrowski, Van Robays.
Three Base Hits: Hamrick, Lillard. Home Runs: Garriott, Maddern. Sacrifice:
Bauers. Stolen Base: Crawford. Time of Game: 2 hr. 31 min. Umpires: War-
neke, Ford, Powell, Somers.

Los Angeles	004	032	000	9 – 13 – 0
Oakland	010	001	143	10 – 14 – 0

Game Five.

The second game was scheduled for nine innings. Four umpires were used in the final round of the playoffs, while only three were used in the opening series. Dutch McCall was on the mound for the Angels and Eddie Malone was back behind the plate. Damon Hayes started for the Oaks but was not involved in the decision. L.A. scored a run in the second when Barton drove in Maddern and then in the fifth, the Angels went up 3–0 when Garriott homered with Stringer aboard. But just as in the opener, the Oaks came back to tie the game. They got one run in the sixth on doubles by Van Robays and Lillard and two runs in the seventh on doubles by Mel Duezabou and Van Robays, followed by Lodigiani's single.

Bill Kelly had to stay with McCall because his pitching staff was exhausted. This turned out to be fortunate for Los Angeles because McCall allowed no more runs. In the eighth inning, the Angels got to Ralph Buxton for four runs that wrapped up the game and the series. Garriott singled, Sauer walked, Maddern got a seeing-eye single into right field, and when Charley Workman juggled the ball, two runs had scored. Barton then hit a homer to make it 7–3.

Los Angeles	AB	R	H	RBI	O	A	E
Garriott CF	5	2	3	2	3	0	0
Schuster SS	3	0	1	0	2	5	0
Sauer RF	3	1	0	0	3	0	0
Maddern LF	4	2	2	0	2	0	0
Ostrowski 3B	4	0	1	0	1	1	0
Barton 1B	4	1	3	3	8	0	0
Stringer 2B	3	1	1	0	2	1	0
Malone C	3	0	0	0	6	1	0
McCall P	4	0	0	0	0	1	0
	33	7	11	5	27	9	0
Oakland	**AB**	**R**	**H**	**RBI**	**O**	**A**	**E**
Holder LF	1	0	0	0	1	0	0
Duezabou RF-LF	4	1	1	0	4	0	0
DiMaggio CF	4	0	1	0	0	0	0
Van Robays 1B	4	2	2	1	9	1	0
Lodigiani 2B	5	0	1	1	5	2	0
Lillard 3B	2	0	1	1	0	5	0
Hamrick SS	3	0	1	0	1	3	0
Raimondi C	4	0	0	0	7	1	0
Hayes P	1	0	0	0	0	0	0
Workman RF	3	0	0	0	0	0	1

Oakland	AB	R	H	RBI	O	A	E
Burnett[a]	1	0	0	0	0	0	0
Buxton P	0	0	0	0	0	0	0
T. Hafey P	1	0	0	0	0	0	0
	33	3	7	3	27	12	1

(a) Batted for Hayes in the sixth.

Pitching Records	IP	H	R	ER	SO	BB
McCall	9	7	3	3	6	8
Hayes (L)	6	7	3	3	2	1
Buxton	2	4	4	4	3	0
T. Hafey	1	0	0	0	2	0

Left on Base: Los Angeles 3, Oakland 11. Two Base Hits: Maddern, Van Robays 2, Lillard, Duezabou. Home Runs: Garriott, Barton. Sacrifices: Malone, Stringer. Double Plays: Hamrick to Lodigiani to Van Robays; Lodigiani to Hamrick to Van Robays. Time of Game: 1 hr. 50 min. Umpires: Ford, Powell, Somers, Warneke.

Los Angeles	010	020	040	7 – 11 – 0
Oakland	000	001	200	3 – 7 – ?

This was the only time the Angels ever won the playoffs; in fact, they never won a series in the postseason again. Bad times were ahead for this franchise. In two years they would be in the cellar and have several poor years while attention in Los Angeles turned to their very successful local rival, the Hollywood Stars. It would be nine years before the Angels won another pennant. But 1947 was a year to celebrate. The Angels split the newly enhanced sum of $30,000, half of which was for winning the pennant and the other half for the playoffs. With 29 players and coaches sharing this, it came to $1,034 a man, or about $4,639 in current dollars. The Oaks divided $10,000 into 32 shares, or about $312.50 apiece, which would be worth about $1,400 in current dollars. The Portland and San Francisco teams each earned $5,000, but the number of shares was not mentioned.

Key Players on the 1947 Playoff Teams

Los Angeles. *Pitchers:* Cliff Chambers, Jess Dobernic (shared team's MVP), Red Adams, Red Lynn, Bill Fleming and Russ Bauers.

Position Players: Clarence Maddern, Johnny Ostrowski (shared MVP), Eddie Sauer, Lou Stringer, Bill Schuster and Eddie Malone.

San Francisco. *Pitchers:* Bob Chesnes, Jack Brewer, Bill Werle and Al Lien. *Position Players:* Joe Brovia, Ted Jennings, Ray Orteig and Don White.

Portland. *Pitchers:* Ad Liska, Jake Mooty, Tommy Bridges, Roy Helser and Jack Salveson. *Position Players:* George Vico, John Lazor, Ford Mullen, Mayo Smith, and Harvey Storey.

Oakland. *Pitchers:* Gene Beardon, Damon Hayes, Floyd Speer, and Will Hafey. *Position Players:* Hershel Martin, Mel Duezabou, Maurice Van Robays, Brooks Holder, Billy Raimondi and Dario Lodigiani.

1948

The Oakland Oaks won the pennant for the first time in 21 years, and then won their first playoff series. This was the third and last year Casey Stengel managed this team before he became the Yankee manager. Known affectionately as the "Nine Old Men," this Oak team had to struggle to stay ahead of the Seals, who led the league by seven games in late June. This season had an ironic twist: Two years earlier Oakland lost its lead to San Francisco when its star player, Les Scarsella, went down with an operation, while in 1948, it was the Seals that lost the services of the league's batting champion, Gene Woodling, that may have cost the Seals the pennant.

Attendance for the 1948 season dropped 10 percent from 1947 but the 3,661,166 fans who did attend in 1948 surpassed all but the 1946 and 1947 seasons. One factor that accounted for some of the decline was the fire that destroyed Edmonds Field, Sacramento, in July, causing the Solons to finish the season on the road. This meant that when one of the Bay Area teams or L.A. or Hollywood were scheduled to play in Sacramento after the fire, the Solons would play in that team's park, causing the local rivals to be home at the same time, something that otherwise did not happen. In addition, there was a big flood in the Portland area that destroyed a lot of homes, including some used by the Beaver players, which distracted fans.

Only the San Diego Padres showed an increase in attendance over 1947, largely due to their slugger, Jack Graham, who had 46 home runs by mid–July, but was beaned by Red Adams, and played very little after that. Without Graham, the Padres sunk to seventh place.

The intense Oakland–San Francisco rivalry became more heated on the night of August 14, when the Oaks scored two runs in the top of the ninth at Seals Stadium to take a one run lead. But in the last of the ninth, Oak reliever Ralph Buxton got caught with pine tar in his mitt while retiring the Seals. Lefty O'Doul successfully protested, but league president Rowland ordered only the last of the ninth to be replayed and not the entire game.

The Seals argued it would be hard to get the two teams together to play a half inning but the problem was solved the last week of the season when the

The 1948 opening-day Oakland batting order (from left to right): Brooks Holder, left field; Merrill Combs, third base; Lloyd Christopher, center field; Les Scarsella, right field; Nick Etten, first base; Ed Samcoff, second base; Ray Hamrick, shortstop; Bill Raimondi, catcher; and Will "Junior" Hafey, the starting pitcher (Doug Mc-Williams collection).

schedule called for the Seals to be home against Seattle and the Oaks to be in Sacramento. Because of the fire, the latter series was played in Oakland, so the Oaks and Sacs took Tuesday night off, and the Oaks put on their visiting uniforms, took a bus over to Seals Stadium, had 10 minutes of fielding practice, and retired the same three batters that Buxton did on August 14, and left the park before the regular Rainier-Seal game.

Oakland did not clinch the pennant until the last day of the season when they beat Sacramento in the first game of the doubleheader. The Seals, after losing the first two games of the final series to Seattle, won the last five in a row, but they could not overtake the Oaks.

The Seals were the preseason favorites to win the pennant, and with a healthy Woodling, they might have. Lefty O'Doul had his team train in Hawaii, travel first class and stay in better hotels than the other PCL clubs, hoping to convince his players they were as well off as if they were in the major leagues.

The third place Los Angeles Angels had a lot of home run power but lacked good pitching. Their parent Chicago Cubs took three of their star players — Chambers, Dobernic and Maddern — and sent very little in return. The Angels got to within three games of the lead in late July, but the Cubs called up pitcher Doyle Lade and promised to send L.A. a replacement but they never did. The Angels dropped to ten games behind the second place Seals, but were nine games ahead of fourth place Seattle.

The Seattle Rainiers, now managed by their former hero, Jo Jo White, finished under .500 for the third year in a row, but this time it was good enough to make the first division. After being as high as second place in early June, thcy slumped into the second division, but got hot in August and passed up Portland, finishing four games ahead of the fifth place Beavers. At one point during the last week of the season, the Rainiers had 93 wins and 90 losses, but lost the last five games of the year to the Seals, ending up at 93–95, and thus became the second team to make the playoffs with a losing record. But Seattle lost their best hitter, Neil Sheridan, in early September when he was recalled by the Red Sox.

The PCL owners were concerned about the dropoff in attendance after Labor Day, especially since professional football began earlier than the college game. The Hollywood Stars postponed a game on Thursday night, September 2, to avoid a conflict with the game between the Los Angeles Rams and Washington Redskins. The Coast League teams now had to compete for newspaper space and sports broadcasts not only with football, but also the tight American League pennant race that ended in a tie between Cleveland and Boston. The playoffs suffered even more than in 1947.

Skipper Lefty O'Doul of the 1949 San Francisco Seals (Dick Dobbins collection).

The Oakland–Los Angeles Series

This series was a pitcher's nightmare but a hitter's paradise. These two teams clubbed each other for 121 runs, 172 hits and 29 home runs in six games. During the regular season the Angels were the only team to have an edge on the champion Oaks, winning 13 and losing 12, just as in 1947, the Oaks were the only team to have an edge on the pennant winning Angels.

Game One.

This series opened on Wednesday night, September 29, at Oaks Park. Only 2,466 came out to see the Angels draw first blood with a 10–9 victory. Johnny Ostrowski hit a two-run homer off loser Charley Gassaway in the first, but the Oaks came storming back against starter Dewey Adkins with five runs. George Metkovitch hit a three-run homer and Dario Lodigiani hit a two-run homer. Each team got a run in the third but the Angels knocked Gassaway out of the game in the fourth when they scored four runs to take a 7–6 lead. The big blow was a three-run double by Bill Schuster, who scored four runs in this game. Rube Novotney singled in a run in the fifth but Metkovitch, who went 4-for-4, hit another homer the next inning to make it 8–7. Albie Glossop put the Angels up 10–7 with his two-run eighth inning homer that proved to be the winning blow. In the last of the ninth, Les Scarsella hit a two-run homer off his former teammate, Tom Hafey, but the Oaks fell one run short. In the eighth, Will Hafey of the Oaks fouled out as a pinch hitter against his brother.

Los Angeles	AB	R	H	RBI	O	A	E
Schuster SS	4	4	3	3	1	4	1
Glossop 2B	4	1	2	1	3	3	0
Ostrowski 3B	5	1	1	3	2	1	0
Aberson RF-LF	5	0	0	1	0	0	0
Dallesandro LF	3	1	0	0	0	0	1
Sauer CF-RF	5	0	1	0	3	0	0
Sanford 1B	4	1	2	0	7	3	0
Novotney C	5	1	1	1	8	0	0
Adkins P	1	0	0	0	0	0	0
T. Hafey P	2	1	0	0	2	0	0
Garriott CF	0	0	0	0	1	0	0
	38	10	10	9	27	11	2

Oakland	AB	R	H	RBI	O	A	E
Combs SS	4	1	1	0	3	5	0
Lavagetto 3B	5	1	1	0	0	1	1
Metkovitch CF	4	2	4	4	5	0	0
Etten 1B	5	0	0	0	10	2	0
Scarsella RF	5	2	2	2	2	0	0
Holder LF	4	2	2	0	4	0	0
Lodigiani 2B	4	1	2	2	1	3	1
Fernandes C	4	0	0	0	2	0	0
Gassaway P	2	0	0	0	0	0	0

Oakland	AB	R	H	RBI	O	A	E
Speer P	0	0	0	0	0	0	0
Van Robays[a]	1	0	0	0	0	0	0
Tost P	0	0	0	0	0	0	0
W. Hafey[b]	1	0	0	0	0	0	0
Wilkie P	0	0	0	0	0	0	0
	39	9	12	8	27	11	2

(a) Batted for Speer in the sixth.
(b) Batted for Tost in the eighth.

Pitching Records	IP	H	R	ER	SO	BB
Adkins	2.2	9	6	2	6	0
T. Hafey (W)	6.1	3	3	3	2	3
Gassaway (L)	3.1	6	7	5	1	3
Speer	2.2	1	1	1	0	1
Tost	2	2	2	2	1	1
Wilkie	1	1	0	0	0	1

Two Base Hits: Schuster 2. Home Runs: Ostrowski, Metkovitch 2, Lodigiani, Glossop, Scarsella. Stolen Base: Sauer. Double Plays: Ostrowski to Glossop to Sanford; Lavagetto to Lodigiani to Etten. Time of Game: 2 hr. 25 min. Umpires: Ford, Warneke, Somers.

Los Angeles	201	410	020	10 – 10 – 2
Oakland	501	001	002	9 – 12 – 2

Game Two.

An even smaller crowd of 1,509 came out on Thursday night and saw the Angels go up two games to none in this series with a 9–7 win. Red Lynn faced Jack Salveson but neither was involved in the decision. A 1–0 L.A. lead was wiped out in the second when Eddie Fernandes homered with fellow ex–Angel Lloyd Christopher on base. The Angels got to Salveson for four runs in the third, the big blow a three-run homer by the former football player, Cliff Aberson. Oakland cut the lead to 5–3 in their half of the third on Merrill Combs' homer and then forged ahead 7–5 with four runs in the fifth inning. With Salveson and Lodigiani on base with two outs, the Oaks got four straight run-scoring singles from Nick Etten, Les Scarsella, Lloyd Christopher and Billy Martin, chasing Red Lynn. The Angels came right back to tie it on Eddie Lukon's two-run homer in the sixth and then got the winning runs in the eighth when the PCL's 1939 batting champion, Dominic Dallesandro, hit a two-run homer, giving the visitors a 9–7 win. Don Carlson got the win, pitching over four innings of shutout ball, for the only decent relief job the Angels were to get in this series. Ralph "Pine Tar" Buxton, who gave up Dallesandro's homer, took the loss.

Los Angeles	AB	H	RBI	O	A	E
Schuster SS	4	2	0	6	2	0
Glossop 2B	4	1	1	4	4	0
Ostrowski 3B	5	1	1	0	2	0
Aberson RF	3	2	3	0	0	0
Dallesandro LF	4	2	2	3	0	0
Sauer CF	4	1	0	2	0	1
Lukon 1B	4	2	2	6	0	0
Malone C	4	1	0	6	1	0
Lynn P	2	0	0	0	1	0
Carlson P	2	0	0	0	0	0
	36	12	9	27	10	1

Oakland	AB	H	RBI	O	A	E
Combs SS	4	2	1	1	3	0
Lodigiani 3B	4	1	0	0	0	0
Metkovitch CF	5	0	0	2	0	0
Etten 1B	5	2	1	12	0	0
Scarsella RF	4	2	1	1	0	0
Christopher LF	4	2	0	3	0	0
Martin 2B	4	1	2	4	4	0
Fernandes C	3	1	2	4	1	0
Salveson P	2	0	0	0	0	0
Buxton P	0	0	0	0	1	0
Holder [a]	1	1	0	0	0	0
W. Hafey P	0	0	0	0	1	0
	36	12	7	27	10	0

(a) Batted for Buxton in the eighth.

Pitching Records	IP	H	R	ER	SO	BB
Lynn	4.2	8	7	7	3	3
Carlson (W)	4.1	4	0	0	3	2
Salveson	6	10	7	7	2	1
Buxton (L)	2	2	2	2	2	2
W. Hafey	1	0	0	0	1	0

Left on Base: Los Angeles 3, Oakland 8. Two Base Hits: Schuster, Glossop, Aberson. Home Runs: Fernandes, Combs, Aberson, Lukon, Dallesandro.

The 1948 Oakland Oaks won the Pacific Coast League championship. Members were *Top Row, left to right:* Lou Tost, Harry Lavagetto, Les Scarsella, Jack Salveson, Nick Etten, Les Webber, Ernie Lombardi, Thornton Lee, Loyd Christopher, Will Hafey. *Middle Row:* Bill Raimondi, Brooks Holder, Mel Duezabou, John Babich, Casey Stengel, Dario Lodigiani, Ralph Buxton, Merrill Combs, Aldon Wilke, Floyd Speer. *Bottom Row:* Ed Fernandez, George Metkovich, Ray Hamrick, Billy Martin, Chuck Symonds, Maurice Van Robays, Earl Jones, Charlie Gassaway (Doug McWilliam's collection).

Double Plays: Martin to Etten; Combs to Martin to Etten; Martin to Combs to Etten; Glossop to Schuster to Lukon. Umpires: Warneke, Somers, Ford.

Los Angeles	104	002	020	9	–	12	–	1
Oakland	021	040	000	7	–	12	–	0

Game Three.

On Friday night, October 1, only 1,962 fans showed up for what could have been the last home game for the champion Oaks in 1948. It was not, but with the home team trailing two games to none, it certainly was a possibility. Lee Anthony faced the Oaks' Earl Jones but each was followed by three relievers in this 11 inning game. The Oaks went ahead with two in the first when Metkovitch hit a two-run homer, but the Angels tied it in the third on solo homers by pitcher Lee Anthony and Albie Glossop. The Oaks retook the lead with two runs in the fourth on singles by Combs, pitcher Earl Jones and Martin, and a fielder's choice. They increased the lead to 5–2 in the fifth on

Metkovitch's triple and Etten's fly ball. But L.A. quickly tied it in the sixth when Aberson got on base on Martin's error and Dallesandro homered. Then Sauer singled, Jack Sanford walked, and Malone singled in the tying run. Ostrowski's homer put L.A. up 6–5 in the seventh, but the Oaks came to tie it in the last of the seventh and would have had another run if Scarsella had not missed third base, trying to score on Combs' single. In the eighth, the Angels went back on top 7–6 when Lefty Louie Tost balked in a run. Lynn, in relief, almost had the game nailed down that would have put his team up three games to none, but with two outs in the ninth, he served up a home run ball to his former teammate, Lloyd Christopher, tying it up 7–7. In the top of the 11th, Aberson hit a two-run homer, but again the Angel relievers could not hold the lead. Metkovitch opened the last half with a single, Dewey Adkins came in and walked Etten, but retired Scarsella. Combs singled in one run and Christopher doubled in the tying run. Eddie Fernandes was passed to load the bases, but pitcher Will Hafey also walked to force in the winning run.

Los Angeles	AB	R	H	RBI	O	A	E
Schuster SS	6	0	2	0	3	3	0
Glossop 2B	6	1	2	1	3	5	1
Ostrowski 3B	5	2	2	1	2	1	0
Aberson RF	5	2	1	2	2	1	0
Dallesandro LF	5	1	3	2	3	1	0
Sauer CF	6	1	2	0	2	1	0
Sanford 1B	2	0	0	0	5	1	0
Malone C	4	0	1	1	6	2	0
Anthony P	3	1	1	1	1	0	0
Bauers P	0	0	0	0	0	0	0
Garriott[a]	0	1	0	0	0	0	0
Lynn P	1	0	0	0	0	0	0
Adkins P	0	0	0	0	0	0	0
Lukon 1B	2	0	1	0	4	0	0
	45	9	15	8	31[b]	15	1

(a) Batted for Bauers in the eighth.
(b) One out when winning run scored.

Oakland	AB	R	H	RBI	O	A	E
Martin 2B	4	1	3	1	4	0	1
Lodigiani 3B	5	0	1	1	3	4	0
Metkovitch CF	4	4	3	2	4	0	0
Etten 1B	5	0	1	1	7	1	0
Scarsella RF	6	0	3	1	3	0	0
Combs SS	6	2	3	1	1	3	0

Oakland	AB	R	H	RBI	O	A	E
Christopher LF	6	1	3	2	5	1	0
Fernandes C	4	1	0	0	6	1	0
Jones P	2	0	1	0	0	0	0
Speer P	0	0	0	0	0	2	0
Tost P	0	0	0	0	0	0	0
W. Hafey P	2	0	1	1	0	0	0
Holder[a]	1	0	0	0	0	0	0
Lavagetto 3B	0	0	0	0	0	0	0
Duezabou[b]	0	1	0	0	0	0	0
	45	10	19	10	33	12	1

(a) Batted for Lodigiani in the 10th.
(b) Ran for Etten in the 11th.

Pitching Records	IP	H	R	ER	SO	BB
Anthony	4.2	12	4	5	5	3
Bauers	2.1	3	2	1	0	0
Lynn	3+	2	1	2	1	1
Adkins (L)	0.1	2	3	2	0	2
Jones	5+	6	3	4	2	3
Speer	2.1	3	3	2	1	1
Tost	0+	0	1	0	0	0
W. Hafey (W)	3.2	6	2	2	1	1

Balk: Tost. Two Base Hit: Christopher. Three Base Hit: Metkovitch. Home Runs: Anthony, Glossop, Dallesandro, Ostrowski, Aberson. Metkovitch, Christopher. Time of Game: 3 hr. 2 min. Umpires: Ford, Warneke, Somers.

Los Angeles	002	003	110	02	9 – 15 – 1
Oakland	200	210	101	03	10 – 19 – 1

The teams traveled to Los Angeles on Saturday, October 2, allowing college football to have center stage that day. In Berkeley, 54,000 saw California beat St. Mary's 20–0. California was to go undefeated that season and play in the Rose Bowl. At the Los Angeles Coliseum, UCLA beat Idaho 28–12 before 21,024. But on Sunday, the 3rd, the Rams and Philadelphia Eagles game competed directly with the playoffs, which were held only one mile away. A crowd of 36,884 saw the Rams come back from a 28–0 deficit and tie the Eagles 28–28 in the Coliseum.

Game Four.

A crowd of 9,450, which was the largest of this series, saw the Angels lose a doubleheader to fall behind three games to two. But it was the way the Angels lost these games that hurt their fans. In the opener, Eddie Sauer, who was given an award for being the team's MVP in 1948, hit a three-run homer off Charley Gassaway in the fourth inning to give his team a 3–0 lead. Oakland got a run off starter Don Carlson in the fifth, so it was 3–1 going into the eighth when the Oaks struck for three runs. Fernandes doubled, then pinch hitter Cookie Lavagetto singled him home, and with two outs, Metkovitch doubled, putting runners at second and third. Red Adams relieved Carlson and walked Etten, loading the bases. Scarsella singled in two runs to put the Oaks up 4–3. In the ninth, Brooks Holder homered with Lou Tost aboard to make the final 6–3. Floyd Speer, who followed Gassaway, got credit for the win.

Oakland	AB	R	H	RBI	O	A	E
Martin 2B	3	0	0	0	3	0	0
Lodigiani 3B	5	0	0	0	2	2	0
Metkovitch CF	5	1	3	0	5	0	0
Etten 1B	3	0	1	0	8	1	0
Scarsella RF-1B	4	0	1	2	0	0	0
Combs SS	4	0	0	0	1	6	0
Christopher LF	4	0	0	0	0	0	0
Fernandes C	3	1	2	0	7	0	0
Gassaway P	1	0	0	0	0	0	0
W. Hafey[a]	1	0	1	1	0	0	0
Wilkie[b]	0	0	0	0	0	0	0
Speer P	0	0	0	0	0	1	0
Holder RF[c]	2	1	1	2	0	0	0
Duezabou[d]	0	1	0	0	0	0	0
Lavagetto 3B[e]	2	1	2	1	0	1	0
Lombardi C	0	0	0	0	1	0	0
Tost P	1	1	1	0	0	0	0
	38	6	12	6	27	11	0

(a) Batted for Gassaway in the fifth.
(b) Ran for W. Hafey in the fifth.
(c) Batted for Speer in the eighth.
(d) Ran for Fernandes in the eighth.
(e) Batted for Martin in the eighth.

Los Angeles	AB	R	H	RBI	O	A	E
Schuster SS	4	0	1	0	2	0	0
Glossop 2B	4	0	0	0	0	2	0

Los Angeles	AB	R	H	RBI	O	A	E
Ostrowski 3B	4	0	1	0	1	0	0
Aberson RF	4	1	2	0	1	0	0
Dallesandro LF	3	1	1	0	5	0	0
Sauer CF	4	1	2	3	6	0	0
Sanford 1B	4	0	1	0	6	1	0
Novotney C	3	0	0	0	5	1	1
Carlson P	3	0	0	0	1	0	0
Adams P	0	0	0	0	0	0	0
Malone[a]	1	0	0	0	0	0	0
T. Hafey[b]	1	0	0	0	0	0	0
	35	3	8	3	27	4	1

(a) Batted for Novotney in the ninth.
(b) Batted for Adams in the ninth.

Pitching Records	IP	H	R	ER	SO	BB
Gassaway	4	6	3	3	2	1
Speer (W)	3	2	0	0	4	0
Tost	2	0	0	0	0	1
Carlson (L)	7.2	8	2	4	4	0
Adams	1.1	4	4	2	0	1

Two Base Hits: Dallesandro, Etten, Aberson, Fernandes 2, Metkovitch, Lavagetto. Home Runs: Sauer, Holder.

Oakland	000	010	032	6 – 12 – 0
Los Angeles	000	300	000	3 – 8 – 1

Game Five.

This game defies description. The Oaks won this nine inning game 23–15, using 21 of their 23 players, including seven pitchers on the mound plus two others in pinch hit or pinch run situations. The Angels used six pitchers and blew leads of 8–3 and 14–6. In addition to the 38 runs scored, there were 43 hits, 27 by Oakland, 11 walks, 9 doubles, 2 triples, and 7 homers, two of which were grand slams by Johnny Ostrowski in a losing cause. To top it off, the Angels pulled a triple play when Schuster speared a line drive, stepped on second and fired to Lukon at first to nail the runner. Oakland got 16 runs in the last three innings to make mince meat of the Angel relievers, who sorely missed their 1947 bullpen ace, Jess Dobernic. The big doubleheader win did not please *Oakland Tribune* writer Alan Ward, who called this 23–15 game "bush league." He felt poor pitching and the lively ball had robbed the home run of its dignity.

He also felt doubleheaders were too long and too tiring, and he again used this forum to campaign against continuing the playoffs.

Oakland	AB	R	H	RBI	O	A	E
Combs SS	5	4	1	0	2	5	0
Lavagetto 3B	5	3	3	4	1	2	0
Metkovitch CF	7	2	4	2	6	0	0
Etten 1B	6	2	3	4	7	0	0
Holder RF	1	0	0	0	0	0	0
Christopher LF	2	2	2	0	1	0	0
Lodigiani 2B	5	3	1	0	4	2	0
Lombardi C	6	2	4	2	5	0	0
Salveson P	1	0	0	0	0	0	0
Jones P	0	0	0	0	0	0	0
Duezabou RF-LF	5	1	3	1	1	0	0
Van Robays [a]	1	0	0	0	0	0	0
Wilkie P	0	0	0	0	0	0	0
Scarsella RF	5	2	2	3	0	0	0
Tost P	1	0	1	0	0	0	0
Gassaway P	0	0	0	0	0	0	0
W. Hafey [b]	1	0	1	1	0	0	0
Speer [c]	0	0	0	0	0	0	0
Webber P	1	0	1	0	0	0	0
Martin 2B	1	2	1	0	0	0	0
Buxton P	1	0	0	0	0	0	0
	54	23	27	17	27	9	0

(a) Batted for Jones in the fourth.
(b) Batted for Gassaway in the sixth.
(c) Ran for W. Hafey in the sixth.

Los Angeles	AB	R	H	RBI	O	A	E
Schuster SS	4	2	2	1	7	2	1
Glossop 2B	4	2	1	1	0	0	0
Ostrowski 3B	5	2	3	8	1	1	0
Aberson RF	4	1	2	1	2	0	1
Dallesandro LF	5	0	0	0	2	0	0
Sauer CF	5	1	2	0	3	0	1
Lukon 1B	5	2	2	2	7	4	0
Malone C	5	3	3	1	5	0	0
T. Hafey P	0	0	0	0	0	0	0
Kleine P	1	1	0	1	0	0	0
Anthony P	2	1	1	0	0	1	0

Los Angeles	AB	R	H	RBI	O	A	E
Lanfranconi P	0	0	0	0	0	1	0
Lynn P	0	0	0	0	0	0	0
Bauers P	0	0	0	0	0	0	0
Garriott [a]	1	0	0	0	0	0	0
	41	15	16	15	27	9	3

(a) Batted for Bauers in the ninth.

Pitching Records	IP	H	R	ER	SO	BB
Salveson	1.1	6	6	6	2	1
Jones	0.2	0	0	0	0	1
Wilkie	1+	3	2	2	1	1
Tost	1+	4	2	2	1	1
Gassaway	2.0	1	4	1	0	0
Webber (W)	1.1	2	1	1	1	1
Buxton	1.2	0	0	0	1	0
T. Hafey	1.2	4	3	2	1	3
Kleine	1.2	5	2	3	2	1
Anthony	2.2	7	4	4	0	0
Lanfranconi	0.2	1	3	2	0	1
Lynn (L)	1.0	5	4	3	0	1
Bauers	1.1	5	7	4	1	1

Triple Play: Schuster to Lukon. Hit by Pitcher: Kleine by Salveson. Two Base Hits: Aberson, Christopher 2, Lombardi 2, Combs, Lukon, Malone, Metkovitch. Three Base Hits: Malone, Schuster. Home Runs: Lukon, Ostrowski 2, Lavagetto 2, Scarsella, Aberson. Umpires: Warneke, Somers, Ford.

Oakland	031	201	574	23 – 27 – 0
Los Angeles	062	060	010	15 – 16 – 3

Game Six.

On Monday night, October 4, the Angels showed their fans that they were not through blowing big leads. A crowd of 2,955 saw them take a 5–0 lead after three innings, and a 9–2 lead after six innings, only to lose in the 10th by a score of 11–9. The only pitcher to go nine innings in this series, Dewey Adkins, lost the game in the 10th before he was relieved by Lee Anthony. Will Hafey started for the Oaks but got knocked out in the fifth, when L.A. was up 8–2. Oakland closed the gap to 9–7 with five runs in the seventh inning, all off Adkins because Bill Kelly had no confidence in his relievers. Les Scarsella hit a grand slam homer for four of those five runs that inning. Cookie Lavagetto's two-run single tied the game in the eighth and then in the 10th, Holder, Lavagetto, and Metkovitch singled for one run and Etten's fly ball scored the second and final run of the series. Ralph Buxton, who pitched the last three innings, got credit for the win.

Oakland	AB	R	H	RBI	O	A	E
Holder LF-RF	3	2	3	0	3	0	1
Lavagetto 3B	6	0	3	3	2	4	0
Metkovitch CF	6	0	1	1	5	0	0
Etten 1B	4	2	0	1	6	1	0
Scarsella RF	6	2	3	4	1	0	0
Combs SS	5	0	1	0	1	1	0
Lodigiani 2B-3B	5	0	2	2	0	0	0
Fernandes C	4	1	2	0	8	0	0
W. Hafey P	2	0	1	0	0	0	0
Jones P	0	0	0	0	0	0	0
Salveson P	1	1	1	0	0	0	0
Van Robays[a]	0	1	0	0	0	0	0
Duezabou[b]	0	1	0	0	0	0	0
Lombardi C	1	0	0	0	3	0	0
Buxton P	1	0	0	0	1	0	0
Martin 2B[c]	0	1	0	0	0	0	0
Christopher LF	0	0	0	0	0	0	0
	44	11	17	11	30	6	1

(a) Batted for Salveson in the eighth.
(b) Ran for Fernandes in the eighth.
(c) Ran for Lavagetto in the eighth.

Los Angeles	AB	R	H	RBI	O	A	E
Schuster SS	5	1	1	1	3	2	0
Glossop 2B	6	0	1	0	1	2	0
Ostrowski 3B	5	0	0	0	1	1	0
Aberson RF	5	1	1	0	1	0	0
Dallesandro LF	4	3	3	2	0	0	0
Sauer CF	5	2	3	1	7	0	0
Lukon 1B	3	2	1	1	6	3	0
Novotney C	5	0	2	3	10	1	0
Adkins P	5	0	0	0	1	1	0
Anthony P	0	0	0	0	0	0	0
	43	9	12	8	30	10	0

Pitching Records	IP	H	R	ER	SO	BB
W. Hafey	4+	9	7	7	4	4
Jones	1+	1	1	0	2	1
Salveson	2	2	1	0	0	3
Buxton (W)	3	0	0	0	3	1
Adkins (L)	9.2	17	11	11	9	2
Anthony	0.1	0	0	0	0	0

Two Base Hits: Sauer 2, Scarsella, Salveson. Home runs: Dallesandro, Scarsella. Umpires: Ford, Warneke, Somers.

Oakland	000	200	520	2	11 – 17 – 1
Los Angeles	005	031	000	0	9 – 12 – 0

Had the Angels been able to win one of the three games played at Wrigley Field, it would have complicated the city of Oakland's plans for a victory celebration, honoring the Oaks for their first pennant in 21 years. The players flew home in two planes on Tuesday morning, October 5, put on their uniforms, and paraded from Oaks Park in Emeryville to the Oakland City Hall in open-top cars. Each player was awarded a gold wrist watch, engraved "Oakland Oaks, PCL Champions, 1948." That evening, the players were feted at a banquet at the Leamington Hotel and given Halliburton airplane luggage. Hundreds of people were turned away that night, yet few fans attended the playoff games. Before the playoffs, Casey Stengel was given a new Cadillac which he parked across the street from Oaks Park the night the playoffs opened. He locked it but left the lights on.

The Seattle–San Francisco Series

During the regular season, the Seals won 16 and lost 12 to the Rainiers, winning the last five games in the season to take the edge. These teams left San Francisco and went up to Seattle to start the playoffs because Oakland was opening the postseason at home, thus avoiding having the Bay Area teams home at the same time. The Seals were dealt a severe blow when the league's top hitter, Gene Woodling, had to go to Akron, Ohio, because his father died. So, again, the loss of Woodling was to prove damaging. In addition, pitcher Jack Brewer was left in San Francisco because of pleurisy. On the other hand, Seattle missed the bat of former Seal Neil Sheridan who was recalled by Boston, and were limited to one catcher, 41-year-old Rollie Hemsley, because Mickey Grasso was hurt and unable to play in this series. The Seals refused to allow

Seattle to use catcher Jack Warren, who joined the team too late for the play-offs.

Game One.

A crowd of 4,219 came to Sick's Stadium on Wednesday night, September 29, to see the first playoff game held on this field in three years. Grumpy Guy Fletcher held the Seals to just one run on four hits, beating Con Dempsey. The "mature" Rainers got to Dempsey for two runs in the second when 41-year-old "Indian Bob" Johnson walked and stole second and scored on 38-year-old Lamar "Skeeter" Newsome's single. Newsome went to second on the throw home and scored on 41-year-old Rollie Hemsley's single. The Seals' only run came in the fourth when Hugh Luby singled, Mickey Rocco doubled and Joe Brovia hit a scoring fly ball. Seattle's final run came in the sixth when manager Jo Jo White and Hillis Layne singled, Earl Rapp was safe on Rocco's error, and Bob Johnson hit a long fly.

San Francisco	AB	R	H	RBI	O	A	E
Tobin CF	4	0	0	0	2	0	0
Luby 2B	4	1	1	0	2	1	0
Rocco 1B	4	0	1	0	5	0	1
Brovia RF	4	0	0	1	2	0	0
Shofner 3B	4	0	1	0	0	0	0
Restelli LF	3	0	0	0	4	0	0
Nicely SS	3	0	0	0	5	2	0
Howell C	3	0	1	0	4	2	0
Dempsey P	2	0	0	0	0	2	0
Orteig[a]	0	0	0	0	0	0	0
Trower[b]	0	0	0	0	0	0	0
Soriano P	0	0	0	0	0	0	0
	31	1	4	1	24	7	1

(a) Batted for Dempsey in the eighth.
(b) Ran for Orteig in the eighth.

Seattle	AB	R	H	RBI	O	A	E
Ramsey CF	4	0	0	0	2	0	0
White RF	4	1	1	0	3	0	0
Layne 3B	4	0	1	0	0	3	0
Rapp LF	4	0	1	0	3	1	0
Johnson 1B	2	1	0	1	11	0	0
York 2B	3	0	0	0	1	4	0

Seattle	AB	R	H	RBI	O	A	E
Newsome SS	3	1	1	1	3	1	0
Hemsley C	2	0	2	1	3	0	0
Fletcher P	3	0	0	0	1	1	0
	29	3	6	3	27	10	0

Pitching Records	IP	H	R	ER	SO	BB
Dempsey (L)	7	6	3	2	2	2
Soriano	1	0	0	0	0	0
Fletcher	9	4	1	1	2	1

Two Base Hits: Shofner, Rocco. Stolen Base: Johnson. Double Play: Howell to Nicely to Rocco. Time of Game: 1 hr. 43 min. Umpires: Engeln, Gordon, Orr.

San Francisco	000	100	000	1 – 4 – 1
Seattle	020	001	00x	3 – 6 – 0

Game Two.

On Thursday night, September 30, the Rainiers went up two games to none when Charley Schanz pitched a four-hit shutout before 4,473 fans. This game took only an hour and 43 minutes. Old Bob Johnson was Seattle's hero, hitting a solo homer in the fifth and singling in the seventh, and coming around to score on Tony York's single. Bill Werle gave up six hits in a losing cause.

San Francisco	AB	R	H	RBI	O	A	E
Tobin CF	3	0	0	0	0	0	0
Luby 2B	2	0	0	0	2	3	0
Rocco 1B	4	0	0	0	13	0	0
Brovia RF	4	0	0	0	1	0	0
Shofner 3B	4	0	2	0	1	5	0
Restelli LF	4	0	1	0	1	0	0
Nicely SS	4	0	1	0	1	3	0
Leonard C	2	0	0	0	2	0	0
Werle P	3	0	0	0	1	5	0
Trower[a]	0	0	0	0	0	0	0
Howell C	1	0	0	0	2	0	1
	31	0	4	0	24	16	1

(a) Ran for Leonard in the seventh.

Seattle	AB	R	H	RBI	O	A	E
Ramsey CF	4	0	0	0	0	0	0
White RF	4	0	1	0	3	0	0
Layne 3B	3	0	0	0	2	1	0
Johnson 1B	3	2	2	1	14	3	0
Rapp LF	1	0	0	0	0	0	0
York 2B	3	0	2	1	2	4	0
Newsome SS	3	0	0	0	3	6	0
Hemsley C	3	0	1	0	1	1	0
Schanz P	3	0	0	0	2	3	0
	27	2	6	2	27	18	0

Pitching Records	IP	H	R	ER	SO	BB
Werle	8	6	2	2	3	1
Schanz	9	4	0	0	1	1

Wild Pitch: Werle. Two Base Hits: Nicely, Hemsley. Home Run: Johnson. Stolen Base: Ramsey. Double Plays: Shofner to Rocco; Nicely to Luby to Rocco. Time of Game: 1 hr. 43 min. Umpires: Gordon, Orr, Engeln.

San Francisco	000	000	000	0 – 4 – 1
Seattle	000	010	10x	2 – 6 – 0

Game Three.

A crowd of 8,313, the largest of the series, went out to Sick's Stadium on Friday night, October 1, perhaps thinking that this would be the last game played in Seattle in 1948. It was, not because Seattle lost the opening round, but because of the uncertain weather in Seattle in October. Al Lien, with relief help from Dewey Soriano, defeated High Herm Besse 4–3 to reduce the Seals deficit to one game in this series. Trailing 1–0 going into the sixth, the Seals struck for four runs after two were out. Dino Restelli singled, Ray Orteig walked, Ben Guintini singled in one run, Roy Nicely doubled in two more, and after Dixie Howell was passed, Al Lien drove in the fourth run. Lien gave up two runs in the last of the sixth on RBI singles by Newsome and Hemsley, but Seattle fell one run short.

San Francisco	AB	H	RBI	O	A	E
Tobin CF	4	0	0	4	0	0
Luby 2B	3	0	0	2	3	0
Rocco 1B	3	0	0	12	1	0
Restelli LF	4	1	0	1	1	0

San Francisco	AB	H	RBI	O	A	E
Orteig 3B	2	1	0	0	3	0
Guintini RF	4	2	1	1	0	0
Nicely SS	3	1	2	5	3	0
Howell C	2	0	0	2	0	0
Lien P	3	1	1	0	3	1
Shofner 3B	1	0	0	0	1	0
Soriano P	1	0	0	0	1	0
	30	6	4	27	16	1

Seattle	AB	H	RBI	O	A	E
Ramsey CF	4	1	0	3	1	0
White RF	4	0	0	3	0	0
Layne 3B	4	0	0	0	2	0
Johnson 1B	4	2	0	6	1	0
Rapp LF	3	1	0	0	0	0
York 2B	4	0	0	2	2	0
Newsome SS	5	3	1	5	2	1
Hemsley C	4	2	1	6	2	0
Besse P	1	0	1	0	2	0
Mohr[a]	1	0	0	0	0	0
Hall P	0	0	0	0	1	0
Russo[b]	0	0	0	0	0	0
Richardson 1B	0	0	0	2	0	0
O'Neill[c]	1	0	0	0	0	0
	35	9	3	27	13	1

(a) *Batted for Besse in the sixth.*
(b) *Ran for Johnson in the eighth.*
(c) *Batted for Hall in the ninth.*

Pitching Records	IP	H	R	ER	SO	BB
Lien (W)	7.1	9	3	3	1	1
Soriano	1.2	0	0	0	0	0
Besse (L)	6	5	4	4	4	5
Hall	3	1	0	0	1	0

Wild Pitch: Besse. Left on Base: San Francisco 7, Seattle 7. Two Base Hits: Orteig, Nicely. Sacrifices: Besse, Nicely, Rapp. Stolen Base: Luby. Umpires: Orr, Engeln, Gordon.

San Francisco	000	004	000	4 – 6 – 1
Seattle	000	012	000	3 – 9 – 1

Game Four.

The teams traveled to San Francisco on Saturday and resumed the series with a doubleheader on Sunday, October 3, at Seals Stadium. Only 4,258 fans showed up for these games while 32,500 were at Kezar Stadium to see Nevada beat USF 26–7. In the opener, Guy Fletcher faced Cliff Melton but neither pitcher got the decision. The Seals got a run in the first but Seattle tied it in the fourth. Each team scored two in the seventh but the Seals got a run off reliever Bob Hall to take a 4–3 lead into the ninth. Seattle then rocked Dewey Soriano for five runs, giving the visitors an 8–4 win. Bob Johnson got two hits, including a homer, while driving in two runs. Hillis Layne and Tony York also drove in 2 runs and each got a double. Dixie Howell homered for the losing Seals, while Hugh Luby hit a pair of doubles.

Seattle	AB	R	H	RBI	O	A	E
Ramsey CF	5	0	1	0	2	0	1
White RF	4	1	1	0	2	0	0
Layne 3B	5	1	1	2	0	2	0
Johnson 1B	4	2	2	2	7	1	0
Rapp LF	4	0	1	0	4	0	0
York 2B	5	1	1	2	3	3	0
Newsome SS	5	1	2	1	3	2	0
Hemsley C	5	1	3	0	6	1	0
Fletcher P	2	1	0	0	0	0	0
Hall P	2	0	0	0	0	0	0
	41	8	12	7	27	9	1

San Francisco	AB	R	H	RBI	O	A	E
Tobin CF	4	2	2	0	2	2	0
Luby 2B	2	0	2	1	5	3	0
Rocco 1B	4	0	0	1	8	0	0
Brovia RF	4	0	2	0	2	0	0
Shofner 3B	4	0	1	0	1	0	2
Restelli LF	4	0	0	1	2	0	0
Nicely SS	4	0	1	0	3	7	2
Howell C	4	1	2	1	4	1	0
Melton P	2	0	0	0	0	2	0
Orteig[a]	1	0	0	0	0	0	0
Soriano P	0	0	0	0	0	1	0
Trower[b]	0	1	0	0	0	0	0
Guintini RF	0	0	0	0	0	0	0

San Francisco	AB	R	H	RBI	O	A	E
Mackie[c]	1	0	0	0	0	0	0
	34	4	10	4	27	16	4

(a) *Batted for Melton in the seventh.*
(b) *Ran for Brovia in the eighth.*
(c) *Batted for Soriano in the ninth.*

Pitching Records	IP	H	R	ER	SO	BB
Fletcher	7	8	3	3	5	1
Hall (W)	2	2	1	1	0	0
Melton	7	7	3	3	3	2
Soriano (L)	2	5	5	2	0	1

Two Base Hits: Luby 2, Tobin, Layne, York. Double Plays: Nicely to Luby to Rocco 2. Time of Game: 2 hr. 20 min. Umpires: Engeln, Gordon, Ford.

Seattle	000	100	205	8	–	12	– 1
San Francisco	100	000	210	4	–	10	– 4

Game Five.

The second game of the doubleheader was scheduled for nine innings, but went 11. Bob Hall again got the win, this time in relief of Herb Karpel. Kenny Gables was tagged with the loss in relief of Con Dempsey. The Seals got two in the third but the Rainiers tied it with two in the sixth. Seattle got two more in the eighth, taking a 4–2 lead into the last of the ninth when the Seals rallied for two runs to send the game into extra innings. In the ninth, Restelli singled, Orteig tripled and Nicely singled. Then in the 11th, pitcher Bob Hall singled, Jo Jo White walked, Layne singled in one run and Johnson doubled in the final two runs of the series.

Seattle	AB	R	H	RBI	O	A	E
Ramsey CF	5	0	2	0	2	0	0
White RF	5	1	2	0	2	0	0
Layne 3B	6	1	1	1	0	3	0
Rapp LF	6	2	3	0	6	0	0
Johnson 1B	4	1	2	2	14	1	0
York 2B	5	1	1	0	0	3	0
Newsome SS	5	0	1	3	4	1	0
Hemsley C	5	0	1	1	5	0	0
Karpel P	4	0	0	0	0	2	0

Seattle	AB	R	H	RBI	O	A	E
Hall P	1	1	1	0	0	1	0
	46	7	14	7	33	11	0

San Francisco	AB	R	H	RBI	O	A	E
Tobin CF	5	1	1	1	4	0	0
Luby 2B	5	0	0	0	2	4	0
Rocco 1B	5	0	1	1	9	3	0
Restelli LF	5	1	1	0	8	0	0
Orteig 3B	4	1	3	1	2	1	0
Guintini RF	4	0	0	0	1	0	0
Nicely SS	4	0	1	0	3	3	0
Howell C	2	1	1	0	2	0	0
Dempsey P	2	0	0	0	1	2	0
Shofner 3B	1	0	0	0	0	1	0
Brovia RF	1	0	0	0	1	0	0
Leonard C	1	0	0	0	0	0	1
Gables P	0	0	0	0	0	0	0
Mackie[a]	1	0	0	0	0	0	0
	40	4	8	3	33	14	1

(a) Batted for Gables in the 11th.

Pitching Records	IP	H	R	ER	SO	BB
Karpel	8.1	8	4	4	3	1
Hall (W)	2.2	0	0	0	0	0
Dempsey	8	11	4	4	2	3
Gables (L)	3	3	3	3	0	1

Wild Pitch: Dempsey. Left on Base: Seattle 8, San Francisco 5. Two Base Hits: Ramsey, Johnson 2, White, Rapp, Tobin, Orteig. Three Base Hit: Orteig. Time of Game: 2 hr. 26 min. Umpires: Ford, Engeln, Gordon.

Seattle	000	002	020	03	7 – 14 – 0
San Francisco	002	000	002	00	4 – 8 – 1

Even though Seattle finished under .500, they were now in the final round of the playoffs. They had to wait in San Francisco Sunday and Monday nights to find if their opponent would be Oakland or Los Angeles. Because of Oakland's pennant winning celebration on Tuesday night, the final series opened at Oaks Park on Wednesday, October 6, the same day the World Series started at Braves Field in Boston.

The Final Series: Oakland vs. Seattle

A Wednesday night crowd of 3,896 at Oaks Park saw Seattle take the opening game 8–4, as Charley Shanz got the win with relief help from Herb Karpel. Bill Ramsey led off the game with a triple off loser Charley Gassaway. Layne's infield out scored Ramsey. In the third, Seattle went up 4–0 with a three-run outburst. Ramsey got an infield hit, Layne doubled him to third, Johnson was passed to load the bases, but Earl Rapp came through with a two-run single. Tony York singled in Johnson to make it 4–0. The Rainiers got another run off reliever Floyd Speer in the seventh when Johnson singled in Layne. But in the last half, Brooks Holder hit a grand slam homer to cut Seattle's lead to 5–4. However, in the top of the eighth, Lefty Louie Tost gave up three runs on run-scoring singles by Newsome, Hemsley and White, putting the game out of reach.

Seattle	AB	R	H	RBI	O	A	E
Ramsey CF	5	2	3	0	2	0	0
White RF	5	0	1	1	1	0	0
Layne 3B	4	2	2	1	1	1	0
Johnson 1B	4	1	3	1	8	1	1
Rapp LF	5	0	1	2	7	0	0
York 2B	5	1	2	1	1	3	0
Newsome SS	5	1	1	1	2	2	0
Hemsley C	4	1	1	1	5	0	0
Schanz P	3	0	0	0	0	1	0
Karpel P	0	0	0	0	0	0	0
	40	8	14	8	27	8	1

Oakland	AB	R	H	RBI	O	A	E
Holder LF	4	1	2	4	2	0	0
Combs SS	4	0	1	0	2	3	0
Metkovitch CF	4	0	0	0	1	0	0
Etten 1B	4	0	1	0	11	1	0
Scarsella RF	4	0	2	0	3	0	0
Fernandes C	3	0	0	0	4	0	0
Lodigiani 3B-2B	3	1	0	0	2	4	0
Martin 2B	1	0	0	0	1	1	0
Gassaway P	1	0	0	0	1	1	0
Hafey[a]	1	0	1	0	0	0	0
Wilkie[b]	0	0	0	0	0	0	0
Speer P	0	0	0	0	0	0	0

Oakland	AB	R	H	RBI	O	A	E
Duezabou LF[c]	1	1	0	0	0	0	0
Lavagetto 3B[d]	1	1	1	0	0	1	0
Tost P	0	0	0	0	0	1	0
Lombardi C	1	0	0	0	0	0	0
Christopher[e]	1	0	0	0	0	0	0
Van Robays[f]	1	0	0	0	0	0	0
	34	4	8	4	27	12	0

(a) *Batted for Gassaway in the sixth.*
(b) *Ran for Hafey in the sixth.*
(c) *Batted for Fernandez in the seventh.*
(d) *Batted for Martin in the seventh.*
(e) *Batted for Speer in the seventh.*
(f) *Batted for Tost in the ninth.*

Pitching Records	IP	H	R	ER	SO	BB
Schanz (W)	6+	7	4	4	1	3
Karpel	3	1	0	0	3	0
Gassaway (L)	6	8	4	4	2	1
Speer	1	1	1	0	1	1
Tost	2	5	3	3	1	0

Passed Ball: Fernandes. Two Base Hits: Layne, Newsome. Three Base Hit: Ramsey. Home Run: Holder. Double Plays: Schanz to Newsome to Johnson; Johnson to Hemsley. Time of Game: 2 hr. 6 min. Umpires: Ford, Somers. Orr, Gordon.

Seattle	103	000	130	8 – 14 – 1
Oakland	000	000	400	4 – 8 – 0

Game Two.

On Thursday night, October 7, 3,280 fans turned out to see the Oaks even the series with a 10–4 win. Oakland's hero was 40-year-old Ernie Lombardi, who went 4-for-5, including two doubles and a homer. Earl Jones, who was relieved by Jack Salveson, beat Herman Besse who needed relief help from Dick Barrett and Marius Russo. Each team got two runs in the first, but Oakland went ahead for good in the second when Lombardi doubled, took third on a wild pitch, and scored on pitcher Jones' single. The Oaks got three more in the third when Christopher doubled, Lombardi singled, and Merrill Combs homered. Bob Johnson's two-run homer in the sixth cut the lead to 6–4 but Oakland scored one in the sixth, two in the seventh, and one in the eighth to make it 10–4. Lombardi's homer was a solo shot in the seventh, and he doubled in the eighth and scored on Comb's double.

Seattle	AB	R	H	RBI	O	A	E
White CF	3	0	1	0	6	1	0
Layne 3B	4	0	0	0	0	0	0
Warren RF	4	2	1	0	1	0	0
Johnson 1B	4	2	2	3	10	1	0
Rapp LF	4	0	1	1	1	0	0
York 2B	4	0	1	0	2	3	0
Newsome SS	3	0	0	0	1	1	1
Hemsley C	3	0	2	0	1	0	0
Besse P	0	0	0	0	0	0	0
Barrett P	1	0	0	0	0	0	0
Richardson[a]	1	0	0	0	0	0	0
Russo P	2	0	0	0	0	1	0
O'Neil SS	1	0	1	0	1	0	0
Grasso C	0	0	0	0	0	1	0
Mohr 1B	0	0	0	0	1	0	0
	34	4	9	4	24	8	1

(a) Batted for Barrett in the fifth.

Oakland	AB	R	H	RBI	O	A	E
Metkovitch CF	5	1	0	0	4	0	0
Lavagetto 3B	5	0	2	0	0	0	0
Duezabou RF	1	1	1	1	0	0	0
Etten 1B	4	1	2	0	6	1	0
Christopher LF	2	1	1	1	1	0	0
Lodigiani 2B	5	0	0	0	4	4	0
Lombardi C	5	4	4	3	7	1	0
Combs SS	4	1	2	3	1	3	1
Jones P	2	0	1	1	0	0	0
Scarsella RF	4	0	2	0	2	0	0
Holder LF	3	0	2	0	2	0	0
Martin 2B	0	0	0	0	0	0	0
Salveson P	1	1	1	0	0	0	0
	41	10	18	9	27	9	1

Pitching Records	IP	H	R	ER	SO	BB
Besse (L)	1.2	5	3	3	1	1
Barrett	2.1	5	3	3	0	0

Pitching Records	IP	H	R	ER	SO	BB
Russo	4	8	4	0	0	0
Jones (W)	7	8	4	4	2	0
Salveson	2	1	0	0	0	0

Hit by Pitcher: Etten by Russo; Salveson by Russo. Wild Pitch: Besse. Two Base Hits: Johnson, Lombardi 2, Christopher, Lavagetto, Holder, Salveson, Combs, Warren. Home Runs: Lombardi, Combs, Johnson. Double Plays: Lodigiani to Etten; Johnson unassisted. Time of Game: 2 hr. 2 min. Umpires: Gordon, Orr, Ford, Somers.

Seattle	200	002	000	4 – 9 – 1
Oakland	213	001	21x	10 – 18 – 1

Game Three.

On Friday night, October 8, a crowd of 5,045 saw the Oaks take a 2–1 lead in the series with a come-from-behind win, 5–3. Both pitchers, Bob Hall and Will Hafey, went the route despite 11 walks in the game, eight by loser Hall. Seattle scored two in the fourth when White and Rapp walked, and Johnson doubled them both home. Oakland tied it in the sixth in much the same way. Metkovich and Etten walked, then Scarsella singled in one and Combs the other. The tie was broken in the last of the eighth when Etten doubled, Scarsella was passed but Combs received an unintentional walk. Billy Martin then tripled them in to make it 5–2. Seattle got a run in the ninth but fell short.

Seattle	AB	R	H	RBI	O	A	E
Mohr RF	4	0	1	0	1	0	0
White CF	3	1	2	0	1	0	0
Layne 3B	4	0	0	0	1	4	1
Rapp LF	3	1	0	0	1	0	0
Johnson 1B	4	0	1	3	12	1	0
York 2B	4	1	0	0	4	8	0
Newsome SS	3	0	1	0	0	1	0
Grasso C	4	0	1	0	4	0	0
Hall P	3	0	0	0	0	1	0
Warren[a]	1	0	0	0	0	0	0
	33	3	6	3	24	15	1

(a) Batted for Hall in the ninth.

Oakland	AB	R	H	RBI	O	A	E
Holder LF	3	0	1	0	3	0	0
Lodigiani 3B	4	0	0	0	2	3	1

Oakland	AB	R	H	RBI	O	A	E
Metkovitch CF	3	1	0	0	1	0	0
Etten 1B	3	2	1	0	13	1	0
Scarsella RF	3	1	1	1	2	0	0
Combs SS	2	1	1	1	1	3	0
Martin 2B	4	0	2	3	2	3	0
Lombardi C	3	0	0	0	2	0	0
Hafey P	3	0	0	0	1	2	0
	28	5	6	5	27	12	1

Pitching Records	IP	H	R	ER	SO	BB
Hall	8	6	5	5	3	8
Hafey	9	6	3	2	2	3

Two Base Hits: Johnson, Etten. Three Base Hit: Martin. Double Plays: Layne to York to Johnson; Hafey to Combs to Etten. Time of Game: 1 hr. 50 min. Umpires: Orr, Ford, Somers, Gordon.

Seattle	000	200	001	3 – 6 – 1
Oakland	000	002	03x	5 – 6 – 1

Game Four.

The teams took Saturday the 9th off while fans turned their attention to college football. At Berkeley, 66,000 saw California beat Wisconsin 40–14, and at Palo Alto, Santa Clara beat Stanford 27–14. On Sunday, October 10, a doubleheader was played before 6,624 at Oaks Park in which Seattle was given the privilege of being the home team. This did not help, as the Oaks swept the twin bill to win their first Governor's Cup.

Brooks Holder hit Guy Fletcher's first pitch for a home run and the rout was on, as the Oaks got three in the first, two in the third, two more in the sixth, on their way to an 11–1 victory. Nick Etten hit two homers and went 4-for-5, while driving in five runs for the "visiting" Oaks. Kewpie Dick Barrett and Steve Peek followed Fletcher to the mound and took their lumps. Lou Tost went the route for Oakland.

Oakland	AB	R	H	RBI	O	A	E
Holder LF	5	2	3	1	2	0	0
Lodigiani 3B	6	3	4	0	2	2	0
Metkovitch CF	5	2	1	0	5	0	0
Etten 1B	5	3	4	5	10	1	0
Scarsella RF	3	1	2	1	2	0	0

Oakland	AB	R	H	RBI	O	A	E
Duezabou RF	1	0	0	0	0	0	0
Combs SS	5	0	1	0	2	3	0
Martin 2B	4	0	1	2	1	5	0
Fernandes C	2	0	0	0	2	0	0
Tost P	5	0	0	1	1	1	0
	41	11	16	10	27	12	0

Seattle	AB	R	H	RBI	O	A	E
Ramsey CF	2	0	0	0	0	0	0
Mohr CF	2	0	1	0	1	0	0
White RF	5	0	0	0	3	0	0
Layne 3B	4	0	0	0	1	2	0
Johnson 1B	3	0	0	0	9	0	0
Besse 1B	1	0	0	0	3	0	0
Rapp LF	4	0	1	0	2	0	1
York 2B	2	0	0	0	1	3	0
Peek P	1	0	1	0	0	1	0
Newsome SS	3	0	0	0	1	3	0
Hemsley C	3	1	1	0	4	2	0
Fletcher P	0	0	0	0	0	1	0
Barrett P	1	0	0	0	0	1	0
O'Neil SS	2	0	1	1	2	0	0
	33	1	5	1	27	13	1

Pitching Records	IP	H	R	ER	SO	BB
Tost	9	5	1	1	1	0
Fletcher (L)	2+	7	4	5	0	1
Barrett	2	4	3	2	1	5
Peek	5	5	4	4	1	3

Wild Pitch: Barrett. Hit by Pitcher: Scarsella by Fletcher. Two Base Hits: Holder, Lodigiani, Peek. Three Base Hit: O'Neil. Home Runs: Holder, Etten 2. Time of Game: 1 hr. 50 min. Umpires: Orr, Ford, Somers, Gordon.

Oakland	302	002	103	11 – 16 – 0
Seattle	000	001	000	1 – 5 – 1

Game Five.

Jack Salveson became the third straight Oakland pitcher to go the distance with a 4–1 win over loser Charley Schanz. Salveson also was the hitting

star, going 3-for-4 with a double and two runs batted in. Merrill Combs, who
went 2-for-4 with a double, drove in the Oaks' other two runs. By coincidence,
Salveson and Lombardi formed the battery on opening day of 1948 for Sacramento, the team that finished last, and on this last day of the season, they
formed the battery for Oakland, the team that finished first. Also coinciden-
tally, Lombardi broke into baseball with Oakland's 1927 pennant winning
team and bowed out of the game with Oakland's next pennant winning club
in 1948.

Oakland	AB	R	H	RBI	O	A	E
Holder LF	5	0	1	0	2	0	0
Lodigiani 3B	5	0	2	0	1	0	0
Metkovitch CF	5	0	0	0	2	0	0
Etten 1B	2	1	0	0	8	1	0
Scarsella RF	4	1	2	0	0	0	0
Combs SS	4	1	2	2	4	4	0
Martin 2B	4	1	1	0	2	2	0
Lombardi C	3	0	1	0	8	0	0
Salveson P	4	0	3	2	0	2	0
Duezabou LF	1	0	0	0	0	0	0
	37	4	12	4	27	9	0

Seattle	AB	R	H	RBI	O	A	E
Mohr CF	4	0	2	1	1	0	0
White RF	4	0	1	0	2	0	0
Layne 3B	4	0	2	0	0	0	0
Rapp LF	4	0	0	0	2	0	0
Johnson 1B	4	0	0	0	11	0	0
York 2B	3	0	1	0	3	4	0
Newsome SS	4	1	2	0	5	4	0
Grasso C	4	0	1	0	3	0	0
Schanz P	2	0	0	0	0	0	0
Warren[a]	1	0	0	0	0	0	0
Besse P	0	0	0	0	0	1	0
Hemsley[b]	1	0	0	0	0	0	0
	35	1	9	1	27	9	o

(a) Batted for Schanz in the seventh.
(b) Batted for Besse in the ninth.

Pitching Records	IP	H	R	ER	SO	BB
Salveson	9	9	1	1	8	1

Pitching Records	IP	H	R	ER	SO	BB
Schanz (L)	7	12	4	4	2	3
Besse	2	0	0	0	0	1

Two Base Hits: Lodigiani, Layne, Lombardi, Salveson, Combs. Double Plays: Layne to York to Johnson; York to Newsome to Johnson; Salveson to Combs to Etten. Time of Game: 1 hr. 46 min. Umpires: Gordon, Orr, Ford, Somers.

Oakland	020	000	200	4 – 12 – 0
Seattle	000	000	100	1 – 9 – 0

The Oaks divided $30,000 for taking the pennant and the playoffs. With about 28 shares, this came to about $1,071 per man, or about $4,446 in current funds. Seattle got $10,000 which would come to $357 if it also included 28 shares. This would be worth about $1,482 today. The Angels and Seals each divided $5,000, which would come to half of what fourth place Seattle earned. Of course, the Oaks and Rainiers got two extra weeks' salary while the Angels and Seals only one.

Key Players on 1948 Playoff Teams

Oakland. *Pitchers*: Lou Tost, Jack Salveson, Earl Jones, Charlie Gassaway, Will Hafey and Floyd Speer.
> *Position Players:* Lloyd Christopher, George Metkovitch, Nick Etten, Les Scarsella, Dario Lodigiani, Cookie Lavagetto, Ernie Lombardi and Bill Raimondi (injured).

San Francisco. *Pitchers:* Con Dempsey, Al Lien, Bill Werle, Ken Gables, Cliff Melton, and Jack Brewer (ill, out of playoffs).
> *Postion Players:* Gene Woodling (league batting champ, unavailable for playoffs), Jackie Tobin, Joe Brovia, Dino Restelli, Ray Orteig, Mickey Rocco, Dixie Howell, and Hugh Luby.

Los Angeles. *Pitchers:* Red Lynn, Don Carlson, Red Adams, Dewey Adkins and Lee Anthony.
> *Position Players:* Cliff Aberson, Eddie Sauer (team's MVP), Dominic Dallesandro, Johnny Ostrowski, and Eddie Malone.

Seattle. *Pitchers:* Guy Fletcher, Bob Hall, Charley Shanz, and Herb Karpel.
> *Position Players:* Neil Sheridan (recalled by Red Sox), Bill Ramsey, Jo Jo White, Bob Johnson, Hillis Layne, Earl Rapp, Lamar Newsome, and Mickey Grasso (injured for first playoff series).

1949

In 1949 the Hollywood Stars finally shined. This was their 12th season since moving south from San Francisco, but until 1949, they had only two first division finishes and were eliminated each time in the first round of the playoffs. But this year, they won it all, becoming the last of the eight teams to win the playoffs.

The Stars were managed by Fred Haney, former manager of the Browns, who had been a popular baseball announcer from 1943 to 1948 in the Los Angeles area. The success of Hollywood this season was mainly due to the working agreement they secured with the Brooklyn Dodgers, that had a lot of talent to send to them. Outfielder Irv Noren was the league's MVP and a major reason Hollywood won the pennant.

The second place Oakland Oaks were now managed by former Reds manager and recent Yankee coach Charley Dressen. The Oaks, with league batting champion Artie Wilson at short, closed to within two games of Hollywood with nine to play, but then lost a crucial doubleheader to the last place Angels, while the Stars were taking two from the Seals. The Stars thus had a four game lead going into the last week of the season and easily clinched the pennant.

The surprise team of 1949 was the Sacramento Solons managed by the former skipper of the Detroit Tigers, Del Baker. The improvement over 1948 was remarkable. Going from a last place team, forced to finish its season on the road, this club played in a rebuilt but uncovered Edmonds Field and set an all-time attendance mark for Sacramento at 447,556. They swept Seattle in a seven game series in August and later got to within three games of the front-running Stars, before Hollywood beat them in a key series. The Sacs' outfielders all hit over .300 but they lost the services of their slugging first baseman, Walt Dropo, with a broken leg, which hurt them in the playoffs.

For the first time since the playoffs started in 1936, there was a tie for fourth place, necessitating a one game tie-breaker between San Diego and Seattle, which the Padres won. Seattle was the preseason favorite to cop the flag but proved to be such a disappointment that manager Jo Jo White was fired in mid-season and replaced by Bill Lawrence. The Padres, just as the

Billy Martin of the 1949 Oakland Oaks
(Doug McWilliams collection).

other first division finishers, had a new manager, Bucky Harris, who had managed at Washington and had just been fired by the Yankees. Of all these first division managers, Del Baker was the only one not to return to the majors to manage again.

The Padres were the best draw in the league early in the season because of their slugging first baseman, Luke Easter, who bashed 25 homers and hit .363 before being hurt, and then called up to the Cleveland Indians. After his departure, the Padres had to scramble to make the first division, falling into a tie with Seattle on the last day of the season, but were no threat to third place Sacramento.

The league attendance for 1949 was 3,751,929, almost a 2.5 percent increase over 1948, making it the third highest year in history behind 1947 and 1946. This was achieved despite the fact that both Los Angeles and San Francisco, the teams with the two largest parks, had huge decreases because they finished eighth and seventh respectively.

The Tie-Breaking Game for Fourth Place

After the Padres won a doubleheader from the Angels on the last day of the season, they had to wait until they found out that Seattle, who had lost the opener of its doubleheader with Hollywood, managed to win its nightcap, causing the two clubs to end up tied for fourth place. The tie-breaking game was held at Lane Field, San Diego, on Monday night, September 26, but Seattle was allowed to bat last.

An overflow crowd of 10,930 came out to Lane Field to see their Padres battle to finish in the first division, supporting Seal owner Charles Graham's view that the benefit of the playoffs comes during the regular season as teams fight to get into them. Red Adams started for San Diego against Rugger

Ardizoia, who was pitching with one day's rest. The batting star for the Padres was Minnie Minoso, who went 4-for-5 with a homer, a double and four runs batted in. Minoso scored on a passed ball in the first, singled in two runs in the fifth, homered in the eighth, and singled in the tying runs in the ninth. Meanwhile, Seattle chased Adams with four runs in the last of the second on doubles by Tony York and Frank Coleman. Lyman Linde, Jesse Flores and Bob Savage followed Adams, with Flores getting the win. The Padres entered the top of the ninth trailing 6–4. After Dee Moore singled, the tiring Ardizoia was replaced by Denny Galehouse, who had won the opening game of the 1944 World Series for the Browns. This, however, was not Denny's night. After retiring Whitey Wietelmann, he walked pinch hitter Dain Clay, and then dropped a throw at first on Bobby Wilson's grounder, loading the

Darib Lodigani is greeted by George Metkovich after touching homeplate (Doug McWilliam's collection).

bases. Minoso drove in two runs with a single, and when the ball was misplayed in right field, Wilson scored the lead run. Al Rosen singled in Minoso, and after Max West singled Rosen to third, he scored on Harvey Storey's fly ball. Bob Savage set the Rainiers down in the last of the ninth to send the Padres into the playoffs for the first time since 1942.

San Diego	AB	R	H	RBI	O	A	E
Wilson 2B	5	1	0	1	6	1	0
Minoso CF	5	3	4	4	4	0	0
Rosen 1B	5	1	1	1	5	1	0
West RF	4	0	1	0	2	0	0
Storey 3B	5	0	2	1	1	0	0
Clark RF	5	0	0	0	4	0	0
Moore C	4	0	1	0	2	1	0

San Diego	AB	R	H	RBI	O	A	E
Wietelmann SS	4	1	2	0	1	5	0
C. Adams P	0	0	0	0	0	0	0
Linde P	1	1	1	0	1	1	0
B. Adams[a]	1	0	0	0	0	0	0
Flores P	0	0	0	0	0	0	0
Barr[b]	0	1	0	0	0	0	0
Clay[c]	0	1	0	0	0	0	0
Ritchey C	0	0	0	0	1	0	0
Savage P	0	0	0	0	0	0	0
	39	9	12	7	27	9	0

(a) Batted for Linde in the seventh.
(b) Batted for Flores in the ninth.
(c) Ran for Moore in the ninth.

Seattle	AB	R	H	RBI	O	A	E
Mohr CF	3	2	3	0	3	0	0
Layne 3B	4	1	3	1	1	3	1
Coleman RF	5	0	1	1	4	0	1
Becker 1B	1	0	0	0	9	1	0
Neill LF	3	1	0	0	1	0	0
Warren C	4	1	1	0	2	0	0
York 2B	5	1	2	1	3	3	0
Schuster SS	4	0	1	1	3	6	0
Ardizoia P	3	0	0	0	0	1	0
Grasso C	1	0	1	1	1	0	0
Ramsey CF	2	0	0	0	0	0	1
Galehouse P	0	0	0	0	0	0	1
Sheridan[a]	1	0	0	0	0	0	0
	36	6	12	5	27	14	4

(a) Batted for Galehouse in the ninth.

Pitching Records	IP	H	R	ER	SO	BB
C. Adams	1.2	5	4	4	1	2
Linde	4.1	6	1	1	1	4
Flores (W)	2	1	1	1	0	3
Savage	1	0	0	0	1	0
Ardizoia	8+	9	4	5	3	2
Galehouse (L)	1	3	5	2	0	1

Left on Base: San Diego 13, Seattle 6. Passed Ball: Warren. Two Base Hits: Minoso, York, Coleman, Linde. Home Run: Minoso. Sacrifice: Ardizoia. Stolen Base: Minoso. Double Plays: Ardizoia to Schuster to Becker; Wietelmann to Rosen; Wietelmann to Wilson to Rosen; York to Schuster to Becker. Time of Game: 2 hr. 58 min. Umpires: Ford, Powell, Mutart, Cunningham.

San Diego	100	020	015	9 – 12 – 0
Seattle	040	001	010	6 – 12 – 4

The Hollywood-Sacramento Series

This series began at Gilmore Field on Wednesday night, September 28, before 3,726 fans. The Solons worked out at home on Tuesday and took the night train to Los Angeles, arriving the morning of the game. During the regular season, Hollywood beat Sacramento 15 times and lost 11.

Game One.

This game was one of wasted opportunities for the Solons. They got 13 hits in the first six innings but scored only three runs and it came back to haunt them. Mal Mallette faced the Stars' Willy Ramsdell but neither got the decision. In the third, singles by Len Ratto, Al White, and Ralph Hodgin plated a run but the next three batters struck out, with Joe Marty being ejected for arguing. In the fourth, Pete Coscarart and Mallette singled, and Ratto squeezed Coscarart home but Mallette was picked off second base, cutting the inning short. In the sixth, the Sacs went up 3–0 when Ratto singled in Joe Grace. But in the eighth, Malette's shutout went by the boards when Frank Kelleher doubled home two runs to cut the lead to 3–2. Reliever Don Johnson retired the side that inning but in the last of the ninth, he gave up the tying run on singles to Chuck Stevens, Mike Sandlock and pinch hitter George Genovese. Jean Pierre Roy pitched shutout ball over three extra innings, and then in the last of the 12th, the Solons were the victims of a bad break and some sloppy fielding. Johnny O'Neil hit a hard smash off Johnson's shin, causing him to leave the game. Jess Dobernic came in and threw too late to second on Irv Noren's bunt. Kelleher walked to load the bases and Dobernic then uncorked a wild pitch, allowing O'Neil to score the winning run.

Sacramento	AB	R	H	RBI	O	A	E
Ratto SS	6	1	3	2	4	4	0
A. White CF-LF	6	0	2	0	4	0	0

Sacramento	AB	R	H	RBI	O	A	E
Hodgin LF-RF	6	0	3	1	3	1	0
Marty RF	2	0	0	0	0	0	0
Tabor 3B	6	0	1	0	2	3	0
Grace 1B	6	1	1	0	14	0	0
Coscarart 2B	4	1	2	0	3	4	0
Raimondi C	5	0	2	0	3	1	0
Mallette P	4	0	1	0	0	3	0
Wilson CF	3	0	1	0	0	0	0
Johnson P	1	0	0	0	0	0	0
Dobernic P	0	0	0	0	0	0	0
	49	3	16	3	33[a]	16	0

(a) None out when winning run scored.

Hollywood	AB	R	H	RBI	O	A	E
Handley 2B	5	0	0	0	2	3	0
O'Neil SS	5	1	2	0	5	3	1
Noren CF	5	1	1	0	1	0	0
Kelleher LF	4	0	2	2	3	0	0
Franklin RF	3	0	1	0	0	0	0
Baxes 3B	5	0	1	0	2	2	0
Stevens 1B	5	1	1	0	9	6	0
Sandlock C	4	0	1	0	9	1	0
Ramsdell P	1	0	0	0	3	1	0
Fallon[a]	1	1	1	0	0	0	0
Gorman RF[b]	2	0	1	0	1	0	0
Salveson P	0	0	0	0	0	0	0
Genovese[c]	1	0	1	1	0	0	0
Roy P	1	0	1	0	1	1	0
	42	4	13	3	36	17	1

(a) Batted for Ramsdell in the eighth.
(b) Batted for Franklin in the eighth.
(c) Batted for Salveson in the ninth.

Pitching Records	IP	H	R	ER	SO	BB
Mallette	7.2	7	2	2	2	3
Johnson (L)	3.1	5	1	2	1	1
Dobernic	0+	0	1	0	0	1
Ramsdell	8	13	3	3	7	1
Salveson	1	1	0	0	1	1
Roy (W)	3	2	0	0	0	0

Passed Ball: Sandlock. Wild Pitch: Dobernic. Left on Base: Sacramento 12, Hollywood 12. Two Base Hits: Franklin, Grace, Kelleher. Sacrifice: Ramsdell, Noren. Stolen Base: Coscarart. Double Plays: Mallette to Ratto to Grace; Handley to O'Neil to Stevens. Time of Game: 3hr. 1 minute. Umpires: Engeln, Ford, Barbour.

Sacramento	000	101	000	000	3 – 16 – 0
Hollywood	000	000	021	001	4 – 13 – 1

Game Two.

These games were recreated back to the capital city and Solons fans had better news on Thursday night, the 29th, as Sacramento evened the series with a 4–2 win in 10 innings. A crowd of 3,350 saw the second straight extra inning game in which the two starters, Orval Grove and Gordon Maltzberger, each pitched eight innings without getting the decision. The Stars broke a scoreless tie in the sixth when Maltzberger looped a single that scored Mike Sandlock. Three singles and an error allowed the Sacs to take the lead in the eighth. Grace and Coscarart singled, and when Jim Baxes muffed the throw to third, Grace scored and the tying run went to second. Bill Raimondi then singled in the lead run. But in the last of the ninth, a walk and two singles loaded the bases, causing Del Baker to bring in Frankie Dasso. Kelleher's fly tied the game, but Ed Oliver lost it for the Stars in the 10th. George Genovese made his second and third errors of the game, allowing the Sacs to get two unearned runs. Joe Marty's single and Jim Tabor's fly ball got them home.

Sacramento	AB	R	H	RBI	O	A	E
Ratto SS	5	1	0	0	0	2	0
A. White CF	4	0	2	0	3	0	0
Hodgin LF	5	1	1	0	5	0	0
Marty RF	5	0	1	1	0	0	0
Tabor 3B	5	0	1	1	0	1	0
Grace 1B	4	1	2	0	11	2	0
Coscarart 2B	4	1	2	0	2	6	0
Raimondi C	3	0	1	1	6	0	0
Grove P	3	0	0	0	2	3	0
Dasso P	0	0	0	0	1	0	0
	38	4	10	3	30	14	0

Hollywood	AB	R	H	RBI	O	A	E
Genovese SS	4	0	0	0	3	2	3
Handley 2B	5	0	1	1	3	2	0

Managers Del Baker and Charlie Dressen confer prior to a 1949 contest (Doug Mc-William's collection).

Hollywood	AB	R	H	RBI	O	A	E
Noren CF	3	1	0	0	5	1	0
Gorman RF	4	0	2	0	2	0	0
Stevens 1B	2	0	0	0	11	0	0
Kelleher LF	4	0	1	1	1	0	0
Baxes 3B	4	0	0	0	1	7	1
Sandlock C	4	1	1	0	4	2	0
Maltzberger P	2	0	1	0	0	0	0
Franklin[a]	1	0	0	0	0	0	0
Oliver P	0	0	0	0	0	0	0
J. White[b]	1	0	0	0	0	0	0
	34	2	6	2	30	14	4

(a) Batted for Matzberger in the eighth.
(b) Batted for Oliver in the tenth.

Pitching Records	IP	H	R	ER	SO	BB
Grove	8	6	1	2	6	2
Dasso (W)	2	0	1	0	0	0

Pitching Records	IP	H	R	ER	SO	BB
Maltzberger	8	9	2	2	3	0
Oliver (L)	2	1	2	0	1	1

Left on Base: Sacramento 7, Hollywood 6. Two Base Hits: Sandlock, Tabor. Sacrifices: Grove, Stevens 2, A. White. Stolen Base: Handley. Double Plays: Tabor to Coscarart to Grace; Baxes to Stevens; Noren to Handley. Time of Game: 2 hr. 25 min. Umpires: Ford, Barbour, Engeln.

Sacramento	000	000	200	2	4 –	10 –	0
Hollywood	000	001	001	0	2 –	6 –	4

Game Three.

On Friday night, September 30, 3,164 fans went to Gilmore Field to see Hollywood take the series lead with a 5–1 win, while over at the Coliseum, 43,137 saw UCLA, under its new coach, Red Sanders, upset Oregon 35–27. George "Pinky" Woods had a relatively easy time beating Ken Holcombe, whose bad throw helped Hollywood score two runs in the first, which was all Woods needed. After Genovese singled, Holcombe picked up Gene Handley's bunt and threw it into right field, allowing Genovese to score, and putting Handley at second, from where he scored on Herb Gorman's single. A walk and singles by Gorman and Stevens made it 3–0 in the third, and Kelleher's two-run homer in the eighth accounted for the final two runs. Woods lost his shutout in the fifth when Grace tripled and scored on a ground out.

Sacramento	AB	R	H	RBI	O	A	E
Ratto SS	4	0	1	0	2	1	0
A. White CF	4	0	1	0	1	0	0
Hodgin LF	4	0	1	0	1	0	0
Marty RF	4	0	2	0	1	0	0
Tabor 3B	4	0	0	0	0	3	0
Grace 1B	4	1	1	0	13	0	0
Coscarart 2B	2	0	1	0	0	5	0
Raimondi C	3	0	0	1	5	0	0
Holcombe P	1	0	0	0	0	1	1
Wilson[a]	1	0	0	0	0	0	0
Conger P	1	0	0	0	1	2	1
	32	1	7	1	24	12	2

(a) Batted for Holcombe in the fifth.

Hollywood	AB	R	H	RBI	O	A	E
Genovese SS	4	1	1	0	2	6	0
Handley 2B	3	1	1	0	0	5	0
Noren CF	2	1	0	0	3	2	0
Gorman RF	4	1	3	1	1	0	0
Stevens 1B	4	0	1	1	15	0	0
Kelleher LF	4	1	2	2	2	0	0
Baxes 3B	3	0	1	0	0	2	0
Sandlock C	3	0	0	0	4	0	0
Woods P	4	0	0	0	0	1	0
	31	5	9	4	27	16	0

Pitching Records	IP	H	R	ER	SO	BB
Holcombe (L)	4	5	3	2	3	2
Conger	4	4	2	2	1	1
Woods	9	7	1	1	2	1

Passed Ball: Raimondi. Left on Base: Sacramento: 5, Hollywood 7. Two Base Hits: Kelleher, Stevens. Three Base Hit: Grace. Home Run: Kelleher. Sacrifices: Sandlock, Noren. Double Plays: Noren to Stevens; Coscarart to Ratto to Grace. Time of Game: 1 hr. 45 min. Umpires: Barbour, Engeln, Ford.

Sacramento	000	010	000	1 – 7 – 2
Hollywood	201	000	02x	5 – 9 – 0

Game Four.

The series was resumed on Saturday night, October 1, at Edmonds Field, after the two teams rode the S.P. Daylight all day, arriving less than an hour before the 8:15 P.M. start. Without a major college football game to distract them, 6,889 Sacramento fans turned out to see Bob Gillespie face the Stars' Glenn Moulder. After giving up an unearned run in the third, the Sacs came right back to take a 3–1 when Hodgin singled in Ratto, Marty doubled in Hodgin and Handley's throwing error allowed Marty to score. But Hollywood tied it in the sixth when Baxes doubled, Al Unser walked, and relief pitcher Jean Pierre Roy came through with a run-scoring single. Noren's groundout later scored Unser. Roy became the hitting hero in the seventh when his single scored two runs which made the difference. Kelleher doubled, Baxes walked and Unser sacrificed them along for his pitcher. After walking Al White in the last of the ninth, Haney took Roy out and brought in Jack Salveson, who gave up a double to Hodgin, putting the tying run on second with no one out. But the only run Sacramento scored came on Marty's fly ball.

Hollywood	AB	R	H	RBI	O	A	E
Genovese SS	4	0	0	0	1	0	0
Handley 2B	5	1	2	0	4	3	1
Noren CF	4	0	0	1	5	0	0
Gorman RF	2	0	2	0	1	0	0
Stevens 1B	4	0	0	1	8	1	0
Kelleher LF	4	1	1	0	4	0	0
Baxes 3B	4	2	2	0	1	7	0
Unser C	3	1	0	0	2	0	0
Moulder P	2	0	1	0	1	0	1
Roy P	3	0	2	3	0	0	0
Salveson P	0	0	0	0	0	0	0
	35	5	10	5	27	11	2

Sacramento	AB	R	H	RBI	O	A	E
Ratto SS	4	1	2	0	4	1	1
A. White CF	4	1	0	0	4	0	0
Hodgin LF	5	1	3	1	2	1	0
Marty RF	4	1	2	2	3	0	0
Tabor 3B	3	0	0	0	2	0	0
Grace 1B	5	0	0	0	2	4	0
Coscarart 2B	3	0	0	0	4	1	2
Raimondi C	3	0	0	0	4	1	0
Gillespie P	2	0	0	0	2	0	0
Dobernic P	0	0	0	0	0	0	0
Marsh[a]	1	0	1	0	0	0	0
Freitas P	0	0	0	0	0	0	0
	34	4	8	3	27	8	3

(a) Batted for Dobernic in the eighth.

Pitching Records	R	ER	SO	BB
Moulder	3	2	2	5
Roy (W)	0	1	0	2
Salveson	1	0	0	0
Gillespie	5	4	2	7
Dobernic	0	0	1	1
Freitas	0	0	0	0

Left on Base: Hollywood 13, Sacramento 11. Two Base Hits: Marty, Baxes, Kelleher, Hodgin. Sacrifices: Gillespie, Unser, Gorman. Stolen Base: Ratto. Double Plays: Baxes to Handley to Stevens; Handley to Stevens. Time of Game: 2 hr. 39 min. Umpires: Engeln, Ford, Barbour.

| Hollywood | 001 | 002 | 200 | 5 – 10 – 2 |
| Sacramento | 003 | 000 | 001 | 4 – 8 – 3 |

Game Five.

A doubleheader was scheduled for Sunday night, the 2nd, but only one game was needed as the Stars nipped the Sacs, 2–1, to end the series. With no roof on the new stands, the Solons played all their games at night. Willy Ramsdell gave up a homer to Jim Tabor in the second for the Sacs' only run. The Stars got to Frankie Dasso for two in the sixth when Noren singled and Gorman doubled him to third. Stevens grounded to Joe Grace who threw too late to the plate, allowing the tying run to score. Kelleher's fly ball got the decisive run home. This was the last time Sacramento was in the playoffs.

Hollywood	AB	R	H	RBI	O	A	E
Genovese SS	5	0	1	0	5	0	0
Handley 2B	4	0	2	0	2	4	1
Noren CF	5	1	1	0	2	0	0
Gorman RF	3	1	1	0	2	0	0
Stevens 1B	4	0	0	1	8	1	0
Kelleher LF	4	0	1	1	3	0	0
Baxes 3B	4	0	1	0	0	3	0
Sandlock C	3	0	0	0	4	1	0
Ramsdell P	4	0	0	0	1	2	0
	36	2	7	2	27	11	1

Sacramento	AB	R	H	RBI	O	A	E
Ratto SS	4	0	0	0	1	2	0
A. White CF	4	0	1	0	2	0	0
Hodgin LF	4	0	0	0	2	0	0
Marty RF	3	0	0	0	2	0	0
Tabor 3B	4	1	2	1	1	3	1
Grace 1B	3	0	1	0	12	2	0
Coscarart 2B	3	0	1	0	1	2	1
Raimondi C	4	0	1	0	4	0	0
Dasso P	3	0	1	0	2	2	0
Wilson [a]	0	0	0	0	0	0	0
Johnson P	0	0	0	0	0	0	0
Outlaw [b]	0	0	0	0	0	0	0
	32	1	7	1	27	11	2

(a) *Batted for Dasso in the eighth.*
(b) *Ran for Marty in the ninth.*

Pitching Records	IP	H	R	ER	SO	BB
Ramsdell	9	7	1	1	4	3
Dasso (L)	8	6	2	2	2	2
Johnson	1	1	0	0	1	0

Left on Base: Hollywood 10, Sacramento 7. Two Base Hits: Gorman, Noren, Tabor, Handley. Home Run: Tabor. Double Plays: Genovese unassisted; Baxes to Handley to Stevens. Time of Game: 2 hr. 10 min. Umpires: Ford, Barbour, Engeln.

Hollywood	000	002	000	2 – 6 – 1
Sacramento	010	000	000	1 – 7 – 2

Because the Oakland–San Diego series was not settled until Monday night, the Stars remained in Sacramento until Tuesday morning to see if they should fly to San Diego or take the train to Oakland for the final round. The Stars wanted to finish the final series at home. Del Baker resigned after the playoffs and managed San Diego in 1950.

The San Diego–Oakland Series

These two teams split evenly the 26 times they met during the season. Their second place finish permitted the Oaks to open at home, but the enthusiasm just was not there. Alan Ward of *The Oakland Tribune* again blasted the playoffs and quoted Oaks' owner Brick Laws as saying he hoped they would not draw, so they could be discontinued. Padre owner Bill Starr also said he was going to vote against them even though San Diego fans turned out rather well for the postseason games.

Game One.

Only 1,814 fans were at Oaks Park on Wednesday night, September 28, to see Oakland pound the Padres 13–3. The Oaks got two in the first and five in both the second and third innings to lead 12–0, making it easy for Milo Candini, who went the route. Red Adams, Al Jurisich and Tom Kipp were hammered before Junior Thompson retired the side in the third. Dick Kryhowski hit a two-run homer in the first and Don Padgett hit a solo shot in the eighth.

In the second, Lloyd Christopher tripled, Billy Martin doubled, and Jackie Jensen, Candini and Padgett all hit singles, while Al Rosen committed an error. In the third, two walks, four singles and a double plated five more runs. Besides the local radio broadcast, these games were recreated back to San Diego.

San Diego	AB	R	H	RBI	O	A	E
B. Wilson 2B	5	1	2	1	0	4	0
Minoso CF	4	0	0	0	4	0	0
Rosen 1B	4	0	1	0	7	0	1
West RF	2	0	0	1	3	0	0
Storey 3B	4	0	0	0	2	0	0
Clark LF	4	1	1	0	2	0	0
Moore C	4	1	2	1	3	1	0
Wietelmann SS	3	0	1	0	3	3	1
C. Adams P	0	0	0	0	0	1	0
Jurisich P	0	0	0	0	0	1	0
Clay[a]	1	0	0	0	0	0	0
Kipp P	0	0	0	0	0	1	0
J. Thompson P	2	0	0	0	0	1	0
B. Adams[b]	1	0	0	0	0	0	0
	34	3	7	3	24	12	2

(a) Batted for Jurisich in the third.
(b) Batted for J. Thompson in the ninth.

Oakland	AB	R	H	RBI	O	A	E
A. Wilson SS	4	2	1	0	1	7	1
Lavagetto 3B	4	0	2	3	0	1	0
Rapp RF	5	2	1	1	2	0	0
Kryhowski 1B	5	2	3	3	10	1	0
Padgett C	5	1	3	1	4	0	0
Christopher CF	5	1	2	1	2	0	0
Jensen LF	4	1	2	1	1	0	0
Martin 2B	4	2	1	0	6	2	0
Candini P	4	2	1	1	1	0	0
Woods 3B	1	0	0	0	0	1	0
	41	13	16	11	27	12	1

Pitching Records	IP	H	R	ER	SO	BB
C. Adams (L)	1+	7	5	7	0	0
Jurisich	1	2	2	0	0	0
Kipp	0.2	5	4	5	0	2

Pitching Records	IP	H	R	ER	SO	BB
J. Thompson	5.1	2	2	1	3	1
Candini	9	7	3	3	4	3

Passed Ball: Padgett. Left on Base: San Diego 7, Oakland 8. Two Base Hits: Martin, Padgett, Rapp, Rosen, Clark. Three Base Hit: Christopher. Home Runs: Kryhoski, Padgett. Double Play: A. Wilson to Martin to Kryhoski. Time of Game: 1 hr. 50 min. Umpires: Somers, Gordon, Orr.

San Diego	000	010	011	3 – 7 – 2	
Oakland	255	000	01x	13 – 16 – 1	

Game Two.

While the Oakland papers devoted most of their sports coverage to the tight major league races that went down to the final day, and to the upcoming Michigan at Stanford and California at Oregon State football games, the Oaks and Padres drew even a smaller crowd of 1,248 fans on Thursday night, which featured San Diego winning 9–6 to tie the series. "Kewpie" Dick Barrett faced Earl Harrist of the Oaks, who was given special permission to play in the first round because the Padres wanted to use Allie Clark, both of whom joined their teams after the deadline.

San Diego led 6–1 after three innings, scoring three in the first on a walk, Minoso's single, Rosen's double and a ground out, and three in the third on Harvey Storey's three-run homer. The Padres led 7–2 going into the last of the sixth, but Oakland chased Barrett with Kryhowski's three-run homer, but Bob Savage relieved and held Oakland to just one run afterwards. San Diego got its final two runs in the eighth off reliever Forest Thompson. Both these teams had relief pitchers named Thompson — Forest for Oakland and Junior for San Diego — and both had infielders named Wilson — Bobby for San Diego and Artie for Oakland. Artie had a bad night, making three errors, two in the eighth, that led to two unearned runs.

San Diego	AB	R	H	RBI	O	A	E
B. Wilson 2B	2	2	2	0	3	6	0
Minoso CF	4	1	1	1	4	0	0
Rosen 1B	4	2	2	3	8	1	0
West RF	3	1	0	0	1	0	0
Storey 3B	3	1	1	4	1	1	0
Clark LF	5	0	1	1	5	0	0
Moore C	4	0	0	0	1	0	0
Wietelmann SS	5	1	1	0	4	4	0

Billy Martin of the 1949 Oakland Oaks takes a batting practice cut (Doug McWilliam's collection).

San Diego	AB	R	H	RBI	O	A	E
Barrett P	2	0	0	0	0	0	0
Savage P	1	1	0	0	0	0	0
	33	9	8	9	27	12	0

Oakland	AB	R	H	RBI	O	A	E
A. Wilson SS	4	1	3	0	2	2	3
Lavagetto 3B	4	1	2	1	1	1	0
Rapp RF	5	1	1	0	1	0	0
Kryhoski 1B	3	1	2	4	9	1	0
Padgett C	4	0	1	0	8	1	1
Christopher CF	4	1	1	0	2	0	0
Jensen LF	4	0	0	0	1	0	0
Martin 2B	3	1	1	0	3	3	0
Harrist P	0	0	0	0	0	0	0
Jones P	0	0	0	0	0	1	0

Oakland	AB	R	H	RBI	O	A	E
Duezabou[a]	1	0	1	1	0	0	0
Cecil P	0	0	0	0	0	0	0
Van Robays[b]	1	0	0	0	0	0	0
F. Thompson P	0	0	0	0	0	0	0
Woods[c]	1	0	0	0	0	0	0
	34	6	12	6	27	9	4

(a) Batted for Jones in the sixth.
(b) Batted for Cecil in the sixth.
(c) Batted for F. Thompson in the ninth.

Pitching Records	IP	H	R	ER	SO	BB
Barrett (W)	5	8	5	5	0	3
Savage	4	4	1	1	0	0
Harrist (L)	3	5	6	6	5	3
Jones	2	1	0	0	1	2
Cecil	2	1	1	1	1	1
F. Thompson	2	1	2	1	0	0

Hit by Pitcher: Minoso by Cecil; Martin by Savage; West by F. Thompson. Wild Pitch: Harrist. Left on Base: San Diego 8, Oakland 7. Two Base Hits: Rosen, Christopher. Home Runs: Storey, Kryhoski. Double Plays: Wietelmann to B. Wilson to Rosen 2; A. Wilson to Martin to Kryhoski. Time of Game 2 hr. 27 min. Umpires: Gordon, Orr and Somers.

San Diego	303	001	020	9 – 8 – 0
Oakland	100	013	100	6 – 12 – 4

Game Three.

The 1,787 fans that came out Friday night, September 30, to see the last game played at Oaks Park in 1949 got a thrill as their Oaks overcame a 4–0 deficit to beat San Diego 6–5 in 10 innings. Lyman Linde started for the Padres and pitched nine innings, but it was Jake Mooty, the ex–Beaver, who lost it in the 10th when he gave up Billy Martin's game-winning homer. Charlie Gassaway started for Oakland but gave up four of the five Padre runs, before leaving after five, trailing 4–0. Max West went 4-for-5 with a homer and a triple in a losing cause. Dick Kryhowski singled in one Oak run in the seventh, when they cut the lead to 5–3. After Oakland got a run in the eighth, to make it a one-run game, Kyrhowski blasted a game tying homer in the last of the ninth to send it into extra innings. Forest Thompson, who pitched two scoreless innings, got the win when Billy Martin homered in the 10th.

San Diego	AB	R	H	RBI	O	A	E
B. Wilson 2B	5	0	2	0	1	3	0
Minoso CF	5	1	0	0	1	0	0
Rosen 1B	5	2	2	0	12	0	0
West RF	5	2	4	2	0	0	0
Storey 3B	5	0	2	2	3	3	0
Clark lF	4	0	0	0	3	0	0
Moore C	5	0	1	0	5	0	0
Wietelmann SS	3	0	1	0	2	3	1
Linde P	2	0	0	0	0	0	0
C. Adams[a]	0	0	0	0	0	0	0
Mooty P	0	0	0	0	0	0	0
	39	5	12	4	27[b]	9	1

(a) Batted for Linde in the tenth.
(b) None out when winning run scored.

Oakland	AB	R	H	RBI	O	A	E
A. Wilson SS	4	1	1	1	2	4	1
Lavagetto 3B	5	0	1	0	0	3	0
Rapp RF	4	1	2	1	1	0	0
Kryhoski 1B	4	2	2	2	9	3	0
Padgett C	5	0	2	1	6	0	1
Christopher CF	5	0	1	0	2	0	0
Duezabou LF	5	0	1	0	4	0	0
Martin 2B	4	2	2	1	6	2	0
Gassaway P	1	0	0	0	0	0	0
Jensen[a]	1	0	0	0	0	0	0
Tote P	0	0	0	0	0	0	0
Van Robays[b]	1	0	0	0	0	0	0
Tost P	0	0	0	0	0	0	0
Woods[c]	0	0	0	0	0	0	0
F. Thompson P	0	0	0	0	0	0	0
	39	6	12	6	30	12	2

(a) Batted for Gassaway in the fifth.
(b) Batted for Tote in the sixth.
(c) Batted for Tost in the eighth.

Pitching Records	IP	H	R	ER	SO	BB
Linde	9	11	5	2	2	4
Mooty (L)	0+	1	1	1	0	0

Pitching Records	IP	H	R	ER	SO	BB
Gassaway	5	6	4	3	2	2
Tote	1	2	0	0	0	0
Tost	2	2	1	1	3	0
F. Thompson (W)	2	2	0	0	0	1

Balk: Linde. Hit by Pitcher: Woods by Linde. Left on Base: San Diego 10, Oakland 11. Two Base Hits: A. Wilson, Rapp 2, Rosen, Christopher, Padgett. Three Base Hits: B. Wilson, Martin, West. Home Runs: West, Kryhoski, Martin. Sacrifices: Linde 2. Stolen Base: Moore. Double Plays: Martin to Kryhoski; B. Wilson to Wietelmann to Rosen; Kryhoski to A. Wilson to Kryhoski. Time of Game: 2 hr. 32 min. Umpires: Orr, Somers, Gordon.

San Diego	201	010	100	0	5 – 12 – 1
Oakland	000	010	211	1	6 – 12 – 2

Game Four.

Because San Diego did not have major college football, there was no off day on Saturday, October 1. Both clubs flew to San Diego and played that night before 6,430 fans at Lane Field. Jesse Flores pitched a complete game victory for San Diego even though he gave up six runs, ten hits and two walks. Frank Nelson started for Oakland and escaped defeat despite twice giving up two-run leads. Forest Thompson gave up two runs in the seventh, which put the Padres up 6–4, a lead they never surrendered. Harvey Storey went 3-for-5 with two doubles, a homer and five RBIs. Allie Clark and Al Rosen also homered for San Diego while Christopher hit one for Oakland. Artie Wilson had another bad night for Oakland, going 0-for-5 and making two errors in the eighth inning when the Padres plated four unearned runs, which gave them a 10–5 lead going into the ninth. Since Oakland scored one in the ninth, those unearned runs proved to be decisive.

Oakland	AB	R	H	RBI	O	A	E
A. Wilson SS	5	1	0	0	0	5	2
Lavagetto 3B	4	1	3	1	0	1	0
Rapp RF	5	1	2	1	3	0	0
Kryhoski 1B	4	1	1	0	11	0	0
Christopher CF	4	2	2	2	4	0	0
Duezabou LF	4	0	1	1	2	0	0
Martin 2B	4	0	0	1	1	1	0
Kerr C	3	0	1	0	3	1	0
Nelson P	2	0	0	0	0	2	0
Woods[a]	1	0	0	0	0	0	0
F. Thompson P	0	0	0	0	0	0	0

Oakland	AB	R	H	RBI	O	A	E
Toolson P	0	0	0	0	0	0	0
Tost P	0	0	0	0	0	0	0
Tote P	0	0	0	0	0	0	0
Van Robays [b]	1	0	0	0	0	0	0
Padgett [c]	0	0	0	0	0	0	0
	37	6	10	6	24	10	2

(a) *Batted for Nelson in the seventh.*
(b) *Batted for Kerr in the ninth.*
(c) *Batted for Tote in the ninth.*

San Diego	AB	R	H	RBI	O	A	E
R. Wilson 2B	5	1	2	0	3	6	1
Minoso CF	4	2	0	0	1	0	0
Rosen 1B	4	3	2	1	13	0	0
West RF	4	1	1	1	0	0	0
Storey 3B	5	2	3	5	0	2	0
Clark LF	3	1	2	1	1	0	0
Moore C	5	0	1	1	8	1	0
Wietelmann SS	4	0	1	0	1	5	0
Flores P	4	0	0	0	0	1	0
	38	10	12	9	27	15	1

Pitching Records	IP	H	R	ER	SO	BB
Nelson	6	7	4	4	2	2
F. Thompson (L)	0.1	2	1	2	0	0
Toolson	1+	2	1	0	0	2
Tost	0.1	0	0	0	1	0
Tote	0.1	1	4	0	0	1
Flores	9	10	6	5	7	2

Hit by Pitcher: Minoso by F. Thompson. Wild Pitch: Tost. Left on Base: Oakland 6, San Diego 10. Two Base Hits: Rapp 2, Storey 2, Lavagetto. Home Runs: Rosen, Christopher, Storey, Clark. Double Play: Moore to R. Wilson to Moore. Time of Game: 2 hr. 17 min. Umpires: Somers, Gordon, Orr.

Oakland	011	002	011	6 – 10 – 2
San Diego	000	202	24x	10 – 12 – 1

Game Five.

A Sunday crowd of 6,641 went to Lane Field hoping to see the Padres take a doubleheader to win the series, but after an easy victory in the opener, the Padres lost the nightcap, forcing a seventh game on Monday.

In the opener, Al Jurisich was staked to an early 6–0 lead and coasted to a 10–1 victory. Harvey Storey got three doubles in four at-bats and drove in four runs and scored two. Al Rosen hit a three-run homer off starter Earl Harrist but had to leave the game with an injured leg that restricted him to pinch hitting duties the rest of the playoffs.

Oakland	AB	R	H	RBI	O	A	E
A. Wilson SS	4	1	1	0	0	4	1
Lavagetto 3B	4	0	1	1	1	0	0
Rapp RF-CF	4	0	1	0	9	0	0
Kryhoski 1B	4	0	1	0	6	1	0
Padgett C	4	0	0	0	4	0	0
Christopher CF	0	0	0	0	1	0	0
Duezabou LF-RF	4	0	0	0	0	0	1
Martin 2B	4	0	2	0	3	1	0
Harrist P	2	0	1	0	0	0	0
Jensen LF	3	0	0	0	0	0	0
Woods[a]	1	0	0	0	0	0	0
Jones P	0	0	0	0	0	0	0
Hamrick 2B	0	0	0	0	0	0	0
	34	1	7	1	24	6	2

(a) Batted for Harrist in the seventh.

San Diego	AB	R	H	RBI	O	A	E
B. Wilson 2B	3	2	0	0	0	5	0
Minoso CF	4	1	0	0	3	0	0
Rosen 1B	2	2	1	3	8	0	0
West RF-1B	4	2	2	1	3	1	0
Storey 3B	4	2	3	4	1	0	0
Clark LF	4	0	1	1	1	0	0
Moore C	4	0	1	0	7	1	0
Wietelmann SS	4	0	1	0	2	3	1
Jurisich P	3	1	2	0	1	1	0
B. Adams RF	2	0	0	0	1	0	0
	34	10	11	9	27	11	1

Pitching Records	IP	H	R	ER	SO	BB
Harrist (L)	6	7	7	7	2	2
Jones	2	4	3	3	2	1
Jurisich	9	7	1	1	4	1

Wild Pitch: Jones. Hit by Pitcher: Rosen by Harrist. Left on Base: Oakland 7, San Diego 5. Two Base Hits: Storey 3, Kryhoski, Martin, A. Wilson. Home Run: Rosen. Sacrifice: Jurisch. Stolen Base: Minoso. Double Plays: Matin to Kryhoski; B. Wilson to Wietelmann to West. Time of Game: 2 hr. 16 min. Umpires: Gordon, Orr, Somers.

Oakland	000	000	010	1 –	7 –	2
San Diego	330	010	30x	10 –	11 –	1

Game Six.

Milo Candini and Red Adams faced each other in this nine inning nightcap, just as they had in game one and the results were the same. Buster Adams' homer in the second was the only run Candini gave up, while Dick Kryhowski's three-run homer off Red Adams in the third was more than enough for the Oaks. Jack Jensen, former California football star, went 3-for-4 with a homer and two RBIs.

Oakland	AB	R	H	RBI	O	A	E
A. Wilson SS	5	1	2	0	2	3	0
Lavagetto 3B	5	1	1	0	0	3	0
Rapp CF	2	2	2	0	6	0	0
Kryhoski 1B	3	1	1	3	9	0	0
Duezabou RF	5	0	2	0	1	0	0
Jensen LF	4	1	3	2	1	0	0
Martin 2B	5	0	0	0	1	0	1
Kerr C	4	0	2	0	7	0	0
Candini P	3	0	0	0	0	1	0
	36	6	13	5	27	7	1

San Diego	AB	R	H	RBI	O	A	E
R. Wilson 2B	4	0	0	0	3	0	0
Minoso CF	4	0	1	0	2	0	0
Clark LF	4	0	0	0	2	0	0
West 1B	3	0	0	0	5	2	0
Storey 3B	4	0	2	0	2	2	0
B. Adams RF	4	1	2	1	4	0	0
Moore C	4	0	0	0	5	2	0
Wietelmann SS	3	0	0	0	3	1	0
C. Adams P	1	0	0	0	0	1	1
Savage P	1	0	0	0	1	1	0
Clay[a]	1	0	0	0	0	0	0

Oakland	AB	R	H	RBI	O	A	E
J. Thompson P	0	0	0	0	0	0	0
	33	1	5	1	27	9	1

(a) *Batted for Savage in the eighth.*

Pitching Records	IP	H	R	ER	SO	BB
Candini	9	5	1	1	7	1
C. Adams (L)	2+	3	4	4	1	4
Savage	6	9	2	2	3	1
J. Thompson	1	1	0	0	1	0

Wild Pitch: C. Adams. Hit by Pitcher: Kryhoski by J. Thompson. Left on Base: Oakland 10, San Diego 6. Two Base Hits: Storey, Minoso, Duezabou. Home Runs: B. Adams, Kryhoski, Jensen. Sacrifice: Candini. Stolen Base: A. Wilson. Double Play: West to Wietelmann to R. Wilson. Time of Game: 2 hr. 1 min. Umpires: Orr, Somers, Gordon.

Oakland	103	001	100	6 – 13 – 1
San Diego	010	000	000	1 – 5 – 1

Game Seven.

On Monday night, October 3, 6,445 fans turned out to see the Padres blow the Oaks out of the playoffs with a lopsided 18–2 win. Dick Barrett, who was 43 years old, had an easy time of it while Charley Gassaway failed to survive the first inning as San Diego scored four runs. The Oaks used seven pitchers in a futile effort to stem the onslaught. Minnie Minoso went 5-for-5 with a walk, six runs scored and three batted in. Harvey Storey drove in four runs while going 3-for-5. Allie Clark went 4-for-4 with a homer in his last playoff game because Hollywood would not let him play in the finals.

Oakland	AB	R	H	RBI	O	A	E
A. Wilson SS	4	0	2	2	0	3	1
Lavagetto 3B	3	0	0	0	1	3	1
Rapp RF	4	0	0	0	0	1	0
Kryhoski 1B	4	0	1	0	7	1	1
Padgett C	4	0	1	0	5	1	1
Duezabou RF	4	0	0	0	4	0	0
Jensen LF	2	1	1	0	0	0	0
Martin 2B	2	0	1	0	6	3	1
Gassaway P	0	0	0	0	0	0	0
Harrist P	0	0	0	0	0	0	0

Oakland	AB	R	H	RBI	O	A	E
Cecil P	0	0	0	0	0	0	0
Van Robays[a]	1	0	0	0	0	0	0
Nelson P	0	0	0	0	0	0	0
Christopher[b]	1	0	1	0	0	0	0
F. Thompson[c]	0	1	0	0	0	0	0
Toolson P	0	0	0	0	0	0	0
Tote P	0	0	0	0	0	0	0
Tost P	1	0	0	0	0	1	0
Woods 3B	1	0	0	0	1	0	0
	31	2	7	2	24	13	5

(a) *Batted for Cecil in the third.*
(b) *Batted for Toolson in the sixth.*
(c) *Ran for Christopher in the sixth.*

San Diego	AB	R	H	RBI	O	A	E
B. Wilson 2B	4	3	0	0	2	4	0
Minoso CF	5	6	5	3	3	0	0
Clark LF	4	3	4	4	1	0	0
West 1B	5	1	3	3	13	2	1
Storey 3B	5	1	3	4	2	0	0
C. Adams RF	5	0	0	0	1	0	0
Moore C	3	1	0	0	1	1	0
Wietelmann SS	4	1	1	1	2	7	0
Barrett P	3	1	1	0	1	1	0
Clay RF[a]	1	1	0	0	1	0	0
	39	18	17	15	27	15	1

a *Ran for Clark in the sixth.*

Pitching Records	IP	H	R	ER	SO	BB
Gassaway (L)	0.2	2	4	2	1	2
Harrist	0.2	3	2	1	0	0
Cecil	0.2	0	0	0	1	0
Nelson	2.1	6	6	6	0	3
Toolson	0.2	0	0	0	0	0
Tote	1	3	5	5	0	5
Tost	2	3	1	1	3	0
Barrett	9	7	2	2	2	2

Hit by Pitcher: Moore by Gassaway. Wild Pitches: Cecil, Nelson. Left on Base: Oakland 4, San Diego 9. Two Base Hits: West, Minoso, Clark. Home Run:

Clark. Sacrifices: Barrett, Nelson. Double Plays: Wietelmann to B. Wilson to West 2; A. Wilson to Martin to Kryhoski 2. Time of Game: 2 hr. 38 min. Umpires: Somers, Gordon, Orr.

Oakland	000	001	010	2	7	5
San Diego	420	245	01x	18	17	1

This was the last series the Padres won in the playoffs and the last time any series went seven games. The final round of 1949 went only six games and in the two remaining years, a shorter format was used.

The Final Series: Hollywood vs. San Diego

Hollywood flew to San Diego on Tuesday morning, October 4, to start this series that evening. There was no off day for the Padres who were now without Allie Clark and had only limited use of Al Rosen. Bucky Harris was upset with Fred Haney for not letting Clark be used.

Game One.

A crowd of 4,051, which was smaller than any that Oakland drew at Lane Field, saw their Padres take the lead in this series with a 6–1 win. Lyman Linde pitched a four-hitter, beating Gordon Maltzberger. After Herb Gorman's single gave Hollywood a brief 1–0 lead in the second, San Diego erased it immediately with three of their own in the last half, on four singles and a sacrifice, which chased Maltzberger. Max West doubled home a fourth run in the fifth and homered with Buster Adams on base in the seventh to make the final 6–1.

Hollywood	AB	R	H	RBI	O	A	E
Geneovese SS	3	0	0	0	1	6	0
Handley 2B	4	0	0	0	5	3	1
Noren CF	4	0	0	0	1	0	0
Gorman RF	3	1	2	1	0	0	0
Stevens 1B	4	0	1	0	13	3	0
Kelleher LF	4	0	1	0	1	0	0
Baxes 3B	3	0	0	0	0	4	0
Sandlock C	3	0	0	0	3	0	0
Maltzberger P	0	0	0	0	0	0	0
Oliver P	1	0	0	0	0	1	0

Hollywood	AB	R	H	RBI	O	A	E
Fallon[a]	1	0	0	0	0	0	0
Roy P	1	0	0	0	0	1	0
	31	1	4	1	24	18	1

(a) Batted for Oliver in the sixth.

San Diego	AB	R	H	RBI	O	A	E
Wilson 2B	5	0	2	2	2	3	0
Minoso CF	4	1	0	0	5	0	0
B. Adams RF	3	1	1	0	2	0	0
West 1B	4	1	3	2	9	0	1
Storey 3B	4	0	1	0	0	3	0
Clay LF	4	1	1	0	3	0	0
Moore C	4	1	1	0	3	0	0
Wietelmann SS	4	1	2	1	3	5	0
Linde P	2	0	0	0	0	0	0
	34	6	11	5	27	11	1

Pitching Records	IP	H	R	ER	SO	BB
Maltzberger (L)	1.1	6	3	3	0	0
Oliver	3.2	3	1	0	2	0
Roy	3	2	2	2	1	2
Linde	9	4	1	1	3	2

Left on Base: Hollywood 5, San Diego 7. Home Runs: Gorman, West. Sacrifice: Linde. Double Play: Wilson to Wietelmann to West. Time of Game: 1 hr. 56 min. Umpires: Engeln, Orr, Barbour, Somers.

Hollywood	010	000	000	1	–	4	– 1
San Diego	030	010	20x	6	–	11	– 1

Game Two.

On Wednesday, October 5, a crowd of 6,731 saw the Padres take a 2–0 lead in the series with an 8–5 win. This was the day the World Series started so attention was diverted from the playoffs. Jesse Flores, with relief help from Bob Savage, beat Pinky Woods, who was chased in the five-run fifth inning.

Opposite page: Irv Noren (left), the PCL's 1949 Most Valuable Player, and Frank Kelleher give manager Fred Haney a victory ride after winning the Stars' first pennant since the team moved south from San Francisco after the 1937 season.

Buster Adams hit three solo homers for the Padres but the crucial blow was Minoso's three-run homer in the fifth that put San Diego up 7–1. Jim Baxes hit a two-run homer off Bob Savage in the eighth in a losing cause.

Hollywood	AB	H	RBI	O	A	E
Genovese SS	5	0	0	2	5	0
Handley 2B	5	3	0	3	1	0
Noren CF	4	2	0	7	0	0
Gorman RF	5	1	1	2	0	0
Stevens 1B	4	1	0	5	0	0
Kelleher LF	3	1	1	1	0	0
Baxes 3B	4	3	2	2	1	0
Sandlock C	3	0	0	2	0	0
Woods P	2	1	0	0	0	0
Shallock P	1	0	0	0	0	0
White ᵃ	1	0	0	0	0	0
Olsen P	0	0	0	0	0	0
	37	12	4	24	7	0

(a) *Batted for Shallock in the eighth.*

San Diego	AB	H	RBI	O	A	E
Wilson 2B	4	2	0	3	6	0
Minoso CF	3	1	3	4	0	0
B. Adams RF	3	3	3	2	1	0
West 1B	4	1	0	8	0	0
Storey 3B	4	2	0	0	0	0
Clay LF	4	1	1	3	0	0
Moore C	4	1	0	6	0	0
Wietelmann SS	4	1	0	1	3	0
Flores P	3	0	0	0	0	0
Savage P	1	0	0	0	0	0
	34	12	7	27	10	0

Pitching Records	IP	H	R	ER	SO	BB
Woods (L)	4.1	9	6	7	2	0
Shallock	2.2	3	2	1	0	0
Olsen	1	0	0	0	0	0
Flores (W)	7	10	2	2	4	2
Savage	2	2	3	3	1	1

Hit by Pitcher: Minoso by Woods. Left on Base: Hollywood 2, San Diego 4. Two Base Hits: Gorman, Wilson. Home Runs: B. Adams 3, Minoso, Baxes.

Sacrifice: B. Adams. Stolen Base: Handley. Double Plays: Genovese to Handley to Stevens 2; Wilson to Wietelmann to West. Time of Game: 1 hr. 58 min. Umpires: Orr, Barbour, Somers, Engeln.

Hollywood	001	000	130	5 – 12 – 0
San Diego	100	150	10x	8 – 12 – 0

Game Three.

A crowd of 8,783, the largest to see any 1949 playoff game, saw the last game of the year at Lane Field as the Stars, behind Willie "The Knuck" Ramsdell, beat Al Jurisich 6–4. Ramsdell's poor control of the knuckleball cost him a run in the fourth when he walked West, who stole second on a knuckler, and came around to score on two wild pitches. But the Stars went ahead to stay in the fifth when Irv Noren doubled in Ramsdell and Handley. Hollywood put it out of reach with three seventh inning runs on a double, two walks and two singles. Minoso's two-run homer in the eighth brought the Padres to within two runs.

Hollywood	AB	H	RBI	O	A	E
Genovese SS	4	1	0	1	4	0
Handley 2B	4	2	1	3	6	0
Noren CF	4	2	3	3	0	0
Gorman RF	4	2	1	0	0	0
Stevens 1B	4	1	1	11	0	1
Kelleher LF	4	1	0	0	0	0
Baxes 3B	4	0	0	0	0	0
Sandlock C	3	2	0	9	1	0
Ramsdell P	4	0	0	0	3	0
	35	11	6	27	14	1

San Diego	AB	H	RBI	O	A	E
Wilson 2B	3	0	0	3	3	0
Minoso CF	4	1	2	3	1	0
B. Adams RF	4	1	0	1	0	0
West 1B	2	0	0	8	5	0
Storey 3B	4	1	0	2	3	0
Clay LF	4	2	0	4	0	0
Moore C	4	2	0	2	1	0
Wietelmann SS	4	1	0	3	2	1
Jurisich P	2	0	0	1	0	0
Mesner[a]	1	1	0	0	0	0

San Diego	AB	H	RBI	O	A	E
Thompson P	0	0	0	0	1	0
C. Adams[b]	0	0	0	0	0	0
Rosen[c]	1	0	0	0	0	0
	33	9	2	27	16	1

(a) Batted for Jurisich in the eighth.
(b) Ran for Moore in the ninth.
(c) Batted for Thompson in the ninth.

Pitching Records	IP	H	R	ER	SO	BB
Ramsdell	9	9	4	3	7	3
Jurisich (L)	8	9	5	5	2	5
Thompson	1	2	1	1	1	2

Left on Base: Hollywood 8, San Diego 5. Two Base Hits: Handley 2, Noren, B. Adams, Genovese. Home Run: Minoso. Double Plays: Genovese to Handley to Stevens 3; Storey to Wilson to West to Wietelmann. Time of Game: 2 hr. 22 min. Umpires: Somers, Barbour, Engeln, Orr.

Hollywood	000	020	301	6 – 11 – 1
San Diego	000	100	021	4 – 9 – 1

Game Four.

The series moved to Gilmore Field on Friday night, October 7, but only 3,461 shivering fans were there on a brisk windy night to see the Stars tie the series with a 7–4 win. A few yards away, 4,000 equally cold fans saw Loyola beat Fresno State 52–13 at Gilmore Stadium with the wind kicking up dust storms. This wind made fly balls hard to catch and some fell for extra-base hits. Glenn Moulder started against Red Adams but neither lasted very long. The Padres jumped ahead with three runs in the first with Dain Clay's single driving in two of those runs. But the Stars blasted Red Adams for four runs in their half of the first with triples by Genovese and Gorman and doubles by Handley and Stevens. Both starters were lifted for pinch hitters in the second with Jack Salveson coming on and getting the win for Hollywood, before being relieved by Jean Pierre Roy. Bob Savage and Tom Kipp finished up for the Padres, with Savage yielding three runs over six innings.

San Diego	AB	R	H	RBI	O	A	E
Wilson 2B	5	1	2	0	2	2	0
Minoso CF	5	1	0	0	4	0	0
B. Adams RF	4	0	1	0	1	0	0

This team picture of the 1949 champion Hollywood Stars was taken in their visiting uniforms at Wrigley Field, Los Angeles, perhaps to "rub it in" on the last place Angels.

San Diego	AB	R	H	RBI	O	A	E
West 1B	2	1	1	0	10	1	0
Storey 3B	5	1	2	1	1	2	0
Clay LF	4	0	1	2	1	0	0
Moore C	4	0	1	0	3	2	0
Wietelmann SS	3	0	2	1	2	2	1
C. Adams P	0	0	0	0	0	0	0
Mesner[a]	1	0	0	0	0	0	0
Savage P	1	0	0	0	0	2	0
Rosen[b]	1	0	0	0	0	0	0
Kipp P	0	0	0	0	0	1	0
	35	4	10	4	24	12	1

(a) Batted for C. Adams in the second.
(b) Batted for Savage in the eighth.

Hollywood	AB	R	H	RBI	O	A	E
Genovese SS	4	1	3	1	3	1	0
Handley 2B	5	1	2	2	3	1	2
Noren CF	3	1	0	0	2	0	0
Gorman RF	5	1	2	2	5	0	0

Hollywood	AB	R	H	RBI	O	A	E
Stevens 1B	4	1	2	1	5	0	0
Kelleher LF	4	0	1	0	1	0	0
Baxes 3B	4	1	3	1	1	4	1
Unser C	3	1	1	0	7	2	0
Moulder P	0	0	0	0	0	0	0
Fallon[a]	1	0	0	0	0	0	0
Salveson P	2	0	1	0	0	0	0
Roy P	0	0	0	0	0	1	0
White RF	0	0	0	0	0	0	0
	35	7	15	7	27	9	3

(a) *Batted for Moulder in the second.*

Pitching Records	IP	H	R	ER	SO	BB
C. Adams (L)	1	4	4	4	0	1
Savage	6	10	3	2	1	0
Kipp	1	1	0	0	2	1
Moulder	2	3	3	0	1	1
Salveson (W)	5.1	6	0	1	4	1
Roy	1.2	1	1	0	2	1

Hit by Pitcher: Noren by Kipp. Left on Base: San Diego 10, Hollywood 9. Two Base Hits: Handley, Stevens, Moore. Three Base Hits: Genovese, Gorman, B. Adams. Sacrifices: B. Adams, Savage, Unser, Genovese. Double Plays: Unser to Genovese; Baxes to Stevens; Genovese to Handley to Stevens; Moore to Storey; West to Weitelmann; Moore to West. Time of Game: 2 hr. 24 min. Umpires: Barbour, Engeln, Orr, Somers.

San Diego	300	000	010	4 – 10 – 1
Hollywood	400	101	10x	7 – 15 – 3

Game Five.

A very small crowd of 1,951 went to Gilmore Field on Saturday night, October 8, to see the Stars win their third straight game, 7–0, as Gordon Maltzberger beat Dick Barrett, who was rapped for five runs in the first inning. Earlier that afternoon at the Coliseum, 62,877 saw USC tie Ohio State, 13–13. Ohio State won the Rose Bowl that season. Gorman, Baxes and Sandlock each drove in two runs.

San Diego	AB	R	H	RBI	O	A
Wilson 2B	4	0	0	0	0	3
Minoso CF	4	0	0	0	3	0

San Diego	AB	R	H	RBI	O	A
B. Adams CF	3	0	3	0	1	0
West 1B	4	0	1	0	8	1
Storey 3B	4	0	1	0	2	1
Clay LF	4	0	1	0	2	0
Moore C	0	0	0	0	0	0
Wietelmann SS	4	0	0	0	0	1
Barrett P	1	0	0	0	0	1
Ritchey C	4	0	2	0	8	0
Mesner [a]	0	0	0	0	0	0
Mooty P	0	0	0	0	0	0
Rosen [b]	1	0	0	0	0	0
Kipp P	0	0	0	0	0	1
	33	0	8	0	24	8

(a) *Batted for Barrett in the sixth.*
(b) *Batted for Mooty in the eighth.*

Hollywood	AB	R	H	RBI	O	A
Genovese SS	5	1	1	0	2	5
Handley 2B	5	1	2	0	5	5
Noren CF	5	0	0	0	6	0
Gorman RF	4	1	1	2	1	0
Stevens 1B	3	2	2	0	6	1
Kelleher LF	2	2	2	1	0	0
Baxes 3B	4	0	2	2	0	2
Sandlock C	3	0	1	2	6	0
Maltzberger P	3	0	0	0	1	0
Oliver P	1	0	0	0	0	0
	35	7	11	7	27	13

Pitching Records	IP	H	R	ER	SO	BB
Barrett (L)	5	8	7	6	3	3
Mooty	1	1	0	0	1	0
Kipp	2	2	0	0	3	1
Maltzberger (W)	7	5	0	0	5	2
Oliver	2	3	0	0	1	0

Left on Base: San Diego 8, Hollywood 8. Two Base Hits: B. Adams, Gorman, Kelleher. Double Plays: Wietelmann to West to Storey; Handley to Genovese to Stevens; Genovese to Handley to Stevens; Baxes to Handley to Stevens. Time of Game: 2hr. 5 min. Umpires: Engeln, Orr, Somers, Barbour.

San Diego	000	000	000	0 – 8 – 2
Hollywood	500	020	00x	7 – 7 – 2

Game Six.

On Sunday, October 9, the Pacific Coast League season came to an end the same day the World Series was over. A crowd of 2,730 saw Hollywood win the only game needed to win the series, four games to two, with an 8–4 win. A doubleheader would have been played if San Diego had won this game. Two other local sporting events outdrew this game. There were 3,100 at Wrigley Field to see a team of Negro League all stars play a team from the Mexican League, and there were 16,757 at the Coliseum to see the Los Angeles Dons beat the Buffalo Bills, 42–28.

Willie Ramsdell faced Lyman Linde, and a 1–1 tie was broken when Hollywood broke through with four runs in the fourth. Three singles loaded the bases before Linde lost it, and walked in two runs, and then gave up a two-run single to Sandlock. Frank Kelleher's homer in the fifth helped increase the lead to 8–1, allowing Ramsdell to coast.

San Diego	AB	R	H	RBI	O	A	E
Wilson 2B	5	0	3	0	2	1	2
Minoso CF	5	1	2	1	3	0	0
B. Adams RF	4	1	2	1	3	0	0
West 1B	1	1	0	0	5	2	0
Storey 3B	4	1	1	0	2	3	0
Clay LF	4	0	0	0	4	1	0
Ritchey C	2	0	0	0	4	0	0
Wietelmann SS	4	0	0	0	1	1	1
Linde P	2	0	0	0	0	0	0
Jurisich P	0	0	0	0	0	0	0
Mesner [a]	1	0	0	0	0	0	0
Thompson P	0	0	0	0	0	0	0
Rosen [b]	1	0	1	2	0	0	0
C. Adams [c]	0	0	0	0	0	0	0
	33	4	9	4	24	8	3

(a) Batted for Jurisich in the eighth.
(b) Batted for Thompson in the ninth.
(c) Ran for Rosen in the ninth.

Hollywood	AB	R	H	RBI	O	A	R
Genovese SS	4	0	0	0	0	6	0
Handley 2B	5	1	1	1	4	4	0

Hollywood	AB	R	H	RBI	O	A	R
Noren CF	4	2	1	0	3	0	0
Gorman RF	4	2	2	0	0	0	0
Stevens 1B	3	1	1	1	11	0	0
Kelleher LF	2	2	1	3	2	0	0
Baxes 3B	2	0	0	1	2	2	0
Sandlock C	4	0	1	2	5	0	0
Ramsdell P	2	0	0	0	0	0	0
	30	8	7	8	27	12	0

Pitching Records	IP	H	R	ER	SO	BB
Linde (L)	4.1	7	8	7	2	3
Jurisich	2.2	0	0	0	1	1
Thompson	1	0	0	0	1	0
Ramsdell	9	9	4	4	3	5

Left on Base: San Diego 7, Hollywood 6. Two Base Hit: Gorman. Home Runs: Handley, Minoso, Kelleher, B. Adams. Sacrifices: Kelleher, Ramsdell 2. Double Plays: Genovese to Handley to Stevens 3. Time of Game: 2 hr. Umpires: Orr, Somers, Barbour, Engeln.

San Diego	001	001	002	4 – 9 – 3
Hollywood	100	430	00x	8 – 7 – 0

For the fourth year in a row the pennant winner won the playoffs, and it was the third year in a row that the fourth place team was runner-up. Hollywood split its $30,000 into 30 shares, so each man's $1,000 would be worth about $4,200 today. San Diego's $10,000 was divided into 28 shares of $356, which equates to about $1,495 now. Oakland and Sacramento each shared $5,000, which would be about $178 each, or $748 in current funds.

The owners voted at the winter meetings to drop the playoffs after 14 seasons and to reward the top four clubs with prize money according to how they finished. But the 1950 schedule of 200 games lasting until October 8, was a big mistake because attendance dropped off in September. The schedule was shortened in 1951 and the playoffs were revived, but not on a best of seven basis.

While the total attendance of the 1949 playoffs was 69,641, an increase of 19 percent over the 58,450 that saw the 1948 postseason games, the average daily crowd was the lowest of the four postwar years. Because of more doubleheaders in earlier years, there were fewer times tickets were taken than in 1949, which had only one doubleheader. The average crowd was 6,450 in 1946 and fell each postseason, reaching 4,108 in 1949. This low figure was caused by the poor turnouts in Oakland and Hollywood, the two large population centers that had more competition from football than in Sacramento or San Diego.

Key Players on the 1949 Playoff Teams

Hollywood. *Pitchers:* Willard Ramsdell, Pinky Woods, Gordon Maltzberger, Art Shallock, Jack Salveson, and Glenn Moulder.
Position Players: Irv Noren (league's MVP), Herb Gorman, Frank Kelleher, Chuck Stevens, Gene Handley, and Jim Baxes.

Oakland. *Pitchers:* Al Gettel, Lou Tost, Milo Candini, Charlie Gassaway, and Earl Harrist.
Position Players: Artie Wilson (league's batting champion), Earl Rapp, Lloyd Christopher, Dick Kryhowski, Mel Duezabou, and Maurice Van Robays.

Sacramento. *Pitchers:* Ken Holcombe, Frank Dasso, Mal Mallette, and Bob Gillespie.
Position Players: Joe Marty, Ralph Hodgin, Al White, Joe Grace, Jim Tabor, and Walt Dropo (out with broken leg).

San Diego. *Pitchers:* Jesse Flores, Dick Barrett, Tom Kipp, Lyman Linde and Red Adams.
Position Players: Al Rosen, Dee Moore, Harvey Storey, Dain Clay, Allie Clark, Max West, and Luke Easter (recalled by Cleveland).

1951

By 1951, the golden age of Pacific Coast League baseball had passed. Attendance had dropped to less than 2.3 million, which was only 56 percent of the peak year of 1947. After the bad experience of the 200 game schedule in 1950, owners cut the season to 168 games, ending on September 9, and followed it with a shorter version of the playoffs. The first round was best of three, and the final, the best of five games.

Several owners lost money in 1950 but the players were happy with the longer season, getting over six months' pay. In addition, $80,000 prize money was set aside for the first division finishers, with the champion Oaks getting half that sum without playing any postseason games. But in 1951, players were paid for a shorter season and no set amount was promised for the playoffs. Instead, the league set aside 1 cent from each admission to be divided ⅓ to the pennant winner, ⅓ to the playoff winner, ⅙ to the final round loser and 1/12 to each first round loser. This final sum of $22,820 was slightly over a fourth of the 1950 reward money.

The drop in attendance was especially discouraging because the 1951 race was tight, with only five games separating the first six clubs in mid–June. For the first time since 1935, an all split season format was tried, rather than the week-long series that the league was noted for. Owners hoped that a balanced schedule would make the league seem more like the majors and that bringing a new team to town twice a week, instead of once, would increase fan interest. Instead, it just increased airline travel costs.

The Seattle Rainiers, managed by the famous Rogers Hornsby, won their first pennant in ten years, and also won the playoffs for the fourth time. After struggling in April and May, the Rainiers got hot in June and took the lead for good by the end of that month. They played at a torrid .774 pace from June 22 to July 22, and took four out of five games in a series with Hollywood, their closest pursuer. Center fielder Jim Rivera had a sensational year for Seattle, winning the batting title and was voted the league's MVP.

The second place Hollywood Stars were still managed by Fred Haney, but now had a working agreement with the Pittsburgh Pirates instead of the Brooklyn Dodgers, because Branch Rickey, who was a close friend of Haney, moved to the Pittsburgh front office. The Stars floundered until mid–June and then straightened themselves out, and played good ball but could not get closer than three games to the front-running Rainiers.

The Los Angeles Angels, under their new manager Stan Hack, finished third after two dismal seasons of finishing eighth and seventh, respectively. The Angels' parent, the Chicago Cubs, acquired another AAA farm team, Springfield, Massachusetts, of the International League, but this diluted the limited talent the Cubs had to send to L.A. The Angels lacked good pitching but had a lot of home run power, which was ideally suited for Wrigley Field. Max West hit 35 homers for the Angels while Chuck Connors, later of movie and TV fame, hit 22 in half a season, before the Cubs recalled him, and sent Dee Fondy, who had a fine half-season, hitting 11 homers. Despite finishing eight games behind Hollywood, the Angels outdrew their local rivals because fans enjoyed the home run power.

The surprise team of 1951 was Portland, which was predicted to finish near the bottom but ended up fourth. The Beavers were managed by Bill Sweeney, who resigned after the season. Portland was in first place in mid–May but fell back in June, and later had to struggle to stay ahead of Oakland for the first division. They clinched fourth place on the next-to-last day of the season, which brought them to the .500 mark, but then they lost the September 9, doubleheader to Oakland, to finish at 83-85. Thus, they were the third and last team to make the playoffs with a losing record, which did not set well with L.H. Gregory of *The Portland Oregonian*. Gregory argued that Sweeney should have used his ace, Marino Pieretti, on the last day of the season to avoid a losing record, rather than save him for the playoffs, which Gregory felt were of less importance. The writer pointed out that Sweeney managed Hollywood in 1941, a team that also finished fourth with a losing record.

Seattle owner Emil Sick felt that the money in the playoff pool was insufficient to reward his fine team so he generously announced a "team appreciation night" on Thursday, September 6, the day after the Rainiers clinched the pennant. All the gate receipts would be given to the Seattle players as a token of appreciation for the city's first pennant in a decade. A crowd of 10,063 turned out, and $7,066 was turned over to the players.

The Seattle–Los Angeles Series

This was the third time that the Angels finished the regular season in Seattle and opened the playoffs there, the others being 1939 and 1943. All games were scheduled for Seattle because the first round was only two out of three.

The Rainiers were playing at a .600 pace until the last week of the season, when they lost three of four to the Angels, finishing at .598. Warren Hacker of the Angels pitched a no-hitter for one of these three wins. But over the whole season, Seattle had won the season series from each of its opponents, beating L.A. 15 times and losing 8.

Game One.

The series opened Tuesday night, September 11, before 3,583 fans which included league president Clarence "Pants" Rowland, who was on hand to present Jim Rivera the Charles Graham Award as the league's MVP and batting champion. Hector "Skinny" Brown pitched a four-hit shutout, winning over Bill Moisan. Brown also drove in four runs with a double and a triple. His triple with the bases loaded in the fourth drove in three runs and broke a scoreless tie, and his double in the eighth put some frosting on the cake. Gordon Goldsberry went 4-for-5 and drove in a run. The honored Jim Rivera went 1-for-5, a run scoring triple in the eighth.

Los Angeles	AB	R	H	RBI	O	A	E
Baker SS	4	0	0	0	1	0	0
Hollis 2B	4	0	1	0	3	2	0
Fondy 1B	4	0	0	0	6	0	0
West RF	3	0	1	0	2	1	0
Layton LF	3	0	0	0	4	0	0
T. Davis 3B	3	0	1	0	2	2	0
Peden C	3	0	0	0	5	0	1
Talbot CF	3	0	1	0	1	0	0
Moisan P	2	0	0	0	0	2	0
Baczewski P	1	0	0	0	0	2	0
	30	0	4	0	24	9	1

Seattle	AB	R	H	RBI	O	A	E
Albright SS	5	0	1	0	0	5	0
Goldsberry 1B	5	1	4	1	13	0	0
Rivera CF	5	0	1	1	4	0	0
Judnich LF	5	1	2	0	2	0	0
Lyons RF	3	1	2	1	3	0	0
Erautt C	3	0	0	0	3	0	0
Krsnich 3B	3	2	2	0	1	2	0
Hamner 2B	3	1	1	0	1	2	0
Brown P	3	1	2	4	0	4	0
	35	7	15	7	27	13	0

Pitching Records	IP	H	R	ER	SO	BB
Moisan (L)	5	8	4	4	2	2
Baczewski	3	7	3	3	2	0
Brown	9	4	0	0	3	0

Left on Base: Los Angeles 3, Seattle 9. Two Base Hits: Lyons, Brown. Three Base Hits: Brown, Rivera. Sacrifices: Erautt, Brown, Hamner. Stolen Base: Talbot. Double Play: Krsnich to Hamner to Goldsberry. Time of Game: 1 hr. 47 min. Umpires: Somers, Runge, Carlucci.

Los Angeles	000	000	000	0 –	4 –	1
Seattle	000	310	03x	7 –	15 –	0

Game Two.

On Wednesday night, September 12, another small crowd of 3,368 saw Warren Hacker beat 20-game winner Marvin Grissom, 5–2, to even the series. The Angels scored a run without a hit in the first and the game remained hitless until the fifth. In the top half, Bobby Dant and Bobby Talbot singled, Hacker sacrificed, and Gene Baker got a two-out double to score them both. In the last half, Walter Judnich got an infield single, which was Seattle's first hit off Hacker in 13 innings. Judnich scored on Joe Erautt's double. L.A. increased the lead to 5–1 in the ninth, one of the runs coming in on Hacker's double. Judnich homered for Seattle's second run in the last half.

Los Angeles	AB	H	RBI	O	A	E
Baker SS	5	1	2	2	2	0
Hollis 2B	3	0	0	3	3	0
Fondy 1B	4	0	0	8	0	0
West RF	4	0	0	1	0	0
Layton LF	4	1	0	2	0	0
T. Davis 3B	4	0	0	1	1	0
Dant C	4	2	0	7	0	0
Talbot CF	4	2	0	3	0	0
Hacker P	3	1	1	0	3	0
	35	7	3	27	9	0

Seattle	AB	H	RBI	O	A	E
Albright SS	3	0	0	1	1	1
Goldsberry 1B	4	1	0	10	0	0
Rivera CF	4	0	0	3	2	0
Judnich LF	4	3	1	2	0	0

Seattle	AB	H	RBI	O	A	E
Lyons RF	4	0	0	1	0	0
Erautt C	3	2	1	3	0	0
Krsnich 3B-SS	3	0	0	3	3	0
Hamner 2B	3	0	0	4	6	0
Grissom P	1	0	0	0	0	0
Montalvo[a]	1	0	0	0	0	0
Clavert P	0	0	0	0	1	0
Christie[b]	1	0	0	0	0	0
J. Davis P	0	0	0	0	0	0
Vico 3B[c]	1	0	0	0	0	0
	32	6	2	27	13	1

(a) *Batted for Grissom in the sixth.*
(b) *Batted for Calvert in the eighth.*
(c) *Batted for Albright in the eighth.*

Pitching Records	IP	H	R	ER	SO	BB
Hacker	9	6	2	2	7	0
Grissom (L)	6	4	3	2	2	1
Calvert	2	2	0	0	1	0
J. Davis	1	1	2	0	0	0

Hit by Pitcher: Hollis by Grissom. Left on Base: Los Angeles 6, Seattle 3. Two Base Hits: Baker, Erautt, Hacker. Home Run: Judnich. Double Plays: Rivera to Albright to Hamner to Goldsberry; Baker to Hollis to Fondy. Time of Game: 1 hr. 51 min. Umpires: Runge, Carlucci, Somers.

Los Angeles	100	020	002	5 – 7 – 0
Seattle	000	010	001	2 – 6 – 1

Game Three.

On Thursday night, September 13, a very small crowd of 2,928 saw the Rainiers eliminate the Angels with a 3–1 win. Doyle Lade started against Charley Schanz but neither got the decision. The Angels committed five errors and threw two wild pitches. It was scoreless until the last of the sixth when Judnich reached base on an error, went to third on Al Lyons' single, and scored on Lade's wild pitch. But L.A. tied it in the seventh when Les Layton doubled and scored on pinch hitter Les Peden's single. Hector Brown, with only one day's rest, relieved at that point and slammed the door on the Angels. In the last of the seventh, Jackie Albright tripled off loser Bob Spicer and scored on Goldsberry's fly ball. Judnich later doubled and scored on Lyons' single for an insurance run. This was the Angels' last playoff appearance.

Los Angeles	AB	R	H	RBI	O	A	E
Baker SS	3	0	1	0	3	4	1
Hollis 2B	4	0	1	0	1	2	1
Fondy 1B	1	0	0	0	2	0	0
West RF-1B	4	0	0	0	4	3	1
Layton LF	4	1	1	0	0	1	0
T. Davis 3B	3	0	1	0	2	2	1
Dant C	2	0	0	0	5	1	1
Talbot CF	2	0	0	0	1	0	0
Lade P	2	0	0	0	2	0	0
Neill RF	3	0	1	0	1	0	0
Spicer P	1	0	0	0	1	1	0
Peden C[a]	2	0	1	1	2	0	0
	31	1	6	1	24	14	5

(a) Batted for Dant in the seventh.

Seattle	AB	R	H	RBI	O	A	E
Albright SS	5	1	1	0	2	0	0
Goldsberry 1B	3	0	0	1	5	0	0
Rivera CF	3	0	0	0	4	1	0
Judnich LF	4	2	2	0	3	0	0
Lyons RF	3	0	2	1	2	0	0
Erautt C	3	0	0	0	7	0	0
Krsnich 3B	3	0	1	0	2	5	0
Hamner 2B	4	0	2	0	2	1	0
Schanz P	3	0	0	0	0	1	0
Brown P	1	0	0	0	0	0	0
	32	3	8	2	27	8	0

Pitching Records	IP	H	R	ER	SO	BB
Lade	5.2	3	1	0	2	4
Spicer (L)	2.1	5	2	2	2	0
Schanz	6.1	6	1	1	4	3
Brown (L)	2.2	0	0	0	1	0

Wild Pitches: Lade 2. Passed Ball: Dant. Hit by Pitcher: Rivera by Lade. Left on Base: Los Angeles 6, Seattle 10. Two Base Hits: Hamner, Hollis, Layton, Judnich. Three Base Hit: Albright. Stolen Base: Hamner. Double Play: Krsnich to Hamner to Goldsberry. Time of Game: 1 hr. 59 min. Umpires: Carlucci, Somers, Runge.

Los Angeles	000	000	100	1 – 6 – 5
Seattle	000	001	20x	3 – 8 – 0

The Hollywood-Portland Series

The Beavers flew to Los Angeles on Monday to start the playoffs on Tuesday night, September 11, at Gilmore Field. During the regular season, Hollywood beat Portland 16 times and lost only 8 to them.

Game One.

A small crowd of 1,858 fans turned out but they weren't kept long. It took just an hour and 38 minutes for Ben Wade to stop Portland on five hits, as Hollywood won 6–2. Marino Pieretti, who was saved for this occasion, was jolted for four runs in the first on singles by Chuck Stevens, George Schmees and Dino Restelli and then a big homer by Frank Kelleher. This lead went to 6–0 in the fifth on an error which was followed by doubles by Stevens and Schmees. Portland's two runs in the seventh were anticlimatic.

Portland	AB	R	H	RBI	O	A	E
White RF	4	0	0	0	1	0	0
Basinski 2B	4	1	2	0	3	6	0
Thomas 3B	3	1	0	0	0	3	1
Brovia LF	4	0	1	0	1	0	0
Holder CF	3	0	0	1	3	0	0
Austin SS	3	0	1	1	2	3	0
Rossi C	3	0	0	0	4	0	0
LaFata 1B	3	0	1	0	10	1	0
Pieretti P	1	0	0	0	0	0	0
Ward P	0	0	0	0	0	0	0
Gladstone[a]	1	0	0	0	0	0	0
Creel P	0	0	0	0	0	0	0
Barr[b]	1	0	0	0	0	0	0
Drilling P	0	0	0	0	0	0	0
	30	2	5	2	24	13	1

(a) Batted for Ward in the sixth.
(b) Batted for Creel in the eighth.

Hollywood	AB	R	H	RBI	O	A	E
Handley 2B	0	0	0	0	0	0	0
Stringer 3B-2B	3	0	0	0	2	2	0
Stevens 1B	4	2	3	1	8	0	0
Schmees RF	3	1	2	1	0	0	0

Hollywood	AB	R	H	RBI	O	A	E
Restelli CF	4	1	1	1	5	0	0
Kelleher LF	4	1	1	3	3	0	0
Sandlock C	4	0	0	0	5	0	0
O'Neil SS	2	0	0	0	2	2	0
Wade P	3	0	0	0	0	3	0
Conaster RF[a]	1	0	1	0	2	0	0
Franklin 3B[b]	2	1	0	0	0	3	0
	30	6	8	6	27	10	0

(a) Ran for Schmees in the fifth.
(b) Ran for Handley in the second.

Pitching Records	IP	H	R	ER	SO	BB
Pieretti (L)	4.1	7	6	5	3	2
Ward	0.2	0	0	0	0	0
Creel	2	0	0	0	0	0
Drilling	1	1	0	0	0	0
Wade	9	5	2	2	5	1

Hit by Pitcher: Handley by Pieretti. Left on Base: Portland 2, Hollywood 4. Two Base Hits: Stevens, Schmees, Basinski. Home Run: Kelleher. Sacrifice: Stevens. Stolen Base: Restelli. Double Plays: Basinski to LaFata to Austin; Thomas to Basinski to LaFata; Franklin to Stringer to Thomas; Stringer to O'Neil to Stevens. Time of Game: 1 hr. 35 min. Umpires: Doran, Mutart, Bentz.

Portland	000	000	200	2 – 5 – 1
Hollywood	400	020	00x	6 – 8 – 0

Game Two.

An even smaller crowd of 1,599 came to Gilmore Field on Wednesday night, September 12, to see the Stars eliminate the Beavers with a 7–4 win. Pinky Woods started against Red Adams but Gordon Maltzberger got the win and Portland's third pitcher, Larry Ward, who followed Lyman Linde to the mound, took the loss. Hollywood went up 3–0 in the third when Lou Stringer and Murray Franklin both homered, Chuck Stevens was hit by a pitch, and came around to score on Schmees' double. But this lead vanished in the fourth when the Beavers struck for four runs. Woods walked four men, forcing in a run, and then gave up a pinch single to Eddie Bahr, which tied the game. Maltzberger was greeted by Don White's single which put Portland up 4–3, but that was all the scoring for the Oregonians. Kelleher homered in the fourth to tie it, and Schmees homered in the fifth to put Hollywood up for good in the fifth. The Stars got insurance runs in the sixth and seventh, making it easier for Maltzberger. This was the last playoff series Hollywood won and the last playoff appearance for Portland.

Portland	AB	R	H	RBI	O	A	E
White RF	5	0	1	1	3	0	0
Basinski 2B	5	0	0	0	5	1	0
Brovia LF	3	0	2	0	2	0	0
Thomas 3B	2	1	0	0	2	2	0
Holder CF	3	1	1	0	3	0	0
Austin SS	4	1	0	0	3	1	0
Rossi C	4	1	1	1	2	0	0
LaFata 1B	3	0	0	0	4	1	0
Adams P	1	0	0	0	0	1	0
Linde P	0	0	0	0	0	0	0
Barr[a]	1	0	1	2	0	0	0
Ward P	1	0	0	0	0	1	0
Brockman[b]	1	0	0	0	0	0	0
	33	4	6	4	24	7	0

(a) Batted for Linde in the fourth.
(b) Batted for Ward in the ninth.

Hollywood	AB	R	H	RBI	0	A	E
Stringer 2B	4	1	2	2	1	2	0
Franklin 3B	4	1	1	1	1	4	0
Stevens 1B	3	2	1	0	12	1	0
Schmees RF	3	1	2	2	2	0	0
Restelli CF	3	0	0	0	1	0	0
Kelleher LF	4	1	1	2	2	0	0
Sandlock C	3	0	0	0	4	0	0
O'Neil SS	3	1	1	0	3	3	0
Woods P	1	0	0	0	0	1	0
Maltzberger P	1	0	0	0	1	0	0
	29	7	8	7	· 27	11	0

Pitching Records	AB	R	H	ER	SO	BB
Adams	2.2	3	3	3	0	1
Linde	0.1	0	0	0	0	0
Ward (L)	5	5	4	4	2	4

Pitching Records	AB	R	H	ER	SO	BB
Woods	3.2	2	3	4	0	5
Maltzberger (W)	5.1	4	1	0	4	0

Hit by Pitcher: Stevens by Adams. Wild Pitch: Adams. Left on Base: Portland 7, Hollywood 7. Two Base Hits: Schmees, Brovia. Home Runs: Stringer, Franklin, Kelleher, Schmees. Sacrifices: Franklin, Maltzberger. Time of Game: 1 hr. 53 min. Umpires: Mutart, Bentz, Mora.

Portland	000	400	000	4 – 6 – 0		
Hollywood	003	111	10x	7 – 8 – 0		

The Stars had to wait at home until Friday morning to see if they were going to play Seattle or the Angels. An Angel-Hollywood final series probably would have drawn large crowds, because even with league attendance down, these two rivals brought the fans out. The Stars were the only team in the league the Angels did not meet in the playoffs.

The Final Series: Seattle vs. Hollywood

This series called for the first two games to be in Seattle, Saturday night and Sunday afternoon, September 15 and 16, and then the rest to be played at Gilmore Field beginning Monday night, with no off day for travel, because the clubs now used air travel. The college football season had not started yet so the Rainiers were not competing with the Huskies, but Seattle fans were already mourning the loss of Washington's star quarterback, Don Heinrich, who was lost for the season.

Game One.

Ben Wade, who beat Portland in the opening round, was overmatched this time by Seattle's Bob Hall, who pitched a four-hit shutout. A Saturday night crowd of 9,189, which was the largest of the 1951 playoffs, saw Walter Judnich break the scoreless tie in the fourth with a home run. Later in the same inning, singles by Joe Erautt, Rocky Krsnich, and Wes Hamner plated the second run. Seattle got its third run in the fifth when Jim Rivera doubled and scored on Al Lyons' single.

Hollywood	AB	R	H	RBI	O	A	E
Stringer 2B	4	0	0	0	2	2	0
Franklin 3B	3	0	0	0	2	0	0

Hollywood	AB	R	H	RBI	O	A	E
Stevens 1B	4	0	2	0	4	0	0
Schmees RF	4	0	0	0	3	0	0
Restelli CF	4	0	0	0	1	0	0
Kelleher LF	3	0	0	0	4	0	0
Sandlock C	3	0	1	0	5	3	0
O'Neil SS	3	0	0	0	3	3	0
Wade P	2	0	1	0	0	1	0
Lindell[a]	1	0	0	0	0	0	0
Landeck P	0	0	0	0	0	0	0
	31	0	4	0	24	7	0

(a) Batted for Wade in the eighth.

Seattle	AB	R	H	RBI	O	A	E
Albright SS	4	0	0	0	2	0	0
Goldsberry 1B	4	0	0	0	3	0	0
Rivera CF	3	1	1	0	5	0	0
Judnich LF	2	1	1	1	4	0	0
Lyons RF	4	0	1	1	2	0	0
Erautt C	4	1	2	0	7	0	0
Krsnich 3B	3	0	1	0	2	3	0
Hamner 2B	3	0	2	1	2	1	0
Hall P	3	0	0	0	0	0	0
	30	3	8	3	27	4	0

Pitching Records	IP	H	R	ER	SO	BB
Wade (L)	7	8	3	3	4	3
Landeck	1	0	0	0	1	0
Hall	9	4	0	0	6	1

Left on Base: Hollywood 5, Seattle 6. Two Base Hits: Stevens 2, Rivera. Three Base Hit: Sandlock. Home Run: Judnich. Double Play: Stringer to O'Neil. Time of Game: 1 hr. 50 min. Umpires: Somers, Runge, Carlucci.

Hollywood	000	000	000	0 – 4 – 0
Seattle	000	210	00x	3 – 8 – 0

Game Two.

The Sunday afternoon crowd of 6,411 saw the last game the champion Rainiers played at Sick's Stadium in 1951, but went home disappointed as

Hollywood squared the series at a game apiece. Johnny Lindell, former Yankee World Series star, pitched a seven-hitter beating Marv Grissom, who was having trouble in the playoffs. The Stars scored their first run in the third when Chuck Stevens singled in Lou Stringer. They increased their lead to 3–0 in the fifth when Stringer homered and Schmees later singled in Murray Franklin. Hollywood's last run came in the seventh when Kelleher doubled in Dino Restelli. Lindell, who was voted the Stars' most valuable and popular player, lost his shutout in the ninth when Judnich singled in Goldsberry. These games were recreated to the L.A. area.

Hollywood	AB	R	H	RBI	O	A	E
Stringer 2B	5	2	3	1	4	4	0
Franklin 3B	4	1	1	0	0	1	0
Stevens 1B	4	0	1	1	11	3	0
Schmees RF	5	0	2	1	1	0	0
Restelli CF	5	1	2	0	1	0	0
Kelleher LF	4	0	2	1	0	0	0
Sandlock C	4	0	0	0	4	0	0
O'Neil SS	3	0	1	0	2	6	0
Lindell P	4	0	1	0	4	1	0
Conaster CF	0	0	0	0	0	0	0
	38	4	13	4	27	15	0

Seattle	AB	R	H	RBI	O	A	E
Albright SS	4	0	2	0	2	2	0
Goldsberry 1B	4	1	1	0	10	1	0
Rivera CF	4	0	1	0	4	0	0
Judnich LF	3	0	1	1	4	0	0
Lyons RF	3	0	1	0	1	0	0
Erautt C	4	0	1	0	3	0	0
Krsnich 3B	3	0	0	0	1	5	0
Hamner 2B	2	0	0	0	1	2	0
Grissom P	1	0	0	0	1	1	0
Vico [a]	1	0	0	0	0	0	0
Calvert P	0	0	0	0	0	1	0
Montalvo [b]	1	0	0	0	0	0	0
Del Ducca P	0	0	0	0	0	0	0
	30	1	7	1	27	12	0

(a) Batted for Grissom in the fifth.
(b) Batted for Calvert in the eighth.

Pitching Records	IP	H	R	ER	SO	BB
Lindell	9	7	1	1	4	3
Grissom (L)	5	7	3	3	0	3
Calvert	3	5	1	1	2	0
Del Ducca	1	1	0	0	0	0

Left on Base: Hollywood 11, Seattle 5. Two Base Hits: Kelleher 2. Home Run: Stringer. Sacrifice: Stevens. Stolen Base: Stringer. Double Plays: O'Neil to Stevens 2; O'Neil to Stringer to Stevens; Lindell to Stringer to O'Neil to Stevens; Krsnich to Goldsberry. Time of Game: 2 hr. 1 min. Umpires: Runge, Carlucci, Somers.

Hollywood	001	020	100	4 – 13 – 0	
Seattle	000	000	001	1 – 7 – 0	

Game Three.

The two teams flew to Los Angeles on Sunday night and resumed the series on Monday evening, September 17, at Gilmore Field before 3,678 fans. Hector "Skinny" Brown continued to weave his playoff magic by shutting out the Stars, 3–0, on 6 hits. This was Brown's third appearance in seven days without yielding a run. Seattle scored its first run in the fifth off loser George "Pinky" Woods, when Rocky Krsnich singled and was able to score on a double by Wes Hamner, but only because Kelleher was slow to come up with the ball and Johnny O'Neil bobbled the ball for an error. Nevertheless, Hamner was given an RBI on the play. It was still a 1–0 game in the eighth when Alex Garbowski singled, Rivera walked and Judnich singled off Stringer's glove, allowing Garbowski to score. After Lyons walked to load the bases, Rivera scored as Erautt hit into a force play. This game was recreated back to Seattle.

Seattle	AB	R	H	RBI	O	A	E
Garbowski SS	5	1	2	0	1	5	0
Vico 1B	2	0	0	0	11	0	0
Rivera CF	3	1	0	0	5	0	0
Judnich LF	4	0	1	1	2	0	0
Lyons RF	3	0	0	0	2	0	0
Erautt C	4	0	0	1	3	1	0
Krsnich 3B	4	1	1	0	0	3	0
Hamner 2B	4	0	2	1	3	6	0
Brown P	4	0	2	0	0	3	0
	33	3	8	3	27	18	0

Hollywood	AB	R	H	RBI	O	A	E
Stringer 2B	4	0	0	0	5	3	1
Franklin 3B	4	0	0	0	0	2	0
Stevens 1B	3	0	0	0	11	0	0
Schmees RF	2	0	0	0	1	0	0
Restelli CF	4	0	3	0	4	0	0
Kelleher LF	4	0	1	0	2	0	0
Sandlock C	3	0	1	0	3	0	0
O'Neil SS	3	0	1	0	1	6	1
Woods P	2	0	0	0	0	3	0
Lindell[a]	1	0	0	0	0	0	0
Maltzberger P	0	0	0	0	0	0	0
	30	0	6	0	27	14	2

(a) Batted for Woods in the eighth.

Pitching Records	IP	H	R	ER	SO	BB
Brown	9	6	0	0	3	2
Woods (L)	8	6	3	3	3	4
Maltzberger	1	2	0	0	0	0

Hit by Pitcher: Stevens by Brown. Left on Base: Seattle 9, Hollywood 6. Two Base Hit: Hamner. Sacrifice: Vico 2. Stolen Base: Kelleher. Double Plays: O'Neil to Stringer to Stevens; Garbowski to Hamner to Vico 2. Time of Game: 2 hr. 5 min. Umpires: Somers, Doran, Mutart, Runge.

Seattle	000	010	020	3	– 8 –	0
Hollywood	000	000	000	0	– 6 –	2

Game Four.

A crowd of 3,975 on Tuesday, September 18, saw Hollywood forestall elimination with an exciting ninth inning victory in a game that saw four home runs. Bob Hall went the distance and hit a two-run homer but still lost. Jack Salveson, who relieved starter Ben Wade, got the win. It was frustrating for Hornsby's boys, who left 12 runners on base. Hollywood scored the first run in the bottom of the first when Franklin singled and scored on George Schmees' double. Seattle quickly tied it in the second on Joe Eratt's homer. Lou Stringer's third inning homer put the Stars up 2–1 in the third, but Seattle again came back swiftly, this time when Bob Hall hit a two-run homer in the fourth to give himself a 3–2 lead. But Murray Franklin's fifth inning homer tied the game and it remained 3–3 until the last of the ninth. Dino Restelli got to second on Rocky Krsnich's throwing error, Kelleher was put on base, but Mike Sandlock bunted into a force play at third. Johnny O'Neal then singled to left and Walter Judnich's throw beat Kelleher to the plate, but big Frank jarred the ball loose from Joe Erautt for an error, allowing the Stars to tie the series at two games each. As in previous years, the final playoff series employed four umpires.

Seattle	AB	R	H	RBI	O	A	E
Garbowski SS	2	0	0	0	1	2	0
Goldsberry 1B	4	0	2	0	8	1	0
Rivera CF	4	0	2	0	8	0	0
Judnich LF	3	0	0	0	2	1	0
Lyons RF	4	0	0	0	1	0	0
Erautt C	5	1	1	1	1	1	1
Krsnich 3B	4	0	0	0	3	1	1
Hamner 2B	4	1	2	0	1	2	0
Hall P	4	1	3	2	0	0	0
	34	3	10	3	25[a]	8	2

(a) One out when winning run scored.

Hollywood	AB	R	H	RBI	O	A	E
Stringer 2B	4	1	1	1	4	1	0
Franklin 3B	4	2	2	1	0	1	0
Stevens 1B	4	0	0	0	7	0	0
Schmees RF	4	0	2	1	3	0	0
Restelli CF	2	0	0	0	5	1	0
Kelleher LF	2	1	0	0	1	0	0
Sandlock C	4	0	0	0	3	1	0
O'Neil SS	4	0	1	0	4	4	0
Wade P	1	0	0	0	0	1	1
Genovese[a]	1	0	0	0	0	0	0
Salveson P	1	0	0	0	0	1	0
	31	4	6	3	27	10	1

(a) Batted for Wade in the fifth.

Pitching Records	IP	H	R	ER	SO	BB
Hall	8.1	6	4	3	1	3
Wade	5	7	3	3	2	2
Salveson	4	3	0	0	0	4

Left on Base: Seattle 12, Hollywood 6. Two Base Hit: Schmees. Home Runs: Erautt, Stringer, Hall, Franklin. Sacrifices: Garbowski, Goldsberry, Restelli.

Double Plays: Restelli to Sandlock; O'Neil to Stevens. Time of Game: 2 hr. 2 min. Umpires: Doran, Mutart, Runge, Somers.

Seattle	010	200	000	3	–	10	–	2
Hollywood	101	010	001	4	–	6	–	1

Game Five.

On Wednesday September 19, a Gilmore Field crowd of 6,166 saw Seattle beat Hollywood, 9–2, to win its fourth Governor's Cup, tying San Francisco as the only teams to win that many. This was the fifth time in a row that the pennant winner won the playoffs, and the fifth time that the final round was between the first and second place teams, and just as in 1936, 1940, 1941 and 1946, the pennant winner came out the winner. This was also Seattle's last playoff series.

Marv Grissom started against Johnny Lindell, each working on two days' rest. Hollywood broke the scoreless tie in the last of the fifth when Lindell and Stringer both singled and Murray Franklin doubled them home. Seattle cut this lead to 2–1 in the sixth when Garbowski singled in Hamner. Reliever Paul Calvert retired the Stars in the sixth but was lifted for a hitter in the seventh, when the roof fell in on the tiring Lindell. Erautt tripled, Krsnich walked and pinch hitter George Vico singled in the tying run. Vico took second on Lindell's wild pitch, but Krsnich held third. Gordon Maltzberger relieved at this point but gave up a two-run single to Jackie Albright, hitting for winning pitcher Calvert. After Goldsberry doubled, Stringer's error allowed Seattle to score the fourth run of the inning.

Rogers Hornsby then called on Skinny Brown again, and it was curtains for Hollywood. Brown retired the last nine Stars in a row, for a total of 23⅔ scoreless innings pitched in the 1951 playoffs. The Rainiers increased their 5–2 lead with a run in the eighth and three more in the ninth, to make it a one-sided affair.

Seattle	AB	H	RBI	O	A	E
Garbowski SS	5	2	1	2	2	0
Goldsberry 1B	4	1	0	11	0	0
Rivera CF	5	3	1	2	0	1
Judnich LF	5	3	1	1	0	0
Lyons RF	5	1	0	3	0	1
Erautt C	5	1	1	6	1	0
Krsnich 3B	4	1	1	2	2	0
Hamner 2B	2	1	0	0	2	0
Grissom P	1	0	0	0	0	0

Seattle	AB	H	RBI	O	A	E
Montalvo [a]	1	0	0	0	0	0
Calvert P	0	0	0	0	0	0
Vico [b]	1	1	1	0	0	0
Albright 2B [c]	2	1	2	0	1	0
Brown P	0	0	0	0	1	0
	40	15	8	27	9	2

(a) *Batted for Grissom in the sixth.*
(b) *Batted for Hamner in the seventh.*
(c) *Batted Calvert in the seventh.*

Hollywood	AB	H	RBI	O	A	E
Stringer 2B	4	2	0	4	2	1
Franklin 3B	4	1	2	0	2	0
Stevens 1B	4	0	0	10	0	0
Schmees RF	4	0	0	2	0	0
Restelli CF	3	2	0	0	0	0
Kelleher LF	4	1	0	4	1	0
Sandlock C	4	0	0	7	1	0
O'Neil SS	3	0	0	0	7	0
Lindell P	2	1	0	0	1	0
Maltzberger P	0	0	0	0	0	0
Handley [a]	0	0	0	0	0	0
Lombardi P	0	0	0	0	1	0
Hood P	0	0	0	0	0	0
Malone [b]	1	0	0	0	0	0
Conaster CF	1	0	0	0	0	0
	34	7	2	27	15	1

(a) *Batted for Maltzberger in the seventh.*
(b) *Batted for Hood in the ninth.*

Pitching Records	IP	H	R	ER	SO	BB
Grissom	5	6	2	1	3	1
Calvert (W)	1	1	0	0	1	0
Brown	3	0	0	0	2	0
Lindell (L)	6.1	7	2	4	4	1
Maltzberger	0.2	2	3	0	0	0
Lombardi	1.1	5	3	4	2	1
Hood	0.2	1	1	0	0	0

Wild Pitches: Lindell, Hood. Left on Base: Seattle 7, Hollywood 7. Two Base Hits: Goldsberry, Judnich, Krsnich, Rivera 2. Three Base Hit: Erautt. Sacrifice:

Goldsberry. Time of Game: 2 hr. 20 min. Umpires: Mutart, Runge, Doran, Somers.

Seattle	000	001	413	9	– 15	– 2
Hollywood	000	020	000	2	– 7	– 1

By winning the pennant and playoffs, the Rainiers received $15,213 from the pool of $22,820. When the $7,066 that Mr. Sick donated from the player appreciation night is added in, the Seattle players and coaches divided $22,279, which came to $891 per man. This would amount to $3,427 in current funds. This was a little over half what the 1950 Oakland players received, and the Oaks did not have to play any postseason games. The runner up Stars received $3,803, or about $152 per player, which would now be worth about $585. The Angels and Beavers each divided $1,901, or $76 per man, which would be worth close to $292 now.

The playoffs were dropped again after the 1951 season. The owners had to deal with the problem of the San Francisco Seals, a club that finished last and suffered at the gate. Seal owner Paul Fagan wanted to sell the team, blaming the broadcast of major league games into the Bay Area for his plight. But fans in Los Angeles and San Francisco wanted to have major league baseball and were becoming dissatisfied with minor league ball. The owners also tried to get Coast League players to sign contracts that would make it more difficult for major league teams to draft them, but most younger players opposed this because they wanted a chance to play at the top level.

Key Players on 1951 Playoff Teams

Seattle. *Pitchers:* Hector Brown, Marvin Grissom, Jim Davis, Charlie Schanz, Bob Hall, and Al Lyons.
    Position Players: Jim Rivera (league's MVP and batting champion), Walter Judnich, Joe Erautt, Rocco Krsnich, and Al Lyons (who also pitched).

Hollywood. *Pitchers:* Ben Wade, Jack Salveson, Johnny Lindell, George "Pinky" Woods, Wally Hood and Vic Lombardi.
    Position Players: Frank Kelleher, George Schmees, Chuck Stevens, Lou Stringer, Dino Restelli, Gene Handley, and Johnny Lindell (who also pitched and was team's MVP).

Los Angeles. *Pitchers:* Dewey Adkins, Bill Moisan, Warren Hacker, Bob Spicer, Doyle Lade, Herman Besse and Jess Dobernic.
    Position Players: Chuck Connors (first half of season), Dee Fondy (second

half of season), Max West, Les Layton, Leon Brinkopf (team's MVP), Gene Baker and Jack Hollis.

Portland. *Pitchers:* Marino Pieretti, Red Adams, Red Lynn, Bob Drilling, and Lyman Linde.

Position Players: Leo Thomas, Brooks Holder, Joe Brovia, Joe Rossi, Frankie Austin and Eddie Basinski.

1954

After two seasons with no playoffs, the Pacific Coast League reinstated them for the 1954 season, but they were not a success. The race ended in a tie between San Diego and Hollywood, which made the playoffs especially anticlimactic. Even with this second tie in the pennant race, league attendance was only 1,773,643, which was about 44 percent of the banner year of 1947 and even less than the war years of 1944 and 1945. Because of the financial distress, the league reduced the player limit to 21 players, only 5 of which could be on loan from the major leagues.

The San Diego Padres, managed for the third and final year by Lefty O'Doul, won the tie-breaker game with Hollywood to win the pennant. After Padres won that game, *The San Diego Union* proclaimed, "Padres Win Their First Pennant After 19 Seasons." Apparently, no one wanted to claim the Padres' 1937 pennant that was won in the playoffs.

Hollywood, managed by Bobby Bragan in his second of three seasons, was going for its third pennant in a row. The Stars led the race from early June on until the Padres caught them at the end. A key blow to Hollywood's pennant chances occurred at Gilmore Field on August 11. Carlos Bernier, an outfielder hitting .313 with six homers, slapped umpire Chris Valenti after being called out on strikes. Bernier was suspended for the rest of the season, which hurt the Stars' offense.

During the last week of the season, Hollywood was at Portland and San Diego was at Los Angeles. After Saturday's games, the race was tied going into the final Sunday doubleheader. Both contenders lost their openers, making the seven-inning nightcap crucial. O'Doul was strapped for pitchers, having lost Cliff Chambers in mid-season while Eddie Erautt and Cliff Fannin both came up with dead arms. So he turned to Al Lyons, who played center field in the opening game and was the goat when his hesitation on the base path cost the Padres a run in regulation, and hence the game, since the Angels won it in extra innings. Lyons, who had only relieved but never started, became the hero as he beat L.A. 7–3. Meanwhile in Portland, Bragan turned to Roger Bowman for the second game. Bowman, one of two 20-game winners in the league,

Charley Dressen managed the 1954 Oakland Oaks to the playoffs championships (Doug McWilliams collection).

was knocked out of the box in the first inning by the Beavers on Saturday. But this time, Bowman pitched a perfect game in that nightcap to send the Stars into the tie-breaker game.

If Hollywood's doubleheader at Portland had been rained out, they would have won the pennant because San Diego split their two games. The Stars' record would have been 100–66 or .602 percentage, while the Padres would have finished at 101–67 or .601. The Coast League did not require postponed games to be made up after the season ended.

The other two first division spots went to Oakland and San Francisco. The Oaks were again piloted by Charley Dressen, who had managed at Brooklyn the past three years but left over a contract dispute. The Oaks were in the first division all season, but after June they were no threat to catch the two front runners.

The Seals were managed by Tommy Heath, who was in his third year, after following Lefty O'Doul who had held the post for 17 years. San Francisco played six more games than fifth place Seattle, and clinched fourth place by percentage points on Thursday of the final week. But the Seals continued to win, finishing four games ahead of the Rainiers, thereby ending the season at the .500 mark, being the second club to make the playoffs with that record. The other was the 1939 Sacramento Solons.

The Tie-Breaker Game.

San Diego won the toss and so this game was played at Lane Field on Monday night, September 13, before an overflow crowd of 11,471 fans. George "Red" Munger started for Hollywood while O'Doul let the players decide whom to start for the Padres. They picked Lefty Bob Kerrigan over the right-hander Theolic Smith. This proved to be a wise choice, along with another even more important one. The "forgotten man," Bob Elliott, formerly of the Boston Braves, was inserted at third base instead of Milt Smith.

Earl Rapp played a key role on the 1954 San Diego Padres (photo by Doug McWilliams).

In the last of the second, Bob Elliott came up with Luke Easter on base and hit a homer off Red Munger, putting the Padres up 2–1. After Hollywood tied it 2–2 in the third, the Padres knocked Munger and a reliever out of the game in the last of the fourth when they scored four runs, which put the game out of reach. Earl Rapp singled with one out, bringing in Lino Dinoso to face Easter. He walked Easter and gave up a run-scoring single to Harry Elliott, the league's batting champion. Mel Queen relieved Dinoso and gave up a three-run home run to Bob Elliott, making it 6–2. Bob Elliott, who was to succeed O'Doul as manager of the Padres in 1955, stated that these two homers gave him a bigger thrill than the one he hit at Braves Field on September 26, 1948, that won the pennant for Boston. He also hit two homers in the fifth game of the 1948 World Series at Cleveland.

Hollywood	AB	R	H	RBI	O	A	E
D. Smith SS	5	1	1	0	1	3	0
Walls RF	4	0	2	0	2	0	0
Lohrke 3B	4	1	1	0	0	4	0
Kelleher LF	4	0	1	2	4	0	0
Phillips 1B	4	0	0	0	11	0	0
Basgall 2B	4	0	2	0	1	1	0
Saffell CF	4	0	1	0	2	0	0
Bragan C	4	0	1	0	3	0	0
Munger P	2	0	0	0	0	2	0
Donoso P	0	0	0	0	0	0	0
Queen P	0	0	0	0	0	0	0
Walsh P	0	0	0	0	0	0	0
Del Greco[a]	1	0	0	0	0	0	0

The 1954 Oakland Oaks finished in third place, 16 games behind the champion San Diego Padres but beat the Padres in the first round of the playoffs, and then beat their cross bay rivals, the Seals, to win the last playoffs ever held. *Top Row, left to right:* "Red" Adams (trainer), Bill Howerton (right field), Gene Hermanski (outfield), Lou Landini (catcher), Allen Gettel (pitcher), Chris Van Cuyk (pitcher), Jim Atkins (pitcher), Ernie Broglio (pitcher), Pete Milne (left field). *Middle Row:* Sam Chapman (center field), Piper Davis (utility), Jim Marshall (1st base), Harry Lavagetto (coach), Charlie Dressen (manager), Ronnie Samford (2nd base), Leonard Neal (catcher), Harry Nicholas (pitcher). *Bottom Row:* George Bamberger (pitcher), Don Ferrarese (pitcher), John Jorgensen (3rd base), Russ Rose (shortstop), Joe Unfried (outfield), Hal White (pitcher), Arthur Cuitti (outfield).

Hollywood	AB	R	H	RBI	O	A	E
O'Donnell P	0	0	0	0	0	1	0
Wolfe[b]	0	0	0	0	0	0	0
Malone C	0	0	0	0	0	0	0
	36	2	9	2	24	11	0

(a) *Batted for Walsh in the eighth.*
(b) *Ran for Bragan in the eighth.*

San Diego	AB	R	H	RBI	O	A	E
Federoff 2B	4	1	1	0	3	0	0
Peterson SS	3	0	0	0	3	0	0
Sisler LF	4	0	0	0	2	0	0
Rapp RF	3	1	1	1	3	0	0
Easter 1B	2	2	0	0	5	1	0
H. Elliott CF-LF	4	1	1	1	5	0	0
B. Elliott 3B	2	2	2	5	2	3	0

San Diego	AB	R	H	RBI	O	A	E
Sandlock C	4	0	2	0	3	0	0
Kerrigan P	2	0	0	0	0	0	1
M. Smith 3B[a]	1	0	1	0	1	0	0
Faber CF[b]	0	0	0	0	0	0	0
	29	7	8	7	27	4	1

(a) Ran for B. Elliott in the sixth.
(b) Ran for Sisler in the seventh.

Pitching Records	IP	H	R	ER	SO	BB
Munger (L)	3.1	2	2	3	1	1
Donoso	0+	1	1	2	0	1
Queen	2.2	3	3	1	2	0
Walsh	1	1	1	1	0	1
O'Donnell	1	1	0	0	0	0
Kerrigan	9	9	2	2	3	3

Hit by Pitcher: B. Elliott by Queen. Left on Base: Hollywood 12, San Diego 4. Two Base Hits: Lohrke, Basgall. Home Runs: B. Elliott 2. Sacrifices: Lohrke, Kerrigan, Rapp (Fly). Time of Game: 2 hr. 44 min. Umpires: Ford, Pelekoudas, Carlucci, Ashford.

Hollywood	101	000	000	2	–	9	– 0
San Diego	020	400	10x	7	–	8	– 1

As mentioned earlier, O'Doul managed in the only other tie-breaker game that decided the pennant in 1947, when his Seals lost to the Angels. Bob Kerrigan, who won for Lefty in 1954, beat the Seals in the final game in 1947, forcing that fatal game at Los Angeles.

The Oakland–San Diego Series

Unfortunately for the Padres, there was no off day between their pennant winning game and the start of the playoffs. Even though the Padres beat Oakland 16 of 24 times in the regular season, they were in no mood to take them, or anyone else, on after their great celebrations Monday night and Tuesday afternoon. After the game on Monday night, the whole team was feted at the San Diego Club, at which some adult beverages were served. Then on Tuesday, a crowd of 35,000 gathered along a parade route from Lane Field to the Plaza downtown, where the mayor spoke and Padre announcer Al Schuss introduced

Pitcher George Bamberger of the 1954 Oakland Oaks (photo by Doug McWilliams).

each player to the cheering multitudes. This was not the way to prepare for a game.

Game One.

The Oaks waited until Tuesday morning to fly to San Diego because neither they nor the Seals knew whom they were to play until after the tiebreaker game. The adoring San Diego crowds somehow did not make their way to Lane Field on this Tuesday night, September 14, to see their Padres, with Lloyd Dickey taking on Oakland and George Bamberger. Only 1,767 were in the stands when the Oaks' Jim Marshall hit a first inning homer to give his team an early lead. Then in the second, Oakland increased this lead to 2–0 when Art Cuitti, "The Crocket Rocket," singled and scored on singles by Sam Chapman and Lenny Neal. The Padres cut the lead to 2–1 in the fourth when Harry Elliott doubled and scored on Walt Pocekay's single. With both pitchers going all the way, the score remained tied until the top of the ninth when Chapman got aboard on Milt Smith's error and came home on Lenny Neal's two-run homer. Neal drove in three of the Oaks' four runs.

Oakland	AB	R	H	RBI	O	A	E
Rose SS	5	0	2	0	1	0	0
Jorgensen 3B	4	0	1	0	1	4	0
Marshall 1B	5	1	1	1	6	1	0
Davis 2B	3	0	1	0	2	2	0
Cutti RF	1	1	1	0	0	0	0
Hermanski RF	2	0	0	0	1	0	0
Chapman CF	4	1	1	0	7	0	0
Neal C	4	1	2	3	7	0	0

Oakland	AB	R	H	RBI	O	A	E
Unfried LF	4	0	0	0	1	0	0
Bamberger P	4	0	1	0	1	2	0
	36	4	10	4	27	9	0

San Diego	AB	R	H	RBI	O	A	E
Federoff 2B	3	0	0	0	4	3	0
Peterson SS	4	0	1	0	2	2	0
Sisler LF	3	0	0	0	1	0	0
Faber CF	0	0	0	0	2	0	0
Rapp RF	4	0	2	0	3	0	0
Easter 1B	4	0	0	0	7	1	0
H. Elliott CF-LF	4	1	1	0	5	0	0
M. Smith 3B	3	0	0	0	1	0	1
Poceekay C	3	0	1	1	2	0	0
Dickey P	3	0	0	0	0	1	0
	31	1	5	1	27	7	1

Pitching Records	IP	H	R	ER	SO	BB
Bamberger	9	5	1	1	7	1
Dickey	9	10	4	4	1	0

Hit by Pitcher: Federoff by Bamberger. Left on Base: Oakland 7, San Diego 5. Passed Ball: Pocekay. Two Base Hit: H. Elliott. Home Runs: Marshall, Neal. Double Play: Jorgensen to Davis to Marshall. Time of Game: 2 hr. 4 min. Umpires: Carlucci, Ashford, Ford.

Oakland	110	000	002	4 – 10 – 0
San Diego	000	100	000	1 – 5 – 1

Game Two.

An even smaller crowd of 1,330 came out on Wednesday night, September 15, and saw the last game in Lane Field in 1954 as the Oaks eliminated the champion Padres in extra innings. Little Don Ferrarese started for Oakland against Theolic Smith, but neither got the decision. Ferrarese kept the Padres hitless until the fifth and scoreless until the seventh. He was staked to a 1–0 lead on John "Spider" Jorgensen's fourth inning homer. But in the last of the seventh, the Padres broke through with three runs to take the lead. Al Lyons singled, Milt Smith walked, then Monday's hero, Bob Elliott, hit for Pocekay and singled in the tying run. Johnny Merson pinch hit for Theolic Smith and got a single on a squeeze bunt, putting the Padres up 2–1. After Ferrarese walked Al Federoff to load the bases, he was replaced by Ernie Brolio, who walked in the third run of the inning, but the Padres left the bases loaded.

O'Doul moved Al Lyons from the outfield to pitch in the eighth, and he retired Oakland without a run but in the ninth, he squandered the lead. Jorgensen singled off Dick Sisler's glove and Jim Marshall blooped a single over third. Both runners moved up on Gene Hermanski's infield out, and then Pete Milne's infield single scored one run and Piper Davis' single scored the tying run. Neither team scored in the 10th, with Chris Van Cuyk, "The Wisconsin Dutchman," pitching for Oakland and Bill Thomason for the Padres. After two were out in the top of the 11th, Hermanski doubled, Milne was passed, but Piper Davis drew a walk. Then Sam Chapman, who 17 years earlier led the California Bears to a Rose Bowl win, hit a grand slam homer, ending the Padres' season.

Oakland	AB	R	H	RBI	O	A	E
Rose SS	5	0	1	0	3	2	0
Jorgensen 3B	4	2	3	1	2	3	0
Marshall 1B	4	1	1	0	7	0	0
Hermanski LF	5	1	1	0	1	0	0
Millne RF	3	1	1	1	2	0	0
Davis 2B	4	1	1	1	3	2	0
Chapman CF	5	1	1	4	3	0	0
Neal C	2	0	0	0	10	0	0
Ferrarese P	2	0	0	0	0	0	0
Howerton[a]	1	0	1	0	0	0	0
Brolio P	0	0	0	0	0	0	0
Cuitti[b]	1	0	0	0	0	0	0
Landini C	2	0	0	0	2	0	0
Van Cuyk P	1	0	0	0	0	1	0
	39	7	10	7	33	8	0

(a) Batted for Neal in the eighth.
(b) Batted for Brolio in the eighth.

San Diego	AB	R	H	RBI	O	A	E
Federoff 2B	5	0	1	0	3	4	0
Peterson SS	2	0	0	1	5	3	0
H. Elliott LF	5	0	1	0	1	1	0
Rapp RF	5	0	0	0	7	0	0
Lyons CF-P	4	1	1	0	1	1	0
Sisler 1B	4	0	1	0	10	0	0
M. Smith 3B	4	1	2	0	1	2	0
Sandlock C	2	0	0	0	1	0	0

San Diego	AB	R	H	RBI	O	A	E
Pocekay C	2	0	0	0	4	0	0
T. Smith P	2	0	0	0	0	0	0
B. Elliott[a]	1	0	1	1	0	0	0
Dickey[b]	0	1	0	0	0	0	0
Faber CF	2	0	1	0	0	0	0
Merson[c]	1	0	1	1	0	0	0
Thomason P	1	0	0	0	0	1	0
	40	3	9	3	33	12	0

(a) *Batted for Sandlock in the seventh.*
(b) *Ran for B. Elliott in the seventh.*
(c) *Batted for T. Smith in the seventh.*

Pitching Records	IP	H	R	ER	SO	BB
Ferrarese	6.1	5	2	3	9	5
Brolio	0.2	0	1	0	0	1
Van Cuyk (W)	4	4	0	0	2	0
T. Smith	7	2	1	1	1	3
Lyons	2+	6	2	2	1	0
Thomason (L)	2	2	4	4	3	2

Left on Base: Oakland 4, San Diego 10. Two Base Hit: Hermanski. Home Runs: Jorgensen, Chapman. Double Plays: Federoff to Peterson to Sisler; Rose to Marshall; Peterson to Federoff to Sisler; Jorgensen to Marshall. Time of Game: 2 hr. 15 min. Umpires: Ashford, Ford, Carlucci.

Oakland	000	100	002	04	7 – 10 – 0
San Diego	000	000	300	00	3 – 9 – 0

San Diego sportswriter Jack Murphy called these playoffs "meaningless" after an exciting pennant race. Another writer, Phil Collier, expressed anger over making San Diego start the playoffs with no off day after a big celebration. Both these managers moved on after the season, Dressen to the Washington Senators and O'Doul to the Oakland Oaks, becoming the last manager in Oakland history, as Lefty moved with the team to Vancouver for the 1956 season.

The San Francisco–Hollywood Series

The disappointed Stars were in no better frame of mind to play the Seals, a team they beat 16 of 24 times during the season, than the celebrating Padres were to play the Oaks, but for obviously different reasons. Looking up into the stands at Gilmore Field on Tuesday night, September 14, did not inspire the Hollywood players – only 694 fans were there, which was the smallest crowd of the year.

Game One.

George O'Donnell went the route for Hollywood, beating Eddie Chandler, who was followed by Frank Hiller and Tony Ponce. Chandler walked nine, which hurt him. In the second, he walked Jack Phillips and "Lucky" Jack Lohrke. Phillips scored when Mike Baxes let Monty Basgall's grounder go through him. But Chandler himself scored the tying run in the third when he singled and came around on base hits by Jim Moran and Dave Melton. The Stars went ahead 2–1 in the last of the third on Tommy Saffell's homer, but the Seals got even in the fourth when Sal Taormina homered. But Hollywood put the game away in the fifth when they scored three runs on only one hit. Shortstop Leo Righetti's error made two of those runs unearned. Ex-Star Chuck Stevens homered for the Seals' last run in the ninth, to make the final score 5–3.

San Francisco	AB	R	H	RBI	E
Moran 2B	5	0	3	0	0
Beard CF	5	0	1	0	0
Melton RF	4	0	2	1	0
Westlake 1B	3	0	0	0	0
Taormina LF	4	1	2	1	0
Baxes 3B	4	0	1	0	2
Righetti SS	4	0	0	0	1
Tornay C	3	0	0	0	0
Chandler P	2	1	1	0	0
Hiller P	0	0	0	0	0
Ponce P	0	0	0	0	0
Zuvela[a]	1	0	0	0	0
Cheso[b]	1	0	0	0	0
Stevens[c]	1	1	1	1	0
	37	3	11	3	3

(a) Batted for Hiller in the seventh.
(b) Batted for Tornay in the ninth.
(c) Batted for Ponce in the ninth.

Hollywood	AB	R	H	RBI	E
Smith SS	4	0	2	0	1
Saffell CF	4	2	2	1	0

Hollywood	AB	R	H	RBI	E	
Walls RF	4	1	1	0	0	
Kelleher LF	4	0	1	0	0	
Phillips 1B	1	2	0	0	0	
Lohrke 3B	2	0	1	0	0	
Basgall 2B	3	0	0	1	0	
Mangan C	4	0	0	0	0	
O'Donnell P	4	0	0	0	0	
	30	5	7	2	1	

Pitching Records	IP	H	R	ER	SO	BB
Chandler (L)	4.1	4	4	2	1	9
Hiller	1.2	0	0	0	1	0
Ponce	2	3	0	0	1	0
O'Donnell	9	11	3	3	7	1

Home Runs: Taormina, Saffell Stevens. Double Plays: Basgall to Phillips. Bases unassisted: Basgall to Phillips. Umpires: Somers, Mutart, Pelakoudas.

San Francisco	001	100	001	3 – 11 – 3	
Hollywood	011	030	00x	5 – 7 – 2	

Game Two.

An even smaller crowd of 626 came out on Wednesday night, the 15th, and saw the Seals tie the series with a 7–0 win. These games were broadcast back to San Francisco. Elmer Singleton, who was 0–4 against Hollywood during the season, pitched a seven-hit shutout. Jim Walsh started and lost for the Stars, being relieved by Ed Wolfe, Forest Main and Mel Queen. Catcher Nini Tornay of the Seals went 4-for-5, with a double, driving in three runs. First baseman Jim Westlake singled and homered, also driving in three runs. It was 2–0 in the fifth when the Seals broke through for four runs, two of which came on Westlake's homer.

San Francisco	AB	R	H	RBI	E
Moran 2B	5	0	0	1	0
Beard CF	4	1	1	0	0
Melton RF	4	1	2	0	0
Westlake 1B	4	1	2	3	0
Taormina LF	4	1	0	0	0
Baxes 3B	4	2	2	0	0
Righetti SS	5	1	3	0	1

San Francisco	AB	R	H	RBI	E
Tornay C	5	0	4	3	0
Singleton P	4	0	2	0	0
	39	7	16	7	1

Hollywood	AB	R	H	RBI	E
Smith SS	4	0	1	0	1
Saffell CF	3	0	0	0	0
Walls RF	4	0	1	0	0
Kelleher LF	4	0	1	0	0
Phillips 1B	4	0	2	0	0
Basgall 2B	4	0	1	0	0
Lohrke 3B	4	0	0	0	0
Mangan C	3	0	1	0	1
Walsh P	0	0	0	0	0
Wolfe P	0	0	0	0	0
Main P	1	0	0	0	0
Malone[a]	1	0	0	0	0
Queen P	0	0	0	0	0
	32	0	7	0	2

(a) Batted for Main in the eighth.

Pitching Records	R	ER	SO	BB
Singleton	0	0	4	1
Walsh (L)	2	2	0	1
Wolfe	2	3	0	1
Main	2	0	1	1
Queen	1	1	0	0

Two Base Hits: Beard, Tornay. Home Run: Westlake. Double Plays: Smith to Basgall; Righetti to Moran to Westlake. Umpires: Mutart, Pelakoudas, Somers.

San Francisco	001	140	001	7 – 16 – 1
Hollywood	000	000	000	0 – 7 – 2

Game Three.

On Thursday night, September 16, the crowd fell even lower, to 467, making it three straight nights the Stars set season lows. This was the nadir, because it was the last game at Gilmore Field in 1954 as the Seals eliminated Hollywood with a 4–3 win. *San Francisco Examiner* writer Prescott Sullivan wrote that the Coast League has a dead duck on its hands, but has not gotten around to bury it. Al Wolf of *The Los Angeles Times* asked rhetorically, "Who revised these playoffs anyway?"

Ken Holcombe faced Roger "No-Hit" Bowman in this deciding game, and Holcombe was staked to a 1–0 lead in the first when Dave Melton drove in Jim Moran. That lead held up until the last of the seventh when Jack Phillips, who was voted the league's MVP, homered to tie it. But in the top of the eighth, Bowman ran into trouble. He hit Melton and walked Jim Westlake. Bob "Deep" DiPietro singled in a run to put the Seals up 2–1. Mike Baxes singled in the second run, and when the ball got through centerfielder Tommy Saffell, a third run also scored, which proved to be the decider. In the last of the eighth, Lee Walls singled in two runs off reliever Bob Muncrief, but the Stars came up a run short.

San Francisco	AB	R	H	RBI	E
Moran 2B	3	1	1	0	0
Beard CF	2	0	0	0	0
Melton RF	3	1	1	1	0
Westlake 1B	3	1	0	0	0
DiPietro LF	4	1	1	1	0
Baxes 3B	3	0	1	1	0
Righetti SS	2	0	0	0	0
Tornay C	3	0	0	0	0
Holcombe P	3	0	0	0	0
Zabala P	0	0	0	0	0
Muncrief P	1	0	0	0	0
	29	4	4	3	0

Hollywood	AB	R	H	RBI	E
Smith SS	3	1	0	0	0
Saffell CF	3	0	0	0	1
Long RF-LF	4	0	0	0	1
Walls LF-CF-RF	4	0	1	2	0
Phillips 1B	4	1	2	1	0
Basgall 2B	4	0	1	0	0
Lohrke 3B	4	0	0	0	0
Mangan C	4	0	1	0	0
Bowman P	2	0	1	0	0
Donoso P	0	0	0	0	0
Kelleher LF[a]	1	0	0	0	0
Malone[b]	1	1	1	0	0
	34	3	7	3	2

(a) Batted for Saffell in the eighth.
(b) Batted for Bowman in the eighth.

Pitching Records	IP	H	R	ER	SO	BB
Holcombe (W)	7+	5	1	3	2	1
Zabala	0+	1	0	0	0	0
Muncrief	2	1	2	0	0	0
Bowman (L)	8	4	4	3	4	5
Donoso	1	0	0	0	0	0

Home Run: Phillips. Stolen Base: Melton. Time of Game: 2 hr. 6 min. Umpires: Pelekoudas, Somers, Mutart.

San Francisco	100	000	030	4	– 4	– 0
Hollywood	000	000	120	3	– 7	– 2

The Final Series: Oakland vs. San Francisco

The Oaks had a day off before this series but the Seals did not. They flew home after beating Hollywood on Thursday night and had to play a doubleheader at Oaks Park on Friday night, September 17. Had Hollywood won, this series would also have started in Oakland because USC was playing Washington State on Friday night in Los Angeles.

Game One.

This doubleheader began at 6:30 P.M. with four umpires but before only 1,727 fans. This was the fourth time these two rivals met in the playoffs but never drew the large crowds that they did when playing during the season. Frank Hiller of the Seals faced Allen "Two Gun" Gettel. The Seals had a 3–0 lead erased in the last of the fourth when Spider Jorgensen homered with Russ Rose on base. Jim Marshall followed with a game tying homer. The game remained tied until the last of the eighth when Pete Milne doubled and scored on Len Neal's single off loser Al Lien.

San Francisco	AB	R	H	RBI	E
Moran 2B	3	0	0	0	0
Beard CF	3	0	2	1	0
Melton RF	3	0	0	0	0
Westlake LF	2	1	0	0	0

San Francisco	AB	R	H	RBI	E
Taormina LF	3	1	1	0	0
Baxes 3B	3	0	1	0	0
Righetti SS	2	0	0	0	0
Tornay C	2	1	1	1	0
Hiller P	1	0	0	0	0
Lien P	1	0	0	0	0
Bradford P	0	0	0	0	0
	23	3	5	2	0

Oakland	AB	R	H	RBI	E
Rose SS	3	1	2	0	0
Jorgensen 3B	2	1	2	1	0
Marshall 1B	2	1	1	1	0
Hermanski LF	3	0	0	0	0
Milne RF	3	1	1	0	0
Davis 2B	2	0	0	0	0
Chapman CF	3	0	1	0	0
Neal C	3	0	1	1	0
Gettel P	2	0	0	0	0
	23	4	8	3	0

Pitching Records	R	ER	SO	BB
Hiller	3	3	0	0
Lien (L)	1	1	0	2
Bradford	0	0	1	0
Gettel	3	3	2	3

Two Base Hits: Beard, Taormina, Rose, Milne. Home Runs: Jorgensen, Marshall. Sacrifices: Hiller, Jorgensen. Double Plays: Moran to Righetti to Westlake; Baxes to Righetti to Westlake. Time of Game: 1 hr. 22 min. Umpires: Ford, Somers, Mutart, Carlucci.

San Francisco	001	200	000	3 – 5 – 0
Oakland	000	300	01x	4 – 8 – 0

Game Two.

In the nine-inning nightcap, Tony Ponce faced George Bamberger but neither got the decision as a total of 15 runs, 23 hits, and 6 home runs made this a hitter's game The Seals got solo homers from Teddy Beard, Dave Melton, and Jim Westlake, and had leads of 3–0, 3–2, 6–2, 6–4, and 7–4 before the Oaks came up with four runs in the seventh to take an 8–7 lead which they never relinquished. In the last of the sixth, Piper Davis' two-run homer off Bob Muncrief cut the Seal lead to 6–4. The Seals got their seventh and last run in the seventh off Ernie Broglio, who had come on in the fifth and allowed the Seals three runs that inning. But in the last of the seventh, Joe Unfried batted for Broglio and singled, and Rose singled, so Tommy Heath brought in Adrian Zabala to face Spider Jorgensen. The Spider bit him, blasting a three-run homer to tie the game. Jim Marshall then homered to put the Oaks up for good, 8–7. Dressen called on reliever Harry Nicholas, who pitched two scoreless innings to save the game, but the win went to Broglio, who was pitcher of record when Jorgensen and Marshall went deep.

San Francisco	AB	R	H	RBI	E
Moran 2B	5	0	0	0	0
Beard CF	4	2	1	1	0
Melton RF	5	3	4	1	0
Westlake 1B	4	1	2	1	0
Taormina LF	4	1	2	0	0
Baxes 3B	4	0	1	0	0
Righetti SS	4	0	1	1	0
Tiesiera C	4	0	1	0	0
Ponce P	1	0	0	0	0
Muncrief P	2	0	0	0	0
Zabala P	0	0	0	0	0
Stevens[a]	1	0	0	0	0
Bradford P	0	0	0	0	0
	38	7	12	4	0

(a) Batted for Zabala in the eighth.

Oakland	AB	R	H	RBI	E
Rose SS	5	1	1	0	0
Jorgensen 3B	4	1	1	3	1
Marshall 1B	4	1	1	1	0
Hermanski LF	4	1	2	0	0
Milne RF	4	2	2	0	0
Davis 2B	3	1	2	2	0
Chapman CF	4	0	1	0	0
Landini C	3	0	0	1	0
Bamberger P	1	0	0	0	0
Howerton[a]	1	0	0	0	0
Broglio P	0	0	0	0	0

Oakland	AB	R	H	RBI	E
Unfried [b]	1	1	1	0	0
Nicholas P	1	0	0	0	0
	35	8	11	7	1

(a) *Batted for Bamberger in the fourth.*
(b) *Batted for Broglio in the seventh.*

Pitching Records	R	ER	SO	BB
Ponce	2	2	1	0
Muncrief	3	3	1	0
Zabala (L)	3	3	0	1
Bradford	0	0	0	0
Bamberger	3	3	0	0
Broglio (W)	4	4	0	1
Nicholas	0	0	1	0

Wild Pitch: Bamberger. Two Base Hits: Righetti, Westlake. Home Runs: Beard, Melton, Westlake, Jorgensen, Davis, Marshall. Double Play: Davis to Rose to Marshall. Umpires: Somers, Mutart, Carlucci, Ford.

San Francisco	100	230	100	7 – 12 – 0
Oakland	000	202	40x	8 – 11 – 1

Game Three.

The teams took Saturday, September 18, off, because Oklahoma came to Berkeley and beat California, 27–13, before 58,000 fans. But the Oaks and Seals did not even have Friday night to themselves because Stanford beat College of Pacific in Stockton 13–12 before 28,000 and the radio broadcast of that game knocked the playoffs off the air. But this final game on Sunday the 19th, was on radio in the Bay Area.

The fans were promised a doubleheader and they got one, but the seven-inning second game was an exhibition because the Oaks won the opener to sweep the Seals, and won the final Governor's Cup. A crowd of 4,954 saw Don Ferrarese shut out the Seals and Elmer Singleton, 2–0. Ferrarese scored the first run in the third when he singled, was sacrificed by Rose, and scored on Jim Marshall's single. Oakland's last run came in the fourth when Milne walked, went to third on Davis' single, and scored on Chapman's single.

Oakland	AB	R	H	RBI	E
Rose SS	4	0	2	0	0
Jorgensen 3B	3	0	0	0	0

Oakland	AB	R	H	RBI	E
Marshall 1B	3	0	2	1	0
Hermanski LF	4	0	0	0	0
Milne RF	3	1	0	0	0
Davis 2B	4	0	3	0	0
Chapman CF	4	0	2	1	0
Neal C	4	0	0	0	0
Ferrarese P	4	1	1	0	0
	33	2	10	2	0

San Francisco	AB	R	H	RBI	E
Moran 2B	4	0	1	0	0
Beard CF	3	0	0	0	0
Melton RF	4	0	1	0	0
Westlake 1B	4	0	1	0	0
DiPietro LF	4	0	0	0	0
Baxes 3B	3	0	1	0	0
Righetti SS	3	0	1	0	0
Tornay C	3	0	0	0	0
Singleton P	1	0	0	0	1
Cheso [a]	0	0	0	0	0
Chandler P	0	0	0	0	0
	29	0	5	0	1

(a) Batted for Singleton in the eighth.

Pitching Records	IP	H	R	ER	SO	BB
Ferrarese	9	5	0	0	7	2
Singleton (L)	8	9	2	2	1	4
Chandler	1	1	0	0	0	0

Two Base Hit: Westlake. Sacrifice: Beard. Double Plays: Melton to Moran to Westlake; Righetti to Moran to Westlake; Jorgensen to Davis to Marshall. Time of Game: 1 hr. 54 min. Umpires: Mutart, Carlucci, Somers, Ford.

Oakland	001	100	000	2 – 10 – 0
San Francisco	000	000	000	0 – 5 – 1

Just as in Los Angeles in 1943, after Seattle swept the Angels, a meaningless second game was played, and just as in 1943, the team that was swept won the exhibition game. The Seals won 5–4 with many players moving from position to position.

As in 1951, the owners set aside 1 cent from each admission to reward the pennant winner and playoff teams. San Diego got ⅓ for winning the pennant, and ¹⁄₁₂ more when eliminated in the opening round, so their ⁵⁄₁₂ of $17,736 amounted to $7,390. If 23 shares were distributed, each man would get $321, or about $1,193 in current funds. The Oaks got ⅓ or $5,912, which would come to $257 per man, or about $955 currently. The Seals received ⅙ or $2,956, or about $128 per man, which would now be worth close to $476. But Hollywood, who led most of the way, and was defeated in the tie-breaker game, got only $1,478, or $64 per man, which would be worth about $238 today.

At least the Padres received more than the third-place Oaks, but in some years, the pennant winner received less than the team that won the Cup. This happened in 1938, 1939, 1942, 1943 and 1945.

The owners met right after the season in Los Angeles and voted to drop the playoffs for good. Thus, the "dead duck" was finally buried. The owners also voted on a measure that never came to pass: If a tie for the pennant were to occur in the future, it would be determined by a two out of three series.

Key Players on the 1954 Playoff Teams

San Diego. *Pitchers:* Bill Wight (league's best won-lost percentage and lowest ERA), Bob Kerrigan, Lloyd Dickey, Eddie Erautt (injured), Bill Thomason and Al Lyons (also an outfielder).

Position Players: Harry Elliott (league's batting champ), Earl Rapp, Dick Sisler, Al Federoff, Buddy Peterson and Luke Easter (good drawing card).

Hollywood. *Pitchers:* Roger Bowman, Lino Dinoso, George Munger, Mel Queen, Jim Walsh, and Ed Wolfe.

Position Players: Jack Phillips (league's MVP), Dick Smith, Dale Long, Lee Walls, Bobby Del Greco, and Tommy Saffell.

Oakland. *Pitchers:* Don Ferrarese, George Bamberger, and Allen Gettel.

Position Players: Jim Marshall, John Jorgensen, Art Cuitti, Sam Chapman, Piper Davis, Len Neal and Pete Milne.

San Francisco. *Pitchers:* Ken Holcombe, Frank Hiller, Adrian Zabala, Elmer Singleton and Tony Ponce.

Position Players: Teddy Beard, Dave Melton, Jim Moran, Jim Westlake, Bob DiPietro, Sal Taormina and Will Tiesiera.

EPILOGUE

This book has documented the controversy and struggle the Coast League officials went through from the late 1930s through the mid 1950s in deciding whether or not to keep the playoffs. The first obstacle was deciding that the pennant winner should not be determined in the playoffs but in the regular season. Later, it became clear that a close exciting pennant race used up so much fan enthusiasm that little was left for the playoffs, as in 1954, 1948, 1947 and 1942. But when the race was not close, as in 1943, 1944, and 1945, the public seemed to enjoy postseason play. When a pennant winner was eliminated in the first round, as the 1939 Seattle, the 1943 Los Angeles, the 1945 Portland and 1954 San Diego teams, it left a sour taste in the mouths of those teams' fans. The season for many was ruined. On the other hand, the playoff winner gave its fans a late season thrill they otherwise would not have had. The team that seemed to gain the most fan enthusiasm from their playoff wins were the San Francisco teams of 1943, 1944 and 1945. The Oakland team of 1954 certainly did not gain much.

This book also covered the problems encountered by the playoffs competing for fan interest and sports page coverage with college and professional football. This problem got worse in the 1950s when television became very popular and when fans in the L.A. area and Bay Area yearned for major league baseball. By 1954, Milwaukee and Baltimore got major league teams and Kansas City was on the verge.

The view of Charles Graham of the Seals seemed to hold true that the benefit of the playoffs comes during the regular season as teams struggle to get into the first division. The packed house in San Diego in 1949 for the Padre-Rainier tie-breaker shows that fans did care about their team making the playoffs. All eight clubs won at least one Cup, with Seattle and San Francisco winning four each, and Oakland and Sacramento winning two each. The other four teams each won it once. The table below shows the number of postseason series each team won from the others.

	Sea.	Por.	Sac.	Oak.	SF.	LA.	Hol.	SD.
Seattle	—	1	2	1	1	4	2	0
Portland	1	—	0	1	1	0	0	0
Sacramento	0	0	—	0	2	2	0	1
Oakland	1	0	0	—	2	2	0	2
San Francisco	3	1	1	2	—	1	2	0
Los Angeles	1	2	0	1	0	—	0	2
Hollywood	0	1	1	0	0	0	—	1
San Diego	0	1	1	1	0	0	0	—

It is unfortunate Los Angeles and Hollywood never met in the playoffs because they drew very well against each other. The two teams played a best of five series for third place after the 1955 season and the fans did support it enthusiastically.

APPENDIX: RECORDS, STANDINGS, AND PRIZE MONEY

Playoff Records of PCL Teams

	Won	Lost Final	Lost Opener
Seattle	4	3	3
Portland	1	1	5
Sacramento	2	1	4
Oakland	2	3	3
San Francisco	4	2	4
Los Angeles	1	4	5
Hollywood	1	1	3
San Diego	1	1	5

Individual Series Won by Each Team

	Won	Lost	Never Played
Seattle	11	6	San Diego
Portland	3	6	Sacramento
Sacramento	5	5	Portland, Oakland
Oakland	7	6	Sacramento, Hollywood
San Francisco	10	6	San Diego
Los Angeles	6	9	Hollywood
Hollywood	3	4	Los Angeles, Oakland
San Diego	3	6	San Francisco, Seattle

Place in Standings of Playoff Winner

First	8 — 1936, 1940, 1941, 1946, 1947, 1948, 1949, 1951
Second	1 — 1943
Third	5 — 1937, 1938, 1942, 1944, 1954
Fourth	2 — 1939, 1945

Place in Standings of Final Round Loser

First	1 — 1944
Second	7 — 1936, 1940, 1941, 1942, 1945, 1946, 1951
Third	2 — 1939, 1943
Fourth	6 — 1937, 1938, 1947, 1948, 1949, 1954

Place in Standings of Teams in Final Round

1 vs. 2	5 times — 1936, 1940, 1941, 1946, 1951 (first place team won each time)
1 vs. 3	1 time — 1944 (third place team won)
1 vs. 4	3 times — 1947, 1948, 1949 (first place team won each time)
2 vs. 3	2 times — 1942, 1943 (#3 won in 1942; #2 won in 1943)
2 vs. 4	1 time — 1945 (fourth place team won)
3 vs. 4	4 times — 1937, 1938, 1939, 1954 (fourth won only in 1939)

Prize Money Awarded Each Year

Boldface *indicates a playoff winner.*
Number in parentheses represents team's place in standings.

Year	Total	By Team		
1936	$10,000	**Portland**	(1)	$5500
		Oakland	(2)	$2000
		San Diego	(2)	$1250
		Seattle	(4)	$1250
1937	$10,000	Sacramento	(1)	$3750
		San Francisco	(2)	$1250

Year	Total	By Team		
		San Diego	(3)	$3000
		Portland	(4)	$2000
1938	$12,500	Los Angeles	(1)	$3750
		Seattle	(2)	$1250
		Sacramento	(3)	$5000
		San Francisco	(4)	$2500
1939	$12,500	Seattle	(1)	$3750
		San Francisco	(2)	$1250
		Los Angeles	(3)	$2500
		Sacramento	(4)	$5000
1940	$12,500	**Seattle**	(1)	$7500
		Los Angeles	(2)	$2500
		Oakland	(3)	$1250
		San Diego	(4)	$1250
1941	$12,500	**Seattle**	(1)	$7500
		Sacramento	(2)	$2500
		San Diego	(3)	$1250
		Hollywood	(4)	$1250
1942	$12,500	Sacramento	(1)	$3750
		Los Angeles	(2)	$2500
		Seattle	(3)	$5000
		San Diego	(4)	$1250
1943	$12,500	Los Angeles	(1)	$3750
		San Francisco	(2)	$5000
		Seattle	(3)	$2500
		Portland	(4)	$1250
1944	$12,500	Los Angeles	(1)	$5000
		Portland	(2)	$1250
		San Francisco	(3)	$5000
		Oakland	(3)	$1250
1945	$25,000	Portland	(1)	$7500
		Seattle	(2)	$5000
		Sacramento	(3)	$2500
		San Francisco	(4)	$10,000
1946	$25,000	**San Francisco**	(1)	$15,000
		Oakland	(2)	$5,000
		Hollywood	(3)	$2500
		Los Angeles	(4)	$2500

Year	Total	By Team		
1947	$50,000	**Los Angeles**	(1)	$30,000
		San Francisco	(2)	$5000
		Portland	(3)	$5000
		Oakland	(4)	$10,000
1948	$50,000	**Oakland**	(1)	$30,000
		San Francisco	(2)	$5,000
		Los Angeles	(3)	$5,000
		Seattle	(4)	$10,000
1949	$50,000	**Hollywood**	(1)	$30,000
		Oakland	(2)	$5,000
		Sacramento	(3)	$5,000
		San Diego	(4)	$10,000
1951	$22,820*	**Seattle**	(1)	$15,213
		Hollywood	(2)	$3,803
		Los Angeles	(3)	$1,902
		Portland	(4)	$1,902
1954	$17,736	San Diego	(1)	$7390
		Hollywood	(2)	$1478
		Oakland	(3)	$5912
		San Francisco	(4)	$2956

In 1951, Seattle held a "players appreciation" night after they clinched the pennant and all gate proceeds were added to the Seattle players' prize money.

INDEX

465